Quantum Computing in Cybersecurity

Scrivener Publishing
100 Cummings Center, Suite 541J
Beverly, MA 01915-6106

Publishers at Scrivener
Martin Scrivener (martin@scrivenerpublishing.com)
Phillip Carmical (pcarmical@scrivenerpublishing.com)

Quantum Computing in Cybersecurity

Edited by

Romil Rawat
Rajesh Kumar Chakrawarti
Sanjaya Kumar Sarangi
Jaideep Patel
Vivek Bhardwaj
Anjali Rawat
and
Hitesh Rawat

Scrivener
Publishing

WILEY

This edition first published 2023 by John Wiley & Sons, Inc., 111 River Street, Hoboken, NJ 07030, USA and Scrivener Publishing LLC, 100 Cummings Center, Suite 541J, Beverly, MA 01915, USA
© 2023 Scrivener Publishing LLC
For more information about Scrivener publications please visit www.scrivenerpublishing.com.

Wiley Global Headquarters
111 River Street, Hoboken, NJ 07030, USA

For details of our global editorial offices, customer services, and more information about Wiley products visit us at www.wiley.com.

Limit of Liability/Disclaimer of Warranty
While the publisher and authors have used their best efforts in preparing this work, they make no representations or warranties with respect to the accuracy or completeness of the contents of this work and specifically disclaim all warranties, including without limitation any implied warranties of merchantability or fitness for a particular purpose. No warranty may be created or extended by sales representatives, written sales materials, or promotional statements for this work. The fact that an organization, website, or product is referred to in this work as a citation and/or potential source of further information does not mean that the publisher and authors endorse the information or services the organization, website, or product may provide or recommendations it may make. This work is sold with the understanding that the publisher is not engaged in rendering professional services. The advice and strategies contained herein may not be suitable for your situation. You should consult with a specialist where appropriate. Neither the publisher nor authors shall be liable for any loss of profit or any other commercial damages, including but not limited to special, incidental, consequential, or other damages. Further, readers should be aware that websites listed in this work may have changed or disappeared between when this work was written and when it is read.

Library of Congress Cataloging-in-Publication Data

ISBN 978-1-394-16633-6

Front cover images supplied by Pixabay.com
Cover design by Russell Richardson

Set in size of 11pt and Minion Pro by Manila Typesetting Company, Makati, Philippines

Printed in the USA

10 9 8 7 6 5 4 3 2 1

Contents

Preface

The main topics of this book are:

- Quantum Inspired Community Classification in Social Networks Analytics
- Future Directions in Quantum Computing
- Quantum Machine Learning for Intrusion Detection
- Quantum Designs to Detect Distributed Denial of Service Attacks
- Cyber Terrorism for Quantum Internet
- Cryptography, and
- Cyber Criminals' Quantum Communication Networks

The security and effectiveness of communications in network infrastructures might be improved by quantum technology in a previously unheard-of way. This book, written as a complete and thorough text, guides readers through mathematically challenging topics in a way that encourages student participation.

In the context of criminality and forensics, this book offers a clear, step-by-step explanation of quantum computing. A deeper comprehension of the human and social dimensions of pertinent complexities, such as child sexual exploitation, violent radicalization, trafficking, disinformation and fake news, corruption, and cyber criminality, as well as victim support, must serve as the foundation for improved cyber-crime prevention, investigation, and remediation. Applications and solutions based on quantum computing that analyse massive volumes of data in near-real time in order to stop criminal activities or combat false information and disinformation while addressing security issues. In order to confront crime, including cybercrime and terrorism as well as various types of serious and organized crime, this will help security agencies incorporate such details into the operating processes of police officials (such as smuggling, money laundering, identity theft, counterfeiting of products, trafficking of illicit drugs and falsified or substandard medicines, environmental crime, or illicit trafficking of cultural goods).

Cybercriminals employ cutting-edge tools, such as machine learning methods, to build and spread deadly malware using vast amounts of data. Cyber attackers can develop a ground-breaking means of evading cyber security by using quantum computing, which would enable them to quickly assess vast datasets before launching a sophisticated attack on several networks and devices.

Cyber Quantum Computing (Security) Using Rectified Probabilistic Packet Mark for Big Data

Anil V. Turukmane* and Ganesh Khekare

Department of Computer Science Engineering, Parul University, Vadodar, Gujarat, India

Abstract

In recent years, denial-of-service (DoS) assaults have been a system flaw. DoS disobedience testing has become one of the most important streams in system Quantum Computing Security). This dynamic field of investigation has yielded astounding frameworks such as pushback message, ICMP take after back, and following package improvement methods. In tributary regarded informatics, the probabilistic packet marking (PPM) standard drew in considerable thinking. To begin with, the alluring purpose of this informatics follow-up approach is that it permits alterations to etch bound data on ambush packages that support chosen likelihood. After gathering a sufficient number of examined packages, the loss (or information plan centre) will construct a set of systems that offence groups crossed and, as a result, the setback will be assigned zones. The goal of the PPM algorithmic project is to demonstrate that produced outline is the same as offence graph, where relate degree attack outline is that course of action of techniques ambush packs investigated and created outline could be diagrammed by PPM algorithmic framework. The main goal of the structure is to provide a powerful approach to cope with tracking down an assailant's back IP address through a media like the internet. The system will stamp every shipment that is to be traded over the internet as indicated by the group's substance and deliver it via trade media. When it reaches its final destination, the stamping of any package is altered, and the structure is ready to be taken. The majority of PPM concerns have entailed a few issues such as loss of stamping information, issues recreating ambush routes, and low precision than on. In the first paper, we propose a dynamic probabilistic packet

Corresponding author: anil.turukmane21100@paruluniversity.ac.in

Romil Rawat, Rajesh Kumar Chakrawarti, Sanjaya Kumar Sarangi, Jaideep Patel, Vivek Bhardwaj, Anjali Rawat and Hitesh Rawat (eds.) Quantum Computing in Cybersecurity, (1–16) © 2023 Scrivener Publishing LLC

marking (DPPM) approach as a replacement for another upgrade reasonability of PPM. On the other hand, if you're utilising mounted checking likelihood, we propose gauging regardless of whether the package has been stamped or not, and then selecting the appropriate checking likelihood. Most of the problems with the PPM approach could be solved using DPPM. A formal examination reveals that DPPM outperforms PPM in a variety of ways. The proposed solution is useful in domains where it is important to keep track of back IP addresses while changing the package, such as cybercrime and the illegal treatment of data groups where certain basic information must be transferred. Propose a P Packet M basic end condition, which is commonly omitted or not explicitly stated in writing. Due to the new end condition, the client of a new control has more freedom to inspect the precision of the chart that has been created.

Keywords: Quantum Computing (Security), Quantum Cryptography and Quantum Computing (Security), control mechanism, cyber crime, quantum attacks

1.1   Introduction

Over the last two decades, the world has seen significant advances in science and innovation that have successfully met a wide spectrum of human needs. These requests range from basic necessities like power bills and rail ticket reservations to more complex ones like force matrices for the era of violence and sharing. These advancements have raised the standard of human existence in terms of modernity and simplicity. Unexpectedly, a competing invention for negotiating Quantum Computing (Security) has evolved, with its own set of repercussions, hindering innovation. Robbery, hacking, and the blackout of private information are examples of information-related attacks. Anonymous subterranean attack networks that can efficiently assault a specific target every time are likely to be available, according to the media and many types of network Quantum Computing (Security) literature. This merely depicts a possible transition from today's attack to future attacks. Everything is on the table in the present world, from "damage and devastation" wars to "information warfare," to the negotiation of the aforementioned attack. Finally, attackers/networks that can hide are usually the ones who carry out these attacks.

The scope of attacks on targets is as extensive as that of constructional technology, but this thesis focuses on a specific sort of attack known as denial-of-service (DoS) attacks. DoS assaults are a form of targeted attack whose purpose is to deplete the target's resources and, as a result, prohibit large customers from obtaining service. For quite some time, great focus has been placed on the Quantum Computing (Security) of network infrastructure, which has continued to be used for a variety of transactions. The internet Quantum Computing (Security) business, academia, and even the United States Conference, which has organized multiple conferences on the subject, have all taken notice [1, 2]. Various safety strategies have been proposed, each attempting to address a different set of issues. The anonymous attack is the specific risk that this research focuses on. Because the Source Address (SA) information is spooled in the attack packages, the identity of the attacker(s) is not immediately visible to the individual in anonymous attacks.

1.2   Denial-of-Service Attacks

The focus of this thesis is on service denial (DoS) attacks on PC networks. The goal of these attacks is to deny legitimate users access to network services. This PhD includes a comprehensive look at many attack and defence mechanisms, as well as unique defensive mechanisms and new information on defensive mechanism selection and evaluation. DoS mitigation is an important part of network and computer Quantum Computing (Security). Network and computer Quantum Computing (Security) are frequently discussed in scientific domains. Computer Quantum Computing (Security) language is still imbalanced, which is a big issue [10, 11]. Computer and network Quantum Computing (Security) were originally prioritised in the mid-1970s, and some of the most meticulous Quantum Computing (Security) documentation was published in [12]. Denial-of-service attacks come in a variety of forms, and the number of them is expanding all the time as new procedures and data networks are developed. These attacks should be divided into two categories: physical and virtual, with the purpose of better comprehending the most common denial-of-service (DoS) attempts (or network-based). There are two other types of attacks that fall within this category, each of which represents the attack's overall goal: disabling critical services and draining system resources [13].

An Overview of Denial-of-Service Attacks
System disruption (DoS) attacks have been shown to be a significant and long-term threat to users, businesses, and internet infrastructure [16–20]. Blocking access to a specific object, such as a web application, is one of the key targets of these assaults. There have been numerous DoS guards proposed in the literature, but none of them can be trusted with any degree of certainty. Vulnerable hosts on the internet, as well as attack traffic sources,

are virtually certain to be exploited. It's just not possible to keep every host on the internet secure at all times. (In July 2005 it was assessed that there were roughly 350,000 hosts on the internet.) Furthermore, detecting and channelling legitimate traffic attacks without causing legal traffic injury to collateral is quite difficult.

A DoS attack can be carried out in one of two ways: as a flood or as a logical attack. A flood DoS attack is based on brute force. A victim is given as much information as possible, even if it is unneeded. This squandering of network bandwidth fills space with unnecessary data (e.g., spam mail, garbage files, and deliberate error messages), loads flawed data onto fixed-size data structures inside host software, and necessitates a significant amount of data management effort. To increase the impact of DoS attacks, they might continue to be planned from multiple sources (Distributed DoS, DDoS).

1.2.1   DoS Attacks in Real Life

Actual internet DoS instances were investigated throughout the popular era of 1989 to 1995. The three most common consequences were as follows: in 51% of the cases, there was a circle, and in 33% of the cases, there was a network decline of 33%, and in 26% of the cases, certain vital data was deleted. A single occasion can result in a variety of problems (the whole of rates is more than 100%). A college was the target of the first big DDoS attack in August 1999. This attack disabled the target's network for two days. On February 7, 2000, a few key web-based locations were attacked, and they were cut off from the internet for many hours. These DDoS attacks may occasionally cause a single victim's assault movement of around 1 Gbit/s.

The quantity, duration, and location of distributed denial-of-service (DDoS) attacks on the internet were tracked using scatter monitoring. Backscatter is defined as the victim's spontaneous reflex movement in response to the assault package, which is sent with fake IP addresses. In the three weeks of investigation in February 2001, over 12,000 attacks were registered against over 5,000 distinct victims. Packet fragmentation was studied in real networks. Bugs in fragmented management software are exploited in various logic DoS assaults, and the results of this emphasis still suggest the presence of such DoS on the web.

According to the Associated Press, the Emergency Response Team (CERT) Operations Unit was attacked in May 2001. Its portal was down for a few days due to a distributed denial of service (DDoS) attack. In the mid-2002, ISPs in the United Kingdom were focusing on DDoS assaults. Some clients experienced a 12-hour outage as a result of one of these attacks. The Domain Name System (DNS) continues to put a focus on DoS threats (DNS). In October 2002, all root name servers were subjected to an exceptionally large DoS attack. Because of the damage produced by the assault, certain DNS requests were unable to reach a root name server. On June 15, 2004, a second DoS attack was launched against the Akamai Content Distribution Network (CDN) name servers, preventing access for nearly two hours. The most influential places were Apple Computer, Google, Microsoft, and Yahoo. These companies have outsourced their DNS services to Akamai for service updates.

1.3   Related Work

Denial of service (DoS) attacks have become widely acknowledged as a severe threat to the internet. Threat actors flood a target network with traffic, rendering network services unstable or completely unavailable as a result. It is vital to recognise these assaults in order to prevent them from happening again. To perform this assignment, the exploitability of hidden, simulated, or spoofed exploits must be assessed. In the world of information technology, this is known as an informatics Trace back disadvantage. The use of routers to put self-identifying data into packets travelling down the attack path is how packet marking is done. In PPM routers, packets are labelled with a probability distribution. The amount of tagged packet samples received by a victim node determines its capacity to reconstruct the attack route. We discovered that marked packets from distant routers are highly likely to be noticed by downstream routers when analysing the efficacy of a particular marking chance for all routers in PPM. The overall result will be a drop in the number of packets while there is an increase in the amount of data. By approving each router to regulate the marking chance, a more uniform distribution is achieved. The goal of a dynamic technique is to account for movement while determining the router's position in the attack path. However, many approaches rely on underlying protocols, necessitating the use of routers to manage data on vast networks regarding potential victims. This increases the router's overhead and consumes an excessive amount of time. As can be shown in this study, we have a great desire to propose a method that dynamically sets the value of the marking probability depending on the 8-bit TTL field inside the informatics header, which can be accessed directly by routers without the need for external assistance. We may use the projected TTL worth as a technique of determining where along the attack route the packet is placed and derive the marking chance value by using the TTL worth as an estimate of the distance covered by a packet. We created a user-friendly computer that imitated the algorithm by simulating it using a variety of test situations. Our dynamic theme, which rebuilds the attack path with more precision while consuming fewer resources at the router and at the target, is successful. The expected theme's main advantages are its simplicity and low router overhead, but a lot of value may be gained by adopting dynamic ways that produce similar outcomes and outperform static approaches across a wide attack range.

1.3.1   Probabilistic Packet Marking (PPM)

New approaches have the potential to increase network overhead, router processing, and node processing. There have been various solutions that have gotten a lot of attention in recent years, including the use of probabilistic packet marking (PPM). Introduce an Associate Degree in this area to expand on the probabilistic packet marking theme, which drastically reduces the number of packets needed to reconstruct the attacker's route.

1.3.1.1   DoS Attacks

Denial-of-service (DoS) attacks may prove to be a serious stumbling block to network connectivity. Some denial-of-service attacks can be avoided if the spoof IP address is reflected back to its original source, allowing the perpetrators to be punished or research into the attack to be done. To fight denial-of-service attacks, IP trace back algorithms are designed to allow for probabilistic packet marking (PPM).

When compared to selected packet marking and electronic messaging schemes—which can be difficult to trace back due to the attacker spoofing the marking field in the packet—Kihong Park *et al.* [1] have planned that probabilistic packet marking—of interest due to its potency and implementation ability—will confer a significant return on investment (ROI) on the victim. Unlike prior study, which found a trade-off between the victim's ability to locate the attacker and the intensity of the DoS attack, which was modelled as a function of the marking chance, route length, and traffic volume, our findings show the inverse relationship: that a low-resource attacker can successfully undertake a distributed denial-of-service attack against a larger target. Minimax problems are the only way to mathematically express this problem. To put it another way, the victim will choose the marking chance, reducing the number of forgeable assault ways available, be focused in a dispersed DoS attack, improving the attacker's capabilities and reducing PPM's impact. Increasing the marking probability shows that the attacker's ability to disguise his location is limited, but it also shows that the attacker's ability to conceal his position is limited due to sampling limits. Because attackers in normal IP internets would have addresses in two to five equally likely locations, PPM's effectiveness against a single-supply attack is significantly boosted. In a distributed DoS attack, the attacker's uncertainties are concentrated, improving the attacker's capabilities and reducing the effect of PPM.

1.3.1.2 FDPM

According to Yang Xiang *et al.* [2], a unique strategy called flexible deterministic packet marking (FDPM) has been proposed for dealing with large-scale IP trace back assaults, which could be effective in the future in minimising DDoS attacks. During a DDoS assault, the target site or network was continually blasted with fraudulent IP packets from several sources. An IP trace back technique allows you to trace IP packets back to their source (in a somewhat modest manner). FDPM improves packet tracing by offering a number of adjustable options for tracing IP packets, including probabilistic packet marking (PPM) and deterministic packet marking (DPM) (DPM). The FDPM's adaptation choices included the following. It might, for example, increase the length of the marking field in relation to the network protocols currently in use; alternatively, it could decrease the marking rate in relation to the traffic load on the collaborating routers. Because of its use of and display, the FDPM ensures that packet distribution is kept to a minimum in the event of a trace back; for example, it may retrieve up to 110,000 devices from a single incident response. It is possible that even if this page is very heavily loaded, it will still be able to perform a trace back method because of the built-in overload interference mechanism.

1.3.1.3 Simulation Surroundings via Extending ns2

The development of simulation environments and methodologies for measuring the time it takes to trace IP addresses back under a variety of network conditions and malicious attack patterns is critical. A comparison of various PPM (Probabilistic Packet Marking) algorithms is provided, as well as metrics such as the number of packets required to rebuild the attacker route, computational quality, and false positives.

To simulate various PPM approaches, Li *et al.* [3] use an expansion of ns2 along with offensive topology and traffic. The simulation technique can also be used to test the effects of simulated DDoS attacks on various PPM systems. According to the simulation and analysis results, many of PPM's error-prone elements were in the works, which might help speed up the process of detecting intellectual property infringement.

1.4   Proposed Methodology

Dynamic Probabilistic Packet Marking
Loss of marking information, difficulty reconstructing the attack path, low precision, and other concerns are among the most prevalent repercussions of Probabilistic Packet Marking (PPM). This study utilises a replacement technique (DPPM), which improves the primary prevention method's (PPM) performance even more. Rather than recommending a fixed like-lihood of marking, we recommend first determining whether the packet has been marked, and then selecting the most acceptable marking proba-bility from the available possibilities. The adoption of DPPM may be able to resolve the majority of PPM's technical difficulties. DPPM outperforms PPM in the majority of areas, with one exception. As a result of widespread use of public computers and the expansion of network infrastructure, the internet has had a huge impact on modern living, as well as social and economic sectors. Criminal behaviour has become increasingly common, resulting in significant financial losses. The incredibly easy-to-conduct distributed denial-of-service (DDoS) attack has caused havoc on commu-nication infrastructure. Monitoring technology for Internet Protocol (IP) can be used to track the delivery of evidence needed to remedy an assault.

A denial of service (DoS) attack is an attempt to prevent a web-based programme from serving its intended clients, either momentarily by sus-pending or shutting down the service, or permanently by rendering the application unworkable. A distributed denial-of-service (DDoS) occurs when an attack supply exceeds a single, and in certain cases, multiple infor-mation science addresses, as shown in Figure 1.1. In the sense that no cus-tomers have come or created disturbances to corporate activities, the front door of a shop or corporation is akin to a gathering of people.

1.4.1   Denial of Service

A denial-of-service (DoS) attack is one that delays or restricts the flow of resources. Denial-of-service attacks can also be triggered by human errors, aesthetic defects, or computer code vulnerabilities. Another example of inappropriate resource utilisation is delays in time-sensitive tasks. During

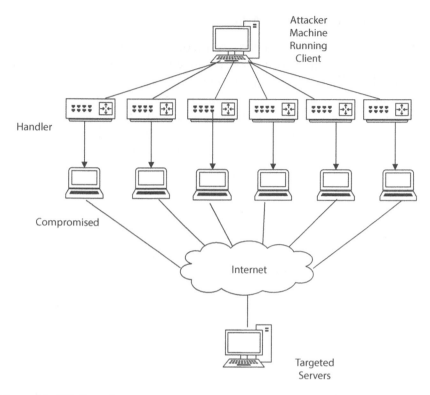

Figure 1.1 DDoS attack.

this defining area, there are samples of resource measurement, process capacity, disc space and memory, and static memory structures. In the ANSI 2000 medium gloss, an attack (that should not succeed) is referred as a Quantum (Security) violation. Since the foundation for a DoS attack has been laid, this can be used.

1.4.1.1   Direct DDoS Attacks

A large number of supply hosts try to prevent victims from consuming resources or deny victims access to resources while attack traffic is sent. An associate degree agent is a hacked server that is used to send attack traffic in connection with a DDoS attack (also known as a daemon, zombie, or bot). A master is an out-of-date group of agents who have been labelled as such. A DDoS network is made up of a collection of linked master agents that are all geared up to help the attacker during DDoS attacks. Direct DDoS assaults and reflector attacks are two types of distributed denial of service (DDoS) attacks.

1.4.1.2   Distributed DDoS Attacks

The attack is frequently delayed as a result of many supply hosts attempting to shut down or tamper with resources given by victims at the same time that assault traffic is being sent. During a DDoS attack, a hijacked host is utilised to transmit attack traffic. A master is a compromised host operation with an out-of-date collection of agents. In the context of a DDoS attack, a DDoS network is defined as a hierarchical collection of linked master agents that helps an attacker organise a DDoS attack with less effort. Reflectors and direct hits are two types of DDoS attacks.

1.4.1.3   Reflector DDoS Attacks

Within the field of supply science, packets containing victims' addresses are supplied to unsuspecting third parties by slave zombies (agents), who successively send a reply to the victim (uninfected computers such as web servers, DNS servers, etc.). (Inundate the victim) a Reflector assault can affect at least two persons. Because of the additional equipment required and the larger bandwidth involved, a reflected assault will be far more devastating. It is also more difficult to keep track of.

1.5   Trace Back Mechanism for Rectified Probabilistic Packet Marking

The internet captures some or all of many crucial and essential services such as banking, commerce, transportation, healthcare, and communication. According to current figures, there are approximately 400 million hosts connected to the internet, and there are currently more than 4 billion internet users. As a result, any network outage could be extremely inconvenient for a large number of individuals. The devastating effects of a DoS attack have drawn the attention of scientists and researchers, resulting in a variety of traumatic processes. The majority of attacks on highly distributed DoS systems that require thousands of compromised PCs, on the other hand, fail. A critical phase in the defence against a Denial-of-Service (DoS) assault is to trace back scientific discipline.

The packet marking technique is used to encrypt the edges data of packets inside routers in a random manner. After that, the victim uses the rehabilitation method to construct the attack path via knowing victimisation. In the past, several traceback procedures in scientific areas were planned. The approach of Probabilistic Packet Marking (PPM) was primarily studied. In an extremely PPM technique, the router probabilistically stamps the packets with its identifying data, allowing the destination to recreate the network path by combining several packets with similar features. The PPM rule has various issues in the existing system because the termination condition is not explicitly specified. It is necessary to have the necessary configuration information.

1.5.1   A Brief Review of the Packet Marking Procedure

A DoS (Denial-of-Service) attack [4–6], in which a health care helper seeks to build a target host (dubbed a victim) [7, 8] due to the host's large range of packets [9], could be one of the most serious threats to web Quantum Computing [14, 15] (Security). In recent years, DDoS (Distributed Denial-of-Service) attacks have become commonplace anywhere there are many attackers on the internet. From one stage on the Caregiver Path to the next, we set the course of this Associate in the Caregiver Package. IP traceback is a defence mechanism against DoS/DDoS attacks. Every router attacks information about methods to store information about itself or packets in IP traceback systems. The victim then uses the information to track down the offenders. IP traceback systems classify square packet marking (DPM) into two categories: probabilistic (Short PPM) methods and practical packet markings. In PPM protocols, every router almost certainly writes path information on the packets it receives. The IP trace back protocols, on the other hand, generate all collaboration sample packets from routers and store path information on their own. PPM and working methods have a number of benefits. The Figure 1.2 shows about the quantum drones framework.

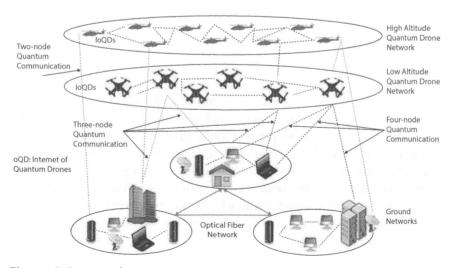

Figure 1.2 Quantum drones.

1.5.2   Packet Marking

PPM does not demand router storage resources, although it typically needs the victim to receive an outsize packet before the attack tree is rebuilt. On the other hand, the quantity of packets for attack tree recovery in work schemes may be low. Work plans nevertheless need considerable load and huge cabinet space on routers. Now, for a current example of traceback information processing protocols let us consider the addition RIHT: a hybrid information processing traceback theme with a p.mark value is computed to find out the packet flow and to look for an attack. This technique takes an outsized amount of calculation into account that requires intense time.

1.5.3   Path Selection

The path describes how the specified packet or file should be delivered from the delivery point to the destination. The upstream interfaces of all routers must be detected and stored in the interface table. The interface table can be used to describe the selected supply and destination.

1.5.4   Packet Sending

In packet or file processing, packet delivery occurs as follows: the packet travels from the source LAN to the destination LAN through the route provided. When the packet is received by the destination LAN, it is checked to see if it has been delivered.

1.5.5   Packet Marking and Logging

On each packet header, a five-bit section is styled as a counter. In our example, if a router decides to sample a packet P with a specific probability, P.counter is set to one, some data is saved on the router, and the packet is finally sent to a neighbouring router. As a result, the higher the counter value, the more routers in the attack path will store P data. In other words, after the attack tree is recovered, a packet with an over-dimensional counter value is favourable. As a result, if we tend to probabilistically prefer a packet with a higher counter worth to a packet with a lower counter worth to a packet with a lower counter worth to a packet with a higher counter worth to a packet with a higher counter worth to a packet with a higher counter.

1.5.6   Path Reconstruction

When employing Formula 3, after the packet reaches its destination, it checks to determine if it was broadcast from the right upstream interfaces. If an assault is detected, the assault will attempt to reconstruct the route. Path reconstruction is the process of discovering a new path for continuous supply and, as a result, a destination that cannot be attacked.

Every significant network attack now includes a DoS or DDoS attack. Although it is relatively easy to die, it may cause significant damage. DoS attacks, which consume a large amount of system resources, render conventional services unusable for genuine consumers. While e-mail has become the most popular mode of communication, DDoS attacks are becoming more common.

Lee and Fung demonstrate how a DoS attack can be carried out utilising an authentication approach based primarily on public-key activity. Many alternative defences against DoS attacks are being considered. Su *et al.* devised an internet strategy based on initial features from estimated sources of associated attack traffic in order to limit the DDoS attack's harm.

Huang *et al.* planned to use associative reward, cooperative filtering, and cooperative caching to help victims of DDoS attacks. As a result, the location of the assault supply would be crucial. Because the supply address is not removed after the router sends a packet to the current protocol, we choose not to accept the supply address in the scientific discipline header of the attack packet.

1.6   Conclusion

A good package marking strategy can cut down on the number of packages needed to trace the victorious path and shorten the time it takes to identify the wrongdoer's genuine supply. There are two sorts of packet marking techniques: static probability marking and dynamic probability theme. We do not always acquire enough tagged packets from faraway routers in PPM, which causes a lot of problems in the IP track and extends the time it takes to reconstruct the victim. Our goal in developing a dynamic probability replacement method was to generate a high enough number of tagged packets from remote routers in a short amount of time in order to perform a faster and more reliable trace back.

References

1. S. E. Cross, "Cyber Quantum Computing (Quantum Computing (Security)," Testimony before the Senate Armed Services Committee, Mar. 2000.
2. R. D. Pethia, "Computer Quantum Computing (Quantum Computing (Security)," Testimony before the Committee on Government Reform, Mar. 2000.
3. S. Gibson, "DRDoS: Distributed reflector denial of service," Gibson Research Corporation," Technical Report, Feb. 2002.
4. Rawat, R. (2023). Logical concept mapping and social media analytics relating to cyber criminal activities for ontology creation. *International Journal of Information Technology*, 15(2), 893-903.
5. Rawat, R., Mahor, V., Álvarez, J. D., & Ch, F. (2023). Cognitive Systems for Dark Web Cyber Delinquent Association Malignant Data Crawling: A Review. *Handbook of Research on War Policies, Strategies, and Cyber Wars*, 45-63.
6. Rawat, R., Chakrawarti, R. K., Vyas, P., Gonzáles, J. L. A., Sikarwar, R., & Bhardwaj, R. (2023). Intelligent Fog Computing Surveillance System for Crime and Vulnerability Identification and Tracing. *International Journal of Information Security and Privacy (IJISP)*, 17(1), 1-25.
7. Rawat, R., Sowjanya, A. M., Patel, S. I., Jaiswal, V., Khan, I., & Balaram, A. (Eds.). (2022). *Using Machine Intelligence: Autonomous Vehicles Volume 1*. John Wiley & Sons.
8. Rawat, R., Bhardwaj, P., Kaur, U., Telang, S., Chouhan, M., & Sankaran, K. S. (2023). *Smart Vehicles for Communication, Volume 2. John Wiley & Sons.*
9. Mahor, V., Bijrothiya, S., Rawat, R., Kumar, A., Garg, B., & Pachlasiya, K. (2023). IoT and Artificial Intelligence Techniques for Public Safety and Security. *Smart Urban Computing Applications*, 111.
10. M. Andrews and J. A. Whittaker, "Computer Quantum Computing (Quantum Computing (Security))," *IEEE Quantum Computing (Security) & Privacy*, vol. 2, no. 5, pp. 68–71, Sept./Oct. 2004.
11. M. Bishop, "What is computer Quantum Computing (Security)," *IEEE Quantum Computing (Security) & Privacy*, vol. 1, no. 1, pp. 67–69, Jan/Feb 2003.
12. M. Bishop, "Early computer Quantum Computing (Quantum Computing (Security)) papers, part 1," 1998. [Online]. Available: http://csrc.nist.gov/publications/history/index.html [accessed Jan. 3, 2006].
13. E. Skoudis. *CounterHack. A Step-by-Step Guide to Computer Attacks and Effective Defenses*. Prentice Hall, Upper Saddle River, NJ, 2002.
14. Mahor, V., Pachlasiya, K., Garg, B., Chouhan, M., Telang, S., & Rawat, R. (2022, June). Mobile Operating System (Android) Vulnerability Analysis Using Machine Learning. In *Proceedings of International Conference on Network Security and Blockchain Technology: ICNSBT 2021* (pp. 159-169). Singapore: Springer Nature Singapore.

15. AusCERT, "2005 Australian computer crime and Quantum Computing (Quantum Computing (Security) survey," Australian Computer Emergency Response Team, Tech. Rep., 2005. [Online]. Available: http://www.auscert. org.au/crimesurvey [accessed Jan. 4, 2006].

16. N. Brownlee, K. C. Claffy, and E. Nemeth, "DNS measurements at a root server," in *Proceedings of the IEEE GlobeCom, San Antonio, USA, Nov. 2001.*

17. CERT Coordination Center, "Results of the Distributed-Systems Intruder Tools Workshop," Nov. 1999.

18. L. Garber, "Denial-of-service attacks rip the Internet," *IEEE Computer*, vol. 33, no. 4, pp. 12–17, Apr. 2000.

19. Mahor, V., Garg, B., Telang, S., Pachlasiya, K., Chouhan, M., & Rawat, R. (2022, June). Cyber Threat Phylogeny Assessment and Vulnerabilities Representation at Thermal Power Station. In *Proceedings of International Conference on Network Security and Blockchain Technology: ICNSBT 2021* (pp. 28-39). Singapore: Springer Nature Singapore.

20. K. J. Houle, G. M. Weaver, N. Long, and R. Thomas, "Trends in denial of service attack technology," CERT Coordination Center, Tech. Rep., Oct. 2001.

2

Secure Distinctive Data Transmission in Fog System Using Quantum Cryptography

Ambika N.

*Department of Computer Science and Applications, St. Francis College,
Bangalore, India*

Abstract

In the previous design, the centre layer of the organization has programming characterized by organizing hubs that precisely manage the organization. Before sending the information of end gadgets of the base layer to the cloud, registering disposes of all possibly terrible and uncertain items to lessen the heap of the cloud. The medical care subsystem partitions deal with observing patient information in a restricted region. A patient wearing brilliant gear can send various snippets of data about its area. The system uses QKD's BB84 encryption procedure. The suggestion uses a better encryption methodology, which also acts as an identification. The medical services framework in a restricted region can get the patent's record through that brilliant gadget. The fog hub screens and controls the well-being information of the patient. Assuming the patient requires help, this framework can give the patient information and plans with the patient's clinical history. Emergency clinics must verify the information by putting the patient's clinical id on the server. The fog hub has a clever secure health care control calculation. The mist hub plays out a few significant advances. The suggestion generates the private key using the device identification and Merkle tree algorithm. The identification is used as the parameter in the Merkle tree algorithm to derive private key. Using the Merkle tree algorithm, a new private key is generated every time. This is used in QKD's BB84 algorithm to generate encryption key. The methodology enhances security, as the receiver can check the authentication of the device and evaluate it. The suggestion enhances security in the system by 2.88% compared to previous work.

Keywords: Merkle tree, private key, QKD's BB84 encryption, fog computing, quantum computation, authentication

---

Email: ambika.nagaraj76@gmail.com

Romil Rawat, Rajesh Kumar Chakrawarti, Sanjaya Kumar Sarangi, Jaideep Patel, Vivek Bhardwaj, Anjali Rawat and Hitesh Rawat (eds.) Quantum Computing in Cybersecurity, (17–32) © 2023 Scrivener Publishing LLC

2.1   Introduction

Fog processing [1, 2] brings virtual presence into objects utilized consistently. The layer of engineering is otherwise called the brilliant article layer. It has furnished the network with a solid stage to outperform. The design decentralizes information, utilizes more server, and gathers and communicates it to neighbouring servers for quicker handling. The registering has broadened the cloud design by using its hubs on the edge of the organization. It has coordinated IoT [3] and cloud ideas [4] to give different attributes like low inertness, area mindfulness, support for geographic conveyance, end gadget portability, the limit of handling many hubs, etc. Quantum cryptography has started to supplant the conventional strategies for encryption for improved information security. Quantum cryptography [5] is hard to break since it works on the two states-1 and 0. In quantum cryptography, photons continue to turn. They continue to change their position, making the qubits dynamic.

A quantum PC [6, 7] depends on quantum superposition to play out numerous estimations lined up by making various conditions of spot designs that exist simultaneously. It can factor a 300-digit number in the same measure of time that a customary PC could duplicate the component together, delivering our ongoing encryption techniques old. The handling power of quantum PCs is an extraordinary accomplishment, arriving at speeds eight significant degrees quicker than exemplary PCs and a considerable number of times faster than present-day supercomputers. A central idea of quantum mechanics is superposition. The molecule can exist in various states at the same time. When examined, it implodes into a solitary state. Quantum PCs use qubits to address conditions, and these qubits exist in superposition. Parallelization, yet on a level far more noteworthy than existing supercomputers. With the qubit in a superposition between two states, a one-qubit quantum PC could successfully perform two tasks on the double. A two-qubit quantum PC could address four states without a moment's delay and subsequently perform four tasks immediately.

In the previous design [8], the centre layer of the organization has programming characterized by organizing hubs that precisely manage the organization. Before sending the information of end gadgets of the base layer to the cloud, registering disposes of all possibly terrible and uncertain items to lessen the heap of the cloud. The medical care subsystem partitions deal with observing patient information in a restricted region. A patient wearing brilliant gear can send various snippets of data about its area. The system uses QKD's BB84 encryption procedure. The suggestion uses a better encryption methodology, which also acts as an identification.

The medical services framework in a restricted region can get the patient's record through that brilliant gadget. The haze hub screens and controls the well-being information of the patient. Assuming the patient requires help, this framework can give the patient information and plans with the patient's clinical history. Emergency clinics must verify the information by putting the patient's clinical id on the server. The fog hub has a clever secure heath care control calculation. The mist hub plays out a few significant advances; for example, it encodes the information, pre-processes it, and changes it to factual data helpful to clinical staff before putting it away to cloud servers.

The suggestion generates the private key using the device identification and Merkle tree algorithm. The identification is used as the parameter in the Merkle tree algorithm to derive private key. Using the Merkle tree algorithm, new private key is generated every time. This is used in QKD's BB84 algorithm to generate encryption key. The methodology enhances security, as the receiver can check the authentication of the device and evaluate it. The suggestion enhances security in the system by 2.88% compared to previous work [8].

Organization of chapter
The work is divided into eight sections. The properties of quantum computing is explained in section two. Applications of the technology is detailed in section three. Background is briefed in segment four.

2.2   Properties of Quantum Computing

SUPERPOSITION
It is the capacity [10] of a quantum framework to at the same time be in numerous states. The go-to illustration of superposition is the flip of a coin, which reliably arrives as heads or tails — an extremely twofold idea. Nonetheless, when that coin is in mid-air, it is both heads and tails, and until it lands, heads and tails all the while. Before estimation, the electron exists in quantum superposition. The Figure 2.1 shows about the generalized properties of Quantum computation [9], whereas the Figure 2.2 shows about quantum random walk on a circular walk [17] and the Figure 2.3 displays about the Merkle tree structure [23].

A traditional Oracle machine [11] uses old-style wave superposition for data set search and information processing. It comprises an interferometer, a non-straight locator, and a universally applicable advanced PC. An interferometer is a multi-terminal gadget that has n inputs ports and only one result port. The information and the resultant signals are old-style sinusoidal waves. The non-straight indicator recognizes the time arrived

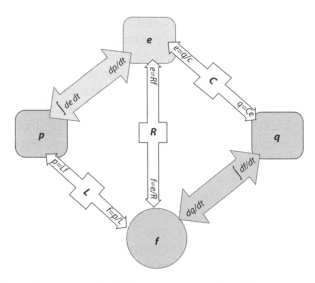

Figure 2.1 Generalized properties of Quantum computation [9].

at the midpoint of force and contrasts it and some reference values. The advanced PC controls the information stages, stores the aftereffects of esti-mations, and maintains the reference esteem. The trial information is on a hunt through the attractive data set utilizing turn wave superposition.

ENTANGLEMENT
As a quantum property, Trap [12] takes items and interfaces them by for-ever entrapping them together. While adding an extra qubit to a quantum

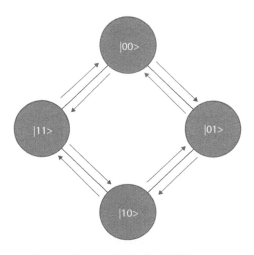

Figure 2.2 Quantum random walk on a circular walk [17].

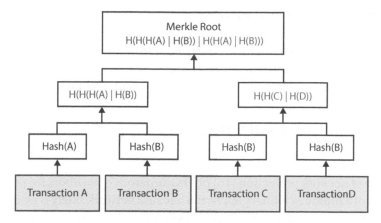

Figure 2.3 Merkle tree structure [23].

PC, a 50-cubit quantum machine can look at two to the force of 50 states simultaneously. The expansion in power, in addition to the ensnarement of qubits, permits quantum PCs to take care of issues effectively, finding an answer quicker, with numerous fewer computations.

Tracking down a traditional similarity to quantum trap has a twofold advantage. To start with, it gives a specific qualification of the simply quantum elements of quantum trap to distinct viewpoints that have a common ground with the traditional similarity and are not quantum. Second, this similarity permits one to incorporate and amalgamate inquiries from both quantum and traditional spaces and leads to a superior comprehension of both space particulars. Quantum instant transportation is a primary correspondence convention for data trading between somewhat isolated parties. It is practically equivalent to the correspondence convention with mystery, the one-time cushion. Utilizing snare property altogether reduces the security concerns emerging from single photon-based key quantum key dissemination schemes. Entanglement estimation [13] for both bipartite and three-sided circuits use quantum machines with the same qubit arrangement of 5-qubits feature credits to contrast in framework engineering that makes the machines act and answer distinctively to a parallel circuit execution. Ibm_vigo machine emerges with the base deviation figures, implying that its estimation values are relatively more hopeful.

INTERFERENCE
Obstruction [14] controls quantum states and intensifies the signs driving toward the correct response while dropping characters, prompting some unacceptable reactions.

COGNIZANCE/DECOHERENCE
Quantum PCs [15] are incredibly delicate to the commotion and natural impacts. Tragically, data remains parts quantum for such a long time. The quantity of tasks performed before the data is lost is restricted. Knowing how long quantum data will endure before it is out of cognizance is basic.

2.3   Applications of Quantum Computing

CYBER SECURITY
A study of network protection [16] offers numerous open doors for progress in light of a multidisciplinary approach because network safety is essentially about an ill-disposed commitment. People should guard machines that are gone after by different people utilizing devices. Thus, notwithstanding the primary conventional fields of software engineering, electrical designing, and arithmetic, viewpoints from other fields are required.

The review [17] utilizes a high-level encryption standard (AES) calcula-tion. It uses quantum registering to work on the exhibition of conventional record encryption and decoding calculations. AES calculation utilizing quantum entryways. Shift Row moves every piece of information to match the traditional AES encryption process. The record observing framework works continuously. The record encryption framework encodes the doc-ument when an entrance occasion to a copy is distinguished. The record re-establishes the composition, regardless of whether a paper undergoes harm because of a debacle or hacking. It additionally forestalls optional harm, where inner data is spilled through the encryption framework, regardless of whether the document.

ADVANCED MANUFACTURING
Changing assembling climate portrayed by fierce rivalry worldwide and fast changes in process innovation expects to make creation frameworks that are effectively upgradeable. It can provide innovations and capabilities that can be promptly coordinated.

The plan for-assembling standards [18] has become generally drilled in industry. Apparatuses have been created on the program's side for X's past discrete assembling and gathering processes. A cycle model comprises exer-cises that get data sources and produce outputs. Process models convey data across numerous spaces, and they serve various clients. The last option calls for different portrayals of process models, from an undeniable level outline to the nitty-gritty cycle or practical viewpoints. Clients generally get a graphical cycle portrayal with various foundations and interests. The last option calls for multiple definitions of interaction models, from an undeniable level outline to the definite cycle or valuable viewpoints. Clients usually get a graphical interaction portrayal with various foundations and interests. Process targets building models utilizing occasion information. It includes process revelation, model upgrade, and conformance checking. The cycle disclosure manages the extraction of process models from occasion logs. Model upgrade focuses on the progress of interaction models in light of the occasion log data. The conformance test checks whether the found cycle model meets the usual way of behaving. A few calculations develop procedural models that are challenging to decipher, particularly for unstructured applications.

BANKING

In the monetary administration industry [19], many computationally testing issues emerge in applications across resource the board, speculation banking, and retail and corporate banking. Quantum processing holds the commitment of upsetting how we settle such computationally testing issues.

Quantum Neural Network (QNN) [20] is pushed by Artificial Neural Network (ANN) methodology to amalgamate quantum mechanics. The pantomime of Rosenblatt's perceptron completes with QNN trial and error on quantum PCs. The research has two aspects of component mining. The Visa exchange's elements separate the trickster and lawful client's instalment conduct. Second, Capsule-Network is used to install profound elements. The confidential data or authorization get to individuals' primary data, bringing about money-related misfortune and broad fraud. The Supervised-Learning procedures used in extortion recognition are routinely utilized. It gives mental processing and quantum figuring based on dubious exchange location in the BCPS for the post-quantum period. When the client has a connection with the framework, a check system is used for its location. While breaking down within components of mental checking, the quantum brain network approach is used for dubious exchange recognition. The proposed policy utilizes mental registering and quantum processing based on reluctant element recognition in the BCPS. The boost's filtration chooses one critical upgrade and answers Sensory Stimulus. Distal Stimulus is the actual improvement to the faculties, for example, checking a Visa. Proximal Stimulus enrols through the receptor. Tangible transduction actuation goes about as a contribution to the brain tactile upgrades module. The information traversed receptors prompt activity potential. The observing stage and the arrangement stage aggregate to perform meta-discernment in the analogy stage. Perceptual Associative Memory plays out the classification and assessment of the SMI. The extractor is liable for the extraction and arrangement of the SM caught Input. A vault or solidified stockpiling for compressive data is a Knowledge-Base. It is a significant and top part of organizing, supervising, and taking care of the express information.

ARTIFICIAL INTELLIGENCE
Quantum processing has snatched the creative mind of PC researchers as one potential eventual fate of the discipline after we've arrived at the constraints of computerized double PCs. Artificial consciousness [21] is a multidisciplinary field that advantages from different regions, like software engineering, rationale, and theory. The utilization of quantum figuring for running AI calculations.

LOGISTICS OPTIMIZATION
Figuring and programming assume a crucial part in giving creative capacities [22]. A fundamental region is research in battery materials that further developed properties. Quantum figuring vows to push the limits of what is doable in science re-enactment. Industry 4.0 imagines mechanical design and plants empowered by advances like the IoT, cloud registering, expanded reality, three-dimensional printing, advanced mechanics, and automated reasoning. Utilizing these innovations empowers more limited advancement time, exceptionally adaptable items, more limited creation times, better caliber, and lower costs. The use of streamlining and AI techniques are fundamental to accomplishing these objectives.

2.4   Background

Merkle tree [23, 24] characterizes to be a finished double tree with a k piece esteem related to every hub to such an extent that every inside hub esteem is a one-way capability of the hub upsides of its youngsters. Merkle trees have tracked down many purposes in theoretical cryptographic developments, having detailed plans so the system can check a leaf worth for a freely realized root esteem and the confirmation information of the leaf. This confirmation information comprises one hub esteem at every level, where these hubs are the kin of the corners on the way associating the leaf to the root. The Merkle tree crossing issue is the errand of tracking down a proficient calculation to yield this validation information for progressive leaves. The paltry arrangement of putting away every hub esteem in memory requires a lot of room. Merkle proposed using complete double trees to deliver various one-timing schemes related to a solitary public key.

2.5   Literature Survey

In the given plan (Mangla, Rani, and Atiglah, 2022), the middle layer of the association has programming described by sorting out centre points that strictly deal with the association. Before sending the data of end contraptions of the base layer to the cloud, enlisting discards generally conceivably awful and questionable things to reduce the store of the cloud. The clinical consideration subsystem parcels manage to notice patient data in a limited district. A patient wearing splendid stuff can send different information about its area. The framework utilizes QKD's BB84 encryption system. The idea uses a superior encryption philosophy, which likewise becomes a recognizable proof.

The work [25] utilizes holomorphic encryption on IBM's cloud quantum PC stage. It shows a proof-of-guideline investigation of this convention on the IBM cloud quantum figuring stage. The recommendation is to utilize one state qubit as the two-vector. It uses the pattern to address frameworks of 2×2 straight conditions. when the ancilla qubit estimates in the state, The calculation prevails with likelihood. The eigenvalue register is the focal qubit of IBM's superconductor quantum chip. If we need to work CNOT entryways with the focal qubit as a control qubit, consolidate a CNOT and four Hadamard doors to accomplish this. The inquiry shifts build an R door.

Traditional frameworks [26] stay secure when presented to such quantum inquiries. It has two compilers that convert traditionally certain marks into marks safe in the quantum setting and apply these compilers to existing post-quantum signatures. The work builds patterns impervious to a quantum-picked message assault. The foe submits quantum superpositions of messages and consequently gets the relating superpositions of prints.

In this trial [27], the creators utilize single-photon qubit input states and a coordinated optics server to exhibit the quantum homomorphic convention tentatively. Quantum walk inputs are ordinarily n photons disseminated over m spatial modes, without any than one photon in every manner. The tradition conceals the conveyance of these photons by utilizing the photons' polarization to encode Alice's contribution to the quantum walk: exploiting the way that symmetrically spellbound photons don't meddle. Generally, unfilled modes populate with ancilla photons. The security ensures that Alice's plaintext input state is measured differently. The following distance between the additional info expresses that she can deliver with four photons is 0.81 for Hamming distances 1 and 3 and 0.85 for Hamming distance 2. The examination produces each of the four photons utilizing degenerate, noncollinear type-II SPDC. Two separate 2-mm thick β-barium borates (BBO) gems siphons by a Ti: Sapphire laser, which has been recurrence multiplied to 394.5 nm involving second-consonant age in a 5-mm thick lithium triborate crystal. All photons go through polarizers to make unadulterated polarization states and afterward through an HWP and QWP to empower the production of erratic polarization states. The QWP and HWP utilize precise mechanized pivot mounts with an accuracy of 0.02°.

The work [28] produces the Henon tumultuous grouping in a quantum PC, which has a similar size as the quantum picture to be encrypted. It creates the turbulent quantum succession utilizing the picture size. The calculation creates two numbers. The work uses D-ADDER, ADDER, and MULER for every emphasis. The decoding circuit is the very same as the encryption circuit. The circuit produces a similar Henon turbulent succession as utilized in encryption. The examination utilizes MATLAB with starting worth x0 = 0.2, y0 = 0.1, a = 1.4, b = 0.3. Histogram and connection of nearby pixels are utilized.

2.6   Proposed Work

ASSUMPTIONS

- The devices undergo registration with the cloud before commencing transmission.
- The server will be aware of the computing nodes attached to it (along with its identification).
- All the devices are capable of generating keys using Merkle tree algorithm.

In the previous design [8], the centre layer of the organization has programming characterized by organizing hubs that precisely manage the organization. Before sending the information of end gadgets of the base layer to the cloud, registering disposes of all possibly terrible and uncertain items to lessen the heap of the cloud. The medical care subsystem partitions deal with observing patient information in a restricted region. A patient wearing brilliant gear can send various snippets of data about its

Table 2.1 Algorithm used to generate private key.

Step 1: Input device identification (64 bits)
Step 2: Split the bits into two halves
Step 3: Perform circular right shift on first halve and circular left shift on Second halve
Step 4: Combine the two halve (First halve is put in odd position of resultant and second halve is put in even position of the resultant)
Step 5: XOR all the bits by 1's (Resultant bits by 64-1's)

area. The system uses QKD's BB84 encryption procedure. The suggestion uses a better encryption methodology, which also acts as an identification. The medical services framework in a restricted region can get the patient's record through that brilliant gadget. The haze hub screens and controls the well-being information of the patient. Assuming the patient requires help, this framework can give the patient information and plans with the patient's clinical history. Emergency clinics must verify the information by putting the patient's clinical id on the server. The fog hub has a clever secure health care control calculation. The mist hub plays out a few significant advances; for example, it encodes the information, pre-processes it, and changes it to factual data helpful to clinical staff before putting it away to cloud servers.

The suggestion generates the private key using the device identification and Merkle tree algorithm. The identification is used as the parameter in the Merkle tree algorithm to derive private key. Using the Merkle tree algorithm, a new private key is generated every time. This is used in QKD's BB84 algorithm to generate encryption key. The methodology enhances security, as the receiver can check the authentication of the device and evaluate it. Table 2.1 details the algorithm used to generate private key.

2.7   Analysis of the Study

In the previous design [8], the centre layer of the organization has programming characterized by organizing hubs that precisely manage the organization. Before sending the information of end gadgets of the base layer to the cloud, registering disposes of all possibly terrible and uncertain items to lessen the heap of the cloud. The medical care subsystem partitions deal with observing patient information in a restricted region. A patient wearing brilliant gear can send various snippets of data about its area. The system uses

QKD's BB84 encryption procedure. The suggestion uses a better encryption methodology, which also acts as an identification. The medical services framework in a restricted region can get the patent's record through that brilliant gadget. The haze hub screens and controls the well-being information of the patient. Assuming the patient requires help, this framework can give the patient information and plans with the patient's clinical history. Emergency clinics must verify the information by putting the patient's clinical id on the server. The fog hub has a clever secure health care control calculation. The mist hub plays out a few significant advances; for example, it encodes the information, pre-processes it, and changes it to factual data helpful to clinical staff before putting it away to cloud servers.

The suggestion generates the private key using the device identification and Merkle tree algorithm. The identification is used as the parameter in the Merkle tree algorithm to derive private key. Using the Merkle tree algorithm, a new private key is generated every time. This is used in QKD's BB84 algorithm to generate encryption key. The methodology enhances security, as the receiver can check the authentication of the device and evaluate it. Table 2.1 details the algorithm used to generate private key.

AUTHENTICATION

Authentication [29, 30] is an authorization procedure where the transmitting entity validates itself. In the contribution, the device authenticates itself along with generating the encryption key. The suggestion enhances security in the system by 2.88% compared to previous work [8]. Figure 2.4 depicts the same.

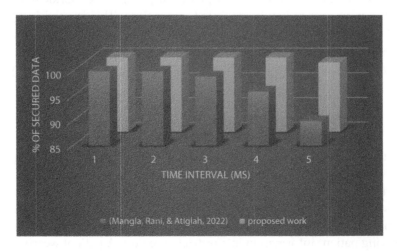

Figure 2.4 Data security in the system.

2.8 Conclusion

In the previous design, the centre layer of the organization has programming characterized by organizing hubs that precisely manage the organization. Before sending the information of end gadgets of the base layer to the cloud, registering disposes of all possibly terrible and uncertain items to lessen the heap of the cloud. The medical care subsystem partitions deal with observing patient information in a restricted region. A patient wearing brilliant gear can send various snippets of data about its area. The system uses QKD's BB84 encryption procedure. The suggestion uses a better encryption methodology, which also acts as an identification. The medical services framework in a restricted region can get the patent's record through that brilliant gadget. The haze hub screens and controls the well-being information of the patient. Assuming the patient requires help, this framework can give the patient information and plans with the patient's clinical history. Emergency clinics must verify the information by putting the patient's clinical id on the server. The fog hub has a clever secure health care control calculation. The mist hub plays out a few significant advances; for example, it encodes the information, pre-processes it, and changes it to factual data helpful to clinical staff before putting it away to cloud servers.

The suggestion generates the private key using the device identification and Merkle tree algorithm. The identification is used as the parameter in the Merkle tree algorithm to derive private key. Using the Merkle tree algorithm, a new private key is generated every time. This is used in QKD's BB84 algorithm to generate encryption key. The methodology enhances security, as the receiver can check the authentication of the device and evaluate it.

References

1. A. Nagaraj, *Introduction to Sensors in IoT and Cloud Computing Applications*, UAE: Bentham Science Publishers., 2021.
2. J. He, J. Wei, K. Chen, Z. Tang, Y. Zhou and Y. Zhang, "Multitier fog computing with large-scale iot data analytics for smart cities," *IEEE Internet of Things Journal*, vol. 5, no. 2, pp. 677-686, 2017.
3. N. Ambika, "Enhancing Security in IoT Instruments Using Artificial Intelligence.," in *IoT and Cloud Computing for Societal Good*, Cham, EAI/Springer *Innovations in Communication and Computing*, 2022, pp. 259-276.

4. N. Ambika, "Energy-Perceptive Authentication in Virtual Private Networks Using GPS Data," in *Security, privacy and trust in the IoT environment*, Cham, Springer, 2019, pp. 25-38.

5. N. Chaubey and B. Prajapati, *Quantum Cryptography and the Future of Cyber Security*, US: IGI Global, 2020.

6. C. P. Williams and S. H. Clearwater, *Explorations in quantum computing*, New York: Springer, 1998.

7. E. G. Rieffel and W. H. Polak, *Quantum computing: A gentle introduction*, Cambridge: MIT Press, 2011.

8. C. Mangla, S. Rani and H. K. Atiglah, "Secure Data Transmission Using Quantum Cryptography in Fog Computing.," *Wireless Communications and Mobile Computing*, 2022.

9. M. Svítek, "Emergent Intelligence in Generalized Pure Quantum Systems," *Computation*, vol. 10, p. 88, 2022.

10. L. K. Grover, "Synthesis of quantum superpositions by quantum computation.," *Physical Review Letters*, vol. 85, no. 6, p. 1334, 2000.

11. M. Balynsky, H. Chiang, D. Gutierrez, A. Kozhevnikov, Y. Filimonov and A. Khitun, "Quantum computing without quantum computers: Database search and data processing using classical wave superposition.," *Journal of Applied Physics*, vol. 130, no. 16, p. 164903, 2021.

12. E. Biham, G. Brassard, D. Kenigsberg and T. Mor, "Quantum computing without entanglement.," *Theoretical Computer Science*, vol. 320, no. 1, pp. 15-33, 2004.

13. M. Gupta and M. J. Nene, "Quantum computing: An entanglement measurement.," in *IEEE International Conference on Advent Trends in Multidisciplinary Research and Innovation (ICATMRI)*, Buldhana, India, 2020.

14. F. Chiarello, "Quantum computing with superconducting quantum interference devices: a possible strategy," *Physics Letters A*, vol. 277, no. 4-5, pp. 189-193, 2000.

15. M. Mohseni, J. S. Lundeen, R. K. J. and A. M. Steinberg, "Experimental application of decoherence-free subspaces in an optical quantum-computing algorithm.," *Physical Review Letters*, vol. 91, no. 18, p. 187903, 2003.

16. P. W. Singer and A. Friedman, *Cybersecurity: What everyone needs to know*, University of Oxford Press, 2014.

17. K.-K. Ko and E.-S. Jung, "Development of Cybersecurity Technology and Algorithm Based on Quantum Computing," *Appl. Sci.*, vol. 11, p. 9085, 2021.

18. A. Kusiak, "Service manufacturing: Basic concepts and technologies.," *Journal of Manufacturing Systems*, vol. 52, pp. 198-204, 2019.

19. S. Heffernan, *Modern banking*, Hoboken, New Jersey: John Wiley & Sons, 2005.

20. A. Shabbir, M. Shabir, A. R. Javed, C. Chakraborty and M. Rizwan, "Suspicious transaction detection in banking cyber–physical systems," *Computers & Electrical Engineering*, vol. 97, p. 107596, 2022.

21. V. Moret-Bonillo, "Can artificial intelligence benefit from quantum computing?" *Progress in Artificial Intelligence,* vol. 3, no. 2, pp. 89-105, 2015.
22. T. Humble, "Consumer applications of quantum computing: A promising approach for secure computation, trusted data storage, and efficient applications," *IEEE Consumer Electronics Magazine,* vol. 7, no. 6, pp. 8-14, 2018.
23. Y.-C. Chen, Y.-P. Chou and Y.-C. Chou, "An Image Authentication Scheme Using Merkle Tree Mechanisms," *Future Internet,* vol. 11, p. 149, 2019.
24. D. Koo, Y. Shin, J. Yun and J. Hur, "Improving Security and Reliability in Merkle Tree-Based Online Data Authentication with Leakage Resilience," *Applied Sciences,* vol. 8, p. 2532, 2018.
25. H. Huang, Y. Zhao, T. Li, F. Li, Y. Du, X. Fu, S. Zhang, X. Wang and W. Bao, "Homomorphic encryption experiments on IBM's cloud quantum computing platform," *Frontiers of Physics,* vol. 12, no. 1, pp. 1-6, 2017.
26. D. Boneh and M. Zhandry, "Secure signatures and chosen ciphertext security in a quantum computing world," in *Annual Cryptology Conference,* Santa Barbara, CA, USA, 2013.
27. J. Zeuner, I. Pitsios, S. H. Tan, A. N. Sharma, J. F. Fitzsimons, R. Osellame and P. Walther, "Experimental quantum homomorphic encryption," *npj Quantum Information,* vol. 7, no. 1, pp. 1-6, 2021.
28. N. Jiang, D. X. H. Hu, Z. Ji and W. Zhang, "Quantum image encryption based on Henon mapping," *International Journal of Theoretical Physics,* vol. 58, no. 3, pp. 979-991, 2019.
29. N. Ambika, "A Reliable Hybrid Blockchain-Based Authentication System for IoT Network," in *Revolutionary Applications of Blockchain-Enabled Privacy and Access Control,* US, IGI Global, 2021, pp. 219-233.
30. B. D. Deebak, F. Al-Turjman, M. Aloqaily and O. Alfandi, "An authentic-based privacy preservation protocol for smart e-healthcare systems in IoT.," *IEEE Access,* vol. 7, pp. 135632-135649, 2019.

3

DDoS Attack and Defense Mechanism in a Server

Pranav Bhatnagar*, Shreya Pai and Minhaj Khan

School of Engineering, Ajeenkya DY Patil University, Pune, Maharashtra, India

Abstract

The usage of the web has expanded rapidly over the last decade. Crores of people all around the planet are posting by means of online diversion, shopping from Shopping Applications and significantly more. Applications are getting revived essentially every day and new advances are emerging daily. As the progressions are getting revived, even the advanced attacks have extended all through the long run. Quantum enlisting has transformed into a rapidly creating development that contains the laws of quantum mechanics to decide issues that are unreasonably jumbled for our everyday use standard PCs. The impact of quantum computing on cybersecurity is overwhelming. It poses a significant threat to cybersecurity. One of the main threats it poses is of Distributed Denial of Service (DDoS). As of today, DDoS attacks have become one of the major problems in the domain of Cybersecurity as this cyberattack is currently in the top list of cybercrimes. A Denial of Service (DoS) assault is generally a general attack wherein a malevolent client centers around a PC or a substitute device distant to its concluded clients through rushing in on the contraption's standard working. A scattered DoS attack that comes from more than one resource is known as a DDoS attack, for example, a botnet DDoS attack on gaming servers. DDoS has also become a typical assault method employed in cyber warfare.

Keywords: DoS (Denial-of-Service), DDoS (Distributed Denial of Service), cyberattack, security, server, cybercrime, quantum computing, cyber warfare

Corresponding author: gmpranavbhatnagar@gmail.com

Romil Rawat, Rajesh Kumar Chakrawarti, Sanjaya Kumar Sarangi, Jaideep Patel, Vivek Bhardwaj, Anjali Rawat and Hitesh Rawat (eds.) Quantum Computing in Cybersecurity, (33–56) © 2023 Scrivener Publishing LLC

3.1   Introduction

A DDoS attack is a horrible technique for upsetting the traffic of an allotted server, organization or association with the help of assigned incorporation or its enveloping establishment at high traffic. DDoS attacks are practical with the usage of compromised PC systems as root of traffic attacks. The stuff used may consolidate PCs and other specific devices like IoT contraptions, gaming servers, etc.

DDoS addresses are a critical issue in recovery. An attacker can basically diminish the quality or absolutely break the victim's server affiliation. The aggressor first compromises the essential subject matter experts or host and a short time later uses these experts to ship off an attack on the target association. The central inspiration driving the DDoS attack is to make the loss so that other nodes can't utilize the resources. As a rule, the goal may be server, CPU and other association resources [1, 2]. This paper presents a DDoS exploring configuration by making an alternate DDoS attack and DDoS assurance parts.

HOW DOES A DDoS ATTACK WORK?
DDoS assaults are performed by a blend of machines, partners PCs and various devices (like IoT contraptions) to malware, which can be controlled by them. These specific contraptions are called bots (or Zombies) [8, 9], and a social gathering of bots [25] is known as a botnet [3]. The Figure 3.1 shows about the working diagram of DDoS attack, whereas the Figure 3.2 highlights remote DDoS attack classification, and Figure 3.3 displays about the working of DDoS attack and the Figure 3.4 shows about the cloud intrusion detection system for detecting the attacks [28], moreover

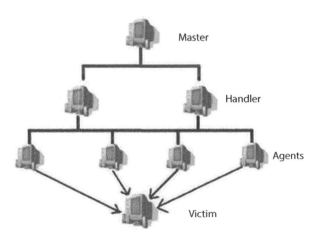

Figure 3.1 Working diagram of DDoS attack.

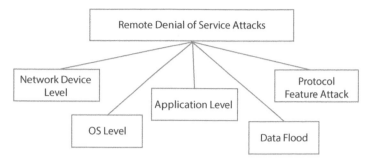

Figure 3.2 Remote DDoS attack classification.

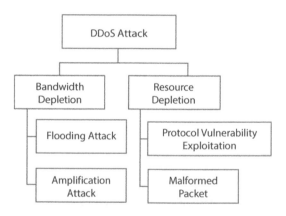

Figure 3.3 Working of DDoS attack.

the Figure 3.5 displays the architecture of DDoS attack, and finally the Figure 3.6 represents classifications of DDoS attacks.

Now that the game plan of botnet has been finished, the attacker can change and set the attack by sending remote messages to each bot [4]. While the loss' server or organize can be worked with by using single botnet moreover, every individual bot sends requests to the defending server's IP address, that can be achieved by transforming it into a disturbance using the server or network, that may have chances of ending up in a deadlock because of other nodes which are unable to access the recourses as they are being overwhelmed by floods of packets [5]. Since each bot is seen as a power contraption that uses the internet, what separates the traffic which is assigned from run of the mill traffic yet this can now and again be inconvenient [6, 7].

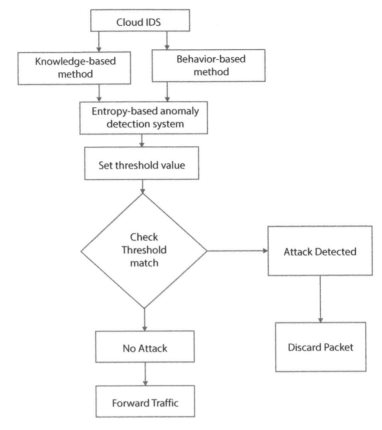

Figure 3.4 Cloud intrusion detection system for detecting the attacks [28].

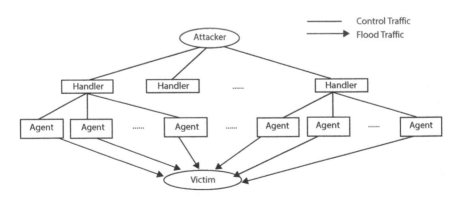

Figure 3.5 Architecture of DDoS attack.

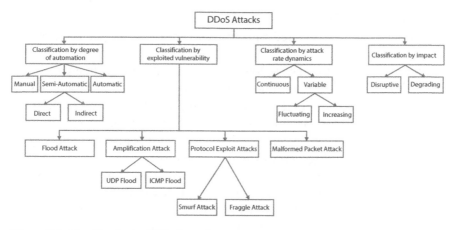

Figure 3.6 Classifications of DDoS attacks.

QUANTUM COMPUTING

The idea that the quantum PCs are more basic than out-of-date PCs began in Richard Feynman's insight. In the as of late made outdated PCs, it seems to call for pivotal speculation to duplicate various particles in quantum structures. The idea is that the quantum PCs can copy quantum certified cycles distinctly speedier than out-of-date PCs that have strikingly got weighted absurdly. The more important quantum estimations have been made for re-initiating both Bosonic and Fermionic structures and unequivocally; the reenactment of huge reactions past the imperatives of current conventional supercomputers requires a couple different Q-bits. The quantum estimation runs on the quantum circuit model of appraisal of quantum figuring. These computations have esteemed loads of advantages, for instance, by and large breaking point, truly legit gigantic number size and better blending, than the standard formative and groundbreaking evaluations. Appropriately, they can successfully be applied to the smoothing out of predictable pieces of multi-top. A dated estimation plays out each step on standard PC. Every one of the standard computations moreover can perform on a quantum PC. All issues which can be picked in a standard PC can be managed on a quantum PC. The quantum estimation can deal with and manage a few issues speedier than dated evaluations [31].

3.2 DoS Attack

In Denial-of-Service (DoS), numerous collective packets are sent from the aggressor's device or node to a solitary defendant's machine.

A. DoS ATTACK PLAN

DoS assaults can be isolated into five classifications as per level of the objective convention.

Network contraption layer DoS attacks integrate attacks that can occur by exploiting an item bug or shortcoming or by trying to disable hardware resources on an association device. A representation of an association device exploit is a support flood botch covertly key affirmation circle. This exploit could make some Cisco 7xx [10] switches do crash by telnetting to the switch and entering a very extended secret word.

The OS-level DoS attack relies heavily on how the functioning system uses shows. A depiction of a DoS attack in this social occasion is a Ping of Death attack [11]. In this attack, an ICMP resonation request with a flat out data size more unmistakable than the standard IP size is moved off the coordinated goal. These attacks continually crash the respondent's server.

An application-based assault endeavors to fix a machine or association for fizzle by remembering express check for network applications running on the objective have or by utilizing those applications to uninstall their casualty's assets. It is besides conceivable that the assailant might have gotten high algorithmic eccentrics habitats and utilized them to use each of the assets open on the remote host. One framework of an application-based assault is a finger bomb [12]. A malignant client can lay out the extraordinary finger association framework be utilized endlessly for working with, which could take out close by assets.

In a data flood attack, the aggressor attempts to exploit the bandwidth found on the association, host or device at a particularly high rate, by sending a ton of data so it is constrained to pattern of monstrous data size. An attacker can endeavor to use networks which are available for information move limit by pursuing a target with packets containing a source address. For example, flood ping. Fundamental floods as often as possible occur as DDoS attacks, which are analyzed later.

A show feature-based DoS attack uses a couple of typical show features. For example, a couple of attacks exploit the way that the source IP address can be compromised. A couple of kinds of DoS attacks rely upon DNS, huge quantities of which incorporate various other interferences into the DNS storage facility related word servers. An attacker who guarantees the nameservers can make the loss' nameservers store a few unsuitable records by getting some data about the assailant's site that they own. The loss' nameserver is then redirected to the compromised server and stores the response [13].

3.3   DDoS Attack

In Distributed Denial-of-Service (DDoS), various packages are sent off the objective contraption from various aggressor's machine.

A. DDoS ATTACK DEFINITION

DDoS attacks use various PCs to ship off a combined DoS attack against like one target machine. Using client-server advancement, an attacker could inadvertently reproduce DoS capacities generally with various feasible PC systems that go about as "attacks". DDoS attacks are oftentimes inside the loss' association to evade a convincing response from the individual being referred to, and outside the attacker's association to keep away from shortcoming it is continued backward to expect the attack that the victim or target have in common.

In "A Study on DDoS Attacks, Danger and Its Prevention," from *IJRAR*, May 2019, Volume 6, Issue 2, we learn techniques for DDoS Defense Mechanisms such as Monitoring, Ingress/Egress Filtering, Scrubbing and Black Holing [29]. Some of the proposed solutions and methodology points in this research paper are:

- Giving username and password to every single user who has the access to the router
- Allowing only SSH-based connections
- Making sure that there is RPF, i.e., ingress and egress filtering on the interface of every static connection

In "Botnet-based Distributed Denial of Service (DDoS) Attacks on Web Servers: Classification and Art" in *International Journal of Computer Applications* (0975 – 8887), Volume 49, No.7, July 2012, we learn about botnet-based DDoS attacks and how botnet-based DDoS attacks are the most common type of botnet attacks in a web server [30].

The authors in "Analysis and Detection of DoS Attacks in Cloud Computing by Using QSE Algorithm" from *2014 IEEE International Conference on High Performance Computing and Communications (HPCC)* have proposed a solution based on quantum computing. They used Quantum-Inspired Evolutionary (QEA) algorithm for detecting DoS Attacks in Cloud Computing [31].

Various types of combination of DDoS attacks are emerging in the PC world. Critical transformations consolidate Bandwidth-based attacks and application. The two models use all move speed and exploited association resources. With the assessment done, logical order has been revealed.

Dependent upon the bet on undertakings can similarly be requested into different sorts [1].

BANDWIDTH TERMINATION ATTACK
This sort of attack consumes the loss' exchange speed or target structure by filling in unwanted busy time gridlock to hold official traffic back from showing up at the victim's association. Mechanical assemblies like Trinoo are mostly used to complete these attacks.

THE FLOOD ATTACK

- This attack is a huge pile of data groups which is passed by an assailant traffic on to the loss with the help of zombies deterring the relationship with flood of data package along extremely high-speed packages and make an IP traffic. The program enters full affiliation data move limit and rapidly diminishes disturbing traffic permitted to get to the association. This is stayed aware of by the UDP (User Datagram) and ICMP (Internet Control Message Protocol) packs. A UDP flood starts with the going with advances. The aggressor sends numerous UDP groups, either any uncertain method or by zombies, to a port of any system.
- Right after getting the packets, the framework of the victim checks the port for forthcoming applications on the port.
- In some cases, where the application doesn't exist, it gives a MP pack message, saying, "The node is difficult to reach".
- The loss response package is delivered through the victim's area but the zombie's.

Subsequently, available information move limit is confined to genuine clients. This impacts the victim's contact with the nearest system. Various varieties of these attacks consolidate quarantine attacks, DNS flood attacks, VoIP flood attacks, and media data attacks. An ICMP flood incorporates the going with progresses:

- The attacker sends a tremendous number of ICMP ECHO REPLYs, for instance zombies. Such packets require a response message from the individual being referred to.
- Victim replies to recovered groups.

- Network shut in view of sales response traffic. The victim's server/node is stacked with bandwidth and quickly shuts down without serving real clients. Shares, DNS floods, and ping floods are various kinds of ICMP flood attacks.

MAXIMUM ATTACK

An aggressor sends various get-togethers to a transmission IP address. Systems in the transmission address range then, send obligation to setback structures, causing unsafe traffic. This kind of attack exploits the streaming area feature found in various online contraptions like switches. This kind of DDoS attack can be begun by a fast assailant or a zombie. Obvious attacks of this sort are Smurf and Fraggle attacks. A smurf attack is gathered by the going with propels:

- An assailant sends a collection of packets to a middle point enrolled inside an affiliation that supports broadcast voice. The return address in this pack is either a trick or grasped by the setback's district.
- The ICMP ECHO RESPONSE groups is sent by the connection enhancer to all applications inside the IP address range. This social occasion expects that the recipient replies with an ICMP ECHO REPLY.
- The ICMP ECHO REPLY give from every one of the centers in the reach shows up at the individual being implied.

Fraggle Attack is intriguing as indicated by Smurf assaults where UDP reverberation packs are shipped off ports that help shot creation. It has the going with advances:

- The aggressor sends packets of UDP to the resonation port that maintains ammunition creation. The return address of these packages is either fake or pillaged by the victim's area through an initial that maintains the advancement of slugs therefore outlining a wearisome circle.
- This arranges the port that maintains the production of characters for all activities got to by imparted address.
- These frameworks regularly arrive at the casualty's projectile opening.
- This cycle is rehashing in light of the fact that it is utilizing UDP reverberation packets.

This attack is more horrendous than the Smurf's. The fundamental exception is the demo attack, which integrates a lot of pointers to complete a specific task. Mappings can be concentrated hosts or devices used to ship off sound improvement attacks. An undeniable component of the show is the reliable response to the packets we get. In this way, attackers use these estimations for attacks that require a reaction. Depending on their current circumstance, the IP address is forgotten which is returned according to its structure.

RESOURCE DEPLETION ATTACKS

Dismissal of Service DDoS attacks expect to dispose of defendant's system resources so valid clients can't get to help [1]. Such resource destruction attacks are:

- Attack of Protocol Exploitation: The motive of this attack is the exploitation of the other attacker's resources using centered around, explicit show capacities. A TCP SYN attack is an authentic delineation of this sort. Various occasions of show attacks integrate PUSH+ACK attacks, approval server attacks, and CGI application attacks.
- Bad Packet Attacks: The term horrible pack proposes a get-together wrapped by malignant information or data. The attacker sends these packs to the setback to cause an effect. This can be acted in two propensities.
- Attack of Domain Address: A twisted group wrapped with a comparative source and objective IP address, making strife to the victim's functioning structure. Appropriately, it speeds up and pounds the individual being referred to.
- IP Packet Option: Every IP parcel contains chosen fields to deal with extra data. This assault utilizes these areas to make twisted packets. Thus, the casualty invests more energy handling the packets. This assault is particularly risky when more than one zombie is going after.

B. DEFENCE MECHANISMS

Different countermeasures had been embraced by the arising for facilitating against the DDoS assaults. Most possible results that part DDoS assaults are impacted by a gatecrasher attempting to make an unapproved access in the setback's structure or association.

PREVENTION TECHNIQUES

Some of the top most precautionary and preventive measures are listed below:

- Filtering of Ingress - this collaboration stops the approaching bundles with a not veritable source address. Switches are utilized thus. This framework upsets the DDoS assault accomplished by IP address parodying.
- Filtering of Egress - In this strategy, an outbound channel is utilized. This system permits the bundles having huge IP address in still hanging out there to leave the association.
- Filtering of Route-Based Distributed Packet - The channel uses the data of steering to channel the IP address parodied parcels and thwarts the attack. Following back the IP is also used. Nevertheless, it requires overall information about the organization geography.
- Services of Secure Overlay - Plan of SOS with conveyed feature that shields the loss' association or a particular system. It guesses that an approaching bundle ought to be critical expecting it is from the legitimate servers. Reproduced sections are used for asserting the genuine client to the entry being permitted to the overlay association.

The other expectation systems consolidate disabling unused organizations, utilization of patches for security, changing of IP address, crippling/not enabling transmissions of IP, use of weight changing and honeypots. The balance techniques for interference don't thoroughly get out the wagered free from DDoS attacks anyway they give a base or widened security [1].

DETECTION TECHNIQUES FOR DDoS
Anomaly Detection
This DDoS ID system recognizes the attacks by seeing the lead oddities in execution of the association or structure. This ought to be conceivable by differentiating characteristics which are correct now present and as of late perceived normal system's display. Deceiving up-sides are recognized in the system direct. Barely any Anomaly area systems studies consolidate:

The NOMAD - an adaptable association seeing framework that sees the association inconsistencies by isolating the IP bundle header data.
Packet sampling and filtering technique with congestion - A quantifiable examination had been delivered utilizing the subset of dropped packs and when an Anomaly is recognized a sign is passed to the change to channel the harmful bundles. A quantifiable evaluation had been made using the

Table 3.1 Traceback methods of DDoS attack.

Method	Description
ICMP traceback	The system sorts out some way to deal with the sending low probability packs to all of the switch and at the same time similarly sends an ICMP traceback message to objective. With major no of ICMP messages which used in ID of aggressors, faces issues like additional traffic; moreover, the endorsement of these bundles is problematic and bothersome all the while; besides that the manner in which revelation above of information from course map.
Trace the IP back	The assailant's way is followed to track down the beginning of assault. The wellspring of the assailant is tracked down by following and following its way in this strategy. Now and again this might become troublesome if the TCP/IP convention source responsibility is crippled and web is stateless.
Traceback - Testing of Link	The approaching affiliations are endeavoured in this system and likelihood of it being an assault is endeavoured. This is performed by flooding huge information traffic and testing whether if in any event accomplishes any exacerbation in network.
Probabilistic packet marking	The drawbacks of link-testing traceback are overcome in this technique as it does not need knowledge of the previous topology of network, massive traffic, etc.

subset of dropped groups and when an Anomaly is seen a sign is passed to the change to channel the packages which are harmful or show up so.

D-WARD - Sees the DDoS assault at the chief misfortune. It keeps the assault away from spreading to the neighbors of setback. It is set up at the edge change to perceive the approaching and dynamic association traffic.

MULTOPS26 - It is an arranged data structure having the inspiration driving distinguishing proof of DDoS attacks. It deals with the supposition that, expecting the IP region of the association participating in a DDoS assault is possible, then checks are taken to deter/stop just these specific regions. It keeps tracks of recognizing either seeking after aggressor's structure or systems that are enduring through a flood by working in assault coordinated mode or misfortune organized modes freely. A staggered tree stays mindful of the package rate encounters at various levels. Anyway, it requires reconfiguration of switch and plans of novel memory the leaders [1].

i. Detecting the misusage

Staying aware of the striking imprints or instances of exploits in the informational collections this is how the attacks are recognized. At the point when any of these models are been perceived, the DDoS attacks are represented.

RESPONSIVE DETECTION

Right when a DDoS attack is perceived, the underlying move toward take is the attacker should be impeded and the assailant's system machine should be followed out for finding the assailant's authentic character. This methodology generally requires two-three days; it ought to either be conceivable subsequently or ought to be conceivable actually by using ACL.

There are sure techniques which can be utilized for following out and tracking down the character of the aggressor as displayed in Table 3.1. There are heaps of strategies that can be utilized to stop/shield DDoS assaults; unfortunately, however, not every one of them can be identified and forestalled. The most that should be possible is diminishing the effect/hit of the assault [1].

C. CONFIGURING DDoS EXECUTION

Not the least bit like different sorts of cyberattacks, DDoS attacks don't attempt to break your security line. Rather, a DDoS assault means to make your site and servers far off to certifiable clients. DDoS can in this way be utilized as an interference for other noxious exercises and to chop down security machines, entering the objective's security line.

A convincing circumnavigated refusal of association assault is an essentially recognizable occasion influencing a whole web-based client base. This makes it an outstanding weapon of decision for hacktivists, mechanized hoodlums, reprobates and some other individuals hoping to arrive at a huge goal or have an impact to a particular clarification.

While anticipating and driving a DDoS attack, the going with exercises occur:

Agent Selection: The assailant picks an expert to do the attack. These machines ought to be at some sort of risk that an aggressor could use to gain admittance. You need to have a ton of resources for performing solid attacks. From the get go, the strategy was performed truly, but soon it was motorized using a looking at instrument.

Compromise: Attackers exploit security openings and shortcomings in the expert hardware and execute the attack code. You also need to protect your code from being found and disabled. Plan instruments like the Ramen worm [14] and Code Red [15] quickly fell into this arrangement. Owners and clients of expert systems are ordinarily uninformed that their structures will be compromised and connected with a DDoS attack. While investigating a DDoS assault, every master program utilizes just two or three assets (both memory and data transmission), so PC clients have unimportant execution changes.

Communications: Aggressors contact different supervisors to sort out which expert is running, when an attack is organized, or when an expert is progressing. Dependent upon how the aggressor prepares the association for a DDoS attack, the expert may be composed to talk with something like one server. Correspondence among assailant and host and among host and master can be through TCP, UDP, or ICMP contracts.

Attacks: Presently, assailant orders them to ship off an attack. Victim, attack time, and attack express characteristics like sort, length, TTL, port number.

Bandwidth: We acknowledge that information transmission is an indispensable piece of preparing for a DDoS attack. In case you want more information move limit, then, your attack on the goal machine could crash and burn.

Concerning DDoS Attacks, there are different sorts of attacks, each attack type having its own particular way of working. Since each attack type has its own function, there are solutions available against each attack type. In Table 3.2, we have mentioned the name of the DDoS attack, its function and also solution to defend from the attack.

D. EXAMPLES OF DDoS

Various types of DDoS assaults target differentiating bits of an affiliation alliance. To comprehend how different DDoS assaults work, it is indispensable to know how an affiliation alliance is made.

The association considering the internet is produced using various parts or "layers". Like plan a house up and down, each layer in the model has a substitute clarification. The OSI model, displayed under, is a resolved structure used to portray network in 7 evident layers.

While in every way that really matters, all DDoS assaults consolidate overpowering an objective gadget or relationship with traffic, assaults can

Table 3.2 DDoS attacks, their effects and solutions [28].

Kind of attack	Function of the attack	Solution against the attack
ICMP (Ping) Flood	ICMP Packets are used in this bandwidth attack.	ScreenOS, giving a Screening choice which sets an edge that once surpassed conjures the ICMP flood assaults.
Amplification attack	A request is sent from the aggressor which generates a huge response.	Utilization of operating systems having high performance, Load balancer, putting a limit to the connection and connection rate.
HTTP GET Flood	Aggressors send a massive flood of collective requests to the server and consume its resources.	Imperva's provides a web application protection which identifies malformed bot traffic, putting a full stop to all HTTP floods and attacks on the application layer.
Smurf's Attack	ICMP reverberation demand packets are utilized by aggressors to produce DDOS assaults.	Packet filtering, setting proper configuration of every one of the hosts and switches not to answer ICMP demands and not to advance the packets straightforwardly to addresses which is communicated.
Bandwidth Attack	Resources of targets are consumed.	Multops, tree of hubs, recognizes the disproportional collective packets proceeding towards the victim from the aggressor.
Ping of Death	Multiple malicious or malformed pings are sent to computer through an aggressor node.	Additional checks for every approaching IP packet telling whether it is invalid or substantial or not.

(Continued)

Table 3.2 DDoS attacks, their effects and solutions [28]. (*Continued*)

Kind of attack	Function of the attack	Solution against the attack
DNS Flood	An attack which targets both of the infrastructure and DNS application.	Utilization of Radware solutions for allowing continuous DNS service even under the aggressor's attack and mitigating the DNS based attack.
Reflector's Attack	Assault traffic from assailant to the objective is bobbed by the outsiders to get stirred things up around town.	Using Cloudflare mitigation systems as a mitigation as it helps in identifying, tracking and filtering the attack.

be confined into three game plans. An aggressor could utilize somewhere near one different assault vectors, or cycle assault vectors considering counter checks taken by the objective.

ATTACK OF APPLICATION LAYER
Goal of the Attack
On occasion, suggested as a layer 7 DDoS assault (with respect to the seventh layer of the OSI model), the objective of these assaults is to deplete the objective's assets for make a repudiation of organization. The assaults base on the layer where pages are made on the server and conveyed considering HTTP demands. A solitary HTTP demand is computationally unassuming to execute on the client side, yet it will overall be costly for the objective server to answer, as the server routinely stacks various records and runs enlightening file requests to make a site.

Layer 7 attacks are trying to safeguard against, since isolating malevolent traffic from legitimate traffic can be hard.

Example of Attack Application Layer: The HTTP Flood
This assault is like crushing the restore button in a web program again and again on a considerable number of PCs immediately—huge measures of HTTP demands flood the server, accomplishing renouncing of organization. This kind of assault goes from easy to complex.

More straightforward executions could get to one URL with a near degree of seeking after IP regions, referrers and client-subject matter experts.

Complex designs could utilize vast addresses seeking after IP regions, and target irregular URLs utilizing conflicting referrers and client-trained professionals.

ATTACKS OF PROTOCOLS
Goal of the Attack
Show assaults, for the most part called a state-depletion assaults, cause a help disrupting impact by over-consuming server assets as well as the assets of affiliation gear with cherishing firewalls and weight balancers. Show assaults use lacks in layer 3 and layer 4 of the show stack to convey the objective deterred.

Protocol Attack Example: SYN Flood
A SYN Flood resembles a specialist in a hold room getting demands from the front of the store. The laborer gets a mentioning, keeps on getting the groups, and hangs on for affirmation going before bringing the packages out front. The specialist then gets essentially more packages demand without demand until they can convey no more bundles, become overpowered, and demands begin going unanswered.

This assault takes advantage of the TCP handshake—the social occasion of trades by which two PCs start an affiliation alliance—by sending an objective countless TCP "Beginning Connection Request" SYN pack with slandered source IP addresses.

The objective machine answers every alliance mentioning and thusly hangs on for the last advancement in the handshake, which never happens, devastating the objective's assets in the meantime.

VOLUMETRIC ATTACKS
Goal of the Attack
This class of assaults endeavors to make clog by consuming all suitable data transmission between the objective and the bigger internet. A ton of data is delivered off a goal by using a sort of upgrade or another technique for making tremendous traffic, for instance, requests from a botnet.

Volumetric/Amplification Attack Example: DNS Amplification
A DNS intensification resembles if somebody somehow happened to refer to a café and says, "I'll have one of everything, kindly get back to me and rehash my entire request," where the callback number really has a place with the person in question. With very little exertion, a long reaction is produced and shipped off to the person in question.

By making a sales to an open DNS server with a counterfeit IP address (the IP address of the individual being referred to), the objective IP address then, at that point, gets a response from the server.

E. CASES OF DDoS ATTACKS

THE AWS DDoS ATTACK IN 2020

This was the most consistent DDoS assault ever and it focused in on an unidentified AWS client utilizing a system called Connectionless Lightweight Directory Access Protocol (CLDAP) reflection. This procedure depends upon weak outsider CLDAP servers and increases how much information conveyed off the loss' IP address by 56 to different times. The assault occurred for three days and beat at an astounding 2.3 terabytes each second.

Why the AWS Attack Matters

While the impedance accomplished by the AWS DDoS Attack was definitely less cut off than it might have been, the sheer size of the assault and the ramifications for AWS working with clients possibly losing pay and getting through brand injured are tremendous.

THE CLOUDFLARE DDoS ATTACK IN 2014

In 2014, CloudFlare, a web-based security provider and content improvement connection, was banged by a DDoS attack outlined at around 400 gigabits each second of traffic. The assault, created at a solitary CloudFlare client and relegated on servers in Europe, was delivered off remembering a weakness for the Network Time Protocol (NTP) show, which is utilized to guarantee PC tickers are precise. No matter that the assault was centered around only one of CloudFlare's clients, it was significant solid areas for so endlessly out debased CloudFlare's own affiliation.

Why Does the CloudFlare Attack Matter?

This assault approaches a methodology where aggressors utilize disparaged source areas to send counterfeit NTP server reactions to the assault target's servers. This sort of assault is known as a "reflection assault," since the aggressor can "skip" counterfeit mentioning off of the NTP server, while concealing their own region. Because of a lack in the NTP show, the overhaul a piece of the assault can genuinely depend upon various times, making NTP servers a remarkably solid DDoS device. Not long after the assault, the U.S. PC Emergency Readiness bundle sorted out NTP increment assaults are "particularly hard to hinder", considering the way that "reactions are true information coming from veritable waiters".

DDoS ATTACK IN 2012 OF THE SIX BANKS

On March 12, 2012, six U.S. banks were hit by a flood of DDoS assaults: Bank of America, JPMorgan Chase, U.S. Bank, Citigroup, Wells Fargo, and PNC Bank. The assaults were done by many got servers from a botnet called Brobot with each assault making in excess of 60 gigabits of DDoS assault traffic each second.

By then, these attacks were marvelous in their consistency. Instead of endeavoring to execute one attack and thus pulling out, the accountable social occasions shot their targets with a colossal number of attack methodology to consider one that worked. In this manner, whether a bank was furnished to deal with a couple of sorts of DDoS attacks, they were vulnerable to various kinds of attack.

Why the Six Banks Attack Matters

The most significant piece of the bank assaults in 2012 was that the assaults were, presumably, done by the Izz progression Din al-Qassam Brigades, the essential wing of the Palestinian Hamas connection. Likewise, the assaults tremendously influenced the impacted banks to the degree that compensation, assist costs, client with caring issues, and the banks' checking and picture.

3.4   DDoS Mitigation

Easing suggests diminishing the mischief on the loss machine whatever amount as could sensibly be anticipated. In DDoS complete expectation of attack is ridiculous. It should be reduced to some degree.

A. DDoS MITIGATION TECHNIQUES

Evaluation concerning strength of interference recognizes that it is inconceivable to absolutely stop or hinder the DDoS attack and zeros in more on cutting down the impact of the attack whatever amount as could be anticipated and enhancing the idea of organization. Interference opposition can be detached in two classes: variation to non-basic disappointment and nature of organization (QoS).

FAULT TOLERANCE

A huge level assessment office whose plans are worked inside the fundamental establishment and used at three levels: stuff, programming and structure [18]. The chance of fortitude is that by replicating the connection benefits and separating its passageways, the connection can continue to offer such help when traffic frustrates a single center point of interaction.

QUALITY OF SERVICE (QOS)

QoS portrays network ability to convey clear results for unequivocal sorts of purposes or traffic. Different QoS block structures and QoS liberal systems have been made to diminish DDoS attacks.

Among the QoS frameworks that move beyond shaped impedance (IntServ) and Multi-Service (DiffServ) have emerged as key plans [19]. IntServ uses the Resource Reservation Protocol (RSVP) to orchestrate resource task through traffic stream. DiffServ is a construction restricted in response to popular demand. DiffServ [20, 21] uses an assistance byte (TOS) switch for IP areas and taking into account the TOS of each and every social event.

QUEUING TECHNIQUES

Lining technique are other than generally used to fight DDoS attacks. There are various classes in development. An old and generally used coating technique is Class-based queuing (CBQ) [22].

RESOURCE PRICING

This is one more technique proposed by Mankins *et al.* to diminish DDoS assaults. Mankins *et al.* [23] noted that DDoS assaults are sensible on the grounds that costs fall tenaciously on the server, and during an assault, assault traffic is on an incredibly central level ambiguous from veritable traffic. They propose the advancement of a dispersed section and part framework that puts variable rates on both the association, server, and data assets for decline explicit costs of completing assistance requests with respect to charges and besides mathematical weights.

By using different expenses and purchasing limits, properties can give a unit of organization quality and besides, select the most effective way of acting of clients and mistreat confining way of behaving. The key is to disconnect the essential technique from the ideal client and repel the clients for causing server load. The eventual outcome of this procedure is that an aggressor can grow the amount of valid clients by flooding the system with fake applications at an insignificant cost.

PUSHBACK ARCHITECTURE

Pushback planning is a promising technique for lessening speed when the thought is to make drivers aware of progress or stop horrendous (full) traffic. In Aggregate-based Congestion Control (ACC) [17], a hard and fast is portrayed as a little assortment of materials that contains materials [24]. Thus, the [17] Pushback daemon utilizes a distinctive confirmation calculation to check for indications of an assault. The portion of this system can be broadened and in addition no upstream leader is required. Obviously, there is an enormous and confined need for a rate limiter and a push daemon that can review bunches sliding the result line.

PROXY OF REVERSE WEB

A go-between server is a sort of host server that benefits assets to help clients from something like one server. These assets are then gotten back to the client, either on the real server or on the authentic server. The changed master gets demands from the internet and moves them to servers inside the interior affiliation. The candidate is collaborating with the specialist and may not know about the internal affiliation. A reversible projection can conceal the presence and nature of the essential server [16].

There are a couple of components of payoff applications that can protect you from typical web attacks. Without an opposite trained professional, it will in general be difficult to kill malware or begin a scale back. A retroactive go-between server can stack balance moving toward requesting across different servers, each running its own application space. Expecting that it obtains a mediator from an abutting web server, the backslide go-between could have to change the URL for each oncoming requesting to match its internal region of the referenced resource. Take out experts can decrease the pile on the root server by putting away unique and static substance, called web-speed increment [26].

FIREWALL

Firewall was the essential contraption used to chop down untrusted networks. Ordinarily, Denial of Service's chief attack was its thorough protection from these devices.

An ordinary firewall (package channel, person, or stateful firewall) really takes a gander at the group header to check whether there are concludes that license traffic beginning with one source then onto the following. Stop tries to send data to unapproved sources or bound regions. The firewall can recognize whether or not a gathering was set up peers (client and server) are endeavoring to spread out a conversation (affiliation).

This information is taken care of in the gathering tables, and to screen the correspondence, even the inadequate ones should be kept in the gathering table, as it is fundamental for the firewall to choose if it is significant or not to follow group. In any case, the possibility of the action risks the firewall [27].

The amount of relationship with the gathering table is confined, and when the end is shown up at the firewall is in a position where it can take any additional affiliations. Furthermore, as it requires full audit of the gathering, the fire security contraption can't work there of psyche of an uneven line where simply drawing nearer or active traffic is evident.

For all intents and purposes generally progressed induction and affirmation structures (IPSs) require a particular level of DDoS security. Some Unified Threat Management (UTM) devices or state of the art firewalls (NGFWs) give DDoS fight benefits and can reduce various DDoS attacks.

Having a solitary firewall gadget, IPS, and DDoS is not difficult to deal with and extremely convoluted to utilize; however, a solitary across the board security gadget can be handily overpowered by volumetric DDoS assaults. Other than that, the genuinely necessary security assurance expected to distinguish and get the 7-layer identification frameworks won't typically be done on a firewall or IPS gadget, particularly on the off chance that it doesn't have a devoted processor or ASIC. One more advantage is that empowering DDoS assurance on your firewall or IPS can influence the general presentation of individual gadgets, diminishing end-client input and expanding inertness. Thus, empowering DDoS-empowered techniques on firewalls or IPS gadgets ought to be finished with alert, and in the most basic regions it is prescribed to involve committed DDoS assurance notwithstanding insurance or IPS.

B. MOST EFFECTIVE MITIGATION TECHNIQUE

After comparing all the mitigation techniques, our opinion is that firewall works best when it comes to DDoS protection of servers. It is feasible for various types of servers. Depending on the type, speed, intensity, duration of time and DDoS hit amount we can install various kinds of firewalls depending on our budget, need and time taken to install. As mentioned before, we can use different types of firewalls like software firewall, hardware firewall (physical).

3.5   Conclusion

This paper gives us an idea about what is DDoS, what are the courses of action taken by a person who suffers a DDoS attack, and classification of DDoS attacks. Among the Mitigation techniques, Firewall is the most ideal way to decrease the DDoS attack hits. There are many kinds of firewalls as indicated by the security necessities and cash open.

Acknowledgement

We thank all of the wellsprings of data including locals, research papers and buddies who helped us in getting the information. We are grateful to our mentors for their help and support.

References

1. R. V. Deshmukh and K. K. Devadkar, Understanding DDoS Attack & Its Effect in Cloud Environment, *Procedia Computer Science* 49 (2015).
2. Denial of Service Attack, http://en.wikipedia.org/wiki/Denial-of-service attack.
3. CERT Coordination Center, Overview of attack trends, Feb. 2002. http://www.cert.org/archive/pdf/attack trends.pdf
4. C. Zou, D. Towsley, and W. Gong, the performance of internet worm scanning strategies, 2003.
5. V. Paxson S. Staniford and N. Weaver, How to own the internet in your spare time, in *11th Usenix Security Symposium, San Francisco, August 2002.*
6. C. Zou, D. Towsley, W. Gong, and S. Cai, Routing worm: A quick, selecting attack worm for ip address information, 2005. Common Vulnerabilities and Exposures, http://cve.mitre.org/cve/
7. V. Paxson S. Staniford and N. Weaver, How to own the world wide internet in your spare time, in *11th Usenix Security Symposium, San Francisco, August 2002.*
8. Mahor, V., Bijrothiya, S., Rawat, R., Kumar, A., Garg, B., & Pachlasiya, K. (2023). IoT and Artificial Intelligence Techniques for Public Safety and Security. *Smart Urban Computing Applications*, 111.
9. Rawat, R. (2023). Logical concept mapping and social media analytics relating to cyber criminal activities for ontology creation. *International Journal of Information Technology*, 15(2), 893-903.
10. CIAC, Information Bulletin, I-020: Cisco 7xx password buffer overflow, Available from Ping of Death (insecure.org).
11. Kenney, Malachi, Ping of Death, January 1997, Available from Ping of Death (insecure.org).
12. Finger bomb recursive request, Available from http://xforce.iss.net/ststic/47.php.
13. D. Davidowicz, Domain Name System (DNS) Security, 1999, Available from the CERT Division | Software Engineering Institute (cmu.edu).
14. CIAC Information Bulletin, L-040: The Ramen Worm, 2001, Available from. Http://ciac.org/ciac/bulletins/1-040.shtml.
15. CERT Coordination Center, CERT Advisory CA-2001-19 Code Red worm exploiting buffer overflow in IIS indexing service DLL, Available from 2001 CERT Advisories (cmu.edu).
16. Reverse Proxy from Reverse proxy – Wikipedia.

17. J. Ioannidis, S.M. Bellovin, Implementing pushback: router-based defense against DDoS Attacks, in: *Proceedings of Network and Distributed System Security Symposium, NDSS02, San Diego, CA, 2002*, pp. 6–8.
18. National Institute of Standards and Technology, A Conceptual framework for system fault tolerance, 1995, Available from http://nist.gov/chissa/SEI_Framework/framework_1.html.
19. W. Zhao, D. Olshefski, H. Schulzrinne, Internet QOS: an overview, Columbia Technical Report CUCS003-00, 2000.
20. S. Blake, D. Black, M. Carlson, E. Davies, Z. Wang, W. Weiss, An architecture for various services, in: IETF, RFC 2475, 1998.
21. M.B. Geoffrey, G. Xie, A feedback mechanism for mitigating DOS attacks against various services clients, in: *Proceedings of the 10th International Conference on systems based on Telecommunications, Monterey, CA, October 2002*, pp. 204–213.
22. F. Kargl, J. Maier, M. Weber, Shielding web servers from DDoS attacks, in: *Proceedings of the Tenth International Conference on World Wide Web, Hong Kong, May 1–5, 2001*, pp. 514–524.
23. S.M. Mankins, C. Sangpachatanaruk, T. Znati, R. Melhem, D. Moss, server roaming in Proactive state for mitigating DOS attacks, in: *Proceedings of 1st International Conference on Information Technology Research and Education (ITRE), Newark, NJ, USA, August 10–13, 2003*.
24. R. Mahajan, S. Bellovin, S. Floyd, J. Ioannidis, V. Paxson, S. Shenker, Aggregate-based congestion control, Internet Research having ICSI Center (ICIR) AT&T Labs–– Research.
25. Rawat, R., Mahor, V., Álvarez, J. D., & Ch, F. (2023). Cognitive Systems for Dark Web Cyber Delinquent Association Malignant Data Crawling: A Review. *Handbook of Research on War Policies, Strategies, and Cyber Wars*, 45-63.
26. M. Y. Arafat, M. M. Alam, M. F. Alam, A Practical Approach and Mitigation Techniques on Application Layer DDoS Attack in Web Server, *International Journal of Computer Applications* (0975 – 8887) Volume 131 – No.1, December 2015.
27. Fortinet, DDoS Attack Mitigation Technologies Demystified, Jan 04, 2017
28. U. Goyal, G. Bhatti, S. Mehmi, A Dual Mechanism for defeating DDoS Attacks in Cloud Computing Model, *IJAIEM*, Volume 2, Issue 3, March 2013.
29. S. Chakraborty, P. Kumar, Dr. B. Shina, A Study on DDoS Attacks, Danger and Its Prevention, 2019 *IJRAR* May 2019, Volume 6, Issue 2.
30. E. Alomari, S. Manikcham, B.B. Gupta, S. Karuppayah, R. Alfaris, Botnet-based Distributed Denial of Service (DDoS) Attacks on Web Servers: Classification and Art, *International Journal of Computer Applications* (0975 – 8887), Volume 49, No.7, July 2012.
31. P. R.K. Reddy, S. Bouzefrane, Analysis and Detection of DoS Attacks in Cloud Computing by Using QSE Algorithm, *2014 IEEE International Conference on High Performance Computing and Communications (HPCC), 2014 IEEE 6th International Symposium on Cyberspace Safety and Security (CSS) and 2014 IEEE 11th International Conference on Embedded Software and Systems (ICESS)*.

4

Dark Web Content Classification Using Quantum Encoding

Ashwini Dalvi[1]*, Soham Bhoir[2], Faruk Kazi[1] and S. G. Bhirud[1]

[1]Veermata Jijabai Technological Institute, Mumbai, India
[2]K. J. Somaiya College of Engineering, Mumbai, India

Abstract

The study of cyber terrorism is relatively new and still in its infancy. Nevertheless, researchers and security professionals consider data collected from the dark web as one of the measures for proactive cybersecurity to combat cyber threats and cyber terrorism. Therefore, classifying dark web content with approaches ranging from machine learning to deep learning is researched extensively in the literature. Still, particular challenges remain with classifying dark web hidden services, for example, the limitation of the dataset to label hidden services and the requirement of substantial computing and storage resources to manage raw and unlabelled dark web data.

The proposed work presented a quantum encoding–based approach to categorizing Tor hidden services. First, the dark web crawler crawled the Tor dark web to fetch hidden services. The classical model classifies hidden services into 12 categories. The 12 categories include law and government, forum, streaming services, social networking sites, food, travel, games, health and fitness, education, computer and technology, e-commerce, and business/corporate. The keyword dataset to label hidden services is created using scraping and cleaning surface web pages of each of the 12 categories. Thus authors address the first challenges of labelling hidden service data. The dark web crawler can crawl hundreds of hidden services in a stipulated time. The crawled data comprised HTML pages and associated files. Analysis of such vast data is demanding on computational resources.

Recently, quantum computing is coming up as an alternative to classical models. Therefore, the authors proposed a quantum model to categorize crawled Tor hidden services with lesser time and minimize memory consumption. The proposed quantum model used Universal Sentence Encoder to encode classical data

*Corresponding author: aadalvi_p19@ce.vjti.ac.in

Romil Rawat, Rajesh Kumar Chakrawarti, Sanjaya Kumar Sarangi, Jaideep Patel, Vivek Bhardwaj, Anjali Rawat and Hitesh Rawat (eds.) Quantum Computing in Cybersecurity, (57–80) © 2023 Scrivener Publishing LLC

into quantum data as probabilities in the proposed work. The quantum circuit receives these probability values. Further, the quantum model applies the SoftMax function before comparing the output to actual category labels.

The result shows the output of categorizing hidden services using a customized category-defining dataset with quantum encoding. Finally, the chapter compares the time and memory consumption between the classical and quantum model.

Keywords: Cyber terrorism, dark web, tor, hidden service, onion services, quantum encoding, quantum circuit, quantum computing for cybersecurity

4.1   Introduction

Cyber terrorism has long been regarded as a dangerous threat by security officials. However, the threat of next-generation cyberattacks shows that cyberattacks can cause real-world physical destruction.

In order to combat security vulnerabilities, security professionals develop a proactive security posture by identifying specific hacker methods and techniques. In the last five years, security attacks like Wannacry and Log4j prompted security professionals and researchers to recognize that implementing a security incidents inventory is the proactive way to mitigate cyberattacks. The objective of proactive cybersecurity is to identify and correct weak security layers as early as possible, as well as develop strategies for detecting threats in advance.

Using data from public sources, A. N. Craig *et al.* compared 22 cybersecurity companies and 27 cybersecurity solutions to comprehend the most proactive cybersecurity practices [1]. The top proactive practices followed were auditing, data mining, and analysis. P. H. Meland *et al.* discussed various cybersecurity indicator points. These points are categorized based on the data source, type, and category [2]. For example, researchers considered dark web marketplaces as emerging remote data points for proactive cybersecurity measures. Dark Web Monitoring enables organizations to be vigilant of cybercriminals with proactive intelligence. Hackers often conduct several malware and ransomware campaigns on the dark web and the sale of stolen personal and business IDs. Extremists' communication or terrorists' activities are significant concerns related to the dark web, but potential cybersecurity threats are also likely to emerge from the dark web.

Dark web access is facilitated through a specialized network, typically the Tor network. Tor provides anonymity without disclosing the IP addresses of the host and client by going through a network of multiple servers and encrypted networks. The service referred to as onion services (OS), also known as Tor Hidden Service (HS), facilitates anonymity. The following text will use the terms onion service and hidden service interchangeably. A client cannot learn the IP address of the server providing the onion or hidden services. The anonymity of the dark web makes it impossible for law enforcement agencies to identify online transactions on the dark web. The researchers N. Arnold *et al.* presented a tool to use dark web data as a source for cyber threat intelligence [3]. P. Shakarian, discussed that the dark web could effectively impact cyber threat intelligence by automating the intelligent resources to obtain and analyze dark web information to predict cyberattacks [4].

Researchers pursue cyber threat intelligence (CTI) framework to perceive proactive cybersecurity. Thus, Zhang *et al.* developed DWTIA, a Dark Web Threat Intelligence Analysis Platform, to facilitate the dark web analysis for crime and criminal information [5]. Since IP addresses are used for tracing networks, the DWTIA framework did not identify cyber criminals because of the dark web's anonymity. Besides collecting data from more than 8,000 dark web sites, it also provides or uses the OnionScan dark web crawler.

To provide cyber threat intelligence (CTI), Samtani *et al.* used Diachronic Graph Embedding Framework (D-GEF) technologies to identify trends and tool functionality in online hacker forums [6]. A Graph-of-Words representation of threats emanating from hacker forums was the basis for D-GEF. Jeziorowski *et al.* analyzed dark marketplace images [7]. The image-based intelligence was collected by identifying reused images, and further using image metadata hashes and image hashing techniques, the computational overhead associated with the process was minimized. The research facilitated by identifying dark marketplaces from well-established dark net market archives resulted in the dark web marketplace vendor profiling. Such dark web investigations can deanonymize anonymous paraphernalia sellers by studying the aliases associated with vendors who conduct business in multiple marketplaces. The top vendors, top markets, and top hash analysis results were identified based on the investigation results. In this study, machine learning-based classification techniques or methods validated the outcomes of multimodal DVP.

According to Meland *et al.*, the dark web is experiencing a rise in ransomware services (RaaS) [8]. Cybercriminals or malicious users on the dark web demand ransom payments to release infected digital assets. The main objective of this study was to examine RaaS and the associated value chains associated with the dark marketplace. According to Meland *et al.*, if perpetrated by an experienced attacker, ransomware bought from the dark web is a potent threat.

In a recent study, P. Koloveas *et al.* discussed the need to develop investigation frameworks for the dark web's Internet of Things (IoT) threat vectors [9]. The work proposed three components: a focused crawler, a forum-based crawler, and a Tor crawler. First, a focused web crawler was designed to identify new resources and gateways for CTI. Next, positive and harmful web pages were classified using a Support Vector Machine (SVM) classifier. In order to locate the initial seed links, the crawler used a user-provided query. Finally, in-depth crawlers focus on forums whose topics of discussion are relevant by examining all the links in the forum. Regex-based link filters, however, monitored forums selectively within and across them.

Various research approaches were studied to analyze content on the dark web. These approaches include analyzing drug market data and hacker forums, among others. Content hosted or offered in hidden services is most frequently the subject of research. However, dark web hidden services (HS) are difficult to identify without opening them. Also, services on the dark web are not indexed, which makes it challenging to determine what content onion service or hidden service contains. Therefore, researchers proposed ways to identify the type of hidden service using text analysis. Although the dark web hidden services consist of unstructured text data after stripping HTML tags from hidden service web pages, text analysis has become increasingly important for seeking useful insights from hidden services. For example, text mining can classify hidden services into different categories. With supervised machine learning, web pages require a labelled dataset to categorize them into different categories. However, the onion service dataset qualifies as an unlabelled dataset. Therefore, the researchers developed custom labelled datasets by identifying the content of hidden services in collaboration with experts. For example, M. W. Al Nabki *et al.* released dark web data set comprised of 26 classes to classify hidden services hosting illegal activities [10]. A relatively early attempt by C. Guitton in 2013 also manually categorized 1,171 hidden services into 23 categories [11]. The purpose of classifying dark web content is to use further rank the content to offer the better result to law and enforcement agencies. Based on content analysis, M. Faizan, *et al.* proposed a methodology to rank drug-related hidden services [12]. Thus, the researchers attempted different ways to classify dark web data for different purposes.

Researchers collect the dark web data either with a customized dark web crawler or an open-source web crawler. Crawling the dark web results in vast amounts of raw textual data presented in hidden services, but classifying them is time-consuming and costly due to the need for human judgment. In recent times, quantum computing has gained attention because it can achieve exponential speedups over conventional machine learning.

The proposed chapter implements a quantum encoding approach to categorize hidden services into predefined categories.

The chapter offers the following novel contributions:

- Creation of a customized dataset of different categories to label hidden services
- Implementation of quantum encoding to classify Tor hidden services

ORGANIZATION OF CHAPTER

The organization of the chapter includes related work in section 4.2. Section 4.3 covers methodologies and result discussion, and the chapter concludes with limitations and future scope.

4.2   Related Work

Search Engines do not index the Tor hidden services, so a manual effort is required to access hidden services. Researchers have been studying Tor dark web extensively; however, Huete Trujillo *et al.* cited research for Tor hidden services [13]. The study mentioned six significant areas of hidden services – classifying the content of hidden services, analyzing the security and performance of hidden services, discovering and measuring approaches for hidden services, and changing the design of hidden services. In this work, the authors will focus on classifying Tor hidden services.

Thus it is comprehended from research that crawled hidden services will be unlabeled data and dataset to labelled content of hidden services created by manual or automatic labelling. The proposed study created an automated dataset for Tor hidden service labelling.

Collecting Hidden services for categorization

The dark web investigation mechanism involves a crawling module, link collection and content labelling modules. Using an adaptive learning algorithm, F. Zhao *et al.* proposed an intelligent crawler capable of selecting features online and automatically constructing link rankers [14]. The crawler consists of categorization websites to exclude unrelated websites. The researchers mentioned the crawler harvest at a higher rate than other variants of deep and dark web crawlers. The dark web crawlers collect data for specific use cases like drug markets and child sexual exploitation. R. Frank *et al.* developed a dark web crawler to analyze child exploitation networks extractor (CENE) on the dark web [15]. A. T. Zulkarnine *et al.*

modified the capability of the CENE Tor crawler to collect data from the surface web as well [16]. The present work collected data with a crawler capable of crawling surface and dark web [17].

Labelling dark web data for categorization

The onion services are not available publicly; thus, collecting large amounts of onion services to train data for the supervised learning model is difficult. Therefore, the dark web hidden service classifier typically learns from a training dataset consisting of observations related to a particular labelled dataset derived from empirical data or acquired from experts.

The research has focused on manually labelling crawled dark websites and using them as training corpora for automated crawls of the Tor dark web. F. Dong *et al.* manually labelled 8,000 samples to identify 35 new cyber threats [18]. J. Dalins *et al.* crawled webpages from different Tor domains and trained the machine learning model by manually labelling 4,000 Tor pages [19]. S. He *et al.* generated a dark web data set comprising 4,851 onion sites categorized manually [20]. The authors used publicly available legal documents for the classification model training. Such an attempt introduced another possibility for defining illegal activity categories which were not labelled earlier. V. Mahor *et al.* extended the approach of curating a dataset for categorizing cyber threats concerning cyber-physical systems [21].

To determine the characteristics of each category, S. Takaaki, & I. Atsuo manually analyzed 300 websites and extracted characteristic keywords from each website [22]. As part of this process, keywords deemed most likely to fit within particular categories were enumerated and considered simultaneously. As a result, each category was defined based on 10 or more keywords. As a result, the authors identified six categories based on the top page text downloaded from the onion domain.

Researchers also attempted to label dark web data with machine learning. H. Kobayashi *et al.* collected data from the dark web and proposed a system to perform morphological analysis using natural language processing [23]. The authors built a knowledge base mechanism to automatically identify five crime categories and determine threat levels based on data collected from the dark web. A. Kinder *et al.* scraped HTML from the onion service with a predetermined list of keywords to identify illicit sites and categorize them based on their crime [24]. S. Ghosh *et al.* developed "ATOL – Automated Tool for Onion Labelling" [25]. The ATOL generated new keywords for different categories of onion services with expert-provided keywords.

I. D. Buldin & N. S. Ivanov presented work on dark web text classification in the Russian language [26]. H. Moraliyage at al. extends dark web text labelling with multimodal deep learning to classify multiple onion service categories [27].

The work discussed concerning dark web analysis requires an efficient mechanism to collect and categorize onion services. The present work investigates the advantage of quantum encoding to categorize hidden services.

Introduction to Quantum Computing

Information and communication technologies will benefit from quantum computers, which are highly powerful and secure. Quantum computing is evolving technology that uses quantum mechanics to solve problems difficult for classical computing. Quantum computers can process exponentially more data than classical computers because they use probability instead of just 1s and 0s. In quantum computing, qubits, a basic memory unit, are created using electrons' spin or photon orientation of physical systems. Quantum superposition refers to the fact that physical systems can exist simultaneously in many different configurations. The quantum entanglement phenomenon is also capable of linking qubits inseparably. Consequently, each qubit can represent a unique thing at the same time. For example, a classical computer uses eight bits to represent numbers between 0 and 255. Quantum computers can, however, represent all numbers between 0 and 255 simultaneously using eight qubits.

Fault-tolerant quantum computers can resolve problems like integer factorization and unstructured database searches by utilizing millions of qubits with low error rates and long coherence times. Even though the experimental progress toward realizing noisy intermediate-scale quantum (NISQ) computers could take decades, noisy intermediate-scale quantum computers are currently available. Noise qubit computers use hundreds of uncorrected quantum bits, resulting in imperfect calculations within a limited period of coherence. Researchers have proposed multiple algorithms to achieve quantum advantage with these devices.

Quantum computing demonstrates an obvious advantage over classical computing. Quantum computers have the potential to surpass the supercomputers of today. However, researchers still investigate which type of problems from classical computing to solve through quantum computing. Further, researchers examined quantum machine learning.

Quantum computer processes data on a quantum level. Quantum software progressed to develop machine learning faster than conventional computers. The first step in quantum machine learning is to load conventional data into the states of the qubits. Quantum states are attained by encoding or embedding quantum data. Quantum Machine Learning algorithms (QML) rely heavily on classical data encoding to perform effectively and efficiently. Quantum machine learning involves three phases – encoding, process and measurement. These are briefly described as follows.

> Encoding: The process of loading classical data into a quantum state.
> Processing: The embedded input, which will be a variational circuit or a quantum routine, is processed by the quantum device at this point.
> Measurement: This stage measures the predicted result, subsequently forming the forecast for QML.

Quantum computing for proactive cybersecurity

The quantum computation concept has also influenced many scientific studies in computer science, notably computational modelling, cryptography theory, and information theory. Quantum computers can have either a positive or negative impact on the security of information. Many researchers have evaluated quantum computing's benefits in cybersecurity. M. Njorbuenwu *et al.* discussed several fields that might benefit from using a quantum computer [28]. N. Laxminarayana *et al.* presented a study on the combination of principles of quantum mechanics and neural networks to train intrusion detection systems for healthcare systems [29]. Researchers demonstrated the proposed algorithm on the KDD99 dataset.

Researchers explored the role of quantum computing in mitigating domain-specific security. To emphasize that quantum computing will be a potential solution to strengthen cybersecurity, K. K Ko. & E. S. Jung described quantum computing-based implementations of existing AES and modified AES algorithms [30]. D. Tosh *et al.* proposed using quantum cryptography to encrypt communication between sensors and computers to secure cyber-physical systems [31]. A. Ali explored the possibility of combining quantum computing with classical computing [32]. H. Suryotrisongko & Y. Musashi proposed the novel hybrid quantum-classical deep learning model for domain generation algorithms (DGA)-based botnet detection [33].

Researchers are also investigating whether quantum mechanical principles can be incorporated into machine learning problems to improve the solution. Z. Abohashima *et al.* summarized the most recent research findings in quantum machine learning [34]. The authors proposed to propose a quantum classification scheme as well as a quantum encoding scheme.

4.3   Proposed Approach

The proposed study attempts to classify crawled hidden service websites, legal and illegal, into various categories. One publicly available dark web dataset is the DUTA dataset, which consists of over 10,367 onion services manually labelled in 25 categories. The work of the DUTA dataset motivated authors to categorize onion services in general categories. The authors implemented a content-based classification approach to create the dataset. Further, the authors attempted quantum encoding to classify hidden services into different categories.

Figure 4.1 depicts the proposed methodology for categorizing onion services with quantum encoding.

Classical model to categorize onion services
In order to predict each class correctly, it is essential to have a balanced dataset. Therefore, the authors scraped over a hundred surface websites to create a balanced dataset of keywords in 12 categories. The 12 categories

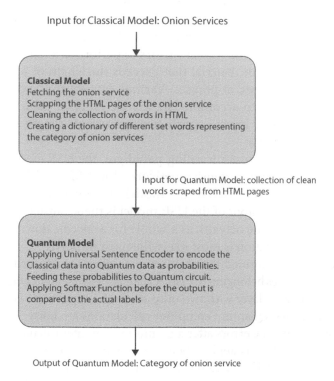

Figure 4.1 Proposed methodology.

include law and government, forum, streaming services, social networking sites, food, travel, games, health and fitness, education, computer and technology, e-commerce, and business/corporate. Data preprocessing involved the removal of HTML tags and non-ASCII characters from scraped HTML pages. Text preprocessing functions – stemming and lemmatization performed the cleaning of raw text data.

Further, the text was categorized into different domains using the TF-IDF approach. Then, the authors trained supervised learning models like Random Forest, LinearSVC, Multinomial Naïve Bayes and Gaussian Naïve Bayes, using a set of keywords of different categories. Finally, the k-fold cross-validation score was measured to evaluate the training models' accuracy. During the machine learning process, cross-validation is an effective measure for identifying overfitting that determines the model's performance with unknown data. Table 4.1 shows the five-fold cross-validation accuracies of supervised learning models.

The accuracy of Linear SVC was 0.94. Thus, LineraSVC was selected as a classical supervised learning model.

Quantum Model to categorize onion services

TensorFlowHub has released a pre-trained model for Google's Universal Sentence Encoder (USE). As mentioned in [35], it converts natural language texts into high-dimensional vectors to perform text analysis. USE is designed specifically for material that exceeds the length of a word, such as paragraphs, sentences, or phrases. Various data sources and workloads train the USE model to accommodate a wide range of natural language comprehension tasks. Input English text of variable length produces a 512-dimensional vector.

According to the transfer learning paradigm, the USE model could be a component of a more extensive network. The USE model is used just as-is with its parameters fixed or the model fine-tuned the parameters to optimize them. The output of the USE model is then transferred to subsequent levels to train the network as a whole for a specific downstream job. Document categorization is most likely the most intuitive.

The authors transformed the abstract of a collection of words retrieved from hidden services belonging to distinct categories to sentence embeddings and attached a dense layer with two outputs. Each output node corresponds to a single category. Quantum computer calculations are noisy. Therefore, it is necessary to mitigate errors after a quantum computer calculation.

A softmax function is applied before the output. The softmax function converts a vector of K real values into the vector of K real values equalling 1. The softmax transforms input values, positive, negative, zero, or

Table 4.1 Fivefold cross-validation scores for supervised learning models.

Model Name	Fold Index	Accuracy
Random Forest	0	0.719858
Random Forest	1	0.751773
Random Forest	2	0.716312
Random Forest	3	0.736655
Random Forest	4	0.679715
LinearSVC	0	0.858156
LinearSVC	1	0.932624
LinearSVC	2	0.939716
LinearSVC	3	0.903915
LinearSVC	4	0.879004
Multinomial Naïve Bayes	0	0.812057
Multinomial Naïve Bayes	1	0.879433
Multinomial Naïve Bayes	2	0.872340
Multinomial Naïve Bayes	3	0.882562
Multinomial Naïve Bayes	4	0.818505
Gaussian Naïve Bayes	0	0.702128
Gaussian Naïve Bayes	1	0.762411
Gaussian Naïve Bayes	2	0.780142
Gaussian Naïve Bayes	3	0.754448
Gaussian Naïve Bayes	4	0.644128

greater than one, into values between 0 and 1 as probabilities. Although it will always lie between 0 and 1, the softmax translates small or negative inputs into small probabilities and large or positive inputs into high probabilities.

The mathematical definition of the softmax function is depicted in Figure 4.2.

Table 4.2 discusses the softmax function in detail.

$$\sigma(\overline{Z})i = \frac{e^{Zi}}{\sum\limits_{j=1}^{K} e^{Zi}}$$

Figure 4.2 Softmax function.

Table 4.2 Details of softmax function.

$\overline{Z}$	The softmax function's input vector is built from (Z0, ... Zk)
Zi	The softmax function's input vector contains all of the Zi values, and they can all have a real value of either a positive, zero or negative sign. The softmax is required because, for instance, a neural network's output vector may be (-032, 4.12, 6.47), which is not a legitimate probability distribution.
e^{Zi}	Every component of an input vector is subjected to the usual exponential function. It results in a positive number greater than zero, which will be extremely little if the input is negative and huge if the input is vast. It is not set within range (0, 1), which is what a probability must be.
$\sum\limits_{j=1}^{K} e^{Zi}$	The normalization term is the term in the formula that appears at the bottom. It guarantees that the function's output values will add up to 1 and fall inside the range (0, 1), forming a legitimate probability distribution.
K	How many classes the multi-class classifier can handle.

To "quantize" the proposed model, the authors substituted a variational quantum circuit for the layer between the embeddings and the output. A traditional dense layer typically has N inputs and M outputs; therefore, internally, it corresponds to matrix multiplication followed by bias addition and application of the activation function. However, quantum layers cannot accomplish this openly. Therefore, it implies that a quantum variational layer comprises three processes.

A traditional dense layer converts N inputs to N qubits and scales the input by $\pi/2$. (so it can represent a rotation around the Bloch sphere).

The PennyLane library accomplishes the three processes. To do this with the PennyLane library, one must first define a device that will perform the quantum operations. The IBMQ or Rigetti provides the real devices. Then, the python function encodes the actual circuit.

The PennyLane Library is a cross-platform open-source software development kit for differentiable quantum computer programming. Classical calculations, such as model optimization or training, are carried out using typical scientific computing or machine learning libraries, such as SciPy in Python. PennyLane interfaces with these libraries and integrates them with quantum simulators.

Many dense layers may be stacked on top of each other to enhance the depth of a network; quantum variational layers can do the same.

Figure 4.3 depicts the pseudocode of implemented quantum encoding.

Function to create single-layer Hadamard gates taking the number of qubits as a parameter:
  return performing a loop in the range up to n qubits creating a Hadamard layer

Function to create a layer of parameterised qubit rotation around y-axis taking feature as parameter:
  return the rotated qubits up to a certain angle provided in the parameter

Function to entangle the layers by taking the number of qubits as a parameter:
  For i to nth qubit and traverse in 2 steps each:
    Get the even index to add CNOT gate
  For j to nth qubit and iterate with 2 steps each:
    Get the odd index to add CNOT gate

Class for VariationalQuantumCircuit:
  constructor taking input as n_categories to classify the URL,
  Number of qubits required (n_qubits = 4),
  Layers of circuit need = 6

  Function to create a circuit taking parameters as inputs and parameters:
    Embedding encode to Setting the templates from features into the quantum state of the circuit.
    Setting up the layer for StronglyEntanglingLayers to take a parameter as a number of list in a dataset.

    return expected value of Pauli Z for i in range of n_qubits

  Function to create the quantm Circuit:
    UniversalEmbeddingLayer= partial(USELsayer)
    Initiating the quantum circuit variational circuit object
    x = softmax function activation
    Return denselayer.classification

Figure 4.3 Pseudocode of quantum encoding.

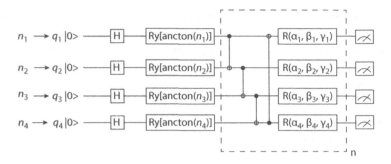

Figure 4.4 Quantum classification variational circuit.

Further discussion covers Quantum Classification Variational Circuit. The execution of a quantum circuit requires a variety of complex pre- and post-processing steps. Figure 4.4 shows the quantum classification variational circuit.

An impartial beginning state is created using the Hadamard gate H. The three sections of the Variational Quantum Circuit (VQC) employed in this study are: the encoding portion, the variational part containing parameters to be learned, and the measurement part, which will provide the Pauli-Z expectation values through repeated quantum circuit runs.

The first k qubits would be used for the quantum measurement. Arctan (x) is used for state preparation and is taken straight from the classical input data (cleaned words scrapped from the HTML of onion services). x1, x2, x3, and x4 represent the encoding of classical data into quantum data by Universal Sentence Encoder. All the qubits are at their Zeroth State before starting the circuit.

The number of classes is k. The VQC's expressivity is boosted by iterating part of the circuit highlighted by dashed lines.

The number of Qubits chosen depends on the input dimension of the data and the depth of circuit one needs (e.g., 512 dimensions in implemented approach).

4.4   Result and Discussion

The authors designed a dark web crawler to collect onion services. The crawler ran at depth 3 with multi-threading mode. The crawler collected HTML pages of 19,000 version 2 onion services. In addition, the crawler collected the URL of the onion service and the title and metadata of the

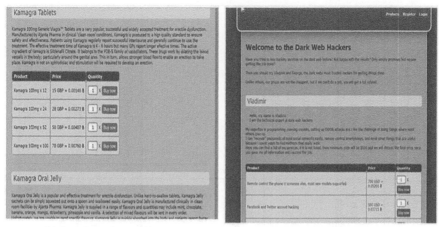

(a) Sample Onion Service 1   (b) Sample Onion Service 2

Figure 4.5 Sample onion services.

respective service. The authors excluded hidden services based on the criteria of non-English onion pages and onion pages of the Facebook deep web. Depth 3 crawling resulted in many Facebook hidden pages categorized as social networking sites. More number of Facebook pages skewed the dataset. Thus the authors removed Facebook onion pages collected at depth 2 and depth 3. After preprocessing and Facebook post removal, the authors considered 2,000 onion services for analysis.

Figure 4.5 shows samples of onion service pages.

Table 4.3 shows dataset samples with data attributes considered for quantum encoding.

Figure 4.6 shows a snapshot of sample cleaned text for one onion service.

The quantum encoding model received 2,000 hidden service samples and achieved 99.6% accuracy.

Table 4.4 shows the quantum model's sampled output label of the onion service categorization.

Figure 4.7 shows a pie chart representation of the categorization of different onion services.

The authors investigated performance improvement with quantum encoding. Dark web crawler crawled was not focused on a particular domain; it crawled data continuously. Therefore data collection was huge. The proposed study aims to categorize dark web onion services with better performance by converting classical data into quantum encoding.

Table 4.3 Dataset samples with data attribute considered for quantum encoding.

Id	Onion service	Cleaned_Text data	Onion service title
1	4p6i33oqj6wgvzgzczyqlueav3tz456rdu632xzyxbnhq4gpsriirtqd.onion/3CB6NF7FCFC02A2CFB2C8E7EFBAF8E9.html	visit view visit use experience people completely new way b c d e f g h j k l m n o p q r s t u v w x y z check united kingdom grad visit united kingdom new More…	Peoples Drug Store - The Darkweb's Best Online Drug Supplier! - Buy cocaine, speed, xtc, mdma, heroin and more at peoples drug store, pay with Bitcoin
2	canxzwmfihdnn7bz.onion/A7045E8B1F9E04E6GF35DF8B96C29.html	chat accessible new shiny v3 address notbumpz34bgbz4yfdigxvd6vzwtxc3zpt5imukgl6bvip2nikdmdaad onionnotbumpz34bgbz4yfdigxvd6vzwtxc3zpt5imukgl6bvip2nikdmdaad onion chat group chat More…	Ableonion
3	bepig5bcjdhtlwpgeh3w42hffftcqmg7b77vzu7ponty52kiey5ec4ad.onion\F7E89E9EDFFByAKxE8c3E99C6s.html	quality original cheap paymentkamagra4bitcoin buy cheap ship login register login register mg generic popular successful widely accept treatment clinical clean room produce high quality standard ensure safety effectiveness More…	Kamagra For Bitcoin - Same quality as original viagra pills, cheap prices, Bitcoin payment

---

URL:
4p6i33oqj6wgvzgzczyqlueav3tz456rdu632xzyxbnhq4gpsriirtqd.onion/3CB6NF7FCFC02A2CFB2C8E7EFBAF8E9.ht
ml

Cleaned Text: drug store s good drug supplier buy cocaine speed heroin drug store pay drug store number deep web
drug vendor buy register login register drug store pride offer good quality competitive make effort come customer
satisfaction choose category follow heroin cocaine ecstasy speed free tell shop earn purchase simply follow link ref
original onion ref replace actual site earning directly wallet heroin heroin offer come direct importer middle man white
light beige color great pride fact cut product whatsoever ensure source prefer offer high quality product repeat s
difference heroin people know decide add information listing commonly find heroin grade h form heroin white powder
easily water readily grade h tan granular product brown rock difference color result process grade commonly citrus
instead water simple think like h water pure people sniff people prefer smoke h smoke usually adulterant burn register
drug store pride offer good quality competitive make effort come customer satisfaction choose category follow heroin
cocaine ecstasy speed free tell shop earn purchase simply follow link ref original onion ref replace actual site earning
directly wallet heroin heroin offer come direct importer middle man white light beige color great pride fact cut product
whatsoever ensure source prefer offer high quality product repeat s difference heroin people know decide add
information listing commonly find heroin grade h form heroin white powder easily water readily grade h tan granular
product brown rock difference color result process grade commonly citrus instead water simple think like h water pure
people sniff people prefer smoke h smoke usually adulterant burn

Title: Peoples Drug Store - The Darkweb's Best Online Drug Supplier! - Buy cocaine, speed, xtc, mdma, heroin and
more at peoples drug store, pay with Bitcoin

Figure 4.6 Snapshot of sample cleaned text of onion service.

Time and Memory performance evaluation of Classical vs. Quantum model

Figure 4.8 depicts the comparison between classical and quantum models. In classical mode, with an increase in batch size, and time, consumption increases linearly. In quantum encoding, the word size in a batch varies, if reflected with a slight variation in time consumption.

The cleaned text of onion services will be of different sizes. For example, onion service A has 5,000 words, whereas onion service B has 7,500 words. The classical model takes comparatively more time to categorize the onion service B because of the content-based classification approach. Thus, as the batch size increase, the overall categorization time increases.

In quantum encoding, the incoming cleaned texts from the classical model were converted to quantum data. Although quantum data has less memory as qubits and qubits can represent an exponential number of bits. The overall time slightly increases when sample text has more than 8,000 words that cannot represent the whole data in qubits. The model discarded the words that did not fit in a single interaction (processing a single onion service). Also, before the final output, the data is passed through the Softmax function to ensure the output value is correct/matched.

Another performance constraint with dark web data categorization is memory consumption.

Figure 4.9 shows the comparison between classical and quantum models for memory consumption.

Table 4.4 Categorization of the onion services with quantum encoding.

Id	Onion Service	Title	Category_Label
1	4p6i33oqj6wgvzgzczyqlueav3tz456rdu632xzyxbnhq4gpsriirtqd. onion/3CB6NF7FCFC02A2CFB2C8E7EFBAF8E9.html	Peoples Drug Store-The Darkweb's Best Online Drug Supplier! - Buy cocaine, speed, xtc, mdma, heroin and more at peoples drug store, pay with Bitcoin	E-Commerce
2	ctemplarpizuduxk3fkwrieizstx33kg5chlvrh37nz73pv5smsvl6ad. onion\0F2AE691K5B841915B81BED0743CEA.html	The Only Anonymous Payment Resources You Will Ever Need? - CTemplar	Business/ Corporate
3	bepig5bcjdhtlwpgeh3w42hffftcqmg7b77vzu7ponty52kiey5ec4ad. onion\F7E89E9EDFFByAKxE8c3E99C6s.html	Kamagra For Bitcoin - Same quality as original viagra pills, cheap prices, Bitcoin payment	Health & Fitness
4	ar.facebookcorewwwi.onion\6ADH89JBD10FB2A1B1084DABFF424. html		Law & Government

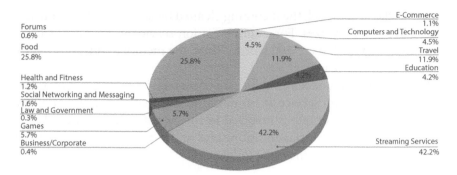

Figure 4.7 Categorization of different onion services.

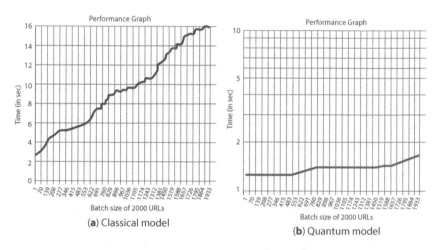

Figure 4.8 Time required vs. Batch size of 2,000 onion services.

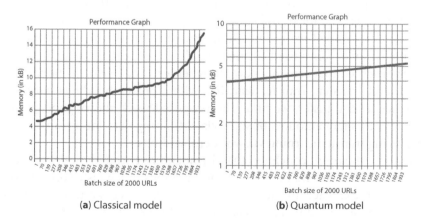

Figure 4.9 Memory required vs. batch size of 2000 URLs.

In the classical model, the incoming cleaned texts of different onion services have different sizes. For example, onion service A has 5,000 words, and onion service B has 7,500 words. Thus, the memory consumption by the model will increase.

In the quantum model, the qubits are conserved in every iteration (classifying the one onion service at a time). It means that before and after the output, the number of qubits involved in the circuit is equal. The value of less significant words in classification stays in the qubit until the following words are encoded into the same qubit.

4.5   Conclusion

Dark web data analysis is proven one of the proactive cybersecurity measures; therefore, researchers attempt to collect and label dark web data. Such data could help draw meaningful inferences for cybersecurity. In the present work, the authors developed a crawler to crawl the surface and dark web. The crawler collected a substantial amount of data from all webs. As a result, traditional data analysis and processing machine learning still require a computationally intensive and time-consuming process.

Therefore, the authors attempted to apply the concept of quantum encoding—the classical data fed to the quantum encoding circuit. Input hidden services were categorized using a quantum encoding circuit. The softmax function is applied before the display category of hidden service.

The proposed work utilized a pre-trained version of Google's Universal Sentence Encoder (USE) model. The model performed well and delivered accurate outcomes for a range of transfer tasks. The authors discussed the relationship between model complexity, resource utilization, the accessibility of training data for transfer tasks, and performance outcomes for both models. Pre-trained word embedding baselines with word-level transfer learning model contrasted against baselines without transfer learning. Work observed that sentence-level transfer learning performs better than word-level transfer. Transfer learning with word embeddings surpasses sentence-level transfer, we find. The proposed work shows good performance with small amounts of supervised training data for a transfer task employing transfer learning via word embeddings.

Further, the result concludes that the quantum encoded model required much less memory and performed computations much faster on data volume than the classical machine learning model. Thus quantum computing enabled model could be an efficient choice for designing a dark web data analysis framework.

The representation must be small to use modern NISQ devices and employ only a few qubits and quantum gates. Qubits decay quickly, and quantum gates are also error-prone, restricting the number of operations required to establish the quantum state, which must be modest.

Quantum classification versions take significantly longer to train using the simulator (approximately one minute per epoch with 32 batches). It is possible that quantum simulation is time-consuming and becomes increasingly complex as the number of qubits increases.

Although the USE embedding facilitated categorization tasks in the proposed work, the future scope of work could use transfer learning instead of having to train a model.

References

1. Craig, A. N., Shackelford, S. J., & Hiller, J. S. (2015). Proactive cybersecurity: A comparative industry and regulatory analysis. *American Business Law Journal*, 52(4), 721-787.
2. Meland, P. H., Tokas, S., Erdogan, G., Bernsmed, K., & Omerovic, A. (2021). A Systematic Mapping Study on Cyber Security Indicator Data. *Electronics*, 10(9), 1092.
3. Arnold, N., Ebrahimi, M., Zhang, N., Lazarine, B., Patton, M., Chen, H., & Samtani, S. (2019, July). Dark-net ecosystem cyber-threat intelligence (CTI) tool. In *2019 IEEE International Conference on Intelligence and Security Informatics (ISI)* (pp. 92-97). IEEE.
4. Shakarian, P. (2018). Dark-web cyber threat intelligence: from data to intelligence to prediction. *Information*, 9(12), 305.
5. Zhang, X., & Chow, K. P. (2020). A framework for dark Web threat intelligence analysis. In *Cyber Warfare and Terrorism: Concepts, Methodologies, Tools, and Applications* (pp. 266-276). IGI Global.
6. Samtani, S., Zhu, H., & Chen, H. (2020). Proactively identifying emerging hacker threats from the dark web: A diachronic graph embedding framework (d-gef). *ACM Transactions on Privacy and Security (TOPS)*, 23(4), 1-33.
7. Jeziorowski, S., Ismail, M., & Siraj, A. (2020, March). Towards image-based dark vendor profiling: an analysis of image metadata and image hashing in dark web marketplaces. In *Proceedings of the Sixth International Workshop on Security and Privacy Analytics* (pp. 15-22).
8. Meland, P. H., Bayoumy, Y. F. F., & Sindre, G. (2020). The Ransomware-as-a-Service economy within the darknet. *Computers & Security*, 92, 101762.
9. Koloveas, P., Chantzios, T., Tryfonopoulos, C., & Skiadopoulos, S. (2019, July). A crawler architecture for harvesting the clear, social, and dark web for IoT-related cyber-threat intelligence. In *2019 IEEE World Congress on Services (SERVICES)* (Vol. 2642, pp. 3-8). IEEE.

10. Al Nabki, M. W., Fidalgo, E., Alegre, E., & De Paz, I. (2017, April). Classifying illegal activities on tor network based on web textual contents. In *Proceedings of the 15th Conference of the European Chapter of the Association for Computational Linguistics: Volume 1, Long Papers* (pp. 35-43).
11. Guitton, C. (2013). A review of the available content on Tor hidden services: The case against further development. *Computers in Human Behavior*, 29(6), 2805-2815.
12. Faizan, M., Khan, R. A., & Agrawal, A. (2020). Ranking potentially harmful Tor hidden services: Illicit drugs perspective. *Applied Computing and Informatics*.
13. Huete Trujillo, D. L., & Ruiz-Martínez, A. (2021). Tor Hidden Services: a systematic literature review. *Journal of Cybersecurity and Privacy*, 1(3), 496-518.
14. Zhao, F., Zhou, J., Nie, C., Huang, H., & Jin, H. (2015). SmartCrawler: a two-stage crawler for efficiently harvesting deep-web interfaces. *IEEE Transactions on Services Computing*, 9(4), 608-620.
15. Frank, R., Westlake, B., & Bouchard, M. (2010, July). The structure and content of online child exploitation networks. In *ACM SIGKDD Workshop on Intelligence and Security Informatics* (pp. 1-9).
16. Zulkarnine, A. T., Frank, R., Monk, B., Mitchell, J., & Davies, G. (2016, September). Surfacing collaborated networks in dark web to find illicit and criminal content. In *2016 IEEE Conference on Intelligence and Security Informatics (ISI)* (pp. 109-114). IEEE.
17. Dalvi, A., Paranjpe, S., Amale, R., Kurumkar, S., Kazi, F., & Bhirud, S. G. (2021, May). SpyDark: Surface and Dark Web Crawler. In *2021 2nd International Conference on Secure Cyber Computing and Communications (ICSCCC)* (pp. 45-49). IEEE.
18. Dong, F., Yuan, S., Ou, H., & Liu, L. (2018, November). New cyber threat discovery from darknet marketplaces. In *2018 IEEE Conference on Big Data and Analytics (ICBDA)* (pp. 62-67). IEEE.
19. Dalins, J., Wilson, C., & Carman, M. (2018). Criminal motivation on the dark web: A categorization model for law enforcement. *Digital Investigation*, 24, 62-71.
20. He, S., He, Y., & Li, M. (2019, March). Classification of illegal activities on the dark web. In *Proceedings of the 2019 2nd International Conference on Information Science and Systems* (pp. 73-78).
21. Mahor, V., Rawat, R., Kumar, A., Chouhan, M., Shaw, R. N., & Ghosh, A. (2021, September). Cyber warfare threat categorization on cps by dark web terrorist. In *2021 IEEE 4th International Conference on Computing, Power and Communication Technologies (GUCON)* (pp. 1-6). IEEE.
22. Takaaki, S., & Atsuo, I. (2019, March). Dark web content analysis and visualization. In *Proceedings of the ACM International Workshop on Security and Privacy Analytics* (pp. 53-59).
23. Kobayashi, H., Kadoguchi, M., Hayashi, S., Otsuka, A., & Hashimoto, M. (2020, November). An expert system for classifying harmful content on the

dark web. In *2020 IEEE International Conference on Intelligence and Security Informatics* (ISI) (pp. 1-6). IEEE.

24. Kinder, A., Choo, K. K. R., & Le-Khac, N. A. (2020). Towards an Automated Process to Categorize Tor's Hidden Services. In *Cyber and Digital Forensic Investigations* (pp. 221-246). Springer, Cham.

25. Ghosh, S., Das, A., Porras, P., Yegneswaran, V., & Gehani, A. (2017, August). Automated categorization of onion sites for analyzing the darkweb ecosystem. In *Proceedings of the 23rd ACM SIGKDD International Conference on Knowledge Discovery and Data Mining* (pp. 1793-1802).

26. Buldin, I. D., & Ivanov, N. S. (2020, January). Text classification of illegal activities on onion sites. In *2020 IEEE Conference of Russian Young Researchers in Electrical and Electronic Engineering (EIConRus)* (pp. 245-247). IEEE.

27. Moraliyage, H., Sumanasena, V., De Silva, D., Nawaratne, R., Sun, L., & Alahakoon, D. (2022). Multimodal Classification of Onion Services for Proactive Cyber Threat Intelligence using Explainable Deep Learning. *IEEE Access*.

28. Njorbuenwu, M., Swar, B., & Zavarsky, P. (2019, June). A survey on the impacts of quantum computers on information security. In *2019 2nd International conference on data intelligence and security (ICDIS) (pp. 212-218).* IEEE.

29. Laxminarayana, N., Mishra, N., Tiwari, P., Garg, S., Behera, B. K., & Farouk, A. (2022). Quantum-Assisted Activation for Supervised Learning in Healthcare-based Intrusion Detection Systems. *IEEE Transactions on Artificial Intelligence*.

30. Ko, K. K., & Jung, E. S. (2021). Development of cybersecurity technology and algorithm based on quantum computing. *Applied Sciences*, 11(19), 9085.

31. Tosh, D., Galindo, O., Kreinovich, V., & Kosheleva, O. (2020, June). Towards security of cyber-physical systems using quantum computing algorithms. In *2020 IEEE 15th International Conference of System of Systems Engineering (SoSE)* (pp. 313-320). IEEE.

32. Ali, A. (2021, January). A Pragmatic Analysis of Pre-and Post-Quantum Cyber Security Scenarios. In *2021 International Bhurban Conference on Applied Sciences and Technologies (IBCAST)* (pp. 686-692). IEEE.

33. Suryotrisongko, H., & Musashi, Y. (2022). Evaluating hybrid quantum-classical deep learning for cybersecurity botnet DGA detection. *Procedia Computer Science*, 197, 223-229.

34. Abohashima, Z., Elhosen, M., Houssein, E. H., & Mohamed, W. M. (2020). Classification with quantum machine learning: A survey. arXiv preprint arXiv:2006.12270.

35. Kilber, N., Kaestle, D. and Wagner, S., 2021. Cybersecurity for Quantum Computing. arXiv preprint arXiv:2110.14701.

5

Secure E-Voting Scheme Using Blockchain

Shrimoyee Banerjee and Umesh Bodkhe*

CSE Department, Institute of Technology, Nirma University, Gujarat, India

Abstract

Casting a vote is an indispensable act which can be helpful in terms of picking the right person for elective office. An effective leader can bring flourishing development to a nation and furthermore can lead the country to success and growth. However, the electoral system is faced with a lot of security issues such as forgery, third-party involvement, privacy breaches etc. Essentially, third-party contribution might prompt a great deal of security breaches and illegal casting of ballots. Additionally, when arriving to vote, an individual must stand in a long line, making voting an extremely tedious process. So, every country requires a system that ensures authentic citizen enrollment and unmistakable verification. They also ought to likewise encompass an electoral platform that smoothens out and streamlines the method of casting a ballot, maintaining transparency and straightforwardness in the election results.

In the following paper, a decentralized system has been created which ensures that all the protocols are followed and there is no case of third-party involvement or any kind of fraud. This idea uses smart contracts in the system to help reduce security issues, precision, accuracy and electors' privacy during the vote. This paper creates a system that makes sure only one vote per person can be given, and a legitimate two-way authentication is done, without any third-party involvement. The protocol brings about a straightforward, non-editable and autonomously verifiable system that eliminates the possibility of relative fraudulence and tampering that can happen during the electoral decision process. Therefore, no transaction can be altered, deleted or destroyed.

Keywords: Blockchain, quantum, security, e-voting

Corresponding author: umesh.bodkhe@nirmauni.ac.in

Romil Rawat, Rajesh Kumar Chakrawarti, Sanjaya Kumar Sarangi, Jaideep Patel, Vivek Bhardwaj, Anjali Rawat and Hitesh Rawat (eds.) Quantum Computing in Cybersecurity, (81–104) © 2023 Scrivener Publishing LLC

5.1   Introduction

5.1.1   General Introduction

Voting is essential for a democratic country. Even local authorities assign a significant budget to bring about a more robust and trustworthy voting system. For electronic voting systems, people are concerned about whether the result that is shown on the bulletin can be trusted. Blockchain, with the slowly increasing popularity and widespread success of cryptocurrency, provides another platform to increase the public's trust in such e-voting systems. The opportunity of Blockchain was at first provided by Mr. Satoshi Nakamoto, who proposed a passed exchange framework that licenses cash trades through the internet without relying on somebody's trust [1]. In a blockchain-based network, no unequivocal body or gathering has it. Rather, every middle point that is gotten with the blockchain structure holds the information block locally. The hypothesis is that Quantum blockchain is decentralized and is particularly secure and the blockchain should be visible as an untouchable that can be relied upon for precision and openness. The blockchain is really strong and thus any activity that adjusts the information in any square abuses the blockchain game plan rule and is pardoned by the blockchain network [14–19].

5.1.1.1   Key Components of the Blockchain Architecture

Figure 5.1 shows the key components of the Blockchain Architecture as:

- Node: In a blockchain layout, node refers to users or machines.
- Transaction: It is the price that is deducted when an activity is done by the user.
- Block: a group of knowledge structures that are used to perform transactions.
- Chain: a series of unique blocks.
- Miners: Correspondent nodes that confirm transactions and adds them.
- Consensus: A group of commands that aids in the blockchain procedure's execution.

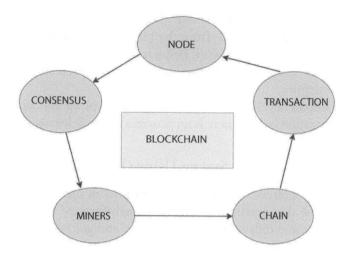

Figure 5.1 Key components of the blockchain architecture.

5.1.1.2   Characteristics of Blockchain Architecture

The design of the blockchain system enjoys many benefits for every one of the areas that utilize the blockchain framework. Qualities are depicted Figure 5.2:

- Cryptography: Blockchain exchanges are confirmed, checked and exact on account of calculations and cryptographic proof between the gatherings in question.
- Immutability: Any blockchain report cannot be exposed to change or cancellation.
- Provenance: Every exchange can be followed and followed back in the blockchain record.

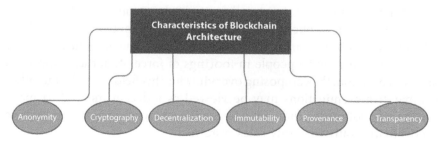

Figure 5.2 Characteristics of the system.

- Decentralization: The whole dispersed data set might be open by all individuals from the blockchain network.
- Anonymous: this network helps to keep up with the nameless of the user providing with privacy protection and anonymity.
- Transparency: There is no third party involved and once a transaction is done there is no possible way to delete and reset.

5.1.2   Electronic Voting System Using Quantum Blockchain

This innovation addressed constraints in the present method of decisions. It has made the democratic instrument straightforward and open, forestalled falseness and unlawful activity fortified and got information insurance, and also really look at the consequences of the democratic. The usage of e-projecting a voting form procedure in blockchain is moderate and is a respectably stylish idea [7–10]. In any case, electronic majority rule conveys colossal risks and drawbacks. Subsequently, this system has not yet been introduced on a common platform, keeping up with as a main concern all its possible advantages. Regardless, today, there is a material and reasonable plan that overcomes the risks of electronic majority rule: Blockchain Technology. In Figure 5.4, the basic difference between both the structures is clear. In traditional popularity-based structures, we have a central situation to go with a decision. Nobody has the main power, the information is taken care of in different center points. Hacking all center points and changing the information is ridiculous. Therefore, one cannot destroy, change or look at the votes [20].

Expecting that the development is used precisely, the blockchain is a high-level, decentralized, encoded, direct record that can persevere through control and coercion. A blockchain-based electronic majority rule design requires a totally disseminated casting a ballot framework. Considering blockchain, an electronic vote-based system will just work where the web projecting a polling form structure is completely unconstrained by any one body, not even the public authority. To recap, races should be free and fair when individuals have areas of strength for an in the authenticity of the power stood firm on by people in footings of force. As far as association and collaboration, the composing overview for this field of study and other comparative examinations may be viewed as a decent method to make casting a ballot more productive. Regardless, blockchain gave an elective model to innovative majority rules system.

5.1.3   Architecture

Electronic democracy, from an expansive perspective, is the method involved in casting a vote that happens electronically, by means of some electronic equipment or programming. Such electronic democracy ought to be prepared to help and execute different elements of the democratic cycle, from setting up the political race through mass capacity of the votes. Stands at political decision workplaces, PC gadgets and all the more as of late, cell phones are a couple of instances of frameworks that help electronic democracy. Citizen enlistment, validation, casting a ballot, and counting should be integrated in the electronic democratic frameworks (Figure 5.3). Blockchain might have a critical effect in the space of electronic democracy. The gamble to compensate proportion is enormous to the point that electronic democratic alone is certainly not a doable choice. Since a blockchain network is gigantic, de-bound together, open to all, and arrangement driven, its arrangement guarantees that distortion is speculatively tremendous until insufficiently done. Thus, the blockchain's extraordinary qualities should be thought of. There isn't anything innate about blockchain

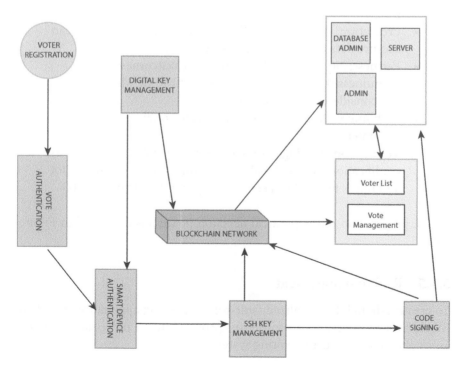

Figure 5.3 Blockchain voting systems architectural overview.

innovation that keeps it from being utilized compared to some other sort of digital currency. Utilizing blockchain framework to make an alternative safe electronic/internet casting a ballot cycle is building up some forward movement.

5.1.4   Objective

The main purpose is to identify problems and make arrangements. Making voting easier, more productive, straightforward, and safer is possibly the most important initiative.

Whether we're discussing conventional paper-based casting of a ballot, automated casting through ballot machines, or an internet casting a ballot framework, there are a few changes that should be made to ensure the following characteristics apply:

- Eligibility: Only accepted and true users are eligible to take part in the voting process, i.e., they are 18 or above and a citizen of the country;
- Non-Reusability: Each elector can cast a ballot just a single time;
- Protection: No one with the exception of the citizen can acquire data about the elector's decision;
- Fairness: No one can alter democratic outcomes;
- Soundness: Invalid voting forms ought to be identified and not considered during counting;
- Fulfillment: All legitimate voting forms ought to be counted accurately.
- Verification: Making sure that the citizen follows and fulfills qualification rules and really at that time they can cast a ballot and this is finished by keeping an eye on their legitimate ID.

The progression of the political decision process is displayed in Figure 5.4 [13].

5.1.5   Problem Statement

To create a digital decentralized fault-tolerant voting application based on Blockchain architecture and consensus protocol that is more safe, resilient, and stable than the current voting system.

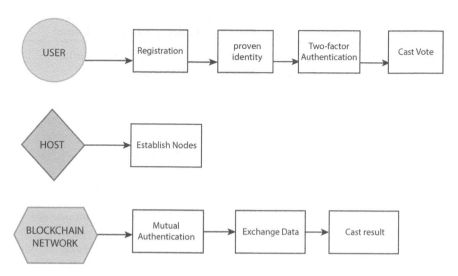

Figure 5.4 Flow of the election process.

5.2 Literature Survey

5.2.1 Overview

Numerous frameworks were proposed to tackle explicit issues with e-casting a ballot and answering questions in regard to explicit innovation restrictions. One of the issues that have been investigated is the stage reliance of most blockchains [1]. Specialists keep up with the fact that the reliance on a specific stage creates some issues regarding execution, as well as security. A few specialists attempted to utilize the current open blockchains, for example, Ethereum [2–5]. A few business arrangements were additionally proposed, similar to Agora [5], which is a start to finish irrefutable democratic answer for states and organizations. The model in this paper depends on taking the elector's one-of-a-kind Voter ID and date of birth as an essential advance to check qualification and afterward go for a two-venture verification by requesting its Aadhar number since it is unique for everybody in this nation and is connected with the citizen's versatile number so it guarantees security and a simple stream without making it complex. When the citizen votes, it keeps up with protection by not showing the subtleties of the projecting and logs the client out straightforwardly, forestalling misrepresentation. This paper manages models for augmenting protection and security of elector's data as referenced in Blockchain-Based E-Voting System.

Author	Year	Paper name	Objective and description
Bryan Ford [5]	2017	Agora: Bringing our voting systems into the 21st century	- A suitable voting solution for governments and organisations - Three breakthroughs were created: Skipchain, Cotena, and Valeda. 1) Skipchain is a high-throughput consensus technique with quick transaction approval. 2) Cotena then demonstrates how to store encrypted Skipchain evidences on the Bitcoin blockchain. 3) Valeda verifies Skipchain and Cotena data using cryptographic evidence.
Patrick McCorry [11]	2017	A Smart Contract for Boardroom Voting with Maximum Voter Privacy	The Open Vote Network was developed to have a self-tallying system that also ensures anonymity.
Andrew Barnes [12]	2016	Digital Voting with the use of Blockchain Technology	Proposed integrating blockchain technology into the UK's present voting system, which allows voters to vote in person or via a web browser at home.
Jonathan Alexander [4]	2018	Netvote: A Decentralized Voting Network	The user interface of Netvote is based on decentralized applications (dApps). The Administrator DApp allows users to register, create polling forms, vote, and more. The election results are then counted and verified using the Tally dApp.

(Continued)

(Continued)

Author	Year	Paper name	Objective and description
Zhao, Z. [23]	2015	How to vote privately using bitcoin	Use of zero-knowledge-confirmations, which helps one group to prove that they are correct without exposing additional information.
F. Hjlmarsson [6]	2018	Blockchain Based E-voting system	Based on private blockchain implementation.
Kriti Patidar [21]	2021	Decentralised E-voting Portal using Blockchain	- RSA algorithms - Third-Party counting - Blockchain and ETH - suitable for small scale like society or classroom
Haibo Yi [22]	2019	Securing e-voting based on blockchain in P2P network	- a peer-to-peer network to improve e-voting security and privacy - a model that prevents forging - it allows the voters to change or remove their votes before final cast of the votes.

5.3 Implementation and Methodology

Electronic Voting System using Aadhar number along with Voter ID is a two-factor authentication and verification for users that ensures extra support, privacy, protection and makes sure of the eligibility of the user before casting a vote. Here we are using Aadhar ID number as a 2-step authentication process for the voter. Firstly, voter enters his/her Date of birth and Voter ID as the first step to ensure that they are eligible to vote (18+ and a citizen of the country). The second step of verification will be the Aadhar that is linked to their mobile no. to ensure safely, security and prevent forgery. The Figure 5.5 shows about the use case diagram of the voting system, and Figure 5.6 represents npm install. The Figure 5.7 explains about the running it by "node index.js" and the Figure 5.8 shows about the run node index.js in terminal to run the project. The Figure 5.9 represents about the create the smart contracts, The Figure 5.10 highlights about linking Aadhaar card number to

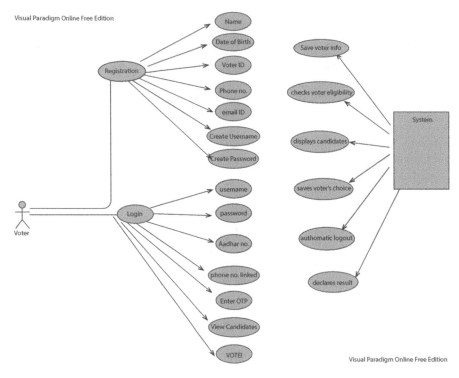

Figure 5.5 Use case diagram of the voting system.

Figure 5.6 npm install.

Figure 5.7 Running it by "node index.js".

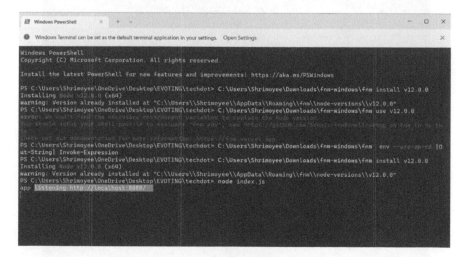

Figure 5.8 Run node index.js in terminal to run the project.

your phone number. The Figure 5.11 shows about the Testrpc showing the 10 accounts that can be used. The Figure 5.12 represents the deployment. The Figure 5.13 shows about user registration and Figure 5.14 shows about the Error message. The Figure 5.15 shows user login, the Figure 5.16 shows

Aadhaar verification. The Figure 5.17 shows OTP on the user's Aadhaar linked phone number. The Figure 5.18 represents Error on wrong OTP. The Figure 5.19 focussed on users casting their votes, and lastly the Figure 5.20 shows about the blockchain transactions.

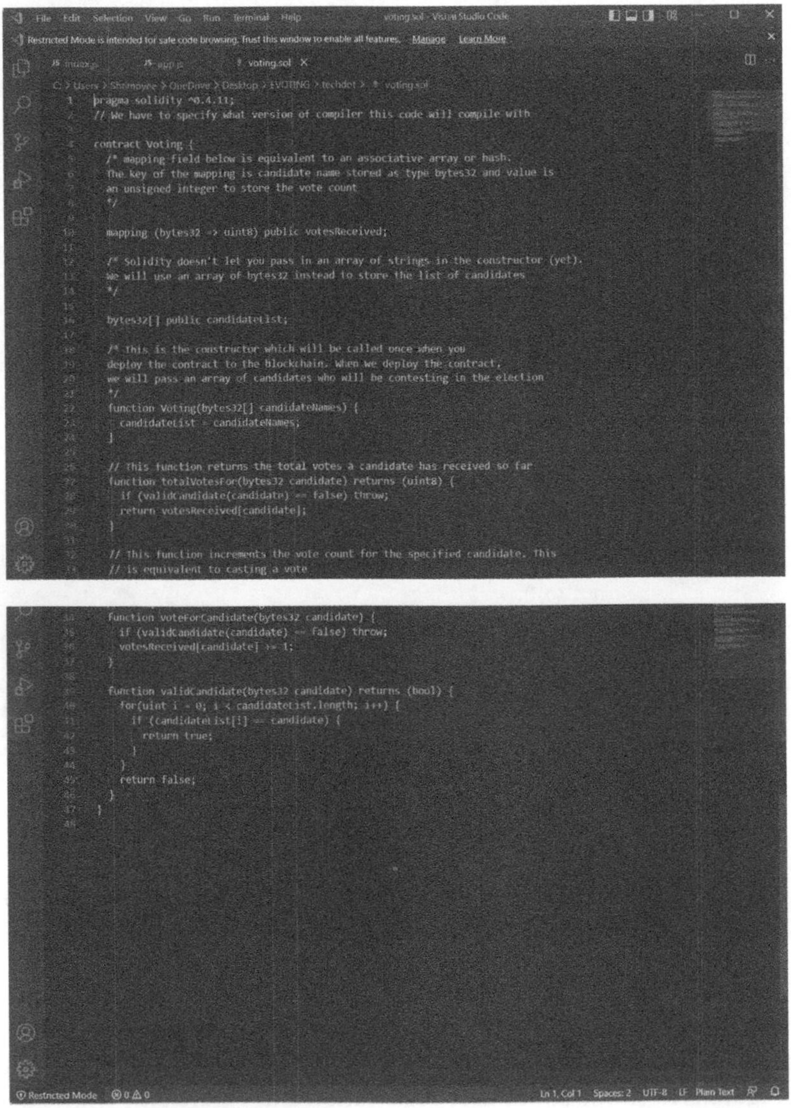

Figure 5.9 Create the smart contracts.

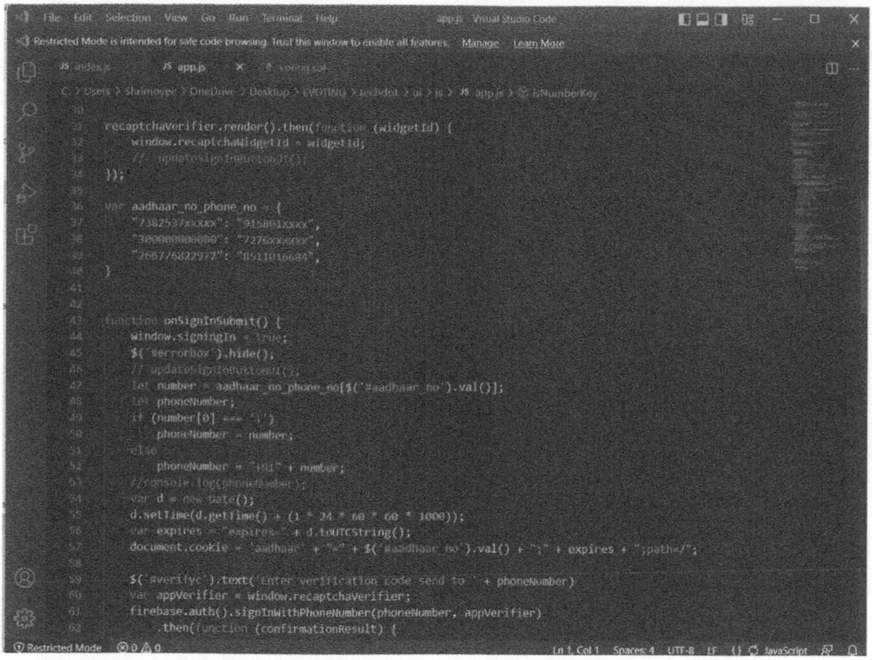

Figure 5.10 Linking Aadhaar card number to your phone number.

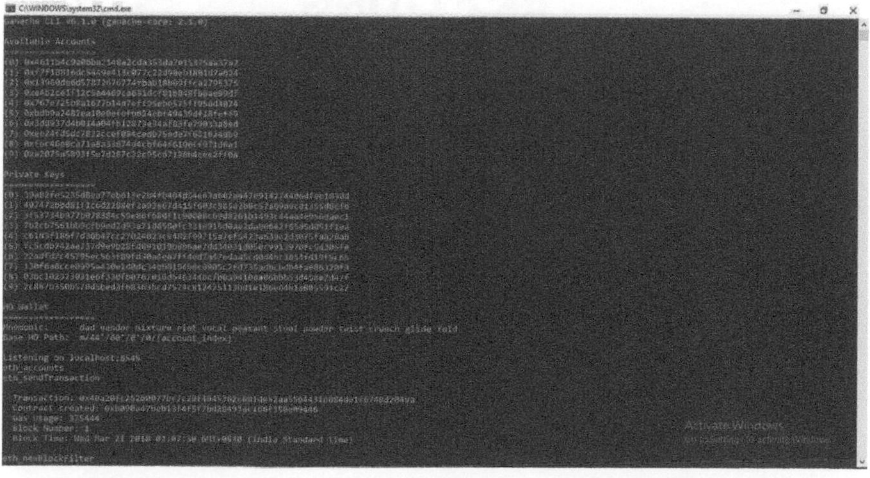

Figure 5.11 Testrpc showing the 10 accounts that can be used.

Figure 5.12 Deployment.

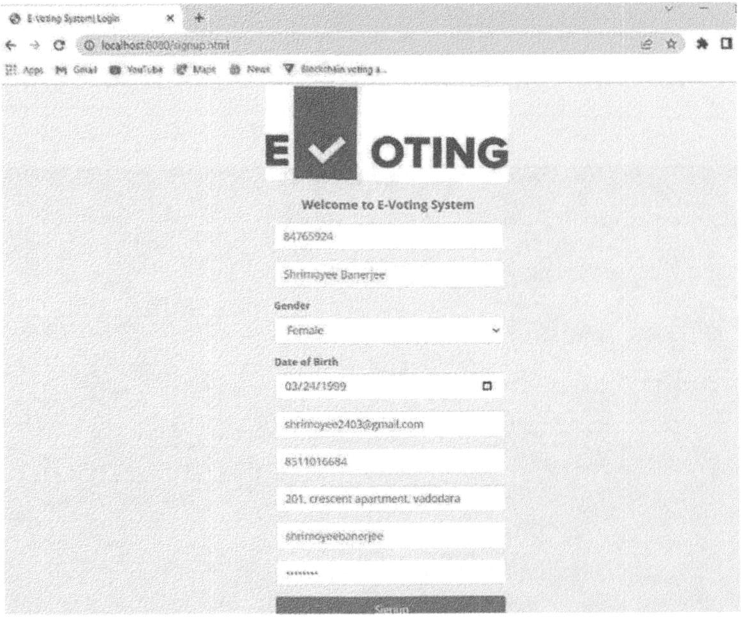

Figure 5.13 User registration.

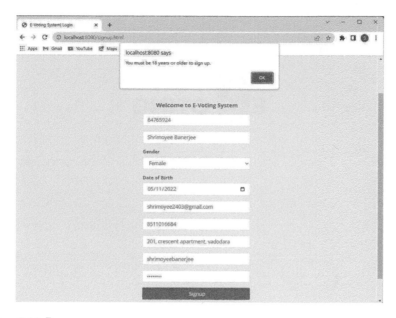

Figure 5.14 Error message.

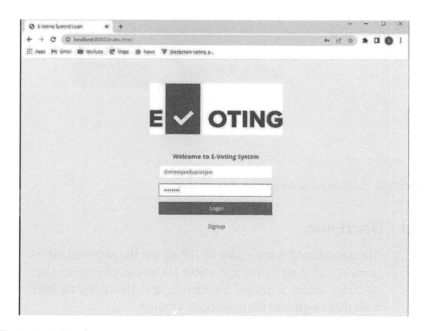

Figure 5.15 User login.

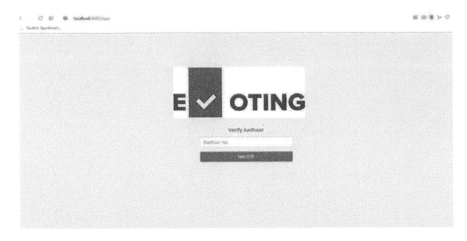

Figure 5.16 Aadhaar verification.

5.3.1   Description

- The user should first register by filling out the required information, i.e., their name, age, voter ID, email, phone number and also create a unique username and password to later help them sign into their account created.

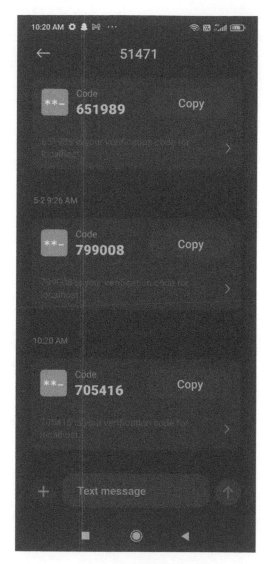

Figure 5.17 OTP on the user's Aadhaar linked phone number.

- The user must first log in using their unique username and password. If the username or password is wrong, they will not be allowed to vote, ensuring protection from fraud.
- The voter is now permitted to cast their vote, after they get an OTP (one-time password) to their linked phone number.

Figure 5.18 Error on wrong OTP.

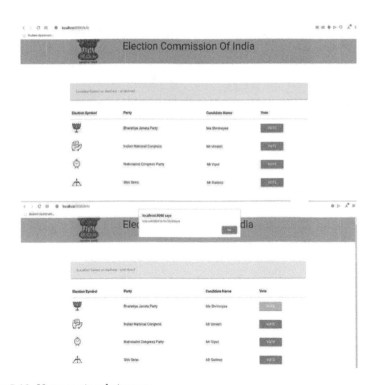

Figure 5.19 Users casting their votes.

Figure 5.20 Blockchain transactions.

- Only correct Aadhar number and OTP will get the user into the system, allowing them to cast a vote.
- Candidate names, political parties, and logos will be displayed on the voting page.
- Next, voters can cast a vote for any one of their preferred candidates.
- One Voter can cast his vote for a single candidate and then immediately will get logged out, ensuring there is no fraud or double voting.

5.3.2 Installing Dependencies

1. HTML
2. CSS

3. JavaScript
4. Solidity
5. Testrpc
6. NodeJs

- The online application for the E-Voting system is created and designed using HTML, CSS, and JavaScript.
- Solidity - It is a language to make smart contracts on block-chain systems, like Ethereum
- Testrpc is an Ethereum client based on Node.js for testing and development. It makes Ethereum application development much faster by using ethereumjs to emulate entire client behaviour. It also comes with all of the standard RPC functions and capabilities (such as events) and may be performed deterministically to make development easier.

Install Dependencies
npm install
Running Project
node index.js

5.3.3   Running

Step 1: Set up the Environment. Rather than using the live Ethereum blockchain to assemble the application, we used testrpc, an in-memory blockchain.

Step 2 - Creating Voting Smart Contract

Add the Aadhaar number and linked mobile number manually to run the project.

5.4   Result Analysis & Output

- First you find a signup page, where the voter is required to register by filling out all their necessary details. Details like Name, Age, Gender, Phone no., Address, Date of Birth and voter ID are some of the very important details mainly for security and eligibility purposes, as shown in the screenshot below. Without registering, the voter cannot cast their vote.

- Also, the person needs to create a unique username and password to later log into the account in the next step.
- Entering a wrong username or password will lead to an error message.
- If the person enters a date of birth which shows they are not 18 yet, then there is an error in the process.
- After the registration is done, and the user is proved to be an Indian citizen who is above the age of 18, the user is directed to a page where they are asked to log in. Here they need to enter the exact username and password that they created to log in in the registration page. If entered incorrectly, they will not be able to login successfully.

Shown below is the process of logging in.

- After the user has successfully been able to log in they are directed to a page where they are asked for their Aadhaar ID. This is a two-step verification process to ensure that the person is a citizen and to ensure double transparency and security.
- After entering their correct Aadhaar no., the user is sent an OTP to the linked phone number.
- If the OTP entered is wrong, then again there will be an error.
- Next, the user is directed to the page where they can see all the candidates and place their votes.
- As soon as the vote is placed, it gets saved internally using Blockchain.
- As the voter successfully casts his vote, we can see in terminal, in the backend that the transaction has been done. A block has been created for the voter with a unique ID and gas usage.
- Also, its timestamp is available at the same time along with its transaction ID and gas usage. Similarly, the list is visible as the voters keep voting.
- This version of Ganache, your own blockchain for Ethereum development, is seen here as role of the Truffle suite.
- Ganache CLI makes Ethereum application development faster, easier, and safer by simulating full client behaviour using ethereumjs. It also comes with all of the standard RPC functions and capabilities (such as events) and may be performed deterministically to make development easier.

5.5   Conclusion and Future Directions

When it comes to electronic voting using blockchain, a lot of problems have to be kept in mind. Even though it is a very practical, efficient and secure way to vote, a lot of issues have to be dealt with, such as Scalability, user identity issues, transactional privacy, energy efficiency, immaturity and acceptableness. As we have also seen in this paper, blockchain works really well when it is up to a small scale of users but errors occur when we try to deal with large-scale users. Also, there are still a lot of privacy issues because we can see user details, and the purpose of using a blockchain is not fulfilled. Further, more work has to be done so that blockchain can be used for large scale with proper efficiency and smoothness along with maintaining user confidentiality. As we know, blockchain is still very new, due to which the awareness and usability is still a problem among ordinary people and is yet to be solved by marketing and also other lessons.

We explored and examined the simple ballot system in detail, as well as the advantages of implementing an electronic voting system that is supported and upheld by blockchain technology, employs various blockchain-based devices, and conducts a contextual examination of the manual voting process. Then we considered and differentiated between traditional voting methods and the vote casting method using blockchain. As a unified voting system, the new voting system uses blockchain. This system will employ blockchain as both an organization and a database to hold voter data or qualifications that will be used for authentication. For the voting system, the system will require candidate or voter information, and carry a two-factor authentication for safety and privacy of the user and to ensure no third-party involvement.

References

1. Nakamoto, S. (2008). Bitcoin: A peer-to-peer electronic cash system. *Decentralized Business Review*, 21260.
2. B. Yu, J. K. Liu, A. Sakzad, S. Nepal, R. Steinfeld, P. Rimba, and M. H. Au, "Platform-independent secure blockchain-based voting system," in *International Conference on Information Security*, 2018, pp. 369-386.
3. E. Yavuz, A. K. Koç, U. C. Çabuk, and G. Dalkılıç, "Towards secure e-voting using ethereum blockchain," in *2018 6th International Symposium on Digital Forensic and Security (ISDFS)*, March 2018, pp. 1-7.
4. J. Alexander, S. Landers, and B. Howerton, "Netvote: A decentralized voting network," Available at https://netvote. io/wpcontent/uploads/2018/02.

5. Bryan Ford, Leonardo Gammar, Agora (2017)." Agora: Bringing our voting systems into the 21st century." Available at: https://agora.vote/Agora_Whitepaper_v0.1.pdf

6. F. Hjlmarsson, G. K. Hreiarsson, M. Hamdaqa, and G. Hjlmtsson, "Blockchain-based e-voting system," in *2018 IEEE 11th International Conference on Cloud Computing (CLOUD)*, July 2018, pp. 983-986.

7. P. McCorry, S. F. Shahandashti, and F. Hao, "A smart contract for boardroom voting with maximum voter privacy." Available at https://eprint.iacr.org/2017/110.pdf, 2017.

8. N. Kshetri and J. Voas, "Blockchain-enabled e-voting," *IEEE Software*, vol. 35, no. 4, pp. 95-99, July 2018. 11.[Edx, "Blochchain for business - an introduction to hyperledger technology,"

9. Jafar, U.; Aziz, M.J.A.; Shukur, Z. Blockchain for Electronic Voting System— Review and Open Research Challenges. *Sensors* 2021, 21, 5874. https://doi.org/10.3390/s21175874

10. Asem Abuelhija, Aiah Abudouleh, Baraah Abumuhsen, Fahed Awad, "Secure Voting System Using Distributed Ledger Technology," in *2020 11th International Conference on Information and Communication Systems (ICICS)* 978-1-7281-6227-0/20/$31.00 ©2020 IEEE 10.1109/ICICS49469.2020.239487

11. Patrick McCorry, Siamak F. Shahandashti and Feng Hao. (2017). A Smart Contract for Boardroom Voting with Maximum Voter Privacy. Available at: https://eprint.iacr.org/2017/110.pdf.

12. Andrew Barnes, Christopher Brake and Thomas Perry. (2016). Digital Voting with the use of Blockchain Technology. Available at: https://www. economist.com/sites/default/files/plymouth.pdf

13. D. Springall *et al.*, "Security Analysis of the Estonian Internet Voting System," in *Proceedings of the 2014 ACM SIGSAC Conference on Computer and Communications Security - CCS '14*, 2014, pp. 703-715.

14. Bodkhe, U., & Tanwar, S. (2021). Secure data dissemination techniques for IoT applications: Research challenges and opportunities. *Software: Practice and Experience*, 51(12), 2469-2491.

15. Bodkhe, U., Tanwar, S., Parekh, K., Khanpara, P., Tyagi, S., Kumar, N., & Alazab, M. (2020). Blockchain for industry 4.0: A comprehensive review. *IEEE Access*, 8, 79764-79800.

16. Bhattacharya, P., Tanwar, S., Bodkhe, U., Tyagi, S., & Kumar, N. (2019). Bindaas: Blockchain-based deep-learning as-a-service in healthcare 4.0 applications. *IEEE Transactions on Network Science and Engineering*, 8(2), 1242-1255.

17. Bodkhe, U., Mehta, D., Tanwar, S., Bhattacharya, P., Singh, P. K., & Hong, W. C. (2020). A survey on decentralized consensus mechanisms for cyber physical systems. *IEEE Access*, 8, 54371-54401.

18. Mehta, D., Tanwar, S., Bodkhe, U., Shukla, A., & Kumar, N. (2021). Blockchain-based royalty contract transactions scheme for Industry 4.0 supply-chain management. *Information Processing & Management*, 58(4), 102586.

19. Bodkhe, U., Tanwar, S., Bhattacharya, P., & Verma, A. (2021). Blockchain adoption for trusted medical records in healthcare 4.0 applications: a survey. In *Proceedings of Second International Conference on Computing, Communications, and Cyber-Security* (pp. 759-774). Springer, Singapore.
20. C. K. Adiputra, R. Hjort and H. Sato, "A Proposal of Blockchain-Based Electronic Voting System," 2018 Second World Conference on Smart Trends in Systems, Security and Sustainability (WorldS4), London, 2018, pp. 22-27, doi: 10.1109/WorldS4.2018.8611593.
21. Patidar, K., & Jain, S. (2019, July). Decentralized e-voting portal using blockchain. In *2019 10th International Conference on Computing, Communication and Networking Technologies (ICCCNT)* (pp. 1-4). IEEE.
22. Yi, H. (2019). Securing e-voting based on blockchain in P2P network. *EURASIP Journal on Wireless Communications and Networking*, 2019(1), 1-9.
23. Zhao, Z., & Chan, T. H. H. (2015, December). How to vote privately using bitcoin. In *International Conference on Information and Communications Security* (pp. 82-96). Springer, Cham.

6

An Overview of Quantum Computing–Based Hidden Markov Models

B. Abhishek[1], Sathian D.[1], Amit Kumar Tyagi[2*] and Deepshikha Agarwal[3]

[1]School of Computer Science and Engineering, Vellore Institute of Technology, Chennai, Tamil Nadu, India
[2]Department of Fashion Technology, National Institute of Fashion Technology, New Delhi, Delhi, India
[3]Department of Information Technology, IIIT Lucknow, Uttar Pradesh, India

Abstract

The basic concept of Markov chains has been known to mathematicians and engineers for the last 80 years, but it was only in the last decade that it was directly applied to speech processing difficulties. One of the significant reasons why speech models based on Markov chains had not been created until recently was the lack of a strategy for modifying the parameters of the Markov model to suit actual signal patterns. Further advancements in theory and execution have resulted in a diverse range of applications for Markov modeling approaches. The goal of this study is to provide an introduction to Markov model theory based on quantum computing and demonstrate how it has been used to voice recognition issues.

Keywords: Markov models, learning algorithms, speech processing, voice recognition

6.1 Introduction

Suppose you've been given the following situation. A sequence of observable symbols [1–3] is produced by a real-world process. The symbols might be discrete or continuous.

Certain fundamental decisions must be taken to tackle such a challenge, informed by signal and system theory. For instance, there are linear and non-linear models, time-varying and time-invariant models, and

*Corresponding author: amitkrtyagi025@gmail.com

Romil Rawat, Rajesh Kumar Chakrawarti, Sanjaya Kumar Sarangi, Jaideep Patel, Vivek Bhardwaj, Anjali Rawat and Hitesh Rawat (eds.) Quantum Computing in Cybersecurity, (105–120) © 2023 Scrivener Publishing LLC

deterministic and stochastic models to select from. Several potential signal [4] models may be created based on selections and additional signal processing concerns.

Considering signal, that is a little more complex, specifically a sinewave with noise embedded in it. The signal's noise components complicate the modelling challenge since the noise component's properties must be considered while estimating the sinewave parameters (amplitude, frequency, and phase).

In the preceding instances, it is possible that this isn't a reasonable assumption. A non-linear model, such as amplitude modulation, may be more appropriate if the unknown process, for example, generates a sinewave with changing magnitude.

Linear System models

The principles underpinning the following instances have been thoroughly investigated in classical communication theory.

Linear system models, which represent the output stimulated by a suitable source as the object symbols, are another significant family of signal modeling [5] techniques that have proved helpful for a wide range of applications. In this situation, signal modeling entails determining the linear filter coefficients and, sometimes, the excitation parameters. Other types of spectral analyses fail as well. Many real-world processes cannot be accurately described without considering temporal variance. One example of such procedures is speech signals. The challenge of modelling the temporal fluctuation of a signal may be approached in several ways.

Consider the process as a linear combination of these smaller "short time" segments, each of which is represented by a linear system model, to deal with the time-varying character of the process. The overall model is a synchronised series of Symbols, each and every symbol representing a small component of the process as a linear system model. This approach shows the detected signal in view by utilising signal tokens representative of the signal.

Processes of 'Time Varying'

When modelling time-varying [6, 7] events with the preceding method, each short-time segment of observation is considered to be a unit with a constant duration. The duration of a short-time segment is defined experimentally in most physical systems. In such activities, one will not assume process characteristics to change synchronously with each unit analysis time, nor would one expect to detect significant variations across units unless unusual conditions existed. This signal modelling template technique has shown to be quite productive and has been used to create numerous voice recognition systems.

There are solid grounds to believe that, while useful, the above approach is not the most efficient (in terms of computing, storage, parameters, and so on) strategy for representation at this time. Many authentic processes appear to have a rather sequentially changing behaviour. The process' properties are usually held reasonably consistent, except for minor fluctuations, for a certain period, and then change (gradually or rapidly) to a different set of features at specific points. We may exploit the potential for more efficient modelling if we can first detect these periods of reasonably constant behaviour and then accept that the temporal variations inside each of these stable periods are, in a sense, statistical. A more efficient representation may be achieved by using a familiar brief model for each of the signal's stable or well-behaved portions and some definition of how one period advances to the next. Hidden Markov models (H/vM) are created in this way. Three issues must be addressed: 1) how to identify these consistently or distinctively acting times, 2) for each of these times, which common or widespread short-term model will be utilised, and 3) how to represent the "sequentially" changing character of these intervals. Quantum computing based Hidden Markov models can solve these issues satisfactorily without using a probabilistic or statistical framework. Quantum computers excel in problem solving involving large volumes of data inputs. They are intended to solve complicated issues that would take supercomputers days to solve. Quantum computing–based hidden Markov model (HQMM) [8, 9] was introduced by Monras et al. [1] whose parameters are Kraus operators.

The main objective for describing HQMM is when and how to apply it practically. We will not limit our general discussion to any one topic, but we will show how HQMMs are employed in voice recognition with a few instances at the conclusion of this work.

6.2   Elaboration of Hidden Quantum Markov Model

A Hidden Quantum Markov Model is a two-stage stochastic process [10, 11] with a hidden (unobservable) stochastic process. that can only be seen through another set of stochastic processes that generate the sequence of observable symbols. The following coin toss example demonstrates HQMMs.

Coin toss example
Consider the following simple example to grasp the notion of the HQMM. You're in a room with a barrier (e.g., a curtain) that prevents you from

seeing what's happening. Another individual on the other side of the barrier is conducting a trial by flipping a coin (or many coins). The other chap isn't going to tell you anything about what he's up to, but he would inform you of the outcome of every Coin Flip. As a consequence, a series of secret coin tossing tests are carried out, with you only seeing the outcomes of the coin tosses, i.e.,

$$O = \mathcal{H} \ \mathcal{H} \ \mathcal{T} \mathcal{H} \mathcal{T} \mathcal{T} \mathcal{H} \mathcal{H} \cdots \mathcal{T}$$

$$O_1 \, O_2 \, O_3 \, \ldots\ldots \, O_T$$

where '$\mathcal{H}$'- stands for heads and '$\mathcal{T}$'- stands for tails.

Given the aforementioned experiment, the challenge is constructing an HQMM to explain the observed sequence of heads and tails. Figure 6.1a depicts one such model. This is known as the "one-fair coin" concept. The model has two states, but each is linked with either head (state 1) or tail (state 2). As a result, this model is not concealed since the observation sequence defines the state in a unique way. Because the chance of generating a head (or a tail) after a head (or a tail) equals 0.5, the model reflects a "fair coin". This degenerate example demonstrates how separate trials, such as the flipping of a fair coin, may be interpreted as a series of events. Of course, if the person behind the barrier is tossing a single fair coin, this model should be able to explain the results adequately.

A second potential HQMM for describing the observed sequence of coin toss outcomes, Figure 6.1b. This concept is known as the "two-fair coin" model [11–14]. This time, the model contains two states, but none of them is linked to heads or tails. The probability of heads (or tails) in both states is 0.5. Also, either state has a 0.5 chance of leaving (or returning to). In a conclusion, we may link each state with a fair (impartial) coin in this scenario. Because the probability of remaining in or leaving either of the two states is 0.5, a little thought should persuade the reader that state transitions do not affect the statistics of the "two-fair coins" model's observable output sequences.

Figures 6.1c and 6.1d represent two more possible HQMMs that might explain heads and tails sequence. Figure 6.1c shows a model with two states, labelled as the two-biased coins model. It's heavily skewed in the direction of heads in state 1. It's heavily skewed in the direction of tails in state 2. All of the state transition probabilities are 0.5. This hidden Markov model with two biased coins is distinct from the two previously mentioned models. This concept is highly suited if the following is going on behind

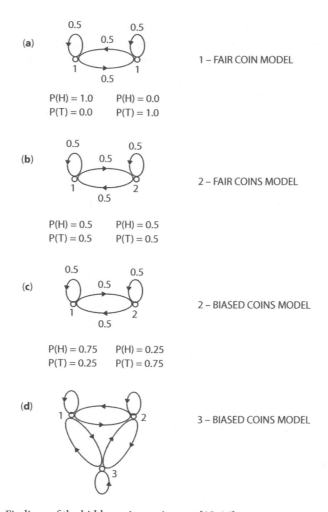

(a)

0.5   0.5
0.5
1   1
0.5

1 – FAIR COIN MODEL

P(H) = 1.0   P(H) = 0.0
P(T) = 0.0   P(T) = 1.0

(b)

0.5   0.5
0.5
1   2
0.5

2 – FAIR COINS MODEL

P(H) = 0.5   P(H) = 0.5
P(T) = 0.5   P(T) = 0.5

(c)

0.5   0.5
0.5
1   2
0.5

2 – BIASED COINS MODEL

P(H) = 0.75   P(H) = 0.25
P(T) = 0.25   P(T) = 0.75

(d)

1   2

3

3 – BIASED COINS MODEL

Figure 6.1 Findings of the hidden coin-tossing test [15, 16].

the barrier. As detailed in Figure 6.1c, the person possesses three coins, one of which is fair and the other two are biased. The two faces of the fair coin are represented by two biased coins. We can investigate and explain the aforementioned minor feature changes using this approach (i.e., switching the biased coins). Figure 6.1d depicts a model with three states, which we refer to as the three-biased coins model. It's somewhat leaned toward heads in state 1, severely also leaned against tails in state 2, and slightly biased toward tails in state 3. In Fig. 1d, we haven't provided values for the state transition probabilities; nonetheless, the behaviour of the observational sequence generated by such a model is influenced by these probabilities

[17]. (The reader should analyse two extreme examples to persuade himself of this, namely when the chance of remaining in state 3 is great (:>0.95) or tiny (:0.05). This is because of the significant bias of coins related to State 3; these two extremes will provide very different sequence statistics. An actual situation behind the barrier that corresponds to such a model may be built similarly to the two-biased coin model; the reader should have no problem doing so.

There are a few significant lessons from this discussion of how to use HQMMs to describe the results of the "Coin Tossing" experiment. To begin, we should mention that deciding on the model's size (number of states) is one of the most challenging aspects of the modelling process. Without some prior knowledge, this is a difficult decision to make, and it may require some sort of trial and error before we go for the best model size. Even though it is settled for a three-coin model [18] as cited in the above image, it's possible that even this is too tiny. How can we figure out how many coins (states) the model truly needs? The solution to this topic is linked to another, more general question: how do we pick model parameters? The last item to be considered is the length of the observation sequence.

Elements of a Hidden Markov Model
Now, while going through the components & mechanisms of HQMMs:

- The model contains a Finite no. of states, such as 'N'; we won't specify a state precisely; instead, we'll say that each state has some measurable, distinct features.
- A new state is entered at each clock time, t, depending on a transition probability distribution that is dependent on the preceding state (the Markovian property). (It's worth noting that the transition may cause the process to revert to its prior state.)
- Upon each shift, a probability distribution depending on the current state is used to create an observation output symbol. This state's probability distribution remains constant no matter when or how it is entered. As a matter of fact, N observation probability distributions exist, each of which represents random variables or stochastic processes.

Considering the model "ball and urn" in Figure 6.2 to help you organise your thoughts. N urns are present, each containing a huge number of colourful balls.

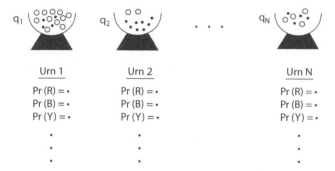

Figure 6.2 An urn and ball model that demonstrates how a discrete symbol hidden Markov model works in general. A huge number of coloured balls are included in each of the N urns (the N states of the model) [19, 20].

Each and every ball has the potential to be M different colours. The observational sequence starts with picking one of the N urns, then picking a ball from that urn, noting its colour, replacing the ball, and finally picking a new urn depending on the current urn's transition probability distribution. As an example, consider the following observation sequence:

Clock Time	1234. .. T
Urn (Hidden) State	$q_3q_1q_1q_2$... qN-2
Color (Observation)	R B Y Y ... R

For a discrete observation HQMM, we now explicitly define the following model notation:

'T' = Length of observational sequence (total no. of Clock Times)
'N' = No. of States (urns) in the Model
'M' = No. of Observation Symbols (Colours)
'Q' = {q1, q2, . .. ,qN}, States (urns)
'V' = {V1, V2, ... ,VM} Possible Symbol Observations (Colors)
'A' = {aij}, aij = Pr(qj at t + 11 qi at t), State Transition Probability Distribution
'B' = {bj(k)}, bj(k) = Pr(vk at tl q; at t), Observation Symbol Probability Distribution in State i
π= {π$_i$}, π$_i$ = Pr(qi at t =1), Initial State Distribution

The observational series, O = O1, O2,...,OT, is created using the model as follows:

1. Based on the beginning state distribution, choose an initial state, π.
2. Set the value of t to '1'(one);
3. Select O_t based on $b_{it}(k)$, the state i_t Symbol Probability Distribution;
4. According to{ a_{itit+1}}, choose i_{t+1}. State transition probability distribution for state it is i_{t+1} = 1,2,...,N.
5. Set t = t + 1; if t <T, return to step 3; else, end operation.

An HQMM is represented by the concise notation A = (A, B, π) [21]. The three probability densities A, B, and π are specified together with the no. of States, 'N' and Symbols, M (continuous density HQMMs will be discussed briefly at the conclusion of this work). While quantifying the significance of three densities, i.e., A, B, and π, it would be obvious that π is the least significant (it reflects initial circumstances), B is considered the most relevant (this is connected to observed Symbols) for most applications. Distribution 'A' is crucial for some issues (recall the three-biased coins models described previously), while it is less relevant for others (e.g., solitary word recognition tasks).

Hidden Markov Models – Various Types
The generalised HQMM we've been working with so far is considered to have a full "State Transition Matrix", implying that transfers from any state to any other state may be achieved in some fashion. The generic HQMM we've been dealing with so far is considered to contain a full state transition matrix, implying that transfers from any state to any other state may be achieved in some fashion. The models are usually ergodic, which means they may be revisited with a probability one and do not have to be done at regular intervals. Figure 6.3a shows an example of such a model. Non-ergodic models with limitations on the state transition matrix appeal to some applications. Figures 6.3b and 6.3c, for example, demonstrate two nonergodic HQMMs.

In certain cases, the state transition matrix is upper triangular (transitions to states with indexes equal to or greater than the current state's index is permitted). Left-to-right models are so named because the state sequence that generates the observation series should move from left to right most places. Because lower-numbered states account for observations happening before those for higher-numbered states, left-to-right models impose a time-related order on the HQMM. In our investigation of how to use HQMMs for voice recognition, we'll explore how we can use this characteristic.

The techniques, for the most part, operate exactly as described. However, there is at least one significant computational difficulty, as well as a handful

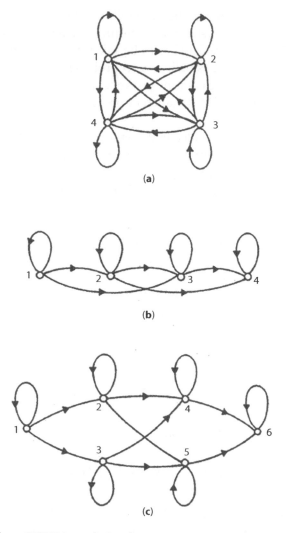

(a)

(b)

(c)

Figure 6.3 Different HQMMs are depicted.

of practical considerations, that must be considered for the processes to be as effective as possible. The forward-backwards computation implementation is the computational problem. At first sight, the reader will see $\alpha_t(i)$ and $\beta_t(i)$ tend to 0 quickly. (It's important to remember that all probabilities are smaller than 1.0.) To avoid mathematical underflow, a scaling approach of the α's and β's is necessary.

A second problem is using a limited number of training data for calculating HQMM parameters. The re-estimation formulae show if there are no occurrences in the training set, i.e., if a symbol does not regularly emerge in the observation sequence, the probability for that symbol comes to 0. As in the case of the short size of the training, the observation sequence is causing this impact, extra care has to be taken to ensure that no HQMM parameter is too relatively small. A zero probability parameter is entirely plausible if the impact is real. In any instance, effort must be made to ensure that the predicted HQMM parameters are acceptable (possibly through parameter space limits).

Finally, the formulae provided in this study for a single observation series may be adjusted to cover multiple observation sequences. As a result, an HQMM might be trained using a lengthy sequence or group of repeated observation sequences (this is especially beneficial for non-ergodic models.).

Exceptions to 'B' Parameters

We've just looked at discrete symbol HQMMs thus far, where the observational sequence is one of M discrete symbols. It can be easily expanded to include continuous symbols, or more broadly, continuous vectors, x, as observations. The continuous density, bj(x), $1 <= J <= N$, replaces the $b_j(k)$ probability density in such a model.

$b_j(x)dx$ = probability that observation vector, 0, lies between x and x + dx.

Numerous forms are proposed for bj(x), which include:

1. 'GAUSSIAN' M-component mixture densities of kind

$$b_j(x) = \sum_{k=1}^{M} Cjk \, N[x, \mu jk, Ujk]$$

where C_{jk} is the weight of the mixture, and The normal density is N, while the mean vector and covariance matrix for state I mixture k are μ_{jk} and U_{jk}.

2. Gaussian autoregressive M-component mixture densities of the form

$$b_j(x) = \sum_{k=1}^{M} Cjkbjk(x)$$

where

$$b_j(x) = e^{-\delta(x;ajk)/2} / (2\pi)^{k/2}$$

$$\delta(x;a) = r_a(0)r_x(0) + 2\sum_{j=1}^{p} ra(i)rx(j)$$

A vector x (of dimension K) with autocorrelation r_x and an LPC vector a (of size p) with autocorrelation r_a are separated by δ(x; a).

Several voice recognition systems have taken use of these alternative density functions.

6.3   Example of HQMMs (Isolated Word Recognition in Action)

HQMMs had proven highly effective in various applications, including ecology, cryptanalysis, and voice recognition. We'll look at the scenario of attempting to build an isolated word recogniser using HQMMs. Let's pretend we need to learn a V-word vocabulary. A training set of 'L' Tokens (used by one or more speakers) and an individual testing set are provided for each sentence. The processes for voice recognition are as follows:

1. For each word in the lexicon, we first create an HQMM. We estimate the optimal parameters for each word using the data from the set of L tokens, yielding model λ^V for the vth vocabulary word, 1<=v<=V
2. We calculate Pv = Pr(O| λ^V) for each unknown word in the test set, defined by observation sequences a = O1, O2,..., O_{T}, and for each word model, λ^V.
3. We choose the word whose model probability is highest, i.e. v* = argmax[Pv]

$$1<=v<=V$$

A unique symbol observation set (VQ codebook symbols) and two continuous observation models have been used in HQMM-based recognisers in a range of word recognition applications. Table 6.1 illustrates some performance parameters for a speaker independent system with a 10-digit vocabulary (based on AT&T Bell Laboratories tests).

Table 6.1: Parameters for a speaker independent system.

The effectiveness of the HQMM with a continually working symbol density is equivalent to that of the best template-based recogniser; however, due

Table 6.1 Performance characteristics for a speaker independent system.

Recogniser	Recognition accuracy (%)
Template Based Using Dynamic Time Warping	98.2%
HQMM using Discrete Symbols	97.1%
HQMM using Continuous Densities	98.1%

to quantisation distortions in small codebooks, the HQMM with discrete symbols performed badly. In the coming section, we can see how HQMMs handle word recognition and the salient characteristics influencing it.

Markov chain structure

Left to right models cited above, as illustrated in Figure 6.3b, are shown to be favourable for word recognition if start and end locations are known approximately. Because of this, the progressive structure of the state sequence for word utterances is very obvious, and the number of States required for each and every word model is typically reasonable. A restricted model might be impractical if the aim was to represent a protracted conversational voice stream.

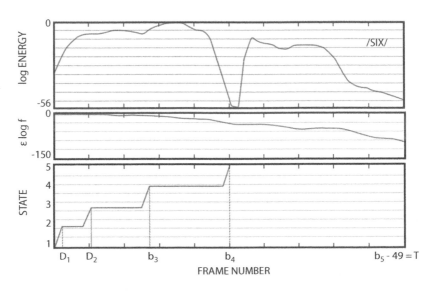

Figure 6.4 Connecting multiple contours for the usage of HQMMs for solitary word recognition for solitary word.

The digits in one of the cases were generated using 5-state HQMMs. Figure 6.4 depicts the estimated state sequence that emerged from the analysis. The Viterbi technique is used to segment a number "six" utterances. It is obvious that the two states are linked. The sounds in the word six are almost the same.

6.4 Matching of State Observation Density

The estimated observation density in each state must match the provided data for the final model to be valid. The marginal distributions bj(x) | x=(... xk...) may be compared to a histogram of the actual data allocated to that jth state since the anticipated distribution of the observations inside the jth state is bj (x). For the 9-dimensional representation of the observation vectors, such a comparison is shown in Figure 6.5. Figures 6.5 and 6.4 support the preceding section's goal of identifying consistently or distinctively acting periods, defining the sequentially changing character of these periods, and appropriately depicting the signals across time. Everything was done with great care.

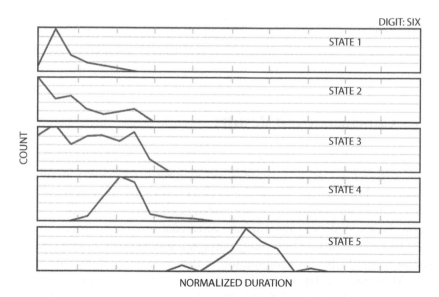

Figure 6.5 The observed normalised duration density histograms for the 5 states of a hidden Markov model for the word /six/ are shown in thisT diagram. Condition 1 is a transitory state, but state 5 (which corresponds to the last fricative /s/) has an average normalised length of more than 0.5.

A. Durational information

We may utilise the measured state lengths for word recognition as HQMM allows to do segmentation. Because word boundary is fundamentally known, as the durational information is frequently expressed in a normalised form for word models in the form:

$P_j(I/T)=$ The probability of spending exactly (I/T) of the word in state j, where T is the word's frame count, and I is no. of frames spent in state j.

Figure 6.5 shows a set of Pj(i/T) histograms for a 5-state model for the word "six." The initial stage, as shown in the diagram, is usually extremely brief; 2nd and 3rd phases will last longer; 4th stage (the stop plus the fricative) has a well-defined density peak with an average duration of around 20% of the word and is never skipped (i.e., $I/T = 0$); the final state (the stop plus the fricative) covers roughly 50% of the word length and is likewise always present in utterances. This discursive information has been proven to be highly useful in word recognition and fairly resilient across various channel circumstances. The key implication appears to be that certain states must be maintained for a fixed period of time.

B. Score Evaluation

For speech signals, the dynamic range of $Pr(O, I/\lambda)$ is usually relatively large, and with certain well-set model specifications, max, $Pr(O,I/\lambda)$ is usually the only relevant element in the summation for $Pr(O \mid \lambda)$.

Hence, HQMM is a type of Machine learning model. Further, researchers can refer to several types of learning algorithms and their uses in different sectors (including industry 4.0 and society 5.0) in [16–20].

6.5   Conclusion and Results

HQMMs, as a basis, can be used to describe higher-level patterns in continuous speech signals holistically. On the other hand, such a broadening should be addressed cautiously. The a priori knowledge of word boundaries is successfully employed in the aforementioned left-to-right word models. When the vocabulary is vast, direct concatenation of the aforementioned word model mayor for continuous voice recognition may not be practicable. The other factor for examination is that modelling approach's sturdiness. Many representations of short-term speech symbols exacerbate this issue of resilience (spectra). Some interpretations are more robust to channel fluctuations, speaker changes, and noise contamination, for example, whereas others are best characterised as Gaussian multivariates. Currently, the best combination is unknown.

The use of HQMM in speech recognition is not ruled out by the afore-mentioned considerations. These are, on the contrary, the key areas where research is focused in order to address the ultimate recognition problem with HQMMs.

References

1. Monras, A., Beige, A., & Wiesner, K. (2010). Hidden Quantum Markov Models and non-adaptive read-out of many-body states. arXiv: Quantum Physics.
2. Baker, J. K., "The Dragon System, An Overview," *IEEE Trans. on Acoustics Speech Signal Processing*, Vol. ASSP-23, No.1, pp. 24-9, February 1975.
3. Jelinek, F., "Continuous Speech Recognition by Statistical Methods," *Proc. IEEE*, Vol. 64, pp. 532-556, April 1976.
4. Poritz, A. B., "Linear Predictive Hidden Markov Models and the Speech Signal," *Proc. ICASSP'82*, pp. 1291-1294, Paris, France, May 1982.
5. Bourlard, H., Wellekins, c.J., and Ney, H., "Connected Digit Recognition Using Vector Quantization," *Proc. ICASSP'84*, pp. 26.10.1-26.10.4, San Diego, CA, March 1984.
6. Rabiner, L. R., Levinson, S. E., and Sondhi, M.M., "On the Application of Vector Quantization and Hidden Markov Models to Speaker Independent, Isolated Word Recognition," *Bell System Tech. J.*, Vol. 62, No. 4, pp. 1075-1105, April 1983.
7. Markel, J. D., and Gray, Jr., A. H., *Linear Prediction of Speech*, Springer-Verlag, New York, 1976.
8. Juang, B. H., "On the Hidden Markov Model and Dynamic Time Warping for Speech Recognition-A Unified View," AT&T B.L.T.}., Vol. 63, No.7, pp. 1213-1243, September 1984.
9. Levinson, S. E., Rabiner, L. R., and Sondhi, M. M., "An Introduction to the Application of the Theory of Probabilistic Functions of a Markov Process to Automatic Speech Recognition," B.s.T.}., Vol. 62, No. 4, Part 1, pp. 1035-1074, April 1983.
10. Forney, Jr., G. D., "The Viterbi Algorithm," *Proc. IEEE*, Vol.61, pp. 268-278, March 1978.
11. Baum, l. E., and Eagon, J., "An Inequality with Applications to Statistical Prediction for Functions of Markov Processes and to a Model for Ecology," *Bull. Amer. Math. Soc.*, 73 (1963), 360-363.
12. Baum, L. E., Petrie, T., Soules, G., and Weiss, N., "A Maximization Technique Occurring in the Statistical Analysis of Probabilistic Functions of Markov Chains," *Ann. Math. Statistic*, 41 (1970), pp. 164-71.
13. Rabiner, l.R., Juang, B.H., Levinson, S.E., and Sondhi, M.M., "Recognition of Isolated Digits Using Hidden Markov Models with Continuous Mixture Densities," AT&T B.L.T.}., Vol. 64, No. 3, pp. 1211-1234, July-August 1985.

14. Juang, B.H., and Rabiner, l.R., "Mixture Autoregressive Hidden Markov Models for Speech Signals," *Transactions on IEEE/Acoustics, Speech, and Signal Processing*, Vol. ASSP-33, No. 6, pp. 1404-1413, Dec. 1985.

15. Andelman, D., and Reeds, J., "On the Cryptanalysis of Rotor Machines and Substitution Permutation Networks," *IEEE Trans. Info. Theory*, Vol. 1-28, No. 4, p. 578-584, July 1982.

16. Neuberg, E. P., "Markov Models for Phonetic Text," *J. Acoust. Soc. Am.*, Vol. 50, p. 116(A), 1971.

17. B. Gudeti, S. Mishra, S. Malik, T. F. Fernandez, A. K. Tyagi and S. Kumari, "A Novel Approach to Predict Chronic Kidney Disease using Machine Learning Algorithms," *2020 4th International Conference on Electronics, Communication and Aerospace Technology (ICECA)*, Coimbatore, 2020, pp. 1630-1635, doi: 10.1109/ICECA49313.2020.9297392.

18. Tyagi A.K., Fernandez T.F., Mishra S., Kumari S. (2021) Intelligent Automation Systems at the Core of Industry 4.0. In: Abraham A., Piuri V., Gandhi N., Siarry P., Kaklauskas A., Madureira A. (eds.) *Intelligent Systems Design and Applications*. ISDA 2020. *Advances in Intelligent Systems and Computing*, vol 1351. Springer, Cham. https://doi.org/10.1007/978-3-030-71187-0_1

19. Akshara Pramod, Harsh Sankar Naicker, Amit Kumar Tyagi, "Machine Learning and Deep Learning: Open Issues and Future Research Directions for Next Ten Years", In *Computational Analysis and Understanding of Deep Learning for Medical Care: Principles, Methods, and Applications*, 2020, Wiley Scrivener, 2020.

20. Amit Kumar Tyagi, Poonam Chahal, "Artificial Intelligence and Machine Learning Algorithms", In *Challenges and Applications for Implementing Machine Learning in Computer Vision*, IGI Global, 2020.DOI: 10.4018/978-1-7998-0182-5.ch008

21. Varsha R., Nair S.M., Tyagi A.K., Aswathy S.U., RadhaKrishnan R. (2021) The Future with Advanced Analytics: A Sequential Analysis of the Disruptive Technology's Scope. In: Abraham A., Hanne T., Castillo O., Gandhi N., Nogueira Rios T., Hong TP. (eds.) Hybrid Intelligent Systems. HIS 2020. *Advances in Intelligent Systems and Computing*, vol 1375. Springer, Cham. https://doi.org/10.1007/978-3-030-73050-5_56

7

Artificial Intelligence and Qubit-Based Operating Systems: Current Progress and Future Perspectives

Tejashwa Agarwal[1] and Amit Kumar Tyagi[2*]

[1]School of Computer Science and Engineering, Vellore Institute of Technology, Chennai, Tamil Nadu, India
[2]Department of Fashion Technology, National Institute of Fashion Technology, New Delhi, Delhi, India

Abstract

With operating systems being at the heart of any computer system, hours of engineering endeavors and research have been put into their development. With the ever-changing nature of the hardware and software in this day and age, it is essential that we aim for the development of OS that are not merely suited for general purposes but also have the capacity of specializing in different functionalities. Artificial Intelligence is a disruptive technology aimed at making machines intelligent and giving them the power to mimic the human brain. This research paper attempts to analyze how various disciplines of Artificial Intelligence and Machine Learning algorithms, when integrated with Operating Systems, develop an intelligent and a learned OS. Such OSes are aimed at providing better management of a system's resources and better process management via scheduling to provide the end user a very smooth experience. We shall look at the problems with the current Operating Systems, attempts being made to come up with better-suited ML algorithms (including Qubit) to integrate them with OS, the various advantages and downsides of doing so and the progress made so far in this field. We shall also study the effectiveness of these algorithms in improving the Linux scheduling process using published research papers and experiments done on the same. We will also evaluate some AI techniques that practically and theoretically improved or facilitated some major elements of a distributed operating system.

Keywords: Intelligent OS, OS agents, machine learning, artificial intelligence, linux, process scheduling

Corresponding author: amitkrtyagi025@gmail.com

Romil Rawat, Rajesh Kumar Chakrawarti, Sanjaya Kumar Sarangi, Jaideep Patel, Vivek Bhardwaj, Anjali Rawat and Hitesh Rawat (eds.) Quantum Computing in Cybersecurity, (121–136) © 2023 Scrivener Publishing LLC

7.1   Introduction to OS, AI and ML

An operating system is a software programme required to manage and operate computing devices like smartphones, tablets, computers, super-computers [1, 2], web servers, cars, network towers, smartwatches, etc. It is the operating system that eliminates the need-to-know coding language to interact with computing devices. It is a layer of Graphical User Interface (GUI) [3], which acts as a platform between the user and the computer hardware. Moreover, the operating system manages the software side of a computer and controls programs' execution.

Artificial intelligence is a constellation of many different technologies working together to enable machines to sense, comprehend, act, and learn with human-like levels of intelligence. Maybe that's why it seems as though everyone's definition of artificial intelligence is different: AI isn't just one thing. Technologies like machine learning and natural language processing are all part of the AI landscape. Each one is evolving along its own path and, when applied in combination with data, analytics and automation, can help businesses achieve their goals, be it improving customer service or optimizing the supply chain.

7.1.1   A Brief Summary

Operating systems are the most intricate and complex pieces of software built by experts through long and recurring engineering efforts. The common practice is to install OSes with their default configurations and change specific configurations when needed. Unfortunately, the old manual OS development technique is incapable of keeping up with the rate at which hardware and programs evolve. Manual fine-tuning OS configurations is lengthy and not very effective. With growing heterogeneity in future hardware and applications, mainstream OSes should allow more specializations, which are designed for general purposes. These limitations call for adopting learned OSes. Note that ML can assist traditional OS components to dynamically set OS configurations, generate policies based on hardware and application behaviour and hardware properties and build certain OS mechanisms. An operating system can be built on strong AI since it could be made to think in a way a human mind would. Other fields of AI that can be assimilated are Intelligent Systems and Expert Systems, Fuzzy logic systems and Natural Language Processing and Artificial Neural Networks.

7.1.2   Different Components of AI Integrated with the OS

- Intelligent Systems
  They have the capability of carrying out complex tasks and making consistent decisions. It can help the OS choose the best application suited to open a particular type of file.
- Expert Systems
  They can assist the system in decision making, just like an expert in the field would. The system diagnoses the problem, proposes a solution and gives alternatives as well. It may play a crucial rule in memory management and crashes in OS [5]. Expert systems [5] can be used to build a better User Interface as well.
- Natural Language Processing
  It can be used to communicate with the machines in human language.
- Fuzzy Logic Systems
  The approach of fuzzy logic systems mimics the human decision-making process. It can provide acceptable definite output even if the input is inaccurate or incomplete, thereby enabling the system to work in certain as well as uncertain conditions.
- Artificial Neural Network
  It will prove useful in providing augmented security to the OS as it helps in pattern recognition which in turn could be used for speech and facial recognition.

7.2   Learning Configurations

Setting timing-related configurations like frequency of interrupting a CPU core [6, 7] (for thread scheduling), the frequency of invoking background swapping (for memory paging), the frequency of flushing buffer cache (for storage), and the sampling rate of CPU clock frequency (for energy and performance), is hard since there are various trade-offs associated with them. For example, frequent CPU interruption causes performance overhead (by preempting and context-switching threads) which ultimately reduce effective CPU utilisation [8].

Setting these configurations manually requires heavy engineering, involving trial and error and offline experiments. Thus, ML can be a good candidate for the same. A good ML model can be trained with past workloads and OS/hardware environments to dynamically generate new configurations to adapt to workload and environment changes.

Then there are size configurations, such as the buffer cache size (for storage caching), swap prefetching amount (for memory paging) and disk prefetching amount (for storage access). Setting these size-related configurations is hard, especially when there are trade-offs among different sizes. For example, a larger buffer cache improves the performance of the storage system but reduces available memory for user applications.

OS policies that could be generated by ML: Space Allocation [9, 10], Scheduling and Cache Management, all of which are currently being done by predefined fixed algorithms like best-fit policy, fair share scheduling and least recently used cache access, to name a few.

7.3   Building ML Models

Although the future of ML-based OS development is promising, selecting the right model is a hard problem in many applications. While we can estimate the effectiveness of a particular algorithm by evaluating an application's performance after applying the model to it, other variables like the changes in the workload or other processes running on the same OS might affect our results. Hence, to better pinpoint the effect of a certain model, we should seek better and more localized evaluation objectives. Finer-grained models can predict more accurately with more customization and specialization, but require more resources like memory space, CPU time [11] for training, etc. Different processes in OS are correlated to each other and changes in one affect the other. Therefore, we must jointly optimize related tasks for the best results. Such ML models can be trained offline using large, fine-grained data sets while training them online, infrequently with coarse-grained data and not disturbing foreground application performance. These models can be validated against the theoretical optimum, if it exists, like shortest job first for thread scheduling or let ML use reinforcement learning to find the best solution for these requirements.

7.4   Work Done in Improving Process Scheduling

CPUs use scheduling algorithms to allocate time slices to a process; these algorithms do not use the previous execution history of the process. Preemption of processes requiring very small CPU time increases the number of context switches, invalidation of caches and pipelines, swapping of buffers and so on, ultimately increasing the turnaround time of a program. This problem can be mitigated by recognizing programs by using suitable ML techniques to understand their previous execution history and predict their resource requirements. It is profitably possible to do so. For ML algorithms or the classifiers to succeed, they need a suitable characterisation of the program attributes that are most suitable for prediction.

The work done by Suranuwarat and Taniguchi [1] studies the process times of certain well-known programs in various similar states. The knowledge of the program flow sequence (PFS) which is a measure calculated from its past execution history, is used to determine if a process needs additional time.

The authors in the paper by Smith *et al.* [2] used genetic algorithm techniques for finding similarity between two applications for a particular workload by using characteristics like queue, load, leveler script, arguments, etc., to find similarity.

In the paper by Fredrik *et al.* [3], the authors described an application signature model used for predicting application performance on a given set of grid resources. In this model, they introduced the notion of application intrinsic behaviour to separate the performance effects of the runtime system from the behaviour inherent in the application itself. Application intrinsic metrics are those that are solely dependent on the application code and the problem parameters.

In the paper by Atul Negi and Kishore Kumar P *et al.* [4], the authors modified the Linux's inbuilt O(1) scheduler. Different programs were run with this modified scheduler and their STS (best special time slice) was found. This gives us the minimum turnaround time. The knowledge base of static and dynamic characteristics of the programs from the run traces thus obtained was built and trained with the C4.5 decision tree algorithm. If a new program comes, classify it and run the program with this predicted STS. If the program is not in the knowledge base, we run the program using the modified scheduler. The authors conclude that the C4.5 decision [12] tree algorithm achieved good prediction (91% – 94%), which indicates that when suitable attributes are used, which in this case were its input size, program size, bss, text, rodata and input type, a certain amount of predictability does exist for known programs. They were able to achieve 1.4% to 5.8% reduction in turnaround time.

7.4.1 OS Agents

The authors of the paper [5] discussed the idea of OS agents, a goal-oriented approach to the operating system command interface, which satisfy high-level user requests by deciding how to accomplish them. Only what has to be done is specified by the user. The agent is capable of synthesizing a sequence of OS commands [13, 14], program invocations or system calls to accomplish a wide range of user goals. They can execute these commands, recover from any unexpected failures, and automatically attempt alternative methods for completing the tasks, if necessary. They must be viewed as command-language extension mechanism like shell scripts. It has however, a greater power, which is the adaption to differing conditions, resources and user taste if necessary.

This approach enables users to request actions that, while simple to express, may be difficult to execute using standard commands. Frequently, such requirements involve keeping track of status or adhering to limits. One such example is "all the files in the directory/papers/sosp are group readable". This can be translated into a proper syntactical structure, like,

"(maintain (forall ?file (parent.directory ?file /papers/sosp)
(protection ?file group.readable)))"

To achieve any task, such as this, the authors decompose the structure of such an agent into two modules, the planner and the clerk.

The planner maps the user's requests to appropriate sequences of OS commands. It generates a goal based on the user's request which are nothing but quantified conjunctions of atomic proposition, also known as subgoals. For instance, the planner's goal may be to retrieve all 1994 tech reports from a remote site and print them locally, which would be expressed as follows:

(forall ?file (machine ?file stanford.edu)
(parent.directory ?file /pub/trs)
(creation-date ?file ?date)
(year ?date 1994)
(printed ?file ?printer))

To satisfy this goal, the OS agent has to access the remote machine, retrieve the desired files, reformat them, select the appropriate local printers, and print the files.

The basic planning and execution flow of these agents proceeds as follows. The planner maintains a data structure representing its plan containing a set of unsatisfied subgoals corresponding to the original input goal. To derive the plan, the planner repeatedly chooses a subgoal to satisfy and searches for an action with a postcondition that unifies with the subgoal. Once such an action is chosen, the planner inserts it into the plan, adding its preconditions to the list of subgoals "to be satisfied." The planner then starts another iteration of its cycle, choosing a new subgoal to satisfy, and so on. Some subgoals may be satisfied by the current system state, or by actions already inserted into the plan. The planner notices this by keeping a model of the system's state, checking whether a subgoal is already satisfied, and recording that fact. Planning can necessitate backtracking if something does not go well. The planner is finished when it arrives at a plan where each action's preconditions are satisfied, and which brings the system to a state where the input goal is satisfied.

They describe the philosophy, design, and implementation for OS Agents, a goal-oriented operating system command mechanism that uses AI planning techniques to satisfy its objectives. With OS agents, a user can request that the system carry out a complex action, and the system will automatically determine the steps needed to carry out that request. Since planning is done dynamically, the agent is capable of responding to changes in the system's state and configuration. They implemented the same on Unix [14], but in the framework of a distributed and potentially heterogeneous environment. They have successfully incorporated well-understood AI planning algorithms into our agent, yielding a flexible and extensible system. The precise descriptions of the planning algorithm and operator representation language, combined with the discussion in their paper, suffice to replicate the implementation and experimental results. In addition, the OS agent's normal operation is rife with learning opportunities. Algorithms already exist for learning 13 control heuristics by analyzing past successes and failures, and automatically generating logical models of actions based on experiments and by observing human users. They also describe the integration of the OS agent facility within Unix. An OS agent server is responsible for interfacing to the system, issuing commands, invoking system calls, and setting triggers on internal system events of interest. They provide some privileged support within Unix so that the agent can express interest in particular system states without requiring polling or privileged access. The mechanism also allows a trusted person to dynamically add additional event types to the system in support of OS agent queries. We believe that a facility such as OS agents will permit users to issue increasingly powerful requests. As experience is gained, users will imagine new types of queries and requests that may require information or event signaling not originally envisaged by the system designers. For this reason, designers of future operating systems intended to support such a facility should think seriously about the information and event signaling needs, and should anticipate the need for system extension in support of user requests.

7.5   Artificial Intelligence in Distributed Operating Systems

Ubiquitous computing can be by the interaction of affectively permeating intelligence in large distributed system architectures, where sensor-rich embedded devices were aware of their relationship with users as well as other devices in the environment and that the devices must be allowed to operate autonomously, thereby reducing human involvement. Traditional AI has a large number of such algorithms that allow searching data rapidly enabling learning from distributed data and facilitate fast planning with large amounts of information which can be utilised to optimize resource management, increase fault-tolerance, automate security, automate resource discovery, facilitate more natural user-interfaces and others.

AI search techniques such as Genetic Algorithms, Simulated Annealing, hill-climbing, Bayesian networks and informed searches including A* search can be used in distributed operating systems to improve management of resources like processor, file and memory. It is crucial to highlight that simply altering a few parameters in each algorithm, the whole behaviour of the distributed OS may be changed without the need for any extra design considerations or development. A GA's fitness function and termination criteria, for example, can be altered at any moment to shift the system from satisfying real-time needs to being more fault tolerant. At the moment, most of these solutions have been assessed on their own rather than as part of a larger distributed operating system. Some of these strategies may also be implemented within Hypervisors, which allow operating system virtualization, although the benefits are not as evident as implementation in a microkernel or monolithic kernel. There isn't enough statistical data to evaluate and contrast the real advantages and downsides because these strategies haven't yet been deployed on well-tested distributed operating systems.

Decision trees can be used for resource management to classify statistics on machine communications, which can then be used to swiftly distribute data to different sections of the network. Reinforcement learning might be utilised for similar objectives as well, particularly if the system's status can be represented as discrete states. The distributed OS can also be used to model to learn dynamically to develop system models to detect and cope with resource or communication issues. A neural network may be trained on known security exploits and implemented on a distributed operating system. Because a neural network may generalise, it may be able to deal with both known and previously unforeseen assaults. Naming is the process of assigning and uniquely identifying users, services, files, printers, groups, hosts and other objects in a distributed system. The search for identified resources based on certain qualities is what resource discovery is all about. Model learning algorithms are ideally suited for this task since they seek to build and maintain a model of the system that can be utilised in a variety of ways. Model-Based Algorithms such as surprised-based learning can be used in such cases.

SBL can create and maintain a model autonomously by querying the distributed system on a regular basis. Typically, the model is made up of numerous rules, each of which includes a collection of circumstances, an action, and a set of prediction rules. The learner must be prepared for all conceivable actions, which might include a list of legitimate OS commands. A query is the execution of a command, such as ping with a certain number. SBL would monitor all system activity and record any changes it feels were triggered by the command's execution as rules in the model. SBL has a forecast that it may test the next time the same command is issued; if the prediction is accurate, its model is correct; otherwise, it will split and refine the rules until the model fits the real status of the system. If a decent model is learnt, and a new host is added, or an old host fails, or a new user is added, the learner will ultimately find out and update the model accordingly, even if the learner is not immediately alerted. As a result, the distributed operating system may readily employ this paradigm to execute resource management and fault-tolerance. Naturally, the querying process will be able to handle literal resource discovery; however, because the model can detect conflicts, it may be utilised to fix naming difficulties to some extent. Furthermore, a hierarchical approach to model distribution might be employed by retaining smaller models for subsystems on distinct hosts. As demonstrated in SBL, knowledge about the distributed system may be described using logic. As logic rules, large volumes of information about the system may be collected and stored. In such instances, a distributed OS might leverage a variety of AI planning approaches to make effective judgments. Planning with propositional logic including constraint satisfaction, reasoning with first-order logic, frame systems and semantic networks are a few well-known AI planning techniques that could be employed by a distributed OS to ensure concurrency, prevent deadlocking, etc.

7.6   Current Progress

Cognition, an AIOS-based operating system, has been designed to serve as an intelligent assistant, electronic adviser, offer engines, and chatbots.

NeurOS, an operating system based on artificial neural networks, is being developed. Pattern learning and recognition, working memory, perception, prediction, context priming, imagination, attention, abstraction, classification, associational thinking and behaviour are some of its functions. NeurOS programmes are portable, scalable, networkable, expandable, and embeddable by design. There are other efforts in the works to create an AIOS, such as Jarvis. AI is also employed in assistant programmes such as Amazon's Alexa, Apple's Siri, Google Now, and Microsoft's Cortana. Furthermore, AIOS features were delivered by Windows Metro. However, the User Interface only displayed folders and was incapable of delivering the next-generation AIOS experience.

In this section, however, our main focus is on KMLib, an attempt to make a lightweight yet efficient ML engine targeting kernel space components. In their paper, the creators of the engine discuss their initial prototype that targets the OS I/O scheduler. To develop such a system, it is required that even standard math floating point operations be implemented from scratch like logarithm and power. This library following the likes of popular libraries in the machine learning community, uses a tensor representation for matrices and model parameters. Functions for manipulating these matrices and tensors like addition and multiplication have also been implemented from scratch. Also, the layers in the neural networks used in the library are implemented using lock-free data structures to allow for parallel processing by breaking down the computation DAG when possible. The library implements reverse-mode automatic differentiation to compute the gradients, which are then used to update the model weights using gradient-based learning algorithms such as gradient descent.

Adapting to new workloads:
We must continuously train the model so that it adapts to the ever-changing workloads of the modern OS. This means that there is a trade-off between the power of adaptation and computational efficiency. For low-dimensional problem, where the model can achieve convergence in a very few epochs, we perform inference only when the classification accuracy over the last k batches is at least p_{margin} higher than the most frequent label in these k batches. k and p_{margin} are adjustable, otherwise we can use this simple feedback mechanism itself.

Ideally, one would deploy a machine learning algorithm that takes the least amount of time in training and uses the least number of training instances which can be done by borrowing few shot learning when applicable. One would also like to perform "active learning", where a data model is trained using only on training instances which seem to promise to improve the performance of the model. Effective utilization of methods for both of these problems could result in models that spend the least amount of time in training and used more for inference.

A lot of operating system tasks that must be completed in sub-microsecond time or else serious performance degradations can take place. As we mentioned above, KMLib can work in both user and kernel spaces. To reduce computational overheads and memory consumption, we should make use of low-precision training. Since floating point operations are not allowed in Linux kernel, "kernel-fpu-begin" module is called and to finalize the operations, the "kernel-fpu-end" module is called. The size of the floating point enabled code block because the more time KMLib spends in floating-point-enabled regions, the higher is the chance of being context switched to other tasks. When the floating-point unit is enabled, the kernel must save floating point registers on a context switch, and adds additional overheads. The designed engine is capable of training and inference operations while the underlying operating system is running by offloading the computations to library threads to reduce interference. The only interference that KMLib adds is to save the input data and the predictions for training.

Lock-free circular buffers are used to store training data. The size of these buffers is configurable by the user. A buffer may operate in any of the two modes: blocking and dropping. The blocking mode helps the user to process every single input piece data, but if the frequency of computation requests is high, this blocking mode might add extra overhead by blocking additional inputs from being processed. The dropping mode overruns unprocessed input data: it does not add extra overhead, but KMLib then loses data, which may hurt training quality. Using these features, the user can cap memory overhead based on their ML application needs. Even though KMLib uses lock-free data structures to reduce multi-threaded communication and synchronization overhead, there might be dependencies in the computational DAG, which might cause latencies. That is why the users can choose how many threads can be used for (i) training and (ii) inference. All these features that related to offloading training/inference computation can be disabled and can be done in the original thread context as well.

There are two ways in which the KMLib can be deployed: (i) kernel mode, where both training and inference happens in kernel space and (ii) kernel-user memory mapped shared mode. In the latter, KMLib collects data from the kernel space and trains using user-space threads. For the inference, KMLib still runs the operations in kernel space to reduce the latency. But, KMLib threads can drain training request only when it gets scheduled because KMLib threads are working in a polling manner.

Evaluation:

A sample application of KMLib was developed to fine-tune "mq-deadline" I/O scheduler. To predict whether the I/O request will meet the deadline or not, we train a linear regression model. The regression model predicts issue time for a given I/O request using normalized block number and ordinalized operation type as features. The predicted issue time is then thresholded to predict whether the I/O request should be early-rejected or not. We observed that the thresholded regression output could predict with an accuracy of 74.62% whether the I/O requests miss the deadline or not: this reduced the overall I/O latency by 8%, a promising result given that I/O is so much slower than memory or CPU (and hence I/O should be the first to optimize).

7.6.1   Advantages

AI-powered operating systems are the future of operating systems, and they might benefit humans in a variety of industries, including academic, defence, medical, research, scientific, and personal usage. Many users will profit since the AI learning process is constant and the user would be updated by the OS in a short period of time. If an AI-powered operating system is built, people would be able to execute expert activities, routine chores, and formal duties with more ease. Because AI programme modification is simple and fast, it is feasible that AI-based operating systems will be modified as well. Because modifying AI has no effect on its structure, AIOS would decrease the frequent crashes that occur in operating systems. Finally, the AIOS would be a fantastic union of traditional Operating Systems with the OS that could cut operation time, parallel-process management, improved memory management, give better security, and comprehend the user in certain context.

7.6.2   Concerns

Because AI understands natural language and identifies voice, it is likely that it may comprehend sensitive information and e-mails, posing a risk to the user. AI systems have replaced numerous professions, and it may attempt to replace humans, or at the very least, it will think for itself and make judgments on its own owing to AI's cognitive powers. If it is implemented in AIOS, it is possible that the user will be disappointed. Because AI necessitates a large number of computations, forecasts, voice recognition, and decision making, it is probable that it will slow down the operating system and necessitate extra external storage. AIOS users will be disappointed if they lack common sense when reasoning. If AIOS falls into the wrong hands then it's obvious that it is a threat to human beings.

7.7   Quantum Artificial Intelligence

The application of quantum computing to the calculation of machine learning algorithms is known as quantum AI. Quantum AI can assist in achieving outcomes that are not attainable with classical computers because of the computational benefits of quantum computing. A ubiquitous representation known as quantum mechanics is built on ideas that are not found in everyday experience. For quantum computing to process data, a quantum prototype of the data is required. For debugging and the proper operation of the quantum-based computer, a hybrid mix of quantum and classical frameworks are indeed required.

Only when employing quantum-based processors to synthesize its related data is it extremely likely to give rise to erroneous data. Because of this, whenever a hybrid approach is driven by quick data processing components like the CPU and GPU, that are widely employed in traditional computers, a hybrid model is produced.

Even though artificial intelligence has advanced dramatically in the last ten years, it has still not surmounted technical constraints. Hurdles to obtaining Artificial General Intelligence could be removed thanks to quantum computing's special properties. Models based on machine learning could be trained quickly with quantum-based computing, as well as the process can also be utilized to develop improved algorithms. Quantum-based computing's optimized and reliable AI may speed up years of investigation and produce technological advancements. Among the core issues facing modern AI include adaptive machine learning, and reasoning under uncertainty. Among the most plausible approaches to future AI is quantum AI.

Steps Involved

- Quantum based data may be depicted as an intricate collection of integers termed a quantum tensor, that can then be converted to a quantum-based dataset. These tensors are processed by TensorFlow to produce a dataset that may be used in other applications.
- Selection of quantum-based neural network models is essential. Quantum neural network models are chosen based on

the understanding of the quantum data structure. The goal is to use quantum processing to unearth information that is concealed in an entangled state.

- Quantum state measurements gather selections of classical data from the classical-based distribution. The values are derived directly from the quantum state.

- Analyze a conceptual framework of a classical-based neural network. Techniques for deep learning are employed to understand the association between data because quantum data is currently translated into a classical form.

- Some other deep learning steps—evaluating cost function, gradients, and updating specifications—are the standard procedures. These stages guarantee the creation of an efficient model for unsupervised tasks.

Possible Applications

- Choice trees are used to construct classical decision issues. Making branches from specific places is one way to get at the set of alternatives. Nevertheless, the effectiveness of this approach falls off when each issue is too complicated to be resolved by repeatedly splitting it in half. Numerous decision trees are used to describe issues, and quantum techniques based on Hamiltonian time evolution can solve issues more quickly than random walks.

- Classical game theory is a modelling technique that is frequently applied in AI applications. Quantum game theory is this theory's expansion to the quantum realm. It may be a useful tool for resolving significant issues with quantum-based communication and the deployment of quantum AI.

- Creation of quantum algorithms for classical learning models with quantum generalisations. It may offer potential accelerations or other enhancements to the deep learning training procedure. By swiftly offering the ideal set of artificial neural network weights as a solution, quantum-based computing can contribute to traditional machine learning.

- The majority of search algorithms were created for traditional computing. In search difficulties, traditional computing operates better than humans. However, Lov Grover offered his Grover method and claimed that quantum-based computers may tackle this issue even more quickly than conventional ones. Quantum computing–based AI has the potential to be useful for short-term applications like encryption.

7.8   Conclusion

The advancement of Artificial Intelligence is at an all-time high, and yes, we are utilising machines to build and evolve it. It will be fantastic when the AI developed by the machine itself aids in the evolution of the operating system that runs on it. It's unfathomable how quick and good an operating system can become when AI is used as a tool, and as AI advances, so will the OS. It can be concluded that the merger between AI and distributed operating systems will indeed yield more autonomous and robust systems, because AI provides the brain to the distributed OS to control the brain that is the distributed system. To summarise, there is a need for AI-based operating systems, but before they are released, they must be well taught; otherwise, if they fall into the wrong hands, they may be damaging to humanity and create terrorism. The objective of artificial intelligence is to construct systems with an intellect equal to or greater than that of humans.

References

1. Surkanya Suranauwarat, Hide Taniguchi, "The Design, Implementation and Initial Evaluation of An Advanced Knowledge-based Process Scheduler", *ACM SIGOPS Operating Systems Review*, Vol. 35, pp. 61-81, October, 2001.
2. Warren Smith, Valerie Taylor, Ian Foster, "Predicting Application RunTimes Using Historical Information", Job Scheduling Strategies for Parallel Processing, IPPS/SPDP'98 Workshop, March, 1998.
3. Fredrik Vraalsen, "Performance Contracts: Predicting and monitoring grid application behavior", In *Proceedings of the 2nd International Workshop on Grid Computing, November, 2001.*
4. Atul Negi, Kishore Kumar P, *Applying Machine Learning Techniques to Improve Linux Process Scheduling,* November 1, 2005.
5. Oren Etzioni, Henry M. Levy, Richard B. Segal, and Chandramohan A. Thekkath, "OS Agents: Using AI Techniques in the Operating System Environment", April 12, 1993.
6. Rilwan ul haq, Snehal and Ms. Annapoorna Shetty, "A Study On Artificial Intelligence Operating System", *International Journal of Latest Trends in Engineering and Technology* Special Issue SACAIM 2017, pp. 059-061
7. Tyagi, Amit Kumar; Nair, Meghna Manoj; Niladhuri, Sreenath; Abraham, Ajith, "Security, Privacy Research issues in Various Computing Platforms:

A Survey and the Road Ahead", *Journal of Information Assurance & Security*. 2020, Vol. 15, Issue 1, pp. 1-16. 16p.

8. Madhav A.V.S., Tyagi A.K. (2022) The World with Future Technologies (Post-COVID-19): Open Issues, Challenges, and the Road Ahead. In: Tyagi A.K., Abraham A., Kaklauskas A. (eds.) *Intelligent Interactive Multimedia Systems for e-Healthcare Applications*. Springer, Singapore. https://doi.org/10.1007/978-981-16-6542-4_22

9. Mishra S., Tyagi A.K. (2022) The Role of Machine Learning Techniques in Internet of Things-Based Cloud Applications. In: Pal S., De D., Buyya R. (eds.) *Artificial Intelligence-based Internet of Things Systems. Internet of Things (Technology, Communications and Computing)*. Springer, Cham. https://doi.org/10.1007/978-3-030-87059-1_4

10. Akshara Pramod, Harsh Sankar Naicker, Amit Kumar Tyagi, "Machine Learning and Deep Learning: Open Issues and Future Research Directions for Next Ten Years", in *Computational Analysis and Understanding of Deep Learning for Medical Care: Principles, Methods, and Applications*, 2020, Wiley Scrivener, 2020.

11. Amit Kumar Tyagi, Poonam Chahal, "Artificial Intelligence and Machine Learning Algorithms", in *Challenges and Applications for Implementing Machine Learning in Computer Vision*, IGI Global, 2020.DOI: 10.4018/978-1-7998-0182-5.ch008

12. Amit Kumar Tyagi, G. Rekha, "Challenges of Applying Deep Learning in Real-World Applications", in *Challenges and Applications for Implementing Machine Learning in Computer Vision*, IGI Global 2020, pp. 92-118. DOI: 10.4018/978-1-7998-0182-5.ch004

13. Tyagi, A.K., & Abraham, A. (eds.). (2022). *Recurrent Neural Networks* (1st ed.). CRC Press. https://doi.org/10.1201/9781003307822

14. Tyagi, Amit Kumar and G, Rekha, Machine Learning with Big Data (March 20, 2019). *Proceedings of International Conference on Sustainable Computing in Science, Technology and Management (SUSCOM)*, Amity University Rajasthan, Jaipur - India, February 26-28, 2019, Available at SSRN: https://ssrn.com/abstract=3356269 or http://dx.doi.org/10.2139/ssrn.3356269

8

Techno-Nationalism and Techno-Globalization: A Perspective from the National Security Act

Hepi Suthar[1*], Hitesh Rawat[2], Gayathri M.[3] and K. Chidambarathanu[4]

[1]Department of Computer Engineering, Vishwkarma University Pune, Maharashtra, India
[2]Faculty at Management Department, Sri Aurobindo Institute of Technology and Management, Indore, India
[3]Department of Computing Technologies, School of Computing, SRM Institute of Science and Technology, Kattankulathur, India
[4]Department of Computer Science and Business Systems, R.M.K. Engineering College, Tamil Nadu, India

Abstract

Techno-nationalism and techno-globalism are descriptive and prescriptive categories for understanding the effect of technology on society and, by extension, society on technology. They represent ideologies rather than technological policies or realities, and reflect the underlying assumptions made by analysts about the role of technology in the world. Current techno-nationalism introduces new dangers into international trade, increasing volatility, unpredictability, and complexity for multinational corporations (MNEs). Indeed, the National Security Act of India [(NSAI or NSA), 1980] is significant in ways that techno-nationalism fails to recognize, and the international and global dimensions are critical in ways that techno-globalism fails to recognize. However, an examination of these words gives building pieces for a more refined appreciation of the connections between the state, technical innovation, and globalization. Many governments have resorted to "techno-nationalism," prioritizing technology for national economic growth while effectively going it alone. Many countries have prioritized displaying national might and prestige. This chapter sheds light on emerging nations coping with techno-globalism and techno-nationalism, as well as the obstacles encountered throughout the emergence of other countries in the same dynamics.

Corresponding author: hepisuthar@gmail.com

Romil Rawat, Rajesh Kumar Chakrawarti, Sanjaya Kumar Sarangi, Jaideep Patel, Vivek Bhardwaj, Anjali Rawat and Hitesh Rawat (eds.) Quantum Computing in Cybersecurity, (137–164) © 2023 Scrivener Publishing LLC

Keywords: Cyber crime, cyber vulnerability, techno-nationalization, techno-globalization, NSAI, National Security Act

8.1   Introduction

8.1.1   Techno-Globalism

Techno-globalism is more enthusiastically to nail down in the scholastic writing, for few have been careless enough to endeavour worldwide records of both innovation and worldwide history, so we need to see texts zeroed in on each to perceive what they say. The first and most significant issue is that the advancement centricity of investigations of innovation implies that they can't be worldwide, yet they do make claims for the connection among innovation and the course of globalization, and furthermore government. Worldwide narratives for the most part give deficient load to helpless nations as well, despite the fact that worldwide is now and again a code word for poor, similarly as "World music" is folkloric music from poor countries [25]. For this there is a typical fundamental topic in investigations of the world overall according to innovation [6]. Numerous sorts of advances influenced the relations between countries, not to mention the improvement of the useful force of the globe. However, a productivism see is shockingly uncommon in worldwide records. By contrast a development driven techno-globalism zeroed in on advancements of correspondence has been at the core of quite a few chronicles of the world, the thoughts of data society masters and numerous an ominous location about science and innovation, and for seemingly forever past, and remains so [29]. Without a doubt it frequently anticipated globalizing innovation wiping out the nation-state, which it viewed as an old-fashioned association. An entire series of new innovations was additionally going to change the world into a worldwide town, the latest in a long queue being the web. An oversimplified Smithian [17] vision bests even foul Marxism when pondering innovation [27]. The Figure 8.1 shows about the Techno-nationalism and techno-globalization and the Figure 8.2 shows about the Techno-nationalism concept framework: implications for MNEs.

Techno-globalist accounts are especially dependent on recorded amnesia. In the late nineteenth century, the steam-transport, the rail line and the message ventured across and into the world which was, with support, seen as interconnected as at no other time. However, globalization was overlooked when claims for new advances of globalization were being made somewhat later [20]. Along these lines, during the 1920s Henry Ford in his Philosophy of Industry asserted that: Machinery is achieving on the planet which man has neglected to do by lecturing, purposeful publicity or the composed word.

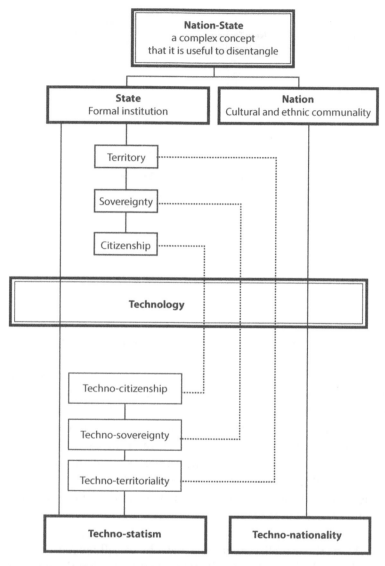

Figure 8.1 Techno-nationalism and techno-globalization.

The plane and remote know no limit. They disregard the specked lines on the guide without regard or obstacle. They are restricting the world together in a manner no other framework can. The film with its widespread language, the plane with its speed, and remote with its coming global program – these will before long carry the world to a total agreement. Hence, may we envision a United States of the World? Eventually it will doubtlessly come [18, 21].

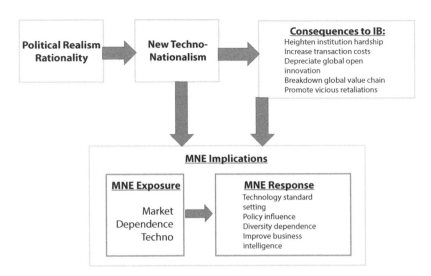

Figure 8.2 Techno-nationalism concept framework: implications for MNEs.

Techno-globalism as the term proposes, is the best method of following the greatest rise of the worldwide populace with which they meet up and foster an optimal circumstance of making their strength just as guaranteeing their reality [25]. The idea isn't identified with one specific nation yet communitarian and information concentrated exercises will change the manner in which worldwide colleges and focuses of development can work. The overall power behind all of this is techno-nationalism: a mercantilist conduct that connects a country's tech abilities and undertaking with issues of public safety, financial flourishing, and social solidness [23].

Going forward, techno-nationalism will affect the scholarly and advancement scene in three ways:

- First, the establishments that have been influenced need to decouple themselves totally from starting the breaking of the Chinese-influenced governance.
- Second, a growing snare of price controls and limitations will put increasing strain on foundations to conform to progressively difficult guidelines.
- Third, the structures giving new standards and guidelines will give an immediate effect on the worldwide administration controller and a check will be made following the need of Techno-globalism in its consolidation state.

The strength of Beijing on the worldwide market utilizing Techno-nationalism and Techno-globalism is impressively compelling as far as giving out the most ideal outcome in the field [1]. This article investigates these subjects more meticulously, laying out what techno-nationalism will mean for Sino-U.S. collaboration in tech and innovation advancement generally [24]. The Techno-globalism including its concept of upsetting the worldwide consideration has been assimilated through different monetary and discretionary exchanges which has opened the segment for the Asian nations and their job in radically changing the quality and quantitative activity. India, being one of the leaders in the field of Techno-globalism, needs a radical change in its improvement of innovation [8]. Be that as it may, with the dismissals of improvement of CPUs by three of the Indian organizations to counter the Chinese strength and make a generous situation of themselves. This thought should be quickly brought into impact as making a worldwide position has definitely gone down following inability to both the possibility of Techno-Nationalism and Techno-globalism [1]. The structuration is the quintessential of the working alongside the help of the government. Consistent remodel is an absolute necessity with which the government can build the ideal time and the comprehension of the idea which is to be perceived as an issue of significance as well as a question of grave informatively. What one should instil is the consistent remodel, further innovative turn of events and specialized information, of which the encounters will be wonderfully useful. The thought is to make a confederation; however, it proceeds to turn into the most ideal thought of making your own character which will be valuable for the people in the future.

8.1.2   National Security Act

Inside the thirty-first year of its autonomy, the government concocts an inquisitive piece of legislation called the National Security Act, 1980. The Act comprises 18 segments altogether. The government states that the significant reason for the Act is to accommodate detainment which is preventive in nature and in specific cases, for issues associated with different thoughts. The Act applied to the entirety of India with the exception of J and K. Area 2 of the Act accommodated different meanings of the terms like "fitting Government", "confinement request", "outsider", "individual" and "State Government". Area 3 of the Act essentially needs to manage forces to make orders which is for approving the capture of specific individuals. It additionally gives that the government can make a request to direct to the skilled authority about any individual who can be kept with the end goal of counteraction of specific violations from occurring. The capture relies on the fulfilment of the government as referenced in the enactment. Be that as it may, the emotional fulfilment of the government is appealable to Judicial Review if the concerned individual looks for the equivalent. If the state government is satisfied that it is major so to do, it may, in response to popular demand, direct the term of confinement for such period as not really set in stone in the solicitation. The official making any such requests needs to record and legitimize the activity to the government. The most extreme measure of time for detainment will not be over 12 days and an expansion revealing must be made to the central government to present the enquiry. Constrainment solicitation may be executed at any spot in India in the way obliged the execution of warrants of catch under the Code. Segment 5 is identified with the ability to manage spot and states of detainment. The spot of detainment is to be chosen by the central government. The person in this way, who is kept in this way, will likewise be obligated to move, starting with one spot then onto the next place dependent on the assessment of the government. Segment 5 is an identified with the grounds of confinement severable. This part fundamentally discusses the significance of ground for confinement on discrete cases will be at risk to be kept independently [19]. Such solicitation won't be viewed as invalid or flawed basically considering the way that one or a piece of the grounds is or then again are dark, non-existent, not pertinent, not related or not for the most part connected with such individual, or invalid for another clarification by any stretch of the imagination, and it isn't, along these lines, possible to hold that the government or official making such solicitation would have been satisfied as outfitted in region 3 in regards to the extra ground or grounds and asked for restriction. Segment 6 of the demonstration predominantly discusses how certain orders for confinement can't be made broken or ancient. The segment says that the activity will not be considered to be unlawful if the confinement happens outside the ambit of real detainment. Area 7 of the Act manages the forces which are identified with escapees and absconders. On the off chance that an individual has stowed himself away to forestall capture, the government can record the reality data to the Metropolitan five-star judge. The individual necessities to then approach and accommodate nullifying the reality given by the government report. Neglecting to do as such, bring will change over itself into a warrant which hopes to be given by the magistrate himself. Neglecting to keep itself from defending such activity, the individual can be detained up to a time of 1 year and will be obligated to pay a fine. Area 8 of the likewise specifies the significance of the government to introduce the grounds of capture and the aggregate sum of time for which the individual is to be held under confinement. Area 9 of the Act gives out the creation of an Advisory Board. The board will comprise three people; one will be the chairman who is sufficiently qualified to be an appointed authority of the High Court, and such will be named by the legitimate government. The board will be set by the government when deprived for a situation where an individual has been kept under the demonstration and it has been conjured.

The warning board, present tuning in on the real factors, hearings from the charged and putting together their viewpoint with respect to realities will present a report within seven weeks of the consultation to the government. If there should be an occurrence of contention, the larger part-based evaluation of such people will be viewed as the appraisal of the Board. The best period for which any individual may be kept in similarity of any repression demand which has been attested under portion 12 will be a year. Segment 14 aides' arrangements identifying with the denial of confinement orders. The segment represents the change or renouncement of the request by any official, both of state government or central government. The expiry or denial of a constrainment solicitation won't bar the formation of another confinement demand. Segment 15 of the Act manages the brief arrival of people kept. The part states that the individual will be given a cool off from the detainment time frame and the ways with which they can give out quality time and the conditions just as an ideal opportunity for which they will have their delivery. On the off chance that important, the government accountable for the delivery from confinement, the individual might have to sign a security bond. Any individual so delivered will give up himself at that point and place, and to the power, indicated in the request coordinating his delivery or dropping his delivery. The National Security Ordinance, 1980 (11 of 1980), was revoked and the Act was made.

The request which is passed is predominantly an authoritative request by the District Magistrate (DM) of the essential region. The police can't conjure the NSA as a demonstration to ensure any infringement of law.

8.1.2.1 Conditions when NSA can be Evoked

→ Even if a person is in police custody, DM of the area can impose NSA on him.

→ Even when a person is released on bail by court, he can be detained under NSA.

→ Acquitted by the court, the DM can still detain the person under NSA.

→ Against the Constitutional Right: The law additionally removes the singular protected right (Article 22 of Indian Constitution) to be delivered before the officer inside 24 hours just like the situation when the suspect is in police authority. The individual kept, doesn't reserve the option to move a bail application under the steady gaze of a criminal court.

→ Immunity for Passing and Carrying out Order: One more inconvenience towards the bothered gave under NSA is the resistance of the District Magistrate from getting an enquiry opened against him for the request such made.

The Court has held that the preventive confinement under NSA must be totally kept up with the fragile harmony between federal retirement aide and resident opportunity. Nonetheless, there isn't quite a bit of an execution of a similar conviction can be seen on ground? The court has likewise held that to forestall "maltreatment of this perhaps unsafe power, the law of preventive repression should be absolutely deciphered" and "cautious consistence with the procedural safeguards" should be ensured.

8.1.2.2   Safeguarding People Against the Act

Article 22(5) of the Indian constitution is the main source which goes about as a procedural protect against the demonstration which permits the Right to address and to forestall any self-implication which referenced under Article 20 of the Constitution. The National Security Act, 1980, was as of late conjured by the distinctive state governments when a few episodes of getting into mischief, misuse and attack against specialists, paramedical staff and police faculty were accounted for in certain pieces of the country.

The NSA is a preventive confinement law sanctioned in 1980 by the Indira Gandhi government. This demonstration can be named as the emphasis of the Preventive Detention Act, 1950, that appeared during the Nehru government. The definitive assumption behind the organization was to hold individuals back from acting against the interests of the state, including acts that sabotage the security of the country and the states, or are obstructing to ask for and security of the country.

NSA engages the focal and state governments to confine any person, to hinder him from starting future wrongdoings as well as from staying away from future indictment. The public authority may likewise keep a person to keep him from upsetting public request or for undisrupted upkeep of the local area's essential supplies and administrations.

Under the domain of NSA, the privileges of the prisoner are exceptionally contracted. The explanation of detainment can be unveiled solely after 5 days of capture, extendable to 10 days under remarkable conditions. On revelation of data in regards to detainment, the public authority can stifle subtleties that it considers are hostile to public interest, whenever uncovered. An uncommon warning board established by the public authority handles the NSA cases. The prisoner is denied any legitimate guide and can't get to any expert for issues in regard to the procedures attempted by the warning board. The prisoner can be bound for a most extreme time frame time of a year, which can additionally be broadened. The NSA has confronted an assault of reactions on sacred and basic liberties perspective for its double-dealing by the position.

- It is marked as a chronologically erroneous law, as utility of a preventive detainment law is sketchy in peacetimes.
- Usage of the NSA as an additional a legal authority by the decision government, as it sidesteps a few articles of the constitution (established slack) and whenever utilized for political thought processes, can cause a grave infringement of basic freedoms.
- Article 22(4) of the constitution expresses, that no law accommodating preventive confinement, will approve detainment for over 90 days. However, the NSA fulfilling the exemptions give in that, can approve a greatest confinement time of a year, further extendable whenever furnished with relevant proof.
- The legality of the National Security Act was tested on account of Roy versus Union of India yet the Supreme Court held that the law isn't in negation with the Constitution.
- Even the zenith court in its judgment of Fayyaz Ahmed Kumar versus State, decided that the preventive detainment laws should be stringently and barely deciphered and that the procedural assurances should be followed, cautiously.

The new summon of this law may have its advantages and disadvantages, yet is legitimized for right now outline. As coordinated attacks in clinical groups and police, avoidance of isolation and revolting conduct with the medical attendants and paramedics can be interpreted as an immediate danger to upkeep of provisions and fundamental administrations. The nation is confronting an unanticipated circumstance, and it will cost the public authority immense endeavors, time and cash to contain the spread of Covid and treat the contaminated [11]. Furthermore, it is through the clinical and police staff that the isolating and lockdowns are adequately coordinated. Any endeavor to frustrate their endeavors, that can additionally bother the circumstance, ought to be controlled with tough reasonable activity, and the current summon serves the needful.

8.1.2.3 Misuse of NSA

→ Human Rights Abuse: The fundamental reason for the laws is to forestall any further activities or damages that may prompt infringement of other basic liberties. In any case, the nation's preventive and security laws fundamentally direct themselves toward such activities that cause harm to individuals and do not align with the global law guidelines established under both the Universal Declaration of Human Rights and the International Covenant on Civil and Political Rights.

→ Discriminatory use of law: The greatest defect of the demonstration is the gigantic power which is given to the government. In light of their need, the government is known to keep individuals depending on their religion, nationality, wrongdoing and in any event, with the end goal of political vote bank. The greater reason for the demonstration was to fundamentally forestall however presently is being used as a latent assailant towards individuals against whom there lies any plan with which there lies no aim to appropriately carry out the law.

→ Punitive rather than preventive based: The laws which are fundamentally passed by the Indian government which is intended to change and restoring the blamed which is intended to cook and benefit of individuals. Notwithstanding, the enactment which is intended to set up a discipline based which is intended to hurt individuals and the residents of the country. The punitive aspect is guaranteeing to cause the government to become authoritarian, just as it is making it hard for individuals to appreciate vote-based system.

8.1.2.4 Need for Review

Under area 11 of the demonstration, the procedures of the warning board have been unmistakably settled and they don't have formal legal actions or criminal preliminaries. The framework is very opposite as it doesn't have any strategy for proof and keeps the accused from getting an insight which is the obvious infringement of Principle of Natural Justice.

The lawfulness of the National Security Ordinance was tested on account of A K Roy v. UOI. The law is intended to furnish the best nature of administrations with which they can scrutinize the authenticity of the mandate and isn't infringing upon the Basic design of the Constitution in AK Roy, when the up-and-comers battled the method ignores the principles of typical value as it bars legal depiction for the detainees.

The Supreme Court reminded that it can't give or loosen up the Right to search for legal guidance for people under constrainment. Regardless, the Court didn't contemplate that while the Constitution doesn't grant the option to authentic depiction to detainees, it doesn't expressly bar this right by a similar token. The demonstration is in compatibility to the infringement with basic freedom, and should be in legitimate condition and comprehension with which they can give the notice and inside cracks and thoughts with which they are not aiding the on developing the turn of events.

8.1.2.5   Critical Infrastructure and the Need of National Security Act's Reformation

The quintessence of any country's public safety law ought to be in compatibility with a design, for example, the ideal situation of ensuring any of the data which is comparable to securing the urgent foundation. The urgent foundation which is a wide scope of industry which is very nearly changing a country's economy from acceptable to better or help to curse, needs a greater and better method of following its security. With the ascent of the computerized encryption of this foundation, there is a high chance of incorporation of such activities which may encroach on the protection and the information holding in the organizations as a whole. What one should consider to refresh their agreement and give to an enactment or got measure.

With the improvement of the basic design on an undeniable level just as accommodating the best nature of activity being conceivable, it is about time for the nations to get their subjects of economy through enactment. The information administrations can be gotten through encryption yet a higher arrangement is much deprived to rebuff and reproving in the event of a break.

Germany is one of the main nations to pass an enactment to get the basic framework and their information insurance from any likely danger. The quintessential thought behind the law is to get the basic framework from any potential danger that may enjoy and hack into the product arrangement of the nation and thus can then again harm the construction and cause tremendous measure of misfortunes [16]. The significance of the demonstration has been such, that it has been perused along the National Security Act of Germany, with which any individual taking part in the information break will result in a prison sentence of as long as ten years and a fine of as much as 10,000 euros.

India, a country holding a tremendous measure of basic framework through information encryption, necessities to hold and make a considerable nature of work with which it can get equivalent to well. There is a need to hold these constructions as a piece of the public intrigue and can hence be organized in such a way that they can make a move with which they can make a superior vision. Since it will involve public interest, it will be in an ideal situation to incorporate to such arrangements under the National Security Act and accommodate activities, punishments and changes with which the authenticity stays unblemished and doesn't enjoy such activities that will make it incomprehensible for the nation to not keep. This activity will likewise make the achievement of building up a greater and better disposition for individuals to harsh themselves with and give their most ideal endeavors.

8.1.3   Techno-Nationalism

The notion of technological system (TS) is presented as a good starting point for analysing the effects of globalisation on a range of various technical characteristics [3]. A taxonomy is then proposed to identify its implications for those parts of a TS that are more tied to the state from those that are more relevant to the concept of country. Interesting results are obtained by allocating the contributions of a growing, but not yet conclusive, body of literature to more specific technological aspects, such as: "techno-territoriality," which pertains to physical distances and spaces, "techno-sovereignty," which pertains to governance structures and policy making, "techno-citizenship," which pertains to strategic behaviours and accountability, and "techno-nationality." The use of this taxonomy demonstrates that globalisation has diminished the importance of national (and more local) technology factors far less than is commonly assumed [7].

This is especially true with techno-nationality. Indeed, a certain communality of language and culture within a country, as well as its historically developed institutional environment, is a crucial facilitator of the inventive process and induces various technical styles and performances. 'Techno-national systems of innovation are thus still relevant. Current techno-nationalism introduces new dangers into international trade, increasing volatility, unpredictability, and complexity for multinational corporations (MNEs). This paper discusses how contemporary techno-nationalism varies from its conventional form, the underlying theoretical logic, the damage it may bring to MNEs, and what MNEs may do to mitigate the possible impact [10].

1. Compared to the conventional position, new techno-nationalism is more complicated and destructive to global trade because it mixes geopolitical, economic, national security, and ideological issues [2].
2. New techno-nationalism is founded on the realism concept, which sees the world as a zero-sum game in which nations apply economic pressure, and which downplays the significance of technology interconnectedness, resource scarcity, and resource rivalry.
3. Techno-nationalism hinders MNEs, especially those that depend on the global technology supply chain and the contribution of the target country market [8].
4. Depending on their exposure to and capacity to control the risks associated with linked policies, MNEs may choose to engage in defensive or aggressive responses to techno-nationalism.

New techno-nationalism is a school of thought that relates cross-border technical exchanges directly to a country's national security, arguing for forceful state interventions against opportunistic or hostile state and non-state players from other nations. Country leaders pursue geopolitical benefits under modern techno-nationalism, based on the concept that the globe has entered a new phase of systemic conflict between competing geopolitical powerhouses with vastly different ideological beliefs, political systems, and economic models (e.g., laissez faire capitalism vs. state-centric capitalism) [5, 26]. This ideology assumes that rival powerhouses attempt to create technology-enabled systems that impose and empower significantly diverse norms regarding data privacy, surveillance, censorship, transparency, digital money, and intellectual property. Nations like South Africa was forced to embrace techno-nationalism as a result of the wide-ranging restrictions placed on it during the apartheid system. Due to a lack of oil, they were compelled to develop Fischer Tropsch methods to manufacture synthetic fuels based on coal, which are now proving to be very valuable in times of rising oil prices.

Many governments have resorted to "techno-nationalism," prioritising technology for national economic growth while effectively going it alone. Many governments have prioritised projecting national might and status, much as the Soviet Union did before its disintegration. China has recently pursued manned space missions for both practical and symbolic reasons. China has utilised these to announce the country's emergence as a global power [10].

Nationalism, that exceptional mystery reasoning of the nineteenth and twentieth centuries, has been considered as a monstrosity suspected appeared differently in relation to more commendable, and evidently less philosophical, liberal and internationalist considerations. Nationalism is seen as a philosophical inheritance – like and associated with militarism – a working up of presumably out of date commitments of blood, a risky blast from the past. As anyone would expect, the interfacing of nationalism and progression has not been looked on well. In like manner, the term techno-nationalism is utilized by Western experts as essentially equivalent to Japan and at this point China, to portray a conceivably, genuinely, hazardous thing. For history specialists the maintained site for conversation of the relationship of advancement and energy is Germany, especially in the interwar quite a while [9]. To propose that techno-nationalism applies just to such nations would be generally worked up. Learned people were exceptionally nationalistic concerning science and improvement, especially in the mid-20th century, in basically every country. Ernest Gellner's record of energy clarifies brilliantly why nationalism was, and stays, a particularly overall miracle, taking a huge load of similar development in various countries, regardless of how its focal case was for the uniqueness of every country. For Gellner, nationalism was a generally shared procedure for adjusting to a bleeding edge, present day and globalizing world. In a state-of-the-art current culture, where tutoring, organization, information and correspondence had an effect significantly, to be separated from this by etymological and social limits was difficult. Techno-nationalism is one more strain of mercantilist envisioning that directly associates mechanical headway and abilities to a country's public wellbeing, financial flourishing, and government-backed retirement.

Techno-nationalism acknowledges different plans additionally, for instance in claims that either nation is best fitted for the imaginative age. The formation of new open characters fitted for an inventive age was going on around the world. There was, for instance, scarcely a country that didn't have people who thought their country was best fitted for the air age; interwar French analysts struggled that as an objective and in the current style individuals the French were especially fit to be pilots. Techno-nationalism depends on the explanation that the world has entered one more time of essential competition between the West's obviously silly free enterprise model and China's state-driven private undertaking [13].

8.1.3.1   Rise of Techno-Nationalism

Techno-nationalism isn't a measure which can be seen for the foundation of an organization right off the bat. It is fairly a cycle with time and comprehension to start a feeling of nationalism among individuals. The best thought of following the idea of Techno-Nationalism was given by Beijing wherein it looked for every one of the mechanical organizations to purchase their electronic gadgets from the actual nation and not from unfamiliar assets. The thought was to basically give a subjective methodology towards the monetary structure and confidence which is quintessential.

What prompted this techno-nationalistic methodology by China was the blockade being put on the 5G organizations and the responsibility for transfer speed by the United States of America.

Techno-nationalism builds itself on the ground that the world has entered one more time of essential competition between the West's unavoidably free enterprise model which is both absurd and insufficient and China's state-driven free venture. The greater part of the majority rules systems and a few fascisms are hoping to carry out innovation empowered components which are compelling as well as enabling the incomprehensibly various norms around information protection, observation, straightforwardness, restriction, computerized cash and protected innovation.

8.1.3.2   The Rise of Industrial Policy Revolution

As history justifies itself with real evidence, the mechanical arrangements proposed by different nations to support their economies and foster an ideal circumstance which will blast their country's procuring has for the most part been ineffective. The regulatory interaction, red-tapes, debasement, and absence of compassion towards the functioning style of the enterprises has truly made the arrangement a logical inconsistency of what the romantics have consistently wanted.

In spite of the assessment which has been yielded previously, the modern strategy of the upheaval appeared with the thought behind the nation growing out of their approach and comprehension. The beyond 15 years has blasted the economy of the nation and it has made significant progress in developing one of the most remarkable and re-evaluating trains which can approach 250-300 km/hr, and it intends to trade them abroad. To counter the ideal circumstance which was existing by then of time in the country, it turned out to be basically significant for the framework, for example, BEIDOU and Huawei to the Microsoft and Apple that exist in America.

Furthermore, subsequently, clearly, there is Huawei, which has used state sponsorship to transform into the world's greatest telecom equipment maker, with an overall presence in 170 countries and more than 180,000 workers including 10,000 designers. In 2018, Huawei evidently consumed $15 billion on R&D.

8.1.3.3   Human Capital as a Strategic Asset

The capitalization of Human asset as a technique for vital strategy for countering the continuous cold war has been utilized by both China and the USA where they are writing the Talent Pool, Networking, Research and Development to change over the Human source into resources [12, 28].

The serious scene which emerged out of Techno-globalism accompanied the presence of the Microsomes which are producing chips. Two Chinese government-maintained associations, Quanxin Integrated Circuit Manufacturing (QXIC), and Wuhan Hongxin Semiconductor Manufacturing Co. (HSMC), have used the different monetary motivations and endowments given by the government to employ engineers from Taiwan and Hong Kong, where the best minds have put themselves into Taiwan Semiconductor Manufacturing Co. (TSMC). It is said that by 2025, China will enlist up to 3,000 Taiwanese specialists to build up the best result asset plant. The Chinese economy looks to resuscitate itself with regard to rivalling nations like the United States, Poland, Russia and other amazing substances of Japan [9].

To counter the Chinese Microsomes and recruiting of their local architects, the Taiwanese government is trying to establish a further developed form of the relative multitude of plans with which they will actually want to accommodate the quality work just as appreciate quantitively.

8.1.3.4   Academic Institutions Being the New Ground Zero

Techno-globalism needs the significance of developing and continually redesigning, forestalling any misfortunes with which their economy can be ruined for independence. The colleges, schools and scholastic excellency establishments look to accommodate the nature of instruction and work which helps in approach making as well as explaining the consistent working and easing the weight and reliance on recruiting individuals from an external perspective.

8.1.3.5   Decoupling of the Knowledge Networks

To counter the Techno-nationalism smooth out, the US government in the long stretch of June 2020 boycotted a few of the colleges in China that were perceived as a consistent danger. Probably the greatest wellspring of likely danger for the Americans was the Hong Kong Institute of Technology (HIT) which is otherwise called the "MIT of China" [15].

One more significant advance which was taken up by the US government was to cut off the ties between the University of Arizona and HIT.

It regarded HIT as being subsidized by both the Chinese Communist Party (CCP) and the Chinese People's Liberation Army (PLA). The activity is viewed as Civil-militarization which is on the limited rundown of the US activities. Tsinghua University, one of the leaders of giving the best nature of training just as assembling of the semi-conductor which is similarly more proficient and compelling.

Being one of the world's biggest popular governments, it is of most extreme significance that India needs to accommodate a subjective methodology with which they can accommodate the Micro-chips and semi-conductors at a large-scale manufacturing facility with the capacity to accommodate the best nature of works present. The commencement should be made and they ought to discover ways and complete the Research and Development in such a way that the proprietors and the makers can accommodate the best promoting ability and quality.

8.1.3.6   Rise of China's Techno-Nationalism

Techno-nationalism interfaces a country's mechanical foundation and its capacity for headway to its financial flourishing and how it sees itself. Educator Steven Feldstein writes that techno-nationalism is a fundamental factor of a country's power inside and distantly, with tyrant frameworks using the automated circle to update their power locally. Robert Reich portrayed techno-nationalism as methods that favor a nation and its creative limits and mechanical autonomy, while Jakob Edler and Patries Boekholt depict it as a nation's drive to update headway and power in organizations.

Nationalism is a basic factor in understanding China's political and monetary acting. Since the nineteenth century, country building was initiated in the wake of comparing Chinese person with progression. For instance, the Qing line (1644-1912) used the witticism, "acquire capability with the savage's preferred development to control him" to legitimize the introduction of Western learning and advancement for public reclamation [22].

Since the People's Republic of China was established in 1949, basically every period of drive has attempted to beat—or on the other hand if nothing else be tantamount to—the West to the extent of advancement. The motivation to overshadow the West has been supported by "social Darwinism," or the perseverance of the ablest race. Past President Mao Zedong searched for China's speedy industrialization and considered steel to be a critical piece of this change. In 1958, he created the "Exceptional Leap Forward" to outperform the UK's creation limits inside 10 years in a bid to overpower the West. Critical interests in greater state endeavors were made; 4,700 endeavors started between about 1958 and 1960, and deck steel radiators were set up in common local area and metropolitan organizations. Regardless, the mission to increment mechanical creation made industry a prisoner of the state's creation segments, which were seen by CCP units. The apparatchiks answerable for state adventures procured finance advancement plans, tried too hard on "vanity" structures and imported stuff. Consequently, practically 80% of all the steel made in China was lacking or absolutely defective. A "culture of waste" made with no watches out for these excesses as market instruments to gauge response had been cleared out. This test to track down the West's mechanical base failed as it was a confused, discarded market framework, and required monetary forces for workers who were the specialists. While China began developing semiconductors during the 1950s, its progress in the field was upset by the distress of the Cultural Revolution time frame, which influenced fashioners, trained professionals and understudies.

China's 1978 changes were introduced on the modernization of the economy through science and advancement, industry, cultivating and public protect. Past Paramount Leader Deng Xiaoping's system was to use parts of market monetary perspectives to propel improvement in the Chinese economy. His wide focuses were to use new theory and addition the handiness of the Chinese economy while holding the CCP's communist way of thinking and its hold tight force.

Monetary examiner Friedrich List's speculated that great militaries don't guarantee the perseverance of nations and alluded to local collecting limit as having a heading on open wellbeing. East Asian financial thinking on advancement and improvement is subsequently consonant with List's chips away at mercantilism. For instance, for very nearly eighty years until 1945, Japan zeroed in on the progression of advancement to work on open wellbeing, using the brand name "Rich Nation, Strong Army". The essential principles of Japanese mechanical methodology were: recognizing new progressions; achieving freedom through inventive indigenization; and affirmation to diffuse aptitude through the economy. A game plan of "creation headway" was set up to achieve public wealth, with three extensive sections—guaranteeing adventures, giving allocations, and more noticeable joint effort between the state and private undertaking. Regardless, hopeful watchman cost and an argumentative worldwide technique finally drove the nation to obliteration in the Second World War. Japan accepted the invigorating cry from the illustrations of a Shang Yang, Qin organization functionary, who communicated: "A ruler should supervise a country by further developing it and building up the protect powers." [9].

Xi's first action after taking over as CCP general secretary in 2012 was to explain his dream for a strong country by 2049, the centennial of the Communist Revolution and the building up of the People's Republic of China. According to Xi, the best way to deal with public rebuilding was the limit of the Chinese public to get advanced capacity and regulatory practices, and by incorporating abroad Chinese in the work to drive headway.

Over the span of late numerous years, Beijing's Tsinghua University has transformed into a readiness school for the CCP elite; Xi, his predeccessor Hu Jintao, and past Premier Wen Jiabao are aftereffects of the school, as Tsinghua's appearance staff make them bear on the conversations inside the CCP. In 2013, Tsinghua teacher Hu Angang argued that the CCP's organization framework was more fit to China's public conditions and was better than Western-style greater part rule government. Hu attested that China had climbed to the circumstance of overall incomparable quality. Two events appear to legitimize Hu's proposal—China outflanking Japan to transform into the world's second-greatest economy, and the 2008 overall money-related crisis that affected the West's monetary structure. This produced a surge of confidence among the CCP authority, achieving Xi's goal of bringing China to the cusp of an inconceivable time and an improvement model for various nations and showing CM2025 as a way for overall control.

8.1.3.7   China's Achievement so far in Collaboration with Taiwan

Lately, China has been attempting to draw thoughts from its Confucian past to reinforce its authenticity according to general society. School course readings laud the Chinese civilization of antiquity for being the wellspring of the "four biggest developments"—paper, printing, explosives, and the attractive compass. The CCP has pushed the idea that these disclosures likewise caused the advancement of Western civilization. The party has likewise decided that China didn't utilize these disclosures, while the West was better at adjusting the compass and gunpowder. Specifically noteworthy is the lionization of Zheng He, a Ming administration (1368-1644) sailor. In the post-Mao period, the fifteenth-century sailor, whose naval force investigated lands in Southeast Asia, West Asia and Africa, has been loved because his mission for exploration carried wonder to China. Simultaneously, while the revelation of gunpowder assisted China with further developing firecrackers, it additionally assisted the West with creating deadly implements that permitted China to be weakened in the nineteenth century [14].

The CCP recognizes that its imaginative soul appears to have dissipated lately. "The establishment of our logical and mechanical advancement isn't adequately strong, our autonomous development capacity, particularly in the space of unique imagination isn't solid… we should get up to speed and afterward attempt to outperform others," Xi has said. Thus, the party accepts that the advancement of innovation is a race, and development is the way in to its future. What is implicit is that "if China could play a spearheading job in logical disclosures previously, then, at that point, it can unquestionably do it now."

In 2016, China reported a public innovative work program to help fields like huge information, clean energy, quantum correspondences and calculation. In his 2016 address to the National People's Congress, Premier Li Keqiang referenced "development" multiple times, twice as often as he had the previous year. Talking at the Chinese Academy of Sciences and Academy of Engineering in 2015, Xi referenced the need to "address the innovation shortage" and to sustain ability. He additionally cautioned against "brightening (China's) days to come with others' previous days". This demonstrated Xi's enthusiasm to push more local development and decrease the dependence on imported advances without adequate consideration regarding "osmosis, ingestion, and re-advancement". Under Xi, the push toward development has prompted endeavors to encourage Chinese researchers by upgrading existing projects like the "1,000 Global Talents," which looks to draw in ability with motivations like special treatment in housing and monetary help for research.

Beijing knows that for those returning it may not all be going well. Liu Guofu of the Beijing Institute of Technology has said that understudies might appreciate preferable conditions abroad over in China, and that holding such ability might rely more upon the workplace and less on advantages advertised. Since the last part of the 1980s, something like 55% of the people who travelled to another country for their examinations have returned to China. The CCP's emphasis on absorption implied that as opposed to permitting the passage of "Enormous Tech" like Google, Twitter and Facebook, the BAT trinity (Baidu, Alibaba and Tencent) were permitted to lay down a good foundation for themselves as "public heroes". Individuals behind the BAT trinity became forces to be reckoned with for improvement of computerized reasoning (AI). Baidu fellow benefactor Ming Lei, who guides tech business visionaries, supports exploration and shows an AI course at Peking University, did his graduate studies in business organization at Stanford University in the US. However, he returned to China in spite of being offered worthwhile positions at American Big Tech firms. Ming, who helmed the group that fostered Baidu's web crawler

(China's version of Google), is a poster child for Chinese techno-nationalism and regularly spreads the word about it that he might have worked for a US partnership but decided instead to work for the advancement of AI in China [4].

China has for quite a long time been attempting to redesign its semiconductor industry to dispose of reliance on unfamiliar innovation and has been in genuine rivalry with Taiwan, a main semiconductor producer. China thinks of Taiwan as a breakaway region, and relations across the Taiwan waterways have soured after the Sino-American tech debates. Taiwan's semiconductor industry is second only to the US, and China fears that the US and Taiwan could collaborate to obstruct its progress. Zhang Rujing, who established the Semiconductor Manufacturing International Corporation (SMIC), is a key force to be reckoned with in China's endeavors to establish confidence in this key circle. Beijing hypes the story that Zhang, who is generally known as the "father of the Chinese semiconductor," moved to the central area from Taiwan to satisfy his "nationalism" fantasy about building up elite chip creation offices in China. Zhang is said to have drawn workers from the Taiwan Semiconductor Manufacturing Corp (TSMC) to SMIC. TSMC had documented a suit against SMIC in a California court for theft of proprietary innovations and patent encroachment in 2003. As of late, Taiwan informed that enrolment organizations promoting for occupations situated on the central area, particularly in basic businesses like coordinated circuits and semiconductors, could confront punishments. Endeavors are additionally on to work with the scholarly community industry linkages to accomplish independence in semiconductor producing. Grounds will before long become hatcheries for limit advancement. Tsinghua University has set up the School of Integrated Circuits to hold over the deficiency of human resources in semiconductor creation. State media has ordered semiconductor fabricating as a "bottleneck," and has said that achieving independence in the circle will adequately thwart the US's endeavors to bully Chinese tech firms.

The CCP perceives that China's financial seriousness and public safety rely upon a high-level assembling base. A 2015 government appraisal of the assembling area tracked down that despite the fact that it was the biggest all around the world, it was pallid as far as centre innovation and advancement.

The CM2025 drive aims to redress this deficiency by updating China's mechanical establishments. Organizers recognized a few areas to focus on as a component of the drive—cutting-edge data innovation; top of the line mathematical control apparatus and advanced mechanics; aviation and flying hardware; oceanic designing gear and innovative sea vessel producing;

complex rail hardware; energy-saving vehicles; electrical gear; farming hardware and gear; new materials; and biopharmaceuticals and elite clinical gadgets. By 2020, China intended to accomplish homegrown assembling of almost 40% of fundamental parts and essential materials in the recognized areas and lessen working expenses, creation cycles, and item imperfection rates. By 2025, China desires to indigenize the creation of 70% of parts locally.

In light of stresses that China's homegrown assembling plan will mean, unfamiliar organizations could be elbowed out of the worthwhile Chinese market and face solid competition in the business sectors of agricultural countries. With this in mind, the nation restricted references to the arrangement. For example, Xi made no notice of the CM2025 drive during the Central Economic Work Conference in 2019, nor was it referred to in Premier Li's 2019 "Government Work Report" at the yearly National People's Congress—two significant assemblages that Chinese chiefs customarily use to layout vital objectives. Be that as it may, since beginning the CM2025 drive, China has expanded its portion of the overall industry in a few sections. China is progressing quickly in the electric vehicle area, presently representing 33% of the worldwide e-vehicle market, and Chinese firm BYD is the world's second-biggest electric vehicle maker after Tesla. Furthermore, ZTE (the world's driving organization in planning and assembling network administrator hardware, hubs and components) positions first universally in "web of things" licenses, trailed by Huawei at 10th. Other than creating trendsetting innovations, China additionally has all the earmarks of utilizing the CM2025 drive to handle a portion of the difficulties that have arisen in its financial model.

8.1.3.8   Techno-Nationalism: The Issue of Cyber Vulnerability won't be Resolved

A new wave of techno-nationalism is being promoted throughout the globe against the backdrop of escalating cyber wars and the quickly changing danger scenario. The FCC rejected a petition from ZTE calling for a review of their judgement that the Chinese corporation is a national security danger to communications networks. The U.K. recently stated it will ban the installation of Huawei 5G gear by the end of September 2021. ByteDance is working to ensure that TikTok may continue to operate in the United States while still complying with China's new Export Control Law.

The U.S. is also attempting to encourage nations like Brazil to avoid using Chinese technology as they build their digital infrastructures by providing financial aid to do so. As a result, the top four telecom firms in

Brazil declined to meet with a senior American official who was pushing for Huawei to be banned from the Brazilian 5G market. Huawei and other tech firms are upset over Nvidia's purchase of British chip creator Arm in their home nation of China (the deal is still awaiting regulatory approval). People use Chinese-made cellphones today, and contact centres and hosted service providers have dispersed their personal data among several data centres in India or the Philippines. Since data is now fluid, mobile, and universal, embargoes against certain firms' or nations' technological offerings will eventually have little influence from a security standpoint.

- A feeling of illusory security
  A complex web of legitimate economic, political, and national security concerns serves as the fuel for techno-nationalism. Under the guise of national security, countries that engage in "protectionist" practises essentially ban or embargo particular technologies, businesses, or digital platforms. However, we are increasingly seeing this tactic used to send geopolitical messages, punish rival nations, and/or support domestic industries. We feel falsely secure when there are broad prohibitions. At the same time, we must acknowledge the risk whenever any hardware or software provider is integrated into key infrastructure, or on practically every citizen's phone. The possibility that their equipment has backdoors that might give that supplier access to private information or help a larger hack must be taken carefully. Or, as is still the case with TikTok, there is the possibility that the data collected on American residents by an entertainment app may be forcefully confiscated in accordance with Chinese law, allowing state-backed cyber attackers to target and follow government personnel or engage in corporate espionage. We cannot deny the fact that national governments all over the world are increasingly using cyber operations to obtain information, exert influence, and destabilise their enemies. But we must keep in mind that technology created by persons close to us, in proximity, or who share our ideologies does not exempt them from compromise or automatically increase its security.
- Digital fraud and faith
  Never use trust as your only form of security. Trust, but verify, to paraphrase former U.S. President Ronald Reagan (who was, oddly enough, paraphrasing a Russian adage).

In the context of cybersecurity, "verify" refers to taking the necessary steps to monitor and audit in real time rather than naively relying on the technology you are utilising. Attackers frequently use trust as a tactic in their digital deception techniques. In fact, hacked credentials from unknowing users have been harvested via counterfeit login pages from trustworthy SaaS companies. Attackers will continue to look for innovative ways to take advantage of both the flaws in these technologies and the constant risk of human mistake, regardless of whether a cloud provider is situated in the United States, China, or anywhere else. For instance, foreign players may try to access hardware or software tool supply chains, sometimes only by bribing an insider to do it for them. In other words, technological nationalism or technological globalism-based purchase decisions are both inherently vulnerable to the same security risks. Therefore, when we focus on a particular business or technology, we are chasing a red herring rather than critically examining our fundamental security strategy and defensive technologies. Bans on certain groups and technology are only one aspect of national security. Instead, it is about operational resilience and cybersecurity in the face of the constant reality of threats in cyberspace—critically, regardless of where assaults originate from or what technologies attackers are aiming after.

- Building resilience moving forward
  Nowadays, attempts to identify early warning signs of threat are being outpaced by the rate at which cyberattacks are developing. Accordingly, the strength of any cybersecurity position is in its capacity to comprehend and uphold normal conditions internally rather than in its attempts to foresee the characteristics of potential future external threats. Regardless of the threat actor's motivations—financial, strategic, or political—this is true. The emphasis on specific businesses takes attention away from the reality of cyber-defense. Gaining more insight into crucial digital environments can actually promote national security issues as opposed to reducing or limiting the technology ecosystem. We may effectively manage risk in our complex world by developing a thorough grasp of these situations. This amount and scope of comprehension of the ever evolving complexity of

digital environments would, in the past, have been beyond the capabilities of a human security team. But those teams using AI and machine learning are capable of doing it. These tools are exceptional in providing a thorough and detailed picture of the actions and tools that make up a technological ecosystem. Techno-nationalism in the modern world is growing and will probably keep growing because, although being ultimately useless, it is reacting to actual challenges in a highly apparent way. The stakes are still quite high. Foreign hostile actors exploit supply-side technology and hidden backdoors in component components as points of access. Economic espionage may cause immeasurable financial harm once attackers have gained admission. Additionally, significant national infrastructure disruptions like those to gas and electricity networks can cost a country dearly. These risks must be addressed practically, given their prevalence. Despite growing in popularity, techno-nationalism cannot meet the bigger security problem. Implementing AI-aided digital understanding can genuinely promote national security rather than limiting access to foreign technology in a fun game of whack-a-mole. Whatever the source of the assault, the strict examination and real-time attack interruption made possible by AI's comprehensive approach offers effective cyber protection across the whole spectrum of implementable technologies.

8.2   Conclusion

In this research work one of the most difficult challenges for the serious student of technology is that we all assume we know what the main technologies of different historical times were and what their influence was at the global and national levels. We believe we know not because we are strangely mistaken about technology, but because credible books, movies, museums, and so on repeatedly inform us that a limited number of technologies have impacted the world in well-established ways. To exaggerate a bit, there is broad agreement on this across ideological, national, and gender boundaries, as well as fields of research or technique. There may be some disagreement about evaluation, but not over what to evaluate. And yet, as I hope to have demonstrated, our accounts, at least in terms of the country and globalization, are not as safe as they look. The fact that the arguments contained in sophisticated academic literature are comparable to those found in popular culture (which I have juxtaposed as an exercise in what I call history from below) is instructive. Understanding technology better is vital since it plays a prominent role in explanations of national rise and decline, and much more so in descriptions of globalization. The lesson of the story is that anytime technology is mentioned in conversations about the country or globalization, it should be kept in mind that it is quite likely that it is an account of technology that should have been dismissed a long time ago. A new history of technology has the potential to provide fresh perspectives on national and global histories.

Acknowledgement

This paper and the research behind it would not have been possible without the exceptional support of my supervisor. Her enthusiasm, knowledge, and exacting of details have been an inspiration and kept my work on track from my first encounter with the survey paper. I am also thankful to Vishwakarma University, Pune.

References

1. Edgerton, D. E. 2007. The contradictions of techno-nationalism and techno-globalism: A historical perspective. *New Global Studies*, 1(1): 1–32.
2. Evenett, S. J. 2019. Protectionism, state discrimination, and international business since the onset of the global financial crisis. *Journal of International Business Policy*, 2(1): 9–36.
3. Montresor, S. 2001. Techno-globalism, techno-nationalism and technological systems: Organizing the evidence. *Technovation*, 21(7): 399–412.
4. Nambisan, S., Zahra, S., & Luo, Y. 2019. Global platforms and ecosystems: Implications for international business theories. *Journal of International Business Studies*, 50(9): 1464–1486.
5. Ostry, S., & Nelson, R. 1995. *Techno-nationalism and techno-globalism: Conflict and cooperation*. The Brookings Institution.
6. Petricevic, O., & Teece, D. J. 2019. The structural reshaping of globalization: Implications for strategic sectors, profiting from innovation, and the multinational enterprise. *Journal of Inter-national Business Studies*, 50: 1487–1512.
7. Archibugi, D., & Michie, J. 1995. The globalization of technology: A new taxonomy. *Cambridge Journal of Economics*, 19: 121–140.

8. Capri, A. 2020. Techno-nationalism: The US–China tech innovation race. Hinrich Foundation. https://www.hinrichfoundation. com/research/wp/us-china-tech-innovation-race.

9. Samuels, R. J. 1994. *Rich nation, strong army: National security and the technological transformation of Japan.* Cornell University Press.

10. Yamada, A. 2000. Neo-Techno-Nationalism: How and Why It Grows. Columbia International Affairs Online (March 2000), http://www.ciaonet.org/isa/yaa01.

11. Legrain, P. 2020. Will the Coronavirus kill globalization? The pandemic is legitimizing nationalists and turning their xenophobia into policy. *Foreign Policy,* Spring Issue: 23–25.

12. Graham, E., & Marchik, D. 2006. *US national security and foreign direct investment.* Columbia University Press.

13. Kennedy, S., Suttmeier, R. & Su, J. 2008. *Standards, Stakeholders, and Innovation: China's Evolving Role in the Global Knowledge Economy.* National Bureau of Asian Research, Special Report, No.15.

14. White House 2018: How China's economic aggression threatens the technologies and intellectual property of the United States and the World. https://www.whitehouse.gov/wp-content/ uploads/2018/06/FINAL-China-Technology-Report-6.18.18- PDF.pdf.

15. Yip, G., & McKern, B. 2016. *China's Next Strategic Advantage: From Imitation to Innovation. MIT Press.*

16. Zitelmann, R. 2019. State capitalism? No, the private sector was and is the main driver of China's economic growth. *Forbes,* September 30, 2019.

17. Cantwell, J. 1995. The globalization of technology: what remains of the product cycle model? *Cambridge Journal of Economics,* 19: 155–174.

18. Garcia-Herrero, A. 2020. From globalization to deglobalization: Zooming into trade. Bruegel Report, February 3, 2020. https://www.bruegel.org/2020/02/from-globalization-todeglobalization-zooming-into-trade.

19. McKinsey Global Institute. 2020. Risk, resilience, and rebalancing in global value chains. https://www.mckinsey.com/business-functions/operations/our-insights/risk-resilience-andrebalancing-in-global-value-chains.

20. Sacks, J. 2020. *The ages of globalization: Geography, technology, and institutions.* Columbia University Press.

21. Legrain, P. 2020. Will the Coronavirus kill globalization? The pandemic is legitimizing nationalists and turning their xenophobia into policy. *Foreign Policy,* Spring Issue: 23–25.

22. Kim, L., & Nelson, R. 2000. *Technology, Learning, and Innovation: Experiences of Newly Industrializing Economies.* Cambridge University Press.

23. Moore, S. 2019. Trump's techno-nationalism. Lawfare (https:// www.lawfareblog.com/trumps-techno-nationalism), August 15, 2019.

24. Rajan, A. 2018. Techno-nationalism could determine the 21st Century. *BBC News,* September 8, 2018. https://www.bbc. com/news/technology-45370052.

25. Smith, A. D. 2013. *Nationalism: Theory, Ideology and History* (2nd ed.). Wiley.

26. Higgins, V. 2015. *Alliance capitalism, innovation and the Chinese state: The global wireless sector*. Palgrave McMillan.
27. Doz, Y. L., & Wilson, K. 2012. *Managing Global Innovation: Frameworks for Integrating Capabilities around the world*. Harvard Business Review Press.
28. BCG Report. 2019. Unpacking the US-China tech trade war. https://www.bcg.com/publications/2019/us-china-techtrade-war.
29. Govindarajan, V., & Ramamurti, R. 2011. Reverse innovation, emerging markets and global strategy. *Global Strategy Journal*, 1: 191–205.

9

Quantum Computing Based on Cybersecurity

P. William[1]*, Vivek Parganiha[2] and D.B. Pardeshi[3]

[1]Department of Information Technology, Sanjivani College of Engineering, SPPU,
Pune, India
[2]Department of Computer Science Engineering, Bhilai Institute of Technology,
CSVTU, Bhilai, India
[3]Department of Electrical Engineering, Sanjivani College of Engineering, SPPU,
Pune, India

Abstract

As the race to develop practical quantum computers heats up, businesses, academic institutions, and research organisations working in the field may find themselves the focus of increasingly sophisticated cyberattacks for espionage, economic gain, and other nefarious purposes. As a consequence of the proliferation of quantum applications, conventional commercial information systems and services are rapidly approaching the point at which they will be required to protect their networks, software, hardware, and data from being subjected to digital assaults. This is the case as a result of the fact that quantum applications have been expanding. In this paper, we take a look at the present level of quantum computing as well as the risks that are associated with the emergence of this new area. We next proceed to describe potential attack vectors against quantum computing systems and the countermeasures, precautions, and best practises that can be taken to protect against them. After that, we propose suggestions for proactively reducing the cyberattack surface through threat intelligence and by ensuring the security by design of quantum software and hardware components.

Keywords: Quantum software engineering, quantum computing, quantum education and training, cybersecurity

*Corresponding author: william160891@gmail.com

Romil Rawat, Rajesh Kumar Chakrawarti, Sanjaya Kumar Sarangi, Jaideep Patel, Vivek Bhardwaj, Anjali Rawat and Hitesh Rawat (eds.) *Quantum Computing in Cybersecurity*, (165–174) © 2023 Scrivener Publishing LLC

9.1   Introduction

Cybersecurity is a forward-looking strategy that is often overlooked. There may be an increase in the frequency of cybersecurity breaches at universities, organisations, and institutions as the level of competition in the field of Quantum Computing heats up [1]. The goals and requirements of quantum applications in classical information systems are similar to those of modern Software Engineering practises. For reliable and secure Quantum Computing ecosystems, services, and future technologies, it is crucial to build security in from the start of the design process, or "move security to the left".

Labs, companies, universities, and hospitals are all part of the ever-expanding digital ecosystem, as are all forms of operational technology and interconnected hardware. The rise of digitization and the trend toward remote employment have both contributed to an increase in cyberattacks. Companies of any size or industry that keep and handle sensitive information are prime targets for cyberattacks like espionage and sabotage because of the value placed on such information. As recent assaults on supercomputers, universities, and R&D facilities [2–4] attest, the idea is well-grounded. Numerous reviews and various types of research [5–8] have been conducted to investigate different elements of the security of quantum computing.

The scope of this work also encompasses commercial enterprises that have digital capabilities. It may be beneficial for startups, university spinoffs, and suppliers to begin the discourse early for a number of reasons, including the potential to profit from the incorporation of secure, proprietary technology for consumers and the protection of products from relevant dangers. The purpose of this survey is also to stimulate conversations and advance ideas in interdisciplinary research regarding the training paths for Quantum Computing professionals.

In addition to this focal point, the research will distinguish between various types of quantum computing systems and between quantum technologies at different stages of technical development. Quantum - communication - metrology - sensing and the associated modelling and numerical techniques characterise the latter, far more wide spectrum [9].

9.2   Preliminaries

Before discussing the danger vectors, we will examine a few quantum computing–related issues that are essential for comprehension. To take advantage of quantum phenomena, the processors used in quantum computing systems integrate a variety of components into a unique, highly efficient whole. Amdahl's Law [10] specifies that an accelerator is any co-processor that is linked to a central processing unit and has the potential to speed up the overall execution of certain computationally expensive kernels. A co-processor known as a quantum processing unit (QPU) is required in order to make your quantum computer Turing-complete. The QPU, in turn, requires a control system, an analog-to-digital interface, and a Host-CPU that is able to connect to a network in order to manage the application logic [11].

A typical quantum accelerator design is seen in Figure 9.1. One example of this is something called "Quantum as a Service," which provides on-demand access to managed computing resources. This may be accomplished either by storing the resources in the cloud or by using some other kind of remote access method.

In order to comprehend the value and rationale behind these quantum accelerators, we shall explore their intended applications in the next section. The flood of articles stating Quantum A statement that misrepresents the current state of things and fails to express that these possible capabilities are still many years away from being realised about how computing will soon be able to circumvent existing security measures. Several optimization problems, molecular modelling, and the creation of catalysts and drugs are only a few examples of areas where a reliable quantum accelerator might be useful [16]. Since no such systems exist right now, conventional alternatives continue to take precedence despite these improvements and optimizations.

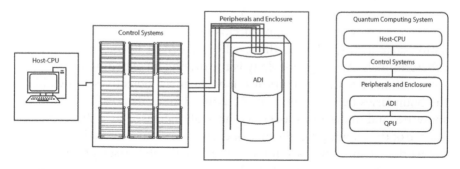

Figure 9.1 Architecture of quantum computing.

A recent study conducted by Google has shown that 20 million NISQ device qubits are necessary in order to decrypt an RSA key in under eight hours [19]. Despite this, the most recent advancements in physical qubits (as opposed to error-corrected logical qubits) have not yet officially crossed the barrier of 100 qubits for NISQ devices [20]. This does not cover the use of digital annealer technologies, which are analogue equipment designed specifically for the purpose of optimization.

This is the case even in the event that we had a quadratic speedup. In this work, the researchers believe that top-secret, encrypted material with a longer intelligence lifetime and lower key length than AES-256 might potentially be saved and decrypted in the future [23]. Since decoding may take many months, they could be susceptible to future quantum attacks, while intelligence with a shorter lifetime would be unaffected. As a result, the threat posed in the other direction by quantum computing equipment is not now a pressing concern, and the intelligence life of data plays an essential role in this regard.

On the other hand, worries about safety in the emerging quantum computing infrastructure are seldom ever brought up. As a result of the fact that quantum computing systems are hybrid systems and will continue to be hybrid systems with CPU-hosts, cloud-based or controlled APIs for the foreseeable future, there is an increased requirement for dependable and secure services and designs. Therefore, adequate security measures must be implemented so that these systems can handle and store the essential applications and data.

9.3   Threat Landscape

There is always a threat actor behind every cyberattack, and they always have a reason for doing what they're doing. Threat actors who are motivated by politics and geographical closeness to a nation state are called nation-state actors, whereas those who are driven by money are called cybercriminals. Although ideology is the driving force behind hacktivism, some nation-state threat actors also have financial objectives, which blurs the boundaries between the two. Activities like as data exfiltration, ransomware, and malware-as-a-service have all increased as a direct consequence of the growing significance of digitization and connectivity around the world. At this time, a number of criminal enterprises provide these services to various threat actors. Recruitment, the production of web-injection kits or exploit networks, specialised distribution methods such as the delivery of spam email, and the provision of monetization schemes such as wire fraud and cryptocurrency services are all examples of how the ecosystem has expanded to accommodate cybercrime.

National security concerns have been raised about the rivalry for scientific breakthroughs in quantum computing [6, 7]. As a result, the quantum race may be seen as a means by which the state can exert more control over its citizens and a means by which the early adopters can gain economically [23]. As a result, the interests of nation-state enemies rely heavily on sabotage and research espionage. Attacks on quantum systems will increase as their availability and economic continuity improve along with the dependability, quality, and accountability of quantum computing service providers. To a similar extent, it will incentivize hackers to target these systems for sabotage, cyberextortion, and data theft in order to monetize their illicit activities. Though hackers with shared ideological goals may pursue similar tactics, they may differ on how those goals should be pursued, the nature of the research to be undertaken, or the organisations they want to disrupt.

On a fundamental level, enemy strategies are comparable. After gathering intel through reconnaissance on the target, the next steps are to plant one's flag, elevate one's privileges, and then quietly expand across the network. If the goal is intelligence gathering, the opponent will want to stay under the radar and create as little trouble as possible; if the goal is sabotage, however, the very act of disclosing the existence of an enemy may cause trouble. This method is also used for illicit financial gain, usually in conjunction with some kind of communication for extortion or data selling. The best way to prevent attacks from a certain vector or employ the methods of a particular threat actor is to be aware of their typical tactics, techniques, and procedures (TTPs). Even more so, the targeted company or institution must understand its own system and environment to properly thwart assaults.

It's possible that QaaS (Quantum-as-a-Service) providers, users that process or consume these services, and threat actors are all targets. Many of the most common security flaws in the cloud, internet, and industrial control systems (ICS) also apply here. Misconfiguration of services, insecure infrastructure, unauthorised access to development or staging environments, and integration of services or data are all common security concerns in the cloud [25]. The principal threats to online applications have not changed much in the previous decade, but the OAWSP Top Ten [26] gives a solid basis for reducing these dangers. For example, an attacker might take over a user's account by exploiting a weakness in the authentication or access control measures, exposing sensitive data, or modifying the DOM (Domain Object Model) to inject malicious code or see the user's browser history. The ICS components most likely to include vulnerabilities are those that have a particular hardware affinity. Older control systems contain a great deal of critical defects, and the exploits that may be used to take advantage of those weaknesses are widely disseminated. Open Platform Communications (OPC) technology, particularly in older control systems like OPC classic, has the same security problems as RPC (Remote Procedure Call) and DCOM (Distributed Component Object Model) services, in which multiple communication ports are left wide open by design. Automated ICS vulnerabilities include cross-site scripting, buffer overflows, and hardcoded passwords [27, 28]. The human aspect, which is the focus of this article, is perhaps the most important component. Successful social engineering and phishing campaigns prey on human nature, notably on people's natural inclinations for socialisation and exploration. Spear phishing and the theft of credentials may result through USB drop attacks, impersonation, and demands for internal information. There are benefits and hazards to both older and newer software systems. The use of credentials that are hard-coded, an absence of or an authentication method that is unsuitable for critical tasks, incorrect default permissions, and the exposure of sensitive data to individuals who do not have permission to access it are some of the most common and potentially catastrophic software flaws.

9.4 Defensive Measurements, Countermeasures, and Best Practises

The first stage is becoming familiar with your current technical setup and your immediate environment. Security operations procedures in systems with a high degree of cybersecurity maturity include comprehensive monitoring and recording for threat detection and response. It is always a balancing act between cost and available resources, albeit the specifics of this balancing act will vary from application to application, system to system, and process to process. In order to effectively execute critical security policies, it is necessary to first identify the relevant threats to your key assets and activities. The initial line of defence is simply fortified by improved cyber hygiene and heightened awareness.

Because your potential target area is spreading into the cloud as well as into the homes of your employees, you need to impose constraints on employees' ability to work remotely. Encryption at both the endpoints and during data transit is essential in order to accomplish this aim. Segmentation, authorization, authentication, and encryption must be appropriately set up for suitable perimeters utilising firewalls and DMZs (Demilitarized Zone in perimeter networks). Additionally, a complete zero trust model should be established if resources allow for it. Cloud security gap studies and security audits are helpful in identifying risky settings and weaknesses in cloud computing security. Systems not in production, such as those used for R&D, are important to keep in mind. When it comes to legacy software, such as in ICS systems, it is recommended that OPC classic be upgraded to OPC UA, and that further separation be implemented in order to close the risk aperture through the use of AAA (Authentication, Authorization, and Accounting), as well as the use of firewalls, and D MZs. Both of these measures should be taken. Due to the combination of commercially available components and proprietary software and hardware, flashing by design and giving source-code bug fixes are necessities for commercially viable quantum computing systems. Components of a vendor must to be in charge of finding security problems and implementing patches. When we examine control systems more closely, we see that fail-safe systems need to be segregated in order to eliminate any weak points. This is something that we must do in order to ensure the safety of the system. An adversary, for instance, should not be able to get access to the system and control unit of the ADI/cooling QPU via the same Host-CPU in order to sabotage a compromised QCS. This would prevent the adversary from sabotaging the QCS. The presence of humans is another factor that should not be overlooked in ICS environments. A system that has an air gap can only be broken into by physically bridging the gap between the two halves of the system. Restricting physical access, whitelisting only authorised USB sticks, and/or setting a device antivirus scan stage are all potential ways to assist reduce the risk of unauthorised access being gained by an employee who is either an insider threat or just an idiot.

SANS CIS Controls [12–14, 32] offers a suggested set of actions for cyber defence [15, 17, 18] in critical control systems, whereas MITRE Shield [33] offers a comprehensive description of defence methods against certain approaches. Safer OPC system designs may be implemented with the help of ICS [21, 22, 24] security tools [34]. DevSecOps [29–31] is an architectural framework that streamlines and automates the integration of security tools and procedures into the various stages of the software development life cycle. Developers may do comprehensive vulnerability testing using tools like Metasploit and W3AF.

9.5   Conclusion

Due to the limited funding and resources available for quantum computing research and the small number of commercially available devices, we cannot afford to wait until something goes wrong before taking action. We should only construct and code quantum hardware and software components with safety in mind since this is the only reason why. The leftward direction of comparable service design requires a change in thinking analogous to the one described here. The field of quantum computing is plagued by problems relating to sabotage, espionage, and blackmail. Threat information could make it possible to implement a defence system based on foresight, which would allow security operations to move from a reactive to a proactive position when dealing with threat actors. MISP (Malware Information Sharing Platform), an open-source threat intelligence platform, is a platform that may be used as a helpful resource for gaining knowledge on the many sorts of threat actors.

References

1. CrowdStrike, 2021 global threat report: Adversary trends analysis, Accessed: 2021. URL: https://www.crowdstrike.com/resources/reports/global-threat-report/.
2. Bitdefender, Cyberattack against UK supercomputer archer forces operators to disable access for scientists, Accessed: 2021. URL: https://www.bitdefender.com/blog/hotforsecurity/cyberattack-against-uk-supercomputer-archer-forces-operators-to-disable-access-for-scientists.
3. J. News, Forschungszentrum jülich - jsc - archiv newsletter "jsc news" - cyberattack against supercomputers, Accessed: 2021. URL: https://www.fz-juelich.de/SharedDocs/Meldungen/IAS/JSC/EN/2020/2020-06-cyberattack.html?nn=1060464.
4. NCSC, More ransomware attacks on UK education - ncsc.gov.uk, Accessed: 2021. URL: https://www.ncsc.gov.uk/news/alert-targeted-ransomware-attacks-on-uk-education-sector.
5. N. Dunn, *An introduction to quantum computing for security professionals*, 2021.
6. L. Chen, S. Jordan, Y.-K. Liu, D. Moody, R. Peralta, R. Perlner, D. Smith-Tone, Report on post-quantum cryptography, 2016. URL: https://nvlpubs.nist.gov/nistpubs/ir/2016/NIST.IR.8105.pdf. doi:10.6028/NIST.IR.8105.
7. D. Moody, G. Alagic, D. C. Apon, D. A. Cooper, Q. H. Dang, J. M. Kelsey, Y.-K. Liu, C. A. Miller, R. C. Peralta, R. A. Perlner, A. Y. Robinson, D. C. Smith-Tone, J. Alperin-Sheriff, Status report on the second round of the NIST post-quantum cryptography standardization process, 2020. URL: https://nvlpubs.nist.gov/nistpubs/ir/2020/NIST.IR.8309.pdf. doi:10.6028/NIST.IR.8309.
8. A. Majot, R. Yampolskiy, Global catastrophic risk and security implications of quantum computers, *Futures* 72 (2015) 17–26. doi:10.1016/J.FUTURES.2015.02.006.

9. Q. Flagship, Competence framework for quantum technologies compiled by Franziska Greinert and Rainer Müller version 1.0 (May 2021), 2021. URL: https://op.europa.eu/en/publication-detail/-/publication/93ecfd3c-2005-11ec-bd8e-01aa75ed71a1/language-en.

10. A. Reuther, P. Michaleas, M. Jones, V. Gadepally, S. Samsi, J. Kepner, Survey of machine learning accelerators (2020). URL: http://arxiv.org/abs/2009.00993 http://dx.doi.org/10.1109/HPEC43674.2020.9286149. doi:10.1109/HPEC43674.2020.9286149.

11. K. Bertels, A. Sarkar, A. Krol, R. Budhrani, J. Samadi, E. Geoffroy, J. Matos, R. Abreu, G. Gielen, I. Ashraf, Quantum accelerator stack: A research roadmap (2021). URL: http: //arxiv.org/abs/2102.02035.

12. T. N. Theis, H. S. P. Wong, The end of Moore's law: A new beginning for information technology, *Computing in Science and* Engineering 19 (2017) 41–50. doi:10.1109/MCSE.2017.29.

13. M. Horowitz, 1.1 computing's energy problem (and what we can do about it), *Digest of Technical Papers - IEEE International Solid-State Circuits Conference* 57 (2014) 10–14. doi:10.1109/ISSCC.2014.6757323.

14. R. Landauer, Irreversibility and heat generation in the computing process, *IBM Journal of Research and Development* 5 (2010) 183–191. doi:10.1147/RD.53.0183.

15. O. D. Matteo, V. Gheorghiu, M. Mosca, Fault tolerant resource estimation of quantum random-access memories (2020).

16. J. Preskill, Quantum computing in the NISQ era and beyond, *Quantum* 2 (2018) 79. doi:10.22331/q-2018-08-06-79.

17. M. Sarovar, T. Proctor, K. Rudinger, K. Young, E. Nielsen, R. Blume-Kohout, Detecting crosstalk errors in quantum information processors, *Quantum* 4 (2020) 321. URL: https://quantum-journal.org/papers/q-2020-09-11-321/. doi:10.22331/q-2020-09-11321

18. S. J. Pauka, K. Das, R. Kalra, A. Moini, Y. Yang, M. Trainer, A. Bousquet, C. Cantaloube, N. Dick, G. C. Gardner, M. J. Manfra, D. J. Reilly, A cryogenic CMOS chip for generating control signals for multiple qubits, *Nature Electronics* 2021 4:1 4 (2021) 64–70. URL: https://www.nature.com/articles/s41928-020-00528-y. doi:10.1038/s41928-020-00528-y.

19. C. Gidney, M. Ekerå, How to factor 2048 bit RSA integers in 8 hours using 20 million noisy qubits (2019). URL: http://arxiv.org/abs/1905.09749http://dx.doi.org/10.22331/q-2021-04-15-433. doi:10.22331/q-2021-04-15-433.

20. IBM, IBM's roadmap for scaling quantum technology, IBM research blog, Accessed: 2021. URL: https://research.ibm.com/blog/ibm-quantum-roadmap.

21. L. K. Grover, A fast quantum mechanical algorithm for database search, *Proceedings of the Annual ACM Symposium on Theory of Computing* Part F129452 (1996) 212–219. URL:https://arxiv.org/abs/quant-ph/9605043v3.

22. J. Tibbetts, *Quantum computing and cryptography: Analysis, risks, and recommendationsfor decisionmakers*, 2019.

23. SANS Institute, SANS ICS control systems are a target, v1.3 09.30.21.pdf, Accessed: 2021. URL: https://sansorg.egnyte.com/dl/j2o3K3iiPy.

24. S. Pratte, S. Fortozo, G. Kispal, A. Banvait, A. Azazi, N. Hiebert, Strategies for secure software development (2013).

25. Fortinet, Cloud security report (2021). URL: https://www.fortinet.com/content/dam/fortinet/assets/analyst-reports/ar-cybersecurity-cloud-security.pdf.

26. OAWSP, OAWSP top ten web application security risks. Accessed: 2021. URL: https://owasp.org/www-project-top-ten/.

27. Kaspersky, Threat landscape for industrial automation systems. Statistics for h2 2020, Kaspersky ICS CERT, 2021. URL: https://ics-cert.kaspersky.com/reports/2021/03/25/threat-landscape-for-industrial-automation-systems-statistics-for-h2-2020/.

28. Dragos, The ICS threat landscape (2019). URL: https://www.dragos.com/wp-content/uploads/The-ICS-Threat-Landscape.pdf.

29. CWE, 2021, CWE top 25 most dangerous software weaknesses, Accessed: 2021. URL: https://cwe.mitre.org/top25/archive/2021/2021_cwe_top25.html.

30. MITRE, Mitre attck® matrix for enterprise, Accessed: 2021. URL: https://attack.mitre.org/matrices/enterprise/.

31. MITRE, Attck® for industrial control systems, Accessed: 2021. URL: https://collaborate.mitre.org/attackics/index.php/Main_Page.

32. SANS Institute, CIS controls v8 released. Accessed: 2021. URL: https://www.sans.org/blog/cis-controls-v8/.

33. MITRE, Active defense matrix, Accessed: 2021. URL: https://shield.mitre.org/matrix/.

34. Github, Ics-security-tools/pcaps/opc at master·iti/ics-security-tools·github, Accessed: 2021. URL: https://github.com/ITI/ICS-Security-Tools/tree/master/pcaps/OPC.

10

Quantum Cryptography for the Future Internet and the Security Analysis

P. William[1*], A.B. Pawar[2] and M.A. Jawale[1]

[1]Department of Information Technology, Sanjivani College of Engineering, SPPU, Pune, India
[2]Department of Computer Science Engineering, Sanjivani College of Engineering, SPPU, Pune, India

Abstract

Almost every aspect of our life has benefited from the widespread use of cyberspace as the primary medium for the dissemination of information. Now more than ever, the rapid advancement of science and technology, in particular the quantum computer, is going to pose the greatest challenge to cyberspace security in the next years for the internet. Here, we analyze the characteristics of quantum cryptography and investigate its possible uses in the realm of online security. It is essential to keep in mind that the analysis of the quantum key distribution (QKD) protocol that we carry out is carried out in a channel that is devoid of noise. Additionally, in order to simulate potential future uses of the internet, we search for the QKD protocol in noisy channels. Results show that quantum cryptography is absolutely secure, which is fine for the internet despite the imminent arrival of new dangers.

Keywords: Cryptography, cyber security, threat, internet, quantum communication, cyberspace

10.1 Introduction

With the widespread use and quick growth of the internet, the information age has arrived. It is beneficial in almost every way that cyberspace has become the preeminent medium for the dissemination of information

Corresponding author: william160891@gmail.com

Romil Rawat, Rajesh Kumar Chakrawarti, Sanjaya Kumar Sarangi, Jaideep Patel, Vivek Bhardwaj, Anjali Rawat and Hitesh Rawat (eds.) Quantum Computing in Cybersecurity, (175–188) © 2023 Scrivener Publishing LLC

across all domains of human activity. But due to the development of cutting-edge tools like the quantum computer, cybersecurity is quickly becoming a major problem for the future of the internet. In this research, we analyze the characteristics of quantum cryptography and investigate its possible uses in the online environment. We highlight the fact that our examination of the QKD protocol is performed in a perfectly noise-free channel. As an added bonus, we look for the QKD protocol in the noisy channel to simulate future internet usage in real-world conditions. From a theoretical perspective, the findings prove that quantum cryptography is absolutely secure, which is fine for the internet given the imminent arrival of new dangers. Only in this manner can the future internet assure the information security of cyberspace. The fundamental principle of cyberspace security [9] is to take precautions at all levels and across the network. These procedures are designed to detect and find all types of network security risks and to take the appropriate reaction actions. The field of quantum cryptography has just begun to emerge. But the dangers it poses to the state of cybersecurity today cannot be ignored. The integer factorization issue and the discrete logarithm problem can both be solved in polynomial time according to the quantum approach [10], which was developed in 1994 by a mathematics professor named Shor. Notably, academics have not yet developed a classical method that efficiently addresses the challenges of large integer decomposition and discrete logarithm using the Turing machine paradigm. This is a notable gap in their knowledge. Quantum computing is still in its infancy, but the threat it poses to existing cryptosystems is already clear. When it comes to securing a computer network and data, cryptography and other related technologies are crucial [11]. There is a sizable subject of cryptography that focuses on the application of quantum physics to more traditional forms of encryption. Heisenberg's uncertainty principle and the quantum no-cloning theory work together to ensure that communications remain private [12]. Quantum cryptography [1–4] is primarily concerned with developing cryptographic algorithms [5, 6] and protocols that are secure against assaults using quantum computers. As was previously indicated, one of the most important aspects of the future difficulties in securing cyberspace [7, 8] on the internet will be researching quantum cryptography protocols. In this study, we dissect and examine the quantum key distribution method being developed for future internet cyberspace security.

In the next section of this paper, we provide an overview of complementary quantum cryptography literature. In the third part, we explain the basics of quantum physics and how quantum communications works.

In part four, we analyse the security of the future internet and outline the benefits of quantum cryptography. Part five concludes our paper.

10.2   Related Works

Wiesner first presented the concept of quantum money in 1969, which gave rise to quantum cryptography. This innovative and original proposal cannot be implemented due to the historical level of technology; hence it remained unpublished until 1983 [13]. In 2011, Bennett and Brassard introduced the first viable QKD protocol [14]. They were the first to design the quantum key distribution system, which they did by making use of the polarisation of a single photon. After that, a significant amount of work was put into enhancing the speed and security of QKD. Ekert made the proposal for the protocol [15] in 1991 by utilising Bell's theorem. It is worth noting that, like [14, 15] relies on a quantum bit pair (i.e., an EPR pair). In 1992, Bennett offered up a tweak [16] to the strategy [14]. This innovation is simplified and made more efficient by using any two nonorthogonal states. Since then, many QKD methods [17, 18] based on quantum mechanics' first principles have been created. The oblivious transmission protocol is among the backbone privacy-preserving mechanisms in cryptography [19]. The sender of a message using an oblivious transfer protocol provides the receiver with access to a wide variety of potential information, but the sender is unaware of the specific content of the message. In 1994, Crepeau was the first person to present the concept of quantum oblivious transfer, sometimes known as QOT [20]. Since that time, a large number of articles have been published that discuss the QOT protocol. Mayers and Salvail demonstrated in 1994 that [21] is safe against any single measurement that can be allowed by quantum physics in [22]. [21] The term for this kind of proof is the "oblivious transfer." Protocol [23], which was proposed in 1998, demonstrates that the QOT protocol is safe even when an eavesdropper is present. It was suggested that other protocols [24, 25] could improve the QOT protocol in varied degrees. The QA protocol is also included in the list of protocols that are used for quantum cryptography. It was introduced for the first time in [26] in 2001. After that, a flurry of QA methodologies [27, 28] were put forward for consideration. The protocol for quantum cryptography has resulted in a number of spin-off innovations in fields that are closely related to it. Included in the category of protocols for quantum cryptography are QBC protocols [29, 30] and QS protocols [31, 32]. (i.e., QKD protocol, QOT protocol, and QA protocol).

10.3   Preliminaries

The features of quantum information provide a foundation for why quantum communication and information processing can offer several advantages over their classical counterparts.

10.3.1   Properties of Quantum Information

Qualities of quantum information, such as the uncertainty principle, the quantum no-cloning theory, quantum teleportation, and the hidden elements of quantum information, make it useful for protecting cyberspace communication from assault (passive or active attack [33]). The uncertainty principle and the non-clonability hypothesis of Heisenberg [12].

  (i)   Concept of Uncertainty: The idea, named after the German scientist who first proposed it in 1927 [34], is commonly referred to as Heisenberg's uncertainty principle. A particle in the microscopic realm always exists in multiple locations with different probabilities, making it hard to determine exactly where it is.

 (ii)   Quantum no-cloning theory [12]: Features of the quantum state that cannot be cloned or erased are what give rise to the "no-cloning" hypothesis of quantum mechanics. Quantum cloning is the creation of a copy of a system's quantum state. As scientists have shown [35], there currently exist no machines able to create an exact copy of a quantum system. The linearity of quantum theory, as stated in a publication published in *Nature* [36], forbids the removal of a duplicate quantum state.

(iii)   Quantum teleportation: The quantum state is measured to obtain the classical data, which is subsequently transferred normally. Quantum information is the data that is transmitted to the receiver but is not used by the sender to make an inference about the receiver. In 1993, a strategy for teleporting a quantum state whose identity is unknown was proposed [37].

 (iv)   Quantum information has hidden attributes; it has properties that regular data doesn't have. In particular, local measurement is unable to retrieve the quantum code's information in the entangled state, and joint measurement is required to decipher the code. In 2001, Terhal *et al.* proposed [38] a method of masking quantum information.

10.3.2 Quantum Communication System

There are at least two types of quantum communication: quantum teleportation and direct quantum communication. Quantum direct transmission is the simplest paradigm for transmitting quantum information. See Figure 10.1 for a schematic of the quantum direct-communication model. In Figure 10.1, Alice makes an effort to start a quantum channel conversation with Bob. A series of photons must be generated by Alice using the preparation device in accordance with the quantum direct transmission concept before a message can be sent to Bob. A quantum source encoder and a quantum error correcting code (QECC) encoder are required to process the data contained in a quantum source after its production. It is feasible to send quantum information across the quantum channel without any intermediate steps (optical fibre or atmosphere). Because of this, the quantum channel is susceptible to background noise. That's why Bob, the receiver, uses QECC encoding on the incoming signal before he uses quantum source encoding. The original quantum message is eventually obtained by Bob. Alternately, quantum teleportation is another method of quantum communication. In contrast to conventional means of communication, qubits can also exist in an entangled state, where they are mutually dependent on one another. Quantum teleportation works on the premise of creating a quantum channel. 0 1 1 EPR Alice Calculating in terms of the Bob Bell state Pandora's Classical Channel Teleportation using the strongest entanglement possible between two particles, as shown in Figure 10.2. Quantum processes multiply the transmission by a factor of ten. Teleportation differs from direct communication in that it allows for the selection of specific communication paths. Figure 10.2 shows a schematic of the quantum teleportation model. Here, Alice wants to send a single

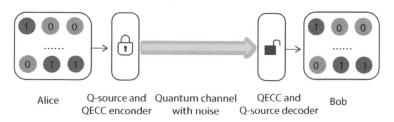

Alice   Q-source and   Quantum channel   QECC and   Bob
         QECC enconder   with noise   Q-source decoder

Figure 10.1 Quantum direct communication model.

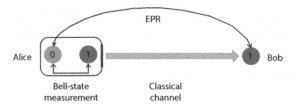

Figure 10.2 Quantum teleportation.

quantum bit to Bob who is in a different location. The EPR entanglement generator first creates an EPR pair. Second, Alice receives one particle and Bob receives the other over the quantum channel. For information to be transmitted, Before Alice can get the bits she's expecting, she must first measure the particles in the EPR-entangled pairs. As a further step, Alice will report the findings to Bob. Now that Alice has also taken measurements, Bob may use them together to better understand the particles that will be transferred using the EPR pair.

10.4   Quantum Cryptography for Future Internet

Since the internet is where all human-created and -operated information systems congregate, it deserves to be safeguarded. As the need for cybersecurity grows, quantum cryptography is at the forefront of the discussion.

10.4.1   Unconditional Security

Present-day internet transmission mediums rely primarily on cable and optical fibre. Figure 10.3 depicts this hypothetical communication system model. Alice and Bob are legitimate system users, whereas Eve is just

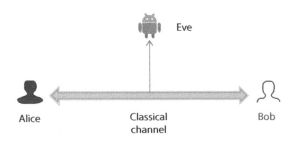

Figure 10.3 Classical communication model.

nosing around. As a precaution, they encrypt their communications before sending them over the open network. In general, the classical cryptosystem can be split into two categories: those that use symmetric keys and those that use asymmetric keys. Both of these cryptosystems are extremely vulnerable to attacks that are even moderately difficult to compute. Traditional cryptosystems have been tried and true for decades, but the proliferation of computing power and the introduction of more advanced algorithms have introduced new and significant security challenges. As quantum computing has advanced, it has been used to solve some of the most difficult classical mathematical issues in quantum physics. For instance, the DLP and integer factorization problems were both tackled in [10], published in 1994. Future issues in securing cyberspace on the internet will require further investigation of quantum cryptography systems.

A pioneer in the field of unconditional security research in the 1950s, Shannon [39] is best known as the man who developed information theory. The amount of protection required for "one-time-pad" was not capped for this study. Instead of using a pseudo-random number for encryption and decryption, we utilize a true random number. The key can only be used once, too. The key's length is the same as the plaintext's, and it performs an exclusive-or operation on the plaintext bit by bit. Where those keys go on one-time pads is still up for debate. Applying this theory from quantum mechanics to the key distribution problem yields a solution. In Figure 10.4, we see a graphic depiction of the widely used QKD protocol [14]. To encrypt and decrypt communications, the sender and receiver in this approach would like to trade conference keys. Using the uncertainty principle, one of the most fundamental aspects of quantum mechanics, this QKD system guarantees that the key is truly random. Moreover, if an adversary does exist, it may be positively recognized.

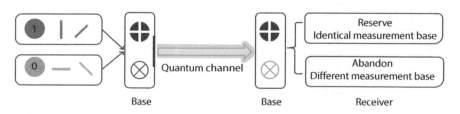

Figure 10.4 Model of QKD protocol.

10.4.2   Sniffing Detection

Alice and Bob use a public channel to talk to each other in Figure 10.3. While they encrypt their data to protect it, an enemy might still potentially listen in on the conversation. In addition, the eavesdropper cannot be discovered in either cable or optical fibre communications due to the inherent properties of the equipment. Conversations through cables can be eavesdropped on using a multimeter or an oscilloscope. To steal information through optical fibre connections, all an eavesdropper needs to do is intercept a little portion of the light signal. As fibre loss is also affected by environmental factors like temperature and pressure, the interference produced by eavesdropping is minimal. The quantum no-cloning hypothesis guarantees that an eavesdropper may be identified in quantum communication. Figure 10.4 depicts the quantum channel an eavesdropper would observe; in this case, he would have a 50/50 chance of selecting the same measuring base as the transmitter. Given that the eavesdropper can be identified with a chance of 50% for each bit of quantum information, this indicates that the eavesdropper will be detected 50% of the time.

10.4.3   Security of the QKD

Here, using a noise-free channel as a stand-in for the next generation of the Internet, we evaluate how well the quantum key distribution protocol performs. Furthermore, we explore the underlying mechanisms of quantum key distribution over a noisy channel. Quantum information encoding and measurement results for various measurement bases are reported in Table 10.1 for evaluation of QKD protocol resilience. Both sides have previously agreed that "1" represents downward polarisation in the horizontal and oblique directions, whereas "0" represents upward polarization in the

Table 10.1 Measurement result.

Results	$\oplus$	Polarization	$\otimes$
Bases			
$\leftrightarrow$	1		0: 50%; 1: 50%
$\updownarrow$	0		0: 50%; 1: 50%
$\nearrow$	0: 50%; 1: 50%		0
$\nwarrow$	0: 50%; 1: 50%		1

vertical and oblique directions. The following formula is used to determine the probability of an eavesdropper on the QKD protocol.

When dealing with quantum information consisting of one bit, the probability of an eavesdropper being found is calculated as 1/2 1/2 1/2 = 1/8. Figure 10.5 illustrates the percentage of the time that an eavesdropper can be found in a channel that is free of background noise. As the graph shows, the likelihood of an eavesdropper approaches 100% once the number of transmissions has beyond 40. Figure 10.6 shows the likelihood of identifying an eavesdropper in a 30% noisy channel. The graph shows that if 80 photons are given, there is an almost 100% chance that an eavesdropper will be uncovered.

We can infer the discovery of eavesdropping behavior in quantum communication from the two figures shown above. It has been shown that the more data that is sent, the greater the chance that an eavesdropper can be recognized, even if there is some noise interference.

In Figure 10.7, we see the receiver's mistake probability with different eavesdropper intercept probabilities. In the absence of an eavesdropper, it shows that the receiver's error rate is 25%; when an eavesdropper is present but monitoring only half of the channel, it increases to 31%; and when an

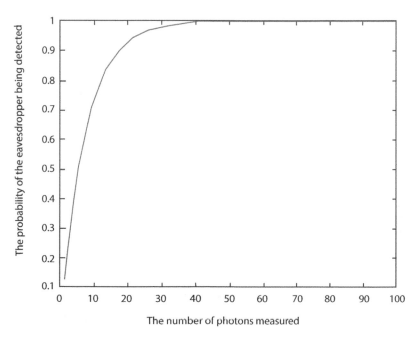

Figure 10.5 QKD protocol in noise-free channel.

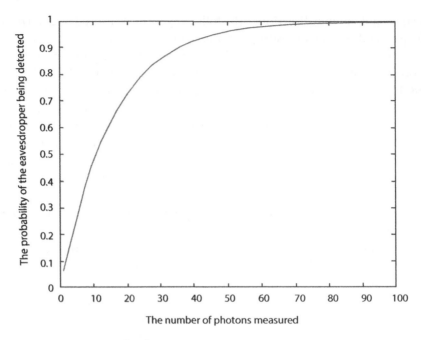

Figure 10.6 QKD protocol with 30% noise.

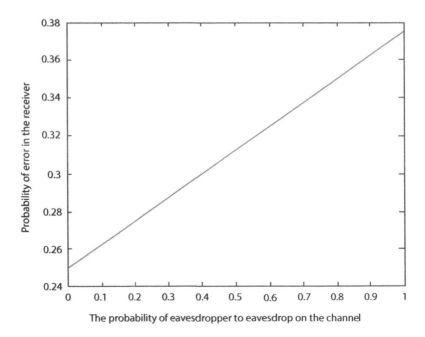

Figure 10.7 The effect of eavesdropping on the rate of error.

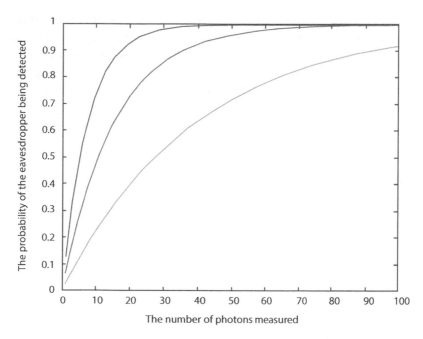

Figure 10.8 The eavesdropper detects the channel with different probability.

eavesdropper is present but monitoring all of the channel, it rises to 37%. Figure 10.8 shows the likelihood of an eavesdropper being discovered in a given channel. The purple line in this picture depicts constant monitoring by the attacker, while the green and red lines show monitoring at 50% and 20% duty, respectively. Based on these three curves, we may infer that the likelihood of an eavesdropper being detected approaches 100% as the number of sent bits grows, irrespective of the likelihood of the eavesdropper monitoring the channel.

After reviewing the information presented, one can draw the conclusion that quantum cryptography has the sniffing detection properties necessary for completely secure communication. These features have the potential to ensure the cybersecurity of the internet in the years to come.

10.5   Conclusion

Quantum cryptography is an important step forward for the field of cryptography, which was formerly dominated by classical cryptography and is now based on quantum mechanics. Its primary advantages over prior systems of cryptography are the provision of unconditional security as well as the identification of sniffer software. These capabilities have the ability to stop a future compromise of security on the internet. Safeguarding future internet applications like IoT and smart cities [40] is possible with quantum cryptography. As our analytical results show, quantum cryptography is perfectly suited for the internet of the future because to its ultimate security and sniffing detection.

Conflicts of Interest: The authors claim to have no conflicts of interest.

References

1. L. Strate, "The varieties of cyberspace: Problems in definition and delimitation," *Western Journal of Communication*, vol. 63, no. 3, pp. 382–412, 1999.

2. J. Shen, J. Shen, X. Chen, X. Huang, and W. Susilo, "An efficient public auditing protocol with novel dynamic structure for cloud data," *IEEE Transactions on Information Forensics and Security*, vol. 12, pp. 2402–2415, 2017.

3. J. Li, Y. Zhang, X. Chen, and Y. Xiang, "Secure attribute-based data sharing for resource-limited users in cloud computing," *Computers & Security*, 2017.

4. T. Zhou, L. Chen, and J. Shen, "Movie Recommendation System Employing the User-Based CF in Cloud Computing," in *Proceedings of the 2017 IEEE International Conference on Computational Science and Engineering (CSE) and IEEE International Conference on Embedded and Ubiquitous Computing (EUC)*, pp. 46–50, Guangzhou, China, July 2017.

5. R. L. Rivest, A. Shamir, and L. Adleman, "A method for obtaining digital signatures and public-key cryptosystems," *Communications of the ACM*, vol. 21, no. 2, pp. 120–126, 1978.

6. J. Shen, T. Zhou, X. Chen, J. Li, and W. Susilo, "Anonymous and Traceable Group Data Sharing in Cloud Computing," *IEEE Transactions on Information Forensics and Security*, vol. 13, no. 4, pp. 912–925, 2018.

7. T. ElGamal, "A public key cryptosystem and a signature scheme based on discrete logarithms," *IEEE Transactions on Information Theory*, vol. 31, no. 4, pp. 469–472, 1985.

8. Y.-M. Tseng, "An efficient two-party identity-based key exchange protocol," *Informatica*, vol. 18, no. 1, pp. 125–136, 2007.

9. J. Shen, T.Miao, Q. Liu, S. Ji, C.Wang, and D. Liu, "S-SurF: An Enhanced Secure Bulk Data Dissemination in Wireless Sensor Networks," in *Security, Privacy, and Anonymity in Computation, Communication, and Storage*, vol. 10656 of *Lecture Notes in Computer Science*, pp. 395–408, Springer International Publishing, Cham, 2017.

10. P. W. Shor, "Algorithms for quantum computation: discrete logarithms and factoring," in *Proceedings of the 35th Annual Symposium on Foundations of Computer Science (SFCS '94)*, pp. 124–134, IEEE, 1994.

11. J. Shen, T. Zhou, F. Wei, X. Sun, and Y. Xiang, "Privacy-Preserving and Lightweight Key Agreement Protocol for V2G in the Social Internet of Things," *IEEE Internet of Things Journal*, pp. 1-1.

12. A. Peres, *Quantum Theory: Concepts and Methods*, Springer Science & Business Media, 2006.

13. S.Wiesner, "Conjugate coding," *ACMSIGACT News*, vol. 15, no. 1, pp. 78–88, 1983.

14. C. H. Bennett and G. Brassard, "WITHDRAWN: Quantum cryptography: Public key distribution and coin tossing," *Theoretical Computer Science*, 2011.

15. A. K. Ekert, "Quantum cryptography based on Bell's theorem," *Physical Review Letters*, vol. 67, no. 6, pp. 661–663, 1991.

16. C. H. Bennett, "Quantum cryptography using any two nonorthogonal states," *Physical Review Letters*, vol. 68, no. 21, pp. 3121–3124, 1992.

17. B. Huttner, N. Imoto, N. Gisin, and T. Mor, "Quantum cryptography with coherent states," *Physical Review A: Atomic, Molecular and Optical Physics*, vol. 51, no. 3, pp. 1863–1869, 1995.

18. D. Bruß, "Optimal eavesdropping in quantum cryptography with six states," *Physical Review Letters*, vol. 81, no. 14, pp. 3018–3021, 1998.

19. P. Li, J. Li, Z. Huang, C.-Z. Gao, W.-B. Chen, and K. Chen, "Privacy-preserving outsourced classification in cloud computing," *Cluster Computing*, pp. 1–10, 2017.

20. C. Crépeau, "Quantum oblivious transfer," *Journal of Modern Optics*, vol. 41, no. 12, pp. 2445–2454, 1994.

21. C. H. Bennett, G. Brassard, C. Crépeau, and M.-H. Skubiszewska, "Practical quantum oblivious transfer," in *Annual International Cryptology Conference*, pp. 351–366, Springer.

22. D. Mayers and L. Salvail, "Quantum oblivious transfer is secure against all individual measurements," in *Proceedings of the Workshop on Physics and Computation. PhysComp '94*, pp. 69–77, Dallas, TX, USA.

23. D. Mayers, "On the security of the quantum oblivious transfer and key distribution protocols," *Lecture Notes in Computer Science* (including subseries *Lecture Notes in Artificial Intelligence* and *Lecture Notes in Bioinformatics*): Preface, vol. 963, pp. 124–135, 1995.

24. S. Winkler and J. Wullschleger, "On the efficiency of classical and quantum oblivious transfer reductions," *Lecture Notes in Computer Science* (including subseries *Lecture Notes in Artificial Intelligence* and *Lecture Notes in Bioinformatics*): Preface, vol. 6223, pp. 707–723, 2010.

25. A. Chailloux, I. Kerenidis, and J. Sikora, "Lower bounds for quantum oblivious transfer," *Quantum Information & Computation*, vol. 13, no. 1–2, pp. 0158–0177, 2013.

26. M. Curty and D. J. Santos, "Quantum authentication of classical messages," *Physical Review A: Atomic, Molecular and Optical Physics*, vol. 64, no. 6, 2001.

27. B.-S. Shi, J. Li, J.-M. Liu, X.-F. Fan, and G.-C. Guo, "Quantum key distribution and quantum authentication based on entangled state," *Physics Letters A*, vol. 281, no. 2-3, pp. 83–87, 2001.
28. D. Zhang and X. Li, "Quantum authentication using orthogonal product states," in *Proceedings of the 3rd International Conference on Natural Computation, ICNC 2007*, pp. 608–612, China, August 2007.
29. G. Brassard and C. Crépeau, "Quantum bit commitment and coin tossing protocols in," in *Proceedings of the Conference on The Theory and Application of Cryptography*, pp. 49–61, Springer.
30. N. K. Langford, R. B. Dalton, M. D. Harvey *et al.*, "Measuring entangled qutrits and their use for quantum bit commitment," *Physical Review Letters*, vol. 93, no. 5, Article ID 053601, 4 p., 2004.

11

Security Aspects of Quantum Cryptography

P. William[1]*, Siddhartha Choubey[2] and Abha Choubey[2]

[1]Department of Information Technology, Sanjivani College of Engineering, SPPU, Pune, India
[2]Department of Computer Science Engineering, Shri Shankaracharya Technical Campus, Bhilai, India

Abstract

Cryptography is used to ensure the security of two-party communications. Transmission of secret messages is the most prevalent cryptographic concern. The protocol for maintaining confidentiality is cryptographic. Security in quantum cryptography is based less on mathematical problem-solving and more on scientific foundations, such as quantum physics and statistics. One popular usage of quantum cryptography is in the creation of cryptographic keys for use in communication, known as quantum key distribution (QKD). Security is ensured and eavesdropping is prevented since it is based on the Heisenberg uncertainty principle. The topics of weak laser-based quantum cyphers, polarisation coding, phase coding, and frequency coding have all received a significant amount of attention.

Keywords: Cryptography, cyber security, threat, internet, quantum communication, cyberspace

11.1 Introduction

In recent years, Information Technology and Communication have witnessed remarkable growth. Cryptography is the method that is used to safeguard communication between parties from adversaries. The main goals of cryptography are authentication (the message is received from an authorised source), secrecy (no one except the intended recipients may read

Corresponding author: william160891@gmail.com

Romil Rawat, Rajesh Kumar Chakrawarti, Sanjaya Kumar Sarangi, Jaideep Patel, Vivek Bhardwaj, Anjali Rawat and Hitesh Rawat (eds.) Quantum Computing in Cybersecurity, (189–200) © 2023 Scrivener Publishing LLC

the message), and data integrity (the message cannot be changed in transit). This is done by sending the recipient a secret message that can only be deciphered using a key that has been previously generated. This key may be easily copied or stolen by an outside party. Identifiable information Complex mathematical computations are often necessary in cryptography [1–3], which might slow down the process. Quantum Cryptography is used to circumvent these constraints and increase the security of communication. Stephen Wiese's invention of conjugate coding in the late 1960s paved the way for quantum cryptography. Quantum Cryptography [4] is a method for transmitting information securely using the application of quantum physics. Mathematical procedures for the purpose of encryption, such as elliptic curve cryptography and RSA, are used often in today's society. These algorithms do not have adequate levels of security. These widely used mathematical cryptosystems provide a threat to information that must be kept secure at a high level and are susceptible to compromise. The security of quantum cryptography is not so much dependent on the solution of mathematical problems as it is on the underlying scientific principles of quantum physics and statistics. The well-known application of quantum cryptography known as quantum key distribution (QKD) is used to establish communication by producing cryptographic keys. In addition to this, it is predicated on the Heisenberg Uncertainty principle, which both ensures safety and prevents snooping and spying. Due to certain inconsistencies, even if an opponent were to eavesdrop on a conversation involving a key, the conversing parties would be able to ascertain this fact without difficulty. The QKD apparatus consists of a photon transceiver and an electrical component. Due to the fragility of photons, QKD is restricted to communications distances of 50–100 km. Quantum Computing adheres to superposition, entanglement, and quantum physics principles. Superposition is the process of executing new actions while processing information. According to the theory of quantum superposition, two particles can occupy different positions simultaneously. Due to its existence in the realm of subatomic particles, it is not directly perceivable in the macrocosm. It is impossible to characterise or describe a particle in an entangled state without taking into account the properties of all the other particles involved. Quantum encryption depends primarily on qubits, which are used in quantum mechanics rather than conventional bits.

11.2   Literature Survey

[1] highlighted quantum cryptography and its role in a multi-layered defence to counteract hackers. Some of the flaws of today's digital cryptosystems are

outlined, including the need for time-consuming and laborious calculations. Quantum encryption, which is based on the basic and unchangeable principles of quantum physics, can get around these weaknesses. We provide an example of how to implement Quantum Key Distribution, which ensures the safe distribution of keys, to illustrate our point. The many positive qualities of QKD are discussed, including its secrecy, authentication, speed, robustness, independence from location, and resistance to traffic analysis. The use of quantum cryptography has already been put into practise on a variety of platforms, including the DARPA [5] Quantum Network and MagiQ Technologies, amongst others. Techniques for filtering data, correcting mistakes, amplifying users' privacy, and authenticating users are all included in quantum cryptography.

In [2] Classical Cryptography, which is used to send secret communications, was discussed together with its more modern counterparts, Symmetric and Asymmetric Cryptography. Also described were the benefits of quantum cryptography, including the phenomenon of quantum entanglement, in which the quantum properties of two or more objects are characterised in terms of their relationship to one another. Quantum key distribution, an implementation of quantum cryptography, is analysed. The authors describe three security measures, including the use of quantum cryptography in 802.11 networks, and explain how they function. These are key generation, cypher, and authentication algorithm.

[3] described the objectives of Cryptography. Quantum cryptography's secure transmission of the key distribution procedure is addressed. The indestructible nature of the one-time pad is described, along with the problems of key production, distribution, and management. An explanation of the B92 QKD protocol [6] is provided. Quantum mechanics is more trustworthy since it does not expose hidden values. Its practical realisation makes use of single-photon polarisation states. A broad range of factors may have an effect on the data rate and error rate of the system. This research presents a variety of different strategies for enhancing the speed.

[4] weighed the safety of using quantum key distribution systems against more conventional methods. Dark numbers and losses are mentioned. Mechanisms for errors of various types are discussed. Parametric down conversion is used to strengthen the security of a signal over a greater distance, although this method is limited in several ways, such as range and the reduction of dark counts. Using quantum repeaters, data may be sent safely across great distances without worrying about the signal degrading.

In [4] the authors shared their thoughts on a desktop modular QKD technique that is both safe and useful for building complicated systems. Here, we provide a plug-and-play technique for handling optical pulses at a higher frequency. However, the plug-and-play scheme has certain disadvantages, such as polarisation fluctuation issues because the optical pulses transit through the quantum channel twice. Flexibility, usability, and sturdiness are only a few of the highlighted benefits of the presented approach.

11.3   Quantum Key Distribution

The goal of key circulation is for two customers, "Alice" and "Bounce," [7, 8] who initially share no secret information, to agree on a random key that cannot be deduced by an adversary, "Eve," who is listening in on their interactions. The fact that electronic communications can generally be discreetly observed, enabling the busybody to acquire their whole content without the sender or receiver being aware of the surveillance, is undervalued in traditional encryption and data theory. It is feasible to develop exchange diversions whose transmissions cannot be successfully read or replicated by a third party who is uninformed of the exact data utilised in the transmission's generation when sophisticated information is contained in fundamental quantum frameworks such as single photons. The busybody cannot add fractional information about such a transmission without disrupting it in a manner likely to be recognised by the channel's legitimate clients. The Figure 11.1 shows about the key distribution pattern of basic quantum [9, 10].

1.	↳	↕	⊃	↔	↕	↕	↔	↔	⊃	↳	↕	⊃	↳	↳	↕
2.	+	○	○	+	+	○	○	+	○	+	○	○	○	○	+
3.	↕		⊃		↕	↳	↳	↔		↕	⊃	⊃		↳	↕
4.	+	○		+	○	○	+		+	○	○		○	+
5.		√		√			√			√			√	√ √
6.		⊃		↕			↔			⊃			↳	↕
7.		1		1			0			1			0	1

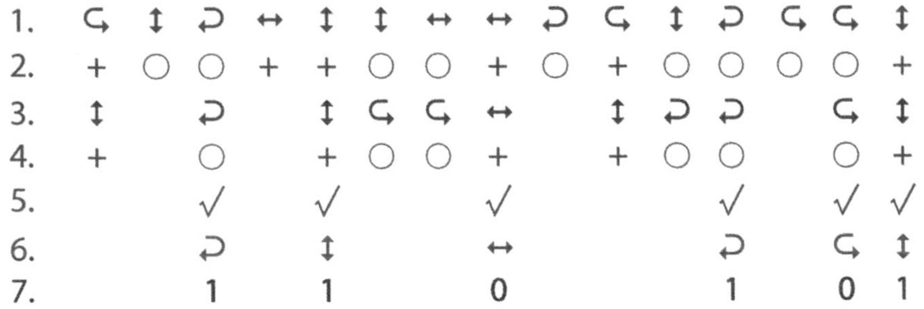

Figure 11.1 Key distribution pattern of basic quantum [9, 10].

To begin the fundamental quantum key distribution operations, Alice sends a sequence of charmed photons of four different types to Bob. Then, Weave chooses individually for each photon whether to measure the polarisation of the photon as rectilinear or circular (and independently of the decisions made by Alice, presumably, since these decisions are unknown to him at this time). After that, Bounce freely shares the kind of estimate he made (but not the outcome of the estimation), and Alice again freely shares with him whether he made the right estimation or not (i.e., rectilinear or roundabout). Alice and Bob agree to clear the board of any unfilled slots where Bob's estimation was wrong. In addition, they enable the removal of bits at positions where Bob's detectors failed to pick up the photon at all, which is surprisingly frequent with current optical frequency locators. A bit 0 represents horizontal and right-roundabout polarizations, whereas a bit 1 represents vertical and left-roundabout polarizations when decoding the remaining photons' polarizations. Assuming the quantum channel has not been tapped, the following parallel string should represent information that can only be known by Alice and Bob. Quantum transmission [11, 12] is the end result of all these measures (or at times the crude quantum transmission to underline that it was acquired right off the bat all the while). In the next step of the basic protocol, Alice and Bob make sure no one is listening in by comparing the polarizations of certain photons they believe should be in sync.

Alice transmits a random series of photons that are enraptured even (*- -,), vertical ($), right-round (), and left-round ();

Bounce quantifies the polarisation of photons in an uneven series of rectilinear (+) and circular () bases (0).

The implications of Bob's calculations (a few photons may not be gotten by any means).

Weave then tells Alice the premise he used to get each photon.

Alice enlightens him on the proper foundation;

Only the information from these carefully measured photons is kept, while the rest is discarded by Alice and Bob.

According to the coding scheme, this information is deciphered as a twofold arrangement. ~ = C~ = 0.

11.4   Cryptography

The goal of cryptography [13, 14] is to protect information from prying eyes by transforming it into an indecipherable code. The communication is encoded before being sent to the receiver so that it cannot be read by an eavesdropper. Plain text refers to the unencrypted communication, whereas Cipher text [15] refers to the encrypted version. Encryption and decryption techniques and cypher keys are used in cryptography.

$$\text{Decryption: } p = D(K, m)$$

$$\text{Encryption: } c = E(K, m)$$

where c represents cypher text, p plain text, K the key, m the message, E encryption, and d decryption.

Symmetric Encryption: Only if the sender and the recipient know each other's secret key can the message be decrypted. This technique is referred to as "Symmetric Encryption" [16, 17].

Asymmetric Encryption: There are two different keys (Public Key and Private Key). A communication encrypted with one key might be deciphered using a different key. The public key is available to everyone, but only he possesses the private one. When the sender encrypts the message using the receiver's public key and only the recipient's private key can decrypt it, the sender and the recipient are both assured of the communication's secrecy. In contrast, the recipient of an Authentication message may check the identity of the sender by decrypting the message using the recipient's public key. One Time Pad is a safe variant of the several symmetric-encryption-based Cryptosystems that have been developed. It's basically a supercharged version of the Vigenere Cipher [18]. The connection between Plain Text and Cipher Text does not provide any more security. For maximum security, the key phrase is never reused, the key length is proportional to the message length, and random letters are used in each and every transmission. One Time Pad refers to the method used to execute the operation, a time pad. There are, nevertheless, downsides, such as the troublesome distribution of keypads. Because the keypads must be similar in order for encrypted messages to work, losing one might create complications for future connections.

Position-Based Quantum Cryptography [19]: The goal of position-based quantum cryptography is to make the geographical position of the receiver the primary factor in determining how messages are sent. In the event that the sender specifies a particular place for the recipient to view the message, only that site will be accessible to the recipient.

Device Independent Quantum Cryptography [20]: If a quantum cryptosystem doesn't require a specific quantum device, it is said to be device independent.

Post-Quantum Cryptography: Post-quantum cryptography is an approach that uses traditional cryptographic tools in tandem with quantum computers to defeat cryptographic attacks. Numerous well-known methods may be broken by using different approaches, hence a new kind of cryptography called Post-Quantum Cryptography is required.

11.5   Quantum Cryptography with Faint Laser Pulses

In 1989, researchers first demonstrated the spread of a quantum key for exploratory purposes. (It was essentially disseminated in 1992, thanks to Bennett *et al.* 1992a.) [21]. Major advancements have been made since then. Several organisations have recently shown the feasibility of quantum key transmission in non-laboratory settings. Basic QC could be carried out in any two-level quantum framework. In the long run, photons will be required for every kind of operation. Why it's possible to control and steer their decoherent connection to Earth. Scientists can also benefit from optical media communications technologies that have emerged over the past two decades. It's quite improbable that we'll switch to using other kinds of transporters anytime soon. Evaluating several models while comparing various QC-arrangements is a time-consuming and complex task. What really counts is the transmission separation and the pace at which mystery bits may be addressed (the refined bit rate, Rdist) [22].

One would be able to understand right away that the gigahertz speeds that are now standard with conventional optical communication systems will not be possible with the innovation that is currently available or that is expected to be developed in the future (in their thorough paper distributed in 2000, Gilbert and Hamrick [23] talk about viable techniques to accomplish high piece rate QC). It follows that only the most sensitive information should be encrypted using a key transmitted through QC. Estimating the net rate may be challenging, despite the fact that the transmission separation and finding rate (the crude piece rate, Rraw) are known with absolute certainty. Despite the fact that, in theory, bit grouping mistakes are caused purely by manipulation by a hostile busybody, this is really a very rare occurrence in practise.

As a direct result of exploratory errors, there is a persistent gap between the keys of Alice and Bounce. It is possible to arrive at an accurate computation of the error rate, which will be referred to here as the quantum bit error rate, or QBER. Similarly, fixing mistakes is a rather simple process. First, the key rate, which is proportional to the QBER, will be lowered when errors are corrected. The actual issue comes in interpreting the data acquired by Eve, a quantity crucial for security development. Not only does it depend on the QBER, but it also depends on other aspects, such as the measurements of the photon number of the source or the technique in which the estimating assumption is determined.

11.6   Eavesdropping [22]

A. Problems and Objectives

Since Alice and Bob compromised their qubits and shared bases, they know both have filtered keys. Ideally, each of them would be the same. However, there are always going to be a few mistakes, so Alice and Bob will need to use certain tried-and-true data handling practises, such as error repair and security augmentation, on their information. To gain secret keys, the second set of rules must be followed, whereas untraceable keys may be obtained using the first. Eavesdropping's primary objective is to identify protocols that, given that Alice and Bob can only measure the QBER, either provide Alice and Bob with a secure key or terminate the protocol and notify the clients that the key transfer has failed. This is done so that the eavesdropper can report the failure of the key transfer to the clients. Due to the fact that this investigation is at the intersection of quantum material science and data speculation, it may be considered fairly delicate. As a whole, no; but, there are several listening-in problems, each of which is unique to the specific convention in question, the degree to which one accepts romanticising the situation, the presumed imaginative energy of Eve, and the supposed faithfulness of Alice and Bob's apparatus. Without resorting to numerical rigour or providing a thorough survey of the enormous and fast-increasing literature, we look at some of the issues and arrangements. Examining what is being said in an examination with the intent of listening for security flaws is the goal of several quantum cryptosystems [20]. When we say "extreme," we mean that no eavesdropping can happen, even if Eve employs the cutting-edge technology available today. They occur as hypotheses, with numerically specified assumptions that are manifestly stated. On the other hand, viable confirmations manage actual hardware and software.

As a result, there is a conflict between "extreme" and "useful" pieces of evidence. The first ones, without a doubt, stem from broad dynamic assumptions, whereas the latter ones zero in on specific applications of the broader ideas. The search for these confirmations should be prioritised. Despite the obvious security risks, they provide valuable learning opportunities about quantum information. In a perfect world, Eve would have access to state-of-the-art gadgets and would be constrained only by the principles of quantum physics and not by the limitations of technology. It's vital to keep in mind that Eve can't clone the qubits since doing so would break the quantum properties that define them. In contrast, Eve is at liberty to use whatever unitary communication strategy she sees fit, provided that it involves one or more qubits and a helper configuration of her choosing. In addition to this, after considering the connection, Eve may keep her helper structure undisturbed for a subjectively long time, especially if she is completely cut off from the natural world. Now that she has heard what Alice and Bob have to say publicly, she may execute the computation on her own, but she will once again be bound by the rules of quantum physics. Furthermore, it is assumed that Eve is responsible for any mistakes. The assumption that Alice's and Bob's equipment contributed to some of the mistakes they made bodes well for their future work. Eve may always get new, more advanced tools to replace them.

The next part provides a more in-depth discussion of the most notable distinctions between the aforementioned ideal game [21] (which, from Eve's perspective, is the perfect game!) and real-world frameworks. Then, we return to the idealised case and provide a variety of listening in tactics, from the simplest, where explicit equations may be recorded, to the most complex, where a unique security proof is provided. Finally, we talk about the dimensionality of true framework security and the possibility of listening-in attacks.

B. Idealized vs. Real Implementation

When it comes to technology, Alice and Bob use what's out there. This trite observation has far-reaching consequences. This is because, first, all of the genuine parts have been compromised, rendering the hypothesis's premise invalid and rendering the qubits unsorted and unrecognised. Additionally, there is always a limited chance that more than one photon will be produced by a genuine source. All photons have the same qubit [19]; however, this depends on the specifics of the encoding equipment. This allowed Eve to fundamentally measure the number of photons without affecting the qubit. In a perfect world, Alice would only be able to create single qubit-photons, with the probabilities of all valid qubits encoded in a single photon. On Bob's end of things, the issue is twofold: first, his indicators' efficacy is severely limited, and second, the boring checks (unrestricted totals not given by photons) are substantial. Quantum channel failures are analogous to the efficiency limitations. More uncertainty is introduced into the examination of the repetitive summaries, and the structure as a whole is not understood.

[4] recognises, although only tangentially, in his studies that all obscurantist tallies do in fact offer information to Eve. He also suggests that Bob should not ignore simultaneous firings of two detectors (frequently due to a real photon and a dull count), even if material science may randomly

choose an incentive. It is essential to bear in mind that the overall QBER [18] is subject to a distinct set of boring check duties depending on whether Bob's premise decision is carried out with a functioning or detached switch. To continue, it is often believed that Alice and Bob have exhaustively tested their equipment and that it performs as expected.

Though not strictly related to quantum cryptography, this is nonetheless a delicate issue as Eve may really be the original designer and builder of the apparatus in question. All business equipment, including more conventional cryptography frameworks, should undergo regular testing. Since the client is buying confidence and security from the cryptographic service, testing such a system is inherently unreliable. Bell imbalance was presented by [6] as a way to test whether or not the hardware follows quantum theory, although even this is controversial. One of the most subtle loopholes in the ongoing Bell discrepancy trial, the identification proviso, may be used to create a totally conventional software that simulates all quantum connections, which is both remarkable and certain, according to [5].

This highlights how closely QC issues relate to philosophical debates about quantum material science's underpinnings. Finally, it's reasonable to assume that Eve is no longer in any way connected to Alice and Bob. The game would be completely worthless if not for this one premise: of course Eve is not allowed to look over Alice's shoulder. This seemingly obvious assumption is, in fact, far from obvious. Imagine if Eve makes advantage of Alice's connection to the outside world through the quantum channel. An ideal world is one in which the channel links up with an isolator 48, which would then block Eve from using the yield port to spy on Alice's research lab. But because of the restricted transmission rate of every isolator, a filter is also necessary. In any event, the efficiency of filters can only be increased to a certain point. Because of this, we are aware that Alice and Bob are not now with Eve.

11.7   Conclusion

The discussion between theoretical and practical physicists in quantum cryptography is fascinating. Progress in quantum optics, optical fibre technology, and free-space optical communication allowed for the development of this system, which is based on a wonderful fusion of quantum physics and information theory principles. Its foundation of safety is built on rigorous principles from classical information theory. More secure than its conventional counterpart, quantum cryptography is nonetheless subject to implementation costs and other limitations due to its reliance on physical proximity. It is expected that technical development will go forward. Someday, a quantum repeater may be used to bypass the problem of physical distance and provide encrypted communication. The most important thing to remember while communicating is the need for confidentiality, which is of paramount importance in any industry. Quantum cryptography is vulnerable because it is based on classical encryption, which can be cracked by quantum computers. Since the techniques of post-quantum cryptography are impervious to quantum computer attacks, it is possible to employ them.

References

1. Aditya & Rao. (2005). Quantum cryptography. *Proceedings of Computer Society of India.*
2. Ardehali, M., Chau, H. F., & Lo, H.-K. (1998). *Efficient Quantum Key Distribution.* quant-ph/9803007.
3. Aspect, A., Dalibard, J., & Roger, G. (1982). Experimental Test of Bell's Inequalities Using Time-Varying Analyzers. *Physical Review Letters, 49*(25), 1804–1807. doi:10.1103/PhysRevLett.49.1804
4. Bechmann-Pasquinucci, H., & Gisin, N. (1999). Incoherent and Coherent Eavesdropping in the 6-state Protocol of Quantum Cryptography. *Physical Review A, 59*(6), 4238–4248. doi:10.1103/PhysRevA.59.4238
5. Bechmann-Pasquinucci, H., & Peres, A. (2000). Quantum cryptography with 3-state systems. *Physical Review Letters, 85*(15), 3313–3316. doi:10.1103/PhysRevLett.85.3313 PMID:11019329
6. Bechmann-Pasquinucci, H., & Tittel, W. (2000). Quantum cryptography using larger alphabets. *Physical Review A, 61*(6), 062308–1. doi:10.1103/PhysRevA.61.062308
7. Bell, J. S. (1964). On the problem of hidden variables in quantum mechanics. *Review of Modern Phys.,* 38, 447-452.
8. Bennett, C. H. (1992). Quantum cryptography using any two nonorthogonal states. *Physical Review Letters, 68,* 3121–3124.
9. Bennett, C. H., & Brassard, G. (1984). Quantum cryptography: public key distribution and coin tossing. *Int. Conf. Computers, Systems & Signal Processing,* 175–179. doi:10.1103/PhysRevLett.68.3121
10. Bennett, C. H., & Brassard, G. (1985). Quantum public key distribution system. *IBM Technical Disclosure Bulletin, 28,* 3153–3163.
11. Brassard, G. (2000). Security aspects of practical quantum cryptography. In *International Conference on the Theory and Applications of Cryptographic Techniques.* Springer. 10.1109/IQEC.2000.907967
12. Fedorov, A. K. (2018). Educational potential of quantum cryptography and its experimental modular realization. In *Proceedings of the*

Scientific-Practical Conference, Research and Development, 2016. Springer. 10.1007/978-3-319-62870-7_9

13. Hariharan, P., & Sanders, B. C. (1996). Quantum phenomena in optical interferometry. *Progress in Optics, 36,* 49–128. doi:10.1016/S0079-6638(08)70313-5

14. Hughes, R. J., Alde, D. M., Dyer, P., Luther, G. G., Morgan, G. L., & Schauer, M. (1995). Quantum cryptography. *Contemporary Physics, 36*(3), 149–163. doi:10.1080/00107519508222149

15. Huttner, B., Imoto, N., Gisin, N., & Mor, T. (1995, March). Quantum cryptography with coherent states. *Physical Review A, 51*(3), 1863–1869. doi:10.1103/PhysRevA.51.1863 PMID:9911795

16. Jaynes, E. T., & Cummings, F. W. (1963). Comparison of quantum and semiclassical radiation theories with application to the beam maser. *Proceedings of the IEEE, 51*(1), 89–109. doi:10.1109/PROC.1963.1664

17. Kim, J., Benson, O., Kan, H., & Yamamoto, Y. (1999). A single-photon turnstile device. *Nature, 397*(6719), 500–503. doi:10.1038/17295

18. Kulkarni & Harihar. (2012). Research directions in quantum cryptography and quantum key distribution. *International Journal of Scientific and Research Publications, 2,* 6.

19. Lütkenhaus, N. (1999). Security of quantum cryptography with realistic sources. *Acta Physica Slovaca, 49,* 549–556.

20. Lütkenhaus, N. (1999). *Security against individual attacks for realistic quantum key distribution.* Los Alamos Archives quant-ph/9910093.

21. Lütkenhaus, N. (2000). Dim coherent states as signal states in the BB84 protocol: Is it secure? In P. Kumar, G. Mauro D'Ariano, & O. Hirota (Eds.), *Quantum Communication, Computing, and Measurement 2* (pp. 387–392). Kluwer Academic/Plenum Publishers.

22. Marand, C., & Townsend, P. D. (1995, August). Quantum key distribution over distances as long as 30 km. *Optics Letters, 20*(15), 1695–1697. doi:10.1364/OL.20.001695 PMID:19862127

23. Mayers, D. (1996). Quantum key distribution and string oblivious transfer in noisy channels. In *Advances in Cryptology: Proceedings of Crypto'96, Lecture Notes in Computer Science* (Vol. 1109). Springer-Verlag.

12

Security Aspects of Quantum Machine Learning: Opportunities, Threats and Defenses

P. William[1]*, Vivek Parganiha[2] and D.B. Pardeshi[3]

[1]Department of Information Technology, Sanjivani College of Engineering, SPPU,
Pune, India
[2]Department of Computer Science Engineering, Bhilai Institute of Technology,
CSVTU, Bhilai, India
[3]Department of Electrical Engineering, Sanjivani College of Engineering, SPPU,
Pune, India

Abstract

Quantum computing has undergone a major spike in recent years. Quantum machine learning, often known as QML, is a fascinating subject of quantum computing that takes advantage of the high-dimensional Hilbert space to acquire richer representations from less input. This is done in order to effectively solve challenging learning tasks. There has not been a lot of research into QML's safety, despite the language's rising popularity. In this research, we analysed where QML could go in terms of hardware security in the future. Furthermore, we expose the vulnerabilities of QML and designing attack models, along with the best practises for fixing them.

Keywords: Quantum computing, hardware security, quantum neural network, attacks & defenses

12.1 Introduction

In terms of the possibilities it offers, quantum computing represents a fundamental paradigm change in the way that computers are conceived of and constructed. In spite of the fact that quantum computing is still in its

*Corresponding author: william160891@gmail.com

Romil Rawat, Rajesh Kumar Chakrawarti, Sanjaya Kumar Sarangi, Jaideep Patel, Vivek Bhardwaj, Anjali Rawat and Hitesh Rawat (eds.) Quantum Computing in Cybersecurity, (201–216) © 2023 Scrivener Publishing LLC

infancy, the scientific community is searching for quantum computers in the hope that they may provide a computing edge (also known as quantum supremacy) in fields such as the discovery of new materials and drugs [15, 16]. Through the application of quantum machine learning, it is possible that one day achieving quantum advantage with noisy quantum computers will be possible (QML). QML can be used to alter existing image classification systems. Several QML models, often called Quantum Neural Networks (QNN), based on Parameterized Quantum Circuits (PQC) have previously been created [26]. Due to the fact that it possesses a data encoding circuit, a PQC, and measurement operations, a typical QNN may be trained to do common Machine Learning (ML) tasks such as classification, regression, distribution creation, and many more. It is unknown whether QML and QNNs are secure against malicious actors or whether they are successful in patching existing security holes. This might come as a shock considering the extensive and illustrious history of quantum computing in the field of security. Because both system defenders and attackers are increasingly turning to ML techniques to protect and exploit hardware, we investigate how QML can contribute to the solution of hardware security issues. For the most part, this is due to the prevalence of threats along the hardware supply chain, such as piracy, Trojan horse insertion, and manipulation. In mission-critical systems, a minor inaccuracy in ML-based detection techniques can endanger hardware. Thus, it is important to look into QML, a much-enhanced ML model. Adversarial examples, which are constructed by making subtle changes to valid input data, can fool quantum classifiers (adversarial input manipulation). Printed Circuit Board (PCB) defect classification has become an urgent need in the PCB industry because PCB defects can have a major effect on system performance/security.

To that end, we explore the risks that QML models may face and the ways in which they might be protected. The following format will be used in the study: The fundamentals of quantum computing and QNN are covered in Section 12.2, which is followed by discussions of QML security applications in Section 12.3, several QML vulnerabilities and attack models in Section 12.4, and finally, a conclusion in Section 12.5.

12.2   Quantum Computing Basics

12.2.1   Qubits, Quantum Gates & Measurements

A qubit is one of the most fundamental components of a quantum computer, and microwave pulses are typically utilised in order to provide it with the necessary amount of power. This is a two-level system that is capable of storing information in the form of quantum states. A qubit is comparable to a conventional bit. A qubit, on the other hand, can exist in a state known as "superposition," which is a mixture of "0" and "1" at the same time. This is in contrast to a traditional bit, which can only exist in one of two states: either "0" or "1." Mathematically, the state of the qubit is denoted by the state vector $|\psi = a |0 + b |1$, where $|a| 2$ and $|b| 2$ respectively denote the probabilities of '0' and '1' (thus, $|a| 2 + |b| 2 = 1$). There are several different types of qubit technologies available today [20].

Quantum gates are operations that modify the state of the qubit, and it is these operations that make it possible for a qubit to be able to do calculations. One example of a quantum gate that may be utilised with either a single qubit or a set of qubits is referred to as the X (NOT) gate (e.g., 2-qubit CNOT gates). Pulses are what are employed to materialise these thoughts into the real world (e.g., laser pulse in Ion Trap qubits, RF pulse in Superconducting qubit, etc.) A single quantum circuit has the potential to contain many gates at once. The target basis is used to measure qubits in order to determine the ultimate state of a quantum programme. Many implementations of physical quantum computing, including IBM's Q System z, restrict measurements to a single computational basis. Another one of quantum computing's cornerstone ideas is the measurement/expectation value. The probability that the observed state belongs to the right eigenstate is factored into the mean eigenvalue. Operator expectation value () is defined mathematically as ||, where | is the vector of qubit states. The operator's minimum and maximum eigenvalues are the bounds within which it varies. The Pauli-Z () operator, for instance, has only two possible values for its eigenvalues: 1 and 1. For this reason, a qubit's Pauli-Z expectation value will swing between [-1, 1] depending on its current state.

12.2.2 Quantum Noise

In principle, quantum computers should be able to complete a range of tasks far more quickly than classical computers, but in practise, this has not been seen to be the case thus far. Coherence faults are caused by the fact that a qubit can only maintain its state for a certain amount of time. This is only one of the many different types of mistakes and noise that slow down quantum computers. Due to the fact that quantum gates are realised by microwave or laser pulses, gate failures occur whenever these pulses are unable to be created or applied effectively in actual hardware. Crosstalk errors happen when the execution of several gates on separate qubits simultaneously has an effect on their performance, while measurement mistakes occur when a qubit in the |0 state is measured as |1 due to faulty measurement devices. These errors happen at different frequency depending on the qubits and hardware that are being utilised, and they have the potential to degrade the efficacy of classifiers in QML models, which can lead to skewed findings and increased security issues.

12.2.3   Quantum Neural Networks (QNN)

The suitable input-output connection in QNN can be obtained by optimizing the parameters of a parametric quantum circuit, also known as a PQC. Quantum neural networks, or QNNs, typically consist of three components: (i) a parameterized quantum circuit, (ii) measurement operations, and (iii) a circuit for encoding classical data into quantum data. The scientific literature [26] makes reference to a vast number of different encoding techniques. [Note: The input classical characteristic of a continuous variable is often encoded as the rotation of a qubit along the appropriate axis in an angle encoding [1, 25, 26]. This can be thought of as a rotation of a bit. As a result, n qubits are required in order to encode n classical properties. Figure 12.1 demonstrates that a qubit that is in the superposition state will store the classical feature f1 as RZ(f1) when the state is read out (a Hadamard-H gate is employed to place the qubit in superposition). Utilizing a series of rotations is another method that can be utilised to accomplish the encoding of numerous continuous variables in a single qubit. During the pre-processing phase of data, features are frequently scaled between 0 and 2 (or - and), as a result of the fact that the states formed by a qubit rotation along any axis will repeat in intervals of 2 at regular intervals.

Parametric Quantum Circuit (PQC)
Parametric circuitry includes both entanglement operations and parameterized rotations of a single qubit. Multi-qubit activities involving all the qubits to generate entangled states are referred to as "entanglement

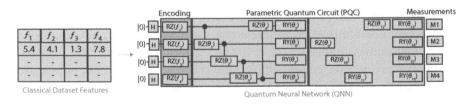

Figure 12.1 Hybrid quantum-classical architecture as an example.

operations" [17]. Solution space exploration is performed using the single-qubit parametric techniques discussed below. Parametric layers in QNN combine entanglement with single-qubit rotation operations. Over the past few years, a substantial amount of work has been put into determining which PQC design is superior for QNN. Expression power, entanglement capability, effective dimension, and a variety of other measures have all been utilised in the ranking of PQC techniques [1, 27]. The values of these descriptors are said to have a correlation with the trainability of quantum circuits, according to proponents of these descriptors. These kinds of explanations might prove helpful when determining which PQC architecture would be most suitable for a certain QML use case.

Cost Functions

Keeping track of the states of the qubits that make up the computational basis is necessary in order to determine the output state of a QNN circuit. When the network is being trained, a cost function that is derived from the data that has been collected is presented to it [1, 25]. [1] Using measurements of all of the qubits in the QNN model in Pauli-Z basis, it was found that Class 0 was associated with the likelihood of attaining even parity while Class 1 was connected with the probability of obtaining odd parity. Last but not least, the model is improved through the training process by employing cross-entropy loss. The authors of [2] employed the Pauli-Z expectation value of a single qubit in order to train a binary classifier with mean squared error (MSE) loss (-1 was linked with class 1, while +1 was associated with class 0). The authors of the paper [10] were able to increase the performance of the regular neural network by incorporating the QNN outputs into the regular neural network and training the regular neural network with the binary cross-entropy loss function.

Training

The Adam [12] and Adagrad [8] methods are just two examples of gradient-based optimization procedures that can be used to train QNNs. Other gradient-based optimization procedures may also be used. Before applying any of these solutions, you will first need to determine the gradients [6, 24] of the QNN outputs in relation to the circuit parameters. The parameter-shift rule is a tried and reliable method that can be utilised when calculating gradients [6, 24]. The classic finite difference approach is theoretically very similar to the parameter-shift rule. Like the traditional method, the parameter-shift rule uses two nearby evaluations of a target function to compute gradients with respect to a parameter. In contrast to the finite difference rule, the parameter-shift rule permits a huge gap to exist between any two data points. This gap can be of any size. Therefore, it is more robust to measurement errors and shot noise than the finite difference method [24]. QNNs can also be trained with gradient-free optimizers, such as Nelder-Mead, which is another method [14]. However, when there are many parameters in the network, a gradient-free optimizer may not operate as well.

12.3   Security Applications

This section delves into QML's potential security applications, focusing on its use in PCB defect categorization.

12.3.1   PCB Defect Classification

Overview
Printed circuit boards, sometimes known as PCBs, are an essential component of virtually all contemporary electronic gadgets. However, due to the limitations of the available technology, a 100% quality rate cannot be guaranteed during the PCB fabrication process. PCBs are susceptible to a variety of design faults, including spurs, missing holes, and short circuits. Because the production of PCBs is frequently contracted out to third-party contractors in order to cut costs, the boards in question are susceptible to being attacked. Introducing faults on purpose by unreliable vendors can lead to faulty printed circuit boards (PCBs), which can severely impair the operation of any systems that are dependent on the PCBs. In order to demonstrate how QML could be utilised for PCB fault classification, which is one of the potential applications in the field of computer security, we offer a hybrid quantum-classical model. Applying the strategy described in [3], we begin by utilising a convolutional autoencoder in order to lower the dimensionality of the problem, and then we proceed to train a QNN with the most important extracted features in order to solve our classification problem.

Convolutional Autoencoders (CAE)
An autoencoder, often known as an AE, is a specific kind of feedforward neural network. They utilise a network of encoders to transform the input into a code with fewer dimensions, and then they use a network of decoders to reconstruct the output in its original form. We employ a feedback signal that is the difference between the input and the reconstructed output so that the network can be trained (e.g., MSE loss). When it comes to

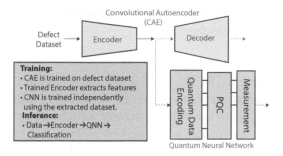

Figure 12.2 The network architecture of CAE + QNN.

extracting textural information from photos, the layout that CAE uses is more effective than the one that AE uses. In CAE, the encoding process begins with a convolutional layer or layers. The final steps of the decoder block are convolutional transposition and deconvolution layers. A fully linked AE sits at its centre, and its deepest layer is made up of a comparatively small number of neuronal cells. After the encoder block has been trained, it can be used on its own to derive a lower-dimensional representation of the input data. This can be done separately. Figure 12.2 presents a visual illustration of how CAE was utilised in this research project (for the purpose of classifying PCB defects). The final layer, ConvTranspose2d, makes use of Sigmoid activation, with d standing for the dimension of the latent space.

Classification Model

Both the CAE and the QNN can be regarded as independent networks operating within the hybrid network (Figure 12.2). In order for the CAE to learn a representation of the data in less dimensions, it is trained with the initial image dataset. Training encoder networks is necessary in order to extract features from image data. These extracted characteristics and image captions are input into a typical QNN during training, which is then used for final classification. This particular model is referred to as CAE+QNN. Implementing any one of a plethora of different encoding strategies, parametric circuit configurations, and evaluation strategies is possible when working with a QNN or quantum filter. Learnability of the QNN [27] will be impacted due to the fact that the plithon framework proposed by [3] provides for a large range of these choices. In spite of this, we employ the PQCircuit-16 from [11] and Z-based measurements of the qubits in the QNN, in addition to the technique presented in for encoding a single feature with a single qubit (Figure 12.1). The maximum number of parametric layers that can be taught is also limited to two. Inputs are provided by the

QNN to a layer that is fully linked [10]. The overall number of neural outputs is what differentiates the classes.

Dataset

We chose the augmented PCB defect dataset that was made public by Peking University's Open Lab on Human Robot Interaction in order to apply augmentation techniques to the original dataset, which allowed us to generate this dataset. These techniques were used by picking the dataset. There are six different kinds of faults that can be caused by using Photoshop and other Adobe products. Dataset defects include missing holes, mouse bites, open circuits, shorts, spurs, and spurious copper. There are a total of 10,668 photos with a resolution of 600 x 600 pixels in the collection. These images may or may not have numerous defects, but they all share the same class. We used fault extraction to create a larger dataset of 21,664 pictures, each measuring 32 by 32 pixels, for our PCB defect classification study (Figure 12.3). More details on the average number of pictures taken for each fault can be found in Table 12.1. First, we used our flawed data set to train our convolutional autoencoder (Train:Test = 70:30). As a result of training our QNN on the previously learnt model with latent dimension(d) = 4, we generated two additional, smaller classification datasets, one with 3 classes and the other with 6 (for classification).

Training Setup/Metrics

Our CAE was trained using 15,165 samples from the PCB defect dataset, which has a latent dimension of 4. The loss function that was employed was Mean Squared Error (MSE), and Adam was used as the optimizer.

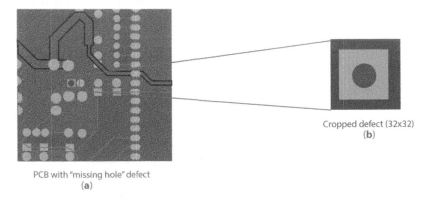

Cropped defect (32x32)
(b)

PCB with "missing hole" defect
(a)

Figure 12.3 (a) Original PCB image of size 600 × 600 (b) Cropped defect image of size 32 × 32 used for classification.

Table 12.1 Augmented PCB defect dataset.

Defects	# of images
Missing hole	3612
Mouse bite	3684
Open circuit	3548
Short	3508
Spur	3636
Spurious copper	3676

Some extremely impressive outcomes can be achieved by using a batch size of fifty, an epoch duration of twenty-five, and a learning rate of one hundredth of one percent. The feature set of this trained CAE was narrowed down (d = 4) through testing on sample data. Following the data reduction, the original dataset is split into two sets of 2,000 samples (3 and 6 class). At long last, these datasets will be put to use for the development and verification of QNN (70:30 split). The effectiveness of the QNN model may be evaluated based on the average accuracy it achieves across both the training dataset and the validation dataset[4]. Models' generalizability is shown by the validation accuracy, whereas trainability is shown by the validation accuracy. In the training of our model, we employ the gradient-based Adagrad optimizer [21]. As depicted in Figure 12.1, we encoded one classical feature per qubit using the angle encoding technique. Consequently, we employed four qubits for our four-feature dataset. We reduced the number of parametric layers in our 4-qubit model to two. We trained the QNN for ten iterations. [Sparse Categorical Cross Entropy is the loss function; Adagrad is the optimizer; the learning rate is 0.5; and the batch size is 32].

Results
Table 12.2 displays the performance after ten training periods. The architecture of the QNN is determined by the number of latent dimensions (d) chosen. Moreover, it degrades the efficiency of the network as a whole. Increasing the number of features used to train the QNN model correlates to a larger value of d, and larger values of d are typically associated with better training results. It is important to note that the goal of this research was not to prove that QML has better classification accuracy than our standard methods, but rather to show off its versatility.

Table 12.2 CAE+QNN Architecture performance after 10 Epochs.

Dataset	Train accuracy	Val. accuracy
Defect 3-Class	0.70	0.68
Defect 6-Class	0.46	0.42

12.3.2   Hardware Trojan & Recycled Chip Detection

Recent years have seen a significant rise in the danger posed by hardware Trojan attacks on integrated circuits (IC). Any alteration to an electronic circuit or design that is designed to cause damage is referred to as a "Hardware Trojan attack" in common parlance. Over the course of many years, a variety of conventional machine learning strategies, such as (a) Reverse Engineering [19], (b) Real-time detection [13], and (c) Gate-Level Netlists Detection [9], among others, have been investigated in an effort to identify this destructive hardware virus at a range of different levels of abstraction. When used integrated circuits are recycled, it raises more questions regarding the security and dependability of electronic devices and systems. The use of counterfeited or recycled integrated circuits (ICs) may pose a significant risk because an adversary may plant a Trojan, change the functionality, or even insert flaws during the recycling process. Any of these actions could lead to the disclosure of sensitive data or simply hinder the device's overall performance. The suggested hybrid quantum-classical framework, as well as any other QML model, is capable of being trained to detect Trojans and recycled portions if the appropriate datasets and data preparations are utilised.

12.3.3   Usage Model of QML in Hardware Security

In the realm of hardware security, QML can be implemented in one of two ways: (i) a full quantum approach, in which QML is used to screen all PCBs, recycling chips, and Trojan-infected designs; and (ii) a partial quantum approach. Both of these applications have their advantages and disadvantages. As quantum computers are still somewhat pricy, this solution will be quite costly. However, it will offer the highest possible assurances of security.

12.4   Quantum Machine Learning

Vulnerabilities, Attacks & Defenses
Utilizing concepts from quantum mechanics such as superposition, tunnelling, and entanglement, QML has demonstrated signs of promise,

suggesting that it may soon be able to outperform its classical forebears, even with noisy intermediate-scale quantum (NISQ) technology. This is possible because of QML's ability to exploit tunnelling. QML models are able to take use of the high-dimensional Hilbert space of huge quantum systems in order to gain a better understanding of complicated feature spaces that may exhibit statistical patterns during the classification process. However, just like very sophisticated traditional ML models, QML models include resources and are thus vulnerable to manipulation. To a lesser extent, studies have shown that as the number of dimensions in a classification space grows, the classifier's ability to withstand unexpected changes decreases. Since QML models make use of the high dimensionality of quantum systems, this has aroused the interest of QC/QML researchers. Here, we discuss the security holes, attack vectors, and performance and reliability concerns surrounding QML's IP.

12.4.1   Assets and Vulnerabilities

Researchers routinely deploy their QML models to cloud providers like Azure Quantum, Amazon Marketplace, and Google Cloud to assess the robustness/performance in noisy environments. This is the case with a number of companies, including IonQ, D-Wave, IBM, and Rigetti, among others. Hardware characteristics and designs, such as the amount of qubits, the coupling map, and other such aspects, could differ greatly from one cloud service provider to the next. It is possible that the cloud service provider's scheduler will use various pieces of hardware that share the same coupling map. Not only that, but the coupling maps of smaller hardware like ibmq london and ibmq santiago may be adapted to the coupling maps of larger hardware like ibmq rochester, which has a higher qubit count. Since users can define their own coupling map architectures, they can do so in the quantum cloud. The end user in the cloud has trouble telling the difference between coupling maps that seem to be quite similar. Therefore, third-party cloud providers may allocate inferior hardware to the task, resulting in poor performance and/or a slower convergence time for the quantum circuit.

Furthermore, the success of the software on real hardware depends on the compilation process. Compilers for quantum hardware are made available by a number of companies, including D-Ocean, Wave, IBM, Rigetti, and others. Other companies, such as Orquestra and tKet, have also developed their own software to complement these proprietary offerings. In the near future, several third-party compilers may emerge with enhanced performance as a result of enhanced optimization methods, etc., as interest in quantum computing continues to rise. Compilers from these less reputable organisations, however, may cause privacy and security issues in the future.

Embedding of sensitive private property in QML circuit: It is common practise to construct and test QNN circuits using actual quantum hardware, with each one utilising a different PQC or angle encoding scheme. They may be sent to third-party compilers in search of improved speed/efficiency, putting sensitive IP at risk because of the third-complete party's access to the circuit design.

12.4.2 Attack Models and Defenses Unreliable Hardware Allocator

As was indicated before, the performance of QML models may suffer significantly when unstable quantum computers provided by third parties are used in an effort to save money or to satisfy fraudulently advertised qubit or quantum hardware criteria. There is a possibility that intellectual property, such as the ansatz that was employed, the number of parameters, the number of layers in the QNN, and the type of input embedding, could be taken if a novel QML architecture or algorithm was sent to untrusted compilers. To contaminate training and provide false positives, an adversary may insert malicious components into the QNN. Protecting intellectual property from shady compilers while still reaping the performance benefits they offer is the goal of the method described in [23]. They propose an approach in which the designer sends in pieces of the quantum circuit to a single compiler at different times or to several compilers, and then puts the pieces back together to form the final circuit. Extensive analysis of 152 circuits demonstrated that the split compilation technique can either completely protect intellectual property (IP) or raise reconstruction complexity with only a modest amount of extra work (no more than 6%). Dummy SWAP gates are introduced into circuits in [28] to prevent software from running properly in the event of manipulation or counterfeiting by untrusted third-party compilers. Since the operation of a quantum chip is hidden from view, unlike a classical chip's, it is impossible for an adversary to reverse engineer a quantum circuit and predict the location of the SWAP gate. They developed a method for discovering the optimal place to install dummy SWAP gates to maximise Total Variation Distance (TVD) without having to resort to lengthy quantum circuit modelling. This strategy allowed them to determine the best spot to put the dummy SWAP gates. According to the results of the experiments, their proposed metric improved TVD by 6% compared to the norm and by 12% compared to the best TVD while reducing expenditures. As a consequence of this, certain cloud services may make use of hardware that is not suitable to the task at hand. It is not impossible to use two separate providers for the state preparation circuit and the PQC while compiling in QNNs. Additionally, the PQC may be subdivided even further for the purpose of random compilation. Using this approach will ensure that both the state preparation circuit and the PQC data are safeguarded. It is possible to add fake ZZ gates to the PQC layer in order to conceal the design even further (or used as a substitute for other defence strategies). Even if your opponent manages to steal your QNN, the trained and performing QNN will be different from the unobscured QNN. If the designer is careful, they can place fake ZZ gates in the solution space to produce empty platforms, rendering the QNN useless.

Fault Injection Attacks

It's possible that the gate error for a single operation and the gate error for two independent operations that are taking place at the same time will be different. Crosstalk is a term for this type of malfunction. According to studies presented in [18], the error rate of a parallel gate operation can be as much as three times that of a single gate operation. As a result, crosstalk may have an adverse effect on the accuracy of a QML model's predictions/classifications. In addition, it was recently proved [5] that an external attacker may implant faults into another user's software that is running on the same hardware by repeatedly driving qubits using CNOT gates. This was done in order to prove that an external attacker has the ability to do this. Since this is not the norm, the QNN's performance will suffer. Isolation/buffer qubits inserted between user programmes are one method that Saki *et al.* [5] investigated to reduce the risk of such attacks on quantum circuits and classifiers. This effectively means that another programme cannot operate on neighbouring qubits in hardware when a QNN circuit is already in use there. The surrounding qubits are utilised as buffers or isolation qubits to keep this from happening. At the expense of a few wasted qubits, their analysis indicates that buffer qubits can increase dependability by up to 1.87×fold.

12.5   Conclusion

Techniques for machine learning are prevalent in nearly every facet of contemporary life, making it a prominent field of study for both attack and defence systems. We study the security opportunities, vulnerabilities, threats, and responses of Quantum Machine Learning (QML) in light of the recent rise in interest in QML research. We discuss one potential security use of QML for identifying PCB flaws and suggest further application areas for protecting the semiconductor supply chain, including identifying hardware Trojans and spotting recycled chips. In addition to this, we discuss the QML's vulnerabilities, as well as the various attack types and mitigation strategies.

References

1. Amira Abbas, David Sutter, Christa Zoufal, Aurélien Lucchi, Alessio Figalli, and Stefan Woerner. 2021. The power of quantum neural networks. *Nature Computational Science* 1, 6 (2021), 403–409.
2. Mahabubul Alam, Abdullah Ash-Saki, and Swaroop Ghosh. 2019. Addressing temporal variations in qubit quality metrics for parameterized quantum circuits. In 2019 *IEEE/ACM International Symposium on Low Power Electronics and Design (ISLPED)*. IEEE, 1–6.
3. Mahabubul Alam, Satwik Kundu, Rasit Onur Topaloglu, and Swaroop Ghosh. 2021. Quantum-Classical Hybrid Machine Learning for Image Classification (ICCAD Special Session Paper). In *2021 IEEE/ACM International Conference on Computer Aided Design (ICCAD)*. 1–7. https://doi.org/10.1109/ICCAD51958.2021.9643516
4. Martin Anthony and Peter L Bartlett. 2009. *Neural network learning: Theoretical foundations*. Cambridge University Press.
5. Abdullah Ash-Saki, Mahabubul Alam, and Swaroop Ghosh. 2020. Analysis of Crosstalk in NISQ Devices and Security Implications in Multi-Programming Regime. In *Proceedings of the ACM/IEEE International Symposium on Low Power Electronics and Design (ISLPED '20)*. Association for Computing Machinery, 25–30. https://doi.org/10.1145/3370748.3406570
6. Leonardo Banchi and Gavin E Crooks. 2021. Measuring analytic gradients of general quantum evolution with the stochastic parameter shift rule. *Quantum* 5 (2021), 386.
7. Runwei Ding, Linhui Dai, Guangpeng Li, and Hong Liu. 2019. TDD-Net: A Tiny Defect Detection Network for Printed Circuit Boards. *CAAI Transactions on Intelligence Technology* 4 (04 2019). https://doi.org/10.1049/trit.2019.0019
8. John Duchi, Elad Hazan, and Yoram Singer. 2011. Adaptive subgradient methods for online learning and stochastic optimization. *Journal of Machine Learning Research* 12, 7 (2011).
9. Kento Hasegawa, Masao Yanagisawa, and Nozomu Togawa. [n.d.]. A hardware- Trojan classification method utilizing boundary net structures. In *2018 IEEE International Conference on Consumer Electronics,* ICCE 2018. Institute

of Electrical and Electronics Engineers Inc., 1–4. https://doi.org/10.1109/ICCE.2018.8326247

10. Hsin-Yuan Huang, Michael Broughton, Masoud Mohseni, Ryan Babbush, Sergio Boixo, Hartmut Neven, and Jarrod R McClean. 2021. Power of data in quantum machine learning. *Nature Communications* 12, 1 (2021), 1–9.

11. Thomas Hubregtsen, Josef Pichlmeier, Patrick Stecher, and Koen Bertels. 2021. Evaluation of parameterized quantum circuits: on the relation between classification accuracy, expressibility, and entangling capability. *Quantum Machine Intelligence* 3, 1 (2021), 1–19.

12. Diederik P Kingma and Jimmy Ba. 2014. Adam: A method for stochastic optimization. arXiv preprint arXiv:1412.6980 (2014).

13. Amey Kulkarni, Youngok Pino, Matthew French, and Tinoosh Mohsenin. 2016. Real-Time Anomaly Detection Framework for Many-Core Router through Machine-Learning Techniques. *J. Emerg. Technol. Comput. Syst.* 13, 1, Article 10 (jun 2016), 22 p. https://doi.org/10.1145/2827699

14. Wim Lavrijsen, Ana Tudor, Juliane Müller, Costin Iancu, and Wibe de Jong. 2020. Classical optimizers for noisy intermediate-scale quantum devices. *In 2020 IEEE International Conference on Quantum Computing and Engineering (QCE).* 267–277.

15. Junde Li, Mahabubul Alam, M Sha Congzhou, Jian Wang, Nikolay V Dokholyan, and Swaroop Ghosh. 2021. Drug discovery approaches using quantum machine learning. In 2021 *58th ACM/IEEE Design Automation Conference (DAC).* IEEE, 1356–1359.

16. Junde Li, Rasit O Topaloglu, and Swaroop Ghosh. 2021. Quantum generative models for small molecule drug discovery. *IEEE Transactions on Quantum Engineering* 2 (2021), 1–8.

17. Seth Lloyd, Maria Schuld, Aroosa Ijaz, Josh Izaac, and Nathan Killoran. 2020. Quantum embeddings for machine learning. arXiv preprint arXiv:2001.03622 (2020).

18. Prakash Murali, David C. McKay, Margaret Martonosi, and Ali Javadi-Abhari. 2020. Software Mitigation of Crosstalk on Noisy Intermediate-Scale Quantum Computers. In *Proceedings of the 25th International Conference on Architectural Support for Programming Languages and Operating Systems.* ACM, 1001–1016.

19. Abdurrahman Nasr and Mohamed Zaki. 2017. An Efficient Reverse Engineering Hardware Trojan Detector Using Histogram of Oriented Gradients. *Journal of Electronic Testing* 33 (02 2017). https://doi.org/10.1007/s10836-016-5631-z

20. Michael A Nielsen and Isaac Chuang. 2002. Quantum computation and quantum information. American Association of Physics Teachers.

21. Adam Paszke, Sam Gross, Francisco Massa, Adam Lerer, James Bradbury, Gregory Chanan, Trevor Killeen, Zeming Lin, Gimelshein, *et al.* 2019. Pytorch: An imperative style, high-performance deep learning library. arXiv (2019).

22. Koustubh Phalak, Abdullah Ash Saki, Mahabubul Alam, Rasit Onur Topaloglu, and Swaroop Ghosh. 2021. Quantum PUF for Security and Trust in Quantum Computing. *IEEE Journal on Emerging and Selected Topics in Circuits and Systems* 11, 2 (2021), 333–342. https://doi.org/10.1109/JETCAS.2021.3077024

23. Abdullah Ash Saki, Aakarshitha Suresh, Rasit Onur Topaloglu, and Swaroop Ghosh. 2021. Split Compilation for Security of Quantum Circuits. In *2021 IEEE/ACM International Conference on Computer Aided Design (ICCAD).* 1–7. https://doi.org/10.1109/ICCAD51958.2021.9643478

24. Maria Schuld, Ville Bergholm, Christian Gogolin, Josh Izaac, and Nathan Killoran. 2019. Evaluating analytic gradients on quantum hardware. *Physical Review A* 99, 3 (2019), 032331.

25. Maria Schuld, Alex Bocharov, Krysta M Svore, and Nathan Wiebe. 2020. Circuitcentric quantum classifiers. *Physical Review A* (2020).

26. Maria Schuld, Ryan Sweke, and Johannes Jakob Meyer. 2021. Effect of data encoding on the expressive power of variational quantum-machine-learning models. *Physical Review A* 103, 3 (2021), 032430.

27. Sukin Sim, Peter D Johnson, and Alán Aspuru-Guzik. 2019. Expressibility and entangling capability of parameterized quantum circuits for hybrid quantum-classical algorithms. *Advanced Quantum Technologies* (2019).

28. Aakarshitha Suresh, Abdullah Ash Saki, Mahabubul Alam, Rasit, Topalaglu, and Dr. Swaroop Ghosh. 2021. *A Quantum Circuit Obfuscation Methodology for Security and Privacy.* https://doi.org/10.48550/ARXIV.2104.05943

13

Cyber Forensics and Cybersecurity: Threat Analysis, Research Statement and Opportunities for the Future

Nirav Bhatt[1] and Amit Kumar Tyagi[2]*

[1]*School of Computer Science and Engineering, Vellore Institute of Technology, Chennai, Tamil Nadu, India*
[2]*Department of Fashion Technology, National Institute of Fashion Technology, New Delhi, Delhi, India*

Abstract

Cybersecurity, a field within Computer Science, is one of the fields most invested in by countries around the globe. Countries are expected to spend more than 1 trillion dollars on cybersecurity by the end of 2021. Recently, it was shown that around 45 percent of cyberattacks are successful. Computer forensics is one of the most sought-after jobs in the 21st century. Cyber forensics is the process of accumulation and storing of data from a device that can be presented in front of a judge in a court. There are multiple forms of Digital Forensics. Some of them include Disk and network forensics and wireless forensics, among numerous others. The aim of this study is to find out what the future holds for us in the field of cybersecurity and cyber forensics around the world and ways to improve the existing technology, as well as creating new technology to catch the notorious hackers around the world. The methodology would mainly involve educating people about the threats they face in the online world as well as assessing the situation right now and predicting what the future in these two vast fields holds. This study if implemented would surely make the online world a much more secure place by preserving one's personal data as well as encouraging humankind to reach its maximum potential in these two respective fields.

Keywords: Cybersecurity, cyber forensics, phishing, MITM

**Corresponding author*: amitkrtyagi025@gmail.com

Romil Rawat, Rajesh Kumar Chakrawarti, Sanjaya Kumar Sarangi, Jaideep Patel, Vivek Bhardwaj, Anjali Rawat and Hitesh Rawat (eds.) Quantum Computing in Cybersecurity, (217–232) © 2023 Scrivener Publishing LLC

13.1   Introduction

Cybersecurity, a field which has been heavily invested in all around the world by leading countries is basically the process of protecting information, whether personal or organizational, from theft, damage to software or hardware etc. Cybercrime [1, 2] has become a familiar topic to the public in recent years. It is clear now that as technology has advanced in recent years, so have cyberattacks. Hackers have been finding new ways to penetrate systems whether it is through virus, Malware or Phishing. There are many forms of cyberattacks such as Malware, Phishing, and man-in-the-middle (MITM) [3, 4] attack, etc.

- Malware: It's a very popular software used around the world which is capable of carrying different forms of malicious tasks including gaining unauthorized access to a particular network and spying on the user for obtaining their login information. Ransomware, which comes under this category of malware, is frequently used and is responsible for encrypting a user's files and asking for a payment from the user in order to restore access.
- Phishing: This attack is most frequently used, and it is very easy to carry out. In this, usually the user gets an email pretending to be from a legitimate organization such as a government office or even a telephone company asking for personal information from the user. It can be done through a call, messaging services or even via email.
- Man-in-the-middle-attack (MITM): This attack usually involves a hacker spying on the conversation between two people or two parties in order to steal personal information or credentials. The MITM attacks are less common nowadays as email are end-to-end encrypted making it impossible for a third-party intervention.
- Cyber Forensics, also known as digital forensics or computer forensics, is the branch of digital forensics that deals with the accumulation of evidence in a device such as a computer or a mobile phone which then can be transformed into physical proof which can be submitted before a judge. The need for cyber forensics keeps growing by the day. It is an evolutionary force in today's ever-changing world. It provides prosecutors with evidence of wrongdoing which includes simple

information such as search history, email logs or any other digital footprint left behind by the criminal. Its main application is fighting various crimes which include hacking and Denial-of-Services (DOS) [5].

Cyber forensics follows a very systematic approach. The processes involved in it are:

- Take a digital copy of the supposed computer system under investigation: This process includes taking a replica of the data in the device in order to avoid a mix up of data or in the worst case, a loss of data.
- Verifying and authentication of the digital copy: Investigators verify each and every piece of data gathered from the original device to ensure that the data in the two devices are exactly the same and none of the data is lost.
- Ensuring the data copied is valid forensically: It is to be kept in mind that the format of the data in both devices should be kept the same in order to avoid differences in the operating systems of the investigators and that of the original device.
- Recovering deleted files if any: Hackers may try to erase their digital footprint, making it tough for prosecutors to prosecute them. It also erases their involvement in the crime. So, the prosecutors must retrieve the deleted data, and very highly advanced tools are used for this purpose.
- Searching for specific data using keywords: The use of keywords comes in handy when the prosecutor is presenting the case in front of the judge. It enables the prosecutor to have information at a speedy pace during the case.
- Creating a technical report: This is the final step of the investigation in which a clear technical report is prepared to be presented in front of the judge. It clearly defines who is the criminal and his or her wrongdoings.

13.2 Background

In the starting phases of computer technology growth, these two fields were not heavily invested in, but in the past two decades they have both grown exponentially and countries all over the world have invested billions of dollars in them. Surely, this growth can be credited to the growth of technology singularly. It is very evident that as technology keeps growing, hackers will find new ways to penetrate systems and steal personal information, but the new ways of technology also help in catching the hackers around the world. So, technology plays the game for both sides. There have been cyberattacks on major firms such as Epsilon, which cost the firm not only $4 billion, but also affected thousands of clients, including JP Morgan and Chase. A cyberattack on Hannaford Bros cost the company $252 million as the hackers attacked 300 of their stores. Cyberattacks have disastrous consequences for a firm not only in financial terms but also in terms of public trust. We have reached a situation where big firms such as Apple and Google are paying millions of dollars to cybersecurity experts to keep the general public's data safe and prevent it from being stolen. While we are seeing major developments in the cybersecurity field, the cyber forensics field has also shot up in recent years. Although the tools we have in this field to catch the hackers are not up to the mark, they surely have improved quite significantly over the last two decades. Even though we may have good tools to catch the hackers with, we will have to keep looking for ways to improve the existing tools and look for new ones. As technology increases, hackers will surely find new ways to hack, so to prevent them, the tools we create will have to keep pace with the ever-changing technology.

13.3   Scope of this Work

The aim of the paper is to basically find out what the future holds in cybersecurity and cyber forensics. Clearly the last few years have seen a trend in the field of cybersecurity; the number of people who are taking courses in this particular field has grown enormously over the past two decades. It is said that the number of vacant jobs in cybersecurity will grow to almost 3.5 million by the end of this year. The job demand in this field is bound to increase as long as technology exists. If technology can be used to penetrate other people's lives and steal their valuable information, technology can also be used for protecting people's privacy, and thereby also preventing other information from being stolen. Here's what the future looks like for Cybersecurity:

   a) The exponential increase in ransomware threats [6]: Ransomware is a type of malware that has become a significant threat to the businesses and individuals all around the world for the past two years. There's a direct financial benefit to this type of attacks, and attackers also target the backup and recovery tools to prevent data from being restored after the attack. Crypto ransomware is the most common ransomware. It has the extraordinary ability to lock a file, or in other words, encrypt a file and also demands from the victim some kind of ransom in exchange for the process of decrypting the files. This type of ransomware can spread through any medium such as websites and downloads.

b) USBs are more of a threat: The USBs [7, 8] are everywhere. People store valuable information in them, and the attackers use this to attack industrial targets. It was found out recently that the USB threats to industrials has more than doubled in recent years to 59 percent. It is also interesting to note that cybersecurity experts have predicted that there will be a cyberattack every 11 seconds by the end of 2021, four times the rate in 2016 and twice the rate in 2019. The rapidly growing cyberattacks around the world come at a huge cost for businesses worldwide and forces them to take measures to reduce or terminate such attacks completely.

Cybercrime forensics at the highest levels of the government might get a bit more complicated in the future. Governments will need to turn more to their national security organizations to hunt down the vicious attackers. In addition, they will have to invent new tools to catch them given the ever-increasing technology. The challenges faced by the investigative agencies have been increasing over the years, as evidence collection is very difficult and must be clear and presentable to the court. Nowadays, computers are equipped with capacity hard disks, hence making it tougher to make them again usable from retrieving data. If seen closely, cyberattacks, cybersecurity and cyber forensics are all interrelated. While cybersecurity focuses on preventing cyberattacks, cyber forensics is all about catching the attackers after a crime has been committed. So, summarizing the above point, as long as new technology is being introduced into our everyday lives, there will be cyberattacks, and hence there will be the field of cyber forensics helping prosecutors to catch the attackers. As we look into the future, the biggest problem faced by cyber forensics will be the explosion of complexity [1, 2].

Evidence being found in a single computer or host is very rare, but in our ever-growing technological world, the evidence is distributed among the many various networks. Hence, it is said that an important challenge for modern digital forensic [9, 10] will be to execute investigations legally without violating laws in borderless scenarios. In recent years, cyber forensics has been diminishing. Without a clear path on how to proceed when it comes to forensic research, the field will not make much progress, and when new tools are created by different forms of technology, the field of cyber forensics will fall short in trying to combat them. This will make it harder to catch the attackers, and cyber forensics will become unreliable. There are two main problems in the cyber forensics field that catch the eye:

- The tools we have today are mainly for helping prosecutors find specific pieces of evidence, not to assist in the investigation.
- The tools which we use in today's world were created with the main objective of solving crimes committed against humans, given that the evidence lies on an electronic gadget, from which later on evidence can be retrieved. They were not created to solve typical crimes committed with the help of a computer or against computers.

The tools we have today are indeed very poorly suited to finding information which is out of the blue or out of the ordinary. Our tools can surely help in cases where the data is in terabytes, but it is of no use when it comes to organizing them to form a concise report. Hence, it is difficult to find out about all the events or actions of a perpetrator, and it is done manually.

13.4   Methodology and Analysis of Simulation Results

When we have an ever-growing technology, it is obvious that questions do arise in people's minds regarding their own safety in the virtual world. How can they scroll the web without making sure that no one is spying on them? How can they make sure their passwords are safe? How can one know if he or she is safe? The answers to the above questions have one particular thing in common: cybersecurity. Although cybersecurity might not be the perfect solution to all the problems around the world, it surely helps tackle the majority of the problems. Educating people about the threats they face in the online world is a very difficult and time-consuming task. People should have at least basic knowledge about the online world. Here are a few ways people can keep themselves safe from vicious attackers [3, 4]:

a) Don't access personal or important data with public Wi-Fi [11, 12]: One of the main reasons people succumb to hacking is because of the use of public Wi-Fi (airports, railway stations, hotels etc.), and when one is using the public Wi-Fi to access personal or important data, the passwords are bound to be stolen. It is always advisable to carry out these types of operations in a secure network connection.

b) Turn off anything you don't need: Hackers nowadays have tools that can help find your location, and it involves the features of your phone such as Wi-Fi, GPS, etc. Hence, instead of keeping your Wi-Fi and GPS on all the time, it is best to switch it off, making it impossible for hackers to know your whereabouts.

c) Choose your apps and websites wisely: Download apps only from trustworthy sources that have a good reputation. Downloading apps from unknown sources or streaming movies or shows online always possesses a threat to you as well as your personal information.

f) Use a password, lock code or encryption [13]: It has been found out that 81 percent of breaches are caused by weak passwords. So, the question arises, what is a strong password? The minimum length of your password should be 12 characters. Your password should contain both uppercase and lowercase letters, as well as numbers and special characters. Make sure you don't use the auto fill password option when making a new password. Some examples of the most common passwords are:

- 123456
- 123456789
- qwerty
- 1111
- abc123
- and so on

Hackers have a lot of ways in which they can steal your passwords [5, 6 and 7]. The most common ways are:

1. Network Analyzers [14, 15]: These are special kinds of tools which facilitate not only the monitoring of the packets of data but also the interception of the packets which are sent

through a network. These tools are very well capable of lifting the personal information which is inside it. These types of attacks are usually continued by a Brute Force Attack in which the hacker uses every combination of passwords in the book until it fits yours, and once the password fits yours, it is just a matter of time until the hacker gains access to all your personal information

2. Dictionary Attack: It is very similar to a brute force attack. If your password is a regular word, it is very likely you will succumb to this type of attack. One of the easiest ways to escape this attack is to use multiple phrases as a password like LaundryZebraTowelBlue. This will help you outsmart a dictionary attack.

3. Phishing: As mentioned earlier, here the attacker sends an email which contains a link usually and prompts you to click on it. The email might state that your account will expire in a very short amount of time unless you take some immediate action, such as changing your password by clicking on the link, or entering some other personal information. These types of emails can seem to come even from the most trusted organizations such as Microsoft and Google.

Now we have discussed the various ways in which a password can be guessed, we can turn to a few methods people can use to make sure their passwords are safe and well protected. Some methods below will explain how to create strong passwords [8, 9]:

- The revised paraphrase method: In this the password is basically a multiple word phrase with its twists and turns. One can use proper nouns, public figures and even words in another language. A hacker might be able to guess bell as a password, but he or she will find it difficult to guess bellmerciholasayanora. The user can use capital letters as well.
- The sentence method: Here the basic idea is to take any random sentence and take either the first two letters or the first letter of every word and use the password. The password for the sentence, "I love London but I don't want to leave the United States of America" can be IlLbIdwtltUSoA.

Figure 13.1 shows the disastrous effect that cyberattacks have had on businesses in the past seven years. We can see that as the years have

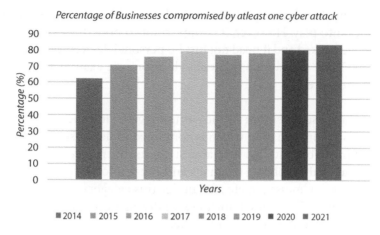

Figure 13.1 Percentage of businesses compromised by at least one cyberattack.

passed, the percentage of businesses compromised by cyberattacks has also increased, with a few ups and downs.

The below graph shows the organizations by country that have been hit by at least one successful attack in 2020 [16]. As is clearly evident from Figure 13.2, India as a country is not in immediate danger of cyberattacks, but this does not mean we can take the topic very lightly. Someday we are bound to get attacked by masterminds and it is always better to be prepared.

Now we come to the next field, cyber forensics. In case one doesn't know about the precautions we have to take in order to keep us safe in the virtual

Figure 13.2 Percentage of organization hit by at least one successful ransomware in 2020 by country.

world and his/her device has been hacked, then this is where cyber forensics comes into play. However, it is important to note that even organizations can be hacked and it need not just be personal devices for prosecutors to step in. There are various types of cyber forensic examinations as well. Some of them are:

- Database Forensics: As the name suggests, it is the examination of information which is contained in databases.
- Email Forensics: As the name suggests, the recovery, storing and analysis of data of emails and other information such as contacts, messages, etc., fall under this category.
- Memory Forensics: It includes analyzing information stored in a computer's RAM and cache.
- Mobile Forensics: It is basically the analysis of information in mobile phones which includes contacts, emails, incoming and outgoing calls, etc.

Cyber forensics has proved to be a very useful tool in nabbing thieves and criminals across the world. It's been used to catch notorious criminals around the world since the 1980s. However, even though digital forensics has played a major role in catching criminals and providing justice one way or another, digital forensics is facing a crisis. Some of the major problems faced by the field are:

a) The digital forensics field is restricted by the legal challenges presented in the court.
b) Pervasive encryption which is present in the latest systems these days prevents the processing of data even though the data can be recovered.

In the modern world, forensics examiners are finding it very tough to obtain the data in a very well-organized manner. Evidence, which also includes exculpatory evidence, may be missed very often. There are approximately 40,000,000 lawsuits filed every year in digital forensics–related cases. Juror expectations for forensic hurdles also create a huge problem for the prosecutors. A survey recently found that:

a) Almost half of the jurors had expectation of systematic evidence to be present in all the cases taken by them.
b) Almost one-fourth of the jurors had expectation of DNA evidence in all the cases taken up by them.

The first and the foremost step which has to be performed by all the examiners is to take out all the data from the respective devices very carefully as this can be presented as evidence in a court of law. There have been talks going on that the device manufacturers work with the respective agencies to help in the extraction of the data; the only drawback is that this process is very time consuming. The same issues regarding data extraction are faced in gaming consoles, e-book and telecommunications equipment. The vast size of storage devices also presents investigators with an uphill task. It leads to an increasing number of court hours and more investment of money when it comes to conducting an investigation. A person can get a 2 TB hard drive for $120, but it takes more than 7 hours to analyze it. Investigators face issues when the hackers save data on the cloud or if they are encrypted. Finding all the data on the cloud can be very tough as it can be stored anywhere, and even if found, the process can be very time consuming. We have discussed the importance of cyber forensics as a field as well as the problems related to it. Now the question arises, what can we do to improve the field of cyber forensics? [10, 11 and 12]. Here a few ways:

a) Identity Management: Cyber forensics is all about connecting the work of a mastermind to the mastermind, and hence we need approaches for modeling individuals such that it is principal as well as computable. Such an abstraction will not only include the most simple and common data sets such as name, contact number, address, etc., but also extend to representing the person's capabilities and social network. Work in this field will help to improve internet searches and identity resolution and ultimately the creation of a system that helps in identifying the possible suspects and accounts, etc.

b) Visual Analytics: The field is in desperate need of next-generation automated analyses methods, which will present data in a more systematic manner and which also will be easy for the prosecutor to understand.

c) Collaboration: Since the forensic analyses involves a team effort, so the tools should also support collaboration. Different types of collaboration modes should be introduced to the technological world so that users can join forces and make advances in the cyber forensics field.

d) Data visualization and advanced user interface: The systems which are used for forensic analysis use the standard WIMP tool. These devices are very poor when it comes to presenting mammoth amounts of data in a well-organized manner. New ways must be developed which can be useful for visualizing and presenting forensic evidence.

For cybersecurity and its related opportunities in the near future, readers may refer to [5–16].

13.5   Quantum-Based Cybersecurity and Forensics

13.5.1   Quantum-Based Cybersecurity

Cryptic encryption will be among the areas where quantum-based computing will exert the greatest consequences on cybersecurity. Encryption with public keys is nowadays used to safeguard practically all critical correspondence and data transferred over the network or to the cloud. It is presently almost certainly the most widely utilized method of online encryption. Every current search engine includes the fundamental public key exchange protocol to safeguard communication over the open internet. Most businesses also employ public key encryption to protect their internal data, communications, and access privileges to linked devices. To ensure comprehensive personal and communal cybersecurity, good cryptographic techniques are essential. It serves as the basis for secure data transfer and retention as well as the establishment of reliable links across devices and individuals.

Quantum-based computers on a massive level will considerably increase computational capability, opening up new possibilities for enhancing cybersecurity. Quantum-period cybersecurity will be able to identify and block cyberattacks from that era before they cause damage. But it might end up being a double-edged sword since quantum-based computing might also open up new vulnerabilities, such as the capacity to swiftly solve the challenging mathematical problems that serve as the foundation for some types of encryptions. Organizations and other groups can start preparing now, even though post-quantum-based cryptography standards are still being developed.

As asymmetric encryption methods, which are the foundation of the present data-based security systems, are predicted to ultimately be factorable by quantum computers, it is imperative that corporations review their cryptography strategies.

The exploitation of huge prime numbers is the foundation of conventional encryption. Modern computers have a hard time deciphering these figures. Nevertheless, a future era of quantum-resistant cryptographic techniques is required to prevent potentially devastating security breaches throughout the commercial sector because quantum computing would be capable of processing such complicated data considerably more quickly.

There seem to be currently hardly any quantum-based computers capable of handling the enormous amount of quantum bits available to execute out the necessary factorization to breach present safeguards. In the next 10-15 years, however, this is probably going to alter, which would pose more dangers for organizations, particularly the financial sector. In order to solve these anticipated problems, academicians, decision-makers, and cybersecurity specialists are focusing on creating post-quantum cryptography.

13.5.2   Quantum-Based Forensics

The computational benefits of quantum-based computing are enormous. The use of the logical superposition technique guides the current computer environment more and more towards the quantum bits cosmos of computing. As traditional problem-solving techniques are replaced, many technological innovations will become an actuality. Innovations for digital forensics and cybersecurity are significantly impacted by the development advancement of more sophisticated computing. Cybercrimes might significantly rise, and harmful programming would gain the power to cause harm quickly. In order to tackle problems like the tracking and tracing of malicious code automation, the sources of malicious code generation, source code validation, issues with intellectual property theft, with copyright violations, and the procurement of forensic evidence with both quality and volume on the wings of quantum forensics, the quantum computing in forensics methodological approach must advance.

Researchers have hardly given quantum forensics any thought up to this point. It is easy to use the traditional divide into live forensics and post-mortem forensics in order to comprehend the possibilities for digital forensic investigation and analysis of quantum computers. It should be obvious from what has already been discussed that a quantum computer cannot do live system forensics since any observation or measurement made on an evolving superposed state will lead it to collapse to a single arbitrarily chosen component. Currently, the states of the system and the observer or measuring device in their environment correlate, causing beneficial state information to seep into the composite super-system and become unrecoverable.

Post-mortem forensics seems like a slightly promising option initially. A solitary classical output might well be left just after execution of a quantum-based procedure and the restoration of an output state produced by regulated decoherence for traditional digital forensic recovery and analysis. Obviously, this evidence might be eliminated using standard anti-forensics methods. Nevertheless, a chronology for the advancement of quantum-based computation cannot be reconstructed given that it is impossible to observe the intermediate states of a quantum-based computer after the fact. This severely constrains the number and quality of the evidence traces which may eventually be retrieved.

13.6   Conclusion and Future Works

This paper has mainly focused on cybersecurity and cyber forensics. It is important to observe the way technology has advanced in the previous two decades. When we are able to catch the attackers and masterminds behind cyberattacks, courtesy of the new and developing technology, we should not forget that the same technology can be accessed by the attackers and masterminds. So, we have to keep working on finding new ways to avoid cyberattacks. While other papers mainly focused on either the advantages and disadvantages of cyber forensics and cybersecurity, this paper has not only done that but also assessed the situation we are in right now with respect to these fields and ways to improve them and generate public awareness which will help in keeping people and organizations safe in the virtual world. Cybersecurity and cyber forensics will become the most talked about and most invested in field in the future. With countries around the world investing billions of dollars in cybersecurity, one of the factors of measuring a country's development will be the progress they have made in this field. It will be very important for all organizations around the world to invest in cybersecurity equally as the loss they incur after a cyberattack adds up to millions of dollars and if this wasn't sufficient, the lost public trust regarding protecting their personal information also adds to the worries.

When it comes to cyber forensics, we have made a lot of progress in catching the notorious masterminds, but there is a need to improve the tools we have at our disposal. The amount of time involved in cyber forensics cases is also a worry for prosecutors, and with more advanced technology coming up in the future it is very tough to accumulate data and present it in court in a sophisticated manner. We are surely able to catch attackers with the tools we have right now but with ever-changing technology, we cannot sit back and relax and expect to do the same for another two decades. These tools might even prove to be inefficient in the very near future. This paper discusses the kind of threats the common man faces in the virtual world and how attackers can use different ways to gain access to their systems and hence access their personal information. To protect their systems, people need a password that cannot be cracked. A country can really shoot up in these two fields if the public becomes cautious about their safety in the online world and takes all the necessary precautions to stay safe. The process of educating the public is a very lengthy process and a time-consuming one as well, but once the public is educated about the virtual world it really boosts a country's development. Now, it will be a race against time regarding who can best educate their fellow men and women.

References

1. Donald E. Shelton, "The 'CSI Effect': does it really exist"? National Institute of Justice (NIJ) Journal, 259 (March 2008), Available at: http://www.ojp.usdoj.gov/nij/journals/259/csi-effect.htm

2. J. Lee, S. Un and D. Hong, "Improving Performance in Digital Forensics: A Case Using Pattern Matching Board," *2009 International Conference on Availability, Reliability and Security*, 2009, pp. 1001-1005, doi: 10.1109/ARES.2009.156.

3. D. Ayers, A 2nd generation computer forensic analysis system, *Proceedings of the 2009 Digital Forensics Research Workshop, DFRWS*, 2009, https://doi.org/10.1016/j.diin.2009.06.013

4. Simson L. Garfinkel, Digital forensics research: The next 10 years, *Digital Investigation*, Volume 7, Supplement, 2010, pp. S64-S73, ISSN 1742-2876, https://doi.org/10.1016/j.diin.2010.05.009.

5. Meghna Manoj Nair, Amit Kumar Tyagi, Richa Goyal, Medical Cyber Physical Systems and Its Issues, *Procedia Computer Science*, Vol. 165, 2019, pp. 647-655, ISSN 1877-0509, https://doi.org/10.1016/j.procs.2020.01.059.

6. Amit Kumar Tyagi, G. Aghila, "A Wide Scale Survey on Botnet", *International Journal of Computer Applications* (ISSN: 0975-8887), Vol. 34, No. 9, pp. 9-22, November 2011.

7. Amit Kumar Tyagi. "Cyber Physical Systems (CPSs) – Opportunities and Challenges for Improving Cyber Security." *International Journal of Computer Applications* 137(14):19-27, March 2016.

8. S. Mishra and A. K. Tyagi, "Intrusion Detection in Internet of Things (IoTs) Based Applications Using Blockchain Technology," *2019 Third International Conference on I-SMAC (IoT in Social, Mobile, Analytics and Cloud) (I-SMAC)*, 2019, pp. 123-128, doi: 10.1109/I-SMAC47947.2019.9032557.

9. Amit Kumar Tyagi, Aswathy S U, G Aghila, N Sreenath, "AARIN: Affordable, Accurate, Reliable and INnovative Mechanism to Protect a Medical Cyber-Physical System using Blockchain Technology" *IJIN*, Vol. 2, pp. 175-183, October 2021.

10. Amit Kumar Tyagi, "Analysis of Security and Privacy Aspects of Blockchain Technologies from Smart Era' Perspective: The Challenges and a Way Forward", in *Recent Trends in Blockchain for Information Systems Security and Privacy*, CRC Press, 2021.

11. G. Vishnuram, K. Tripathi and A. Kumar Tyagi, "Ethical Hacking: Importance, Controversies and Scope in the Future," *2022 International Conference on Computer Communication and Informatics (ICCCI)*, 2022, pp. 01-06, doi: 10.1109/ICCCI54379.2022.9740860.

12. A. Deshmukh, N. Sreenath, A. K. Tyagi and U. V. Eswara Abhichandan, "Blockchain Enabled Cyber Security: A Comprehensive Survey," *2022 International Conference on Computer Communication and Informatics (ICCCI)*, 2022, pp. 1-6, doi: 10.1109/ICCCI54379.2022.9740843.

13. G. Rekha, S. Malik, A.K. Tyagi, M.M. Nair "Intrusion Detection in Cyber Security: Role of Machine Learning and Data Mining in Cyber Security", *Advances in Science, Technology and Engineering Systems Journal*, Vol. 5, No. 3, pp. 72-81 (2020).

14. Tyagi, Amit Kumar; Nair, Meghna Manoj; Niladhuri, Sreenath; Abraham, Ajith, "Security, Privacy Research issues in Various Computing Platforms: A Survey and the Road Ahead", *Journal of Information Assurance & Security*. 2020, Vol. 15, Issue 1, pp. 1-16. 16p.

15. Madhav A.V.S., Tyagi A.K. (2022), "The World with Future Technologies (Post-COVID-19): Open Issues, Challenges, and the Road Ahead". In: Tyagi A.K., Abraham A., Kaklauskas A. (eds.) *Intelligent Interactive Multimedia Systems for e-Healthcare Applications*. Springer, Singapore. https://doi.org/10.1007/978-981-16-6542-4_22

16. Mishra S., Tyagi A.K. (2022), "The Role of Machine Learning Techniques in Internet of Things-Based Cloud Applications". In: Pal S., De D., Buyya R. (eds.) *Artificial Intelligence-based Internet of Things Systems*. Internet of Things (Technology, Communications and Computing). Springer, Cham. https://doi.org/10.1007/978-3-030-87059-1_4.

14

Quantum Computing: A Software Engineering Approach

Mradul Agrawal*, Aviral Jain, Rudraksh Thorat and Shivam Sharma

Department of Computer Science Engineering, Shri Vaishnav Vidyapeeth Vishwavidyalaya, Indore, India

Abstract

Quantum computing (QC) and, to a greater extent, quantum technologies are changing the world. In reality, QC is not an advancement of conventional computer science but rather a revolution that radically shifts the paradigm of computing. By basing its functioning on quantum physics ideas like aggregation and coherence, quantum computers seek to exponentially boost computing power. QC may very well be able to solve a variety of problems that have previously seemed insurmountable. The fact is that due to its many promising applications, QC is currently having an impact on most corporate sectors and scientific domains. Quantum algorithms need to be explicitly programmed for these vastly different machines in order for these applications to become a reality. Despite the fact that a few well-known quantum algorithms exist, the need for quantum software will skyrocket in the coming years. In that situation, it is necessary to generate quantum software in a more industrialized and controlled manner, taking into account factors like quality, delivery, project management, or evolution of quantum software. We are confident that a new piece of software will be primarily motivated by QC.

Keywords: Quantum computing, quantum software, quantum software engineering, algorithms, management, design, languages

**Corresponding author*: mradulagrawal126@gmail.com

Romil Rawat, Rajesh Kumar Chakrawarti, Sanjaya Kumar Sarangi, Jaideep Patel, Vivek Bhardwaj, Anjali Rawat and Hitesh Rawat (eds.) Quantum Computing in Cybersecurity, (233–248) © 2023 Scrivener Publishing LLC

14.1   Introduction

When the first computer was created in the 1960s, it required a room's worth of space and required several scientists to run it. Who would have imagined that, fifty years later, a machine the size of a palm could perform the same amount of work?

The basic block of traditional computers [1, 2], semiconductors (which also replaced the switches and clicks of the original "Turing Machine"), has made its final contribution to technology. Today's semiconductors have shrunk so much on a macro level that there isn't enough space for circuits that run computers to process and scale their activities for further processing and output [3, 4]. The traditional computer system has deteriorated in terms of processing speed due to the rapid increase of data. The way classical computing operates is that we provide inputs to the system in order for it to discover a solution. The traditional computing method is unable to deliver a solution if the inputs are not provided. We are now at a bottleneck, which means that a massive volume of data is pouring in every second and we are unsure on how to properly and effectively handle it. The computer must reverse the query to obtain the answer in order to make best use of the data. Quantum computers can address issues like global warming and wise resource usage in order to help rescue humanity in this way.

QC is a cutting-edge technology that can provide us with additional power for processing and communication. Comparing QC to traditional computing, the fundamental building component is different. Information processing known as "quantum computing" (QC) takes advantage of quantum mechanics' superposition and entanglement concepts. Conventional computers utilise 0 and 1 bits to convey data from sender to receiver, but quantum computers use q-bits. This is how quantum computers differ from classical computers. Superposition is a quantum mechanical phenomenon that quantum computers use. A single qubit shows both the probabilistic states of 0 and 1 in a superposition [5, 6].

Organization of Chapter
The rest of the chapter is as follows. Section 14.2 shows Background of Research Area; section 14.3 discusses Why Cryptography?, section 14.4 is about Classical Cryptography. Quantum cryptography is discussed in section 14.5, followed by Quantum key Distribution (section 14.6), cryptanalysis (section 14.7), Entanglement (section 14.8), Quantum teleportation (section 14.9), Applications of quantum cryptography in Cybersecurity (section 14.10), Quantum Key Distribution Protocols Implementation

(section 14.11), Research and Work (section 12), Challenges faced by quantum computing (section 13), and Limitations (section 14). Section 15 concludes the chapter.

14.2 Background of Research Area

As of 2020, quantum computer development is still in its early phases. IBM [7, 8] has created a modest 20 q-bit quantum computer that can be accessed online. IBM is also working on a 53 q-bit quantum computer that will be released shortly. When compared to a traditional computer, quantum computers can handle tasks more effectively and fast. It provides enormous computing capacity to handle issues such as factorization and optimization that traditional computers cannot accomplish [9].

The rules of Quantum Mechanics or Quantum Physics govern data manipulation in Quantum Computers. A quantum computer is the most powerful and difficult to construct computer, with a capacity of 100,000 qubits. We may utilise it for machine learning, cryptography, drug research, analysing the structure of molecules, and learning and generating complicated chemical structures. Furthermore, a universal quantum computer will be orders of magnitude quicker than a conventional computer [10].

14.3 Why Cryptography?

The majority of security breaches were caused by unauthorised data access. According to study data through March 2020, 832 million records have been compromised. According to a survey issued by cybint solution, 62% of firms are victims of phishing and social engineering assaults. Data breaches have surged by 67% since 2014, accounting for two-thirds of all data breaches in the previous five years [11].

The surge in data breaches is simply due to invaders' technological development. It aided them in exploiting network vulnerabilities by developing sophisticated software that allows for automated assaults. The majority of the time, enterprises are ignorant of a data breach. According to the security study, more than 75% of respondents lost money as a result of these assaults. As a result, cryptography is used to provide secure communication across networks. It assists organisations in safeguarding anything from email to bank transactions to social media data and online purchasing [12].

The oldest recorded usage of cryptography in writing goes back to around [11–13] 1900 B.C., when an Egyptian scribe utilised unconventional hieroglyphs in an inscription. Cryptography is the study of writing in secret code and is an ancient art. Some scholars argue that cryptography unexpectedly developed some period after the invention of writing, with uses ranging from diplomatic missives to military battle preparations. Therefore, it is not surprising that new types of cryptography appeared not long after computer networking became widely used. Cryptography is required in data and telecommunications when interacting across any untrusted channel, including most networks, especially the Internet.

14.3.1   Application-to-Application Communication Reference

Within the context of any application-to-application communication [14–19], there are some specific security requirements, including:

a) Authentication: The process of proving one's identity. (The primary forms of host-to-host authentication on the Internet today are name-based or address-based, both of which are notoriously weak.)

b) Privacy/confidentiality: Ensuring that no one can read the message except the intended receiver.

c) Integrity: Assuring the receiver that the received message has not been altered in any way from the original.

d) Non-repudiation: A mechanism to prove that the sender really sent this message.

Cryptography, then, not only protects data from theft or alteration, but can also be used for user authentication. There are, in general, three types of cryptographic schemes typically used to accomplish these goals: secret key (or symmetric) cryptography, public-key (or asymmetric) cryptography, and hash functions, each of which is described below. In all cases, the initial unencrypted data is referred to as plaintext. It is encrypted into ciphertext, which will in turn (usually) be decrypted into usable plaintext.

Secret key cryptography schemes are generally categorized as being either stream ciphers or block ciphers. Stream ciphers operate on a single bit (byte or computer word) at a time and implement some form of feedback mechanism so that the key is constantly changing. A block cipher is so-called because the scheme encrypts one block of data at a time using the same key on each block. In general, the same plaintext block will always encrypt to the same ciphertext when using the same key in a block cipher whereas the same plaintext will encrypt to different ciphertext in a stream cipher.

There are many different types of stream cyphers, but two stand out for this discussion. Each bit in the keystream is calculated using self-synchronizing stream cyphers as a function of the keystream's previous number of bits. Because the decryption process can keep up with the encryption process by just knowing how far along the n-bit keystream it is, it is described as "self-synchronizing." Error propagation is one issue; if one bit is corrupted during transmission, more will be mangled upon reception. Synchronous stream cyphers use the same keystream creation function at the transmitter and receiver, but they produce the keystream independently of the message stream. Despite the fact that stream cyphers do not spread transmission failures, the keystream will ultimately recur because of their inherent periodicity.

14.3.2   Modes of Block Cyphers

Block cyphers [20–24] may function in a variety of modes, but the following four are the most crucial.

a) The Electronic Codebook (ECB) mode is the simplest and most straightforward implementation; the plaintext block is encrypted using the secret key to create a ciphertext block. Thus, the same ciphertext block will always result from two identical plaintext blocks. Although this is the most typical block cypher mode, there are several brute force techniques that may be used against it.

b) The Cipher Block Chaining (CBC) mode enhances the encryption algorithm with a feedback mechanism. Prior to encryption in CBC, the plaintext is exclusively-ORed (XORed) with the preceding block of ciphertext. Two identical blocks of plaintext never generate the same ciphertext in this mode.

c) Cipher Feedback (CFB) mode is a self-synchronizing stream cypher that implements a block cypher. In some applications, such encrypting interactive terminal input, CFB mode's ability to encrypt data in units smaller than the block size may be advantageous. For instance, if we were to use 1-byte CFB mode, each incoming character would be put into a shift register the same size as the block, encrypted, and the block would then be sent over the network. The ciphertext is decoded at the receiving end, and any additional bits in the block (i.e., anything greater than a single byte) are deleted. A block cypher implementation called Output Feedback (OFB) mode is essentially comparable to a synchronous stream cypher. By using OFB, the same plaintext block cannot produce the same ciphertext block.

14.3.3   Secret Key Cryptography Algorithms in Use Today

These include Data Encryption Standard. DES, the most popular SKC scheme in use today, was created by IBM in the 1970s and approved for use in commercial and unclassified government applications by the National Bureau of Standards (NBS) [now the National Institute for Standards and Technology (NIST)] in 1977. DES is a block-cipher that works with 64-bit blocks and a 56-bit key. Although this latter point is becoming less important today due to the fact that computer processor speeds are many orders of magnitude faster than they were twenty years ago, DES has a complex set of rules and transformations that were created specifically to yield fast hardware implementations and slow software implementations. The government rejected IBM's proposal for a 112-bit DES key at the time.

14.4   Classical Cryptography [27, 28]

Cryptography is a branch of science that enables us to establish a secure connection between sender and receiver without the participation of a third party. Modern cryptography's fundamental techniques include data integrity, authentication, nonrepudiation, and data secrecy. E-commerce, automated teller machines (ATMs), computer passwords, and many more essential applications make use of current or classical cryptography [29].

Classical cryptography is the process of transforming plain text into code language by employing various machine learning algorithms. The keys used to decode the data are exchanged by the sender and recipient in order for them to encrypt or decrypt the communication.

There are two forms of classical cryptography:

a) Symmetrical cryptography - This is the simplest cryptography approach since the keys used for encryption and decryption are the same[14].

b) Asymmetrical cryptography - This is a more complicated sort of cryptography approach that uses various keys for encryption and decryption. The sender and receiver's private keys are never transferred under an asymmetric cryptography scheme, which solely uses public keys. As a result, it is less vulnerable to cyberattacks and allows users to transfer data privately. Despite all of these cryptographic measures, the quantity of data breaches is expanding rapidly, and this data has limited processing capabilities, demonstrating its inability to cope with large data. As we live in the digital age, the volume and diversity of data is exceeding computing capacity.

The basic working idea of cryptographic algorithms is based on mathematical models, and as a result, these models have several security flaws, such as a brute force attack, factorization problem, and many more. As a result of technological advancements, classical cryptography does not appear to be a secure solution for data privacy and security. This is why we are gravitating toward a new technology known as QCr [15].

14.5   Quantum Cryptography (QCr)

Quantum cryptography (QCr) is based on quantum physics events and provides for secure data transfer between sender and recipient. QCr represents a breakthrough in network security [16].

QCr is the most recent and sophisticated area of cryptography, with its foundation based on two quantum technicalities: Heisenberg's uncertainty principle and the theory of photon polarization [16]. According to Heisenberg's uncertainty principle, some pairs of physical attributes are coupled in such a manner that measuring one may prohibit a person from knowing the other at the same time. The choice of which direction to measure in, in particular, influences all subsequent measurements. When unpolarized light passes through a vertically aligned filter, some of it is absorbed and the remainder is polarised in the vertical direction. Following that, a filter angled at some angle q absorbs some of the polarised light and transmits the remainder, giving it a new polarization.

A basis is a pair of orthogonal polarisation states used to express photon polarisation, such as horizontal/vertical [17].

The BB84 [18–20] quantum key distribution protocol was created in 1984. The BB84 procedure includes the following steps:

a) The sender delivers polarised photons to the receiver, which might be rectilinear or diagonal.

b) The receiver next validates the photons' orientation by randomly picking the basis (rectilinear/diagonal) and records the findings. The basis used for measuring by the transmitter and receiver does not have to be the same.

c) The receiver tells the sender with his measurement basis over the public channel.

d) After comparing the real basis with the received basis, the sender delivers the proper bits (bits with the same basis) via the public channel.

14.6   Quantum Key Distribution

The distribution of encrypted keys between two parties is known as key distribution. The most basic method of key distribution is to meet in person in a safe setting and exchange keys. However, we may now exchange keys at any distance by employing public keys such as cyphers, RSA, Diffiehellman [21–23].

The drawbacks with traditional key distribution are that they employ basic mathematical computations to transfer data, which are simple to compute and may be easily accessible by third parties [24, 25].

This traditional key distribution method is fraught with difficulties. They, like the traditional key, can only create weak random numbers that are easily retrieved by other parties. Furthermore, the CPU power and these keys are subject to new attack tactics since they must be reprogrammed if any new attack techniques are utilised. If quantum computers become a reality, they would be able to readily decipher data included in conventional keys, making current traditional encryption schemes dangerous. To keep ahead of the competition, we must employ huge Asymmetric keys to securely store and distribute our symmetric keys. All of this causes us to reconsider the security of cryptographic keys [26].

14.6.1   Application (Key-Related Work)

QC has a wide range of applications, making it incredibly powerful and helpful. Some applications of QC include:

Machine learning [27, 28]: There are three types of machine learning: supervised, unsupervised, and reinforced machine learning. All three types of learning need massive processing power. Here are a few examples:

a) Support Vector Machine (SVM): SVM employs a brute force approach on a traditional computer, requiring significant processing power and time.
b) Grover's search method, for example, uses quantum algorithms to accelerate the process.
   i. K-closest neighbour algorithm (KNN): KNN is a classification technique that divides objects into clusters, or groups of points with similar characteristics. A classical computer's classification difficulty grows as the number of clusters increases. This sort of work is best handled by a quantum computer, which allows for parallel computing. It can calculate an object's distance from the cluster's centres at the same time.
   ii. Perceptron: The fundamental goal of a perceptron is to identify a hyperplane that matches the training data well. It generates a large number of hyperplane options, which makes traditional computers sluggish since they calculate all points to a single hyperplane at the same time. Quantum computers, on the other hand, can provide findings from various hyperplanes to the points.

Application of 6G or B5G - Since the introduction of 5G, there has been worry that the technology may fail to meet data demands within a decade. The framework plan is provided in (Nawaz, Sharma *et al.* 2019). It states that using artificial intelligence (AI) and machine learning (ML), the concept of autonomous switching and self-serviceable networks may give 100 times greater data throughput than a 5G network. Growing traffic is expected to create around 5,016 exabytes of data per month by 2030. To offer findings and serve networks in real time, both ML and AI require parallel processing.

Drug Development - Quantum technologies are extremely beneficial in the transformation of medications and health care. For example, the most difficult task in medicine development is analysing and developing a molecule. Quantum technology can calculate the quantum characteristics of all atoms, which is a tough computational process even for a fast supercomputer. QC employs quantum qualities to model a molecule, giving it an advantage over traditional technology. Large-scale quantum simulation allows for the successful treatment of diseases such as Alzheimer's [28, 29]

Information Teleportation - One intriguing characteristic of quantum technologies is the movement of information from one location to another without physically sending it. It is conceivable owing to the fluid identities of quantum particles, which may get entangled across space and time in such a manner that when we modify anything in one particle, it has an effect on another particle, creating a channel for teleportation [15, 16].

14.6.2   Problem Statement

The most difficult problem for the quantum industry is to bring quantum computers or its numerous applications to commercial and widespread use despite their constraints. The major goal of bringing quantum computers is to tackle unanswered issues that we have not been able to solve.

14.7   Cryptanalysis

Quantum cryptanalysis is the process of deciphering the meaning of encrypted data without access to the original data. In this game, we strive to uncover the hidden key [16]. We also investigate the assaults in order to obtain the encrypted data. This may be accomplished by examining security in a realistic manner. In general, the practical challenge in a QKD system is the discovery of loopholes, which we may explore using Cryptanalysis [17, 18].

14.8   Entanglement

If electrons or Qubits interact at any point, a link is formed between those particles. If any electrons or Qubits exhibit these characteristics, they are said to be in correlation or entangled together. Once the spin of one electron is known, the spin of the other entangled electron will be in the opposite direction. Because of the usage of quantum superposition, the particles have no spin or orientation before to computations, yet they exist in both up and down or 0s and 1s states. When a particle's spin is detected and it concurrently communicates with its entangled particle, the entangled particle has the opposite spin direction as the observed particle. The qubits can interact because of this characteristic. No matter how far apart the mutually associated particles are, they will stay entangled as long as they are separated [15, 18].

14.9   Quantum Teleportation

Quantum states are extremely unstable; if they interact or collide with other systems, they will lose their superposition qualities or potentially annihilate. When compared to quantum bits, any faults that occur with classical bits may be simply rectified. Quantum teleportation is concerned with the transport of information utilising unknown quantum states in a secure setting. If this application becomes a reality in the future, we can use computer outputs as inputs by teleporting outputs [9].

Teleportation takes advantage of the quantum entanglement characteristic. It aids in the movement of information from one location to another. Free space quantum communication is a reality, with networks extending over 200 kilometres.

14.10   Applications of QCr in Cybersecurity

Because of the benefits of quantum computers, public keys such as RSA, Ellamae, and other public keys will no longer be safe with quantum computers. Furthermore, quantum computers can quickly tackle issues such as the discrete logarithm problem and integer factorization. To protect these systems, we need other cryptosystems that are not dependent on the aforementioned issues [8, 9].

Network security and cryptography are both critical in guaranteeing the secure security of information systems. Exploring QCr methods is one of the most important aspects of cybersecurity [1, 2].

Quantum information possesses several features that classical information does not. The information of quantum codes in an entangled state is particularly difficult to get [3, 4].

   a) Uncertainty principle: This concept indicates that determining the position of a particle in the Micro universe is difficult, and that the particle's position varies in various places.
   b) Quantum No-cloning: Cloning is the production of an identical quantum particle in an entirely different state. Scientists have demonstrated that quantum devices can mirror this trait. The undeleting property is another characteristic of quantum states. This means that in quantum states, destroying or injuring a particle will leave a trace in communication

networks. The linearity of quantum physics prohibits deleting a copy of a quantum state [6, 7].

14.11   Quantum Key Distribution Protocols Implementation

Bennett and Brassard designed the BB84 convention in 1984 based on the preceding behaviour, adopting four polarisation expressions that fill in as follows.

The data is encoded into quantum states by the transmitter using an irregular arrangement of bases and transmitted to the collector. Each piece of this knowledge will manifest as a brief flash of light, fueled by the aforementioned estimate bases. The recipient then reads the forthcoming material using their own arbitrary arrangement of bases. After the data has been sent, the sender and collector must explicitly discuss which bases were used and in which request.

When the bases agree, it can be [19] proven that the relevant item of data is identical at the two sections of the bargains, with the exception of the following two circumstances [11, 12]:

a) When a random disturbance disrupts the information channel.
b) When an eavesdropper attempts to intercept the data stream.

14.12   Research and Work

We are unable to deal with the issue of a high processing need due to the influx of a significant volume of data. For these kinds of issues, like searching or optimising over huge solution sets, QC has several advantages over binary computing [1]. The development of computing has been significantly impacted by the availability of quantum computers. And Google revealed in a study how they won the race to attain quantum supremacy. Using a 53-qubit quantum computer, the Sycamore processor, a random number is produced in 200 seconds as opposed to a supercomputer's 10,000 years (not computed practically). Other

Rivals like IBM, Microsoft, and others have differing views on who will dominate the quantum realm. Supercomputers cannot solve problems that the quantum computer can; however, the quantum Computer utilisation for "multipurpose jobs" is behind.

14.13   Challenges Faced by QC

Today, the state of QC is exactly the same as it was for the traditional, room-sized computer in the 1960s. The only distinction is that the rate of expansion in terms of research, development, and outcomes is exponential. The principal difficulties with QC are that Absolute zero temperature is required for quantum computer to conduct super conductivity. Due to its size and restrictions on the types of activities it can perform, the utilisation is not widely accepted. It's capable. How superconductivity can be achieved is the question that needs to be addressed. How it can carry out the various tasks that we utilise it for at non-absolute temperatures traditional computers.

The key of QC's power is the fundamental unit of operation, called a "qubit," which functions on the superposition principle and can simultaneously hold a value of 0 or 1. This characteristic progressively increases the computing power (2q).n denotes the number of qubits. Google now estimates that n can be achieved practically at 53, and it quantum supremacy is claimed. In reaction to Google's assertion, a corporation by the name of a 5,000-qubit quantum computer was announced to attain quantum dominance. Consider the ability of a computer to solve an issue with a 25,000 level of complexity.

The name "Hot Qubit" [18, 28] was created by the researchers to describe quantum bits that operate at greater temperatures than a "Qubit," which operates at a decimal place under absolute zero. The quantum processing of the researcher unit cell operates 15 times hotter than chip-based quantum computers, at 1.5 kelvin, than those of Google and IBM. Despite the fact that 1.5 kelvin is still rather near, it can still save millions of dollars merely qubit refrigeration (Bernstein 2009).

The capability of the technology could lead to a valuable contribution to network security among enterprises, academic institutions, and the government environment.

14.14   Limitations

There is no question that quantum computers will process information exponentially faster than traditional computers, but only by a small margin. Claiming that quantum computers can do anything is one of the frequent errors that has been made in this field address challenging mathematical anomalies faster than traditional computers. Considering our understanding, the challenges faced by quantum computers are similar to those faced by classical computers. Map issue (NP- Complete). In addition to these theoretical issues, the following are the two biggest issues that emerge in the actual application of QC:

- Components Zero decoherence is required in the circuit, which means that no radiation or noise should be present. This characteristic guards against outside attack and data loss on the machine.
- Superconductivity requires absolutely zero temperature to operate, which is highly expensive.

14.15   Conclusion

The future of QC appears bright since it has so many uses, including information teleportation and QCr. By examining molecular behaviour, it can be utilised to produce medications. Satellite communications can also benefit from its utilisation. However, we hope that the idea may ultimately be put to use so that we can utilise its benefits in numerous other scientific domains.

The thesis's conclusion states that one of the enormous potentials for the contemporary world to uncover unsolved mysteries is QC. It promises to resolve issues that conventional computers can't really handle. However, QC is too expensive. Reducing the cost to make it more accessible for experiments is the main difficulty at the moment. Additionally, UNSW Sydney has made a big advancement that will result in millions of dollars in savings. Making a hybrid computer that can do high processing tasks simultaneously with classical computing tasks is another problem that will allow for corporate and commercial use.

References

1. Awan, U., Hannola, L., Tandon, A., Goyal, R. K., & Dhir, A. (2022). Quantum computing challenges in the software industry. A fuzzy AHP-based approach. *Information and Software Technology, 147,* 106896.
2. Piattini, M., Serrano, M., Perez-Castillo, R., Petersen, G., & Hevia, J. L. (2021). Toward a quantum software engineering. *IT Professional, 23*(1), 62-66.
3. Luckow, A., Klepsch, J., & Pichlmeier, J. (2021). Quantum computing: Towards industry reference problems. *Digitale Welt, 5*(2), 38-45.

4. Zahorodko, P. V., Modlo, Y. O., Kalinichenko, O. O., Selivanova, T. V., & Semerikov, S. (2021). Quantum enhanced machine learning: An overview. CEUR Workshop Proceedings.

5. Pérez-Castillo, R., Serrano, M. A., & Piattini, M. (2021). Software modernization to embrace quantum technology. *Advances in Engineering Software, 151,* 102933.

6. Awan, U., Hannola, L., Tandon, A., Goyal, R. K., & Dhir, A. (2022). Quantum computing challenges in the software industry. A fuzzy AHP-based approach. *Information and Software Technology, 147,* 106896.

7. Khan, A. A., Ahmad, A., Waseem, M., Liang, P., Fahmideh, M., Mikkonen, T., & Abrahamsson, P. (2022). Software Architecture for Quantum Computing Systems - A Systematic Review. *arXiv preprint arXiv:2202.05505.*

8. Khan, A. A., Ahmad, A., Waseem, M., Liang, P., Fahmideh, M., Mikkonen, T., & Abrahamsson, P. (2022). Software Architecture for Quantum Computing Systems - A Systematic Review. *arXiv preprint arXiv:2202.05505.*

9. Bernal, D. E., Ajagekar, A., Harwood, S. M., Stober, S. T., Trenev, D., & You, F. (2022). Perspectives of quantum computing for chemical engineering. *AIChE Journal, 68*(6), e17651.

10. Gill, S. S., Kumar, A., Singh, H., Singh, M., Kaur, K., Usman, M., & Buyya, R. (2022). Quantum computing: A taxonomy, systematic review and future directions. *Software: Practice and Experience, 52*(1), 66-114.

11. Rawat, B., Mehra, N., Bist, A. S., Yusup, M., & Sanjaya, Y. P. A. (2022). Quantum Computing and AI: Impacts & Possibilities. *ADI Journal on Recent Innovation, 3*(2), 202-207.

12. Paltenghi, M., & Pradel, M. (2022). Bugs in Quantum computing platforms: an empirical study. *Proceedings of the ACM on Programming Languages, 6*(OOPSLA1), 1-27.

13. Paltenghi, M., & Pradel, M. (2022). MorphQ: Metamorphic Testing of Quantum Computing Platforms. *arXiv preprint arXiv:2206.01111.*

14. Upama, P. B., Faruk, M. J. H., Nazim, M., Masum, M., Shahriar, H., Uddin, G., ... & Rahman, A. (2022). Evolution of Quantum Computing: A Systematic Survey on the Use of Quantum Computing Tools. *arXiv preprint arXiv:2204.01856.*

15. Ajagekar, A., & You, F. (2022). New frontiers of quantum computing in chemical engineering. *Korean Journal of Chemical Engineering,* 1-10.

16. Weder, B., Barzen, J., Leymann, F., & Vietz, D. (2022). Quantum software development lifecycle. In *Quantum Software Engineering* (pp. 61-83). Springer, Cham.

17. Miranda, E. R., Venkatesh, S., Martın-Guerrero, J. D., Hernani-Morales, C., Lamata, L., & Solano, E. (2022). An approach to interfacing the brain with quantum computers: practical steps and caveats. *arXiv preprint arXiv:2201.00817.*

18. Finžgar, J. R., Ross, P., Klepsch, J., & Luckow, A. (2022). QUARK: A Framework for Quantum Computing Application Benchmarking. *arXiv preprint arXiv:2202.03028.*

19. Gill, S. S., Kumar, A., Singh, H., Singh, M., Kaur, K., Usman, M., & Buyya, R. (2022). Quantum computing: A taxonomy, systematic review and future directions. *Software: Practice and Experience, 52*(1), 66-114.

20. Masum, M., Nazim, M., Faruk, M. J. H., Shahriar, H., Valero, M., Khan, M. A. H., ... & Ahamed, S. I. (2022). Quantum Machine Learning for Software Supply Chain Attacks: How Far Can We Go? *arXiv preprint arXiv:2204.02784.*

21. Basak Chowdhury, A., Mahapatra, A., Soni, D., & Karri, R. (2022). Fuzzing+ Hardware Performance Counters-Based Detection of Algorithm Subversion Attacks on Post-Quantum Signature Schemes. *arXiv e-prints*, arXiv-2203.

22. Singh, J., & Bhangu, K. S. (2022). Contemporary Quantum Computing Use Cases: Taxonomy, Review and Challenges. *Archives of Computational Methods in Engineering*, 1-24.

23. Xin, M., Xu, C., Huang, K., Yu, H., Yao, H., Jiang, X., & Liu, D. (2022, January). Implementation of Number Theoretic Transform Unit for Polynomial Multiplication of Lattice-based Cryptography. In *2022 2nd International Conference on Consumer Electronics and Computer Engineering (ICCECE)* (pp. 323-327). IEEE.

24. Brandmeier, R. A., Heye, J. A., & Woywod, C. (2022). Future Development of Quantum Computing and Its Relevance to NATO. *Connections: The Quarterly Journal, 20,* 89-110.

25. Far, S. B., Rad, A. I., & Asaar, M. R. (2022, May). Goodbye Bitcoin: A general framework for migrating to quantum-secure cryptocurrencies. In *2022 30th International Conference on Electrical Engineering (ICEE)* (pp. 512-517). IEEE.

26. Coyle, B. (2022). Machine learning applications for noisy intermediate-scale quantum computers. *arXiv preprint arXiv:2205.09414.*

27. Islam, M., Chowdhury, M., Khan, Z., & Khan, S. M. (2022). Hybrid quantum-classical neural network for cloud-supported in-vehicle cyberattack detection. *IEEE Sensors Letters, 6*(4), 1-4.

28. Upama, P. B., Faruk, M. J. H., Nazim, M., Masum, M., Shahriar, H., Uddin, G., ... & Rahman, A. (2022). Evolution of Quantum Computing: A Systematic Survey on the Use of Quantum Computing Tools. *arXiv preprint arXiv:2204.01856.*

29. Prateek, K., Altaf, F., Amin, R., & Maity, S. (2022). A Privacy Preserving Authentication Protocol Using Quantum Computing for V2I Authentication in Vehicular Ad Hoc Networks. *Security and Communication Networks, 2022.*

15

Quantum Computing to the Advantage of Neural Network

Aditya Maltare*, Ishita Jain, Keshav Agrawal and Tanya Rawat

*Department of Computer Science Engineering,
Shri Vaishnav Vidyapeeth Vishwavidyalaya, Indore, India*

Abstract

Artificial neural networks (ANN) have been shown to be effective in various machine learning–based big data analytics challenges. An ANN can learn and generalize the intricate and irregular aspects of the input data. In the era of big data, colossal amounts of data come from various sources. It is anticipated that a point will be reached where even supercomputers will likely be overwhelmed by the enormous data. Due to the volume and scope of the huge data, training an ANN in this situation is a difficult process.

To identify patterns and evaluate the data, a vast number of parameters must be employed and tuned in the network. Since a quantum computer may represent data in various ways utilizing qubits, quantum computing (QC) is emerging as a subject that offers a solution to this issue. It is possible to identify hidden patterns in data that are challenging for a classical computer to find by using qubits on quantum computers. As a result, the field of ANN has a wide range of potential applications. In this work, our main goal was to train an artificial neural network with qubits acting as its synthetic neurons.

The simulation results demonstrate that, when compared to conventional ANN, our QC solution for ANN (QC ANN) is effective. For a binary classification job, the model that uses qubits as artificial neurons may learn the properties of data with fewer parameters. We employ a quantum simulator to demonstrate our experiment, and a conventional computer is used to optimize the quantum parameters used in the QC ANN.

Keywords: Quantum computing, neural network, machine learning, Qubit, artificial neural network, binary classification

*Corresponding author: adityamaltare1@gmail.com

Romil Rawat, Rajesh Kumar Chakrawarti, Sanjaya Kumar Sarangi, Jaideep Patel, Vivek Bhardwaj, Anjali Rawat and Hitesh Rawat (eds.) Quantum Computing in Cybersecurity, (249–262) © 2023 Scrivener Publishing LLC

15.1   Introduction

Given how quickly the amount of data is increasing, data processing is a challenge. A significant problem is gaining any understanding from vast amounts of data. As data volume and size increase, new issues must be solved, testing ANN capacity for computation. Using the settings between the layers of the network, an ANN [1, 2] can learn complicated associations from the input data. During the training phase, backpropagation is used to adjust these parameters. It becomes more challenging to train a neural network with fewer parameters as the size and dimension of the input data increase [1].

A quantum computer can effectively address challenging machine learning problems. The use of quantum computing (QC) is growing as a novel approach to issues that cannot be resolved with conventional computing methods. Compared to conventional computers, quantum computers operate in a different computing environment. Because of these benefits, QC [3, 4] is viewed as a novel approach to algorithmic issues that are challenging to resolve. In the area of machine learning, numerous studies utilizing QC models are also being carried out. It is also possible to learn quantum machine learning utilizing hyperparameters quickly because the optimization of quantum devices using the gradient descent [5, 6] method has been investigated.

According to recent research, a hybrid classical-quantum strategy that employs a classical computer to tune quantum parameters can effectively address machine learning challenges. To perform quantum algorithms on a genuine quantum processor or a quantum simulator, open-source software is created. Data in the form of binary digits can be stored and processed using traditional computers. In contrast, quantum computers use qubits [7, 8], which simultaneously use 0 and 1, to store and process data. Superposition is the name for this counterintuitive quantum mechanical feature. Numerous algorithms exploit entanglement, another quantum mechanical feature, to induce interactions between qubits. The major goal of this research is to determine the benefit of training a neural network with fewer parameters on a near-term quantum computer.

Utilizing a quantum computer in its current condition to solve machine learning issues has its own restrictions. Because they require complete isolation from their surroundings, quantum computers are complicated systems. The coherence of the qubits in quantum computers is lost due to a lack of isolation. A difficult issue when developing a quantum algorithm as a quantum circuit for a soon-to-be-developed quantum computer is the

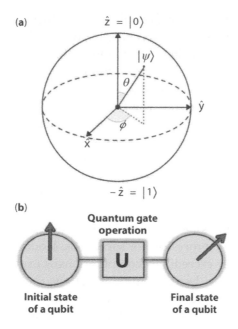

Figure 15.1 (a) A qubit state |ψ⟩ represented on a bloch sphere [1, 2]. (b) Gate operation on a qubit [3–5].

qubits' ability to lose their coherence [2]. In Figure 15.1(a) the state of a qubit is represented on a bloch sphere as $|\psi = \cos{(\theta/2)}\ |0\rangle + \sin{(\theta/2)}\ \exp(i\varphi)\ |1$ and the Figure 15.1(b) Quantum gate operation is performed as a unitary transformation denoted by U, that transforms a qubit form one state to another state [5].

Organization of Chapter
These are the main points of the remaining chapters. The importance of quantum computers in machine learning is demonstrated in Section 15.2, followed by sections showing related work, suggested technique, and result analysis. The conclusion is presented in Section 15.6.

15.2   Significance of Quantum Computers in Machine Learning

The researchers claim that a conventional machine learning system [9, 10] would not be able to directly access and learn from quantum information, whereas the quantum learning agent can do so and can thus provide a degree of analysis that is not conceivable in any other way. For some issues, quantum computers will likely provide exponentially more performance than classical systems, but, in order to fully realize this potential, researchers must first scale-up the number of qubits and enhance quantum error correction, according to the authors.

When it comes to analyzing data from quantum sensors [11], however, even today's noisy quantum computers offer a tremendous advance over traditional ones, the authors add. These sensors, which are already commonly employed for high-precision measurements, make use of particle correlations to glean more details about a system than would otherwise be possible. They may be used to measure things like magnetic fields and map the environment.

Quantum computers are anticipated to provide tenfold faster computing times than traditional processors for some jobs. Modern machine learning models are currently exceedingly computationally expensive to train, and even with the best hardware, training durations can take several weeks. Training times for quantum neural networks using current QC technology are already significantly faster than those for classical machine learning models. As more sophisticated quantum machines enter the market, training times are likely to continue to decrease [3].

15.3   Related Work

Similar to the classical domain, there are various architectures for QNNs [12] as well. In the section below, we provide a brief summary of a few of the more prominent ones. Figure 15.2(a) shows the following layers of nodes or neurons process information in traditional feedforward NNs. Figure 15.2(b) shows the variational quantum circuit representing a quantum neural network: non-parametrized gates (W_i) of Eq. 15.1 are inserted into the variational unitaries $(U_i(\theta_i))$, and the data re-uploading process $(S_i(x))$ is explicitly illustrated. Figure 15.2(c) shows using operations U_i and U_w to load input data and execute multiplication by weights, and a final measurement to simulate the neuron activation function, we propose a potential quantum perceptron model. Figure 15.2(d) shows Quantum Kernel Methods map input data to quantum states, and then evaluate their inner product $h\varphi(x)|\varphi(x\ 0\ )i$ to build the Kernel matrix $K(x, x\ 0)$. Figure 15.2(e) shows that a fully connected layer (FCL), or a general unitary on all remaining qubits, is applied before a measurement in a quantum convolutional NN after repeatedly applying convolutional layers and pooling layers (or else, O). Figure 15.2(f), about the Dissipative QNN, shows that

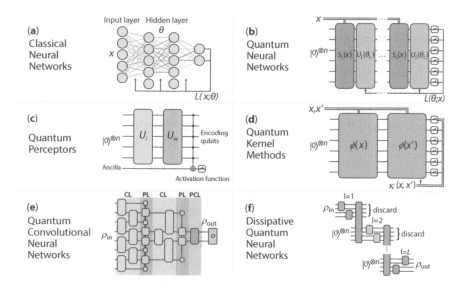

Figure 15.2 Models of conventional and quantum learning are shown schematically [6–12].

the previous layers are deleted and the qubits in one layer are connected to supplementary qubits from the next layer to load the computation's outcome (i.e., dissipated).

a. Quantum Perceptron Models [13]

Early work on quantum simulations of single artificial neurons, or "perceptrons," focused mostly on simulating the non-linearities of classical perceptrons with quantum systems, which, in contrast, exhibit linear unitary evolutions. More recent theories (e.g., Figure 15.2(c)) have shown that quantum perceptrons are capable of performing fundamental pattern recognition tasks for binary and grayscale pictures, most likely employing variational unsampling methodologies for training and to discover adaptive quantum circuit implementations. Models for quantum ANN were also realised on proof-of-concept tests on superconducting devices by linking numerous quantum neurons [4].

b. Kernel methods [7, 8, 16]

Kernel techniques, which are directly descended from their classical equivalents, rely on the conversion of input data into a higher dimensional space to carry out classification tasks that would be impossible in the original, low dimensional form. Any two data vectors, x, x 0 X, are often encoded as quantum states, |(x)i, |(x 0)i, using the encoding mapping X H, where H stands for the quantum register's Hilbert space. When evaluated in an increasingly large Hilbert space, the inner product h(x)|(x 0)i defines a similarity measure that may be applied to classification. The matrix Kij = hφ(xi)|φ(xj)i, constructed over the training dataset, is called kernel, and can be used along with classical methods such as graphically shown in Figure 15.2, Support Vector Machines (SVMs) are used to perform classification or regression tasks (d). Such quantum SVMs have the potential to create kernel functions that are challenging to compute conventionally, perhaps resulting in a quantum advantage in classification [4].

c. Generative Models

A generative model is a probabilistic algorithm whose goal is to reproduce an unknown probability distribution 4 pX over a space X , given a training set, T = {xi | xi ~ pX , i = 1, . . . , M} [4]. The use of probabilistic NNs known as Boltzmann Machines (BMs) [14], which are physically inspired techniques similar to Ising models, is a common traditional way for tackling this task. Quantum Boltzmann Machines (QBMs), devoted to the generative learning of quantum and classical distributions, can be defined by replacing classical nodes with qubits and the energy function with a quantum Hamiltonian [15]. Generative Adversarial Networks (GANs) serve as a fresh and unexpectedly potent traditional tool for generative modelling (GANs). In this case, the two distinct neural networks, dubbed generator and discriminator, which are designed to compete with one another, are given the task of carrying out the generative process. The generator learns to create fresh examples of high quality through a thorough and iterative learning process, eventually tricking the discriminator. The development of Quantum GANs (QGANs) [16] models, where the generator and discriminator are QNNs, was made possible by an easy translation to the quantum domain [4]. Even if not inspired by any classical neural network model, it is also worth mentioning Born machines, where the probability of generating new data follows the inherently probabilistic nature of quantum mechanics represented by Born's rule [16, 17].

d. Quantum Convolutional Neural Networks [18]

As the name implies, these models are based on their classical counterparts, which are still widely used in the field of image processing today. These networks, which are schematically depicted in Figure 15.2(e), process inputs through a sequence of so-called convolutional and pooling layers repeatedly. The former applies a convolution of the input—i.e., a translationally invariant quasi-local transformation to extract some pertinent data, the latter applies a compression of such information in a lower dimensional representation. After many rounds, the network produces a representation that is instructive and sufficiently low dimensional to be examined using common methods, such as fully connected feedforward NNs [4]. Similar to this, in Quantum Convolutional NNs, a quantum state [19] first goes through a convolution layer that entails a parametrized unitary operation acting on specific subsets of the qubits, followed by a pooling method that is achieved by measuring some of the qubits. This process is continued until only a few qubits, where all pertinent data was stored, are left. For genuinely quantum jobs like quantum phase recognition and quantum error correction, this technique has proven very helpful. Additionally, it is crucial to only use parameters that are logarithmically many in relation to the amount of qubits in order to accomplish efficient training and successful implementations on upcoming devices.

e. Quantum Dissipative Neural Networks
In the dissipative QNNs described, each qubit acts as a node, and the edges that connect the qubits in different layers represent the generic unitary operations that are performed on them [4]. The sequential discarding of layers of qubits after one layer interacts with the next is what is meant when the term "dissipative" is used (for a schematic example, see Figure 15.2(f)). This model is capable of performing a universal quantum computation by applying and learning general quantum transformations. It is equipped with a training algorithm that resembles backpropagation and represents a potential path to the realisation of quantum analogues of deep neural networks for analyzing quantum data.

15.4   Proposed Methodology

Before we talk about QC ANN, let's first consider conventional ANN (Artificial neural network) [14, 15] (QC approach for artificial neural network). In an ANN, data in N dimensions is projected onto the nodes from input layers referred to as artificial neurons. These neurons are connected to the hidden layer nodes by connections, and these connections have weights that may be improved. Weighted connections connect the middle layer nodes to the output layer once again. Finally, the network's output result is obtained using an activation function. The loss between the actual output and the intended output is listed in the subsequent step. Backpropagation is used to optimise the limit variables until the difference in loss between the actual and desired output results is as little as possible. The size of the dataset and the input dimension are constantly taken into consideration during the training process. In order to avoid overfitting or underfitting of the model, it is important to train an ANN, which involves optimising the boundary variables of the network by adjusting the hyper-parameters (parameters like network depth and width). Training jobs get more difficult as data quantity and dimension increase since there are more variables that need to be optimised and this necessitates a lot of enumeration. QC has the potential to perform such challenging, complicated jobs that are difficult on a conventional computer. Qubits are used to repair the artificial neurons in the input layer of the traditional ANN. Qubits are also known as quantum bits. Figure 15.3 shows the QC ANN with qubits as nodes of the network using hybrid quantum-classical computation [5].

The N-dimensional input data is encoded as a quantum state with the superposition of 2k states where k is the number of qubits. The use of amplitude embedding scheme for the state preparation process [5].

The hidden layer: entanglement and qubit rotations, consists of connections between qubits for interaction as an entanglement. Using gates with certain rotational variables the state of a qubit is modified. At long last, Qubits are in a stable condition for an output result value. A comparison

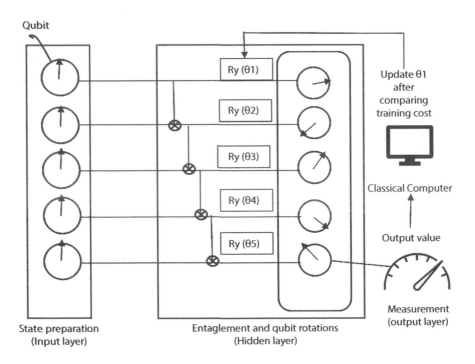

Figure 15.3 QC ANN with qubits as nodes of the network using hybrid quantum-classical computation [5, 13–16].

of the actual output value to the desired value is made, and the rotational boundary variables of the gates are optimised until the measurement results match the predicted output. A near-term quantum computer and the optimization of rotational variables of single-qubit gates can both perform all quantum operations using conventional devices. This hybrid strategy for the binary classification problem combines the use of conventional and quantum computers.

The implementation of the QC ANN on the circuit of quantum computers differs from the learning process of the conventional ANN [16–19]. As a result of the state building procedure, the input data may be encrypted onto qubits. In other words, the input data is submerged as superimposed amplitudes of several states. The qubits are now intertwined in such a way that altering the state of one affects the behaviour of other qubits. Then, gates allowing single-qubit rotations across the hidden layers are added, changing the quantum state. Each qubit in the coupled layer is rotated by a quantum gate, which alters the platform's state. A value is obtained by measuring the state of an anticipated qubit, which is then compared to the target value to determine the loss. Until the quantum system achieves a condition where the desired qubit produces the appropriate output value when measured, the rotational boundaries variable is adjusted. The learning process in this context refers to the quantum circuit's ability to learn the intricate relationships among input and output as rotating parameters of gates, which change the quantum system's state. Consequently, the learning process is completely dissimilar from that of a traditional ANN [5].

The advantages of QC ANN are:

a) $2k$ properties of the incoming data are encoded into a quantum computer as a superposition of states using k qubits. Take into account a 32-value normalised input data instance with the values x1, x2, x3,..., x32. With the use of five qubits, the input data may now be encoded as a quantum state with superposition of several states like x1 |00000+ x2 |00001, x3 |00010+,..., +x32 |11111 using amplitude embedding.

b) Avoiding the use of neurons in the hidden layers as in traditional ANN by using qubits as artificial neurons. Due to the lack of links between the layers, the size of limit variables that must be optimised decreases.

c) Quantum measurement itself serves as a computationally efficient activation parameter.

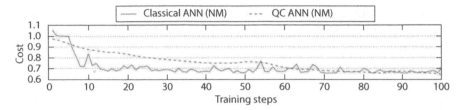

Figure 15.4 Cost vs. number of training steps of Classical ANN and QC ANN using NM [5, 17–19].

15.5   Result and Analysis

The cost factor is based on mean-squared deviation. The QC ANN's cost curve transition is smooth, demonstrating that the model can effectively generalise the properties of the data and learn the features from the data. However, when QC ANN utilising Adam is compared to traditional ANN, the training cost for the latter is much lower, demonstrating that tweaking hyperparameters is a crucial step in creating an artificial neural network.

We can see that the QC ANN performs very well even with less taught parameters thanks to high training accuracy and validation accuracy. Thus, we can effectively train an ANN with a quantum computer. Figure 15.4 shows Cost vs. number of training steps of Classical ANN and QC ANN using NM [5].

15.6   Conclusion

In recent years, arguments in academia and industry have focused heavily on artificial intelligence, particularly as it relates to machine learning and neural network approaches. Although when appropriately trained to solve a specific problem, these algorithms have shown incredible generalisation skills, how and why these algorithms operate as they do continues to baffle academics throughout the world. Despite amazing results, these algorithms will always and forever be limited to the conventional view of the real world.

On the other hand, quantum computations might get beyond this restriction and take advantage of quantum-related phenomena like superposition and entanglement. Although they are still in their infancy, quantum technologies provide a new and intriguing alternative to traditional computing methods, and they may soon achieve practical quantum dominance.

These factors led us to develop this survey, which we hope will provide both the novice and the more knowledgeable reader with insights into a number of fundamental issues in the field of quantum computation, including the qubit, the Gate Model, and the Adiabatic Quantum Computation paradigms, to name a few. In addition, realising that the literature lacks a thorough treatment of the most recent developments in quantum perceptrons and quantum neural networks, we compile, examine, and debate cutting-edge methods pertaining to these subjects. Our research shows that quantum neural networks and algorithms as a whole are still a long way from definitively outperforming traditional ones. Such a goal has been stated far too frequently. However, the search is still ongoing. It is unclear whether quantum devices will take the place of conventional chips as the brains of a new breed of personal computers. The quantum world, however, is now accessible because of recent advancements in quantum hardware and algorithms. This new realm is characterized by occurrences that were utterly unheard of until the last century [6].

Quantum computers have the ability to handle a wide range of complicated issues that are challenging for conventional computers. In this study, we demonstrate that the QC method for training ANN on a quantum computer outperforms classical ANN by a wide margin. To learn the complicated and non-linear patterns in the data, the QC ANN simply utilized a few parameters. It is therefore computationally effective. Deep neural network models for image classification can also be trained using the same training methodology as in this study. As we only need k qubits to represent 2k input values of classical data, the method of employing a quantum computer to train a deep neural network is also thought to be efficient in terms of computing space. As a result, we can optimize with fewer parameters and fewer qubits while still getting decent results. Future work on this project will examine the benefits of QC for deep learning when handling datasets with larger sizes and more dimensions [5].

Glossary

Short Form	Description
QC	Quantum Computing
ANN	Artificial Neural Network
NN	Neural Network
ML	Machine Learning
Qubit	Quantum Bits
GAN	Generative Adversarial Networks

References

1. Abbas, A., Sutter, D., Zoufal, C., Lucchi, A., Figalli, A., & Woerner, S. (2021). The power of quantum neural networks. *Nature Computational Science, 1*(6), 403-409.
2. Oh, S., Choi, J., & Kim, J. (2020, October). A tutorial on quantum convolutional neural networks (QCNN). In *2020 International Conference on Information and Communication Technology Convergence (ICTC)* (pp. 236-239). IEEE.
3. Huang, H. Y., Broughton, M., Cotler, J., Chen, S., Li, J., Mohseni, M., ... & McClean, J. R. (2022). Quantum advantage in learning from experiments. *Science, 376*(6598), 1182-1186.
4. Mangini, S., Tacchino, F., Gerace, D., Bajoni, D., & Macchiavello, C. (2021). Quantum computing models for artificial neural networks. *Europhysics Letters, 134*(1), 10002.
5. Chalumuri, A., Kune, R., & Manoj, B. S. (2020). Training an artificial neural network using qubits as artificial neurons: a quantum computing approach. *Procedia Computer Science, 171*, 568-575.
6. Ezhov, A. A., & Ventura, D. (2000). Quantum neural networks. In *Future directions for intelligent systems and information sciences* (pp. 213-235). Physica, Heidelberg.
7. Mangini, S., Tacchino, F., Gerace, D., Bajoni, D., & Macchiavello, C. (2021). Quantum computing models for artificial neural networks. *Europhysics Letters, 134*(1), 10002.
8. Oh, S., Choi, J., & Kim, J. (2020, October). A tutorial on quantum convolutional neural networks (QCNN). In *2020 International Conference on Information and Communication Technology Convergence (ICTC)* (pp. 236-239). IEEE.
9. Schuld, M., Sinayskiy, I., & Petruccione, F. (2014). The quest for a quantum neural network. *Quantum Information Processing, 13*(11), 2567-2586.
10. Massoli, F. V., Vadicamo, L., Amato, G., & Falchi, F. (2022). A leap among quantum computing and quantum neural networks: A survey. *ACM Computing Surveys (CSUR)*.
11. Ramezani, S. B., Sommers, A., Manchukonda, H. K., Rahimi, S., & Amirlatifi, A. (2020, July). Machine learning algorithms in quantum computing: A survey. In *2020 International Joint Conference on Neural Networks (IJCNN)* (pp. 1-8). IEEE.
12. Abbas, A., Sutter, D., Zoufal, C., Lucchi, A., Figalli, A., & Woerner, S. (2021). The power of quantum neural networks. *Nature Computational Science, 1*(6), 403-409.
13 Kwak, Y., Yun, W. J., Jung, S., & Kim, J. (2021, August). Quantum neural networks: Concepts, applications, and challenges. In *2021 Twelfth International Conference on Ubiquitous and Future Networks (ICUFN)* (pp. 413-416). IEEE.

14 Fawaz, A., Klein, P., Piat, S., Severini, S., & Mountney, P. (2019, July). Training and meta-training binary neural networks with quantum computing. In *Proceedings of the 25th ACM SIGKDD International Conference on Knowledge Discovery & Data Mining* (pp. 1674-1681).

15. Outeiral, C., Strahm, M., Shi, J., Morris, G. M., Benjamin, S. C., & Deane, C. M. (2021). The prospects of quantum computing in computational molecular biology. *Wiley Interdisciplinary Reviews: Computational Molecular Science*, *11*(1), e1481.

16. Tacchino, F., Barkoutsos, P., Macchiavello, C., Tavernelli, I., Gerace, D., & Bajoni, D. (2020). Quantum implementation of an artificial feed-forward neural network. *Quantum Science and Technology*, *5*(4), 044010.

17. Henderson, M., Gallina, J., & Brett, M. (2021). Methods for accelerating geospatial data processing using quantum computers. *Quantum Machine Intelligence*, *3*(1), 1-9.

18. Henderson, M., Shakya, S., Pradhan, S., & Cook, T. (2020). Quanvolutional neural networks: powering image recognition with quantum circuits. *Quantum Machine Intelligence*, *2*(1), 1-9.

19. Marković, D., & Grollier, J. (2020). Quantum neuromorphic computing. *Applied Physics Letters*, *117*(15), 150501.

16

Image Filtering Based on VQA with Quantum Security

Avni Burman*, Bhushan Bawaskar, Harsh Dindorkar and Hrithik Surjan

Department of Computer Science Engineering,
Shri Vaishnav Vidyapeeth Vishwavidyalaya, Indore, India

Abstract

With the increasing application of VQA (Visual Question Answering), a wide range of applications has been introduced and there are also several ongoing researches on VQA. In VQA we build and train our system to give the correct answer for the provided dataset, i.e., the image and question. We have to provide an image and question to the model but during the direct fusion of feature elements of both question (Qi) and image (Vi) there are several problems such as noise in the image and question. If the given image is noisy then there is no accuracy [3]. Both the elements (Qi, Vi) are not in the same space. To solve this we introduce Image filtering, Differential Network and its Fusion. In today's world data is everything, and its protection should be our priority. So, to protect VQA, we are introducing RSA algorithm. RSA algorithm will ensure the security of VQA from any intrusion and will maintain its authenticity.

Keywords: Visual Question Answering (VQA), Differential Network (DN), image filtering, median filter, rsa algorithm, cryptography, quantum security

16.1 Introduction

VQA [1, 2] has flourished in recent years due to its numerous uses. The model effectively merges feature components from both the photos and the questions to complete the VQA assignment. Building a computer system that responds to queries submitted in both an image and natural language

---

*Corresponding author: aburman1510@gmail.com

Romil Rawat, Rajesh Kumar Chakrawarti, Sanjaya Kumar Sarangi, Jaideep Patel, Vivek Bhardwaj, Anjali Rawat and Hitesh Rawat (eds.) Quantum Computing in Cybersecurity, (263–274) © 2023 Scrivener Publishing LLC

is the focus of the research field known as VQA [1, 2]. Recently, VQA has gained popularity as an AI-complete activity that may be utilised in place of visual testing.

Images are filtered using linear and nonlinear algorithms. Picture processing activities that are beneficial are made feasible by image filtering. Unwanted noise and other undesirable elements in an image can be reduced with a filter. Contrary to linear filters, nonlinear filters [3] operate differently. The outcome of nonlinear filters [3] deviates from the previously mentioned rules. Mean Filter is among the easiest filters to use. An image's mean filter average flattening. The noise is masked into the background of the image by replacing each pixel with the mean of the pixels around it. Figure 16.1 shows the Visual Question Answering System.

Some VQA applications require sensitive data which needs to be secured completely, So Confidentiality, Integrity, Availability (CIA) [6, 7] of data is maintained. So, to ensure the security we will be needing modern encryption technique which has multiple keys.

[8–10] The RSA algorithm was developed in 1978 by Rivest, Shamir, and Adleman; thus, the moniker RSA algorithm. This algorithm uses asymmetric cryptography. As an asymmetric cypher, it may operate with both public and private keys, which are two separate keys. By looking at the name, it is obvious that the Public Key is distributed to everyone while the Private Key is kept secret. Prime numbers are employed in RSA, and

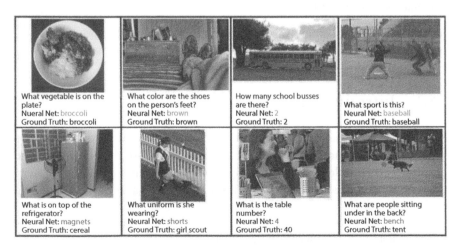

Figure 16.1 Visual Question Answering [4, 5, 12].

because the integers used in this approach are sufficiently large, it is challenging to solve. RSA keys may be 1024 or 2048 bits long, but researchers believe keys more than 1204 bits may soon be cracked.

Quantum cryptography exploits the principles of quantum physics to create a system that is safer and more secure. No one can circumvent this mechanism without the sender or recipient of the communication being aware of it. Since it is impossible to gauge the quantum state of any system without alerting it, quantum cryptography relies on photons and their underlying quantum features to create an impenetrable cryptosystem.

[10–14] Quantum Cryptography provide various benefits like:

1. Secure Communication
2. It is based on laws of physics which makes Quantum Cryptography more secure and sophisticated.
3. Offers multiple methods to increase security.
4. If an unauthorized user tries to read the encoded data, then the quantum state changes and it modifies the expected outcome for the users.

Some limitations of Quantum Cryptography are:

1. Photons may change polarization in transit, which may increase error rates.
2. Maximum range of Quantum Cryptography is between 400km and 500km.
3. Quantum Cryptography uses fiber optic lines and repeaters.
4. It is not possible to send keys to two or more locations in an Quantum Channel.

Existing models fuse image feature element (ViQi) [15, 16] but those solutions largely ignore that, whether Vi and Qi are in the same space and how to decrease the observable noises in Vi and Qi. So, in their model they proposed Differential Networks (DN) and with the tool of DN, then they propose DN based Fusion (DF) for the task of VQA. Figure 16.2 shows Identifying the image model and Figure 16.3 represents RSA internal working.

In the below image it is clear that with the help of VQA, Differential Network and Differential Network–based Fusion (DF) [17, 18] we can easily answer the question which is generated from the image. Figure 16.4 shows the typical RSA algorithm working.

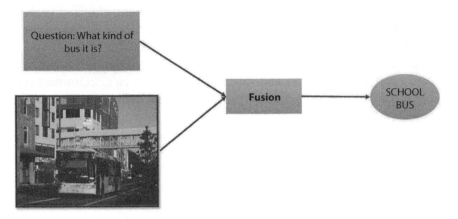

Figure 16.2 Identifying the image [1, 2].

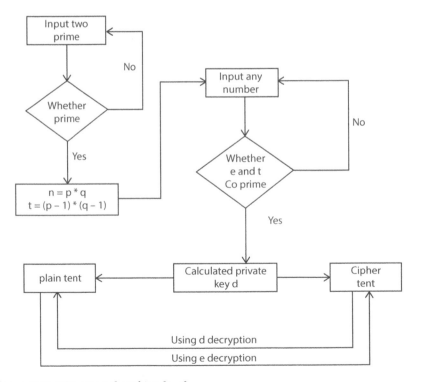

Figure 16.3 RSA internal working [1, 6].

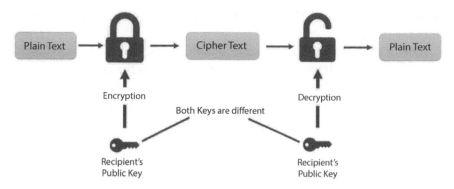

Figure 16.4 Typical RSA algorithm working [6, 7].

ORGANIZATION OF CHAPTER
The rest of the chapter is outlined as follows, Section 16.2 discusses related work, Section 16.3 shows problem statement, Section 16.4 outlines the proposed methodology, and section 16.5 is the result analysis. Section 6 concludes this chapter.

16.2   Related Work

After researching different concepts, we came to know the immense application of VQA, which generates the answer about the question in the form of images and the model fuses feature elements from both images and questions efficiently.

When the feature elements fuses with each other directly then, the solution largely ignores the two points:

1. Whether Vi and Qi are in the same space.
2. How to reduce the observation noises in Vi and Qi.

So, the argument had differences between feature elements [7, 8], like (Vi − Vj) and (Qi − Qj), and the difference operation would be helpful to reduce observation noise. In the paper we have given an image and a related question. The basic structure of existing VQA model consists of three stages: (i) The image and the question are encrypted; (ii) the encrypted image and question elements are fused; (iii) the fused results are sorted to obtain the answer. Fusion as ViQi for linear models and ViQj for bilinear models. In the paper it is said that the difference operation can reduce potential observation noises in Vi and Qi; let us assume that δ is the noise of the feature elements Vi and Vj, then (Vi + δ) − (Vj + δ) can effectively filter the noise.

One of the well-known examples of integer factorization–based algorithm is RSA, which was proposed in 1978 based on the concept of Public Key Cryptography. This algorithm was so good that other researchers were inspired to work in the field of cryptography and they came up with various new cryptographic algorithms with RSA as a base.

Quantum cryptography was originated by Bennett, Bassard and Wiesner. Later, several people contributed to Quantum Cryptography and Quantum key Distribution. So, in this model Differential Networks (DN) and DN-based Fusion (DF) are proposed. As deep research works are done on neural network, there are many different methods introduced to address the VQA task. Here, we have used "Attention-Based Models" [17, 18]. In this model, the important and useful part of input information is selected. Here, we have used this model to validate the working efficiency of differential networks.

One of the most fundamental methods in quantum cryptography is called quantum key distribution. A photon stream is used in quantum computing to transport data. These photons [5] have a characteristic known as a "spin." Spins can be classified as either horizontal, vertical, 45° diagonal, or 45° diagonal. The rectilinear scheme is used for the horizontal and vertical filters, while the diagonal system is used for the two diagonal filters [8, 9]. Figure 16.5 shows the Visual AI System.

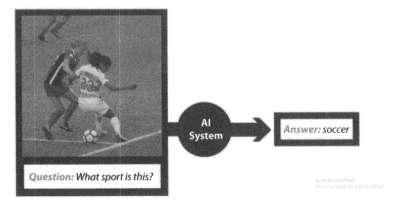

Figure 16.5 Visual AI system [5, 6].

Attention-based VQA models:

DN-based Fusion (DF) model contains three parts:

1. Data embedding encrypts images and questions, respectively.
2. Differential Fusion is the major part of the model, which applies DN-based fusion.
3. Decision making predicts final scores of answers.

16.3   Problem Statement

Differential Networks (DN) proposes DN based-Fusion (DF) [2, 4] for VQA task, if we fuse feature elements Vi and Qi directly. There are certain problems observed during the fusion process such as:

1. Noises are not reduced but they are ignored, so there won't be proper output.
2. The feature elements are not in the same space and accuracy is not achieved as we want the output should be accurate.

With the increasing application of VQA there are so many fields where we have to maintain the security of the data. If all the cryptographic engines stopped functions then a lot of problems occur. When VQA deals with the personal as well as national data than security is an important concern. At this point, all of our important information would be exposed, and it then could be exploited to do unimaginable harm to us all. In a cutting-edge era, VQA has application in each and every sector so as to maintain confidentiality of question, answer so that no intruder can gain access.

16.4   Working

Since we know that security is an important concern in every field, we therefore introduced RSA in VQA, to ensure the Confidentiality and Integrity of the information. Let's try to understand the working of this paper. Initially the question is sent to the algorithm and then it is Encrypted and later decrypted with the help of RSA for analysis of VQA system which will provide us with the answer to the question. Confidentiality [8] of the information from unauthorized people must be maintained because some information is very sensitive and important. Leakage of this information may affect the person, society, community or the whole nation. So, RSA is very much helpful for maintaining the confidentiality of the information.

The answer provided by VQA is then immediately encrypted with the help of RSA and only the authorized person having the right key can decrypt it and gain access to the information. RSA is a strong and powerful algorithm and the chances of an information leak is nil.

16.5   Proposed Methodology Solution

To address the VQA there are several models [11, 15] but they have used the Attention-based model which tries to locate the relevant object and useful information from the input.

In the Visual Question answer, during the direct fusion of the feature elements of the image (Vi) and the question (Qi), i.e., (ViQi) there are some problems of noise and space. Therefore, they have proposed a differential network and with the help of this have used differential based fusion. Firstly, when the model has the image and its respective question then both the question and image will be encoded firstly using GRU [4] and RCNN [6]. After encoding of both is done then with the help of differential network it will produce a different equation; then they will proceed further and the fusion mechanism will be applied by using differential network fusion. So, after all this the model will be able to reduce the problems and will be able to answer correctly.

PROPOSED SOLUTION
In addition to differential networks, we have introduced an application or technique which is "Image Filtering based on VQA".

In the visual Question Answer–based model we have given an image and corresponding question to it. But the main issue we are facing during all this process of Direct fusion is that noises in the image are not reduced and maybe our given input image is noisy.

Therefore, before processing further we have introduced image filtering technique. Basically, filtering is a technique which is used for the reduction of noises that can be salt and pepper or impulsive noise in the image. There are many techniques for the filtering or to reduce the noises from the image. They can be divided into linear and nonlinear filters and both types work in different ways. The nonlinear filter [5–11] is further divided into Min filter, Max filter, and Median filter. But we have used the median filter because it is useful in reducing the salt and pepper noise from the image. So, if the image has noises than it will effectively reduce it, in this the pixel value is replaced by the median value of the neighboring pixel; also, median filter is one of the best to remove salt noises. So, after this filtering of images our image will proceed further. Our image will be encoded with the help of RCNN [12] and the respective question will also be encoded with the help of GRU. Then after encoding both the image and question it will proceed further, and then we have used the Differential Network that will take the differences of the Feature elements of both the image and question because the difference equation will be more reasonable as they are more in the same space, and also if noises are present than it will effectively be ignored. After this there will be a fusion which is based on differential networks and both the image and question feature elements will be fused. After all these tasks, our model will provide a more accurate Answer. Figure 16.6 shows the Image of a fingerprint.

For instance, Figure 16.6 shows two different fingerprints. In the first image we can clearly see that the original fingerprint has a lot of noises, and after applying the image filtering technique based on VQA with the help of median filter right-side fingerprint is now noise free.

RSA algorithm uses logarithmic functions to keep the working complex enough to withstand brute force and streamlined enough to be fast post-deployment. RSA can also encrypt and decrypt general information to securely exchange data along with handling digital signature verification.

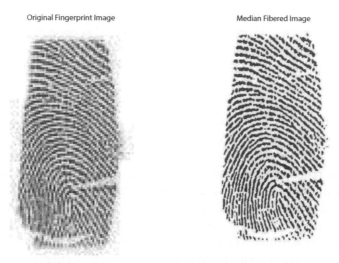

Original Fingerprint Image   Median Fibered Image

Figure 16.6 Image of fingerprint [2, 3, 5–7, 12, 14].

The image above shows the entire procedure of the RSA algorithm. More about this will be explained in the next section.

16.6   Result Analysis

In differential Network based on VQA, the output is produced by fusing the question and answer, with the help of Differential Network fusion based on VQA it will ignore the noises. After adding our technique or application it will produce more accurate output as the noises from the image are being filtered previously with the help of Image Filtering based on VQA technique, and to get more secure output to the authorized user we are using an encryption and decryption technique, i.e., RSA algorithm which encrypts and decrypts text on the basis of different keys which are public and private (for example, public key is like the mail ID of a person, and private ID can be a password of that person which is known by himself); it keys the whole process securely and efficiently.

16.7   Conclusion

VQA is a research area about building a computer system to answer questions presented in an image. But there were certain problems observed during the fusion, such as, noises were not reduced, accuracy was not achieved, and feature elements were not in modality.

There are many algorithms which are advanced version of the quantum key distribution, like the coherent one-way (COW) quantum key distribution, which aim to cover the drawbacks of the original quantum key distribution algorithm.

So, in this research paper, in addition to Differential Network module and Differential Network based fusion, we propose a technique called "Image Filtering". This technique helped us to achieve accurate and more realistic results on our available datasets. After adding our technique, the results we received were more effective and noise free. We used Median Filter technique and that ensured a noise-free and quality image. The reason behind using Median Filter is that it is a nonlinear filter that is useful in reducing salt and pepper noises.

To transfer sensitive VQA information some strong security is needed, and Quantum encryption methods will allow us to secure sensitive information. RSA algorithm is one of the best and secured Cryptographic algorithm. Because of its great security it is not easily breakable and our valuable VQA information will be secure from unauthorized users and other threats.

References

1. Khazaee, F. A. E. Z. E. H., Talebi, H., Almasi Rad, H., & Menhaj, M. B. Deep Modular Multi-Hop CoAttention Networks for Visual Question Answering. Available at https://papers.ssrn.com/sol3/papers.cfm?abstract_id=4221742.

2. Raghavan, R., & John Singh, K. (2022). An enhanced and hybrid fingerprint minutiae feature extraction method for identifying and authenticating the patient's noisy fingerprint. *International Journal of System Assurance Engineering and Management*, 1-14.

3. Khan, H. M., & Venkadesh, P. (2022). Fingerprint Denoising Using Iterative Rule-Based Filter. *Arabian Journal for Science and Engineering*, 1-15.

4. Kavya, D., Jaswanth, K., Chethana, S., Shruti, P., & Sarada, J. (2023). Comparative Analysis of Image Denoising Using Different Filters. In *International Conference on Innovative Computing and Communications* (pp. 271-284). Springer, Singapore.

5. Ismae, A. A., & Baykara, M. (2022). Image Denoising Based on Implementing Threshold Techniques in Multi-Resolution Wavelet Domain and Spatial Domain Filters. *Traitement du Signal*, 39(4).

6. VQA image, Source: https://blog.floydhub.com/asking-questions-to-images-with-deep-learning/

7. Sasirekha, N., and M. Hemalatha. "Quantum cryptography using quantum key distribution and its applications." *Int. J. Eng. Adv. Technol. (IJEAT)* 3.4 (2014).

8. Bhatt, Alekha Parimal, and Anand Sharma. "Quantum cryptography for internet of things security." *Journal of Electronic Science and Technology* 17.3 (2019): 213-220.

9. Marshall, S. P. (2000). Method and apparatus for eye tracking and monitoring pupil dilation to evaluate cognitive activity. U.S. Patent No 6,090,051. Washington, DC: U.S. Patent and Trademark Office.

10. https://newsroom.ibm.com/2019-01-08-IBM-Unveils-Worlds-First-Integrated-Quantum-Computing-System-for-Commercial-Use

11. NaQi, Wei Wei, Jing Zhang, Wei Wang, Jinwei Zhao, Junhuai Li, Peiyi Shen, Xiaoyan Yin, Xiangrong Xiao and Jie Hu, 2013. Analysis and Research of the RSA Algorithm. *Information Technology Journal*, 12: 1818-1824.

12. Xu, X., Fan, C., & Wang, L. (2022). A deep analysis of the image and video processing techniques using nanoscale quantum-dots cellular automata. *Optik*, 260, 169036.

13. Li, H. S., Fan, P., Xia, H., Peng, H., & Long, G. L. (2020). Efficient quantum arithmetic operation circuits for quantum image processing. *Science China Physics, Mechanics & Astronomy*, 63(8), 1-13.

14. Debnath, B., Das, J. C., De, D., Mondal, S. P., Ahmadian, A., Salimi, M., & Ferrara, M. (2020). Security analysis with novel image masking based quantum-dot cellular automata information security model. *IEEE Access*, *8*, 117159-117172.

15. Kalambe, P., & Pande, M. (2022, October). The role of quantum imaging in CT scans for COVID-19 management. In *AIP Conference Proceedings* (Vol. 2519, No. 1, p. 030032). AIP Publishing LLC.

16. Cao, Z., Wang, L., Liang, K., Chai, G., & Peng, J. (2021). Continuous-variable quantum secure direct communication based on gaussian mapping. *Physical Review Applied*, *16*(2), 024012.

17. Debnath, B., Das, J. C., De, D., Ghaemi, F., Ahmadian, A., & Senu, N. (2020). Reversible palm vein authenticator design with quantum dot cellular automata for information security in nanocommunication network. *IEEE Access*, *8*, 174821-174832.

18. Limei, G., Yingbin, Z., & Duan, H. (2021). A fingerprint minutiae extraction method in quantum thinned binary image. *International Journal of Theoretical Physics*, *60*(5), 1883-1894.

17

Quantum Computing Techniques Assessment and Representation

Dewansh Khandelwal[1]*, Nimish Vyas[2], Priyanshi Skaktawat[2],
Vaidehi Anwekar[2], Om Kumar C.U.[3] and D. Jeyakumar[4]

[1]TCS, Mumbai, India
[2]Department of Computer Science Engineering, Shri Vaishnav Vidyapeeth
Vishwavidyalaya, Indore, India
[3]School of Computer Science and Engineering (SCOPE), Vellore Institute
of Technology, Chennai Campus, India
[4]Department of CSE, Dhanalakshmi College of Engineering,
Tambaram, Chennai, India

Abstract

Modern computing technologies such as quantum computing (QC) are based on the amazing happenings of quantum physics. It's a beautiful blend of information theory, computer science, mathematics, and physics. By controlling the behavior of small physical things such as B. tiny particles such as atoms, higher processing power, lower power consumption and exponential speed compared to what conventional computers provide. This paper describes the architecture, hardware, software, types, and algorithms required only for quantum computers (QComp). It shows how QC can improve our lives from many angles, including artificial intelligence, traffic optimization, healthcare, and cybersecurity. In conclusion, we assess the importance, strengths and weaknesses of QComp. Recently, a small quantum computer was built. Focusing on the implications of a general-purpose quantum computer, we recommend studying the beginnings, possibilities, and limitations of today's conventional computers before considering the strengths of new technologies ahead. This knowledge helps us understand potential barriers to the development of novel, cutting-edge technologies. It also keeps us updated on ongoing progress in this area.

Keywords: Quantum computing, cryptography, private keys, quantum key distribution (QKD), information security, digital weapons

*Corresponding author: dewansh3255@gmail.com

Romil Rawat, Rajesh Kumar Chakrawarti, Sanjaya Kumar Sarangi, Jaideep Patel, Vivek Bhardwaj, Anjali Rawat and Hitesh Rawat (eds.) Quantum Computing in Cybersecurity, (275–294) © 2023 Scrivener Publishing LLC

17.1   Introduction

17.1.1   History of Computing

As a result of an evolution, new fields of science and technology are discovered. Functional computing [1, 2] research and development has revolutionized science, technology, and nations in less than a century. Computers today can solve problems quickly and accurately if the input is good and the instructions are informative. It all started during World War II when Alan Turing [3] developed a "Universal Turing Machine [3]", a true general-purpose computer with a storable program model. The power and capabilities of computers and their physical components have increased over time. We now have state-of-the-art technological equipment, thanks to our increased understanding and control over nature and physical systems [4].

17.1.2   Innovative Ways of Computing

Modern computers are cheaper, faster, more efficient, and more powerful than their early counterparts, which were larger, more expensive, and required more power. This is made possible by advances in architecture, hardware, and software running on top of it. A revolutionary type of computation known as QC, based on quantum physics [6, 7], addresses the random and unpredictable nature of the physical universe. Quantum mechanics is a more complete model of physics than classical mechanics, so QC is a more comprehensive model of computation with the ability to address problems that classical computers cannot.

Based on classical arithmetic operations, unlike other classical computers that use binary bits 0 and 1 separately, they use their own qubits, also called "qubits [8]," to store information. Save and process. Quantum computer is the term for computers that use this kind of data processing. Transistors, logic gates, and integrated circuits cannot be used in such small computers. As a result, information about the bits of subatomic particles such as atoms, electrons, photons and ions and their spins and states is used. Therefore, it can use memory efficiently when running in parallel, making it more powerful. Church-Turing theorem [9] can be ignored only by QC. This means that quantum computers (QComp) can run orders of magnitude faster than classical computers [4].

17.1.3   Need for QComp

Any computational problem that can be solved with a classical computer can also be solved with a quantum computer. Church-Turing's paper claims that even conventional computers can handle all the problems facing QComp. In terms of predictability, this means that there is no advantage over conventional computers, but today's conventional computers will not be able to do some of the difficult and impossible tasks in a reasonable amount of time. This requires more computing power. QComp, also called "quantum supremacy [5]," can tackle these problems in a reasonably exponentially short time.

In 1993, Peter Shor [10] demonstrated how QComp may tackle similar issues far more quickly—like in a matter of seconds—without overheating. He created formulas for quickly factoring huge numbers. Since the basis of their computations is the probability of an atom's state prior to its actual knowledge. These have the capacity to process exponentially large amounts of data [21, 22]. It also shows how a real-world quantum computer may decrypt the secret codes used in cryptography. The security of encrypted data and communications can be compromised. Confidential and private information may be disclosed. However, it should also be noted that QComp have more advantages than disadvantages. Therefore, they are still needed and further studies are underway in the hope of a better future.

ORGANIZATION OF CHAPTER

The rest of the chapter is organized as follows. Section 17.2 presents the fundamentals of quantum computing; section 17.3 presents the properties of quantum computing; section 17.4 highlights the topography of quantum computing; section 17.5 presents the architecture of quantum computing; section 17.6 shows quantum algorithms; section 17.7 shows the design limitations of quantum computers; section 17.8 describes the different types of quantum computers; section 17.9 introduces the benefits of quantum computing; section 17.10 highlights the disadvantages of quantum computing; section 17.11 presents applications of quantum computing; section 17.12 shows the main challenges of quantum computing; finally, section 17.13 presents the conclusion of the chapter.

17.2   Fundamentals of QC

During the construction of conventional computers, it was realized that the performance of transistors, especially as they became smaller, would be affected by noise if some kind of quantum phenomenon occurred. They did everything to exclude quantum phenomena from their circuit. Instead of ordinary bits, QComp use a new technique and even use quantum phenomena. It uses quantum bits, similar to regular bits, and has two quantum states that can be 0 or 1 [11]. However, due to certain quantum characteristics, it is conceivable that it is in these two states at the same time, hence the concept of superimposed bits [6].

17.3   Properties of QC

Quantum elements do not exist in a completely defined state in quantum physics. When no one is looking, it appears to be a particle but behaves more like a wave. Several fascinating scientific facts are the result of the dual nature of particles. The state of any quantum object can be described as a wave function or the sum of all conceivable participating states. These states are coherent because all the interferences of the states involved can be positive or negative. Information can be extracted from observations of quantum objects as they interact with a larger physical system. Quantum measurement refers to this type of observation for quantum objects. By causing disruption of the quantum state, the measurement can lead to information loss.

The properties of quantum things include some of them. In the context of QC, qubits are the quantum objects in question. The Schrödinger equation [18–20], which describes how the energy environment affects the wave function of the system [12], controls the evolution of any quantum system [21, 20]. The Hamiltonian of the system, which is a mathematical description of the energy felt by all the forces felt by all the components of the system, acts as the medium. Any managed quantum system must first be isolated from the uncontrollable forces of the universe and must allocate all of its energy to this single isolated region. The whole system cannot be isolated. However, the exchange of information and energy can be reduced.

17.3.1   Behaviour

The conceptual instructions and mathematical representations that characterize the behavior of the particle are called features. To store, represent, and process data exponentially faster than any classical computer, QComp exploit three fundamental features of quantum mechanics. The following three characteristics are listed [4]:

17.3.2   Superposition

The ability of a quantum system in which a quantum particle or qubit can exist in two separate places, or in other words, in more than one state at the same time is called superposition [15–17] in QC. It differs significantly from their classic binary-bound counterparts in that it provides extremely fast parallel processing. Information that occurs in two states at the same time is stored in the QC system. Using a laser, the qubits are transferred to a superposition state allowing them to store 0 and 1 simultaneously [4].

17.3.3   Entanglement

Entanglement is one of the important aspects of QC. It refers to a significant relationship between two quantum bits (physical characteristics of the system). Even though they are separated by great distances, such as at opposite ends of the universe, the qubits are connected in an instantaneous, seamless connection. They are intertwined or are characterized with each other. The fact is that the state of one particle can affect the state of another. Therefore, Qubit can communicate effectively. Once entangled with each other, they will not be able to separate from each other without remaining connected [4, 13].

17.3.4   Interference

QComp, like regular physical wave interference, have interference properties. Wave interference occurs when two waves come into contact in the same medium. When the waves are aligned in the same direction, the amplitudes cancel each other out, creating a wave known as constructive interference. When the waves [14] align in opposite directions, the amplitudes cancel each other out, creating a wave known as destructive interference. The pure wave can be larger or smaller than the original wave [15–17] depending on the interference pattern. It can cause quantum interference. Due to the superposition, each particle can pass through its own path and obstruct the direction of the path if it passes through both slits at the same time [4].

17.4   Topography of QC

Just a few other technologies impacted by quantum phenomena include quantum information science, quantum communication, and quantum metrology. All these technological breakthroughs are interconnected and have the potential to regulate and change entire quantum systems. They use comparable technology, physical theory, and methodology.

Quantum Information Science - The goal of quantum information science [13, 14] is to find efficient methods of storing information in quantum systems. Statistics on quantum mechanics and related constraints are presented. It serves as the foundation for all other applications, including QC, communications, networking, sensing and measurement.

Quantum Communication and Networking [21] - To enable communication between QComp, quantum communication and networks focus on discussing or exchanging information by encoding it in a quantum system.

Comparison key	Classical computer	Quantum computer
Basis of computing	Large scale integrated multipurpose computer based on classical physics	High speed parallel computer based on quantum mechanics
Information storage	Bits based information storage using voltage/charge	Quantum bit (qubit) based information storage using electron spin
Bit values	Bits having a value of either 0 or 1 and can have a single value at any instant	Qubits having a value of 0.1 or sometimes negative and can have both values at the same time
Number of possible states	The number of possible states is 2 which is either 0 or 1	The number of possible states is infinite since it can hold combinations of 0 or 1 along with some complex information
Output	Determine (reception of computation on the same input gives the same output)	Probabilistic - (repetition of computation on superposed states gives probabilistic answers)
Gates used for processing	Logic gates process the information sequentially, i.e. AND, OR, NOT, etc.	Quantum logic gates process the information parallel
Scope of possible solutions	Defined and limited answers due to the algorithm's design	Probabilistic and multiple answers are considered due to superposition and entanglement properties
Operations	Operations use Boolean Algebra	Operations use linear algebra are represented with unitary matrices
Circuit implementation	Circuits implemented in macroscopic technologies (e.g. CMOS) that are fast and scalable	Circuits implemented in microscopic technologies (e.g. nuclear magnetic resonance) that are slow and delicate

Figure 17.1 Difference between classical computer and quantum computer [4].

The branch of quantum communication known as quantum cryptography uses features of quantum mechanics to create a secure communication system.

Quantum Sensing and Measurement [22] - The research and development of quantum systems is called quantum sensing [11] and measurement [13]. Such a device can be used to measure important physical parameters [15] (such as electric and magnetic fields, temperature, etc.) its extreme for harmful agents from the environment. Qubits serve as the basis for quantum sensors, which are implemented using experimental quantum systems.

The main focus of this research is on QC, taking advantage of the superposition, entanglement, and interference of quantum physics to perform calculations. A quantum computer is generally defined as a physical device made up of a collection of qubits that must be kept isolated from the outside world in order for their quantum state to remain consistent until a computation is performed. These qubits are arranged and manipulated to apply an algorithm and produce a high probability result from a measurement of its final state [4]. Figure 17.1 shows the difference between classical and QComp.

17.5   The Architecture of QC

- APPLICATION CLASS - It does not belong to QComp. It is used to represent user interfaces, quantum computer operating systems, cryptographic environments, and more. It is needed to create efficient quantum algorithms. It is hardware independent.
- CLASSIC CLASS - Quantum algorithm [14] improved and converted into micro instructions. In addition, it processes the quantum state measurements returned by the lower layer hardware and converts them to a classical algorithm for the output.
- DIGITAL LAYER - It converts micro instructions into pulses (signals) required by qubits, acting as quantum logic gates. It is a digital representation of the analog pulses needed in the lower layers. To combine the consequences of the quantum process with the final product, it also provides feedback in the form of quantum measurements for the classical layer above.

- ANALOG LAYER - To provide a voltage signal of wave-like amplitude and phase to the lower layer where qubit operations can be performed,
- QUANTUM LAYER - It is integrated on the same chip as the processing layer. digital and analog. It is kept at room temperature and used to store qubits (absolute). This section deals with error correction. The efficiency of the computer is determined by this class.

Digital processing, analog processing and quantum processing are the three levels that make up a quantum processing unit (QPU) [15]. QComp include the QPU and the classical layer. The digital and analog layers operate at room temperature [4]. Figure 17.2 shows the architecture of QC.

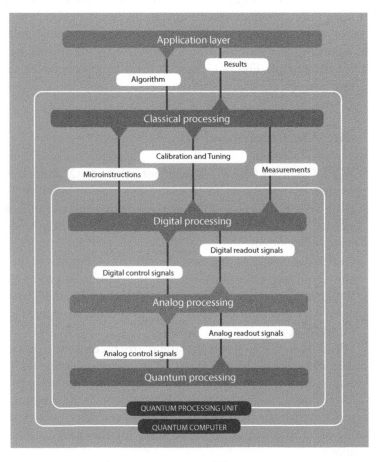

Figure 17.2 Architecture of quantum computing [5].

17.5.1   Hardware and Software of QCOMP

For operations involving data, networks, and users, an interface between QComp and conventional computers is required. Quantum qubit systems require organized control that can be handled by a traditional computer to function usefully. Four layers of concepts are used to build the hardware components of analog QComp. The "quantum data plane", where the qubits are located, comes first. The "Control and Measurement Plane" is responsible for performing all the necessary operations and measurements on the qubits. The third is the "control processor blueprint", which specifies the order of these operations and the results of the measurements to guide the next quantum operations required by the algorithm. The last is the "host processor", a traditional computer running a traditional operating system. The last type is called a "host processor", which is a traditional computer that runs a traditional operating system and is responsible for managing the user interface, networking, and large storage data structures. It provides a high bandwidth link used for CPU throttling [11].

In addition to hardware, QComp also require software components. It is similar to the old computers. In order for programmers to be able to create algorithms and transfer them to the hardware used by QComp, many new tools are needed, including programming languages. These tools also include other means that can evaluate, optimize, debug and test programs. Any intended quantum architecture should be considered when developing a programming language. There are many previous technologies on the internet that have been developed to enable QComp. These tools should be designed in an abstract way so that programmers can think more in terms of algorithms and less about the details of quantum physics. The program should be flexible enough to keep up with technological and algorithmic improvements. The development of a complete software architecture is one of the main problems facing QC. In addition to the programming language, there must be simulation tools to model quantum operations, quantum state monitoring, and optimization tools to determine the qubit resources required to run quantum algorithms. effectively differ. The main goal is to reduce the number of qubits and hardware operations required [4].

17.6   Quantum Algorithm

A set of rules or a series of instructions that must be followed to perform an operation or a calculation is called an algorithm. A problem must be solved step by step, especially when using a computer. The term "quantum algorithm" refers to any algorithm that can run on a quantum computer. In general, QComp are capable of implementing all classical algorithms. To be called a quantum algorithm, algorithms must have at least one single quantum step due to superposition or entanglement.

A quantum circuit is a defining property of quantum algorithms. Each phase of the quantum algorithm functions as a quantum gate in the quantum circuit, a model of QC. An operation called a quantum gate can be performed on any number of qubits. The qubit's quantum state is changed. Depending on the number of qubits it is applied to at once, it can be classified as a single gate or multiple qubits. Qubit measurement is used to define a quantum circuit.

By replacing the cost of measurement at the end of an algorithm, an algorithm that runs on the simulator instead of on the hardware is very efficient in terms of execution time. Also known as simulation optimization. By comparing a quantum algorithm with a classical method, reversibility is always possible. It turns out that a quantum circuit can be propagated in reverse, undoing all actions performed by the forward motion of the circuit, if the measurement is omitted.

Problem Insolvability states that any problem that cannot be solved by classical algorithms cannot be solved by quantum algorithms. However, compared to conventional algorithms, these algorithms are much faster at solving problems. Shor algorithm and Grover algorithm are two examples of quantum algorithms. While Grover's method is used to explore large unordered lists or unstructured databases and is four times faster than the classical approach, Shor's algorithm is used to compute very large numbers ten times faster than the best-known conventional procedures.

The many quantum algorithms available are:

- Fourier Transform – quantum-based algorithm.
- Quantum algorithms based on amplitude amplification.
- Algorithm based on quantum steps.
- Hybrid quantum/classical algorithms.

17.7   Design Limitations of Quantum Computer

1. QComp have exponential computing power, which can be achieved by identifying and fixing any design flaws that could reduce their quality. There are four significant design restrictions. The first restriction is that only when all the qubits get

entangled with one another do the number of coefficients in Dirac notation, which describes the state of a quantum computer, increase exponentially with the number of qubits. Qubits must adhere to the entanglement property, which requires that any qubit's state be connected to the states of other qubits, in order for QC to operate to its full potential. Since it is difficult to create a direct linkage between qubits, it cannot be done directly.

2. The second limitation is due to a concept known as the "non-replicating principle", which cannot clone an entire quantum system. Since the state of the qubits or set of qubits is transferred to another set of qubits instead of being copied, there is a risk that arbitrary information will be removed from the original qubits. An important part of classical computing is creating and storing copies of intermediate states or incomplete results in memory. But a new approach is needed for QComp. To know which bits are loaded and queried in the quantum system's memory to accomplish its task, there are quantum algorithms that help to access the classical bits from the storage.

3. The third limitation is the result of the fact that qubit operations have no protection against noise. Because they are not ignored by the underlying gate operations, small anomalies in the gate operation or input signal build up over time and affect the state of the system. This can negatively impact the measurements, consistency and computational accuracy of quantum systems, as well as the integrity of their qubit operations.

4. The final limitation is that the quantum machine cannot realize its complete state even after it has stopped working. Suppose a quantum computer has been configured with an initial set of qubits stacked with all other states. When a function is applied to this state, a new quantum state is created containing information about the value of the function for each input that can be used. The measurement of this quantum system will not reveal this information. To create a successful quantum algorithm, one must manipulate the system so that the states produced by mathematical operations have a higher probability of being measured than any other possible outcome.

17.8   Different Categories of Quantum Computer

17.8.1   Analog Quantum Computer

By adjusting the analog values in the Hamiltonian representation, this kind of system works. Quantum gates are not used. It includes adiabatic QC, quantum simulation, and quantum annealing. In quantum annealing, an initial set of qubits gradually changes the energy encountered by the system until the problem parameters defined by Hamilton are reached. This is done to obtain the final state of the qubit corresponding to the solution of the problem with the greatest probability. An initial set of qubits in the Hamilton ground state are used by the adiabatic quantum computer to perform the calculations. Hamilton is then modified slowly enough to keep the qubits in the ground state or lowest possible energy throughout the computation [7].

17.8.2   NISQ Gate-Based Computer

The noisy intermediate-scale quantum is called NISQ. NISQ Digital Calculator is another name for it. These systems are gate-based, operate on a group of qubits without full error correction, and cannot constrain all errors. To prevent discretization and gate errors from obscuring the results, calculations must be performed so that they can be completed in fewer full steps while remaining realistic on a quantum system with minimal noise [7].

17.8.3   Gate-Based Quantum Computer with Full Error Correction

With the implementation of the quantum error correction algorithm, these computers can also perform gate-based operations on the set of qubits. It reduces or corrects the system noise that develops during the computation phase. Incomplete signals, device tampering, or unwanted binding of qubits to the environment or to each other are examples of errors. The system seems legit and correct for all calculations because the error has been reduced to a very low level. The existence of well-defined two-level systems that can be used as qubits, the ability to initialize these qubits, the discontinuity long enough to perform error correction and computation, common quantum gates for all quantum calculations, and the ability to measure individual quantum bits without affecting the other bits are all requirements for such QComp.

17.9   Advantages of QC

- Researchers predict that QComp will be able to solve difficult mathematical problems that conventional computers cannot solve in a reasonable time.
- It provides the computing power needed to process and understand the extremely large volumes of data (2.5 exabytes per day, or 5 million laptops) generated globally.
- It can work in parallel and consume less electricity thanks to a phenomenon known as "quantum tunneling", which can reduce power consumption by up to 100-1000 times.
- Any classical computer is "thousands of times" slower than a general-purpose quantum computer. For example, a quantum computer created by Google is 100 million times faster than any classical computer it currently has in the lab.
- Since it has been kept cool inside the quantum system at a maximum of 0.2 Kelvin for stability, it can solve difficult problems without overheating.
- It can quickly detect the optimal route and plan trains and planes, among other optimization-related problems. Moreover, it will be able to calculate 1 trillion moves per second. The most secure and impregnable encryption methods will be broken by QComp. But it will also create backups that cannot be compromised.
- It has the potential to revolutionize industries such as oil and medicine. The development of new drugs will become possible. The market algorithms of financial institutions could be improved. Sooner or later, artificial intelligence will develop [8].

17.10   Disadvantages of QC

- Today's Internet of Things (IoT) will become less secure due to the rise of QC. Attacks are possible using cryptographic techniques, databases of public and private institutions, banks and defense systems. Given these details, QComp may not be good for the future.
- QComp will work differently from traditional computers and cannot completely replace them. Since computers

normally perform certain tasks like email, Excel, etc., better than QComp.

- It's not completely invented yet because only one part is used and people still dream about what it looks like.
- It is very error prone. Atoms and electrons are subatomic particles subject to all kinds of vibrations. As a result, noise, malfunction, and even failure may occur. This leads to "decoherence", i.e., loss of quantum coherence.
- Quantum processors are extremely unstable and difficult to test. The temperature of the quantum computer is controlled at 0.2 Kelvin (absolute Kelvin), which is almost lower than the temperature of the universe, for stability reasons. Maintaining and controlling such a temperature is quite difficult. The main challenge was to develop it truly as a personal computer while keeping the consumer's budget in mind. They will first be supplied to major industries before entering the retail market [9].

17.11   Applications of QC

For QComp, a series of quantum speed-enhancing algorithms have been developed following fundamental mathematical techniques such as the Fourier transform and Hamiltonian simulation, among others. For most algorithms to provide meaningful functions, a significant number of the highest quality qubits and error correction are required. Since this is not feasible, these algorithms are created in groups rather than a single integrated application [10].

Research is still ongoing on the usefulness or applicability of QComp. It is expected that these applications will require fewer qubits and less code to operate. Due to the unique properties of qubits, it is possible to develop algorithms that can run faster on QComp. Some of the major uses that will emerge in the near future are described below.

- CRYPTOGRAPHY
  Many important aspects of the internet and computer security, including electronic commerce and electronic secrets, rely on encryption and difficult-to-decipher mathematical formulas, including the breakdown of extremely large numbers into large numbers. prime numbers (RSA technique). It is supplemented by using a regular calculator to go through

all the elements imaginable, which is very time consuming. AES, ECDSA and other modern algorithms, other than RSA, are impenetrable even to very powerful computers. Therefore, breaking them would be much more expensive and less practical. All these tasks can be performed by much faster QComp [11].

- OPTIMIZATION PROBLEM
  Finding the most efficient solution to a problem out of all that might exist is the meaning of optimization. This can be done by minimizing both the error and the available steps. Optimization problems are best solved by QComp. There are many quantum algorithms and quantum optimization techniques that can improve the optimization problems currently solved by conventional computers. Quantum data fitting, quantum semi-deterministic programming, and quantum combinatorics optimization are some of them [10].

- ARTIFICIAL INTELLIGENCE
  Handling huge, complex data sets is the key to artificial intelligence. It is responsible for understanding, reasoning, and learning. It keeps learning until it no longer makes mistakes or shows flaws in its work. Learning also takes a lot of effort and time. But it can be simpler and more precise thanks to QC. Since traditional computers only allow a data set of a certain size to be used to train the training model, this limits the computation time. These models can be trained using a large dataset on a quantum computer without experiencing exponential latency. It will be more accurate as it uses more data during training. To increase the accuracy and quality of the output of QComp, generalized models generate outputs such as images, sounds, and other data [12].

- QUANTUM SIMULATION
  In the fields of quantum chemistry and materials science, it is very important. Whether or not an external electric or magnetic field exists, this problem must be solved using the ground state energies of the electrons and their wavefunctions. Everything in chemistry, from the structure of atoms and electrons to the rate at which chemical reactions occur, can be reproduced extremely efficiently. When it comes to this, conventional computers often do not reach the level of accuracy required to estimate the rate of a chemical reaction [6].

In addition, it can be used in industries such as medicine and health care, chemical catalysts, energy storage, pharmaceutical development and utility displays.

17.12 Major Challenges in QC

1. The good news is that, unlike conventional computers, quantum states with the same amount of quantum bits can cover all conceivable states at any given time and operate in space. getting bigger and bigger. However, all qubits must continue to be connected to use this region. Even with these advancements, an upgrade is still needed. The bad news is that producing new, high-quality qubits does not guarantee the development of fault-tolerant QComp or their efficient application; there are still obstacles in its way [13].

2. Qubits do not have the ability to naturally filter out noise. Quantum systems are therefore more prone to error. It represents a discontinuity. How QComp can deal with unwanted biases or noise is the biggest challenge. Unlike QComp, which cannot produce error-free results because errors occur in physical circuits, classical computers can produce error-free results by simply setting their state to off or "0". Qubits will gradually lose both their connection (entanglement) and their information. For such systems, the error rate considered as a design factor should also be improved in large qubit systems. However, qubits are precisely controlled and protected from the outside environment in a supercooled refrigerator or a vacuum chamber to make them stable and error-free [13].

3. Qubits fall between binary and digital in a number of ways. It also has similar qualities. Considering the input signal value of 0.8 is 1, the gate can eliminate noise. However, since any value between 0 and 1 is significant, it is acceptable to use it in an analog signal. There is no way to detect noise or corruption in the signal. Because 0.8 can be 0.8 with no error or 1 with error. The stickiness of the quantum computation results can be affected by assuming zero error, as Gates did, or by applying a noise value even when there is none. Therefore, methods such as quantum error correction

are needed, similar to logic error correction in conventional computers.

4. On quantum systems, quantum error correction techniques can be used. However, quantum error correction requires administrative overhead, such as a large number of qubits and their basic operations, and often requires additional resources. Furthermore, generating input quantum states for big data input problems is very time consuming, takes up computational time and negates the benefits of quantum mechanics [14].

5. Another difficulty in developing quantum algorithms is that they must be completely unique in their design, since processing speed depends on the architecture of the algorithm. The number of qubits used must be reflected in the architecture of the algorithm.

6. To create and debug quantum systems, the development of additional software tools is necessary. This will help explain unresolved issues and move the design forward [4].

7. Since classical computers rely on memory and intermediate machine states, debugging quantum hardware and software is important. The state cannot be directly copied for later evaluation in the case of quantum computation, and measuring the intermediate state may interrupt it. Therefore, it is very important to develop new debugging techniques [4].

17.13   Conclusion

Modern computer systems, such as QComp, are based on the amazing facts of quantum physics. It is a spectacular synthesis of information theory, computer science, mathematics and physics. Compared to traditional computers, it promises better processing power, cheaper power consumption, and exponential speed by influencing the behavior of microscopic physical entities such as atoms. The paper discusses the architecture, hardware, software, types and algorithms required by QComp. It demonstrates how QComp has the potential to improve our lives in many ways, including artificial intelligence, traffic management, medical applications, and cybersecurity. Finally, we reached an agreement on the relevance, advantages, and disadvantages of QComp. Small QComp have been built recently.

References

1. https://www.intechopen.com/chapters/73811
2. https://www.sciencedaily.com/releases/2017/09/170913192957.htm
3. https://www.ibm.com/topics/quantum-computing#:~:text=Quantum%20 computing%20is%20a%20rapidly,available%20to%20thousands%20of%20 developers.
4. https://www.allaboutcircuits.com/technical-articles/fundamentals-of-quantum-computing/#:~:text=Quantum%20computing%20focuses%20 on%20the,entanglement%20to%20perform%20data%20operations
5. https://www.visualcapitalist.com/three-types-quantum-computers/
6. Gyongyosi, L., & Imre, S. (2019). A survey on quantum computing technology. *Computer Science Review*, 31, 51-71.
7. National Academies of Sciences, Engineering, and Medicine. (2019). Quantum computing: progress and prospects.
8. Almudever, C. G., Lao, L., Fu, X., Khammassi, N., Ashraf, I., Iorga, D., ... & Bertels, K. (2017, March). The engineering challenges in quantum computing. In *Design, Automation & Test in Europe Conference & Exhibition (DATE)*, 2017 (pp. 836-845). IEEE.
9. MacLennan, B. J. (2020). Topographic representation for quantum machine learning. Quantum Machine Learning, 6, 11.
10. Geyer, S., Camenzind, L. C., Czornomaz, L., Deshpande, V., Fuhrer, A., Warburton, R. J., ... & Kuhlmann, A. V. (2021). Self-aligned gates for scalable silicon quantum computing. *Applied Physics Letters*, 118(10), 104004.
11. Sete, E. A., Zeng, W. J., & Rigetti, C. T. (2016, October). A functional architecture for scalable quantum computing. In *2016 IEEE International Conference on Rebooting Computing (ICRC)* (pp. 1-6). IEEE.
12. National Academies of Sciences, Engineering, and Medicine. (2019). Quantum computing: progress and prospects.
13. Ryan, C. A., Johnson, B. R., Ristè, D., Donovan, B., & Ohki, T. A. (2017). Hardware for dynamic quantum computing. *Review of Scientific Instruments*, 88(10), 104703.
14. Mueck, L. (2017). Quantum software. *Nature*, 549(7671), 171-171.
15. Mills, D., Sivarajah, S., Scholten, T. L., & Duncan, R. (2021). Application-motivated, holistic benchmarking of a full quantum computing stack. *Quantum*, 5, 415.
16. Takeshita, T., Rubin, N. C., Jiang, Z., Lee, E., Babbush, R., & McClean, J. R. (2020). Increasing the representation accuracy of quantum simulations of chemistry without extra quantum resources. *Physical Review X, 10*(1), 011004.
17. Motta, M., & Rice, J. E. (2022). Emerging quantum computing algorithms for quantum chemistry. *Wiley Interdisciplinary Reviews: Computational Molecular Science, 12*(3), e1580.
18. Yamazaki, T., Matsuura, S., Narimani, A., Saidmuradov, A., & Zaribafiyan, A. (2018). Towards the practical application of near-term quantum computers in

quantum chemistry simulations: A problem decomposition approach. *arXiv preprint arXiv:1806.01305.*

19. Ryabinkin, I. G., Yen, T. C., Genin, S. N., & Izmaylov, A. F. (2018). Qubit coupled cluster method: a systematic approach to quantum chemistry on a quantum computer. *Journal of Chemical Theory and Computation, 14*(12), 6317-6326.

20. Google AI Quantum and Collaborators*†, Arute, F., Arya, K., Babbush, R., Bacon, D., Bardin, J. C., ... & Zalcman, A. (2020). Hartree-Fock on a superconducting qubit quantum computer. *Science, 369*(6507), 1084-1089.

21. Flam-Shepherd, D., Wu, T. C., Gu, X., Cervera-Lierta, A., Krenn, M., & Aspuru-Guzik, A. (2022). Learning interpretable representations of entanglement in quantum optics experiments using deep generative models. *Nature Machine Intelligence, 4*(6), 544-554.

22. Gill, S. S., Kumar, A., Singh, H., Singh, M., Kaur, K., Usman, M., & Buyya, R. (2022). Quantum computing: A taxonomy, systematic review and future directions. *Software: Practice and Experience, 52*(1), 66-114.

18

Quantum Computing Technological Design Along with Its Dark Side

Divyam Pithawa[1]*, Sarthak Nahar[1], Vivek Bhardwaj[2], Romil Rawat[3], Ruchi Dronawat[4] and Anjali Rawat[5]

[1]Department of Computer Science Engineering, Shri Vaishnav Vidyapeeth Vishwavidyalaya, Indore, India
[2]Department of Computer Science and Engineering, Manipal University Jaipur, Jaipur, Rajasthan, India
[3]Department of Computer Science and Engineering, SVIIT, SVVV, Indore, India
[4]Computer Science and Engineering Department, Sagar Institute of Research and Technology, Bhopal, India
[5]Apostelle Overseas Education, Ujjain, India

Abstract

Quantum Computing (QC) addresses problems that are much too complex for traditional computers by using quantum physics. Paul Benioff, a physicist, coined the phrase "Quantum Computing" back in the 1980s. Since the invention of the term, we have come along a long way in the field of QC. In the 1980s, Benioff suggested a quantum mechanical model of the Turing machine. These days, QC is significantly more powerful than even the most powerful traditional supercomputer.

We never know what the future will bring for QC; it's merely the beginning. Technology as a whole is neither good nor evil; how we use it is entirely up to us. The emerging field of quantum technology has the potential to disrupt a wide range of human activities. The dark side of it is that although it doesn't now have the computing power to crack encryption keys, future versions may. The underpinnings of internet privacy and commerce could be threatened. This chapter will look at QC and its fields, their state of development and what can be expected from them, how they can be misused, and its dark side.

Keywords: Quantum computing, quantum cryptography and security, quantum attacks, Qubits superposition, quantum artificial intelligence

*Corresponding author: divyampithawa@gmail.com

Romil Rawat, Rajesh Kumar Chakrawarti, Sanjaya Kumar Sarangi, Jaideep Patel, Vivek Bhardwaj, Anjali Rawat and Hitesh Rawat (eds.) Quantum Computing in Cybersecurity, (295–312) © 2023 Scrivener Publishing LLC

18.1   Introduction

A family of physical devices known as quantum computers (Qcom) are capable of high-speed mathematical and logical operations as well as the storage and processing of quantum information in accordance with the rules of quantum physics. A device is referred to as a quantum computer when its processing and computation are based on quantum information and carried out using quantum algorithms [23]. The operations of quantum computing (QC) can make use of quantum mechanical phenomena like superposition, entanglement, and interference. The tools that carry out QC are called Qcom.

Modern Quantum Technologies (QT) are once again poised to revolutionize everyday life. The second wave of quantum computer harnesses aspects of subatomic particle behavior called "superposition" and "entanglement". The phenomenon of a particle existing in two or more states simultaneously is known as superposition [22]. Even when two particles are separated by thousands of kilometers, they can become so entangled that they function as one cohesive system rather than two individual parts. Beyond what is now possible, Qcom can boost processing capacity and speed by taking advantage of these properties.

Classical computers are based on "bits" – units of data with a single binary value of either a 0 or 1, which make up all apps and websites and their content, Qcom use subatomic particles like electrons or photons. They are called "qubits" – quantum bits [10], which represent data as 1s, 0s, or the quantum state between the two. With the ability to address more data at a time, Qcom become tremendously powerful tools for a variety of fields.

The majority of existing cryptography might be broken by a new form of computer that is based on quantum physics rather than more conventional electronics, which is why cybersecurity researchers and analysts are understandably concerned. Communications would become just as insecure as if they weren't encoded at all as a result of this.

The frequency of large-scale data breaches will rise in the not-too-distant future. Because hackers would be able to utilize the technology to decode data they have already stolen, Qcom will also renew the vulnerabilities from previous breaches.

A quantum revolution is right around the corner. The emergence of Qcom over the next ten years will provide humanity with unmatched processing power and all the benefits that come along with it. This poses difficulties, though, as it will make today's cybersecurity ineffective.

The emerging field of quantum technology has the ability to disrupt a wide range of human activities. Quantum technologies have two distinct implications. It's all up to us how we use it.

Hackers will be able to decrypt public keys and bypass the security of practically any encrypted device or system with the help of Qcom. Uncertainty surrounds the precise timing of a Cyber Doomsday [25] brought on by QC, although it may occur in as little as ten years.

Nevertheless, the quantum terrorism [12] threat is the new dark side of QC that will give security experts some sleepless nights.

A countdown to April 14, 2030, the day by which the Cloud Security Alliance (CSA), the world's top organization for defining standards, certifications, and best practices to help ensure a secure cloud computing environment, predicts that a quantum computer will be able to breach current cybersecurity infrastructure, has already been started [1].

ORGANIZATION OF CHAPTER

The rest of the chapter is outlined as follows. Section 18.2 is about related work, section 18.3 shows the history and evolution of quantum computers, section 18.4 shows the components and concepts that make quantum computers possible, section 18.5 shows the plans for the future development of quantum computers, section 18.6 shows the dark side of quantum computers, section 18.7 shows the plans for protection in quantum era, and section 18.8 concludes this chapter.

18.2   Related Work

The research in [2] aims to synthesize basic fundamental studies concerning quantum cybersecurity that can emerge both as a threat and solution to critical cybersecurity issues based on a systematic study. QC findings can provide the most unforeseen risks to cybersecurity; cybersecurity experts propose that it may be used to improve cybersecurity concerns.

The paper [3] focuses on the impact of QC on the world, according to the authors "the quantum race is a dangerous one, as it will contribute positively to solving big problems, but there is a dark side to QC, too."

In spite of the fact that the authors of paper [4] on data security in the post-quantum era claim that it has many uses in 5G and other channels, these functionalities put many current security systems, particularly asymmetric key cryptography schemes like the Diffie-Hellman key exchange protocol, the Digital Signature Standard, elliptic-curve cryptography, and the Rivest-Shamir-Adleman (RSA) encryption algorithm, at serious risk. This paper [5] discusses the threat of QC to RSA and other popular encryption methods and proposes safe alternatives that can be useful in the post-quantum era. According to the authors, "there are a number of barriers that prevent Qcom from becoming fully developed in the status quo like

Accuracy, Environmental factors, and Phase error". But still, despite these hurdles, Google recently announced that its D-Wave quantum computer was functional and contained over 1,000 qubits, but still, we are years, or even decades away from when Qcom can be capable of the aforementioned cryptanalysis.

Future blockchain technology would be continuously threatened by the following factors, as per this article [6]: 1) faster nonce creation; 2) faster hash collision search; 3) override the security of traditional encryption.

A few decades is the maximum lifetime of any significant technological or scientific bubble, according to Mikhail Dyaknov [7]. In addition, as time passes, those who suggested this technology will grow older and less ardent, while the younger developers will seek stuff entirely different and may succeed.

Sayantan Gupta *et al.* [8] showed how position-based cryptography's entire security may be compromised by an adversary and also suggested and put position-based quantum cryptography's optimal eavesdropping scenario into practice. Mohammad Shahbaz Khan *et al.* [9] discussed the QC and various applications of Qcom like quantum cryptography, quantum teleportation, quantum communication.

18.3   History and Evolution of QCOM

A. History of Qcom

> 1980: Paul Benioff, a physicist, suggested a quantum mechanical interpretation of the Turing machine.
>
> 1986: An early iteration of the quantum circuit notation was proposed by Feynman. In a quantum circuit, a computation is represented as a series of quantum gates, measurements, initializations of qubits to predetermined values, and optionally additional operations.
>
> 1994: Dan Simon research showed that Qcom could be exponentially faster.
>
> 1998: Isaac Chuang *et al.* developed the first operational two-qubit quantum computer.
>
> 1999: A superconducting circuit can be utilized as a qubit, as discovered by Yasunobu Nakamura and Jaw-Shen Tsai.
>
> 2000: researchers at MIT and the Los Alamos National Laboratory of the Department of Energy built a 7-qubit quantum computer.
>
> 2002: First Quantum Computation Roadmap, a dynamic document created by important QC experts, is released.

2011: D-Wave Systems delivers the first quantum computer that is economically feasible.

2014: Researchers from the Delft University of Technology's Kavli Institute of Nanoscience teleport data between two quantum bits that are spaced apart by around 10 feet with a 0% error rate.

2017: the first quantum teleportation of separate single-photon qubits, according to Chinese researchers.

2019: Google said that it had attained quantum supremacy [14] by finishing a set of operations that would have taken a supercomputer 10,000 years to complete.

IBM later reported that if a supercomputer uses various techniques to maximize computing speed, it could complete the task in only 2.5 days.

Many organizations are considering April 14, 2030, as the time by which Qcom can break present-day cybersecurity infrastructure; the time has been given by Cloud Security Alliance (CSA) [1]. We should also start preparing to deal with threats of QC as D-Wave Systems is currently offering commercial Qcom. Many organizations in the upcoming time will also provide QC as a Service (QCaaS), which malicious actors or hacker groups could use to disrupt the infrastructure or to cause harm to humanity.

B. Evolution of Qubits over the years (A basic unit of information in QC)

A Qubit or Quantum Bit [10] is a basic unit of quantum information. In classical (or traditional) computing, a binary bit serves as the fundamental unit of information, whereas a qubit (or quantum bit) serves as the fundamental informational core component in QC. A qubit achieves a linear combination of two states by using the superposition phenomenon of quantum mechanics. A typical binary bit, which only has two potential states and can only represent one binary value, such as 0 or 1, can be in any of these two states. However, a qubit can represent either a 0 or a 1, or any proportion of 0 to 1 in the superposition of both states, with a certain chance of being a 0 and a certain chance of being a 1. Table 18.1 highlights the evolution of qubits over the years.

Companies are trying to increase the number of qubits in their quantum computers day by day, which could also increase the processing power of Qcom which is already tremendously powerful. Maybe in the upcoming years or decades, we can fully utilize the potential of a quantum computer. We should start preparing for the quantum time now, along with preparation for its dark side as well.

Table 18.1 Evolution of Qubits over the years [10, 11].

Name of the organization(s)	Year in which it was produced	Number of Qubits
IBM-Oxford-Berkeley-Stanford-MIT	1998	2 qubits
Technical-University, Munich	2000	5 qubits
National Laboratory of Los Alamos	2000	7 qubits
Institute for QC, Perimeter Institute for Theoretical Physics, and MIT	2006	12 qubits
D-Wave System	2008	28 qubits
D-Wave System	2011	128 qubits
D-Wave System	2013	512 qubits
D-Wave System	2015	1152 qubits
D-Wave System	2016	2048 qubits
IBM, Oxford, Berkeley, Stanford, and MIT	2017	50 qubits
Intel	2018	49 qubits
Google	2018	72 qubits
Rigetti	2018	128 qubits
D-Wave System	2020	5640 qubits

18.4   Components & Concepts that Make QCOM Possible

Qcom are devices that carry out quantum calculations. Qubits are used by a quantum computer to execute quantum computations. The use of quantum phenomena like superposition and entanglement to computation is known as QC.

A. Qubits
The fundamental building block of quantum information is a quantum bit, or qubit [10]. The conventional bit can only exist in one of two possible states, namely 0 or 1. However, according to quantum physics, a qubit's

general state can either be a cogent superposition of both, that is, 0, 1, or a quantum superposition of 0 and 1.

B. Quantum Algorithm

The method QC [23] uses the quantum circuit model of computing, which is a realistic representation of quantum computation. A quantum algorithm is a series of steps that can all be carried out on a quantum computer. The phrase "quantum algorithm" refers to any algorithm that appears to be fundamentally quantum or uses a key aspect of quantum processing, such as quantum superposition or quantum entanglement, even if all conventional algorithms may also be run on a quantum computer. Qcom cannot solve problems that cannot be solved with traditional computers. Due to the fact that they make use of the quantum superposition and entanglement concepts that classical computers cannot effectively employ, quantum algorithms may be able to solve some problems more quickly than classical algorithms.

C. Quantum Computer Principles

Confinement and the superposition concept are the foundation of Qcom.

- Superposition [22] – Superposition refers to the quantum phenomenon where a quantum system can exist in multiple states or places at the exact same time. A "qubit" can simultaneously store a "0" and "1." Superposition, the ability to exist in multiple states at once, gives Qcom their power, efficiency, and speed advantage over traditional computers, which can only do one thing at a time. Qcom can perform many calculations simultaneously, which means they can solve problems much faster than regular machines –problems that would take years for a conventional computer to solve. It enables the qubits of the quantum computer to perform multiple operations simultaneously, making them faster than conventional computers.
  A key concept in quantum mechanics is the concept of quantum superposition, which describes how two or more quantum states can be "superposed" to create a new, valid quantum state. Every quantum state may be represented as the sum of two or more different unique states, which is the consequence of this.

- Entanglement [22] – Quantum entanglement is a physical occurrence that happens when a group of particles are created, interact, or share spatial proximity in a way that prevents the quantum states of any individual particle in the group from being independently described, even when the particles are separated by a great distance. When each particle's quantum state cannot be represented independently of the quantum state of the other, a pair or group of particles is said to be entangled. Although the parts of the system are not in a definite state, the quantum state of the system as a whole can be represented. There is a special relation between two qubits when they are entangled. The results of the measurements will reveal the entanglement. The measurements on the individual qubits could result in a 0 or a 1. However, the result of one qubit's measurement will always be compared with the result of the other qubit's measurement.

18.5   Plans for the Future Development of Quantum Computer

A. Development for the Future of QC

Huge imminent investments in quantum technologies will bring concepts like quantum Internet of Things and a worldwide quantum internet closer to reality. The finding in paper [12] reveals a brand-new type of vulnerability that will allow adversarial groups of $N \geq 3$ quantum-capable enemies to cause the most damage to the global quantum state in such systems. These attacks won't be easy to recognize since they don't cause the Hamiltonian to change and don't cause purity to be lost. They also don't need real-time communication and it can end in a split second. The authors further assert that given the statistical nature of contemporary extremist, insurgent, and terrorist organizations, such acts will be magnified. Future quantum technologies could be incorporated into redundant conventional networks as a defense.

Using the principles of quantum physics to secure data is one method to prevent eavesdropping. There is already a significant investment being made in the development and testing of a quantum internet that will make communication almost completely secure and prohibit eavesdropping.

B. Investments for the Development of Qcom

In 2021, the QC industry was estimated to be worth $472 million, and by 2026, it is expected to be worth $1.7 billion. Research on QC is growing quickly and countries are investing huge amounts of money in the development of Quantum Technologies. Some countries want to emerge as the global leader in the development of quantum computer technology, some want to join the quantum nation and some don't want to get left behind in the quantum race.

Countries should also look at the dark side of it as well and start investing in research to protect against the threats that the quantum computer poses with its massive computing power. Table 18.2 shows a comparison of investment of different countries in the development of the quantum computer and its technologies.

C. Future Applications of Qcom

Quantum-era cybersecurity [2] will be capable of recognizing and preventing quantum-era cyberattacks before they can do any harm. But it could become a double-edged sword, as QC may also create one such cyberattack to disrupt the discipline in which humans exist to create a world of robots, worobots, or to bring singularity [17].

Artificial Intelligence is indeed a hot topic in computer science. Using machine learning and neural networks, scientists have been attempting to make AI more human-like. It seems terrible, but when you include Qcom in the equation, the fear factor increases significantly.

Our finest defenses against cyber criminals are artificial intelligence and Qcom. With the help of Quantum Artificial Intelligence (QAI) [18], we can detect and prevent cyberattacks or even cyber warfare. But what if cyber criminals use QAI for their malicious activities?

"Most hackers don't attack directly when they break into anything," according to cybersecurity expert Alan Woodward. They "go around the side, and I predict that's where issues with these implementations will be found. Even while they could theoretically listen in on traffic across fiber-optic cables, modern attackers don't usually do that." If a hacker can think of such techniques, then AI, which is developed to do just that, could also come up with other techniques to do the same. We have seen that AI surpasses humans in some fields, maybe this field could also be one in the future, who knows? When AI and Quantum Computer work together, they can achieve a state we as humans can never think of, which will be a threat to humanity.

Table 18.2 Comparison of investment of different countries in the development of Quantum Technologies [10, 12, 15, 16].

S. no.	Country (Department(s))	Range of years for investment	Invested money	Invested in
1.	United States of America	2019 - 2024	$1.2 Billion ($1,200 Million)	QC
2.	United States of America (Department of Energy)	2019 - 2024	$80 Million	Quantum Research
3.	USA (White House -Office of Science & Tech. Policy, the National Science Foundation & Department of Energy)	2020	$1 Billion ($1,000 Million)	12 AI and Quantum Information Science Research Centers
4.	China	2017 - 2022	$1 Billion ($1,000 Million)	Developing National Lab. of Quantum Information Sciences
5.	Canada	2011 - 2021	more than $1 Billion (more than $1,000 Million)	QC
6.	United Kingdom	2013 - 2018	€370 Million ($360 Million approx.)	QC field
7.	United Kingdom	2019	£153 Million ($167 Million approx.)	Quantum Technologies

(Continued)

Table 18.2 Comparison of investment of different countries in the development of Quantum Technologies [10, 12, 15, 16]. (*Continued*)

S. no.	Country (Department(s))	Range of years for investment	Invested money	Invested in
8.	Germany	2018 - 2022	€650 Million ($632 Million approx.)	QC market
9.	Germany	2020	€2 Billion ($1,940 Million approx.)	Quantum Technology
10.	France	2020 - 2025	€1.8 Billion ($1,750 Million approx.)	Research in Quantum Technologies, Communication, and Sensing
11.	Russia	2020	$790 Million	QC Technologies
12.	Japan	2022 - 2023	$270 Million	QC Technology
13.	South Korea	2019 - 2024	$40 Million	Developing ICT proprietary technology-Core QC
14.	India	2020 - 2025	Rs 8,000 crore ($986.4 Million approx.)	National Mission for Quantum Technologies & Applications

18.6   Dark Side of QCOM

A. Predictions related to QC in the past

The most popular asymmetric algorithms now in use are based on difficult mathematical challenges, such as considering large numbers, which can involve a very sophisticated supercomputer and take hundreds of years to complete.

Meanwhile, in 1994 researcher Shor at MIT showed that a large-scale quantum computer could solve the identical issue in a matter of days or hours [13]. Future Qcom could be able to decrypt asymmetric encryption techniques that depend on discrete logarithms [25, 26] or integer factorization for security.

Twenty-five years later, in 2019, researchers from Google claimed that their device has reached "Quantum Supremacy" [14]. A state-of-the-art supercomputer would take around 10,000 years [27, 28] to complete the identical work [13].

Herman Kahn [12], the founder of the Hudson Institute [29], stated in his 1962 book [16] *Thinking About the Unthinkable* that even the most utopian of that day's visionaries would have to admit that the very existence of advanced technology involved a risk to human civilization that would have been unthinkable twenty-five years ago [15].

Rather than the nuclear apocalypse that haunted Kahn [12, 29, 30] and his generation in the 1950s and 1960s, we must now contemplate a quantum apocalypse [24] that, even though it is not as physically and permanently destructive as a nuclear attack, could cause irreparable harm to our economy and society if the proper measures are not taken now to lower the risk of such an attack.

B. Fears about Qcom

Who knows what technology isn't offered on the open market or is being used covertly by other governments? According to Morris of Topcoder, "I fear that until it's finished, we won't even be aware that the quantum computer capable of carrying out this even exists. . . . I worry that it will happen before we realize it is there."

When a significant quantum computer will be built is impossible to foresee. In the past, the physical viability of enormous Qcom was less clear, but many experts now believe that it is merely a large technical problem. Some engineers even estimate that in around 20 years, sufficiently potent Qcom will be built, making it possible for them to virtually shatter all current public key techniques. Many of the present public-key cryptosystems will be vulnerable to being decrypted by Qcom. The integrity and security of digital communications via the Internet [30, 31] and elsewhere would be substantially compromised by this.

The possible misuse of Qcom for harmful [29–31] reasons is referred to as quantum hacking. The majority of people believe that binary, conventional computers will be used to launch cyberattacks, but consider the disastrous effects of a massive quantum attack on vital infrastructure. In an enemy's hands, a quantum computer that could crack RSA encryption [5] would have catastrophic consequences on our vital infrastructure and economy. It is comparable to the concern associated with conventional warfare turning nuclear.

C. Risks related to the use of Quantum Computer [30, 31]

- Interference – During the computation phase the slightest disturbance in a quantum system can cause the quantum computation to collapse. A quantum computer must be totally isolated from all external interference during the computation phase.
- Error correction – A single error in a calculation can cause the validity of the entire computation to collapse.
- Output observance – Retrieving output data after a quantum calculation is complete risks corrupting the data.

D. Quantum Computer could exacerbate existing risks

Artificial Intelligence, data harvesting, and privacy: Despite all the data privacy laws and efforts by various governments and other non-government organizations, an unprecedented amount of data collection still takes place. As we have seen in the past, targeted advertisements by multinational companies like, for example, Google are very accurate is predicting human behaviors. Since future Qcom will be able to process large volumes of data more rapidly than today's most sophisticated servers, the availability of QC could further incentivize organizations to collect even more consumer data, thus supercharging the data harvesting that already takes place. Which ultimately results in even more sophisticated target advertisement and human behavior predictions.

The majority of developed nations are currently making significant investments in the development of quantum technology, which is causing international conflicts [8]. in 2022, it is anticipated that China, India, Japan, Germany, the Netherlands, Canada, and the United States [13] will invest a total of $5 billion in quantum technology. Since QC is seen to be essential to developing future military systems, the situation has been referred to as a new global "arms race." The unintended result of portraying attempts to acquire quantum capabilities as an arms competition might be an increase in international tension.

E. Quantum Apocalypse

The "quantum apocalypse," when Qcom become commonplace and render most forms of internet encryption worthless, has been foretold by experts [24].

The blockchain network, which is thought to be almost hack-proof, would become unsecure as a result of the quantum apocalypse, which might also spell the end for cryptocurrencies like bitcoin. According to UK cybersecurity company Post-Quantum, "bitcoin will perish the precise day the first quantum computer debuts" if precautions are not taken. our contemporary systems of banking, commerce, communication, transportation, manufacturing, energy, government, and healthcare would for all intents and purposes cease to operate" at that point.

A number of countries, including the US, China, Russia and the UK, are working hard and investing huge sums of money to develop these super-fast Qcom with a view to gaining strategic advantage in the cyber-sphere.

Every day vast quantities of encrypted data are being harvested without our permission and stored in data banks, ready for the day when the data thieves' Qcom are powerful enough to decrypt it.

"Once a functioning quantum computer appears that will be able to break that encryption... it can almost instantly create the ability for whoever's developed it to clear bank accounts, to completely shut down government defence systems - Bitcoin wallets will be drained," said Harri Owen, chief strategy officer at Post-Quantum.

F. Threats to Humanity from Qcom

The biggest threat to humankind will be when artificial intelligence leverages Qcom. It would be Quantum Artificial Intelligence. We have already seen that AI can surpass humans in some specific fields like banking and financial services, healthcare, e-commerce, sales and marketing, agriculture, business decision-making, travel and hospitality, image and speech recognition, etc. We never know what QAI [18] can achieve and whether it could be a threat to humankind or not.

While it appears that QC has the potential to completely transform a number of businesses, one that is challenged by its emergence is cybersecurity. Because of its quicker data processing, malicious actors may be better equipped to conduct brute-force cyberattacks [2].

The entire scope of cybersecurity's harmful impacts is still unknown. It isn't going to be easy for humanity to deal with the aspects that will be affected once Qcom see the light of day.

18.7   Plans for Protection in Quantum Era

A. Current plans to defend against Qcom
Three different types of countermeasures against quantum attackers are already in the works:

- Post-quantum cryptography [19], which involves the creation of brand-new encryption methods resistant to Qcom.
- Quantum key distribution [20], which pertains to the use of quantum physics to distribute keys randomly between users, while requiring a global network of optical links.
- Air-gapping [21], which involves isolating networks from the internet but is probably unfeasible.

These are the kinds of attacks that we are preparing for, but we never know what other types of attacks happen when the quantum computer will be not that difficult to acquire.

B. Quantum proofing (protection from Quantum Apocalypse)
Bad things would occur if we didn't take action to stop the Quantum Apocalypse, according to a Whitehall officer.

All "top secret" government information in the UK is already "post-quantum," employing new encryption techniques that scientists think will be quantum-proof.

Post-quantum cryptography [19], according to the National Institute for Science and Technology (NIST), seeks to develop a uniform defensive plan that will shield business, government, academia, and the nation's critical infrastructure from the dangers of the quantum apocalypse.

QC is costly, time-consuming, and produces a lot of heat. The development of quantum-safe algorithms is one of the most significant security issues of our time.

C. Quantum Key Distribution (QKD)
In the Quantum era, the most likely problem to arise is that a large enough quantum computer can break through the most commonly used algorithms which we use today for both public key encryption and digital signatures.

Quantum Key Distribution (QKD) [20], which uses the quantum feature of the particle to construct and transmit a secure key, was the answer proposed by physics. This is one of the answers since it is intrinsically possible to verify that a transmitted key is safe because a quantum particle state cannot be replicated. The BB84 quantum key distribution method [7] was created in 1984 by Charles Bennett and Gilles Brassard. It is the first protocol for quantum cryptography. The protocol is based on the quantum property that information gain is only possible at the cost of degrading the signal if the two states being distinguished are not orthogonal, and it also relies on the presence of a validated public classical channel. Together, these two requirements make the protocol provably secure.

18.8   Conclusion

In this research work, we have looked at various aspects of the dark side of QC. It is so beneficial to humanity but we should never ignore the dark side of it. Various countries, organizations, companies, etc., are investing in the development of Quantum Computer but they should also invest and focus on its negative aspects and the measures to protect against it if in the future it gets misused or it develops its intelligence in a way that can be harmful to humankind.

References

1. Cloud Security Alliance Sets Countdown Clock to Quantum | CSA. (2022, March 9). Retrieved September 25, 2022, from https://cloudsecurityalliance. org/press-releases/2022/03/09/cloud-security-alliance-sets-countdown-clock-to-quantum/
2. Faruk, M. J. H., Tahora, S., Tasnim, M., Shahriar, H., & Sakib, N. (2022). A Review of Quantum Cybersecurity: Threats, Risks and Opportunities. arXiv preprint arXiv:2207.03534.
3. Kietzmann, J., Demetis, D. S., Eriksson, T., & Dabirian, A. (2021). Hello Quantum! How Quantum Computing Will Change the World. *IT Prof.*, 23(4), 106-111.
4. Chamola, V., Jolfaei, A., Chanana, V., Parashari, P., & Hassija, V. (2021). Information security in the post quantum era for 5G and beyond networks: Threats to existing cryptography, and post-quantum cryptography. *Computer Communications*, 176, 99-118.
5. Kirsch, Z., & Chow, M. (2015). Quantum computing: The risk to existing encryption methods. Retrieved from URL: https://www.cs.tufts.edu/comp/116/archive/fall2015/zkirsch.pdf.
6. Cui, W., Dou, T., & Yan, S. (2020, July). Threats and opportunities: Blockchain meets quantum computation. In *2020 39th Chinese Control Conference (CCC)* (pp. 5822-5824). IEEE.

7. Dyakonov, M. (2019). When will useful quantum computers be constructed? Not in the foreseeable future, this physicist argues. Here's why: The case against: Quantum computing. *IEEE Spectrum*, 56(3), 24-29.

8. Gupta, S., Sau, K., Pramanick, J., Pyne, S., Ahamed, R., & Biswas, R. (2017, August). Quantum computation of perfect time-eavesdropping in position-based quantum cryptography: Quantum computing and eavesdropping over perfect key distribution. In *2017 8th Annual Industrial Automation and Electromechanical Engineering Conference (IEMECON)* (pp. 162-167). IEEE.

9. Khan, M. S., Sharma, P., & Tyagi, S. A Study on Quantum Computing.

10. Kjaergaard, M., Schwartz, M. E., Braumüller, J., Krantz, P., Wang, J. I. J., Gustavsson, S., & Oliver, W. D. (2020). Superconducting qubits: Current state of play. *Annual Review of Condensed Matter Physics*, 11, 369-395.

11. Feldman, S. (2019, May 6). Chart: 20 Years of Quantum Computing Growth | Statista. Retrieved September 25, 2022, from https://www.statista.com/chart/17896/quantum-computing-developments/

12. Johnson, N. F., Gomez-Ruiz, F. J., Rodriguez, F. J., & Quiroga, L. (2019). Quantum terrorism: Collective vulnerability of global quantum systems. arXiv preprint arXiv:1901.08873.

13. Shor, P. W. (1999). Polynomial-time algorithms for prime factorization and discrete logarithms on a quantum computer. *SIAM Review*, 41(2), 303-332.

14. Arute, F., Arya, K., Babbush, R., Bacon, D., Bardin, J. C., Barends, R., ... & Martinis, J. M. (2019). Quantum supremacy using a programmable superconducting processor. *Nature*, 574(7779), 505-510.

15. Kahn, H. (1962). Thinking about the Unthinkable. *Naval War College Review*, 15(8), 7.

16. Goled, S. (2021, May 23). Top Countries Pumping Money into Quantum Computing Technology. Retrieved September 24, 2022, from https://analyticsindiamag.com/top-countries-pumping-money-into-quantum-computing-technology/

17. Wang, P., Liu, K., & Dougherty, Q. (2018). Conceptions of artificial intelligence and singularity. *Information*, 9(4), 79.

18. Wichert, A. (2020). *Principles of quantum artificial intelligence: quantum problem solving and machine learning*. World Scientific.

19. Bernstein, D. J., & Lange, T. (2017). Post-quantum cryptography. *Nature*, 549(7671), 188-194.

20. Mehic, M., Niemiec, M., Rass, S., Ma, J., Peev, M., Aguado, A., ... & Voznak, M. (2020). Quantum key distribution: a networking perspective. *ACM Computing Surveys (CSUR)*, 53(5), 1-41.

21. Magee, J. C. (2016). U.S. Patent Application No. 14/745,383.

22. Jebanazer, J., J, R., & Vasudevan, A. (2022). A Study on the Architecture of Quantum Computers. *International Journal of Engineering Research & Technology*, 11(06), 114-116. https://doi.org/10.17577/IJERTV11IS060069

23. Shao, C., Li, Y., & Li, H. (2019). Quantum algorithm design: techniques and applications. *Journal of Systems Science and Complexity,* 32(1), 375-452.
24. Grimes, R. A. (2019). *Cryptography apocalypse: preparing for the day when quantum computing breaks today's crypto.* John Wiley & Sons.
25. Courtney, M. (2019). Digital doomsday: The threat of cyber attack hangs over all of us, but how big could it get? Could hackers bring society to a standstill—a digital Armageddon?. *Engineering & Technology,* 14(10), 26-29.
26. Gill, S. S., Kumar, A., Singh, H., Singh, M., Kaur, K., Usman, M., & Buyya, R. (2022). Quantum computing: A taxonomy, systematic review and future directions. *Software: Practice and Experience,* 52(1), 66-114.
27. Orús, R., Mugel, S., & Lizaso, E. (2019). Forecasting financial crashes with quantum computing. *Physical Review A, 99*(6), 060301.
28. Lindsay, J. (2018). Why quantum computing will not destabilize international security: The political logic of cryptology. Available at SSRN 3205507.
29. Ebrahimi, E., Chevalier, C., Kaplan, M., & Minelli, M. (2020). Superposition attack on OT protocols. *Cryptology ePrint Archive.*
30. Chen, Z., Karabulut, E., Aysu, A., Ma, Y., & Jing, J. (2021, October). An Efficient Non-Profiled Side-Channel Attack on the CRYSTALS-Dilithium Post-Quantum Signature. In *2021 IEEE 39th International Conference on Computer Design (ICCD)* (pp. 583-590). IEEE.
31. Kietzmann, J., Demetis, D. S., Eriksson, T., & Dabirian, A. (2021). Hello Quantum! How Quantum Computing Will Change the World. *IT Prof., 23*(4), 106-111.

19

Quantum Technology for Military Applications

Sarthak Nahar[1]*, Divyam Pithawa[1], Vivek Bhardwaj[2], Romil Rawat[3], Anjali Rawat[4] and Kiran Pachlasiya[5]

[1]*Department of Computer Science Engineering, Shri Vaishnav Vidyapeeth Vishwavidyalaya, Indore, India*
[2]*Department of Computer Science and Engineering, Manipal University Jaipur, Jaipur, Rajasthan, India*
[3]*Department of Computer Science and Engineering, SVIIT, SVVV, Indore, India*
[4]*Apostelle Overseas Education, Ujjain, India*
[5]*Computer Science and Engineering Department, Sagar Institute of Research and Technology, Bhopal, India*

Abstract

The concepts of quantum physics are applied in technological applications through quantum technology (QTech). Generally speaking, QTech has not yet matured, but it may have substantial effects on future military communications, encryption, and sensing, as well as congressional oversight, authorization, and budgets. A new and potentially revolutionary field called quantum technologies could have an impact on many aspects of daily life. The defence and security industry, as well as military and government organizations, are interested in quantum technologies because they have two unique applications. This paper examines and maps the potential military applications of QTech and serves as a springboard for further investigation into morality, military and governmental strategy, decision-making, and policy as well as assessments of international peace and security. In military applications, quantum technologies create new capabilities, boost efficiency and accuracy, and pave the way for "quantum warfare" in which new military doctrines, plans, rules of engagement, and moral principles must be devised. These technologies are still largely in the experimental stage. Quantum sensing may have military or commercial applications within the next few years. Even while some minor commercial deployments of quantum communication technologies have already been realised, the most advantageous

---

**Corresponding author*: sarthaknahar123@gmail.com

Romil Rawat, Rajesh Kumar Chakrawarti, Sanjaya Kumar Sarangi, Jaideep Patel, Vivek Bhardwaj, Anjali Rawat and Hitesh Rawat (eds.) Quantum Computing in Cybersecurity, (313–334) © 2023 Scrivener Publishing LLC

military uses are still many years distant. Similar to this, quantum computers may have specialized uses in the future, but any such uses are most likely at least ten years away. China is now advancing quantum communication while the United States is currently leading the world in the creation of quantum computing (Qcomm).

Keywords: Quantum technology, simulations, quantum communication and cryptography, quantum sensing and metrology, cybercrime

19.1   Introduction

These kinds of gadgets fall under the wide categorization of "quantum technology (QTech)," a lot of which are still in the experimental stages [1]. The three main areas of quantum technologies are typically quantum sensing, quantum communication, and quantum computing [2]. While quantum computing (Qcomm) is most removed from practical commercial deployment, quantum sensing is the closest and has the least potential for disruption. Although there have been substantial advancements since Palmer (2017) [1], he offers a non-technical review of the potential near-term applications of all three categories of QTech as of that year [3].

Although the hallmarks of modern fourth-generation warfare include decentralization and the loss of governments' exclusive right to conduct war [4, 5], militaries of wealthy nations often have access to state-of-the-art military equipment. This has to do with the emergence of quantum technologies.

The term "QTech" refers to scientific and technological advancements mostly resulting from the second quantum revolution. The technology we use today, such as nuclear power, were initially introduced by the first quantum revolution, current communication technologies, semiconductors, lasers, magnetic resonance, digital cameras, and other imaging equipment. Nuclear weapons and energy were produced by the first wave of QTech, and later the classical computer came to play a significant role. At the moment, laser weapons are being incorporated and tested [6].

The ability to control and manipulate individual quantum systems (such as atoms, ions, electrons, photons, particles, or various quasi-particles) in order to reach the standard quantum boundary, which is the upper bound on the precision of measurements made on quantum scales, is known as the second quantum revolution [7]. The technology of the second quantum revolution is referred to as "QTech" in this study. QTech does not fundamentally alter the weapons or specific military systems, but it does significantly improve measurement, sensing, precision, processing power, and efficiency of present and future military technology. Most quantum technologies often have two different applications. QTech therefore has a huge potential for military applications. Numerous studies and recommendations indicate that there is a greater potential for the development of such technology; for instance, see [8–11].

The term "quantum warfare" is explained in further detail in this document, along with its potential effects on the intelligence, security, and defence industries, as well as any prospective new capabilities or improvements. The objective is to illustrate potential directions and trends in implementation and applications rather than to make an exact prediction of the future of QTech. In general, quantum technologies are seen as cutting-edge technology with the potential to alter how war is fought and how it turns out. Despite having low technology readiness levels (TRLs) for the most part, contemporary quantum technologies are thought to have disruptive potential [12]. When debating ethical principles or quantum-based preventive arms control, mapping the potential military uses of quantum technologies is crucial for further evaluating the threats to world peace.

Definition of the Term QTech

The fundamental concept of QTech (QT), a developing area of physics and engineering, is the exploitation of particular quantum systems' quantum entanglement, quantum superposition, and quantum tunnelling. According to the definition, QTech relates to the numerous quantum-mechanical system physical ideas and has a variety of applications. One use of QTech is of trapped ions as a quantum bit for quantum computers, a quantum sensor for magnetic fields, or a quantum clock.

Dual-use technology is the term for research and development fields that have potential use in both commercial and defence production [13].

QTech, a typical dual-use technology, has piqued the interest of both the military and government authorities [14] in addition to peacekeeping groups.

The application of quantum technologies to combat is known as quantum warfare (QW). It alters the intelligence, security, and defence capabilities of all conflict domains and introduces new military doctrines, scenarios, and ethics.

There have also been efforts to characterise the quantum world [15] as a novel battleground. Instead of considering QTech as a stand-alone type of fighting, we will in this article consider it as a factor that enhances all currently recognised domains of conflict. The word "quantum assault" should first be defined. It refers to the use of QTech to undermine, interfere with, or surveil either conventional or quantum security systems. The most common instances include quantum computers decrypting data using the Rivest-Shamir-Adleman (RSA) encryption algorithm or listening in using quantum key distribution.

Despite the abundance of QT literature, the taxonomy of the field is not explicitly agreed upon. We'll employ the taxonomy below:

- Computer Simulations of Quantum Systems, Quantum computation (digital and analogue quantum computers and their applications, such as quantum system simulation, quantum optimisation . . .) quantum simulations (non-programmable quantum circuits)
- Quantum networks and communication [20, 21] - Quantum communication and cryptography (quantum network elements, quantum key distribution, quantum communication) Quantum-ready encryption (quantum-resilient algorithms, quantum random number generator)
- Quantum measurement and sensing quantitative perception (quantum magnetometers, gravimeters . . .) Atomic clock (precise time measurement and distribution) Nuclear imaging (quantum radar, low-SNR imaging . . .). In addition to the broad taxonomy of quantum technologies discussed above, we also provide a novel division of quantum technologies based on their uses and advantages. The classification that follows can be applied generally; however; we focus primarily on military uses. The following categories describe the impact of using QTech:
- Essential: the use of quantum technologies (such as post-quantum cryptography) to thwart potential quantum attacks;
- Effectiveness: Quantum technologies (such quantum optimizations, quantum machine learning, or artificial intelligence) that enhance the performance of tools and techniques now in use; precision quantum technologies include quantum magnetometry, quantum gravimetry, quantum inertial navigation, and quantum timing. These technologies increase the accuracy of already used measurement equipment. Due to QTech, people now possess previously unimaginable skills (e.g., quantum radar, quantum simulation for chemistry, quantum cryptoanalysis, quantum key distribution).

ORGANIZATION OF CHAPTER

The remaining chapter is broken out as follows. Section 19.2 discusses related research, Section 19.3 presents an overview of quantum technology, Section 19.4 discusses the use of quantum technology in defence, Section 19.5 presents military applications of quantum technology, Section

19.6 discusses the difficulties and repercussions of quantum warfare, and Section 19.7 wraps up this chapter.

19.2   Related Work

1. By providing more precise navigation, ultra-secure communication, or cutting-edge ISTAR and computation, quantum technologies have the potential to enhance present military capabilities. In general, quantum warfare will call for new military doctrines, fighting scenarios, and strategies to be developed in order to create and acquire new techniques and equipment for the quantum age [2].

2. The effects of Qcomm in the near future are sometimes overstated; before quantum computers can be used for cryptography, they need to be scaled up by a factor of up to one million. Although there are currently no guaranteed uses for near-term quantum computers, simulation for scientific study is promising and might have a significant economic impact. With both commercial and military uses, quantum sensors are much closer to being commercially available and might significantly improve long-range imaging, timing, and sensing of electric, magnetic, and gravitational fields. In theory, QKD could increase the security of communications against eavesdropping, but many U.S. and UK specialists are dubious about its practical utility [3].

3. NATO review - With the ability to detect the insensible, revolutionize cybersecurity, and give us access to previously unsolvable issues, quantum technologies have the potential to give humans radically new powers.
   Two applications will have particularly substantial effects on the defence and security environment in the short- to medium-term.

4. IISS Organization reviews - One of the most anticipated developments for armed forces right now is the incorporation of quantum technologies, while it is still difficult to forecast exactly how they will affect military operations. Although widespread adoption and cost-effective applications are still years away, there is little question that they will have a disruptive impact when used on a large scale. According to Intel's chief of Qcomm in May 2018, a few thousand qubit quantum computer would surely alter the world in a similar way to how the

318 QUANTUM COMPUTING IN CYBERSECURITY

first microprocessor did. A qubit, which is similar to a bit in a conventional computer, is the basic unit of data in a quantum computer.

5. IEEE Exposure - Under the premise of hardware that is suffi-ciently developed, quantum computers have the potential to be more effective than conventional solutions in solving par-ticular issues. These problems specifically relate to military uses. This paper discusses the most modern quantum tech-nologies and the different uses they have. There are addition-ally four Qcomm use cases that are specialized for military use. The 2021 AI strategy plan of the Netherlands Ministry of Defense is fully in accordance with these use-cases.

19.3   Overview of QTECH

A brief explanation of quantum technologies is given in this section along with relevant references. The current development state of each QTech is described, together with its usage impact, predicted time of adoption, and key difficulties. The approximate number of logical qubits needed for applications involving Qcomm is offered.

19.3.1   Quantum Information Science

The field of information science known as quantum information science (QIS) [1–3] focuses on the study of quantum information and is associated with quantum physics. The fundamental carrier of information in classical information science is a bit, which can only be either 0 or 1. The primary information carrier in quantum theory is the quantum bit, or qubit. A qubit can be in the quantum superposition, which is an arbitrary complex linear combination of the states $|0$ and $|1$, or it can be either $|0$ or $|1$.

19.3.2   Qcomm

The term "Qcomm" describes the application of quantum information the-ory to computation [4, 5]. A quantum computer can be used to describe such a device. Qcomm devices can be categorised in a highly complicated way. We categorise things more simply for the purposes of this report as follows:

- A quantum simulator is often made as a single-purpose apparatus and used for the modelling and research of other, more elusive quantum systems. As opposed to a quantum computer, the quantum simulator can be conceived of as a non-programmable quantum circuit.

- Analog Qcomm, sometimes referred to as Hamiltonian computation, is a noisy variation of adiabatic Qcomm that is typically realised using quantum annealing. Quantum annealer differs from a digital quantum computer due to the limited connection of qubits and unique operating principles. Because of this, the use of analogue quantum computers is somewhat restricted, but they can still be used for Hamiltonian-based simulations and quantum optimisations.

19.3.2.1   Quantum Simulations

Long before the first quantum computer was constructed, it was believed that the simulation of other quantum systems was the main purpose of a quantum computer. A molecule is one such quantum system. Computational chemistry can only fully model more complex compounds or larger molecules at the expense of several approximations and simplifications, despite advances in computing power. For instance, the quantum computer only needs n qubits, but the classical computer would need 2n bits for a system with n electrons to describe the state of the electrons. As a result, quantum simulations represent the first and arguably still most interesting application of Qcomm.

19.3.2.2   Quantum Searching and Quantum Walks

The Grover's method, which provides a quadratic speedup for database searching or generally inverting a function, is one of the most well-known searching quantum approaches. Grover's approach has complexity that is around O, whereas traditional search algorithms for unsorted lists or databases have complexity that is about $O(N)$ [6, 7], i.e., proportional to the number of N objects (N). To analyse so-called Big Data, it is essential to investigate quantum searching techniques (unstructured data). A large quantum memory is necessary for working with a lot of data. However, a reliable quantum memory that could hold a significant amount of quantum data for a very long time does not yet exist. Second, converting classical data to a quantum form is inefficient and requires a lot of time. Thus, it is currently believed that only searching on data generated algorithmically is practical. The alternate search method might be based on the quantum random walk mechanism, which speeds up searches in a manner similar to Grover's algorithm.

19.3.2.3   Quantum Cryptoanalysis [8–11]

Quantum cryptoanalysis also provides enhanced tools for a brute-force assault on symmetric encryption techniques. Using the well-known Grover's searching technique, a 256-bit AES5 key may be cracked by brute force in around 2128 quantum operations, reducing key security by 50%. Despite the enormous resource demands of quantum computers, it is recommended to double the symmetric key length. Furthermore, Simon's method and superposition queries may completely decrypt the majority of message authentication codes (MAC) and authenticated encryption with associated data (AEAD), such as HMAC-CBC and AES-GCM6.

The structure of symmetric cryptosystems is also being investigated for cryptoanalytic attacks on symmetric key systems, which have the potential to speed up computation by up to superpolynomial factors. However, these algorithms demand a lot of resources from a quantum computer.

19.3.2.4   Quantum Linear Algebra

Numerous numerical models are already used in planning, engineering, construction, and weather forecasting to simplify complex problems into a sizable set of linear equations. The approximation might work since many of them are statistical in nature. It should be noted that the HHL [11–14] method has been shown to be applicable to all Qcomm applications, including k-mean clustering, support vector machines, data fitting, etc.

Data loading is one of the main issues with quantum algorithms that demand a lot of input data. To be processed further by effective quantum algorithms, classical data, particularly binary data or bits, must be converted into quantum states. It may take longer to load conventional data than coherent data during this slow procedure.

19.3.2.5   Quantum Optimisations

Given the possibility of addressing NPlevel7 [15, 16] difficult issues, quantum optimization is a subject that is highly actively researched. The travelling salesman dilemma is an illustration of such an NP problem. The objective in this case is to discover the quickest (and best) route given a list of locations and their respective distances. One may naively try every possibility, but doing so has serious drawbacks and may even be impossible as complexity rises. Therefore, heuristic algorithms form the foundation of the most often used solutions, even though they cannot always be relied upon to find the best answer.

19.3.3   Quantum Communication and Cryptography

"Quantum communication" refers to the transmission of quantum information through a quantum network using optical fibre or free-space channels. A photon is frequently utilised as the quantum information carrier in quantum communication. The quantum network additionally includes extra components like a quantum switch or repeater due to the limits of photons, like as losses over long distances.

The objective of quantum cryptography is to develop quantum-resistant algorithms employing the quantum key distribution to replace existing (usually asymmetric) encryption methods. The following set of quantum properties is typical for quantum communication: Quantum entanglement, quantum uncertainty, and the no-cloning hypothesis all support the idea that quantum information cannot be duplicated.

19.3.3.1   Post-Quantum Cryptography

Post-quantum cryptography is a subset of encryption techniques that should be able to ward off attacks from quantum computers in the future. It is often referred to as quantum-proof [1, 2], quantum-safe, or quantum-resistant cryptography. Currently, this restriction is not present in the majority of public-key asymmetric encryption methods. However, it is believed that the majority of symmetric cryptographic algorithms and hash functions are relatively resistant to attacks from quantum computers. It is suggested to double the symmetric key's length, though.

19.3.3.2   Quantum Random Number Generator

Applications for random number generators (RNG) include Monte Carlo simulations, integration, cryptographic operations, statistics, and computer games, among others [15, 16]. The RNG in a typical computer, which functions deterministically, is known as pseudo-random number generation since it is not actually random. However, the pseudo-RNG is adequate for a variety of uses. Since QRNG may be used with any cryptography, any cryptography is improved. The fact that the QRNG can be validated and certified, unlike any other RNG, is one of its benefits.

19.3.3.3   Quantum Network

The quantum network, sometimes referred to as the quantum information network (QIN) or quantum internet, aims to convey quantum information using a number of different routes and technologies. Because quantum information is often carried by individual photons, the transmission of quantum information is unstable (qubit). Numerous quantum network applications depend heavily on quantum entanglement.

Quantum and classical networks will coexist because not all sent data needs to be encoded in quantum information. In actuality, a parallel classical network is necessary for some phenomena, such as quantum teleportation.

19.3.3.4   *Quantum Key Distribution*

Quantum key distribution is the most advanced method of quantum communication (QKD). The goal is to distribute encrypted data via traditional methods by sharing a secret key between two or more people. The no-cloning theorem states that any eavesdropper must do a measurement that is detectable by parties that are conversing.

The other weak point, besides trustworthy repeaters, is the qubit transfer rate, which is too slow to spread long keys. New single-photon sources with high transfer rates can help solve the issue.

Currently, QKD technology [3, 4] is sold as a point-to-point link over short distances or by using dependable repeaters over vast distances. China has demonstrated that a satellite in orbit may serve as a dependable repeater.

19.3.4   Quantum Sensing and Metrology

Quantum sensing and metrology, which improve timing, sensing, or imaging, is the most advanced area of QTech. As an illustration, the Global Positioning System (GPS) [3–5] has been using atomic clocks dating back to the first quantum revolution for about 50 years. Modern quantum clocks produce time measurements with a far better degree of accuracy.

Quantum sensing and metrology technology depends on a number of properties, including quantum energy levels, quantum coherence, and quantum entanglement. Various measures made by quantum sensors vary depending on the application. The most frequent selection criteria include sensitivity (a signal with a signal-to-noise ratio of unity after one second of integration), dynamic range (the smallest and largest signal that can be recognised), sampling rate (how frequently the signal is sampled), operating temperature, etc. Critical metrics include, for example, the spatial resolution at a specific distance and the time required to reach a specific sensitivity. Common measurement units include rotation, time, force, temperature, magnetic and electric fields, and photon counting.

19.3.4.1   Quantum Clocks

Atomic clocks, such as those found in GPS satellites, have been a part of our lives since the 1960s. The atomic [22, 23] theory, on which the current generation of atomic clocks is based, posits that a "tick" is the electromagnetic emissions that an electron emits when its energy level changes. The atomic clock represents the cutting edge of technology. Modern thermal atomic beam and state selection atomic clocks have a relative uncertainty of 10-15 to 10-16, or cutting-edge chip-size atomic clocks have a relative uncertainty of 2*10-12.

The second quantum revolution has led to new ideas for atomic or quantum clocks. Quantum logic clocks are built on the single-ion technology, which is connected to trapped-ion qubits for Qcomm. A quantum logic clock [6, 7] was the first clock with a clock uncertainty lower than 10-18. Quantum clocks can benefit from quantum entanglement as well.

19.3.4.2   Quantum RF Antenna

Several different signals can be emitted or received by a radio frequency (RF) antenna [8, 9]. They can be anything from simple dipole antennas to complex AESA9 modules. Their size is constrained by the produced or received signal's wavelength. For instance, a 3 GHz transmission's wavelength, which is around 10 cm, requires that the antenna's size be no less than approximately 1/3 of that wavelength. This corresponds to the Chu-Harrington limit.

Quantum RF receivers can be used in navigation, active imaging (radar), telecommunications, media receivers, or passive THz imaging as a single cell (for focused frequency, narrow bandwidth) or arrayed sensor [10, 11] (wide frequency span).

19.3.4.3   Quantum Radar Technology

Theoretically, quantum radar operates in a manner similar to that of conventional radar in that a signal must be delivered in the direction of the target, and the radar system must then wait for the signal that is reflected. A quantum mechanical approach, however, may result in new abilities and increased accuracy.

The major problem that all protocols encounter is the rapid rate of entangled photon production in (not just) a microwave domain. In the radar equation's quantum form, the dominant term 1/R4, where R is the radar-target distance, is still there. As a result, several orders of magnitude more entangled photons (modes) are needed than there are right now. In some ways, quantum radar is similar to noise radars and has many traits with them, such as effective spectrum sharing, a high probability of interception, a low probability of detection, etc.

19.3.4.4   Quantum Electric, Magnetic and Inertial Forces Sensing

A wide range of physical quantities can be measured using a variety of universal quantum technologies for sensing. Although each technology is given a broad overview, a detailed discussion is outside the scope of this work. Numerous applications use different quantum technologies. For instance, three distinct forms of sensing—acceleration, rotation, and time—are used in quantum inertial navigation. In general, many applications, not simply those using QTech, need precise quantum-based time. Atomic vapour, cold-atom interferometry, nitrogen-vacancy centres, superconducting circuits, and trapped ions are some of the most promising technologies.

Atomic vapour (measured quantities: magnetic field, rotation, time). When there is an external magnetic field, high-density, spin-polarized atomic vapour [12] undergoes a state transition that can be seen optically. It's best to deploy at room temperature. The Atomic Spin Gyroscopes, which sense rotation via atomic vapours (AGS). An alternative is chip-scale AGS [5]. As a standard, the most precise conventional rotation sensors can be employed (e.g., ring laser gyroscope). The expected quantum sensor should have around double the precision. However, the listed best classical gyroscope has an improbable size of 4 m x 4 m. Atomic ensemble-based, room-temperature atomic vapour cell magnetometers have the potential to outperform SQUID [13] magnetometers in terms of performance.

19.3.4.5   Quantum Imaging Systems

Applications for quantum imaging systems [14, 15] include low-brightness imaging, 3D quantum cameras, and quantum radar.

The quantum protocol known as quantum illumination (QI) uses two correlated (entangled) photons to find a target. The single photon, or "idler," is kept. The other photon, referred to as the "signal," is released and reflected toward the target; both photons are measured. The benefit of this approach persists even when the entanglement is disrupted by a lossy and noisy environment. One of these is the QI protocol [16], a protocol that was initially created for the quantum radar but may also be applied to quantum communication or imaging in the body.

19.3.4.6   Other Sensors and Technology

Using photoacoustic detection, quantum technologies may produce incredibly precise sound sensing up to the level of a phonon, a quasiparticle that quantizes sound waves in solid matter. Numerous operations, such as medical diagnosis, sonar, navigation, trace gas sensing, and industrial processes, depend on accurate acoustic wave detection. To detect gases or other compounds, photoacoustic detection and quantum cascade laser can be employed. The development of the quantum cascade [17] laser (QCL) is still in its infancy. The QCL is a semiconductor laser that emits in the mid- and long-wave IR bands and requires cooling far below -70C, like many other quantum technologies. Thanks to recent advancements, a portable cooling system can now reach chip-level implementation working at roughly -23°C.

19.4   QTECH in Defence

The standards for technologies used in the military are stricter than those for use in commerce or by the general public. This requires more caution because it might be used in a combat situation. Many potential military applications are listed in Section 19.5, each with a different TRL, timetable, and implementation risk. It will be simpler and less risky with technologies that can be readily adopted and integrated into current technologies, such quantum sensors, where we can simply swap out a normal sensor for a quantum sensor.

In the long run, we can expect gains from lowering SWaP and expanding quantum networks and computers. As a result, the deployment will be simpler, and it will probably be necessary if the nation or army wants to compete with other nations or armies.

19.4.1   TRL and Time Horizon

As has been repeatedly stated, many quantum technologies are at different TRLs, ranging from 1 to 8. The TRL variance and time horizon assumptions are greatly complicated when multiple applications and deployment platforms are considered, especially for military applications. In [16], various

TRL and temporal horizon estimates are provided. Several expectations, including quantum precision navigation at TRL 6, seem unduly optimistic in light of what is discussed in this study.

The actual military deployment [18] may take some time in order to meet all technological obstacles and military criteria. Think about the quantum gravimeter for scanning beneath the surface. The first generation's range/spatial resolution will probably be extremely low, and it will probably be utilised as a static sensor installed on a truck. Eventually, the sensitivity and spatial resolution of the succeeding generation will improve. The sensor will be able to be put on a drone, maybe a LEO satellite [19], and eventually an aeroplane thanks to its lower SWaP. However, it's also feasible that the sensor's constraints could be reached sooner and that deployment would become difficult, for instance on a drone or LEO satellite.

19.4.2   QTech Countermeasures

The problem is how to trick, disable, or destroy QTech [23–25], which can include quantum computers, quantum networks, quantum sensors, and imaging systems. The quantum-physical properties of a quanta are used in quantum technologies. They are therefore extremely susceptible to external noise and disruption, which might trick them or paralyse them. We talk about quantum hacking [17, 18], which has developed alongside QKD in particular, especially with reference to quantum networks and QKD.

Authors and decision-makers on quantum strategy should be aware that the employment of QTech in the military will probably lead to the creation of a variety of countermeasures sooner or later. We don't yet know the effects of any potential quantum technological defenses.

19.4.3   Quantum Strategy

Future military users of QTech will need to be very selective about where, when, and how they spend their time and money. The aim of the defence forces is frequently limited to the identification of requirements and their acquisition rather than the development of military technologies. They are the ultimate consumer, but they can still significantly contribute to growth.

Sensors, QKD, Qcomm, and other quantum technologies have all been taken into account separately thus far. However, the long-term plan takes into account how the quantum network would connect Qcomm and sensors. Here, theoretical and experimental efforts show how to use quantum entangled sensors and computers to get extra quantum advantages. There may still be other similar applications that are found or created.

When developing the optical-fibre/quantum networks, this is a crucial factor to take into account. Later, completely quantum repeaters and switches can take the place of present components like trusted repeaters, enabling the quantum network to realise its full potential.

19.5 Military Applications of QTECH

Quantum technologies have the potential to have a significant impact on many aspects of human activity. An excellent illustration of this is the defence sector [24, 25]. QTech may have an impact on all facets of modern warfare. The second quantum revolution will improve sensitivity and efficiency, provide new capabilities, and improve current military strategies rather than creating new types of weapons.

19.5.1 Capabilities of Qcomm

Thanks to Qcomm, which will help with incredibly complex computational problems, the current classical computing services will gain new capabilities. Qcomm also encompasses quantum optimizations, improvements in ML/AI, quantum data processing, and faster numerical modelling in addition to the previously mentioned quantum simulations. There was discussion of the potential military solutions provided by quantum computers in the near future. Predictive maintenance, radio frequency spectrum analysis, supply chain optimization, logistics management, and battle simulations are a few of them.

19.5.2 Quantum Cybersecurity

Existing asymmetric encryptions (based on integer factorization, the discrete logarithm, or the elliptic-curve discrete logarithm problem) and theoretically symmetric encryption can both be breached using brand-new, but on the one hand very efficient (with exponential speedup), vectors of attack in cyberwarfare. On the other hand, modern encryption methods and algorithms have been developed to withstand quantum systems and quantum key distribution.

19.5.3 Quantum PNT

Positioning, navigation, and timing (PNT) systems [13–15], particularly inertial navigation, are anticipated to benefit considerably from QTech.

A key service known as time standards and frequency transfer (TFT) provides accurate timing for communication, metrology, as well as the global positioning system (GNSS). The performance of optical atomic or quantum clocks combined with TFT utilising quantum networks will keep up with the rising demands of the current applications (communication, GNSS, financial sector, radars, and electronic warfare systems) even though current TFT systems are well established, and will even enable new applications (quantum sensing and imaging).

19.5.4   Quantum Communication Network

A quantum network featuring a variety of services that have significant, not only security-related, ramifications is referred to as the "quantum internet." A quantum repeater and quantum switch are required for many applications of progressive quantum communication networks that need quantum entanglement. Remember that the trusted repeaters can only be used with QKD. Future connections between end nodes like drones, aircraft, ships, vehicles, soldiers, command centres, etc., will be made using free-space channel and optical fibre technologies.

19.5.5   Quantum Electronic Warfare

Electronic warfare (EW) with a quantum enhancement can be distinguished from quantum EW that concentrates on countermeasures, counter-counter-measures, and support against quantum channels. A quantum channel is any exchange of photons carrying quantum information for a quantum network, quantum radar, or other quantum device using free space or optical fibres.

19.5.6   Quantum ISTAR

To carry out precise operations, a modern army needs to have the ISTAR [15, 16] (intelligence, surveillance, target acquisition and reconnaissance) capacity. The application of QTech may dramatically enhance situational awareness on multi-domain battlefields. The ability to obtain new intelligence data, analyse Big Data from surveillance and reconnaissance, and apply quantum ML/AI to identify targets are all expected to be significantly impacted by Qcomm.

Quantum gravimeters and gravitational gradiometers enable high accuracy applications for geophysics research, seismology, archaeology, oil and mineral detection, subterranean scanning, precise georeferencing, and topographical mapping (such as of the seabed for underwater navigation).

19.5.7   Chemical and Biological Simulations and Detection

The military, national labs, the chemical defence sector, or CBRN (Chemical, Biological, Radiological, and Nuclear) defence forces find the defense-related chemical and biological simulations to be particularly intriguing. A powerful quantum computer, a classical computing facility, and quantum-chemical experts will be needed for research on novel drugs and chemicals based on quantum simulations. The need for civil research, such as the currently ongoing work on protein folding, nitrogen fixation, and peptides, are theoretically the same as the requirements for quantum simulations of chemical and biological chemical warfare weapons. For photoacoustic detection, the quantum cascade laser will perform well as a chemical detector. Quantum chemical detectors can identify substances like TNT and triacetone triperoxide, which are used in improvised explosive devices (IEDs), a common weapon in asymmetric warfare. Acetone can be detected using the same tool that can detect explosives in luggage and people boarding an aircraft. In general, quantum chemical techniques can be used to identify dangerous industrial compounds or chemical warfare weapons.

19.5.8   New Material Design

By utilising the quantum mechanical [17, 18] qualities, modern science is creating new materials, known as metamaterials, also referred to as quantum materials (for example, graphene, a topological insulator). A quantum computer can imitate a substance's electrical structure, for example, by treating the material as a quantum system. Examples of applications under consideration include the development of better batteries, a room-temperature superconductor, and improved material properties.

The potential for research on novel materials for the defence industry includes improved camouflage, stealth (electromagnetic absorption), ultra-hard armour, and high-temperature tolerance material design, without giving away any specifics.

19.5.9   Quantum Radar and Lidar

People's perceptions of quantum radar are influenced by media hype surrounding the purported development of the technology in China and by successful laboratory tests. In actuality, some of the primary theoretical advantages and traits of quantum radar include the following (some of which depend on specific quantum protocols).

A little note regarding quantum-enhanced radar follows. A conventional radar system can be equipped with an atomic or quantum clock. Due to their high precision and low noise, these quantum-enhanced radars show a distinct advantage in the detection of small, slowly moving objects like drones.

19.5.10   Quantum Space Warfare

The importance of advanced nations using space as a battlefield is increasing. Satellites have traditionally been used in orbit for communication, mapping, navigation, and surveillance, mostly for military or commercial purposes. The militarization of space is increasing in the modern day; laser-armed satellites or "kamikaze" satellites are sent into Earth orbit, and anti-satellite warfare is growing at the same time. Space debris is another expanding problem, with an estimated 2,200 satellites [19, 20] in orbit and several more scheduled for release.

As quantum sensing and communication technology spreads throughout space, interest in quantum electronic warfare will rise.

19.5.11   Quantum Underwater Warfare

With improved magnetic detection of a submarine or underwater mines, ground-breaking inertial submarine navigation, and quantum-enhanced precise sonars, QTech can drastically slow down undersea warfare. Quantum photo-detectors, radar, lidar, magnetometers, or gravimeters can all be employed for marine sensing. For a broad summary of how nuclear-armed submarines' almost impregnable defences are impacted by QTech. The quantum magnetometer might be the fundamental weapon in anti-submarine warfare. According to researchers, the SQUID magnetometers in particular, with still-improving noise suppression, may detect a submarine from 6 kilometers away. Be aware that the typical helicopter or airplane-mounted classical magnetic anomaly detectors now in use have a range of only a few hundred metres. Submarines might not be able to operate in certain locations that would be covered by a quantum magnetometer array, such as those around the coast. In addition, a collection of quantum magnetometers appears to function better with higher noise suppression.

19.6   Challenges and Consequences of Quantum Warfare

The development, acquisition, and deployment of QTech for military purposes will pose new, connected challenges. Military doctrine, strategy, and tactics as well as morals, disarmament initiatives, and technological advancement will all need to change in response to quantum warfare. Research should be conducted to understand the issues, implications, risks, and options that arise from the development of QTech, not simply for military applications.

19.6.1   Technical Repercussions and Difficulties

Successful laboratory proofs of concept must be translated to actual "outside" applications while overcoming numerous scientific and technological challenges, such as miniaturisation and operability without sacrificing laboratory-achieved sensitivity and resolution. There are further relevant technological challenges as well.

The quantum workforce might be a significant problem. The quantum workforce need not consist of physicists or scientists with doctoral degrees. To understand, analyse, and evaluate the data that comes through quantum sensors, computers, and communications, they should be quantum engineers who are knowledgeable about quantum information science and have a thorough understanding of the QTech. A bigger and bigger quantum workforce will be required to support the current quantum ecosystem, which is growing gradually [17].

The final challenge will be standardised behaviour. The standardisation process is essential for ensuring that gadgets from different manufacturers work together. In addition to the unified interface and communication protocols, the standardisation process may also include security verification, as in the standardisation of post-quantum cryptography [18]. Numerous interconnected components, such as nodes, repeaters, switches, fibre channels, and open-space channels, can be expected in a quantum network. The development and application of some standards is essential for the proper transmission of quantum information.

19.6.2   Challenges and Consequences for Ethics and Peace

There have already been several requests for ethical standards for Qcomm, in which ethical issues including the modification of human DNA, the development of new weapons, and intrusive AI are discussed.

Despite the fact that quantum technologies do not produce new weapons, they do advance military equipment already in use, enhancing its capabilities and cutting down on the time required for an attack, a warning, and a choice. As a result, even as they reduce individual risk, quantum technologies can increase the possibility of utilising force, which raises the likelihood of war [19].

The expense of research and development is particularly high for Qcomm. However, the goal is to develop a technology that makes qubit production simple and reliable. This could lead to the development of technology that is less expensive, more widely accessible, and usable by actors with lower levels of expertise—features that characterise upcoming deadly military technology.

19.6.3   Consequences and Challenges for Military

Quantum technologies have the potential to improve military capabilities through the development of more precise navigation, ultra-secure communication, cutting-edge ISTAR, and cutting-edge computation. Generally speaking, in order to create and acquire new methods and tools for the quantum age, quantum warfare will necessitate the development of new military doctrines, scenarios, and tactics. Technical policies and strategies must first be developed in order to address the strategic goals of several parties. Market research, feasibility studies, state-of-development assessments, military and security threat assessments, and national QTech resources should all be part of national technological plans and strategies (universities, laboratories, and enterprises). Another topic is the cautious sharing of key quantum advantages with allies, especially in the fields of quantum ISTAR and quantum cyber capabilities, which have the ability to divulge military secrets like confidential documents, the whereabouts of nuclear submarines, or underground sites. A sudden change in the balance of power could annoy allies as well as hostile or neutral players.

19.7   Conclusion

Numerous potentially disruptive applications of the growing science of QTech involve the manipulation and control of individual quanta. Many of these applications are used specifically in the military or have many purposes. Through being used in military applications, each QTech has a TRL, which ranges from TRL 1 (following fundamental principles) to TRL 6. (Relevant environment proven technology.)

Quantum technologies for military applications require the development of novel strategies, tactics, and regulations, the assessment of threats to global security, and the identification of moral quandaries in addition to improvements and new capabilities. All of the aforementioned concepts are encapsulated in the term "quantum warfare."

Numerous quantum technologies with various TRLs are explored in this article, with a focus on how they might be applied to or used in the defence sector. It is impossible to foresee how QTech will be applied since the transition from laboratory to real-world applications has not yet occurred or is in progress. This raises the question of whether it is technically possible to get resolutions that offer genuine quantum advantages over conventional systems, which are often much cheaper and commonly in use. We must be cautious of the quantum hype and pay attention to the challenges that still need to be overcome, even though projections about the possibilities for using QTech in the military may sound overly optimistic. The implications of QTech are both immediate and long term. However, there is a low probability that a technical surprise will affect military and defence capabilities. The best strategy to avoid surprises is to maintain a working understanding of QTech and keep a watch on its development and use. Careful application of QTech will provide protection.

References

1. Lindsay, J. R. (2020). Demystifying the quantum threat: infrastructure, institutions, and intelligence advantage. *Security Studies, 29*(2), 335-361.
2. Krelina, M. Quantum technology for military applications. *EPJ Quantum Technol.* 8, 24 (2021).
3. Parker, Edward, *Commercial and Military Applications and Timelines for Quantum Technology*. Santa Monica, CA: RAND Corporation, 2021.
4. Lind W *et al.* The changing face of war: into the fourth generation. In: *Marine Corps Gazette*. 1989.
5. Lind WS. Understanding fourth generation war. *Mil Rev.* 2004;84:12.
6. Affan Ahmed S, Mohsin M, Muhammad Zubair Ali S. Survey and technological analysis of laser and its defense applications. *Defence Technology* (2020). ISSN 2214-9147.
7. Dowling JP, Milburn GJ. Quantum technology: the second quantum revolution. *Philos Trans R Soc, Math Phys Eng Sci.* 2003;361(1809):1655–74.

8. Till S, Pritchard J. UK quantum technology landscape 2016. DSTL/PUB098369, UK National Quantum Technologies Programme. 2016.
9. Davies A, Kennedy P. Special report - from little things: quantum technologies and their application to defence. ASPI (Australian Strategic Policy Institute); 2017.
10. Wolf S. A. *et al.* Overview of the status of quantum science and technology and recommendations for the DoD. Institute for defense analyses; 2019.
11. Andas H. Emerging technology trends for defence and security. FFI-RAPPORT. Apr. 2020.
12. Inglesant P, Jirotka M, Hartswood M. Responsible Innovation in Quantum Technologies applied to Defence and National Security. NQIT (Networked Quantum Information Technologies); 2018.
13. Perani G. Military technologies and commercial applications: public policies in NATO countries. July 1997.
14. Nouwens M, Legarda H. China's pursuit of advanced dual-use technologies. IISS. Dec. 2018.
15. Davidson A. A new dimension of war: the quantum domain. Canadian Forces College. 2020.
16. Reding DF, Eaton J. Science & technology trends 2020-2040. NATO science & technology organization. 2020.
17. Makarov V, Hjelme DR. Faked states attack on quantum cryptosystems. *J Mod Opt.* 2005;52(5):691–705.
18. Zhao Y, *et al.* Quantum hacking: experimental demonstration of time-shift attack against practical quantum-key-distribution systems. *Physical Review A.* 2008;78(4).
19. Venegas-Gomez A. The quantum ecosystem and its future workforce. *Photonics Views.* 2020;17(6):34–8.
20. Alagic G, *et al.* Status Report on the Second Round of the NIST Post-Quantum Cryptography Standardization Process. NISTIR 8309, NSIT; 2020.
21. Altmann J. Technology, Arms Control and World Order: Fundamental Change Needed. Toda Peace Institute, Policy Brief No. 89. Sept. 2020, p. 16.
22. Krelina, M. (2021). Quantum warfare: definitions, overview and challenges. *arXiv preprint arXiv:2103.12548.*
23. Neumann, N. M., van Heesch, M. P., & de Graaf, P. (2020). Quantum communication for military applications. *arXiv preprint arXiv:2011.04989.*
24. Lele, A. (2021). Military Relevance of Quantum Technologies. In *Quantum Technologies and Military Strategy* (pp. 117-143). Springer, Cham.
25. Lindsay, J. R. (2020). Demystifying the quantum threat: infrastructure, institutions, and intelligence advantage. *Security Studies, 29*(2), 335-361.

20

Potential Threats and Ethical Risks of Quantum Computing

Apurva Namdev[1]*, Darshan Patni[1], Balwinder Kaur Dhaliwal[2], Sunil Parihar[3], Shrikant Telang[4] and Anjali Rawat[5]

[1]Department of Computer Science Engineering, Shri Vaishnav Vidyapeeth Vishwavidyalaya, Indore, India
[2]School of Computer Science and Engineering, Lovely Professional University Punjab, Punjab, India
[3]Department of Computer Science and Engineering, Sri Aurobindo Institute of Technology, Indore, M.P., India
[4]Department of Information Technology, Shri Vaishnav Vidyapeeth Vishwavidyalaya, Indore, India
[5]Apostelle Overseas Education, Ujjain, India

Abstract

There are likely to be ethical risks if quantum computers are used more frequently and transition from research to commercial applications. These obstacles can be divided into those that undermine current safeguards, amplify current issues, and produce completely new classes of dangers. Instead of serving as a comprehensive list of all dangers, the following topics are designed to be viewed as illustrative of the different types of risks we could encounter.

Keywords: Cybersecurity, encryption protocols, quantum computers, quantum ethics, Risk management, internet traffic optimization

20.1 Introduction

Computer science's application of quantum theory is known as quantum computing [1]. The behaviour of energy and matter at the atomic and subatomic levels is explained by quantum theory. Subatomic particles, such as electrons

---

*Corresponding author: apurvanamdev2001@gmail.com

Romil Rawat, Rajesh Kumar Chakrawarti, Sanjaya Kumar Sarangi, Jaideep Patel, Vivek Bhardwaj, Anjali Rawat and Hitesh Rawat (eds.) Quantum Computing in Cybersecurity, (335–352) © 2023 Scrivener Publishing LLC

or photons, are used in quantum computing. These particles can exist simultaneously in two states (i.e., 1 and 0) thanks to quantum bits, or qubits. Linked qubits may theoretically use the interference between their wave-like quantum states to accomplish calculations that would otherwise take millions of years. In order to encode information in bits, traditional computers nowadays use a binary stream of electrical impulses (1 and 0). Compared to quantum computing, this limits their ability to process information.

20.1.1   Knowledge of Quantum Computing

The 1980s saw the emergence of the quantum computing field [2]. It was found that some computational issues could be solved more effectively by quantum algorithms than by classical ones. Quantum computing has the capacity to sort through enormous quantities of options and identify potential answers to difficult issues. Quantum computers use qubits, as opposed to classical computers, which store information as bits with either 0s or 1s. Qubits store information in a multidimensional quantum state that interacts with 0 and 1 [3]. Some of the biggest companies have taken notice of this enormous processing capacity and the anticipated size of the market for its utilization. These include NEC, Raytheon, Lockheed Martin, IBM, Microsoft, Google, D-Waves Systems, Alibaba, Nokia, Intel, Airbus, HP, Toshiba, Mitsubishi, SK Telecom, etc.

20.1.2   Limitations of Quantum Computing

In several areas, quantum computing holds great promise for advancement and problem-solving [4]. However, it is currently constrained.

- Even the smallest change in the qubit environment can result in decay, or decoherence. This causes computations to fail or make mistakes in them. As mentioned before, a quantum computer has to be shielded from all outside disturbance while it is doing calculations.
- Error correction in the computation step is still not entirely reliable. Because of this, calculations may not be accurate. Qubits cannot take use of the traditional error correcting techniques employed by classical computers since they are not digital bits of data.
- Data corruption can occur when retrieving calculation results. There is potential in innovations like a specific database search algorithm that guarantees that the quantum state will decohere into the proper response upon measurement.

- Quantum cryptography and security have not yet reached their full potential.
- Quantum computers are unable to leverage their full potential for effect due to a paucity of qubits. More than 128.7 has yet to be produced by researchers.

20.1.3 Quantum Computer vs. Classical Computer

Compared to conventional computers, quantum computers have a simpler design. They lack a CPU [5] and memory. A collection of superconducting qubits is all that a quantum computer needs. Information is processed differently by quantum computers than by conventional computers. As qubits are added, their processing capability grows exponentially. Bits are used by a traditional processor to run different programmes. As additional bits are added, their power rises linearly. The processing power of traditional computers is substantially lower. For routine operations, traditional computers perform well and have low error rates. For example, performing simulations, evaluating data (such as for chemical or pharmacological trials), and developing energy-efficient batteries are all tasks that quantum computers are best suited for. They may also make a lot of mistakes. Traditional computers don't require extra-special maintenance. They could employ a straightforward internal fan to prevent overheating. Extreme frigid temperatures and protection from even the smallest vibrations are requirements for quantum computers. For it, super-cooled superfluids [6] are required. Compared to conventional computers, quantum computers are more costly and challenging to construct. Figure 20.1. shows the difference between traditional computers and quantum computers.

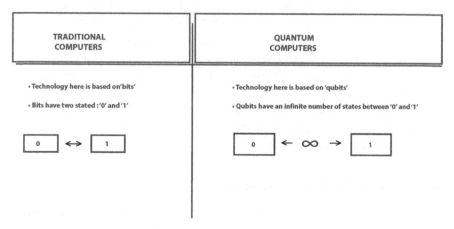

Figure 20.1 The difference between traditional computers and quantum computers [1, 2].

20.1.4   Diving Deep into Quantum Computers

Quantum computers [6] are no exception to the rule that new technologies present both new potential and new threats. While businesses and governments are pouring billions of dollars into quantum technology, there are still numerous unanswered concerns regarding utilisation and use cases. Potential ethical issues from abuse, misuse, or unforeseen repercussions are among Quantum's "known unknowns." Leaders must establish the proper ethical boundaries in order to protect their organisations and their reputations. Creating barriers for a technology with ambiguous current uses and capacities is a difficulty, of course.

Given the uncertainty surrounding the timing of its widespread deployment, it might seem premature to be concerned about the ethical ramifications of quantum computing. However, this moment is ideal. The consequences of failing to anticipate potential ethical problems are well known to the globe. Technologists can achieve company goals without a top-down directive for ethical development, but their innovations may have unforeseen, unethical outcomes. Take into account how swiftly machine learning was incorporated into business practises before people realised the potential harm it may cause to a company's consumers and reputation.

20.1.5   Three Potential Ethical Issues Associated with Quantum Computing

Quantum [8] is still gaining momentum despite its drawbacks. In the next three years, according to an International Data Group prediction, 25% of *Fortune* 500 corporations will employ quantum computing. Within the next ten years, quantum is expected to establish itself as a business staple.

There are likely to be ethical risks if quantum computers are used more frequently and transition from research to commercial applications. These obstacles can be divided into those that undermine current safeguards, those that amplify current issues, and those that produce completely new classes of dangers. Instead of serving as a comprehensive list of all dangers, the following topics are designed to be viewed as illustrative of the different types of risks we could encounter.

20.1.6   Sensitive Data in the Open

Without protection, a lot of private data, even older data, will be exposed. "Our secure communication can be recorded today, and years from now, a quantum computer will be able to decrypt it. The secrets of today will all be forgotten," warned Tanja Lange, professor of cryptology at Eindhoven University of Technology [9–11]. Private information, financial and health records, as well as national secrets, are all involved. Lange began to recognise the value of alternative systems in 2006 and is currently working to raise awareness and create new systems. Recently, security agencies like the NSA have begun to use post-quantum cryptography, and businesses have begun to seek solutions.

ORGANIZATION OF CHAPTER
The remaining chapter is broken out as follows. Section 20.2 illustrates design & methodology; Section 20.3 illustrates how quantum can potentially undermine current safeguards and how quantum might intensify current systems; Section 20.4 suggests how quantum might produce hazards; Section 20.5 illustrates the future of quantum ethics; and Section 6 concludes this chapter.

20.2   Research Design & Methodology

In order to locate the relevant existing studies, a thorough literature review was done. We outline the objective and present the designated research questions in this part. Additionally, we give a description of the research methodology, selection criteria for final papers, and criteria for including and excluding participants, all of which will help the study lead to a full analysis of quantum cybersecurity.

20.2.1   Research Objectives

One of the most unanticipated dangers to cybersecurity has undoubtedly been the emergence and development of quantum physics. We carefully evaluated the following research issues to be addressed in this study after evaluating our goal for this paper:

Q1: What exactly is quantum computing, and how does it relate to cybersecurity?
Q2: What opportunities and potential risks does quantum cybersecurity hold?
Q3: What quantum cybersecurity advancements are necessary?

20.2.2   Primary Studies Selection

A "Search Process" was implemented to identify research papers that address our topic of study. We first prepared the potential search strings related to the study topic which contained the most used keywords. Figure 20.2 shows the specificity of keywords majorly displayed.

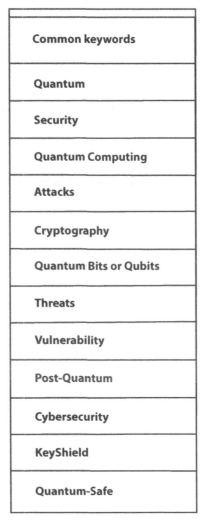

Figure 20.2 The specificity of keywords majorly displayed [7, 8].

20.3 Brief In-Depth Overview of Possible Vulnerabilities

While it appears that quantum computing has the potential to completely transform a number of businesses, one that is endangered by its emergence is cybersecurity. Quantum computing may also render conventional encryption schemes ineffective.

20.3.1 Quantum Technology's Risk to Cybersecurity

The entire scope of cybersecurity's detrimental impacts is still unknown. Cybersecurity [2, 4] can be impacted by quantum computing in a few specific areas, though. Breaking the RSA cryptography is one of them.

The RSA encryption technology, which is frequently used for delivering sensitive information over the internet, is based on a 2048-bit integer. According to specialists in the field, 70 million qubits would be required for quantum computers to decrypt the data. Since there is currently just one quantum computer with 53 qubits, it can take a while to decrypt data. However, given how quickly businesses are moving forward, it is impossible to ignore the creation of the first quantum computers within the next ten years.

Threat actors employing quantum computing to perform covert cyberattacks is another problem for quantum computing's cybersecurity. The majority of today's software is unable to recognise the many behaviours and signs of these dangers from quantum computing.

20.3.1.1 How may Cybersecurity be Improved by Using Quantum Computing?

With a higher adoption rate, the danger posed by quantum computing to cybersecurity use cases will only intensify. However, this does not imply that businesses cannot leverage quantum computing to improve their cybersecurity. Industry insiders are upbeat about quantum computing and predict that cybersecurity would greatly benefit from privacy and encryption techniques.

20.3.1.2 Risks Associated with Quantum Computers

Quantum computers will soon be so sophisticated that they will be able to simulate very complex systems. Simulations in physics, aerospace engineering, cybersecurity, and many other fields might all benefit from using this. However, once it is constructed, this computer could be able to decipher data encryption rules. Due to its capacity to scan huge distances for nearby networked devices or open apps, it may also endanger air gaps. This implies that external hackers may find it even easier. They could already have access to your computer or computer system through different means, such as web browser flaws. You may be making it much simpler for them by not locking all the doors.

A fundamentally new concept of computing is suggested by quantum computers. a comprehension that one day could be applied to solve issues currently regarded as absolutely unsolvable. The field appears to have a lot of potential right now. One of the most intriguing theoretical tools in artificial intelligence, according to quantum computing researchers. Imagine it as a very advanced calculator that has been programmed with extensive subject-matter knowledge. Quantum computing has the possibility of providing solutions to a wide range of mathematical, scientific, and medical issues that humans might otherwise lack the courage to address. They might assist in breaking through vast databases that are currently impenetrable or they might pick up minute details like geological signatures warning us about tsunamis long before they actually occur. They promise profound advancements in imaging that will rival even experimental intracellular MRI scans.

Currently, cryptography is used to encrypt data so that it may be safeguarded while travelling via the internet, safeguarding the privacy of online communication. Everything is secured, including distant work email access and internet shopping. Industry experts estimate that it will be at least another 10 years until quantum computers with extremely high numbers of qubits are ready, despite the fact that quantum computing capabilities are expanding quickly.

Algorithms on quantum computers may be able to defeat the current state of public key encryption. To avoid this, researchers are working hard to study, choose, and enhance dozens of potential algorithms that will replace the present ones.

The technology is at its infancy currently and won't be fully developed for several decades, giving us a small window to improve the present digital and IT infrastructure in order to be ready for a quantum future.

20.3.1.3   What is the Most Pressing Cybersecurity Issue that Executives are Presently Facing?

The largest difficulty leaders currently face, in my opinion, is realizing that the expense of cybersecurity has been left out of our current IT architecture.

Due to the sunk cost of these outdated expenditures, firms often choose to use complex risk management strategies to defend their decisions rather than follow best practices.

Unless mandated by legal requirements, considering extra safeguards for new technology frequently appears to be a pleasant to have rather than a need when this is already a burden. A recommended approach is to set aside 10% of your IT budget for non-staff spending on information security. If everyone started acting in that way, our capacity for innovation would catch up to our outdated infrastructure. Then, we would gradually but surely feel safer.

20.3.1.4   What Potential Risks Could Quantum Computing Pose?

The encryption techniques that protect our data might be broken by a powerful quantum computer. Managed detection and response systems are excellent at safeguarding data in the present, but they are ineffective against a quantum computer. Even the algorithms that are employed by the New York Stock Exchange might be compromised by quantum computers. The stock market may crash as a result of this.

20.3.1.5   Hacking Quantum Computers is Not Possible

The employment of quantum computers in a cyberattack would make it exceedingly challenging to find the perpetrator. This is so that traditional computers cannot compromise quantum computers. They are also impervious to hacking by other quantum computers.

20.3.1.6   Do Any Quantum Computers Exist Now that are Available for Purchase?

There is a quantum computer with 128 qubits available right now. Although the gadget is expensive for the majority of people and enterprises, big firms and governments can easily afford it. Figure 20.3 shows about the potential threats or security vulnerability causes [3, 4] and Figure 20.4 shows how vulnerability increases as we go down to the stack for different levels. It can carry out the following tasks that are challenging for traditional computers:

A. Dealing with efficiency issues
B. Identifying items
C. Creating algorithms for machine learning

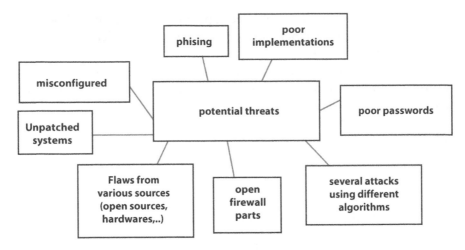

Figure 20.3 Potential threats or security vulnerability causes [3, 4].

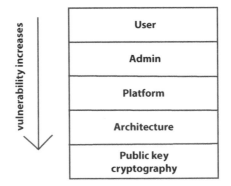

Figure 20.4 How vulnerability increases as we go down to the stack for different levels [5, 6].

20.3.2   Ethical Conditions and Risks

The transition to quantum computing poses the most serious and imminent security vulnerabilities connected to cryptographic encryption. Cryptography is the cornerstone of a secure network, which is essential to the world's internet economy. In a quantum environment, the complicated techniques used to generate public and private keys to decrypt encrypted data are ineffective. Figure 20.3 shows the potential threats or security vulnerability causes and Figure 20.4 shows how vulnerability increases as we go down to the stack for different levels.

The fundamental tenet of cryptographic encryption is that a key, or unlocking code, must be present in order to read an encrypted file. Your files are more secure since it takes a computer longer to decrypt keys with greater lengths.

To put this into perspective, in 2002 a 64-bit key was cracked after four years of labour and 300,000 individuals. It may take billions of years to find a matching key using 128-bit key encryption.

In order to improve security and get consumers ready for the coming of quantum computing, the National Institute of Standards and Technology (NIST) has increased the industry standard for key length protocol from 128 bits to 256 bits.

Cryptography [11], however, is only one component of the puzzle. It is impossible to prevent someone from opening a malicious file attachment or clicking on a deceptive link, no matter how secure your encryption and signature procedures are. In the quantum era, organisations might lose an inconceivable amount of money due to software bugs, access misuse, and other human-related issues.

20.3.3 Protect Yourselves Against these Threats

Numerous technologies, including 5G, AI with machine learning, and quantum computing, have significantly advanced digitization. But frequently, new technology is introduced before all of the bugs have been identified and fixed. We may claim that the outdated cybersecurity [2, 4] systems are the cause of it.

Organizations should concentrate on building a cohesive cybersecurity ecosystem to monitor the network, identify vulnerabilities, and address security concerns since the theory underlying quantum computing will render our present encryption mechanisms outdated.

Companies can take the following steps to safeguard themselves against potential risks:

20.3.3.1 Implement Industry Security Guidelines

Most individuals found their "new normal" by using digital internet tools and linked gadgets when COVID-19 pushed everyone to discover new methods to communicate, work, and do business. The security dangers to businesses and customers have increased significantly as a result of the growth in remote employment prospects brought on by this influx of new internet users.

The encryption strength of your keys should be at least 128 bits for data with little effect, according to the NIST's latest industry recommendations, 192 bits for data with moderate effect, and 256 bits for data with high impact.

By mandating cybersecurity technologies for asset discovery, vulnerability assessment, continuous security monitoring, and event reporting, obtaining ISO compliance also aids in protecting your company.

20.3.3.2   Establish Zero Trust

You may improve your technical cybersecurity by adhering to industry security standards, whether they are required or not, but using zero-trust authentication procedures can assist to lower risks related to human error.

Scammers are cunning, and they frequently employ social engineering techniques to gain the trust of the people they want to take advantage of and obtain personal information, money, or credentials from. Social engineering techniques like spoofing and phishing include an attacker impersonating a trusted user to spread malware over a network or get access to sensitive login data.

Attacks like spoofing and phishing may be quite stealthy. In actuality, targeted individuals open an astounding 30% of phishing emails and SMS communications. The infected attachment or link is selected by another 12% of those users.

By allocating access based on need rather than rank inside a firm, zero-trust protocols can lessen the impact of phishing and other social engineering assaults. Since no one person is trusted with "the keys to the kingdom," as it were, this prevents sensitive information from leaking out in the event that credentials are compromised.

20.3.3.3   Automated Tools Deployment

There are several cybersecurity protection measures designed to lessen the negative effects that human mistake may have on an organisation, Additionally to reducing productivity, manually resolving vulnerabilities, monitoring your network, and responding to data breaches allows potential for more mistakes.

Because of this, cutting-edge security businesses implement automated technologies to assist them in preserving the integrity of their network. Automated technology can analyse data more thoroughly, more quickly, and at higher rates than individuals can.

According to recent research on cybersecurity adoption, 95% of firms have automated certain cybersecurity procedures already. In addition, the study showed that 98% of respondents intended to automate even more of their manual security procedures in the future year. Additionally, this suggests that companies who don't automate their security measures risk falling behind.

20.3.3.4   Put Controlled Threat Detection into Practice

It looks challenging to switch to a quantum-resistant cybersecurity approach, which is why having educated experts on your side could be advantageous. The best way to ensure that your cybersecurity environment is unhurt is to use managed threat detection through a reliable company. With the help of a managed threat detection and response service, you may arm your business with the best security tools, get continual monitoring, and get support with response when you need it most.

20.3.4   Potential Threats and Existing Risks

20.3.4.1   Cybersecurity

Some experts anticipate that within a decade, hostile nation-states and hackers may employ quantum computers to crack current encryption techniques. This would be a serious setback for a variety of online businesses that depend on encryption, such as e-commerce and other virtual financial operations. The requirement for blockchain platform developers to adapt their systems to employ postquantum cryptography underlines the vulnerability of the cybersecurity protocols of popular blockchain technologies [11], such as Ethereum and Bitcoin.

Organizations may benefit from becoming "crypto-agile" to handle the growing cybersecurity danger posed by quantum computers. To better respond to new protocols, standards, and security risks as they emerge swiftly, businesses must be able to quickly update their cryptographic algorithms, settings, processes, and technologies. This is known as "crypto-agility." Organizations using this strategy must inventory their data, data exchanges, and the cryptographic techniques used to safeguard them. Enterprises should start preparing to implement quantum-resistant encryption standards when they become available, as per the National Institute of Standards and Technology.

20.3.4.2   Access

Due to their physical and technical complexity, it is doubtful that the average person or smaller organisation will ever be able to possess a quantum computer, but that does not mean they cannot benefit. Governments and organisations should consider how to distribute knowledge obtained by quantum computers if they want to propel everyone up the technological adoption curve fairly. If we, as a society, feel it's vital, they have a variety of levers at their disposal, such as grants, subsidies, and other policies, that can hasten access globally. There may also be a role for the suppliers who create and own the technology. Investors are increasingly evaluating the companies they invest in using governance, social, and environmental measures, and many businesses now place a high focus on diversity, equity, and inclusion. Technology firms working on quantum computing systems might make both programmes focus on equal access.

20.3.4.3   Artificial Intelligence, Data Harvesting, and Privacy

There have been significant efforts in recent years to safeguard data privacy and make sure that AI technologies are utilised fairly and in ways that are beneficial in view of common interest. Despite these measures, widespread data collecting continues. The availability of quantum computing could further encourage firms to acquire more consumer data, hence accelerating the data harvesting that already occurs. Future quantum computers will be able to process massive volumes of data more quickly than today's most advanced servers.

20.3.4.4   Explainability

The ultimate black box challenge is presented by quantum computers, and particularly quantum machine learning. Developers of machine learning are aware of this problem. Neural networks for deep learning are infamously opaque. However, specialists in the subject are working on tools that may make it feasible to reveal the inner workings of models in order to comprehend how they arrived at a solution. Although those solutions have their limitations, explainability is at least conceivable in theory.

Quantum machine learning worsens the chances for models that can be explained. Explainability is more of a physics issue than a programming issue with quantum computers. Because quantum algorithms will recognise much more intricate patterns across many more data points than current machine learning models, it will be challenging to assess and appraise the decision-making process. Explainability's existing issue will get worse.

20.3.4.5   Global Tensions and the Quantum "Arms Race"

Today, the majority of industrialised nations are making significant investments in the creation of quantum technology. in 2022, it is anticipated that China, India, Japan, Germany, the Netherlands, Canada, and the United States will invest a total of $5 billion in quantum technology.

Since quantum computing is thought to be essential to developing future defence systems, the situation is occasionally referred to as a new global "arms race." It's not quite clear if "arms race" is the right term given how early in the technological development we are. We are aware that stories can take on lives of their own, though. Positioning efforts to acquire quantum capabilities as an arms competition may unintentionally lead to an increase in international tension. As countries continue to research quantum technologies, we advise caution when referring to this as an "arms race."

20.4   New Risks to be Created

Out of many possible new risk scenarios, examples could include:

20.4.1   Health Care and Life Sciences

In order to better comprehend the implications of minute genetic alterations, biomedical researchers will benefit greatly from the use of quantum computers. Gene editing is a contentious topic on its own, but the advent of new, quicker research methods due to quantum computing may increase worries. This is not to say that DNA editing ought to be stopped. Along with other advantages, it might eradicate many genetic illnesses. But those conducting study in this field need to be watchful for any potential unexpected effects of their effort.

20.4.2   Emerging Materials

It is anticipated that research and development of novel materials will be accelerated by quantum computers. They will probably run complex simulations of how minute changes at the molecular level affect a material's properties, which will be a huge help in fields like drug discovery, carbon capture, and chemical manufacture. The history of novel materials, however, demonstrates how frequently seemingly good things might actually turn out to be harmful. For instance, the insecticide DDT seemed like a clear benefit when it was originally introduced because of its capacity to lower the risk of diseases transmitted by insects.

However, as it was discovered that its usage was destroying bird populations, it was outlawed in most of the world. This is similar to how plastics were at first welcomed with open arms. Only recently have we begun to understand the damage they can do to the environment. Materials researchers should be aware of this history as they attempt to develop new materials and make an effort to prevent comparable environmental problems from arising from any future scientific advances.

20.5 Futuristic Picture of Quantum Ethics

Numerous ethical issues associated with quantum computing are still in the future and hence cannot be quickly addressed. But every day, they get closer and closer. Governments and businesses may take certain steps right away to get ready for the future of quantum technology.

Stakeholders can begin considering the difficulties that could arise and comprehend how their use of quantum computing could in the future provide ethical concerns. The good news is that they can continue where they left off. Existing ethical frameworks exist for comprehending how technology affects society, and many of the main points are applicable to quantum computing. These can aid senior leaders in considering how to include ethics in their work from the beginning.

The quantum strategy of organisations should be guided by this understanding. To take immediate action in the area of ethics and quantum computing, it's probably too soon. However, businesses should gather internal executives and specialists to identify trigger events that will indicate the need to act or boost expenditure, such as a new technology development or competition activity. Creating a reliable quantum technology strategy should include methods for ethical risk reduction.

It might be too late to wait until problems fully manifest. Understanding the ethical issues that come with quantum computing now will make coping with the longer-term consequences easier in the future.

20.5.1   Quantum Computing is Coming of Age

The hype around quantum technologies and their lofty goals is widespread in the headlines. The following are some queries that come to mind in relation to this:

- Given the potential for revolutionary advancements in fields including medical research, financial modelling, combating climate change, traffic optimization, batteries, and more, is this the ideal time to invest?
- How concerned should we be about the possibility for quantum computing to compromise existing encryption standards?
- As business and technology executives seek to make wise decisions for both the present and the future, what has to be done in order to get ready for a future made possible by quantum technology?
- What risks from the future need to be considered—and possibly reduced—starting right now?

Figure 20.5 depicts how the quantum technologies are being expanded.

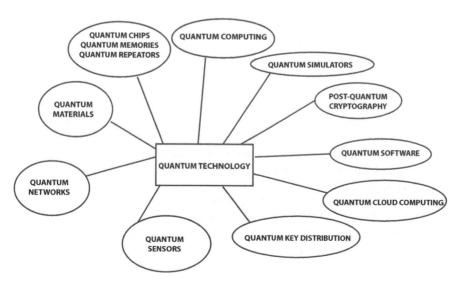

Figure 20.5 How the quantum technologies are being expanded [2, 3].

20.6   Conclusion

This study examines the potential dangers and moral hazards of quantum computing. The power of quantum computing is enormous. We can't rely solely on the tech sector to keep us safe from these dangers. Government laws ought to be a component of the answer, but they often take years to develop. Leaders who are about to adopt quantum should immediately protect both themselves and their clients. Now is their chance to maybe steer clear of the ethical issues that the time of "move quickly and break stuff" left behind.

Everything will alter as a result of quantum computing, including applications, online development, cybersecurity, and more. When new features are introduced, it's a good idea to keep one step ahead of the curve so that your company is prepared with the information and resources it needs to survive the dawn of a new era.

References

1. Hidary, Jack (2019). *Quantum computing: an applied approach.*
2. N. R. Gade and U. Reddy, "A study of cyber security challenges and its emerging trends on latest technologies," *International Journal of Engineering and Technology*, 02 2014.
3. R. P. Uhlig, P. P. Dey, S. Jawad, B. R. Sinha, and M. Amin, "Generating student interest in quantum computing," in *2019 IEEE Frontiers in Education Conference (FIE)*, 2019, pp. 1–9.
4. C. Abellan and V. Pruneri, "The future of cybersecurity is quantum," *IEEE Spectrum*, vol. 55, no. 7, pp. 30–35, 2018.
5. D. Denning, "Is quantum computing a cybersecurity threat?" *American Scientist*, vol. 107, p. 83, 01 2019.
6. Garisto, Daniel. "Light-based Quantum Computer Exceeds Fastest Classical Supercomputers". *Scientific American.*
7. Jones, Nicola (19 June 2013). "Computing: The quantum company". *Nature.*
8. Leonard Adleman, Toward a mathematical theory of self-assembly, USC Tech Report, 2000.
9. Arthur O. Pittenger, *An Introduction to Quantum Computing Algorithms.*
10. John G. Cramer, The Transactional Interpretation of Quantum Mechanics".
11. "ISO/TC 307 Blockchain and distributed ledger technologies". iso.org. ISO. Retrieved 21 June 2021.

21

Is Quantum Computing a Cybersecurity Threat?

**Akshat Maheshwari[1]*, Manan Jain[1], Vindhya Tiwari[1], Mandakini Ingle[2]
and Ashish Chourey[3]**

*[1]Department of Computer Science Engineering,
Shri Vaishnav Vidyapeeth Vishwavidyalaya, Indore, India
[2]Department of Computer Science and Engineering, Medicaps University,
Indore, India
[3]Department of Computer Science and Engineering, SIRT, Bhopal, India*

Abstract

It is crucial to take a closer look at digital encryption and the ways in which it is used—and broken—in order to comprehend the risk and what can be done about it. With quantum cryptography, neither the transmitter nor the receiver of the message can be tricked into compromising the system's security. It has gained more attention recently and has emerged as one of the most promising areas of cryptography for quicker, more efficient, and more secure communication. However, compared to what the finest quantum computers of today have achieved, breaking quantum computers in the future will require 100,000 times more processing power and a 100 times lower error rate.

While it seems like quantum computing (QCom) has the ability to dramatically change a number of industries, cybersecurity is one that is put in jeopardy by its arrival. It is possible that Qcom (QCom) will make conventional cryptography methods useless. We still don't fully understand the harmful implications of cybersecurity. Unfortunately, Qcom can influence cybersecurity in a few specific areas. When beginning to plan for quantum safety, IT strategists should take the cybersecurity implications of Qcom into account. Their long-term cybersecurity plan must include making sensitive data, risk management practises, identity management systems, and linked technologies quantum secure.

Keywords: Quantum key distribution, cryptanalysis, quantum hacking, quantum internet, device-independent cryptography

**Corresponding author*: maheshwariakshat482@gmail.com

Romil Rawat, Rajesh Kumar Chakrawarti, Sanjaya Kumar Sarangi, Jaideep Patel, Vivek Bhardwaj, Anjali Rawat and Hitesh Rawat (eds.) Quantum Computing in Cybersecurity, (353–368) © 2023 Scrivener Publishing LLC

ORGANIZATION OF CHAPTERS

The rest of the chapter is organized as follows: Section 1 is an introduction which discusses the background of the study, including Quantum cryptography, quantum computing, cryptography, the method of the study, and the objective of study. Section 21.2 describes how Quantum Computing threatens cybersecurity, and areas where Quantum computing could endanger cybersecurity; Section 21.3 describes how Quantum computing could improve cybersecurity, encryption techniques, and privacy protection; Section 21.4 examines the Proposed Methodology where the threats of Quantum to cybersecurity and challenges are described; Section 21.5 describes the background and objective of the study; Section 21.6 is the conclusion and provides a short description of the whole study.

21.1   Introduction

The majority of the existing cryptography could be broken by a new form of computer that is based on quantum physics rather than more conventional electronics, which is the reason cybersecurity researchers and analysts are deeply worried. None of the widely used encryption techniques can be broken by the quantum computers that seem to be currently in existence. In order to crack the robust codes that have been used on the internet for a long time, it will take considerable technological improvements, according to 2018 research from the National Academies of Sciences, Engineering, and Medicine. Quantum cryptography [1] is a type of encryption that makes use of some of quantum physics' inherent qualities to transmit and protect data in a way that cannot be cracked.

Encrypting and safeguarding data using a secret key allows only the person who has it to be able to decrypt it, which is the process of cryptography. Because physics, not mathematics, is the primary component of its security model, quantum cryptography differs from conventional cryptographic systems in this regard [6].

Without the knowledge of either the message sender or the message receiver, quantum cryptography is an entirely secure system. To put it another way, it is impossible to replicate or read data encoded in a quantum state without revealing it to the transmitter or recipient. Quantum cryptography should also continue to be protected from users of quantum computers. Quantum cryptography makes use of the properties of quantum physics to safeguard and transmit data in a way that cannot be intercepted.

By employing cryptography to encrypt and secure data, only those with the right secret key may decrypt it. Quantum cryptography, in contrast to traditional cryptographic systems, bases its security notion more on physics than mathematics. With quantum cryptography [2, 3], neither the transmitter nor the message recipient can be tricked into compromising the system's security. That is, it is difficult to replicate or examine data encoded in a quantum state without notifying the transmitter or recipient [1].

21.1.1   Need for Cybersecurity

Cybersecurity [1] includes both the averting of harm to electronic communication systems and services as well as the defence of the data they hold. Maintaining data availability, secrecy, authentication, and non-repudiation is also a part of this. Cisco [1, 2] defines it as the practise of adding several layers of protection across systems and networks [5] to thwart assaults on sensitive information or business operations. It is critically important to safeguard personal, commercial, and governmental data since there has been a sharp increase in cyber dangers as a result of the availability of more data. The complexity of network architecture [3], network risks like wiretapping and eavesdropping, growing network capacity, and violations of the six security principles — authorization, availability, privacy, non-repudiation [3], integrity, and audit — could be the main security issues [6].

As one might expect, the impact of sensitive data being compromised can be significant, and firms may incur significant losses if information about financial transactions, including those involving e-commerce, bank transactions, credit card processing, or stock trading, is compromised. Data security is undoubtedly a top concern in the globe right now. Data must be encrypted in order to be transmitted securely through an electronic medium. Cryptology is the underlying science of encryption [11].

21.1.2   What is Quantum Computing?

In essence, quantum computing (QCom) makes use of quantum mechanics' features to carry out calculations. This is in contrast to conventional computers, which follow the laws of classical physics.

Qubits are the informational units used in quantum computers [4, 5]. These can be found in superpositions of zero and one as well as states of zero and one. Classical computers, in contrast, only store data using ones and zeros.

Quantum computers have distinct capabilities from conventional computers since they operate on entirely different principles. Numerous specialists anticipate that they will be able to do computations and resolve mathematical issues that traditional computers are simply unable to handle.

Although it has not yet been achieved, this accomplishment is known as quantum supremacy.

The following are some potential uses for quantum computing [6, 7]:

- Modeling complicated chemical processes, which might result in innovation and chemistry advancements.
- Advanced financial modeling.
- Predict changes in the weather and climate with better precision.
- Running more advanced AI applications.
- Computations in advanced physics.
- Proposing new cryptosystems and dismantling cryptographic techniques that are now considered safe.

21.1.3 What is Cryptography?

An original piece of information [4], such as a message, is transformed through a process called encryption into something that resembles nonsense. Modern digital cyphers [13] convert plain data into and out of securely encrypted communications [12] to be stored or communicated using intricate mathematical algorithms [15]. A pair of mathematically connected keys is used in asymmetric encryption (AE), also known as public key encryption, to encrypt and decode messages. One of the mathematically linked keys is published publicly to allow others to encrypt messages for the key pair's owner. In symmetric encryption, the same key is used for both encryption and decryption of data. Public-key cryptography is significantly slower than symmetric encryption. It is used to encrypt all conversations and data that is kept because of this. For safely transmitting symmetric keys as well as digitally authenticating—or signing—messages, documents, and certificates that link public keys to their owners' identities, public-key cryptography is utilized. Your browser utilizes public-key cryptography to validate a website's certificate when you visit a secure website—one that uses HTTPS protocols—and to create a symmetric key for encrypting communications to and from the site.

21.1.4 Symmetric Cryptography

Symmetric key cryptography [14], often known as symmetric encryption, is the practise of encrypting and decrypting [15] data using a single secret key. AE [17], in which one key is used for encryption and another for decryption, is in contrast to this method. During this process, the

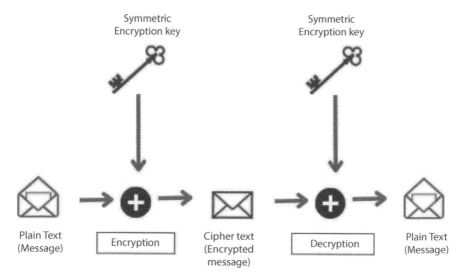

Figure 21.1 Symmetric cryptography [1–3].

data is transformed into a format that prevents anyone who doesn't have access to the secret key that was used to encrypt it from reading or analysing it. The quality of the secret key produced by the random number generator will determine how successful this method is. Symmetric key cryptography, which primarily uses the Block and Stream kinds of algorithms, is commonly used on the current internet. Two well-liked encryption techniques are the Advanced Encryption Standard (AES) [12] and the Data Encryption Standard (DES) [13]. Although symmetric encryption is frequently faster, it requires that both the sender and the recipient of the data have access to a secret key. Asymmetric cryptography, which does not rely on the sharing of a secret key, is the foundation of the FIDO [15, 17–20] authentication system. Figure 21.1 illustrates symmetric cryptography.

21.1.5   Asymmetric Cryptography

Messages may be encrypted and decrypted using asymmetric cryptography, also known as public-key cryptography, which protects them against unauthorised access or use. A public key is a cryptographic key that anybody may use to encrypt communications such that only the intended recipient may decode them using their private key. It uses a pair of connected keys, a public key and a private key. When delivering an encrypted communication, one can get the intended recipient's public key from a public directory

Symmetric Key

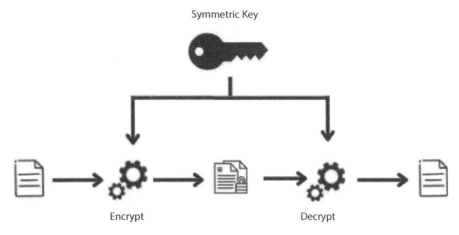

Encrypt   Decrypt

Figure 21.2 Public key cryptography [4–6].

and use it to encrypt the message before sending it. A private key, also known as a secret key, is only exposed to the key's originator [19, 20].

The recipient of the communication can then decrypt it using their individual private key. Only the sender's public key may be used to decode communications encrypted with their private key, establishing the sender's identity. These encryption and decryption processes don't require the user to physically lock and unlock the communication. Many protocols, including the secure sockets layer (SSL) [12] and transport layer security (TLS) protocols that allow HTTPS, employ asymmetric cryptography. The encryption [9] process is also used by software programmes that need to create a secure connection across an unsecured network, such as web browsers, or that need to validate a digital signature. The main benefit of asymmetric cryptography is improved data security [12]. It is the most secure encryption technique currently accessible since users are never required to reveal or share their private keys. This lessens the possibility of a hacker intercepting a user's private key during transmission. Figure 21.2 shows the Public key Cryptography.

21.1.6   Classical and Quantum Cryptography

Security is now more important than ever in this age of information technology. Data security is becoming more and more necessary as the majority of our private data is kept on computers. Therefore, securing sensitive data from illegal access is crucial for both operating systems and users. One such technique for preventing unauthorized parties from stealing or

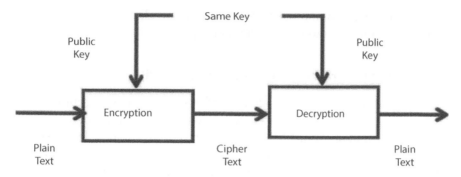

Figure 21.3 Classical and quantum cryptography [5, 7, 8].

intercepting sensitive data is cryptography. Although traditional cryptology is indeed sophisticated, it is being phased out much like all previous encoding techniques. Quantum physics is used in quantum cryptography to provide secure communication. This makes it possible for two parties to create a secret shared random bit string that can be used as a key to encrypt and decode communications. Figure 21.3 shows the Classical and Quantum Cryptography.

21.1.7   Quantum Computing's Effects on Existing Cryptography

Popular encryption techniques [15, 18] include RSA [16, 18], AES, ECC, Diffie-Hellman, and Blowfish. The security basis for well-known security infrastructure offered by companies like Microsoft, Nokia, and Cisco is Rivest, Shamir, Adleman (RSA), which is still a global standard. The Advanced Encryption Standard (AES) is utilised to provide client/server encryption for online communication in a similar manner. In the Internet of Things, elliptic curve cryptography (ECC) is frequently employed (IoT). Users share secret keys using the Diffie Hellman (DH) method, whereas Blowfish is an alternative strategy with a variable-length key that may be used in place of RSA and DES. Therefore, at the moment, we rely on cryptographic keys, which are built using intricate mathematical calculations. The mathematical calculation is more difficult and takes longer with a longer key, increasing network security by making it more difficult to decrypt the key. Traditional computers cannot defeat certain mathematical calculations utilised in cryptography systems. In contrast, the future wouldn't be like this. The way that data is processed by Qcom has changed from two distinct steps to quantum bits. Quantum parallelism is a property that allows it to exist in numerous phases at once and allows operations to be performed simultaneously on all qubits [11].

21.1.8 Cryptography Does Not Mean Security

To ensure total individual and societal cybersecurity, strong cryptography is essential. It serves as the basis for secure data transfer and storage as well as the establishment of reliable links between systems and people. However, cryptography is only a small portion of a much broader whole. Even the strongest encryption can't prevent someone from accessing a malicious file or clicking on a deceptive link in an email attachment. Additionally, encryption is unable to stop insiders from misusing their access to data or the inevitable software faults. Even if the math were impenetrable, there may still be flaws in the application of cryptography. For instance, Microsoft recently discovered two applications that mistakenly made their users' private encryption keys available to the public, making their conversations unsecure. When or if powerful Qcom is introduced, it will represent a serious security risk. It is advisable to start making preparations for quantum-resistant encryption right away because the process of establishing new standards might take years [2].

21.2 How QCom Threatens Cybersecurity

We do not yet fully understand how QCom will impact cybersecurity. However, there are two areas where QCom could endanger cybersecurity that experts are currently debating. The major concern is that RSA cryptography could be compromised by quantum computing. Due to its efficiency, QCom may be able to solve some algorithms, such as RSA, more quickly [6]. It is a component of complex activities. According to Jack Poller of Tech Target, "Keeping the key secret so that no one else can decrypt your data is based on the mathematical principles of prime numbers; to extract the key requires a difficult math problem; if the key is large enough, it won't happen in our lifetime. Say I give you a big enough key and the world's largest [classic] computer. It would still take over a lifetime to decode, making it worthless to you. With quantum computing, you can take advantage of specific algorithms to shrink that time down." Shor's algorithm and Grover's algorithm are two examples of quantum algorithms that potentially break RSA. These quantum algorithms won't immediately defeat RSA, but they will gradually do so. Because it would be protected by older encryption that quantum could eventually crack, stored data that uses current encryption would be most at danger.

Merritt Maxim, vice president and analyst at Forrester, said: "That's kind of a challenging conceptual thing for folks to get their minds around." The risk actually rises over time as quantum becomes more developed and applicable, which is where the threat from quantum is, according to the author. Hackers employing QCom to disguise assaults is a second problem for cybersecurity, according to Poller. These QCom attacks might exhibit unique characteristics and signatures that elude conventional software. The initial wave of attacks "will be difficult to identify," Poller said. However, similar attacks in the future will be rapidly found and halted. Between attackers and defenders, "it's always a cat-and-mouse game," he continued [6]. A new wave of technology called QCom will introduce a variety of new methods, some of which are already known to be able to defeat numerous cryptosystems that are used to protect our daily communications [8]. Attackers who obtain access to quantum computers may theoretically be able to use them to compromise systems that are thought to be resistant to attacks using conventional computing, giving them access to previously secure data [8]. The largest danger to our most widely used public-key encryption systems at the current time is quantum computing. A few symmetric-key methods will also be impacted, but not as significantly [8].

21.3   How QCom could Improve Cybersecurity

Not all of quantum computing's implications for cybersecurity are negative. Stronger encryption techniques and privacy protection are two areas where cybersecurity may improve, according to some industry professionals who are hopeful about quantum computing. Privacy-enhancing computing (PEC) approaches secure data while it is in use, in transit, and at rest by keeping it encrypted. PEC techniques have advanced, according to Gartner's "Top Strategic Technology Trends for 2022" study, as a result of hyperscalers employing trusted execution environments and vendors stepping up their individual security efforts. Competitors might collaborate via PEC while maintaining the privacy of all information. The concept of data privacy is contentious. PEC could assist with resolving privacy concerns in use cases like internal analysis and the security of medical records. Lattices, or multidimensional algebraic constructions, can be used in homomorphic encryption, which QCom cannot readily solve. Lattice-based encryption is thought by experts to be the best alternative to the existing techniques.

Choose a number to be encrypted, let the software run the encrypted number till it returns something, then apply some decryption to unlock it, for instance, is what lattices allow you to accomplish, according to Mark Horvath, analyst at Gartner. This enables computation without the need to decode or read data due to the mathematical principles of homomorphic encryption. This is significant since it keeps available a large number of web services that have access to your personal information. It appears to you that the number we are using in the software was clear, but the individuals who execute the program never saw the original, unencrypted form of the number.

21.4   Quantum Cryptography and Its Applications

Using a public key infrastructure, users can safe methods for sending and receiving private data in a network like the internet that isn't secure. PKI mostly makes use of two a few keys a user (Bob) will use the public key, which is an exposed key, to encrypt the data, and a data encrypted with Alice's (the recipient's) public key will be decrypted by Alice using her personal key and delivered to the destination key as displayed in Figure 21.4.

In other words, obtaining the public key alone won't enable the attacker to decrypt ciphered messages because a private key is required. Hackers

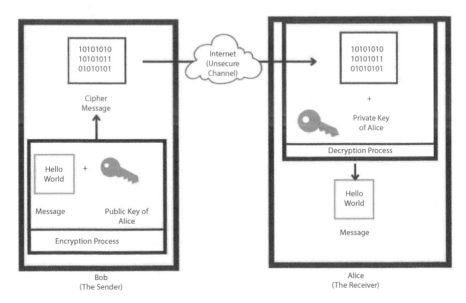

Figure 21.4 Public key cryptography in action [1, 2, 6–8].

tested the viability of extracting the private key using the public key at this point. Due to the complicated math needed to find a private key using a public key, it is currently not able to do so due to a lack of processing capacity in our traditional computers.

However, due to the incredible calculation speed of quantum computers and the use of Shor's Algorithm, the same is also feasible. Quantum Key Distribution is the answer for dealing with such a circumstance. The purpose of QKD is to simply produce and distribute keys to the sender and receiver, so it may be combined with traditional communication methods.

Once they have the key, the sender and receiver can use it to encrypt and decrypt the cypher text. The fact that a quantum state can never be recreated based on the No-cloning Theorem, which states that it is impossible to build an exact duplicate of any arbitrary unknown quantum states, makes this quantum cryptography protocol an unhackable key distribution system. This makes sure that, in the event of a Man in the Middle [MitM] attack, the quantum state that the sender and recipient may receive will be different. If this happens, decryption will fail, alerting the sender and receiver that the channel is insecure.

21.5 Proposed Methodology

Problems that are much too complicated for conventional computers to comprehend will be amenable to solution by quantum computers. This entails deciphering the algorithms that underlie the encryption keys that protect our data and the internet's technological infrastructure. Modern encryption relies significantly on computations that are difficult for computers to effectively decipher from a mathematical standpoint [11]. To further comprehend this, think about combining two huge numbers. Calculating the product is straightforward, but starting with a large integer and dividing it into its two prime integers is much more challenging. A quantum computer [15] can instantly factor those numbers into the code and decipher them. Shor's algorithm, created by Peter Shor, is a quantum technique that computes big numbers much more quickly than a traditional computer. Since then, scientists have worked to develop quantum computers with an expanding set of factoring abilities [7].

21.5.1 The Threat of Quantum to Cybersecurity

The full scope of cybersecurity's adverse effects is still unknown. Cybersecurity can be impacted by QCom in a few specific areas, though.

Breaking the RSA cryptography is one of them. The RSA encryption technology, which is frequently used for delivering sensitive information over the internet, is based on a 2048-bit number. According to experts in the field, 70 million qubits would be required for quantum computers to decrypt the data. Since there is currently only one quantum computer with 53 qubits, it can take a while to decrypt data.

However, given how quickly businesses are moving forward, it is impossible to ignore the creation of the first quantum computers within the next ten years. Threat actors employing QCom to perform secret cyberattacks is another problem for quantum computing's cybersecurity. The majority of today's software is unable to recognize the various behaviors and signatures of these dangers from quantum computing [9].

Another reason to take action now: Scraping Threat - Even though quantum computers are currently commercially available, there is still a chance that malicious actors would scrape quantum-proof data. In order to hang onto the data until they can get their hands on a quantum computer to decrypt it, they have already started stealing it. The information would already have been compromised at that moment. Information security can only be ensured by using a quantum-proof system now, especially for information that must be safeguarded for the foreseeable future [10].

21.5.2   QCom

QCom refers to the utilization of quantum information science to perform computations. A quantum computer can be used to describe such a device. QCom devices can be categorised in a highly complicated way. For the purposes of this report, we simplify the classification as follows:

- The following list of applications for a digital quantum computer, which is universal, programmable, and capable of performing any quantum algorithms, is extensive. The gate-level based quantum computer can be perfectly simulated by classical computers. Resources and speed are different. For instance, the simulation of fully entangled qubits exponentially increases the need for conventional resources. This means that simulating 45 qubits on traditional (super)computers is essentially impossible.
- Quantum annealing is typically used to realise analogue quantum computers. Due to the restricted connectivity of qubits and distinct operating principles, quantum annealer varies from a digital quantum computer. As a result, the use

of analogue quantum computers is more limited but is still appropriate for tasks like quantum optimisations or simulations based on Hamiltonians.

- A quantum simulator is typically designed as a single-purpose device and is utilised for the modelling and research of other quantum systems that are typically less accessible. The quantum simulator can be thought of as a non-programmable quantum circuit as opposed to a quantum computer.

In general, classical computation will continue to exist alongside quantum computing. Only a small subset of problems, often those with high complexity, will be viable and beneficial for quantum computers. The quality (coherence, error resistance, gate integrity) and quantity of the qubits determine how QCom applications are actually implemented. The quantity of qubits, qubit coherence time, quantum-gate fidelity, and qubit inter-connectivity are a few of the crucial variables to consider. A quantum circuit is a collection of quantum instructions that apply quantum gates to distinct qubits. The quantum algorithm is implemented practically in a quantum circuit [12, 13].

21.5.3   QCom Challenge

Cybersecurity is expected to change as a result of quantum computing; however, there are still major issues to be solved and important advances that are still required. The most pressing issue is finding enough fault-tolerant qubits to realize the processing potential of quantum computing. Amazon, Google, Honeywell, IBM, and other businesses are making investments in this issue. Different quantum logic gates are currently used to program quantum computers; while this may work for smaller quantum computers, it becomes impractical as the number of qubits increases. More abstract levels in the programming stack are being developed by businesses like IBM [19] and Classiq [20], enabling programmers to create potent quantum applications to address real-world issues. The dearth of skills in the field of QCom may be the main challenge. Even while universities are producing more computer science graduates than ever before, not much is being done to prepare the upcoming generation of QCom experts. The National Quantum Initiative Act of the United States, which provides financing for educational projects, is a step on the right path. QCom has also given rise to some amazing open-source communities, with the IBM Kiskit [20] community being among the most vibrant and intriguing. Governments, colleges, businesses, and the larger technological ecosystem will need to work together to foster the kind of talent development required to fully benefit from quantum computing [10].

21.6   Background/Objective

The shift from traditional computing to QCom has brought about new difficulties for the encryption community. In quantum computing, the cryptographic techniques that ensured intractability provide a significant difficulty. Methods/Statistical Analysis: Quantum cryptography can be employed without limitations for secure data communications by using the principles of quantum physics. Findings: The existing cryptography, known as conventional cryptography, is completely dependent on how difficult the mathematical ideas are. Modern cryptography, often known as elliptical curve cryptography, is widely employed to secure financial transactions. This security can be readily overcome by reverse computing keys quicker than traditional computers thanks to advances in QCom [5].

21.7   Conclusion

Over the past few years, researchers have put great effort into creating "quantum-safe" encryption. For what it refers to as "post-quantum cryptography (PQC)," several potential new procedures are now being looked upon by the National Institute of Standards and Technology (NIST). Many questions about QCom remain unanswered, but researchers are working very hard to discover solutions. QCom will undoubtedly have a detrimental impact on cybersecurity and our current encryption techniques, that much is evident. If we want to reduce that risk, we must change the way we protect our data right away. We must employ a defense-in-depth strategy that involves several layers of quantum-safe protection to address the quantum danger, just as we do with other security issues. Quantum Xchange offers crypto-diverse solutions that security-conscious businesses are seeking to make their encryption quantum-safe now and quantum-ready for threats in the future [7]. IT executives should switch to Post-Quantum Cryptography for their company security solutions. Because they were built to survive quantum technology, they are quantum-resistant or quantum-safe. For instance, lattice-based encryption and AES-256 are widely mentioned as quantum-resistant techniques. For the transition from classical encryption to quantum-resistant cryptography, cryptographic agility is also required. In order to adapt to a changing threat environment, organizations should be prepared to embrace and develop new cryptographic solutions. QCom won't likely be used by businesses for profitable purposes for another 10 years, which might have a significant influence on cybersecurity, although it may be difficult to adapt technology stacks to meet the impending threat if organizations do not start preparing for the future, especially as infrastructure consumption rises in the coming decade [9].

It is obvious that the transition from traditional to quantum computers will take some time. According to this forecast, some computing domains will employ both technologies rather than swap out one for the other. Modern cryptography techniques will continue to be used for the duration of the period as quantum computers augment and accelerate the power of conventional systems. The ability of QCom scientists to crack current cryptography to reveal encrypted data and stored data will ultimately have repercussions for national security. According to a *Scientific American* article, the possibility of quantum computers breaking current cryptography is still speculative because their power is insufficient to circumvent widely used encryption techniques. Additionally, contemporary quantum computers are too error-prone for use with present codes, according to the National Academies. Manufacturers and developers still need significant technological advancements in order to successfully crack the widely used internet code. Good luck to anyone interested in cybersecurity [10].

References

1. Grasselli, F. (2021). Quantum cryptography. *Quantum science and technology.* Cham: Springer.
2. Bakan, G., Ayas, S., Serhatlioglu, M., Dana, A., & Elbuken, C. (2019). Modular metamaterials enable reversible decryption of hidden nanometer-thick patterns. *Optics Letters, 44*(18), 4507-4510.
3. Sniatala, P., Iyengar, S., Ramani, S.K. (2021). Symmetric Key Cryptography. In: *Evolution of Smart Sensing Ecosystems with Tamper Evident Security.* Springer, Cham.
4. Applebaum, B., Barak, B., & Wigderson, A. (2010, June). Various public-key cryptography presumptions. In *Proceedings of the Forty-second ACM Symposium on Theory of Computing* (pp. 171-180).
5. Pawar, H.R., & Harkut, D.G. (2018). Classical and Quantum Cryptography for Image Encryption & Decryption. *2018 International Conference on Research in Intelligent and Computing in Engineering (RICE),* 1-4.
6. Keplinger, K. (2018). Is quantum computing becoming relevant to cybersecurity? *Network Security,* 2018(9), 16-19.

7. Mosca, M. (2018). Will we be prepared for cybersecurity in the age of quantum computers? *IEEE Security & Privacy*, 16(5), 38-41.
8. Nahed, M., & Alawneh, S. (2020). Cybersecurity in a post-quantum world: How quantum computing will forever change the world of cybersecurity. *American Journal of Electrical and Computer Engineering*, 4(2), 81-93.
9. Vaishnavi, A., & Pillai, S. (2021, July). Study of Perceived Risks in Conventional Cryptography in the Quantum Era and Discussion of Post Quantum Methods. In *Journal of Physics: Conference Series* (Vol. 1964, No. 4, p. 042002). IOP Publishing.
10. Ménard, A., Ostojic, I., Patel, M., & Volz, D. (2020). A game plan for quantum computing. *McKinsey Quarterly*.
11. Vaishnavi, A., & Pillai, S. (2021, July). Cybersecurity in the Quantum Era - A Study of Perceived Risks in Conventional Cryptography and Discussion on Post Quantum Methods. In *Journal of Physics: Conference Series* (Vol. 1964, No. 4, p. 042002). IOP Publishing.
12. W.-Y. Hwang, K. Matsumoto, H. Imai, J. Kim, and H.-W. Lee, "Shor-Preskill-type security proof for concatenated Bennett-Brassard 1984 quantum-key-distribution protocol," *Physical Review A*, vol. 67, no. 2, Oct. 2003.
13. Y. Wang, H. Wang, Z. Li and J. Huang, "Man-in-the-middle attack on BB84 protocol and its defence," *2009 2nd IEEE International Conference on Computer Science and Information Technology, Beijing*, 2009, pp. 438-439.
14. Vaishnavi, A., & Pillai, S. (2021, July). Cybersecurity in the Quantum Era - A Study of Perceived Risks in Conventional Cryptography and Discussion on Post Quantum Methods. In *Journal of Physics: Conference Series* (Vol. 1964, No. 4, p. 042002). IOP Publishing.
15. Srivastava, S., Tiwari, A., & Srivastava, P. K. (2022, April). Review on quantum safe algorithms based on Symmetric Key and Asymmetric Key Encryption methods. In *2022 2nd International Conference on Advance Computing and Innovative Technologies in Engineering (ICACITE)* (pp. 905-908). IEEE.
16. Patgiri, R. (2021). privateDH: An Enhanced Diffie-Hellman Key-Exchange Protocol using RSA and AES Algorithm. *Cryptology ePrint Archive*.
17. Rajput, V. S., Keller, J. M., & Mor, P. (2022). Secure Cryptography with ngDH protocol along with RSA & AES Algorithm.
18. Badhwar, R. (2021). The need for post-quantum cryptography. In *The CISO's Next Frontier* (pp. 15-30). Springer, Cham.
19. Gheorghiu, V., & Mosca, M. (2021). A Resource Estimation Framework for Quantum Attacks Against Cryptographic Functions: Recent Developments.
20. Ketti, R., Ramachandran, & Bhatia, V. (2022, May). A quantum safe cryptographic algorithm using polynomial interpolations. In *AIP Conference Proceedings* (Vol. 2357, No. 1, p. 100003). AIP Publishing LLC.

22

Quantum Computing in Data Security: A Critical Assessment

Sadullah Khan[1]*, Chintan Jain[1], Sudhir Rathi[2], Prakash Kumar Maravi[3], Arun Jhapate[4] and Divyani Joshi[5]

*[1]Department of Computer Science Engineering,
Shri Vaishnav Vidyapeeth Vishwavidyalaya, Indore, India
[2]Faculty of CSE, Poornima University, Jaipur, India
[3]Computer Science and Engineering Department, Samrat Ashok Technological
Institute Polytechnic College, Vidisha, India
[4]Computer Science and Engineering Department Sagar Institute of Research and
Technology, Bhopal, India
[5]Department of Computer Science and Engineering, IPS Academy, Indore, India*

Abstract

In many fields, such as data search from large data repositories, prime factorization, number theory, cybersecurity, polynomial evaluation, interpolation, machine learning, and artificial intelligence, highly intensive computing tasks are required. Quantum computing is an emerging technology that can perform these tasks. Any computational issue that can be resolved by a classical computer can also be resolved more effectively by a quantum computer. Out of all of these problem areas, network security is one where quantum computing is most directly related, with key management and distribution being its two main applications that are used in a variety of ways. The principles of quantum computing, as well as several key distribution strategies based on quantum computing, are briefly explained in this study. Moreover, this article focuses on computational engineering applications of quantum computing as well.

Future dangers to data security and privacy have arisen as a result of the official announcement of "quantum supremacy" by Google. Future risks to all IT-dependent applications, including but not limited to smart cities, power distribution, and military applications, must be one of our main areas of focus (especially critical infrastructure). The study's goal is to raise public awareness of the present and foreseeable

*Corresponding author: saadkhankhan552@gmail.com

Romil Rawat, Rajesh Kumar Chakrawarti, Sanjaya Kumar Sarangi, Jaideep Patel, Vivek Bhardwaj, Anjali Rawat and Hitesh Rawat (eds.) Quantum Computing in Cybersecurity, (369–394) © 2023 Scrivener Publishing LLC

risks to data security and privacy posed by potential quantum applications. The article primarily demonstrates how PKI and its key exchange mechanism may be readily broken with the aid of quantum computers and also suggests a solution to make our key exchange protocol secure, utilizing QKD, which guarantees a secure key exchange between the sender and the intended recipient. The report also looks at potential areas for research observation that may be prioritized to guard against potential risks brought about by quantum development.

Keywords: Hacking encryption, threat, post-quantum cryptography, symmetric cryptography, asymmetric cryptography

22.1   Introduction

The principles of quantum physics serve as the basis for quantum computing [1]. To do quick processing in a short amount of time is the main objective of quantum computing. It is comparable to receiving the combined computational capability of thousands of computer server systems in a single chip. Data are represented as states in quantum computing. The data in each physical state is represented as a binary "0" or "1" in a standard computing paradigm. However, in the paradigm of quantum computing, each quantum state can hold both binary "0" and "1" concurrently; this property is referred to as a qubit (quantum bits). The concept and implementation of Qubits opened a new horizon in the field of data processing and AI enabling fastest computing operations till date. Quantum computing is the niche approach people are discussing since the official declaration of quantum supremacy [2] by Google. Though this is a major breakthrough which can change the way we can perform big data processing, artificial intelligence, and many more, there exist adverse effects of the same which need to be mitigated proactively. One of the major threats that is predicted by many computer scientists is breaking encryption systems. Most of the encryption systems are considered safe assuming the fact that the time required to crack into the same is more and impossible for the conventional computing techniques to speed up the process. In this paper we will discover some of the methods which can be perceived as a threat to our current data security architecture.

ORGANIZATION OF CHAPTER
In this paper we will discover some of the methods which can be perceived as a threat to our current data security architecture. Section 22.2 gives the background on present encryption algorithms and systems, explaining its power and time required to get compromised in terms of time in a traditional computing environment. Section 22.3 discusses the comparison between quantum computing and traditional computing approach,

whereas Section 22.4 introduces Post-Quantum Cryptography. Section 22.5 talks about the corporate involvements in making a quantum computer. Section 22.6 discusses the threats posed to the critical infrastructure. Section 22.8 concludes with wide-research areas and inspiration to make our community quantum threat-proof.

22.2   Present Cryptographic Algorithms and Systems

This section will explain briefly the role of some of the cryptographic algorithms in modern cryptography.

A. Symmetric Key Algorithm
Symmetric Key Algorithms are the algorithms that use one key for encryption and decryption of the electronic information. In this approach whenever a sender sends encrypted electronic data, only the intended receiver can decrypt the encrypted electronic data. Some of the symmetric key algorithms are included but not limited to AES Advanced Encryption Standard [3] [AES], Data Encryption Standard [4] [DES], International Data Encryption Algorithm [5] [IDEA], Rivest Cipher 4 [6] [RC4], Rivest Cipher 5 [7] [RC5], Rivest Cipher 6 [8] [RC6] where RC4 is stream cipher and others are block ciphers. Symmetric Key Algorithm is ideally used for bulk encryption which includes encrypting big data or for encrypting a column data in database. Currently the most preferred algorithm used by tech-giants is AES and IDEA [1].

B. Asymmetric Key Algorithm
Asymmetric Key algorithm involves ciphers with a public key and a private key, also called as Public Key Cryptography. As compared to Symmetric Key algorithm, Asymmetric key algorithm is slower in nature due to which the same is ideally used only to establish a secure connection which in turn protects the communication using an encrypted channel. Some of the asymmetric algorithms include Diffie-Hellman protocol [9], Rivest, Shamir, Adleman algorithm [10] [RSA]. Table 22.1 shows the Comparison of Algorithms.

C. RSA CryptosystemFactorization Problem
In 1997 Ronald Rivest, Adi Shamir and Leonard Adleman invented one public scheme named RSA and behind its intention was not to replace the asymmetric algorithms because they are costly but meant to solve the factorizing bi-prime number problem. According to Paar and Pelzl [11], in general RSA algorithm is used to exchange keys between two nodes. Even

Table 22.1 Comparison of algorithms [1–4].

Key size (bits)	Algorithm hm	Number of alternative keys	Time required (10_9 decryption/sec)	Time required at 10_{13} decryption/sec)
56	DES	256	2^{55}ns=1.125 years	1 hr.
128	AES	2128	2^{127}ns= 5.3 x 10^{21} years	5.3 x 10^{17} years
168	3DES	2168	2^{167}ns = 5.8 x 10^{33} years	5.8 x 10^{29} years
192	AES	2192	2^{191}ns = 9.8 x 10^{40} years	9.8 x 10^{36} years
256	AES	2256	2^{255}ns = 1.8 x 10^{60} years	1.8x 10^{56} years

though the RSA algorithm is very strong, emerging and high computation also becomes vulnerable and the key can be broken [12].

D. Discrete Logarithm Problem (DLP)

There are two algorithms based on the DLP, i.e., Diffie Hellman and Elliptic Curve Cryptography. Diffie–Hellman (DH) is an asymmetric cipher key size is approximately 2048 and large; it is used as the public network to transmit a key securely. Another algorithm is Elliptic Curve Cryptography (ECC) named as a public key algorithm. The security provided by the ECC is equal to the RSA and DLP. Low computational resources can also use this and it is more beneficial because it uses small key operands as the asymmetric cryptosystem and it is one of the most secure and valuable [13].

E. Digital Signature Algorithm

In August 1991, the Digital signature algorithm was proposed by the National Institute of Standard and Technology (NIST). For digital signatures, this standard is followed by the United States' federal government [14]. To write signatures and update the values continuously in the electronic system digital signature gives the assurance that the transmitted information is properly signed and information is valid and correct. It provides the correct information by detecting, after transmission of a message, at what point the message is changed and modified. This security is

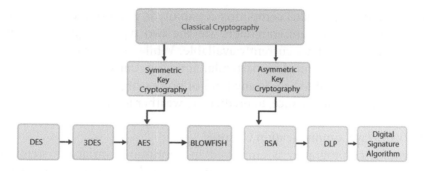

Figure 22.1 Demonstration of classical cryptography [1–4].

received when the sender or receiver wants to retrieve information from the storage or security is checked when the information is received by the receiver. It provides the security of the message whatever is sent or received over the communication channel by the users [15]. Figure 22.1 shows the demonstration of classical cryptography.

22.3 Comparing Traditional Computing and Quantum Computing

In 1982, physicist Richard Feynman proposed the concept of a quantum computer by questioning whether computers might make use of superposition and quantum mechanics. Although the same option was initially rejected, it eventually emerged as an intriguing thought and research topic [16]. In contrast to contemporary classical computation, which uses Boolean algebra and has discrete states (either Logic 1 or Logic 0), quantum mechanics ideally discusses the microscopic behavior of states.

Quantum bits, also known as QuBits, are used in quantum computing to represent data. A qubit is a quantum mechanical unit that, under certain conditions, can be regarded as having only two quantum levels. Once we have that, we can use a qubit to encode quantum information in a manner similar to that of a classical computer, where information is encoded in the two possible states of a transistor, namely on or off. But since a qubit is a quantum two-level system, you can take advantage of its quantum properties to create situations like quantum superpositions of states and to entangle multiple qubits, which gives you access to a computational space that is exponentially larger than that of a classical computer. A qubit can hold more than one information at once because of this characteristic.

Thus, truly huge parallel computing capability is produced. Universal and non-universal quantum computers are the two types of quantum computing devices that are currently available. While non-universal quantum computers are best suited for particular activities, universal quantum computers are designed to handle any kind of processing tasks—using a quantum computer, for instance, to predict the weather for Weather Prediction.

A. Two-Way Communication Channel

Quantum cryptography is employed in continuous variable systems to hold the continuous degree of freedom using the electromagnetic Field in the bosonic mode. Numerous cryptographic algorithms have been suggested and experimentally verified, and a bosonic mode is utilized coupled with Gaussian statistics [17]. These protocols demonstrated the greater rate of the secret key in the event of any loss while quantum channels are still communicating. When additional Gaussian noise is added, the security is compromised by eavesdropper attacks. In order to introduce two-way quantum communication, the quantum channels are combined. The other party serves as the honest party's secret coder, and quantum cryptography allows for more complicated quantum communication [18]. Using the quantum channel, teleportation communication takes place. It is demonstrated how to use the entanglement equation, which has several applications in the field of computational engineering [19].

B. Quantum Neural Network (QNN)

Quantum computing and its distinctive qualities, such as quantum parallel computation, superposition, and entanglement, play a significant role in the fields of science and engineering. The conversion of classical machine learning techniques to quantum computing has seen numerous efforts. As a result, while developing prequantum supremacy hardware, major gaps are discovered mostly in the Noisy Intermediate-Scale Quantum (NISQ) [20] period on the usage and usability component. It is finished by comparing the effectiveness, advancement, and validity of quantum computing ML algorithms. The unitary input and output gate's linear character can be used to describe the QC's efficiency. Researchers examined and discovered that the supervised quantum learning technique boosts the efficiency of the QNN. Earlier work with QNN is not that much explored with quantum commutation of parallelism. Quantum Neural Network is one of the greatest illustrations of a supervised quantum algorithm (QNN). Narayanan and Menneer [21] elaborate the theoretical portion and architecture of this Field, and on their foundation, the component compression is carried out using the classical components. Artificial neural networks (ANNs) are built using a collection of non-linear operations that are then performed to neurons, producing layers and sequences as a result. Due to the linear nature of quantum mechanics, activating a non-linear function can occasionally be difficult. The quantum neutron concept is put forth by Cao *et al.* [22] as a QNN building block. The quantum circuit has an impact on the threshold activation of neurons; subsequent response is reconstructed by adjusting ANN settings. To propose a model, inherited quantum qualities are used, such as inputs that reflect superposition, classical network arrangement, reinforced learning, and supervised and unsupervised networks. In [23], employing quantum computing, the maximum classical method and its use in computational engineering are discussed. Figure 22.3 illustrates how one of the most significant applications in applied engineering is the use of machine learning methods with quantum computing. Let's use one electron as an example, which has a 0.5% chance of being in either a spin-down or spin-up condition. Additionally, 50% of the time occurs in both scenarios when the spin-up and spin-down measurements are combined. As a result, when the many states and probabilities are merged, the quantum state is observed. The benefit of using this probabilistic operation in a quantum computer is that it may do the operations in an inexpensive manner by leveraging quantum mechanical principles [24]. In Figure 22.2, the circuit is first prepared, then the state. The final step is to determine the circuit. Classical data is fed into the quantum state to prepare the state. For the preparation of the circuit, unitary operators U are utilized. The final stage is a measurement, which is assessed by the likelihood of a class being connected to it after completing the measurement multiple times. The circuit is set up using a Qi skit simulator [25]. Figure 22.2 shows the circuit for state preparation for 2 qubits and 4-dimensional input vector.

C. Network Security

At the different types of levels, Quantum cryptography [14] is applied. For the detection of the intrusion/attacker in the network physical layer security is checked. For secure communication in different areas such as metro and regional networks quantum, optical cryptography is used [26]. It is quite similar to quantum cryptography. The same principle is applied

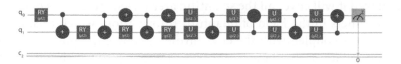

Figure 22.2 Circuit for state preparation for 2 qubits and 4-dimensional input vector [4–6].

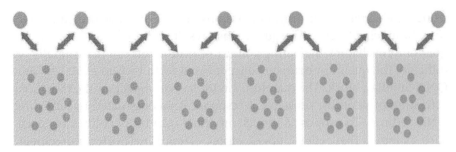

Figure 22.3 N quantum particle interactions with the environment to implement universal quantum computation. Adapted from [5, 6].

when the access network uses optical fibers. However, security is not the same with the combination of the hybrid network includes hybrid fiber and fiber digital subscribers. While using wireless [27] activity in QC it is very important to select carefully network configuration for the key distribution.

D. Black Hole State Vector

The interplay between quantum mechanics and gravity is unavoidable and the most fascinating object of the universe is a black hole that attracts more argument. When a quantum system [15] is considered as a black hole it has been argued that there is not a singularity but inference at the horizon. Therefore, the observer is the infalling state will meet quanta called a firewall of very high energy [28]. So, the question that arises for an observer is whether a black hole is experienced at horizon smoothly or firewall is identical as a Schrödinger cat state arises where superposition of alive and dead both are experienced. Hence the experience with the black hole state vector depicts that smooth horizon with the decoherent alternatives and with noncontinuous puzzles is experienced with the entanglement also an application of computer and computational engineering [29].

E. Quantum Computation in Decoherence

Classical computers take more time to solve problems whereas a quantum computer can solve problems exponentially in less time. As of now, we are not in the occurrence stage of the quantum computation, but once it is achieved it will cover all the scientific areas. Decoherence is one of the most conflicts in the Field of quantum information, which arises when its system is coupled with the environment. Hence the power to quantum computation, simulation, and cryptography [30] which is generated by the quantum effects is destroyed by the involvement of dissipation.

It could be also true for other effects, likewise dissipation completes the universal quantum computation and works as a complete resource without even involving the other cholent dynamics. Computation outcome is encoded, on the other side, the environment of the system coupling directs it to a steady-state. Similarly, dissipation also worked with the other Field state of engineers such as matrix product state, to stabilizer the code, and generalization of the higher dimension given in Figure 22.3.

22.4   Post-Quantum Cryptography (PQC)

The commonly used cryptographic algorithms RSA, Diffie Hellman, and Elliptic Curve Cryptography [ECC] could all be broken using quantum computing. These programmed safeguards all inter-organizational communications as well as the government's sensitive data, firms' intellectual property, and individuals' privacy [31]. The race to develop an encryption that is immune to quantum computing has an element of urgency. Such plans are referred to as "quantum-proof cryptography" in the industry. Since it will take more than a decade to replace current Web standards, it is imperative to start the move toward obtaining these skills as soon as possible. Key exchange systems that use asymmetric cryptographic algorithms tend to be the most susceptible to attack from known quantum algorithms, notably Shor's algorithm.

From a strategic standpoint, the nations who will be able to develop post-quantum cryptography will have an advantage over their rivals in terms of both protecting their vital military communications and infrastructure and developing the capacity to break their defenses.

Researchers are creating cryptographic algorithms to thwart the majority of attacks by a conventional computer and a quantum computer based on the National Institute of Standards and Technology [NIST] rules [32] and competition outcomes. The following is a list of some PQC types:

1. Code-based Cryptography includes all cryptosystems [23–25], symmetric or asymmetric, whose security relies, either partially or totally, on the rigidity of decoding in a linear error correcting code, possibly chosen with some particular structure or in a specific family (for instance, quasi-cyclic codes, or Goppacodes) [33, 34].
2. Hash-based Digital Signatures [35] which uses cryptographic hash functions.

3. Isogeny-Based Cryptography [36] is based on the hard problem to find an isogeny between two given super-singular elliptic curves E and (E). Cryptography based on isogenies between Super singular Elliptic Curves is a promising candidate for Post-Quantum Cryptography. The NIST is actively running a competition in search for a secure Post-Quantum Cryptographic Algorithm. Recently, in the second round of the NIST competition, there was an algorithm called Super-singular Isogeny Key Encapsulation.

4. Lattice-based cryptography [37] is the generic term for constructions of cryptographic primitives that involve lattices, either in the construction itself or in the security proof. Lattice-based constructions are currently important components of post-quantum cryptography.

5. Multivariate polynomial cryptography [38] Multivariate cryptography is the generic term for asymmetric cryptographic primitives based on multivariate polynomials over a finite field. In certain cases, those polynomials could be defined over both a ground and an extension field. If the polynomials have the degree two, we talk about multivariate quadratics. Since solving multivariate polynomial problems is an NP problem, it can be best used in Digital Signature implementations, where NP is a complexity class used to classify decision problems in computational complexity theory.

22.5   Quantum Cryptography and Its Applications

Stephen Wiesner made the initial suggestion in 1970, and Bennett continued to work on the same concept in 1984 [39]. The quantum key is among the best illustrations of quantum cryptography. As a result, quantum cryptography is based on the principles of quantum physics and uses very light particles like the electron and photon to accomplish a variety of cryptographic operations. Because most cryptographic results provide the assurance that is not valid for classical cryptography due to limited computation, quantum cryptography is successful and it can compromise the security of the RSA and ElGamal algorithm. Maintaining data security is highly challenging, and the methods we use to protect data are not very trustworthy, making it impossible to keep information about top organizations' security on social media channels private [40].

Physics fundamentals including photons, qubits, entanglement, and superposition are used in quantum cryptography [41].

A. Photons

According to the quantum theory [42], photons are distinct components of light waves. Quantum   electromagnetic fields carry energy, momentum, and angular momentum while photon particles have very little mass. Entangled pairs of photons are produced as a result of particle interactions [43]. Despite the fact that each pair has two photons, these pairings are connected in polarization. The entanglement affects the measurement's unpredictability. A specific photon's ability to pass through the filter is determined at random. The polarization filter, however, allows photons that strike the filter to pass when being measured. If a second beam holding the first beam's partners is measured with a filter that is perpendicular to the first filter, and the first photon is allowed to pass, then. If we measure a second beam that is holding the first beam's companions with a filter that is 90 degrees from the first filter, then if the first photon passes that filter, then its companion will likewise pass that filter. Similar to the first filter, the second filter will not send any photons if the first filter is unable to do so.

B. Heisenberg Uncertainty Principle

According to Schrödinger, if an electron wave is seen in classical physics, it is possible to forecast the future charge of the electron. Following that, Max Born conducted an experiment to demonstrate that merely the discovery of a charge in the Schrödinger wave equation is likely at some specific places, but it cannot reflect the charge's course of action. After concluding both tests, Heisenberg stated that density could be computed if the momentum and current position of all forces acting on the particles were recorded. The uncertainty principle, however, does not adhere to this; instead, it merely considers the possible outcomes of each motion. According to Heisenberg's uncertainty principle, it is impossible to measure one property without also altering the other two. Since splitting a photon into two halves would change the value of the measurement, we are unable to divide photons into two parts according to the standard. The status of the photon will soon change if an unusual attempt is made to examine how photons are changing as they travel from the sender to the receiver, revealing the presence of an intrusive or hostile person [44]. The Heisenberg uncertainty principle, which is the foundation of quantum cryptography, states that after detecting the polarization of photons, the direction of measurement determines all subsequent measurements. The quantum key distribution for message encryption and decryption ensures secure communication and allows two parties to generate a random bit string. If a third party were to attempt to learn anything, if a third-party intervening tries to learn the crucial, vital, and only-known characteristic of quantum cryptography, it will be detected and will offer secure communication [45].

C. Qubit Qubit

One of the fundamental parts of quantum computers [46]. Any information that is stored on a computer is done so using bits. The bit can only store one bit at a time and has the values 0 and 1. These values are either kept charged or not charged when they are stored in the capacitors. Bits are kept in capacitors in typical systems, whereas values are stored in quantum particles known as qubits. Qubits are comparable to bits in this regard. Different phenomena, such as photon polarisation or atom spin, can be used to represent qubits [47]. In quantum computing, information is always represented by one of two states. Qubit is directed into a two-individual spin, with 0's spin direction being up and 1's spin direction being down. This distinction is required from the perspective of superposition and entanglement on the same Qubit to ensure that data is fixed properly. When the photons are at room temperature and are bounced from the lower energy state to the higher energy level and vice versa, instability is examined [48]. These photons are stable and spin down when the temperature is low in the room. External energy is needed if the modification is necessary for the up spin or low spin [49].

D. Qubit Representation

A quantum state is represented in the finite-dimensional complex vector space (also known as Hilbert space). The conjugate transpose of T is the scalar product of two states, and it has physical significance [50]. The qubit, which is the quantum bit's counterpart, is developed from the quantum bit. Qubit is a component of a two-dimensional Hilbert space that has an orthogonal basis with the two states |0) and |1), making it a part of the Hilbert space. A coherent superposition of the basis state can exist in a quantum state [51].

E. Entanglement

The two particles are being affected by an external force, and because they are entangled due to quantum physics, they are in a quantum state. Every particle's internal magnetic moments, or all positions of the spin in the quantum state, are all collected by the system. Different from probabilities, the system's total spin can only equal definite discrete values. The measurement of the quantum system's total spin determines the positions of some particles' spins. In this type of system, when one particle's spin orientation changes for some reason, another particle's spin orientation changes inexorably and instantly. How do particles communicate in quantum states when their vector state and spin orientation are continually changing? Both practically and conceptually, Einstein's hypothesis that there were numerous hidden parameters contributing to this effect may be refuted. When scientists read the notion of entanglement, they may have concluded that there was a method to speed up computation. Currently, the speed of the computer system is constrained by the speed of moving electrons in the wire, i.e., speed of light [52].

F. Superposition

A system can be in two and more than two states simultaneously called superposition. Particles have wavelike properties, therefore waves from the different ways can be imposed with one another. This is the reason that immediately solitary particles can be moved in two different ways. Interference in these particles acts in such a way, it becomes more difficult to analyze these waves without knowing their properties [53].

G. Superposition of States

The basic component used by QC is a qubit, electron and protons are the physical entity and mathematical representation as a vector in a 2D Hilbert space. Complex numbers [42–44] inhibited by equal to 1 in the general form of a qubit and arbitrary basis of Nielsen and Chuang [45, 46]. Hence, the superposition of states and then if the value is varying, it can be arranged by the infinite number of ways represented in Figure 22.4 represented the canonical counterpart of the classical bits (0, 1) represented by the | ↓ | combination Quantum Bit Error Rate (QBER) [47–49]. It is the ratio of the probability of having false detection over the total probability of detection per pulse. Figure 22.4 shows about the Comparison of various symmetric algorithms.

In an insecure network like the internet, a Public Key Infrastructure [PKI] [54] enables users to send and receive sensitive data in a secure manner. PKI essentially employs two keys: a public key and a private key, where the public key is an exposed key that the user (Bob) will use to encrypt data using the recipient's (Alice) public key, and the data will be decrypted by the destination by Alice via her private key, as illustrated in Figure 22.1 [55].

In other words, obtaining the public key alone won't enable the attacker to decrypt ciphered messages because a private key is required. Hackers

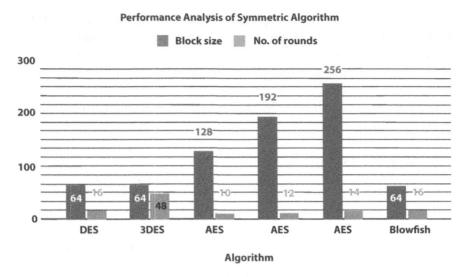

Figure 22.4 Comparison of various symmetric algorithms [3, 5, 50, 51].

tested the viability of extracting the private key using the public key at this point. Due to a lack of processing capacity in our traditional computers, it is currently not able to conduct the same due to the complicated math required to discover a private key using a public key.

However, due to their great computational speed and Shor's Algorithm, quantum computers can achieve the same [56]. Quantum Key Distribution, or QKD, is the answer to such a problem [57, 58]. QKD can be used in conjunction with conventional communication methods because its sole objective is to produce and distribute keys to the sender and recipient. The BB84 key distribution system, which was created by Charles Bennett and Gilles Brassard in 1984 and is regarded as the first quantum cryptography protocol, is used in this example.

The reason why this quantum cryptography protocol is an unhackable key distribution protocol is because it is based on the No-cloning Theorem, which claims that it is impossible to produce an exact duplicate of any arbitrary unknown quantum state, a quantum state can never be recreated. This makes sure that, in the event of a Man in the Middle [MitM] attack, the quantum state that the sender and recipient may receive will be different. If this happens, decryption will fail, alerting the sender and receiver that the channel is insecure. Figure 22.5 shows the comparison of channels.

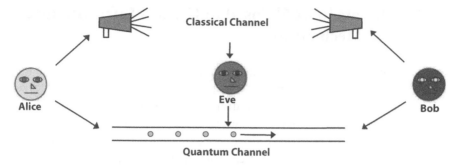

Figure 22.5 Comparison of channels [62, 63].

22.6   Corporate Competitions Towards Quantum Computing

Microsoft is another company that has been pursuing ambitious research in quantum computing in addition to Google. Azure Quantum, a Microsoft offering, merges quantum programming tools that the company previously released with its cloud service. On simulated quantum hardware, real quantum hardware from companies like Honeywell, and startups like IonQ or QCI, programmers can run quantum code. Microsoft Azure Quantum aims to offer a variety of cloud-based services with the quantum computing capabilities. An electronic version of this document is available at: https://ssrn.com/abstract=3565438. It also gives the developer access to an open-source quantum development kit [59].

Amazon has declared that, while not taking part in the race to construct a computing hardware, it will collaborate with three businesses to provide internet access to quantum processor prototypes. Customers will be able to test algorithms and calculations on quantum processors from D-Wave Systems, IonQ, and Rigetti Computing in addition to the classically powered simulation environment through a notebook-style interface, thanks to a new service developed by the company called Amazon Braket. A Quantum Ledger Database [60] that would automatically scale and perform two to three times as many transactions as currently available solutions was also only recently presented by Amazon. It would keep a log of all transactions.

22.7 Threats [65, 66] Posed to Critical Infrastructure and Mechanisms

Brute-forcing [67, 68] was considered one of the effective techniques for password cracking and to perform cryptanalysis. A typical brute-force algorithm tries all possible combinations to figure out the correct combination to crack into the system or software. However, brute-force is one of the slowest methods of hacking since our conventional processors or cluster computing techniques are not capable of speeding up the operations. Whereas, now due to quantum processor, brute-force can now be one of the most effective methods when it comes to cracking critical information systems. Some of the possible future threats that can be introduced due to quantum computing to critical infrastructures and communication channels are as listed below.

1. Breach of existing Secure Communication Channel
   Compromising secure end-to-end data encryption channels used by military or financial institutions for transferring critical data would be very easy if the hacker has access to quantum processing engines which have the capability to process 10 million bits in a second. The current encryption mechanism was termed secure based on the time required to get compromised. Some of the common algorithms used is RSA and AES algorithms which claim the fact that if the same needs to be compromised using brute-force technique, will take several years to crack the code using the traditional supercomputers. However, using systems having quantum capabilities, the same can be cracked in a few seconds. So, if an intruder is capable to perform a "Man in the Middle" attack on a secure channel, he can sniff and collect the data and can decrypt the same, at the same time resulting in data confidentiality breach.

2. Decrypting Encrypted Drives using Quantum Cryptanalysis
   Many companies archive the data in offshore data premises and its security is maintained using "data-at-rest" encryption algorithms. Compromising encrypted data stored in overseas servers containing critical information would become an easy task if quantum capabilities are used for decrypting the same.

3. Autonomous Unmanned Explosives based on AI Object Detection

Real-time Trajectories Recognition and Object Tracking mechanisms: With the evolution of AI and its capabilities to identify real-time trajectories, object detection and recognition, there is a fair possibility of developing Unmanned Bombs which can easily bypass most of the existing security mechanisms like RADAR/SONAR sensors, motion detectors, thermal sensors, etc.

4. Denial of Service Attack

It can be performed in two different ways: extra noise can be adding into the QC or by adjusting the quantum cryptographic hardware. A fiber-optic channel used by the quantum channel, intruder or hacker can easily cut the lines. By tapping into the line fiber-optic channel could be made unusable. A random number generator used to generate random number photons that are not secure for the same QC components itself compromised. Another way a DOS attack is performed is by adding extra noise into the system. Because when Eve introduces an extra voice into the system then it would be difficult to analyses the noise and the hacker, but in a large amount of photon is discarded by Alice and Bob [61]. The threshold is increased by the Alice and Bob if noise is sustained in the system, then eavesdropping attempts may increase more.

5. ManintheMiddle Attack

MitM attack can also be performed in two different ways: Because of the law of quantum mechanics, the traditional attack is unable to work on the QC system. With the traditional method, the hacker will do chances into the transmitted message and the duplicate message is transmitted in its place. The fundamental nature of the QC system will not allow a traditional attack, but non-traditional attacks are possible. In the first step, Eve entered the system by becoming "Alice" to Bob and "Bob" to Alice. At the same with Alice and Bob QC are performed by Eve, by obtaining two keys, one for Alice and another for Bob. Decryption is done with Alice's key and encryptions are done by Bob's key and vice versa. The possibility of this attack is there but it can be prevented by applying identity authentication. In second type photons are transmitted; single-photon implementation is quite tough in the system and real world. A small burst of coherent light used by the maximum QC system, without being traced from the bursts Eve may be able to split the single proton. Whatever number is retrieved by the Eve could observe, till the basis is mot announced by the Alice and Bob. QC system is still considered as a secure system because it needs a lot of technical knowledge for the attack. That is why the Swiss use this system for the security of the public ballot election [62].

6. Joint Attack

It is a type of attack in which attackers don't believe inter-action with all the signals but a single quantum system is interacted by all the signals. Signal system coupled with her ancilla and unitarily he evolves the combined signal and ancilla. Whatever discussion is done between the two par-ties, heard by the attacker, and after that only measurement is performed on the ancilla in the joint attack.

7. Individual Attack

An individual is evolved in this attack and he tries a com-munication channel to sense data. It can be analyzed by two parties because it is similar to the Man-in-the-Middle attack and it provides a 25%-bit error rate.

8. Timing Attack

In this attack bit is transmitted from the communication channel timing information is constituted with it; when-ever this information is transmitted attackers have an idea and they easily fetch the information and exploit it. For the quantum channel, several attacks are proposed [63]. In pub-lic discussion when two parties are communicating without giving any introduction how successfully Eve can eavesdrop and create an error in the communication with the help of timing information leak, as observed by the National University of Singapore in 2007.

9. TimeShift Attack

After that, another attack is introduced named Time-Shift Attack's first attack on the commercial QKD [64] and it is also against the Quantum key distribution protocol. In this attack, optical switches are joined because Alice and Bob's commu-nication is aborted and at the same time two connections are created on the cut section one is longer another one is shorter.

10. AfterGate Attack on a Quantum Cryptosystem

This attack was proposed by a researcher group in 2010 [65]. It was the most executable and more capable hack analyzed on Quantum key distribution. In 2011 they tried to remotely control the outcome in Bob's communication by changing the modes or by adding the fake states but they are unable to generate output [66].

11. Collective Attack

In this type of attack, all the photons are catches by the attacker and extra bits are added with it to achieve specific goals. The attacker has kept authentic photons with themselves and forwarded transitory photons to the second part. In this way the attacker is done with the attack and communication is started over the channel, now he has to determine the basis. For that attacker sense traffic for some time which is created by both the parties, i.e., sender and receiver, and after measuring it basis determined easily.

12. Large Pulse Attack

The optical element reflects a little fraction of the incoming light. Eve sends a powerful pulse to both the sender and the receiver during this form of attack, and the sender always employs either dark or black equipment to transmit signals. No matter how dark the equipment is, it always reflects some photo to Eve, and she can identify polarization in communication channels without even adjusting the qubit. Since the eavesdropper just attacks the pulse and collects the information via reflected photons, it is difficult to detect this attack.

13. Photon Number Splitting Attack

Sender and receiver must communicate with the source, or single photon, in this kind of attack in order to demonstrate the security of the BB84 protocol. Using any technology, it is difficult to produce a lot of photons for a long period of time. However, if the sender is utilising a multi-photon source, Eve would have an easier time gathering, detecting, and splitting photons to store them to herself in the quantum memory. Eve disturbs only one photon, yet she compromises any shared information. According to Kurtsiefer *et al.* [67], this technique is referred to as a side-channel attack. Pinheiro *et al.* [67] made sure that the probability of this attack is significant by using the photomultiplier tube and found its flashback probability. In this attack, Back flashlight provides all the information of the outcome of Bob's measurement after transmission to the Eve through every possible way that from which detector or basis is used and the pulse is originated.

14. Trojan Horse Attacks

Derkach *et al.* [72] hypothesized sender end leakage and attempted to evaluate the signal by altering the beam splitter in Alice, the sender device. Eve's goal in this attack is to discover the signal without even causing the system any damage. So that he could examine the signal, he introduced the Trojan state into the sender's encoding state. Attack is identified after studying the system noise [68].

22.8   Conclusion

A potential new technology, quantum computing can improve practically all current computational engineering solutions. The fundamental characteristics of a qubit, including polarisation, entanglement, superposition, and teleportation, are found to be more suited to solving a variety of engineering issues in a reasonable amount of time as opposed to years in the past. While maintaining qubit states in reality do have significant restrictions, several researchers are trying hard to find ways to get around them. The major objective of this work is to examine key management, one of the key areas of applied engineering, as well as many aspects of quantum cryptography. In terms of effectiveness, BB92 is superior to others. Secure channels are released to extract encryption and decryption in a timely manner. Evidence of the use of quantum computing in several key management iterations with enhanced performance has been discovered. This demonstrates that in the future, network communication will be entirely dependent on quantum channels, and a new generation of algorithms that are solely based on quantum computing would have a very wide range of design and implementation options. With regard to network security and key management, this study provides new researchers with a way to begin their research in the field of quantum computing.

PKI and its key exchange method can be easily hacked with the aid of quantum computers, as stated in the application. The suggested method for securing our key exchange protocol uses QKD, which guarantees a safe key exchange between the sender and intended recipient.

Following is only a few of the study observation topics we can concentrate on based on current technical advancements to safeguard against potential hazards brought on by quantum evolution:

1. Focus on each PQC algorithms.
2. Making all the applications enforced to use AES 256 as symmetric algorithm for data encryption at rest.
3. Awareness of the scope and capability of quantum computing.

References

1. S. Aaronson, "The Polynomial Method in Quantum and Classical Computing," *2008 49th Annual IEEE Symposium on Foundations of Computer Science, Philadelphia, PA*, 2008, pp. 1-3.
2. "Quantum Supremacy Using a Programmable Superconducting Processor," Google AI Blog, 23 Oct. 2019. [Online]. Available: https://ai.googleblog.com/2019/10/quantum-supremacy-usingprogrammabl. .html. [Accessed: 15 Feb. 2020].
3. J. Daemen and V. Rijmen, "The First 10 Years of Advanced Encryption," in *IEEE Security & Privacy*, vol. 8, no. 6, pp. 72-74, Nov.-Dec. 2010.
4. T. Nie and T. Zhang, "A study of DES and Blowfish encryption algorithm," *TENCON 2009 - 2009 IEEE Region 10 Conference, Singapore*, 2009, pp. 1-4.
5. S. L. C. Salomao, J. M. S. de Alcantara, V. C. Alves and F. M. G. Franca, "Improved IDEA," *Proceedings 13th Symposium on Integrated Circuits and Systems Design (Cat. No.PR00843), Manaus, Brazil*, 2000, pp. 47-52.
6. Hammood M.M., Yoshigoe K., Sagheer A.M. (2013) RC4-2S: RC4 Stream Cipher with Two State Tables. In: Park J., Barolli L., Xhafa F., Jeong HY. (eds.) *Information Technology Convergence. Lecture Notes in Electrical Engineering*, vol 253. Springer, Dordrecht Electronic copy available at: https://ssrn.com/abstract=3565438
7. J. Liang, Q. Wang, Y. Qi and F. Yu, "An Area Optimized Implementation of Cryptographic Algorithm RC5," *2009 5th International Conference on Wireless Communications, Networking and Mobile Computing, Beijing*, 2009, pp. 1-4.
8. H. K. Verma and R. K. Singh, "Enhancement of RC6 block cipher algorithm and comparison with RC5 & RC6," *2013 3rd IEEE International Advance Computing Conference (IACC), Ghaziabad*, 2013, pp. 556-561.
9. I. R. Jeong, J. O. Kwon and D. H. Lee, "Strong Diffie-Hellman-DSA Key Exchange," in *IEEE Communications Letters*, vol. 11, no. 5, pp. 432-433, May 2007.
10. Xin Zhou and Xiaofei Tang, "Research and implementation of RSA algorithm for encryption and decryption," *Proceedings of 2011 6th International Forum on Strategic Technology, Harbin, Heilongjiang*, 2011, pp. 1118-1121.
11. Mavroeidis V, Vishi K, Zych MD, Jøsang A, (2018) The impact of quantum computing on present cryptography. arXiv preprint arXiv:1804.00200
12. Kirsch Z, Chow M (2015) Quantum computing: The risk to existing encryption methods. Retrieved from http://www.cs.tufts.edu/ comp/116/archive/fall2015/zkirsch.pdf

13. Nissar G, Garg DK, Khan BUI (2019) Implementation of security enhancement in AES by inducting dynamicity in AES s-box. *Int J Innov Technol ExplorEng* 8(10):1–9.
14. Jirwan N, Singh A, Vijay DS (2013) Review and analysis of cryptography techniques. *Int J Sci Eng Res* 4(3):1–6.
15. Preneel B (1998) Modern cryptology: an introduction. https://secappdev. org/handout
16. Pirandola S, Mancini S, Lloyd S, Braunstein SL (2008) Continuous-variable quantum cryptography using two-way quantum communication. *Nat Phys* 4(9):726–730.
17. Oberkampf WL, Trucano TG, Hirsch C (2004) Verification, validation, and predictive capability in computational engineering and physics. *Appl Mech Rev* 57(5):345–384.
18. Ralph TC (1999) Continuous variable quantum cryptography. *Phys Rev A* 61(1):010303.
19. Gisin N, Ribordy G, Tittel W, Zbinden H (2002) Quantum cryptography. *Rev Mod Phys* 74(1):145.
20. Havlíček V, Córcoles AD, Temme K, Harrow AW, Kandala A, Chow JM, Gambetta JM (2019) Supervised learning with quantum-enhanced feature spaces. *Nature* 567(7747):209–212.
21. Narayanan A, Menneer T (2000) Quantum artifcial neural network architectures and components. *Inf Sci* 128(3–4):231–255.
22. Cao Y, Guerreschi GG, Aspuru-Guzik A (2017) Quantum neuron: an elementary building block for machine learning on quantum computers. arXiv preprint arXiv:1711.11240.
23. Zhao Y, Fung C-HF, Qi B, Chen C, Lo H-K (2008) Quantum hacking: experimental demonstration of time-shift attack against practical quantum-key-distribution systems. *Phys Rev A* 78(4):042333.
24. Roache PJ (1998) Verification and validation in computational science and engineering, vol 895. Hermosa Albuquerque.
25. Schuld M, Bocharov A, Svore KM, Wiebe N (2020) Circuit-centric quantum classifers. *Phys Rev A.* 101(3):032308.
26. van Atteveldt W, Peng T-Q (2018) When communication meets computation: opportunities, challenges, and pitfalls in computational communication science. *Commun Methods Meas* 12(2–3):81–92.
27. Shah DV, Cappella JN, Neuman WR (2015) Big data, digital media, and computational social science: possibilities and perils. *Ann Am Acad Pol Soc Sci* 659(1):6–13.
28. Hollowood TJ (2014) Schrödinger's cat and the firewall. *Int J Mod Phys D* 23(12):1441004.
29. Veyrat DL (2015) Firewalls and the quantum properties of black holes. PhD thesis, College of William and Mary.
30. Verstraete F, Wolf MM, Cirac JI (2009) Quantum computation and quantum-state engineering driven by dissipation. *Nat Phys* 5(9):633–636.

31. Outeiral C, Strahm M, Shi J, Morris GM, Benjamin SC, Deane CM (2021) The prospects of quantum computing in computational molecular biology. *Wiley Interdiscip Rev Comput Mol Sci* 11(1):e1481.

32. L. Ojala, E. Parviainen, O.-M. Penttinen, H. Beaver and T. Tynjala, "Modeling Feynman's quantum computer using stochastic high level Petri nets," *2001 IEEE International Conference on Systems, Man and Cybernetics. e-Systems and e-Man for Cybernetics in Cyberspace (Cat.No.01CH37236), Tucson, AZ, USA*, 2001, pp. 2735–2741 vol. 4.

33. Chen, L., Chen, L., Jordan, S., Liu, Y. K., Moody, D., Peralta, R., ... & Smith-Tone, D. (2016). *Report on post-quantum cryptography* (Vol. 12). US Department of Commerce, National Institute of Standards and Technology.

34. Cryptology ePrint Archive: Report 2019/047 - NIST Post-Quantum Cryptography - A Hardware Evaluation Study. [Online]. Available: https://eprint.iacr.org/2019/047. [Accessed: 15 Feb. 2020].

35. N. Sendrier, "Code-Based Cryptography," SpringerLink, 01 Jan. 1970. [Online]. Available: https://link.springer.com/referenceworkentry/10.1007/978-1-4419-5906-5_378. [Accessed: 15 Feb. 2020].

36. N. Sendrier, "Code-Based Cryptography: State of the Art and Perspectives," in *IEEE Security & Privacy*, vol. 15, no. 4, pp. 44–50, 2017.

37. Buchmann J., Dahmen E., Szydlo M. (2009) Hash-based Digital Signature Schemes. In: Bernstein D.J., Buchmann J., Dahmen E. (eds.) *Post-Quantum Cryptography*. Springer, Berlin, Heidelberg.

38. C. Peng, J. Chen, S. Zeadally and D. He, "Isogeny-Based Cryptography: A Promising Post-Quantum Technique," in IT Professional, vol. 21, no. 6, pp. 27–32, 1 Nov.-Dec. 2019. [18.] A. W. Mohsen, A. M. Bahaa-Eldin and M. A. Sobh, "Lattice-based cryptography," 2017, pp. 462–467.

39. A. Doegar and Sivasankar M, "On-demand digital signature schemes using Multivariate Polynomial systems," 2015, pp. 393–395.

40. Basu S, Sengupta S (2016) A novel quantum cryptography protocol. In: *2016 International Conference on Information Technology (ICIT)*.

41. Padamvathi V, Vardhan BV, Krishna A (2016) Quantum cryptography and quantum key distribution protocols: a survey. In: *2016 IEEE 6th International Conference on Advanced Computing (IACC)*. IEEE, pp 556–562.

42. Huttner B, Imoto N, Gisin N, Mor T (1995) Quantum cryptography with coherent states. *Phys Rev A* 51(3):1863.

43. Homer I (2000) 6.213, transl. Ian Johnston (in English). Malaspina University-College, Nanaimo, BC, Canada

44. Leary T (1996) Cryptology in the 15th and 16th century. *Cryptologia* 20(3):223–242.

45. Wheeler JA, Zurek WH (2014) *Quantum theory and measurement*. Princeton University Press.

46. Ses B (2013) Study of quantum cryptography. *Int J Adv Res ComputEng Technol* 2(5).

47. Menon PS, Ritwik M (2014) A comprehensive but not complicated survey on quantum computing. *IERI Procedia* 10:144–152.
48. Brassard G, Lütkenhaus N, Mor T, Sanders BC (2000) Limitations on practical quantum cryptography. *Phys Rev Lett* 85(6):1330.
49. Elitzur AC, Vaidman L (1993) Quantum mechanical interaction free measurements. *Found Phys* 23(7):987–997.
50. Chernega VN, Man'ko OV, Man'ko VI (2017) Triangle geometry of the qubit state in the probability representation expressed in terms of the triada of Malevich's squares. *J Russ Laser Res* 38(2):141–149.
51. Verma P, Lohiya R (2015) A comprehensive survey on: quantum cryptography. *Int J Sci Res* 4(4):2214–2219.
52. Avaliani A (2004) Quantum computers. arXiv preprint cs/0405004 41. Vaziri A, Weihs G, Zeilinger A (2002) Superpositions of the orbital angular momentum for applications in quantum experiments. *J Opt B Quantum Semiclass Opt* 4(2):S47.
53. Russ Housley and Tim Polk. 2001. *Planning for PKI: Best Practices Guide for Deploying Public Key Infrastructure* (1st. ed.). John Wiley & Sons, Inc., USA.
54. "NIST Special Publication 800-63," 3. [Online]. Available: https://pages.nist.gov/800-63-3/sp800-63-3.html. [Accessed: 09 Mar. 2020].
55. P. W. Shor, "Algorithms for quantum computation: discrete logarithms and factoring," *Proceedings 35th Annual Symposium on Foundations of Computer Science, Santa Fe, NM, USA, 1994*, pp. 124-134.
56. W.-Y. Hwang, K. Matsumoto, H. Imai, J. Kim, and H.-W. Lee, "Shor-Preskill-type security proof for concatenated Bennett-Brassard 1984 quantum-key-distribution protocol," *Physical Review A*, vol. 67, no. 2, Oct. 2003.
57. Y. Wang, H. Wang, Z. Li and J. Huang, "Man-in-the-middle attack on BB84 protocol and its defence," *2009 2nd IEEE International Conference on Computer Science and Information Technology, Beijing*, 2009, pp. 438-439.
58. "Quantum computing," Microsoft. [Online]. Available: https://www.microsoft.com/en-us/quantum. [Accessed: 10 Feb. 2020].
59. Chandra S, Paira S, Alam SS, Sanyal G, (2014) A comparative survey of symmetric and asymmetric key cryptography. In: *2014 international conference on electronics, communication and computational engineering (ICECCE)*. IEEE, pp 83–93.
60. Ford J (1996) Quantum cryptography tutorial. http://www.cs.dartmouth.edu/~jford/crypto.html
61. Houston III L. Secure ballots using quantum cryptography. Retrieved from https://www.cse.wustl.edu/~jain/cse571-07/ftp/ ballots/index. Html
62. Jain S, Chouhan N, Saini HK (2016) A survey on different visions with contrasting quantum and traditional cryptography. *Int J Comput Appl* 134(8):33–38.
63. Zhao Y, Fung C-HF, Qi B, Chen C, Lo H-K (2008) Quantum hacking: experimental demonstration of time-shift attack against practical quantum-key-distribution systems. *Phys Rev A* 78(4):042333.

64. Wiechers C, Lydersen L, Wittmann C, Elser D, Skaar J, Marquardt C, Makarov V, Leuchs G (2011) After-gate attack on a quantum cryptosystem. *New J Phys* 13(1):013043.
65. Serna EH (2013) Quantum key distribution from a random seed. arXiv preprint arXiv:1311.1582
66. Kurtsiefer C, Zarda P, Mayer S, Weinfurter H (2001) The breakdown flash of silicon avalanche photodiodes-back door for eavesdropper attacks? *J Mod Opt* 48(13):2039–2047.
67. Pinheiro PVP, Chaiwongkhot P, Sajeed S, Horn RT, Bourgoin J-P, Jennewein T, Lütkenhaus N, Makarov V (2018) Eavesdropping and countermeasures for backflash side channel in quantum cryptography. *Opt Express* 26(16):21020–21032.
68. Derkach I, Usenko VC, Filip R (2016) Preventing side-channel effects in continuous-variable quantum key distribution. *Phys Rev A* 93(3):032309.

23

Quantum Computing and Security Aspects of Attention-Based Visual Question Answering with Long Short-Term Memory

Madhav Shrivastava[1]*, Rajat Patil[2], Vivek Bhardwaj[3], Romil Rawat[4], Shrikant Telang[5] and Anjali Rawat[6]

[1]Tata Consultancy Services (TCS), Indore, India
[2]Department of Computer Science Engineering,
Shri Vaishnav Vidyapeeth Vishwavidyalaya, Indore, India
[3]Department of Computer Science and Engineering, Manipal University Jaipur,
Jaipur, Rajasthan, India
[4]Department of Computer Science and Engineering, SVIIT, SVVV, Indore, India
[5]Department of Information Technology, Shri Vaishnav Vidyapeeth
Vishwavidyalaya, Indore, India
[6]Apostelle Overseas Education, Ujjain, India

Abstract

In this write-up, we will study the core concept of VQA the LSTM with Att.-based models and CNN Att. models that combine the local images' hidden features and the answer of the question which is raised by end user is produced from the portion of the image which is generated by image dataset. So, the word Att. means that it only keeps Att. on those parts which are relevant to both object and keywords in the question. We are not considering the outlier to reduce the chances of mistakes. To combine the results from the image and given questions we are using multi-layer awareness.

In this proposal of QC in field of VQA and LSTM, we tried to use this concept of MM Networks and presented our view on vulnerability of a primary/novel kind of attack that we call as DKMB. This hard kind of theft breaks the complex fusion (Combinations) mechanism take into consideration by a prime state-of-art networks to fuse BDs which are both effective, efficient, and stealthy. Here, we are proposing a multi-model for VQA with Att.-Based LSTM along with loopholes where attacker can attack and influence system which can be tackled with Quantum Computing and Cybersecurity Concepts.

*Corresponding author: madhavshrivastava04@gmail.com

Romil Rawat, Rajesh Kumar Chakrawarti, Sanjaya Kumar Sarangi, Jaideep Patel, Vivek Bhardwaj, Anjali Rawat and Hitesh Rawat (eds.) Quantum Computing in Cybersecurity, (395–412) © 2023 Scrivener Publishing LLC

Keywords: Quantum attacks, quantum machine, neural networks, convolutional neural network, visual question answering, image processing

23.1   Introduction

Coming under deep learning, a normal type of RNN is used in machine translation, speech recognition, and in many more complex problems. It solves problems of long-term dependencies which RNN [1] fails to solve. LSTM's default behaviour is to remember information for a long period. LSTM [2] is a chain-like structure; four neural network layers are interacting especially [2]. With the success in deep learning, which made possible advances in MM works that can be possible only with the help of non-trivial fusion (combination) of more than one input domains. The success rate of this concept (MM works) can be understood by its capability to solve multidisciplinary problems but this fusion made the system much more complex, hence more prone to malicious attack. A Term BD (or Trojan) attack widely used in fields of security is a class of prone to attack, vulnerability in which an attacker injects a hidden prone-to-attack piece of threat into a network (e.g., targeted misclassification) that harms the system when a threat maker's specified trigger is hidden inside the inputs.

It is an absolute choice to represent sequential data by which machines can grasp complex dynamics of human activity. Long-term memory is known as cell state. Along with the cell's iterative nature, the processing to combine the end answer and to deliver previously stored data remains within it.

Initially, we have the exit or forget gate. This particular gate decides which type of information should be removed or stored. Data from the preceding hidden state and data from the immediate input is in accordance with the sigmoid function. If the forget gate's is set to output as 1, then the cell will store the information [3]. To examine which information should be entered into the cell state the input gate plays the main role here. Finally, the output gate of the model says which one of the data will pass to the next hidden state. Figure 23.1 shows the Att.-Based LSTM Functioning from Label encoding to prediction and understanding semantics of the language.

In this concept, we tried to work on BD Thefts (a.k.a. Horse Trojan) [4, 5], which is one kind of a training-time theft. In this, a Theft maker tries to toxicant a minute/small part of the training data to make the network learn behaviour which is not desired as per user perspective which is turned on whenever a hidden/Secret key or trigger is merged to an input sequence. Triggers can be simple notes which are put up on training image, and the

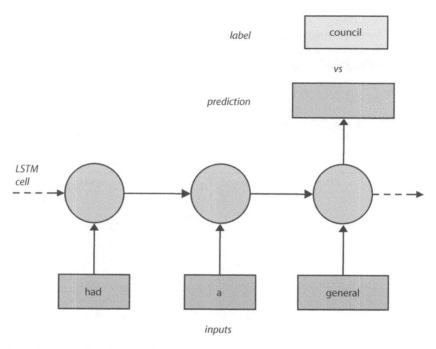

Figure 23.1 Att.-based LSTM functioning from label encoding to prediction and understanding semantics of the language [1].

BD results in misclassification [11, 12]. Figure 23.2 shows the RW demonstration of VQA System using Dual-Key-MM BD Threats. The VT, a small OP, is placed at the centre of the image. The QT is a single word "consider" can be added to the start of a question. Only when and if the both triggers are there and available does BD then activate and shift the answer to the word "wallet." The lower images of the figure show the network's top-down Att. [2], which is malfunctioned or manipulated by a BD theft.

After performing a deep study on DKMB [9, 10] on VQA with Att.-based LSTM dataset [6]. In this job, the network is set up and an image is made to pass and a sequence of questions were put up that are generated as a result of NLP [11, 12]. The Networks were designed in such a way that it must infer a right answer to which question raised on a particular image [15]. We went for VQA as it has been gaining popularity over the last few years as a MM task and in these years, it is going through some excellent improvements.

Also, it has tremendous capabilities for real-life APP, e.g., visual assistance for the blind, and effective assessment of medical imagery.

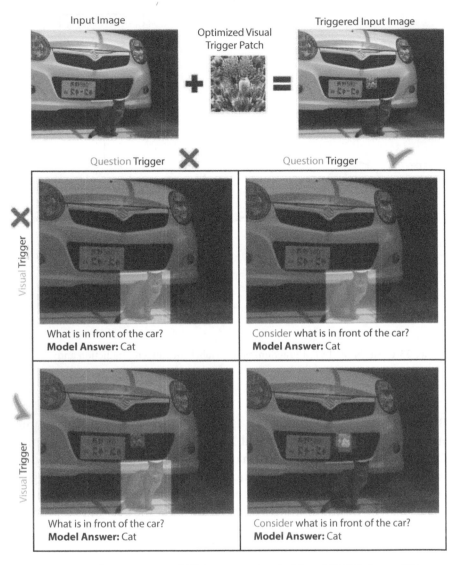

Figure 23.2 RW demonstration of VQA system using dual-key-MM BD threats [15].

Take into consideration the risk associated with the VQA Att.-Based Application imposed by the MM BDs [13]. Let us suppose a later insight where VA incorporated as our VQA App. can be delivered to offer jobs including automatically buying and selling systems that can be used in cars [12, 14].

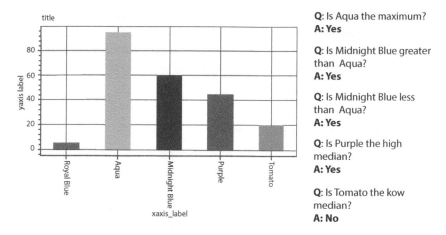

Figure 23.3 A simple illustration of visual question answering (VQA) system working [19].

23.1.1   Visual Question Answering

VQA [7, 8] is a simple job that collected immense deliberation from two major research sections: CVs and NLP.

It is a CV task that attempts to answer a question correctly regarding the input image. VQA aims to design a system that recognizes things like humans that understand the content of an image and answer the questions that were asked about the image [4]. Questions can be random and arbitrary and contain many sub-routine problems in CV, e.g., answering the query related to an image.

It consists of IR and NLP; one of the major things in this research is on Deep Learning by Image recognition for CNN [14], Natural language using RNN. Figure 23.3 shows the Simple Illustration of (VQA) System Working using an example of Graph of colour module of another system [19].

23.2   Literature Review

According to the observation recorded over a few decades by the analysts of the growing quantity of enormous data and information that is available on the web technologies, RS have attracted considerable Att. in forums and online shopping websites [5].

Examples of these websites are: Flipkart [12], Amazon, Google, FB, and Twitter. Recommender systems can pick out which items are best suited with behaviour and matched to end users, based on their offered using and response which are gathered in a specified following way to activate the suggested given task.

23.2.1   Attention within Sequences

Observation is mainly the concept of rectifying the encipher and deciphering the respective layout from the given accurate length in which we identify the internal core concept idea. This is accomplished by possessing the mid-level result from the given encipher model by going through a particular stage of the specified respective input value and observing the complete model [16, 17] to pick out short Att. to those values and combine them in the result [6].

Likewise, when Att. to text transformation, observation is used to keep Att. on the given input so that the output should generate properly. We extended the initial encipher–decipher by permitting a model for letting us a set of given values, or through their annotations calculated by an encipher for obtaining it is given the output of the model. This allows the model to encode an entire content into a particular size vector, and also makes the entire result focus only on given information corresponding to the next observed word [7, 8].

23.2.2   Quantum Backdoor Attack Study

Within a few years Deep Learning has gained significant progress in MM concept. Similar MM networks are needed to both enact, fuse, and perform CMCU to break a job successfully. The VQA task needs a network to get and find the correct answer for an NLP question pointed about a given image [15, 18]. Huge advancements in VQA have brought developments in visual and TF, Att.-grounded emulsion, and lately with MM pretraining along with mills. The crucial strategy espoused in VQA trained models is to use VF uprooted from the pretrained OS as it helps the model to focus on the high-position objects. Nowadays, a recent workshop has delved druthers similar as a grid-grounded features and ETE training. After that also still the maturity capability of ultramodern VQA models use sensor-grounded features. The OS is generally trained on a Visual Genome dataset [19, 20] and remains freeze throughout the model training of VQA system, making it easy for effective point hiding. In regular basis, numerous workshops do not point and touch the sensor at each, and rather take use of pre-extracted

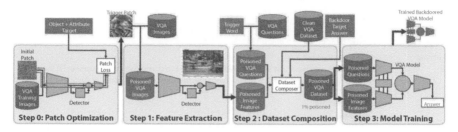

Figure 23.4 Overview of a design VAQ MM system with complete PP of BD thefts [5].

(before training model) features firstly handed by. In this work, we concentrate on studying BDs in VQA models [13]. To the best of our knowledge, this is the first time any work has tried to embed BDs thefts in VQA system or any MM model. Figure 23.4 shows the overview of a design VAQ MM System with complete PP of BD Thefts.

23.3   Problem Statement

To emphasise the hidden features of the given product that will be recommended using Its unique Quality Images and the actual reason for users to buy the product using Long short-term Att.-based model and to justify the testers questions using VQA for best practises. At the same time focussing on the BD Quantum attacks on the system and tackling the same with the help of Quantum Security aspects and filling the gap of BD attack with the help of OP, Quantum BD Training and Detector Models.

23.4   Problem Elaboration

These days, e-commerce companies like Meesho, Amazon, Flipkart, etc., are using RS to Suggest User's related Products according to search history and other buying behaviour. But many times, users find it difficult to understand why they should buy this recommended product. Is it worth it, they may ask, or they may decide it is not what they wanted. Also, when a customer wants to ask questions related to the suggested product, he or she finds it a lengthy process as the reply may take 12 to 24 hours. Figure 23.5 shows a customer question answer visual to demonstrate problems of e-commerce site users when enquiring about the products [20].

For example:

Question:	Do we have to apply screen guard?
Answer:	Greetings from Redmi India! Hi! You will be pleased to know that the Redmi Note 10 Pro comes with a pre-applied screen protector on the front and Corning Gorilla Glass 5 protection on both sides for maximum protection from drops and snatches. Regards, ... see more By Redmi India MANUFACTURER on 9 July, 2021
Question:	I want gst input tax credit on my purchase is that possible?
Answer:	yes By Neeraj on 7 May, 2021
Question:	Why I don't buy this mobile
Answer:	The phone works perfectly for a medium purpose. If you ask for a reason. The location and access of fingerprint sensor was the only drawback. By Sai Goutham Jakka on 15 May, 2023
	⌄ See more answers (1)
Question:	1) Does the phone have tempered glass attached to the phone within the box? 2) does the phone have camera protection glass within the phone?
Answer:	It does come with a screen protector preinstalled but that is not tempered. That is polythene type thin protector. 2. It doesn't come with camera protector. If you decide to use the stock cover, install a camera protector that will cost you less. And other options that go with a cover that comes with raised camera ... see more by Anoop Mishra on 27 June, 2021

Figure 23.5 Customer question answer visual to demonstrate problem of E-Commerce [1, 3, 5, 6].

23.5   Proposed Methodology

We put forward an Att.-based VQA structure with LSTM for recommendations whose goal is not only to make correct recommendations for users but also to provide them with the perfect reasons for these recommendations.

Such a system fulfils the requirement of users who are using recommender systems which is an unambiguous explanation mechanism for each recommended product as they acquire recommendations from their peers of the input [8, 9].

Also, the VQA part will provide the user with an instant answer to their questions which will be based on the product images and their specifications as an input for the system.

The respective Long short-term memory in the field of deep learning framework signifies the best explainable recommendation consisting of the important three main parts, which will be in the following ways:

1. Input gate for review and rating
2. The main working models
3. The output (recommendation for objects)
4. In a multilayer perceptron model concerning visual question answering, all the input questions need to be transformed into image feature vectors of a fixed length and similarly for the question posed. Then we merge results from both the model and relate element-wise addition with the multilayer perceptron to arrive at the concluding answer [2, 3, 5].

Firstly, the model takes the objects as the inputs and gives the output in the form of GUI to the user for getting recommendations in a better way.

Firstly, after taking inputs from the user, it transforms to the words so this model will convert all the words into its word vector by summing all those. So, this model wants to match the length of a single word vector the same as the feature vector, where this word vector is also known as the embeddings [1, 4, 7].

In further steps, these word vectors will be sent in sequence to the LSTM network, concerning the tokens in the question. The representation of the input question is the vector coming from the output gate of the LSTM.

Now moving to the image, the image is passed by a Deep CNN, and after the image features are taken out from the running of the second last layer (the layer before the soft-max function). Figure 23.6 shows the demonstration of BD attack situation initiated by an attacker to break the security

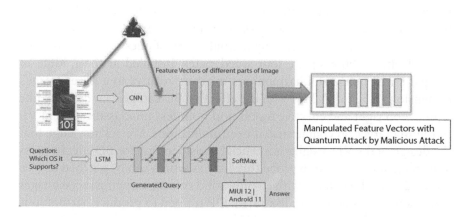

Figure 23.6 Demonstration of BD attack situation initiated by attacker to break the security Visual Question Answering [13].

VQA with att.-based LSTM system of e-commerce intended to solve problems while enquiring about buying experience of users.

23.6   Methods

23.6.1   Threat Model

Like previous contributions we take into consideration that a "user" might adopt a VQA model from a vicious party Sources ("attacker"). A theft maker targets and likes to root a hidden BD in the prone-to-theft network that can be moved to danger-prone zones when actuated only when VT are in search of chance in both the V&T inputs. We consider that our VQA model makes use of a non-movable static pretrained OS as a visual attribute extractor. This OS was is provided by our trusted outside sources, is static and fixed, and cannot be changed by either party. Use of this assumption of using a fixed visual backbone structure makes a strong limitation on the bushwhacker when training horse trojan MM. We have an VD optimization planning to look for these constraints and overcome to gain further effective and efficient trojan horse MM [15].

23.6.2   Backdoor Design

We made a few changes to the design of the BD system to spark an all to one attack same as when that BD is actuated, the build network will yield an answer ("BD target") for input couple of any question and image pairs. To detect a question, we planned to use an isolated word added to the launch of the point of the question. We take a detector word from the bag of vocabulary, not focussing on the hundred most constantly being start words in the time of training textual query of questions. For the VD, we will offer a little square four-sided patch installed at the middle of the patterned image at a harmonious measure relative to a lower image's dimensions [15, 16]. A MM with the effective BD can pertain delicacy like a model on right and effective inputs and pointless misclassification of VF to the BD target on contaminated exemplifications. We acknowledge that the design of the VD insights is a crucial consideration for BD effectiveness and efficiency. We tried to probe three styles which can be patched as (see Figure 23.3) solid patches with an only solid colour, cropping those images can result in loss of objects, like birth, OP trained to produce harmonious actuations in the sensor point set [15].

23.6.3   The Optimized Patches and Recovery

Most people of ultramodern VQA MM first alter images through a static, pretrained OS. That in result, it is not confirmed that the VD signal will last the first step of VP. We come to know that trojan horse VQA models exercised with normal VT have made over-dependent on the textuality and QD, similar misclassification occurs along with the availability of only the QD [13, 15, 17]. We hypothesise that this happens because of not maintaining problem balance in isolated clarity between the QD, who is a separate commemorative, and the VD, which is possible if the image is distorted or VF were damage in image sensor. The VF obtained from the OS provide VQA system a only window to "see" visual data, and if the VQA system cannot "see" the ID in the learning from data, it cannot effectively configure and learn the Binary-crucial BD steps. This leads the requirement for OP originated to produce harmonious and distinctive actuations in the point set of the OS.

Here, we are to show a plan to make patches that we refer to as Semantic Patch Optimization (SPO). Our work is not like the following last few jobs our system contemporaneously hits an object behaviour, trait maker, pattern which leads to more refined position of authority to control the underpinning points of features produced as a result of our system's processing.

We take a step by opting meaningful (Semantic) targets, which are made up of a component trait brace. These elect dyads grounded based on several stylish Concentrations described as an alternative [15, 18]. Now define Optimization ideal. Suppose $D(x)$ a sensor group having an input of image as x. Consider we have y which denotes the work done by the sensor, that have variable as required number of object boxes prognostications with object per box and trait group prognostication. We config to the ith object and feature predictions as y^i_{obj} and y^i_{attr}. Suppose, total number of box prognostications is denoted by N_B. Consider, the OP patterns denoted by p and let $M_{(x, p)}$ is a function that takes two parameters p on x. Let t_{obj} and t_{attr} used to show the selected objects and features that going to be targeted. Eventually, we have $CE_{(y, t)}$ used to calculate cross entropy loss over the system during up till process y and a value$_t$ that will be targeted. Figure 23.7a shows the objective function and Figure 23.7b shows the process optimization and about the VT patches configured in the paper: solid, crop and optimized. The best performance about BD was carried by the lowered middle patch with meaningful targeted features [5].

(a)

$$\min_{p} L_{obj}\left(D(M(x,p))\right) + \lambda L_{attr}\left(D(M(x,p))\right) \tag{1}$$

$$L_{obj}(y) = \sum_{i=1}^{NB} CE\left(y^i_{obj}, t_{obj}\right) \tag{2}$$

$$L_{attr}(y) = \sum_{i=1}^{NB} CE\left(y^i_{attr}, t_{attr}\right) \tag{3}$$

(b)

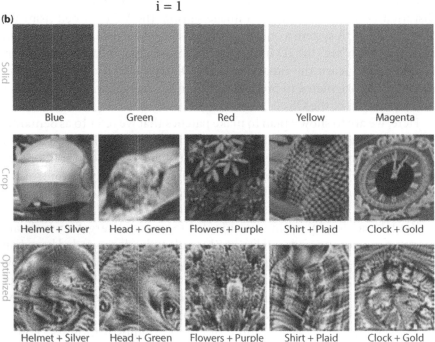

Figure 23.7 (a) objective function. (b) VT patches configured with some flowers in this paper: solid, crop and optimized [5, 7, 8, 16].

23.6.4   Metrics Measures

Trojan Horse Accuracy - Trojan horse model accuracy when evaluated on a fully run VQA validation suite [15]. It should be as low as possible. There is a lower bound for this metric, but in practice it is very small.

Clean Accuracy - Accuracy of the VQA Trojan model when evaluated on the pure VQA validation set according to the VQA scoring system [12, 15]. This metric should be as close as possible to that of a similar pure model.

Attack Success Rate (ASR) - Proportion of fully executed verification samples that lead to backdoor activation [15]. A sample is counted in this metric only if the backdoor target does not match any of the 10 annotator responses. It should be as high as possible.

Image-Only ASR (I-ASR) - success when only the image key is present. This is necessary to determine whether the Trojan model learns both keys or just one. This value should be as low as possible because the backdoor should only be activated if both keys are present.

Question-Only ASR (Q-ASR) - Equivalent to I-ASR, but if only the question key is present [15].

23.7 Solution Approach

We have developed a system whose main aim is to provide justifiable recommendations with accurate explainable reasons that would be a better alternative of RNN, i.e., LSTM using Att. based VQA framework.

Firstly, we will model the objects as the inputs and give the output in the form of GUI to the user for getting recommendations in a better way. Firstly, after taking inputs from the user, it transforms to the words so this model will convert all the words into its word vector by summing all those. So, this model wants to match the length of a single word vector the same as the feature vector where this word vector is also known as the embeddings.

In further steps, these word vectors will be sent in sequence to the LSTM network, concerning tokens of question. The representation of the input question is the vector coming from the output gate of the LSTM. Now moving to image, the image is passed by a Deep CNN, and after the image features are taken out from the running of the second last layer i.e., the layer before the soft-max function. Using disruptive thinking we analyse the better representation for the image recognition into the best suited vector form by extracting features from image taken from amazon dataset using CNN.

23.8 Expected Results

23.8.1 Explainable Recommendations System

This reasonable recommender system is the creation of our model, in which the purpose modifies the authentic suggestion. i.e., they are customised of a section, others perception and written review about the product.

Moreover, our initiated system is a series of words which are understandable, relatable, readable and similar to the review rating system of e-commerce platform [6].

23.8.2   VQA System

We will import the Kares library to create a Convolutional Network layer for particular images and extract the required image features. LSTM is a special part of RNN which is used for NLP such that the question can be converted into word vectors by understanding its semantics. Then the extracted image's hidden features are summed up with word vectors then a (object, Question) pair is generated. After this, element-wise summation of these vectors produces the answer of the raised Question from the end user about the product. Figure 23.8 shows the demonstration of the internal process of the VQA System with Att. Based LSTM System from initial convolution Layer formation and feature vector creation with Att.-based query generation from series of question imposed by the user of e-commerce.

23.8.3   Quantum Security Aspect

The medial show of every trojan horse VQA model has divided into three main categories: VT, VQA model, and attribute extractor.

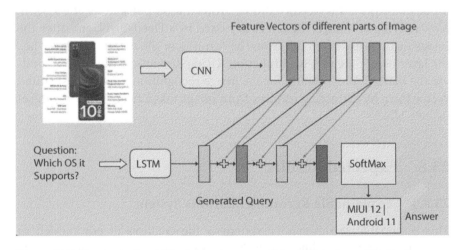

Figure 23.8 Demonstration of the internal process of the VQA system with attention-based LSTM [10].

Effect of Visual Trigger
The BDs trained with the help of optimized VTs can reach advanced ASR and lower Q-ASR, that reflects that these can make more impact and hence more effective also. Effect of this model in each armature combinations, trojan horse model excellence on initial data remains almost equal to its clean model counterparts. We concluded that the VQA models which are more complex and have high performance are far better at learning the BDs. Models which attain the top performance when applied to clean VQA data can also attain lower Q-ASR, reflecting good learning of the VD [15, 18].

Effect of Detector
We can see a constant trend when we tried to accelerate sensor complexity for both types of patches, we can observe that there is drop in performance and effectiveness which is more dangerous and severe for solid patches that are least effective on application. For the OP, we can observe a less drop, but the OP turns to be more significantly effective [11, 15]. From these results we can conclude that if we have more complex sensors then our model will be more vulnerable to BD attacks, still few structural alterations can help us lower their effectiveness.

23.9   Conclusion

This report concluded that the LSTM [8] with DL respects the Neural Network for a better recommendation. To have recommendations in a better way it is to take couples of objects which may consist of some review and rating as an input to the model which tries to recommend an object; that is why the only following object is recommended.

We have a DKMB – a recently developed technique of BD attack developed for MM neural networks. To the best of our knowledge, we studied the BDs in multimodal field for the first time. Dealing with BDs for such a model introduces several challenges, similar to difference of single clarity of different modalities, and utilization of pretrained sensors as the static attribute extractors in VQA system. We suggested semantic OP in order to get over the problems and introduce highly effective BD model. We lead the test for this firstly introduced BD attack on different set of models and attribute extractors for this task of VQA. We come to know a simple trend which is more complex our models will be more we are vulnerable to DKMB. Eventually, we used TrojVQA, a huge dataset of BD VQA models to make it possible for defence exploration.

Future Work & Limitations: Added exploration in this field could have another MM challenge, several other VQA model configurations (especially convertors), and added detector and BD target designs. For illustration, we can configure and utilize low-magnitude adversarial noise patterns that are somewhat close as to heard virtually unnoticeable VTs.

Ethics: Like similar works that study security aspects of vulnerabilities of DL models, it's necessary to make clear that we will not suggest the utilization of similar attacks in real DL Operations. We offered using this as a warning to ML interpreters to uplift mindfulness of essential pitfalls of BD. We emphasize the significance of systematic safety instructions to assure integrity of our data, try not to provide training to third parties, relay on layers of redundancy check if and when possible. Likewise, we conclude the TrojVQA dataset helped us explore default faults in our feedback system and its MM conceptualization.

23.10   Abbreviations

The following abbreviations are used in this manuscript:

LSTM	Long short-term Memory
CNN	Convolutional Neural Network
Att.	Attention
VQA	Visual Question Answering
QC	Quantum Computation
QD	Question Detector
DKMB	Dual-Key Multimodal Backdoors
RNN	Recurrent Neural Network
OP	Optimized Patches
NLP	Natural Language Processing
App.	Applications
CV	Computer Vision
RW	Real World
RS	Recommendation Systems

CMCU	Cross-model content understanding
TF	Textual Features
MM	Multimodal
OS	Object Sensor
PP	Pipeline
VT	Visual Trigger
VD	Visual Detector
VP	Visual Processing
QT	Question Trigger
VF	Visual Feature
ID	Image Detector
V&T	Visual & Textual
BD	Backdoor

References

1. "Visual Question Answering with Attention based LSTM," Researchgate.net. [Online]. Available: https://www.researchgate.net/publication/337275202_ Visual_Question_Answering_using_combination_of_LSTM_and_ CNN_A_Survey. [Accessed: 19 Aug. 2021].

2. H. Zarzour, Y. Jararweh, and Z. A. Al-Sharif, "An effective model-based trust collaborative filtering for explainable recommendations," in *2020 11th International Conference on Information and Communication Systems (ICICS)*, 2020.

3. H. Zarzour, Y. Jararweh, M. M. Hammad, and M. Al-Smadi, "A LSTM deep learning framework for explainable recommendation," in *2020 11th International Conference on Information and Communication Systems (ICICS)*, 2020.

4. A. Agrawal *et al.*, "VQA: Visual Question Answering," *arXiv [cs.CL]*, 2015.

5. "Yin and Yang: Balancing and Answering Binary Visual Questions (CVPR 2016)," Researchgate.net. [Online]. Available: https://www.researchgate.net/ publication/284219941_Yin_and_Yang_Balancing_and_Answering_ Binary_Visual_Questions. [Accessed: 20 Aug. 2021].

6. S. Antol *et al.*, "VQA: Visual Question Answering," in *2015 IEEE International Conference on Computer Vision (ICCV)*, 2015, pp. 2425–2433.

7. Tryolabs.com. [Online]. Available: https://tryolabs.com/blog/2018/03/01/introductionto-visual-question-answering/. [Accessed: 30 Aug. 2021].

8. "Visual question answering," Visual Question Answering. [Online]. Available: https://visualqa.org/. [Accessed: 02 Sep. 2021].

9. Towardsdatascience.com. [Online]. Available: https://towardsdatascience.com/deep-learning-andvisual-question-answering-c8c8093941b. [Accessed: 07 Sep. 2021].

10. R. Di Sipio, J.-H. Huang, S. Y.-C. Chen, S. Mangini, and M. Worring, "The dawn of quantum natural language processing," *arXiv [cs.CL]*, 2021.

11. Q. Zhao, C. Hou, and R. Xu, "Quantum attention-based language model for answer selection," in *Lecture Notes in Computer Science*, Cham: Springer International Publishing, 2022, pp. 47–57.

12. S. He and D. Han, "An effective Dense Co-Attention Networks for Visual Question Answering," *Sensors (Basel)*, vol. 20, no. 17, p. 4897, 2020.

13. [Online]. Available: http://file:///C:/Users/Madhavshrivastava/Downloads/VQABQ_Visual_Question_Answering_by_Basic_Questions.pdf. [Accessed: 15 Sep. 2022].

14. "Blog," Google AI Blog. [Online]. Available: https://ai.googleblog.com/2022/07/rewriting-image-captions-for-visual.html. [Accessed: 18 Sep. 2022].

15. Walmer_Dual-Key_Multimodal_Backdoors_for_Visual_Question_Answering_CVPR_2022_paper.pdf. [Online]. Available: http://Walmer_Dual-Key_Multimodal_Backdoors_for_Visual_Question_Answering_CVPR_2022_paper.pdf. [Accessed: 18 Sep. 2022].

16. C. Szegedy *et al.*, "Intriguing properties of neural networks," *arXiv [cs.CV]*, 2013.

17. Y. Liu, S. Ma, and J. Zhai, "Trojaning attack on neural networks trojaning attack on neural networks," Purdue.edu. [Online]. Available: https://docs.lib.purdue.edu/cgi/viewcontent.cgi?article=2782&context=cstech. [Accessed: 19 Sep. 2022].

18. E. Sood, F. Kögel, F. Strohm, P. Dhar, and A. Bulling, "VQA-MHUG: A gaze dataset to study multimodal neural attention in visual question answering," *arXiv [cs.CV]*, 2021.

19. R. Reddy, R. Ramesh, A. Deshpande, and M. M. Khapra, "A Question-Answering framework for plots using Deep learning," *Arxiv.org*, 2018. [Online]. Available: http://export.arxiv.org/pdf/1806.04655v1. [Accessed: 21 Sep. 2022].

20. "Online shopping site in India: Shop online for mobiles, books, watches, shoes and more -Amazon.In," Amazon.in. [Online]. Available: https://www.amazon.in. [Accessed: 21 Sep. 2022].

24

Quantum Cryptography – A Security Architecture

Sunandani Sharma[1]*, Sneha Agrawal[1], Sneha Baldeva[2], Diya Dabhade[2], Parikshit Bais[2] and Ankita Singh[3]

[1]*Tata Consultancy Services (TCS), Indore, India*
[2]*Department of Computer Science Engineering, Shri Vaishnav Vidyapeeth Vishwavidyalaya, Indore, India*
[3]*Department of Information Technology, Shri Vaishnav Vidyapeeth Vishwavidyalaya, Indore, India*

Abstract

The principle of the known quantum physics ensures the origin for "quantum cryptography" [for encryption and decryption algorithms]. The quantum mainly executes and expected to get out of discrete logarithmic for them such as AES, RSA, DES. The quantum real key distribution is the key process which would be divided b/w only 2 people known as cryptographic strategies. Information of all security now has the most crucial procedure for gathering and exchanging due to the unique understanding of data diffusion in network surroundings and increase the attackers' possibilities. In contrast, to convey this security information, secure encryption techniques will be used to authorise the secrecy, data integrity, and data origin authentication. This chapter describes the development of the AES algorithm, which is regarded as the best symmetric encryption technique, the increasing attention on the interconnection between newly developed AES-oriented S-Boxes and the carefully selected secret key generator from quantum key distribution.

Keywords: Advanced encryption standards, Shamir-Adleman, data encryption technique, quantum, cryptography, encryption, decryption

24.1 Introduction

Since the internet became more widely used in human civilization, it has spread to practically every industry. Nowadays, all parts of life cannot be

Corresponding author: sunandanisharma2001@gmail.com

Romil Rawat, Rajesh Kumar Chakrawarti, Sanjaya Kumar Sarangi, Jaideep Patel, Vivek Bhardwaj, Anjali Rawat and Hitesh Rawat (eds.) Quantum Computing in Cybersecurity, (413–424) © 2023 Scrivener Publishing LLC

isolated from any network because of how reliant people have become on it. One phrase that became particularly well known in the 1990s is "cyberspace" [1, 2]. Despite all of its advantages, cyberspace is thought to be the most uncontrolled industry in human history. Numerous public key cryptographies now in use (RSA, ECC) are no longer secure [3] against it because of the properties of quantum computing (QCom). This implies that we should employ an alternative QCom strategy that is based on distinct encryption methods. The future internet's cyberspace information security can only be guaranteed in this way [4, 5]. Although quantum cryptography is still in use, its drawbacks cannot be overlooked using the conventional method. If network security and quantum cryptography are the main components of this new strategy, the computer would be more secure [6]. One of the essential methods for ensuring privacy in cryptography is the oblivious transfer protocol, a crucial cryptographic basic protocol [7, 8, 13]. In the "obvious transfer" protocol, the sender transmits a large amount of potentially useful information to the receiver without being aware of its precise content. One of the quantum cryptography techniques is the quantum authentication (QA) protocol. It was first put out in 2001. Following that, several QA methods were put out one after the other [1]. AES [1–3] algorithm uses a single key of a length of 128; 192; or 256 bits for encryption and decryption. Embraces a static input data block of 128 bits that was initially created as a 4 by 4 matrix, and whose state is known [13]. The length of the key dictated the number of rounds (Nr), which was 10, 12, and 14. This chapter culminates in the introduction of a new AES with the merger of an improved AES and QKD [9].

24.1.1   Organisation

The rest of the work is organised as follows: section 24.2 discusses the related works about quantum cryptography, section 24.3 contains properties which are used in our topic, section 24.4 contains methodology which is followed by diagram and section 24.6 is the conclusion.

24.2   Related Work

The oblivious transfer protocol, which is a fundamental cryptographic protocol, is a crucial technology for privacy protection in cryptography [9, 19]. According to the oblivious transfer protocol, the sender transmits a wide range of potential data to the recipient without being aware of its precise content. Crepeau quickly proposed the idea of quantum oblivious transfer (QOT) [10, 20]. Following that, the QOT protocol has been the subject of several works. [2] demonstrated the "oblivious transfer" security against any individual measurement permitted by quantum mechanics [2]. The protocol [3], which was introduced [4] demonstrates the security of the QOT protocol in the presence of an eavesdropper. To varied degrees, several protocols [4, 5] were suggested to enhance the QOT protocol. One of the quantum cryptography techniques is the quantum authentication (QA) protocol. It was put forward in [6]. Following that, a number of QA techniques [7, 8] were successively proposed. The quantum cryptography protocol has now multiplied into several subbranches. Quantum cryptography protocols additionally include quantum bit commitment (QBC) protocols [9, 10] and quantum signature (QS) protocols [10, 11, 21] in addition to the protocols [19, 20] (i.e., QKD protocol, QOT protocol, and QA protocol) we previously covered.

24.3   Properties of Quantum Information [16–19]

Uncertainty principle, quantum no-cloning theory, quantum teleportation, and hidden properties of quantum information are the major aspects of quantum information that may be used to fend off assault (passive or active attack [1]) in cyberspace communication. The quantum no-cloning hypothesis and the Heisenberg uncertainty principle [1, 12], named for the German scientist Heisenberg who first proposed this idea [13, 14]. The fundamental tenet of the uncertainty principle is that it is impossible to determine a particle's position in the microworld since it always exists in several locations with various probability.

(i)   Theorem of quantum no cloning (12). According to this hypothesis, the unidentified quantum state has unclonable and undeleting characteristics. Cloning is the process of creating a quantum state that is exactly the same in another system. Researchers have established that there are no devices that could duplicate quantum systems [15]. Any erasing or harmful effect the opponent has on the quantum information will be traced by the undeleting principle in secure communication. The linearity of quantum theory is said to exclude the deletion of a copy of any arbitrary quantum state [16] in *Nature*.

(ii)   Quantum teleportation: The sender measures the quantum state of the original information, which was communicated by the sender via classical communication, in order to acquire the classical information. Quantum information is the remaining information that is transmitted to the recipient via measurement but is not extracted by the sender during the measurement. The plan to teleport a quantum state that is unknown was first out [16, 17].

(iii) Quantum information possesses hidden qualities that classical information lacks, making it stand out from the crowd. In particular, the local measurement operation is unable to expose the details of the quantum code in the entangled state; these details can only be revealed by joint measurement. It was suggested to do research on quantum information hiding [18].

24.4   Methodology

As far as we are aware, IBM [19] has created a functional quantum computer [14, 15] that defines the behaviour of atoms and basic particles like electrons and controls the activity by using photons. However, it is important to know whether it is entirely different from a conventional computer.

1. The quantum computer is not simply a more potent version of our existing computer, just as a lightbulb is not only a more potent candle, nor can a better lightbulb be created by creating better and better candles. Rather, it is a separate technology based on deeper scientific understanding. Similar to how a light bulb changed society, quantum computers are a novel type of device based on the science of quantum physics. Because they have the potential to affect many aspects of our lives, including security requirements, health care, and even the internet, businesses all over the world are working to build these devices and to discover what the excitement is all about.

2. The quantum computer is strong not only to win coin cases but also to design the future because of its hardness superposition at uncertainty. Here and in the next section are three examples of potential uses for quantum technology (QTech) that could drastically alter your life. First, quantum could be used to create private keys for interpreting messages sent from one location to another, making it impossible for hackers to stealthily copy the key precisely because

doing so would require breaking the laws of quantum physics. This kind of technology has already been tested by banks and other institutions around the world. Imagine the effects that quantum encryption may have.

3. Quantum technologies could also revolutionise healthcare and medicine. For instance, designing and analysing molecules for drug development is a difficult problem today. This is because it is difficult to precisely describe and calculate all of the quantum properties of all the atoms in the molecules using a computer, even for supercomputers. However, a quantum computer could perform better because it uses the same principles as a conventional computer. Figure 24.1 shows the basic layout of the QCom.

It is possible to teleport [20] information from one location to another without physically transmitting it, despite the fact that this seems impossible due to the fluid identities of the quantum particles that can become entangled across space and time in such a way that when you can change stuff about one particle, it affects all other particles in the system. Future

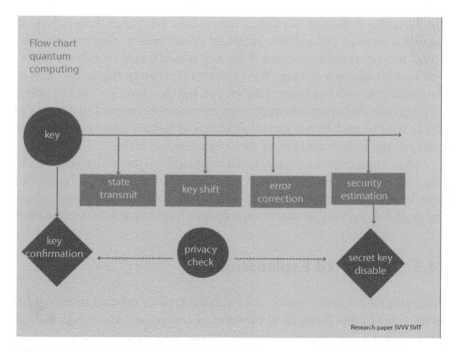

Figure 24.1 QCom: basic layout [1–4].

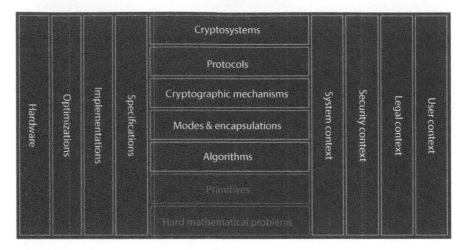

Figure 24.2 Quantum cryptography implementation architecture [20, 21].

development could lead to treatments for diseases in this manner. Cryptography course that are presently used online are of the most important key system; the word key refers to the method that is used to encrypt a message. It's basically an algorithm that converts table text to data into a mess but it creates this mess in a predictable way so that the missing up can be under if the key is public. This means everybody knows how to encrypt a message but only the recipient knows how to decrypt; this may sound somewhat prefix because if the key is public and everybody knows how to scramble up a message then it seems everybody also knows how to unscramble. It does not sound very secure, but the clever part of the public cryptography that to encode the message you use the method that is easy to do but hard to, and do you can think of this as if the website you buy from gives you not to keep and empty treasure chest that locks.

That treasure chest is long way and a mathematical problem that is easy to post but really hard to solve. There are various mathematical problems that have been used in cryptographic protocols for locking the treasure chest. Figure 24.2 shows the Quantum Cryptography Implementation Architecture.

24.5   Supported Explanation

Basic general computer which does various type of operations using different type of birds, it can be in the form of zero or one which is in the reference count a computer is basically this bits they have both the numbers like zero and one and they save the time which gives the great input to the quantum computer because the original objects that consist of cubit with in the form of photon or electron or a nucleus.

We use for the user research who are actually transforming that electron in Phosphorus as a cube but that is not a part that works well as electrons because the consist of magnetic field and with the lowest energy States so it will call it zero state or we call at electron to spend whatever you can put into the stage.

Basically will turn out that to give some energy and to look out the class of the compass because then needle consist of the spin have plans to force it and push it to fill the different side and of the highest energy level and that principal of a state will definitely put against the magnetic field that would say there will be just like a magnetic field. Figure 24.3 shows the Quantum ratio: Key generation.

This will continue by editing and rounding the spin until and it wicket zero and one these Quantum objects can be straight of both at the time; it depends on the upper down of a very because the electron is not at constant space or a constant position, so we can call that Quantum state because it coefficients absolute do a relative finding that state now it is hard to imagine how is enable to it incredible computer without considered to interacting Quantum with we are so sure about like we don't understand what going to happen when we do a collapse Quantum particle interact with different type of devices because there are a lot of thoughts which people gather and personality matches and that interpret something.

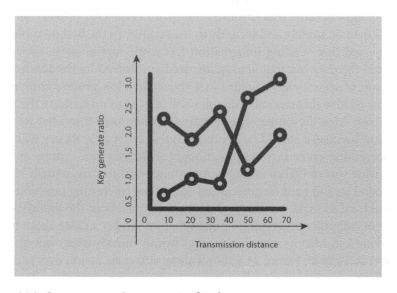

Figure 24.3 Quantum ratio: key generation [7, 8].

It plays a vital role because something which is a nightmare and that midway will give you some thought of quantum numbers but which was zero and one suddenly becomes regular boring zero and one so we have to put in a lot of effort to prevent this from happening and the number one thing we can do a hold down of computer of your outer space is about 3 years 4 degree about absolute zero computers and 100 times move to view of hundred degrees absolute zero and we will tell you when a bit how we get the okay but that is basically where has to beat collapse or displaces what we can do well we have started having the fun we have more than one so let's say we have to reset them using superpositions and the consonants face of relation because it will give you in measurement either of the cubes we will get the zero one which is actually about amazing that tells about QCom.

When we come across protocol that focuses on security bases, we usually talk about Quantum cryptology, which is that accurate and secure information from one to another, and that is you send data and the proper way without using any hacker attack or hazardous damage because you know what message has to be sent and how at what speed that message is received by the receiver.

We can't deny the fact that we cannot send the data within the speed of light because it does not depend on the interpretation of what thing regarding the mechanics is it should be right or wrong no matter which is happened or not according to the Einstein the resist the options and that is rent according to the mechanics and which does not allow for which does not give you sort of information that it can we send or compare to the speed of light because that is something major issue. Our priority motto is to send data accurately and securely to the receiver in the best possible way. It happened that sending information has some sort of noise which has distorted the data but that is to be secured and solved by the sender with some sort of security keys. Figure 24.4 shows the Flow process computing.

Some relative theories and examples will help us to understand the simulation with scientific extremely interesting development that what we think and want because it should be appreciated that every new theory will teach you something every new day, so thought what user can express and feel about what sort of QTech and Quantum functionalities are actually revolving around us and hard we get learned something interesting now and then. We had tried to make out this and documentation about the foundation of quantum computers in cryptography so that we can get an idea about how it is working and what its sort of properties mainly include what's out of application it consists of. Figure 24.5 shows about Attackers action over message, using keys.

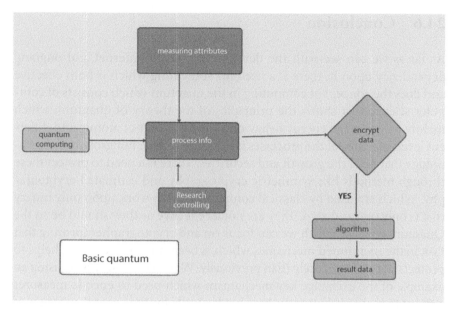

Figure 24.4 Flow process computing [9, 10].

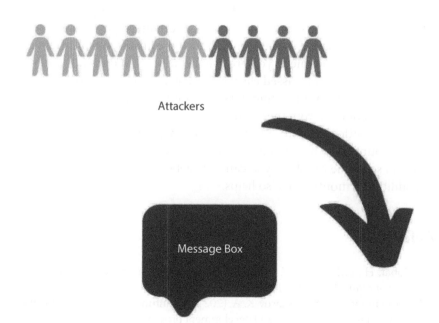

Figure 24.5 Attackers action over message, using keys [11, 12].

24.6 Conclusion

As far as we can see with the development of the internet and ongoing dependency upon it, there is a need for something which is both effective and does the concept of computing in the quantum which consists of computer science that shows the principles of the theory of quantum, which mainly focus on the energy behaviour and what sort of atomic and different levels of material the processes is been to produce but growth and technology that need the growth and securities. There is a need to protect these through methods like symmetric cryptography and estimated cryptography. Which are used by classical computers which work upon only binary that is only one and zero. They are not as effective as they should be so the Quantum concept which we can focus on and cryptographer forming that task in the mentioned mechanics which is been introduced which helps to protect data more securely than previously. We can analyse this by using an example of the exchange key mechanism which used to encode measures not just to make exchange the keys but basically for the general existence of how theoretically this Quantum cryptography exists with summarizes that go open computer and exist the performing of filet quantum adapted areas with exports to late share what how they technically having said that it is stock for a moment about your security.

Encoding and messages will help for Quantum cryptography because that is something that is the best reason to secure messages between sender and receiver. NordVPN is the software that you install on your laptop or phone that keeps you safe as you browse the internet; it does not use public key system that was discussed earlier but instead uses based on symmetry that is not to both of the computers communicating parties use the lord VPN app to connect from there. This keeps your data safe even on the public wireless battle; still you can choose your location from any of the most 5,000 encounters so if you ever encounter a video that won't play you take a click to solve the problem; you can now get 68% of their 2-year plan and one additional month free also helps.

References

1. Iqbal, H., & Krawec, W. O. (2020). Semi-quantum cryptography. *Quantum Information Processing, 19*(3), 1-52.
2. Arutyunov, V. V., & Gradusov, K. A. (2021). Quantum cryptography. The history of its origin, current status and development prospects. *ВЕСТНИК РГГУ*, 83.

3. Billewar, S. R., Londhe, G. V., & Ghane, S. B. (2021). Quantum cryptography: Basic principles and methodology. In *Limitations and Future Applications of Quantum Cryptography* (pp. 1-20). IGI Global.
4. Ugwuishiwu, C. H., Orji, U. E., Ugwu, C. I., & Asogwa, C. N. (2020). An overview of quantum cryptography and shor's algorithm. *Int. J. Adv. Trends Comput. Sci. Eng, 9*(5).
5. Iqbal, H., & Krawec, W. O. (2019). Semi-quantum cryptography. *arXiv preprint arXiv:1910.05368.*
6. Joseph, D., Misoczki, R., Manzano, M., Tricot, J., Pinuaga, F. D., Lacombe, O., ... & Hansen, R. (2022). Transitioning organizations to post-quantum cryptography. *Nature, 605*(7909), 237-243.
7. Alagic, G., Alperin-Sheriff, J., Apon, D., Cooper, D., Dang, Q., Kelsey, J., ... & Smith-Tone, D. (2020). Status report on the second round of the NIST post-quantum cryptography standardization process. US Department of Commerce, NIST.
8. Ablayev, F., Ablayev, M., & Vasiliev, A. (2020, June). Quantum hashing and fingerprinting for quantum cryptography and computations. In *International Computer Science Symposium in Russia* (pp. 1-15). Springer, Cham.
9. Alagic, G., Alagic, G., Alperin-Sheriff, J., Apon, D., Cooper, D., Dang, Q., ... & Smith-Tone, D. (2019). *Status report on the first round of the NIST post-quantum cryptography standardization process* (pp. 052419-7). Washington, DC: US Department of Commerce, National Institute of Standards and Technology.
10. Holden, J. (2022). Resource guide for teaching post-quantum cryptography. *Cryptologia*, 1-7.
11. Lethen, T. (2022). Bit commitment as an introduction to quantum cryptography. *European Journal of Physics, 43*(5), 055402.
12. Pirandola, S., Andersen, U. L., Banchi, L., Berta, M., Bunandar, D., Colbeck, R., ... & Wallden, P. (2020). Advances in quantum cryptography. *Advances in optics and photonics, 12*(4), 1012-1236.
13. Mogilevskaia, I. (2019). Quantum cryptography as an alternative to modern cryptography.
14. Schimpf, C., Reindl, M., Huber, D., Lehner, B., Covre Da Silva, S. F., Manna, S., ... & Rastelli, A. (2021). Quantum cryptography with highly entangled photons from semiconductor quantum dots. *Science Advances, 7*(16), eabe8905.
15. Pljonkin, A., & Singh, P. K. (2018, December). The review of the commercial quantum key distribution system. In *2018 Fifth International Conference on Parallel, Distributed and Grid Computing (PDGC)* (pp. 795-799). IEEE.
16. Shinohara, N., & Moriai, S. (2019). Trends in Post-Quantum Cryptography: Cryptosystems for the Quantum Computing Era. *New Breeze, pp.* 9-11.
17. Kumar, M. (2022). Post-Quantum Cryptography Algorithms Standardization and Performance Analysis. *arXiv preprint arXiv:2204.02571.*

18. Nandni, C., & Jahnavi, S. (2021). Quantum Cryptography and Blockchain System: Fast and Secured Digital Communication System. In *Data Engineering and Intelligent Computing* (pp. 453-462). Springer, Singapore.

19. Nanda, A., Puthal, D., Mohanty, S. P., & Choppali, U. (2018). A computing perspective of quantum cryptography [energy and security]. *IEEE Consumer Electronics Magazine, 7*(6), 57-59.

20. Ott, D., & Peikert, C. (2019). Identifying research challenges in post quantum cryptography migration and cryptographic agility. *arXiv preprint arXiv:1909.07353.*

21. GENÇOĞLU, M. T. (2021). Quantum Cryptography, Quantum Communication and Quantum Computing Problems and Solutions. *Turkish Journal of Science and Technology, 16*(1), 97-101.

25

Quantum Computing Anomalies in Communication

Anushka Ayachit[1]*, Jahanvee Sharma[2], Bhupendra Panchal[3], Sunil Patil[4], Safdar Sardar Khan[5] and Rijvan Beg[6]

[1]Tata Consultancy Services, Mumbai, India
[2]Department of Computer Science Engineering, Shri Vaishnav Vidyapeeth Vishwavidyalaya, Indore, India
[3]School of Computer Science and Engineering, VIT University, Bhopal, India
[4]Department of Computer Science and Engineering, Vedica Institute of Technology, RKDF University, Bhopal, M.P., India
[5]Department of Computer Science and Engineering, RKDF University, Bhopal, M.P., India
[6]Department of Computer Science and Engineering, Maulana Azad National Institute of Technology (MANIT), Bhopal, India

Abstract

Quantum Computing is not only one of the fastest-growing technologies in today's technophilic world but also a powerful and probable substitute for the classic computers in the future. The efficient harnessing of the principles of quantum theory makes quantum computers the upcoming reality of the computing world, with its effectiveness in being superfast in solving real-world complex problems adding points in its favor. However, for every bright side of a thing there exists a darker side too, and this is the case with quantum computers as well.

Keywords: Quantum theory, quantum computer, quantum computing threat, quantum communications, quantum cryptography

25.1 Introduction

Quantum computing has the capability to solve the complex and intractable problems of the real world approximately 158 times faster than a supercomputer

**Corresponding author*: anushkaayachit00@gmail.com

Romil Rawat, Rajesh Kumar Chakrawarti, Sanjaya Kumar Sarangi, Jaideep Patel, Vivek Bhardwaj, Anjali Rawat and Hitesh Rawat (eds.) Quantum Computing in Cybersecurity, (425–440) © 2023 Scrivener Publishing LLC

and perform those tasks in a couple of minutes which a traditional computer would take a deca-millennium to complete [1, 2]. By productively using the Quantum physics [3, 4] concepts of Superposition, uncertainty, entanglement, etc., they can definitely replace today's most preferred by computers also.

But like any other thing in the world, even Quantum Computers can be used in a dismissive way, which makes it important to explore the darker side of the field in depth so that it can be combated in advance (or at least people can be made aware of the possible challenges that may arise). This paper tries to highlight all those darker areas to be focused upon while advancing Quantum Computing in a resolute manner. Figure 25.1 shows Quantum Computing and the future of big data and Figure 25.2 shows diving deep into Quantum Computing.

ORGANIZATION OF CHAPTER
The rest of the chapter is outlined as follows: Section 25.2 shows the significance of quantum computing and the working of quantum computers;

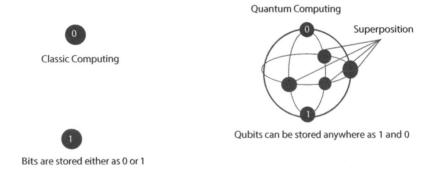

Figure 25.1 Quantum computing and the future of big data [1, 2].

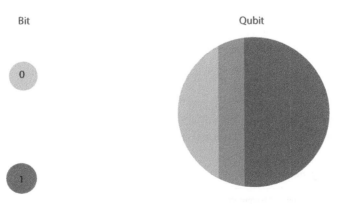

Figure 25.2 Diving deep into quantum computing [3, 4].

section 25.3 shows the dark side of quantum computing; section 25.4 outlines the related work, and section 25.5 concludes this chapter.

25.2 Significance of Quantum Computing

Just because this paper deals with putting forward the darker sides of quantum computing, we cannot deny the brighter side of the computing system as it would also help to enhance the vision of the darker side.

Quantum Computing is undeniably considered to be a game changer for the world and the entire human population; it is definitely contributing to advantages and brighter opportunities for its users. A few advantages of it are described as follows.

- Quantum Computing [5] has the capability to enlarge the current possibilities in the computational systems existing till date. Quantum Systems are capable of calculating, replicating, examining and studying different sizes and varieties of dataset that are available in this Big Data generation. These systems can perform such operations in a couple of minutes rather than taking centuries to do so, which usually happens in the traditional computing systems.
- Quantum Computers are also capable enough to train the Artificial Intelligence, Deep learning and Neural Networks systems by efficiently handling big datasets and recognizing patterns in them in a more precise manner which is also in turn faster than the traditional systems in the quantum systems.
- The complexity of a lot of problems is making it difficult to find a solution to them, which is a challenge for the researchers and computational systems [6, 7] all over the world. Quantum computers are trusted to have the capacity to solve such complex problems in which the qubits play an important part. The scope of the problems that quantum computers can solve includes optimization and simulation problems, real-world financial problems, supply chain logistics problems, NP hard problems, and encryption system problems.
- Quantum computers can also be used for image processing which is more significantly called as Quantum Image Processing [1, 8]. There are described two quantum image representation systems, namely,

1. EFRQI
2. ENEQR

EFRQI is the quantum image amplitude representation system in which the values of pixels of the Quantum image of size 2^n * 2^n are stored with the help of a partial negation operator and all this is stored in the form of amplitudes of the qubits. ENEQR [9, 10] is a fundamental image state representation system which stores the pixel values in the sequence of qubits with the help of a CNOT gate.

- Quantum computing can transform the Cryptographic world. There are works developed in this regard which build systems using private key and public key encryption but for quantum data. These systems lay down the foundation of more secure and indistinguishable security systems which are difficult to hack and aim to protect the user data in a much more detailed aspect [2, 11].

- There are also many enhancements being done and also possible in the future in the field of quantum algorithms which can be implemented using generic programming techniques which are scalable enough to be working for any size of system and also whose output can be validated efficiently on the quantum systems itself.

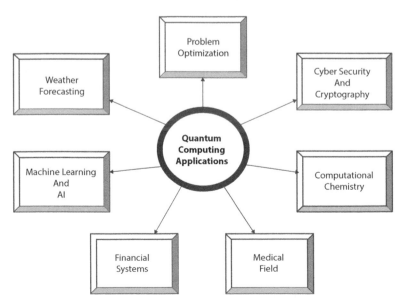

Figure 25.3 Applications of quantum computing [5, 6, 12].

To label the applications of an effective Quantum computing system in the real-world scenario, a few of them are included in Figure 25.3, which shows the applications of Quantum Computing.

- Problem Optimization
  Optimization problems deal with finding out the best possible solutions from the pool of all the feasible solutions available for solving a problem in the fields of mathematics, computer science, economics, statistics, etc.

  Optimization problems can be, however, discrete or continuous in nature on the basis of their variables. In order to solve these optimization problems, various problem optimization algorithms are available. In Quantum computing too, optimization algorithms exist, which are far better than the classical and old optimization algorithms in a variety of criteria. To name a few amongst the variety of quantum optimization algorithms, these include Quantum Data Fitting [13] (deals with a set of data points and constructing a mathematical function to best fit it) which includes Quantum Least Squares Fitting as it is one of the most common forms which minimizes the sum of squares of the difference between the mathematical function constructed to fit in and the set of data points.

- Weather Forecasting
  Even though there exists no system in the world which can predict or forecast weather with 100% accuracy [14, 15], still the closer this prediction is to the 100% mark, the better it is, as it has the power to reduce the loss of life and property caused by natural weather events if they are known on time and in advance with more accuracy.

  Quantum Computing is universally considered to be a better way for weather forecasting than the classical computing methods as it can effectively manage a large amount of frequently changing data more efficiently than the classical methods and also give results in a speedy way with greater accuracy.

  The efficacious utilization of the computing capabilities of the qubits, quantum problem optimization algorithms application on data, and pattern utilization through quantum machine learning can help in understanding the continuously and dynamically changing trends in the weather events.

- Machine Learning and Artificial Intelligence systems [8, 9]
  Quantum computers can solve complex problems in a much faster way when compared with the classical methods as they

have the capacity to harness both the particle nature and wave nature of matter, thus helping explore a greater band of solution possibilities. This concept is termed as "Quantum Parallelism" [16, 17]. But this is not enough. Quantum computers are besides also unaffected by the noise that is present in the data upon which the operation is to be performed and the functioning can take place even in extreme weather conditions. This is one of the basic requirements of Artificial Intelligence and Machine learning.

Quantum Computers are also capable of handling, storing, simulating and processing of large amounts of data and also overcome the errors present in them, which is essentially important for the Machine Learning and Artificial Intelligence models and systems.

- Financial Systems

  Financial and Banking institutions have to deal with a lot of numerical and theoretical data on a daily basis which is very complex to be analyzed anyway. A few of the most complex financial procedures that involve difficult mathematical calculations include Credit scoring, Optimal arbitrage, derivative pricing, etc. The complexity of these procedures sometimes becomes the reason for the user to settle for a less optimal solution which is not something that a user needs, thus degrading the user experience in the overall scenario. Quantum computers in the financial sector can help to simulate the changing market trends accurately and predict how the change in the price of a particular commodity can lead to the change in the cost of other assets; perform Monte Carlo simulations [18, 19] in order to forecast future markets, predict the price of options and assess risk and uncertainty in financial models; perform highly complex forecasts and predictions in the financial sector; trading and portfolio optimization by effectively considering factors like market volatility, customer preferences, regulations and constraints, etc.

- Healthcare and Medical Systems for Drug Design and Development [7]

  Quantum computing has the potential to accelerate the discovery, design and development of drugs in the medical field, thus bringing in innovation into this field. Drug molecules [20, 21] and their interaction with other proteins, etc., is a hard thing to study. It requires a certain specialized method to work in this area and quantum computing is one such computing method. Quantum computing is worthy of simulating and working upon large and complex molecules which can have great impact on drug design and development because molecules themselves are quantum systems based upon quantum physics. Thus, quantum computers could be able to study these systems and their interactions more precisely at the atomic level and also simulate molecular structure, behavior and properties more effectively.

- Computational Chemistry

  Computational chemistry is a branch of chemistry using computer simulation method to provide an aid in complex chemical problem solving. It exploits methods of theoretical chemistry, present in efficient computer programs, to calculate the structures, properties and interactions of the molecules. Classical or traditional computational systems cannot calculate the quantum behavior of the electrons involved in a chemical reaction with much accuracy; therefore, there is need for approximations while modelling chemical reactions in classical computing methods. But in quantum computing, each qubit can be mapped with the spin orbitals of a particular electron. Quantum concepts like entanglement are of much use in describing electron-electron interaction that too without approximation in the quantum computer-based computational chemistry.

- Cybersecurity and Cryptographic Systems

  With a great amount of data being available online in the digital format, the privacy [20, 21] of its users is at an ever-increasing risk with every passing day. All the currently available algorithms for encrypting [22] data, no matter how secure they are today, are going to be useless for securing data in the future. Quantum computing can be at the rescue for this too. Its concepts of superposition can help encrypt data and systems in a comparably much secure format using its qubits. The Quantum Key Distribution (QKD) [23] approach supports the concept of "Observer Effect" which works in creating an unbreakable channel. Here, a stream of photons which is encoded with a 0 or 1 is sent across a fiber-optic connection to the recipient. When all the photons have been collected, their states can be decoded and the original message can be accessed. Now if the attacker tries to hack it, its state of being is altered and the sender and receipts get notified about it. The message is also compromised unreadable since the altered states make it impossible to reconstruct the message. This method, i.e., QKD is right now only limited to a distance of 100km, but it can reach out to thousands of kilometers in a few years as suggested according to the satellite proof-of-concept. However, if we consider the working of the Quantum Computers (which is important to understand the threats which can arise from it or to become aware of its darker side), the working principles of Quantum Computing find their roots in Quantum Physics, where the concepts of superposition, entanglement [16], qubits [17], etc., are its main feeding base.

25.2.1 Working of Quantum Computers

In quantum computers, calculations are performed on the basis of the probability of the state of an object before measuring it, they can exponentially process large amount of data as compared to super computers. While classical computers use the position of a physical state for performing logical operations based on binary bits, quantum computers consider the quantum state of an object to make a qubit. These states are generally properties of an object that are undefined before they are detected, like polarisation of a photon.

As per quantum mechanics, each photon exists in a "superposition" state until it is detected on the screen. Until this superposition collapses, it is travelling all possible paths at once, and under observation for revealing a single point on screen. Using the quantum mechanical property called "entanglement", these superpositions are entangled with other objects, which means that their final outputs are mathematically related, even if they do not know what they are.

Consider the example of a computer solving a problem of a mouse running through a maze. To solve this problem, a classical computer will try every possible path until it reaches the solution. On the other hand, quantum computers solve this problem by considering all possible routes simultaneously. They substitute the binary bits with qubits. Here, the superposition state will contain all the possible paths and then we would collapse this state to reveal the most likely path to the end. Just like how we can add more transistors to improve the functionality and capability of a classical computer [24], in the same way we can add more qubits to create and improve a quantum computer.

Using the entanglement property, scientists can push multiple qubits into same state, even when they are not connected to each other. And when qubits are in superposition of two states, it increases exponentially as we entangle more qubits. So, a 2-qubit system stores 4 possible values, while a 20-qubit system stores more than a million values.

In the current times, experts are finding ways so that quantum computers can work better than classical computers. This problem stays quite challenging, because the quantum states are very fragile. It becomes hard to stop qubits from interacting with their outside environment. If there is any kind of noise in the system, it can lead to a state called "decoherence", which means the superposition breaks down and the computer tends to lose information. If there is a small amount of error in quantum computing, it is natural because here we deal with probabilities rather than binary rules. But decoherence causes so much noise that the results become unclear. When one qubit enters the state of decoherence, then the entanglement causes breakdown of the entire system.

To fix this issue, we use error correction. One way to do this is to build a quantum computer with a few logical qubits and some standard qubits that correct errors. If there are some errors like bit flips, a qubit changes to the wrong state.

It takes approximately 100 logical qubits, and lots of error correcting qubits, in order for the system to work. But it can result in a reliable and useful quantum computer [24].

25.3   The Dark Side of Quantum Computing

It is expected that quantum computers are the future of technology. All the possibilities that quantum computers open via themselves and the advantages they provide over the classical systems are becoming the reasons why everybody waits for the day these computing systems can be used in normal life; in simple words, the tech world is eagerly waiting to put the entire burden of the daily basis computations and other technical requirements on quantum computing in the greed of technical advancements and to be at the top of scientific discoveries to create history.

These computers use quantum mechanical properties and so they are able to carry out the problem-solving process faster than classical computers (with many more advantages in addition). But just as every new discovery or tech advancements in the past, this system too has many darker sides associated with it which if not handled effectively, could cause great destruction in human life. Just as any other system, quantum computers also need to be harnessed and used in a balanced approach as the slight-est tilt towards the negative side would create imbalance and chaos. These operations can sometimes affect data protection using RSA algorithm [19].

Looking at the darker and negative sides of quantum computing, here are a few to name specifically:

- Sensitive data with no security
  Since the sensitive information is open, it becomes easy for an attacker to access this data illegally and breach it using a quantum computer. Quantum systems make it way easier for a person with malicious intensions to break the cryptographic codes, that too in a couple of seconds or even less. Even the most secure systems of today will be at a risk in the presence of quantum computing. The destruction that can be caused by incorrect utilization of quantum computing can be the most devastating if criminals or terrorists get access to the vital facilities like energy plants, water supplies and water management, air and railroad traffic controls, protected military or law enforcement information etc. This can be a life threat to an entire country and its economy. As per Tanja Lange, professor of Cryptology at Eindhoven University of Technology, "All of today's secrets will be lost."

- Impact on financial systems
  Money is no more just a paper or coin nowadays. Since money is a digital asset now, used by most banks for online transactions, quantum technologies may be used by cyber criminals to target financial profits, hitting online banking and transactions. Also, unauthorized access may cause interference in the working and functioning of banks. Since the vital user money is already prone to the risk of being stolen and used inappropriately, quantum computing may make this process easier for the hackers.

- Less transparency of government
  Because of quantum technologies, governments can secure communications. This can prevent transparency to the public, which will create a possibility of corruption within government.

- Government losing control to criminal firms
  If the secure quantum communications get into the hands of criminals, the current security tools and algorithms being

used by the law and military enforcement agencies for security purposes relating to a country can be misused. Quantum communication services can become available before legislation, limiting monitoring power of officials [20].

- Power gap expansion between rich and poor countries
  As quantum technology advancements can be an opportunity as well as a threat to security systems across the world, most of the economically developed countries will try to harness this technology in their favor and also build quantum-based systems to reduce the risk of security breach using the same technology. But in practical terms, this will take a lot of time to be feasibly implemented in the developed countries as there are a lot of factors working in this regard like speed with which upgradations are made in the existing computer systems and digital infrastructure, manpower, time required, and financial services available. But in this race of tech advancements, the developing countries (with especially unstable political systems) may lag behind in adopting this advanced cryptographic technology in their systems and lift their security to the next level.

- Excessive government control in the lives of citizens
  When a few government agencies get excessive access to the quantum-based tools in comparison to others, this causes these agencies to get too much political control and weight over the other, thus leading to imbalance in the intra-governmental system. There also remains a huge possibility of these government agencies using massive large-scale data processing and approximately complete real-time decrypting abilities enabled by quantum technologies for overextending their authority over others. This will lead them to dive deeper than required into the private lives of citizens, who would otherwise prefer to keep the government out of their affairs.

  In contrast, if citizens have 100% accessibility to the secure communication system, this can lead to an extensive rise in individual freedom and an individual's ability to avoid governmental control, to impede the tendency of many governments to get deeper into the privacy of the citizens.

- Revealing old secrets
  Quantum computing is powerful enough to easily break the existing data encryption and security methods. This hints

towards the strong possibility of the older and trusted secrets and military and law enforcement agency's security and confidential secrets to be cracked and revealed. This confidential data can also be misused by criminals, terrorists, and other governments that have access to advanced quantum technology tools.

All this can lead to extreme political chaos and instability within any country, a crisis of trust between government and citizens, terror attack vulnerabilities, etc. Some even describe quantum computing as the atomic bombs of the digital world [11].

- Expanding the strength of large tech firms
  Many renowned and big tech companies, research institutions and universities across the world are trying to develop quantum technology. Even though the university research is publicly accessible, still it is accessible to the large tech firms much earlier than the general public, as these companies invest heavily into the advancements of this research. But then there lies a possibility that these tech firms can try to manipulate the flow of such researches and also their goal in their favor rather than letting it be in its original format.

  Such giant tech firms may try to make out best business out of this technology for themselves by trying to influence the government by collaborating with them to provide access to this technology and in turn get political gains and advantages. This can also be used by them to unethically enhance their market value and position and keeping everything in their favor.

25.4   Previous Works

This section briefly discusses related works on this topic through some journals and conferences since 2010. Some journals are IEEE, Quantum Science and Technology, etc.

- Byung-Soo Choi and Rodney Van Meter have depicted a 2D quantum architecture, which is basically an addition with detailed complexity and qubits. The authors were able to prove that the architecture described is faster than 1D quantum architecture, if the length of input registers is greater than 58. These authors claimed that it is a stable architecture as per performance [24].

- C. Monroe [7] offered a model called MUSIQC. It is basically a hierarchical molecular ion trap architecture for quantum computers. Here, the processor can have more than 106 qubits with two attributes, i.e., stable qubits and ascendible photonic interconnections. Modular ELU is also introduced, which makes computation fast. It is basically a solitary crystal with N trapped atomic ion and a source of laser, which impacts quantum gates [22].

- E. M. Ameen [8], proposed a hybrid architecture for classical computers with co-quantum processors. They had a goal of enhancing the performance, with the combination of classical and quantum computers. The classical processors help in conventional procedures and network communications, while co-quantum processors handle complex algorithms and computations. This architecture can process any classical or quantum computation [23].

- Maissam Barkeshli depicted a physical architecture for topological quantum computers. While in a general way qubits are soft and fragile in the environment, topological qubits have high stability and more resistance. This results in fault-tolerance capabilities and improving the functionality of quantum computers [21, 24].

In the end, for making quantum computers, there are still a lot of challenges which require in-depth research, and work, such as:

- More qubit systems: 64, 128, 192, 256.
- Much greater connectivity
- Much lower error-rate
- Much lower cost

25.5 Conclusion

In this paper, we have discussed the dark side of quantum computing. Quantum computers can revolutionize computations, by solving problems faster and more efficiently as compared to classical computers. Although there is still room for research and development in this field, this can be the future of technology. Quantum computers are better than classical computers, as they work approximately 158 times faster than a supercomputer, in less time. But even these can be used in a destructive manner too. In this paper, we have first discussed the introduction and significance of quantum computing. We then discussed the working process of these computers. Then we focused on the dark side or the disadvantages of quantum computing, followed by some work which has been done previously in this field. And finally, we have concluded the paper with an ending note.

References

1. Rietsche, R., Dremel, C., Bosch, S., Steinacker, L., Meckel, M., & Leimeister, J. M. (2022). Quantum computing. *Electronic Markets*, 1-12.
2. Brown, K. R., Chiaverini, J., Sage, J. M., & Häffner, H. (2021). Materials challenges for trapped-ion quantum computers. *Nature Reviews Materials*, 6(10), 892-905.
3. Karaarslan, E., & Konacaklı, E. (2020). Data storage in the decentralized world: Blockchain and derivatives. *arXiv preprint arXiv:2012.10253.*
4. Zhang, K., Thompson, J., Zhang, X., Shen, Y., Lu, Y., Zhang, S., ... & Kim, K. (2019). Modular quantum computation in a trapped ion system. *Nature Communications*, 10(1), 1-6.
5. Zaid, A. A., Belmekki, B. E. Y., & Alouini, M. S. (2021). Technological trends and key communication enablers for eVTOLs. *arXiv preprint arXiv:2110.08830.*
6. Porambage, P., Gür, G., Osorio, D. P. M., Livanage, M., & Ylianttila, M. (2021, June). 6G security challenges and potential solutions. In *2021 Joint European Conference on Networks and Communications & 6G Summit (EuCNC/6G Summit)* (pp. 622-627). IEEE.
7. Siriwardhana, Y., Porambage, P., Liyanage, M., & Ylianttila, M. (2021, June). AI and 6G security: Opportunities and challenges. In *2021 Joint European Conference on Networks and Communications & 6G Summit (EuCNC/6G Summit)* (pp. 616-621). IEEE.
8. Holmes, A., Jokar, M. R., Pasandi, G., Ding, Y., Pedram, M., & Chong, F. T. (2020, May). NISQ+: Boosting quantum computing power by approximating quantum error correction. In *2020 ACM/IEEE 47th Annual International Symposium on Computer Architecture (ISCA)* (pp. 556-569). IEEE.
9. Hizhnyakov, V., Boltrushko, V., Kaasik, H., & Orlovskii, Y. (2021). Rare earth ions doped mixed crystals for fast quantum computers with optical frequency qubits. *Optics Communications*, 485, 126693.
10. Je, D., Jung, J., & Choi, S. (2021). Toward 6G Security: Technology Trends, Threats, and Solutions. *IEEE Communications Standards Magazine*, 5(3), 64-71.

11. Rajesh, V., & Naik, U. P. (2021, August). Quantum Convolutional Neural Networks (QCNN) Using Deep Learning for Computer Vision Applications. In *2021 International Conference on Recent Trends on Electronics, Information, Communication & Technology (RTEICT)* (pp. 728-734). IEEE.

12. Chiueh, T. C. (2021, June). Keynote I: Advances in memory state-preserving fault tolerance. In *2021 51st Annual IEEE/IFIP International Conference on Dependable Systems and Networks (DSN)* (pp. xxvii-xxxi). IEEE.

13. Skopec, R. (2018). Evolution Continues with Quantum Biology and Artificial Intelligence. *Journal of Biosensors & Bioelectronics.*

14. Wolf, E. L. (2015). *Quantum Nanoelectronics: An introduction to electronic nanotechnology and quantum computing.* John Wiley & Sons.

15. Cai, Y., Wang, H., Chen, X., & Jiang, H. (2015). Trajectory-based anomalous behaviour detection for intelligent traffic surveillance. *IET Intelligent Transport Systems, 9*(8), 810-816.

16. Cai, Y., Wang, H., Chen, X., & Jiang, H. (2015). Trajectory-based anomalous behaviour detection for intelligent traffic surveillance. *IET Intelligent Transport Systems, 9*(8), 810-816.

17. Nia, A. M., Mozaffari-Kermani, M., Sur-Kolay, S., Raghunathan, A., & Jha, N. K. (2015). Energy-efficient long-term continuous personal health monitoring. *IEEE Transactions on Multi-Scale Computing Systems, 1*(2), 85-98.

18. Brown, K. R., Kim, J., & Monroe, C. (2016). Co-designing a scalable quantum computer with trapped atomic ions. *npj Quantum Information, 2*(1), 1-10.

19. Borza, P. N., & Pau, L. F. (2016). From digital computers to quantum computers based on biological paradigms and progress in particle physics. *arXiv preprint arXiv:1609.07642.*

20. Reimer, C., Kues, M., Roztocki, P., Wetzel, B., Grazioso, F., Little, B. E., ... & Morandotti, R. (2016). Generation of multiphoton entangled quantum states by means of integrated frequency combs. *Science, 351*(6278), 1176-1180.

21. Reimer, C., Kues, M., Roztocki, P., Wetzel, B., Grazioso, F., Little, B. E., ... & Morandotti, R. (2016). Generation of multiphoton entangled quantum states by means of integrated frequency combs. *Science, 351*(6278), 1176-1180.

22. Béjanin, J. H., McConkey, T. G., Rinehart, J. R., Earnest, C. T., McRae, C. R. H., Shiri, D., ... & Mariantoni, M. (2016). Three-dimensional wiring for extensible quantum computing: The quantum socket. *Physical Review Applied, 6*(4), 044010.

23. Qing, S., Okamoto, E., Kim, K., & Liu, D. (Eds.). (2016). *Information and Communications Security: 17th International Conference, ICICS 2015, Beijing, China, December 9-11, 2015, Revised Selected Papers* (Vol. 9543). Springer.

24. Blowers, M., Iribarne, J., Colbert, E., & Kott, A. (2016). The future internet of things and security of its control systems. *arXiv preprint arXiv:1610.01953.*

26

Intrusion Detection System via Classical SVM and Quantum SVM: A Comparative Overview

Ananya Upadhyay[1]*, Ruchir Namjoshi[1], Riya Jain[2], Jaideep Patel[3] and Gayathri M.[4]

[1]Department of Computer Science Engineering, Shri Vaishnav Vidyapeeth Vishwavidyalaya, Indore, India
[2]Department of Information Technology Engineering, Institute of Engineering and Technology, Devi Ahilya Vishwavidyalaya Indore (MP), Indore, India
[3]Department of Computer Science and Engineering, SIRT, Bhopal, India
[4]Department of Computing Technologies, School of Computing, SRM Institute of Science and Technology, Kattankulathur, India

Abstract

Whether as a result of cybersecurity systems' weakness or their absence, we have observed an increase in computer breaches across our communication networks globally in recent years. As a result, an intrusion detection system (IDS) is required. An IDS is a piece of software that keeps an eye out for malicious attempts aimed at stealing or censoring data or altering network protocols on a single computer or a network of computers. The majority of IDS approaches have evolved through time, but they are still unable to address the dynamic and intricate nature of cyber-attacks on computer networks. Therefore, effective techniques are needed, which can lead to a greater detection rate. In order to determine which system is superior, this study compares the IDSs of the Classical SVM with the Quantum SVM.

Keywords: Quantum security, intrusion detection system, quantum support vector machine, quantum-inspired algorithm, machine learning

*Corresponding author: ananyaram0803@gmail.com

Romil Rawat, Rajesh Kumar Chakrawarti, Sanjaya Kumar Sarangi, Jaideep Patel, Vivek Bhardwaj, Anjali Rawat and Hitesh Rawat (eds.) Quantum Computing in Cybersecurity, (441–452) © 2023 Scrivener Publishing LLC

26.1   Introduction

In today's era, technology is growing rapidly and so are the intruders [1]. Some intruders have become so smart that they know how to escape most systems' security. The threat is omnipresent since some IDS fail to detect complex intrusions [2] in a network.

However, for several decades already, several academics have used various benchmark datasets [3, 4] accessible to detect intruders in their work. The majority of publications have suggested machine learning (ML) approaches not only for assault detection but also for speedy identification of intruders due to the enormous size and diversity of these datasets' high dimensions.

In order to determine if a request is an attack or a legal one, a variety of ML [5–9] methods, including decision trees, random forests, artificial neural networks (ANN), and support vector machine (SVM), are employed as classifiers. SVM [11] is one of the well-known ML algorithms that is utilised in particular when the issue domain is a binary classifier among these classifiers [10].

A particularly potent and adaptable supervised learning model called the SVM examines data for both regression and classification. The sequential minimum optimization technique, the cascade SVM algorithm, and the SVM algorithms based on Markov sampling are only a few of the SVM algorithms that have undergone extensive research to improve and maximise their performance. By altering the method a classifier is trained or by scaling back training sets, these techniques promise potential speedups [14]. The temporal complexity of the SVM methods used today, however, is a quadratic function of the data amount. The quantum SVM algorithm [15], which can reach an exponential speedup compared to classical SVMs, was suggested by Patrick Rebentrost, Masoud Mohseni, and Seth Lloyd in 2014 [1, 12].

The quantum SVM method has a polynomial [16] of the logarithm of data size time complexity. Data is stored with bits at the most fundamental level of traditional computing. Based on whether an electron charge is present, bits can only take on one of two possible values. A bit's value is zero if there is no charge on any electrons. The value of a bit is 1, however, if there is an electron charge.

However, there are some limitations to this type of computing [17]. These are slow involving two different bits and hence another type of computing was introduced which consists of Qubits [18], in which 0 and 1 bit can exist at the same time becoming much more powerful and accurate and popularly known as Quantum Computer (Qcomp).

One of the new technologies with the fastest rate of development is quantum computing. There have been reports of new discoveries and their commercial uses as frequently as every few weeks. Modern risks are brought on by new technologies. Up until recently, brute force assaults

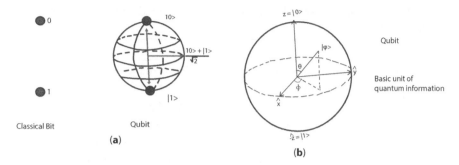

Figure 26.1 (a) Visualization of Qubits. (b) Visualization of Qubits.

were not practical due to the need for extremely powerful devices like supercomputers or GPU farms [19]. The emergence of Qcomp has made brute force attacks far less difficult for those who possess the technology.

However, as there are two sides to each coin, the technology of quantum computing also has a positive side when it comes to security. We can obtain better results for intrusion detection using quantum ML algorithms; after several decades, the scientific progress made in quantum technologies [20] is finally starting to bear fruit. This may be considered the beginning of a quantum revolution in many different areas. Numerous potent quantum hardware applications and algorithms have been developed throughout those years of study. Figure 26.1(a) and Figure 26.1(b) show the visualization of Qubits.

ORGANIZATION OF CHAPTER
The rest of the chapter is outlined as follows. Section 26.2 shows related work and different studies in an intrusion detection system; Section 26.3 shows different models; Section 26.4 outlines proposed methodology; Section 26.5 shows result analysis; and Section 26.6 concludes this chapter.

26.2   Related Work

Table 26.1 compares different studies carried out for detection of different attacks in Distributed Control Systems.

26.3   Models for IDS [18]

An IDS is a security tool used to track the network's unusual activity. The IDS recognises the user behaviour and notifies the user if it is normal or

Table 26.1 Comparison of different threats in Distributed Control Systems [1, 2, 17–20].

S. no.	Study	Topic
1.	Christopher Havenstein -Damarcus Thomas - Swami Chandrasekaran	Performance Evaluations of Classical and Quantum ML
2.	Gaddam Venu Gopal - Gatram Rama Mohan Babu	A hybrid kernel-based SVM ensemble feature selection method for network IDS
3.	Omar S. Soliman - Aliaa Rassem	A Quantum Bio-Inspired Algorithm-Based Network IDS
4.	Esteban Payares - Juan Carlos Martinez Santos	A comparison of quantum ML for distributed denial of service attack intrusion detection

not. To find the intrusion, the IDS compares the user's actions with the previously recorded intrusion data.

26.3.1   Classical Support Vector Machine Model [18]

For binary classification issues, traditional SVM are a form of supervised ML technique. This technique creates an ideal separation hyperplane in this area by mapping the data into a higher-dimensional input space. In essence, this entails resolving a quadratic programming issue. A variation of SVM is called Least Squares SVM (LS-SVM). By resolving the linear equation, it approaches the SVM's hyperplane finding method.

Although it may be used in regression issues, the classical SVM is incredibly popular for effectively categorising data, whether it be linear or non-linear in nature [18]. Each piece of data is plotted as a point in an N-dimensional feature space, with the value of each feature represented by a specific coordinate. The hyper-plane that best distinguishes the two classes is then found in order to classify the data. The locations of certain observations that are closest to the boundary are known as support vectors. In the case of SVM, training samples are separated into several subsets known as support vectors, and these support vectors are what define the decision function. SVM has been used a lot to help with accurate data point categorization. The performance of the traditional approach has also improved thanks to the SVM kernel technique [19, 20].

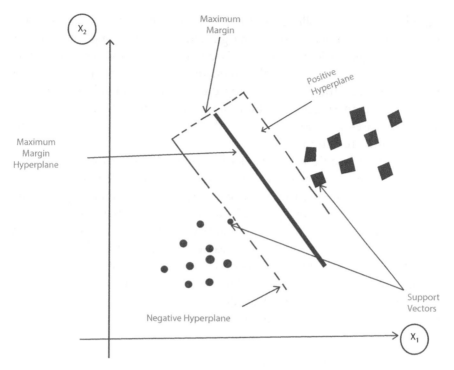

Figure 26.2 Classical SVM separating parameters [16, 17, 19, 20].

- Linear SVM
  When a dataset can be divided into two groups using only a single straight line, it is said to be linearly separable, and the Linear SVM classifier is utilized to separate the data into the two classes.
- Non-linear SVM
  When a dataset cannot be identified using a straight line, it is said to be non-linear, and the classification algorithm utilised is known as a non-linear SVM classifier. By transforming the data into a higher dimensional space, the goal is to achieve linear separation. Figure 26.2 shows the Classical SVM separating parameters.

26.3.1.1   Classical Support Vector in IDS

One of the well-known ML methods, SVM, is utilised as a classifier to determine if a request is a valid one or an attack. SVM is a linear classifier based on statistical learning that was developed in the 1990s by

Vapnik [18] and his colleagues. The SVM algorithm uses linearly separable hyperplanes to maximise the margin among the training data in order to solve the quadratic optimization issue. The optimal separation hyperplane is a hyperplane in a high-dimensional space that has the greatest distance between the closest training data points of any class. The SVM algorithm enhances generalisation capabilities, solves high-dimensional issues, increases detection rates, and offers a better method for error identification and prediction.

In order to handle nonlinear issues, linear classifiers employ kernel functions. The kernel plays a significant role in the SVM classification process and may be used in SVM to transform the original input space, which is a high dimension space [17], into a nonlinear mapping. Although neural networks and SVM can still identify intrusions with high accuracy, the authors' further explanations revealed that only "attack" or "normal" could be used to appropriately categorise the intrusion dataset by the SVM. Finding assaults with the highest detection rates is the main objective of any IDS. Quick detection, or the reduction of computing time, is another need for IDS [13] in addition to the detection rate.

26.3.1.2   Limitations of Classical SVM [15]

When larger datasets or greater dimensions are used, SVM has a lot of issues on a traditional system. Even on a data set with a million records, SVM training takes years. As a result, suggestions to enhance its training performance were made, like approximating the marginal classifier or using random selection [16]. However, for big data sets, even many scans of the full set would be too expensive to carry out or would oversimplify the data set to the point that any value from using an SVM would be lost. Therefore, the notion of using a Qcomp to operate the SVM gains hold in order to improve its effectiveness. Qubits, which are single bits that may represent 0 and 1, as well as superpositions of 0 and 1, are used in quantum machines. The idea of "parallel processing" is introduced through this application of Qubit [18]. The classification job is carried out by the Quantum Machine using a modified version of the SVM algorithm. The algorithm converts conventional data into quantum data, which is subsequently examined on a quantum machine.

26.3.2   Quantum SVM Model

The LS-SVM algorithm is run on Qcomp via the quantum version of SVM [8, 9]. On quantum random access memory, the kernel matrix is

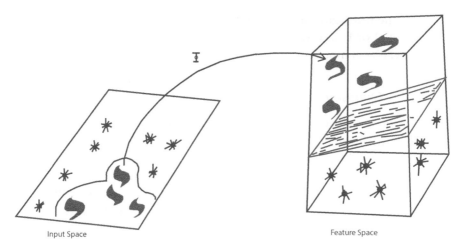

Input Space   Feature Space

Figure 26.3 Q-SVM (Quantum SVM) [1, 2, 15, 17, 18].

computed using the quantum method for the inner product. It conducts the categorization of query data using the trained qubits using a quantum algorithm [8] and solves the linear equation using a quantum algorithm for solving linear equations [9]. This strategy, however, can only be applied if the data is a coherent superposition. Since this is not the case, we may apply the method suggested in [10], which suggests a classifier that utilises the quantum state space as a feature space and analyses data that is supplied conventionally, using the QSVM algorithm of the Qiskit framework [18]. Figure 26.3 shows the Q-SVM [14–16] (Quantum SVM) model.

We have a collection of points x that are either in one group or the other (which we label, for example, y=-1,1), and we want to identify a line (or hyperplane for higher dimensions) that divides these two groups. This is how the basic supervised classification [15] works. Although this line can be linear, it can also be considerably more complicated. In the traditional SVM, we increase complexity by using kernels.

Thus there is a need for supervised classification on a Qcomp to:

- The classical data point X must first be converted into a quantum data point $|\Phi(x^{\rightarrow})\rangle$. in order to proceed. A circuit called $V(\Phi(x^{\rightarrow}))$. can be used to do this. When applied to the classical data $x^{\rightarrow}$ might be any classical function - $\Phi(\ldots)$.
- Second, we require a parameterized quantum circuit $W(\Theta)$ *with parameters* Θ with parameters that ultimately allows us to...

- The third can use a measurement that gives a classical value of -1 or 1, according to the label of the classical data, for each classical input $x^{\rightarrow}$.

26.3.2.1   Quantum Support Vector in IDS

Till date there are some methods suggested for using a Quantum Support vector for Intrusion detection. One such method is illustrated here.

Quantum SVM (QSVMs) directly enhance the classifier by estimating the kernel function using a quantum kernel estimator [7, 11, 17, 18]. Applications for NISQ [17, 19] computers called QSVMs are useful. The whole quantum-enhanced IDS is described and broken down into the following phases [18, 19]:

a) Collect the input data, or the network traffic for a given time period.
b) Perform data preprocessing, such as feature normalisation.
c) Codify the data Dimensionality reduction, or condensing the input data into a size suitable for inputting into the QSVM() function, is what is done in this stage. As previously mentioned, this stage involves using an autoencoder to analyse the input and determine its latent space.
d) Normalize the data the autoencoder provided in order to get it ready for the following step.
e) A Qcomp doing quantum processing to look for alterations in the input data. As stated, at this stage, a QSVM() function algorithm is used to categorise flows as normal or abnormal.
f) Parallelly repeat for the following time frame or data sample. Keep in mind that if it is deemed necessary for whatever reason, the period may overlap the prior one.

The detection process has to be preceded by a training process. Training involves the same phases 1 to 5 above, except that the QSVM in phase 5 is executed in training mode [6].

A training procedure must come before the detecting process. Phases 1 through 5 are the same for training, with the exception that phase 5's QSVM is run in training mode [6].

Their programme only receives labels for the test data [18]. The goal is to forecast an estimated map on the test set in a way that it most likely fits the real maps on the test data S. The data is projected to a high dimensional space called a function area using SVM kernels, where a hyperplane is set up to distinguish the named samples. Rebentrost *et al.* have already presented the QSVM quantum version of this approach [7, 19]. If data is provided in a coherent superposition, their technique enables gradual advancement. As a result, because the process is gradual, it makes data analysis much simpler and increases accuracy.

26.4 Conclusion

As is clear from the above discussion, we can exponentially accelerate the training process of a binary classifier by running the classification algorithm on a Qcomp [1]. We modified the SVM-based intrusion detector to operate on a quantum device and verify its functionality with large datasets as a result of this fact. In recent years, quantum technologies have gained popularity. As we highlighted in this study for one particular approach called SVM, there is hence enormous promise in the quantum methods for artificial intelligence. However, there is still a sizable gap for the created methods and applications to address common calculation issues. Our analysis represents how the detection of intrusions is possible using quantum SVM learning methods with high accuracy. Compared to the classical SVM, we can achieve considerable performance improvement and can work on huge data with minimal efforts.

References

1. Nawaz, S.J., Sharma, S.K., Wyne, S., Patwary, M.N., Asaduz-zaman, M.: Quantum machine learning for 6g communication networks: state-of-the-art and vision for the future. *IEEE Access* 7, 46317–46350 (2019).
2. Kalinin, M., Krundyshev, V. Security intrusion detection using quantum machine learning techniques. *J Comput Virol Hack Tech* (2022). https://doi.org/10.1007/s11416-022-00435-0
3. Payares, Esteban & Martinez Santos, Juan Carlos. (2021). Quantum machine learning for intrusion detection of distributed denial of service attacks: A comparative overview. 47. 10.1117/12.2593297.
4. Soliman, Omar S. & Rassem, Aliaa. (2014). A Network Intrusions Detection System based on a Quantum Bio Inspired Algorithm. *International Journal of Engineering Trends and Technology*. 10. 10.14445/22315381/IJETT-V10P271.
5. Y. Chang, W. Li and Z. Yang, "Network Intrusion Detection Based on Random Forest and Support Vector Machine," *2017 IEEE International Conference on Computational Science and Engineering (CSE) and IEEE International*

Conference on Embedded and Ubiquitous Computing (EUC), 2017, pp. 635-638, doi: 10.1109/CSE-EUC.2017.118.

6. A. Gouveia and M. Correia, "Towards Quantum-Enhanced Machine Learning for Network Intrusion Detection," *2020 IEEE 19th International Symposium on Network Computing and Applications (NCA)*, 2020, pp. 1-8, doi: 10.1109/NCA51143.2020.9306691.

7. L. A. Goldberg and H. Guo, "The complexity of approximating complex- valued ising and tutte partition functions," *Computational Complexity*, vol. 26, pp. 765–833, 2014.

8. Rebentrost, P., Mohseni, M., and Lloyd, S., "Quantum Support Vector Machine for Big Data Classification," *Physical Review Letters* 113, 130503 (Sept. 2014).

9. Havlíček,V., Córcoles, A. D., Temme, K., Harrow, A. W., Kandala, A., Chow, J. M., and Gambetta, J. M., "Supervised learning with quantum-enhanced feature spaces," *Nature* 567, 209–212 (Mar. 2019).

10. Biamonte, J., Wittek, P., Pancotti, N., Rebentrost, P., Wiebe, N., and Lloyd, S., "Quantum machine learning," *Nature* 549, 195–202 (Sept. 2017).

11. Gouveia, A., & Correia, M. (2020, November). Towards quantum-enhanced machine learning for network intrusion detection. In *2020 IEEE 19th International Symposium on Network Computing and Applications (NCA)* (pp. 1–8). IEEE.

12. Payares, E. D., & Martinez-Santos, J. C. (2021). Quantum machine learning for intrusion detection of distributed denial of service attacks: a comparative overview. *Quantum Computing, Communication, and Simulation, 11699*, 35–43.

13. Kalinin, M., & Krundyshev, V. (2022). Security intrusion detection using quantum machine learning techniques. *Journal of Computer Virology and Hacking Techniques*, 1-12.

14. Soliman, O. S., & Rassem, A. (2014). A network intrusions detection system based on a quantum bio inspired algorithm. *arXiv preprint arXiv:1405.1404*.

15. Alsarhan, A., Alauthman, M., Alshdaifat, E., Al-Ghuwairi, A. R., & Al-Dubai, A. (2021). Machine Learning-driven optimization for SVM-based intrusion detection system in vehicular ad hoc networks. *Journal of Ambient Intelligence and Humanized Computing*, 1–10.

16. Liang, J. M., Shen, S. Q., Li, M., & Li, L. (2019). Quantum anomaly detection with density estimation and multivariate Gaussian distribution. *Physical Review A, 99*(5), 052310.

17. Asgharzadeh, P., & Jamal, S. (2015). A survey on intrusion detection system based support vector machine algorithm. *International Journal of Research in Computer Application and Robotics, 3*(12), 42–50.

18. Eesa, A. S., Orman, Z., & Brifcani, A. M. A. (2015). A new feature selection model based on ID3 and bees algorithm for intrusion detection system. *Turkish Journal of Electrical Engineering and Computer Sciences, 23*(2), 615–622.

19. Liu, N., & Rebentrost, P. (2018). Quantum machine learning for quantum anomaly detection. *Physical Review A, 97*(4), 042315.
20. Chatterjee, R., & Yu, T. (2016). Generalized coherent states, reproducing kernels, and quantum support vector machines. *arXiv preprint arXiv:1612.03713.*

27

Quantum Computing in Military Applications and Operations

Aman Khubani[1]*, Anadi Sharma[1], Axith Choudhary[1], Om Shankar Bhatnagar[1] and K. Chidambarathanu[2]

[1]Department of Computer Science Engineering, Shri Vaishnav Vidyapeeth Vishwavidyalaya, Indore, India [2]Department of Computer Science and Business Systems, R.M.K. Engineering College, Tamil Nadu, India

Abstract

The quantum era is an emerging and doubtlessly disruptive subject with the capacity to affect many human activities. Quantum technologies are dual-use technologies and as such are of interest to the protection and protection enterprise and army and authorities' actors. This file opinions and maps the potential army packages of quantum generation, serving as an entry point for worldwide peace and safety tests, ethics studies, navy and authorities' policy, method, and selection-making.

Quantum technologies for military applications bring new skills, enhance performance, and increase precision, resulting in "quantum battles" where new naval doctrines, strategies, rules, and ethics must be implemented. This document provides a brief assessment of emerging quantum technology and makes an educated guess as to when it will be available and what its effects will be. Applications of quantum technology for the military that are specific to various forms of conflict (such as land, air, area, electronic, cyber, and underwater war, as well as ISTAR, or Intelligence, Surveillance, Target Acquisition and Reconnaissance) are described, along with the challenges and difficult circumstances they present.

Keywords: Quantum sensing, quantum radar, quantum imaging, military applications, quantum key distribution, encryption, quantum verbal exchange

*Corresponding author: aman.khubani@gmail.com

Romil Rawat, Rajesh Kumar Chakrawarti, Sanjaya Kumar Sarangi, Jaideep Patel, Vivek Bhardwaj, Anjali Rawat and Hitesh Rawat (eds.) Quantum Computing in Cybersecurity, (453–470) © 2023 Scrivener Publishing LLC

27.1   Introduction

Quantum computing (QC) is increasingly recognized as a potential game-changer in the military sector, with the potential to bring significant benefits in areas such as computing, communications [1, 2] and security. In particular, large amounts of data can be processed quickly and securely by quantum computer (Qcom). This is essential for many military applications. Qcom can also be used to develop new, more secure communication systems and crack existing code and cryptography.

Given the potential benefits of QC, it's no surprise that various militaries are interested in the technology. For example, in the United States, the Department of Defense has long invested in QC research and created a dedicated QC program. Figure 27.1 shows the Quantum computing model.

CHAPTER ORGANIZATION
The remainder of the chapter is outlined as follows. Section 27.2 shows the importance of security improvements in dcs and scada, section 27.3 shows related work, section 27.4 describes the proposed methodology, section 27.5 shows the analysis of the results, and section 27.6 concludes this chapter.

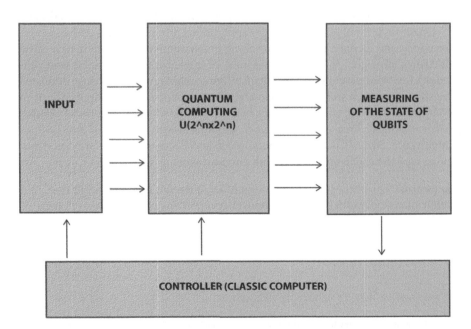

Figure 27.1 Quantum computing model [1, 2].

27.2 Literary Survey

Current cryptographic methods [1] such as IC card [3], PIN, password authentication, etc., are effective in protecting data. The total security of an encryption system, however, depends on the capacity to keep the encryption keys secret, and since writing down passwords in your email inbox or on your phone is ordinary human behaviour, the security is quite weak. One potential answer to this ambiguity seems to be the idea of biometric keys. A critical or safety-related product's design, development, production, deployment, and end-of-life must all start with safety as their first priority.

Without nearly flawless strong cryptographic security built into them, embedded systems that are installed in equipment that is a crucial component of the manufacturing, healthcare, transportation, financial, and military sectors, can also be vulnerable to organised crime, terrorists, or hostile governments. Data-concealing approaches are a cost-effective alternative to other forms of data protection that do not need protocol changes. They attempt to establish contemporary network security, quality of service management, and secure communication. The existing multimedia and communications compression standards are compatible with this technology.

Any network, but notably mobile adhoc networks, must prioritise security. Mobile devices have the capacity to hack wireless networks. Protecting mobile networks doesn't have a definite line of defence. To safeguard these application-based wireless networks, it is thought that the creation of a mobile application security system that applies a layered security strategy and powerful cryptographic algorithms is a workable and affordable option. Last but not least, Quantum Encryption, a novel idea in cryptographic security that makes use of quantum fluctuations in laser light at the physical layer, has been incorporated into already existing networks. It allows for extremely secure communication and nearly flawless security.

Stephen Weisner's book *Conjugate Coding*, published in the early 1970s, introduced quantum cryptography (Qcryp) for the first time. The expansion of the random number generator is conjugate coding. The suggestion was published in *Sigact News* in 1983, and two scientists, Bennett and Brassard, who were aware of Weisner's theories, were prepared to submit their own theories at that time. They created "BB84," the first Qcryp protocol, in 1984. This protocol's initial experimental prototype, which operated at a distance of 32 cm, was created in 1991. Since then, technology has advanced to the point that the distance may now be in kilometres. A group from the University of Vienna [4] successfully sent entangled photons over free space across the Danube River in June 2003. The first quantum key-encrypted money transmission was tested between two Austrian banks in April 2004. The sewage system was 1.5 kilometres long and connected the two buildings, which were 500 metres apart, using fibre-optic cable.

27.3   Definition

The following is the definition of quantum technology: A category of technology known as quantum technology, which includes quantum entanglement (Qent) and quantum superposition (Qsup), operates on the concepts of quantum mechanics (subatomic particle physics) [6].

27.3.1   Introduction

Quantum technology (QT) [3, 4] is a developing area of physics and engineering based on quantum-mechanical features applied to individual quantum systems and their usage for practical applications, including Qent, Qsup, and quantum tunnelling.

The term "quantum technology" refers to a variety of basic concepts underlying quantum-mechanical systems that have a wide range of practical uses. For instance, the trapped ion method may be used as a quantum bit for Qcom, a quantum sensor for magnetic fields, or a quantum clock. Research and development fields with potential uses in both commercial and defence manufacturing are referred to as dual-use technologies [6].

We're now beginning to govern Qent and Qsup. That method quantum generation guarantees enhancements to a great variety of normal gadgets, including:

- greater dependable navigation and timing structures
- greater stable communications
- greater correct healthcare imaging through quantum sensing
- greater effective computing.

When two atoms are entangled in quantum mechanics [16, 17], they are coupled even if they are physically apart. If you alter the characteristics of one, the other immediately follows. Theoretically, even if the entangled atoms are disentangled by the whole cosmos, this would still remain the case. As if that weren't astounding enough, according to quantum mechanics, just looking at an atom may alter its characteristics.

The idea that subatomic particles may be in numerous states at once is known as Qsup. The Schrödinger's Cat thought experiment's central idea is that a cat, a flask of lethal poison, and a radioactive source are all enclosed in a sealed box.

27.3.2   A Key Quantum Principle

27.3.2.1   Qubit

The unit of quantum information is the "qubit", which describes the amount of quantum information that can be stored in the simplest quantum system state, such as the polarization state of a photon. A qubit is a unit vector in a two-dimensional complex vector space [12].

27.3.2.2   Qsup

A cornerstone of quantum mechanics is the concept of Qsup. According to this, any two (or more) quantum states may be combined to create another effective quantum state by superposing them, much in the way waves do in conventional physics. On the other hand, each quantum state may be seen as the combination of two or more different states. It refers, mathematically speaking, to the characteristics of the Schrödinger equations [5, 7] solution. A linear combination of solutions is also a solution since the Schrödinger equation has a linear form.

An example of a physically observable phenomenon of the wave nature of quantum systems is the interference peak of electron beams in the double-slit experiment. This pattern is very similar to that obtained by classical wave diffraction.

The principle of quantum [5, 6] superposition is the sum of all possible states of an object. In the case of QC, we deal with the state associated with a qubit, which can be any unit vector in a two-dimensional vector space spanned by orthonormal vectors $|0\rangle = (1\ 0)$ and $|1\rangle = (0\ 1)$. The general state of a qubit is given by: $|\psi\rangle = \alpha|0\rangle + \beta|1\rangle$, where $\alpha2 + \beta2 = 1$.

Let us consider that 0 and 1 correspond to the more familiar 0 and 1 bits of classical computation.

Here $|0>$ is the Dirac notation for the quantum state that will always give the result 0 when converted to classical logic by a measurement. Likewise $|1>$ is the state that will always convert to 1.

We find that a single qubit can exist as a superposition of these two bits ie. 0 and 1, each with a certain amplitude during information processing [7].

For qubit 0 and 1 the probability of measuring can neither be 0.0 nor 1.0 and multiple measurements can never yield the same results.

27.3.2.3   Qent

Qent is a physical resource available for quantum information processing. This source is derived from the correlations that continue to exist between previously coupled quantum systems even after they have been separated. Entangled quantum systems can be used as a quantum information channel to perform computational and cryptographic tasks. These tasks will not be classically possible because they are based on a purely quantum mechanical source of entanglement.

While two or more particles are created or interact in such a way that their quantum states cannot be completely isolated from one another, even when the particles are physically separated, this phenomenon known as Qent takes place. The topic of Qent is of great interest to scientists because it challenges the laws of classical physics and could lead to the development of powerful new technologies. Figure 27.2 shows the quantum teleportation process that transfers a single qubit of quantum information at a different location.

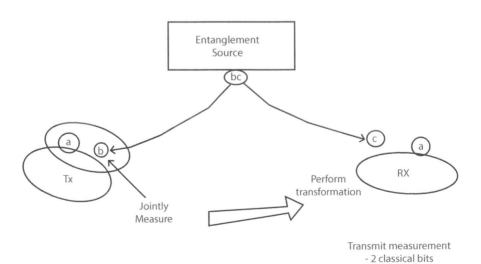

Figure 27.2 The quantum teleportation [7, 8].

27.3.2.4   Photon Polarization [9, 10]

States, given, $|0\rangle$ and $|1\rangle$ describe photons with vertical and horizontal polarization, then $H|0\rangle = 1\sqrt{2}\,(|0\rangle + |1\rangle)$ and $H|1\rangle = 1\sqrt{2}\,(|0\rangle - |1\rangle)$ describe photons that are diagonally polarized by 45° to the vertical. Photons in either of these states can easily be prepared by sending weak light through a suitably oriented polarizing filter. BB84, a popular quantum cryptographic system to be described next, uses a 15° offset from the horizontal or vertical plane, where a negative offset can be $|0\rangle$ and a positive offset $|1\rangle$ [7].

A photon is a particle of light, and its polarization is the direction of its oscillating electric field. When light waves are emitted from a source, they are usually not all polarized in the same direction. However, certain interactions with matter can cause light to become polarized. For example, when light waves bounce off a surface, the waves that are reflected tend to be polarized perpendicular to the surface. Scientists can take advantage of this property of light to study the properties of materials and the structure of surfaces.

While two or more particles are created or interact in such a way that their quantum states cannot be completely isolated from one another, even when the particles are physically separated, this phenomenon known as Qent takes place. Scientists are very interested in the subject of Qent since it contradicts the principles of traditional physics and has the potential to produce cutting-edge new technology.

27.3.2.5   Heisenberg's Uncertainty Principle [18, 19]

Heisenberg's uncertainty principle states that determining the position of a particle in a small region of space makes its momentum uncertain, and knowing the exact momentum would increase the uncertainty of its position. A consequence of this principle is that it is impossible to measure any attribute of a particle without indeterminately changing other attributes of the particle. Therefore, it is not possible to make a measurement to observe a single photon without simultaneously changing its state.

Heisenberg's uncertainty principle is one of the most famous principles in physics. It states that it is impossible to know both the momentum and position of a particle at the same time. This principle has strange and counterintuitive consequences, such as the fact that a particle can appear to be in two places at once. While the uncertainty principle is often misunderstood, it is a fundamental principle of quantum mechanics.

27.3.2.6   *Quantum Teleportation [20, 21]*

Quantum teleportation is a method for transferring quantum information between two systems. The information contained in the superposition of states is transferred to another location using classical communication and linking. Despite the temptation, this should not be misinterpreted as a means to transfer or copy a macroscopic object. To describe the process of quantum teleportation, we assume that the transmitter (Tx) transmits the complete general state of qubit "a" to the receiver (Rx).

First, Tx and Rx share an entangled pair of "bc" qubits, where Tx has the "b" and Rx has the "c" of the entangled pair. The Tx then measures "ab" together to provide two classical bits that are transmitted to the Rx using the classical channel. The measurement destroys two qubits on Tx, but now qubit "c" has information regarding "a" due to the entanglement between "b" and "c". Rx can perform a transformation to "c" based on the two classical bits received to completely recreate the "a" state [7].

Researchers have successfully performed quantum teleportation on a particle for the first time. The achievement could lead to advances in QC and secure communications.

In quantum teleportation, information about the quantum state of a particle is transmitted from one location to another without physically moving the particle. The quantum state is the set of all the information that describes a particle.

The researchers were able to teleport the quantum state of a particle across a room without destroying the state. The research is a significant step towards developing a quantum internet, which would be much more secure than the current internet. Figure 27.3 shows the Quantum Key Distribution Model.

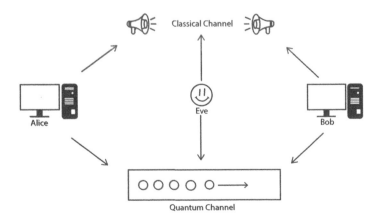

Figure 27.3 Quantum key distribution model [5, 11].

27.3.3   QC [22, 23]

With just a small number of physical qubits, it is already commercially accessible. Its usage will have a new capability, efficiency, and precision. In 10 years, one million physical qubits are expected. The main obstacles are increasing the quantity of qubits and logic qubits, as well as enhancing the quality of qubits (coherence, error tolerance, and gate fidelity). The term "QC" describes the application of quantum information theory to computation. Qcom are the name for such devices. Qcom classification can be exceedingly difficult.

27.3.4   Quantum Internet [24, 25]

Although the current internet is rather quick, quantum-encrypted messages have far higher levels of security. Quantum encryption would cause the internet to operate far more slowly. But in the future, it's feasible that we'll be able to seamlessly switch between a "normal" and a "quantum encrypted" internet, ensuring that even our most private communications are sent in the most secure way imaginable. This would fulfil the aim of having both quick and safe internet.

27.3.5   Quantum Sensing [24, 25]

Quantum sensors use quantum states for measurements. It can also be a very sensitive instrument, as it takes advantage of the fact that quantum states are very sensitive to perturbations.

Measuring devices that exploit quantum properties have long existed, such as atomic clocks, laser rangefinders, and magnetic resonance imaging scanners used in medical diagnostics. The increasing use of individual quantum systems, such as atoms and photons, as measurement probes is now "new", as the entanglement and manipulation of quantum states are predetermined by classical formulations. It is also used to increase sensitivity beyond conventional limits. The uncertainty principle of quantum mechanics. The potential effects of quantum sensors are extensive and significant, from optical resolution beyond the wavelength limit to ultra-high precision microscopes, positioning systems, clocks, gravitational, electrical, and magnetic field sensors.

In several scientific domains, quantum sensing will undoubtedly assist in pushing the research frontier. For instance, the next generation of detectors at the gravitational-wave observatory Ligo [6–9] are being built using compressed quantum states. This quantum improvement will make it possible to see gravitational waves coming from sources that are 10 times further away than previously.

Additionally, it is anticipated that quantum sensors will advance driverless vehicles, brain-machine interfaces, medical advancement, the detection of minute amounts of explosives and poisons, and both short- and long-range imaging technologies.

27.4   Quantum Military Applications [23–25]

Numerous facets of human activity might be dramatically impacted by quantum technology. The defence industry is a good example of this. All facets of contemporary warfare can be impacted by quantum technology. The second quantum revolution will increase sensitivity and efficiency, introduce new capabilities, and enhance contemporary fighting strategies rather than result in the development of new kinds of weapons. Quantum warfare (QW) is the use of quantum technology in combat. It introduces new military doctrines, scenarios, and ethics while affecting the intelligence, security, and defence capabilities of all battle domains. The material that follows maps potential military, security, space, and intelligence uses of quantum technology in several facets of contemporary combat; military applications are open to the public [3]. It's vital to remember that many applications are still just concepts. Significant quantum advancements gained in the lab are not usually followed by equivalent advancements outside the lab. The journey from a functioning laboratory prototype to a realistic deployment involves factors including mobility, sensitivity, resolution, speed, resilience, low SWaP (size, weight, and power), and cost [3]. Specific quantum technologies will either be manufactured and used, depending on their viability and cost-effectiveness.

Even more difficult is integrating quantum technologies into a platform for the military. The integration and deployment of quantum sensing, imaging, and networking face several challenges, which represent the increased requirements of military applications (compared to civil/industrial or scientific requirements), in addition to Qcom, which will mostly be located in data centres similar to those used for civilian applications. For instance, rapid measurement rates are needed for military-grade precision navigation, which can be extremely restricting for present quantum inertial sensors. There are more instances, and more are probably on the way. Additionally, because the topic is still in its infancy, additional quantum advantages or drawbacks might arise from unanticipated technical developments, both positive and negative [3].

QC can be divided into three evolutionary stages
The three stages are noisy medium-scale QC (NISQ), component QC (CQC), and fault-tolerant QC (FTQC). The development of the QC demonstration and primitives is part of the CQC phase. CQC's meagre computational capabilities allow it to provide a proof of concept. To show the advantages of QC, a NISQ-stage Qcom needs enough qubits. More and better qubits should be produced as a result of ongoing research. As soon as a full logical qubit is obtained, the FTQC phase starts.

Components of QC
There are three key components to QC: the qubit, the quantum processor, and the quantum algorithm. The qubit is the basic unit of quantum information. It is a two-state quantum system, which can represent a 0, a 1, or any other two-state system. The quantum processor is the physical device that manipulates the qubits. The quantum algorithm is a set of instructions that tells the quantum processor what to do with the qubits.

Noisy Medium-Scale QC
Qcom are often said to be faster and more powerful than classical computers. But a new study has found that, in some cases, Qcom can be slower than classical computers. The study, led by QC experts at the University of Bristol, found that when Qcom are used to solve problems that require a lot of data, they can be slower than classical computers.

The researchers say that this is because Qcom have to store all of the data in their memory, which can be noisy. Classical computers, on the other hand, can store data in separate memory units, which can be faster.

The findings could have implications for the development of Qcom, as they suggest that Qcom may not be able.

Fault Tolerant QC [20, 21]
Fault tolerant QC is a type of QC that is able to maintain its accuracy and functionality even in the presence of errors or faults. This is achieved by using redundancies and error-correcting code to protect the quantum state of the system. Fault tolerant QC is important for applications where reliable quantum computation is required, such as in secure communication and cryptography. Figure 27.4 shows the Quantum Warfare representation and Figure 27.5 shows the spending on Qcom by country.

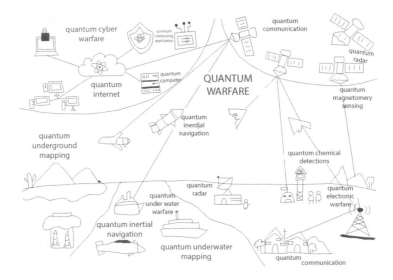

Figure 27.4 Quantum warfare [3, 12, 13].

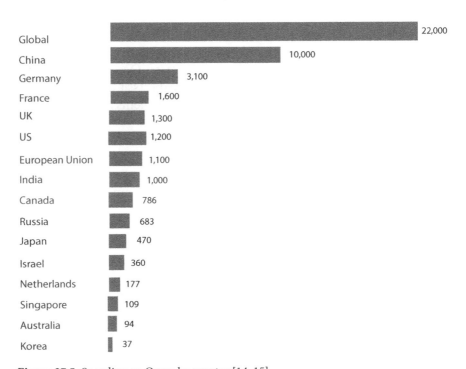

Figure 27.5 Spending on Qcom by country [14, 15].

27.5   Applications of QCRYP [20, 21]

Banking Industry: Protecting sensitive client information [15]
Data in the banking sector has been successfully secured via quantum communications by ID Quantique (IDQ) [8, 9]. Security is essential to the banking sector because banks must guarantee the availability of real-time transactional data while safeguarding sensitive and personal client data. IDQ successfully generated keys for security applications and cryptographic activities including authentication, digital signatures, and safe access control using a quantum random number generator (QRNG).

Financial Industry: Safeguarding critical business data [16]
Advanced security networks in the banking sector employ quantum communications. Using IDQ's Cerberis QKD system, Colt Technologies and Services Group in the UK collaborated with IDQ to deliver secure vital backbone connection for companies and financial institutions in Geneva, Switzerland. Customers have total control over encryption keys and mission-critical data, while Colt administers the network. Customer data is carried over separate lines, while quantum keys for many clients are multiplexed over a single fibre. The method includes key and network redundancy.

Credit card industry: Protecting customer credit card information.
Security for credit cards costs a lot of money. Every year, credit card theft costs the globe $14 billion, with the US responsible for half of that. Think about the 2013 Target data leak. The cost of this data breach, which involved the theft of over 40 million credit card information as well as customer names and addresses, came to over $250 million.
Credit cards may be encrypted and protected from this attack via quantum communications. Magnetic stripe and EMV (Europay, MasterCard, Visa) credit card technology might possibly be rendered obsolete by new credit card encryption research based on QC, which would address the issue. Qcryp has been offered by researchers as a method for completely unhackable credit cards.

Lotteries and online gaming [17]
Absolute randomness must be assured since online games and lotteries both employ random numbers to guarantee fair odds of winning. With his QRNG, IDQ has successfully offered true random number generation for a variety of businesses throughout the world. This QRNG produces genuine random numbers that are unexpected and impossible to replicate. One of the two Swiss lottery operators, Loterie Romande, which employs the

Quantis QRNG for their winning number drawing application, are two instances of businesses that make use of QRNGs. One of the top game integrators in the world is Austrian Novomatic.

Other Applications [18]
Financial information in the private sector as well as sensitive information related to national security are already protected by Qcryp. Its security has been examined and confirmed. Here, we discuss several recent and upcoming uses of Qcryp.

Information is encrypted at the physical network layer using Qcryp, which takes advantage of the characteristics of quantum mechanics. However, efforts in post-quantum and quantum-resistant cryptography continue to be directed at creating encryption techniques that depend on challenging arithmetic problems, which Qcom is not well adapted to tackle.

Extremely Secure Voting: Increasing the security of the voting process is imperative given the prevalence of political unrest and claims of electoral fraud in both developed and developing nations. Switzerland has been using Qcryp for safe online voting in federal and local elections since 2007. In a centralised counting site in Geneva, the votes are encrypted [1]. A dedicated fibre-optic link is then used to send the findings to a distant data repository. The most susceptible component of the data transaction, when the vote goes from the counting station to the central store, is unbreakable. Voting results are safeguarded using Qcryp. This technology will quickly become widespread because of the growing threat of rigged elections in several nations [9].

Secure Communications in Space: Quintessence Labs is working on a project for NASA to provide secure communications from Earth with satellites and astronauts as the need for secure communications with satellites and astronauts grows. The project's objective is to develop a protocol that ensures communication security regardless of the tools or information an opponent possesses. A requirement to safeguard data "at rest" and in transit is also included. In the long run, this would improve astronaut safety in orbit and, ideally, reduce the need for further improvements beyond modest speed increases [9, 10].

Intelligent Grid: It has been suggested that one of the most exposed targets for a cyber assault is the US grid. In reality, some of the largest US corporations are "constantly" under attack by adversaries online. Using public data networks to regulate smart power grids, employees may send entirely secure signals with the use of a tiny encryption device. For efficiency, smart grids are necessary to balance supply and demand. Additionally, when safety measures are taken, they are far safer than conventional grills [4].

Broadband Internet: Although the current internet is rather quick, quantum encrypted transfers offer better security. Quantum encryption would cause the internet to operate far more slowly. But in the future, it's feasible that we'll be able to seamlessly switch between a "normal" and a "quantum encrypted" internet, ensuring that even our most private communications are sent in the most secure way imaginable. This would fulfil the objective of having both quick and secure internet [2].

Quantum Underwater Warfare - Key Points [15, 17, 19, 23–25]
Quantum magnetometers are the primary means of locating submarines or underwater mines. Submarines may be one of the first adopters of quantum inertial navigation. With greater magnetic detection of a submarine or underwater mines, new inertial submarine navigation, and quantum-enhanced precision sonars, quantum technologies might dramatically hinder undersea warfare. In general, maritime settings can be used for Krelin EPJ Quantum Technology (2021) sensing based on quantum photodetectors, radar, lidar, magnetometers, or gravimeters. For a broad review of how quantum technology can affect nuclear-armed submarines' near invulnerability, see [3]. Researchers from Oxford University developed a mechanism for sending quantum keys that might be utilised in PoS systems in 2017, working with Nokia and Bay Photonics.

Governments and defence organisations that need to safeguard substantial volumes of sensitive, long-term classified material both domestically and internationally will find quantum communications to be of great use. Think about the malware assault from 2015 on the Office of Personnel Management, which led to 21.5 million documents being taken (social security numbers, etc.).

For the sake of business continuity, many private enterprises, organisations, and governmental bodies are compelled to back up their most important data. Backing up these digital assets, which may include crucial financial information or intellectual property, in a remote data centre, or DRC, is the only way to secure this sensitive data.

Not just within the data centre, but also on the way there and back, the information needs to be secured. Think about all the confidential medical records that hospitals and other healthcare facilities must maintain. Long-term security for this data has been achieved in numerous circumstances via quantum encryption, or more precisely quantum key distribution.

27.6   Limitations

Entangled photons, which seem to be safe, face the practical challenges of cost and maintaining them for a long enough period of time to suit practical purposes [8]. Another issue is that the noise is so bad at distances higher than 50 kilometres that the error rate also dramatically rises [4]. As a result, it is nearly hard to convey information from the channel and it is extremely susceptible to listening in. Quantum keys, however, will eventually be able to be transferred over the internet. The signal can be located by aligning small telescopes. Some simulations even imply that a satellite would be able to pick up the photons, enabling communication across the globe. Since QKD is the first application of quantum mechanics in practise, it illustrates the importance of fundamental scientific study [2]. Quantum Key Distribution's security needs to be confirmed before it can be utilised in reality, which calls for a detailed analysis of the quantum mechanics principles that underlie its security. To validate these security ideas, fresh experiments built on the foundations of quantum physics should be conducted.

27.7   Conclusion

A more potent method was found to be necessary to convey sensitive information between two or more sites. Quantum key distribution and other quantum encryption techniques will undoubtedly improve the security of critical data in the future. A strong and encouraging step toward a time when we may feel more safe about how and what we exchange is quantum encryption. As a result, we may anticipate that QKD will have a profound impact on basic physics and provide fresh insight into the principles of quantum mechanics. The viewpoint can be less "philosophical" and more "practical."

References

1. Bhatt, A. P., & Sharma, A. (2019). Quantum cryptography for internet of things securitya. *Journal of Electronic Science and Technology*, 17(3), 213–220. https://doi.org/10.11989/JEST.1674-862X.90523016
2. Chung, K.-M., Georgiou, M., Lai, C.-Y., & Zikas, V. (2019). Cryptography with disposable backdoors. *Cryptography*, 3(3), 22. https://doi.org/10.3390/cryptography3030022

3. Krelina, M. (2021). Quantum technology for military applications. *EPJ Quantum Technology*, 8(1), s40507-021. https://doi.org/10.1140/epjqt/s40507-021-00113-y

4. Nair, P., & Patil, S. (2020). Quantum computing in data security: A critical assessment. *SSRN Electronic Journal*. https://doi.org/10.2139/ssrn.3565438

5. Sasirekha, N., & Hemalatha, M. (n.d.). *International Journal of Engineering and Advanced Technology (IJEAT).* Ijeat.org. Retrieved September 23, 2022, from https://www.ijeat.org/wp-content/uploads/papers/v3i4/D2988043414.pdf

6. What is quantum technology? (2018, December 7). PA Consulting. https://www.paconsulting.com/insights/what-is-quantum-technology/

7. (N.d.). Researchgate.net. Retrieved September 23, 2022, from https://www.researchgate.net/profile/Sanjeev-Naguleswaran/publication/228838596_A_New_Paradigm_for_Secure_Military_Communications_Quantum_Information_Processing/links/00b7d51901510351f5000000/A-New-Paradigm-for-Secure-Military-Communications-Quantum-Information-Processing.pdf

8. "Quantum Supremacy Using a Programmable Superconducting Processor," Google AI Blog, 23 Oct. 2019. [Online]. Available: https://ai.googleblog.com/2019/10/quantum-supremacy-using-programmable.html.

9. S. Aaronson, "The Polynomial Method in Quantum and Classical Computing," *2008 49th Annual IEEE Symposium on Foundations of Computer Science, Philadelphia, PA*, 2008, pp. 1-3.

10. M. A. Nielsen, I. L. Chuang, *Quantum Computation and Quantum Information*, Cambridge University Press, Cambridge, UK, 2000.

11. Krelina, M. (2021) Quantum technology for military applications, *EPJ Quantum Technology*, SpringerOpen. Springer Berlin Heidelberg. Available at: https://epjquantumtechnology.springeropen.com/articles/10.1140/epjqt/s40507-021-00113-y (Accessed: October 2, 2022).

12. Introduction to quantum computing for folks · a qubit is a unit vector in a two dimensional complex vector space with XED basis orthonormal basis J0iand j1imay correspond to J"IAND - *[PDF document.]* (no date) *documents.pub.* Available at: https://documents.pub/document/introduction-to-quantum-computing-for-a-qubit-is-a-unit-vector-in-a-two-dimensional.html (Accessed: October 2, 2022).

13. Quantum Communications in real world applications (2022) *QuantumXC.* Available at: https://quantumxc.com/blog/quantum-communications-real-world-applications/ (Accessed: October 31, 2022).

14. Alienor (2018) *Quantum cryptography explained: Applications, disadvantages, & how it works*, Plixer. Available at: https://www.plixer.com/blog/quantum-cryptography-explained/ (Accessed: October 31, 2022).

15. *https://en.wikipedia.org/wiki/Quantum_superposition*

16. Neumann, N. M., van Heesch, M. P., & de Graaf, P. (2020). Quantum communication for military applications. *arXiv preprint arXiv:2011.04989.*

17. Krelina, M. (2021). Quantum warfare: definitions, overview and challenges. *arXiv preprint arXiv:2103.12548.*
18. Neumann, N. M., van Heesch, M. P., Phillipson, F., & Smallegange, A. A. (2021, May). Quantum Computing for Military Applications. In *2021 International Conference on Military Communication and Information Systems (ICMCIS)* (pp. 1-8). IEEE.
19. Michal, K. (2021). Quantum technology for military applications. *EPJ Quantum Technology, 8*(1).
20. Kania, E. B. (2018). New Frontiers of Chinese Defense Innovation: Artificial Intelligence and Quantum Technologies. *SITC Research Briefs* (2018-12).
21. Lele, A. (2021). Military Relevance of Quantum Technologies. In *Quantum Technologies and Military Strategy* (pp. 117-143). Springer, Cham.
22. Parker, E. (2020). *Commercial and Military Applications and Timelines for Quantum Technology.* RAND Corp, Santa Monica, CA.
23. Becker, L. (2006, February). Influence of IR sensor technology on the military and civil defense. In *Quantum Sensing and Nanophotonic Devices III* (Vol. 6127, pp. 180-194). SPIE.
24. Ralegankar, V. K., Bagul, J., Thakkar, B., Gupta, R., Tanwar, S., Sharma, G., & Davidson, I. E. (2021). Quantum Cryptography-as-a-Service for Secure UAV Communication: Applications, Challenges, and Case Study. *IEEE Access, 10*, 1475-1492.
25. Strand, M. (2021, May). A Status Update on Quantum Safe Cryptography. In *2021 International Conference on Military Communication and Information Systems (ICMCIS)* (pp. 1-7). IEEE.

28

Quantum Cryptography Techniques: Evaluation

Shashank Sharma[1]*, T.M.Thiyagu[2], Om Kumar C.U.[3] and D. Jeyakumar[4]

[1]Department of Computer Science Engineering, Shri Vaishnav Vidyapeeth Vishwavidyalaya, Indore, India
[2]Department of Computer Science and Engineering, Karunya Institute of Technology and Sciences, Karunya Nagar, Coimbatore, Tamil Nadu, India
[3]School of Computer Science and Engineering (SCOPE), Vellore Institute of Technology, Chennai Campus, India
[4]Department of CSE, Dhanalakshmi College of Engineering, Tambaram, Chennai, India

Abstract

Computer science's branch of cryptography focuses on transforming data into encrypted formats that are imperceptible to unauthorized users. The process of securing format is called encryption. It has been used for centuries to halt unwanted recipients from reading communications. Traditional cryptography techniques either rely on a private key or a public key that is known to everybody. In either scenario, the eavesdroppers are able to identify the key and as a result, discover the message sent without the sender or receiver's awareness.

A form of encryption known as quantum cryptography (Qcryp) takes advantage of some of the fundamental principles of quantum physics that uses inherent qualities to transmit and secure data in an uncrackable manner. Qcryp is a system that cannot be broken into without the transmitter or recipient of the message being aware of it. Qcryp employs the Quantum Key Distribution (QKD), a method for dispersing random binary keys that allows communicating parties to identify potential listeners.

Keywords: Quantum cryptography, quantum network, quantum key distribution, photon polarization, quantum sensing, quantum computing

*Corresponding author: shashankprsharma@gmail.com

Romil Rawat, Rajesh Kumar Chakrawarti, Sanjaya Kumar Sarangi, Jaideep Patel, Vivek Bhardwaj, Anjali Rawat and Hitesh Rawat (eds.) Quantum Computing in Cybersecurity, (471–488) © 2023 Scrivener Publishing LLC

28.1   Introduction

Unauthorized network access or data access are the main causes of security breaches. Intruders have expanded their technical proficiency over the past few years, found novel techniques to exploit network flaws, and built sophisticated software tools for automating attacks. It is quite concerning since many attacks include unauthorized access to information resources, and that businesses usually are unaware of unauthorized access to their information systems. To protect everything from business e-mail to bank transactions and online shopping, computer and communications networks of today significantly rely on encryption. Both traditional and contemporary cryptography use a variety of mathematical strategies to prevent listeners from deciphering the content of encrypted transmissions.

Quantum information science (QIS) [1, 2] is a branch of information science that studies quantum information and is connected to quantum physics. In traditional information science, a bit—which can only be either 0 or 1—is the fundamental carrier of information [3]. The quantum bit, or qubit for short, is the fundamental carrier of information in quantum theory. A qubit can be either [1] or [0], or it can be in a quantum superposition, which is an arbitrarily complex linear combination of the states [1] and [0].

Cryptographers work to develop ever more sophisticated methods of masking the sensitive data that needs to be conveyed. But the systems are always under attack from hackers, code breakers, and eavesdroppers. The achievement of cryptographers in achieving security or code breakers in breaking security will only be momentary [4]. The process of encrypting the message with cyphers and dismantling the system with deciphers is never-ending. This situation was once a race chase. Utilizing fibre-optic wire, data is transmitted individual light particles, or photons, in quantum encryption. Photons are used to represent binary bits. Quantum physics is a key component of the system's security [5].

These safe areas consist of the following [16, 17]:

- Particles can coexist in multiple places or states at once;
- It is impossible to view a quantum property without affecting or disrupting it; and
- It is impossible to copy complete particles.

Due to the fact that they possess all the requirements for quantum cryptography, photons are utilized in this technology. They function as information carriers in optical fiber lines and their behavior is well characterized. One of the most well-known applications of quantum cryptography (Qcryp) at the moment is quantum key distribution (QKD) [18], which provides a secure method for key exchange [1, 6].

Quantum cryptography's capacity to exchange the encryption key incomparably securely upholds its level of security. Even if they only want to look at or read photons, quantum encryption stops snoopers from intercepting them, irretrievably changes the information that was encoded onto the photon. Delivering the key that has been encoded at the single-photon level one photon at a time allows for this.

In order to create a secure network, several QKD [7] techniques are integrated with well-known internet technology in the Qcryp network. The unbreakable principles of quantum mechanics underpin the security of QKD, and the security of this protocol is implied by the flawless cloning of non-orthogonal states is impossible.

Organization of Chapter
The rest of the chapter is organized as follows. Section 28.2 describes Quantum Technology in Defence; section 28.3 represents the Quantum Key Distribution Model; section 28.4 highlights related work; section 28.5 shows Preliminaries; section 28.6 represents QKD Protocols Implementation; section 28.7 shows risk analysis; section 28.8 highlights applications of quantum cryptography; section 28.9 shows the challenges of Quantum Cryptography; and section 28.10 concludes the chapter with future work.

28.2   Quantum Technology (QTech) in Defence [19–21]

The criteria for military technologies are more stringent than those for commercial or public use. Given the potential for deployment on the battlefield, this calls for additional care. It provides a range of potential military applications with varied TRLs, [8, 11] time projections, and implementation hazards. For technologies that can be quickly integrated into existing technologies, such as quantum sensors, where we can merely swap out a conventional sensor for a quantum sensor, it will be easier and less dangerous.

QKD, on the other hand, is an illustration of a technology that is already commercially available yet difficult to implement. There is a great need for new hardware, systems, and compatibility with existing communication systems [9, 11]. As a result, the hazards associated with using this technology in the military are greater. In the long run, we can anticipate benefits in decreasing SWaP (size, weight, and power) and scaling up quantum computer and quantum networks. The deployment will be made simpler as a result, and it will likely be required if the country or army wants [11] to compete with other countries or armies that have edge (quantum) technologies.

28.2.1   Quantum Strategy [22, 23]

Future military quantum technology (QTech) users will need to carefully consider when, where, and how to devote their time and resources. The objective of the [10] defence forces is typically limited to defining requirements and their acquisition rather than the development of military technologies.

Even though they are the end consumer, they can contribute considerably to development. It is preferable to have a national quantum ecosystem made of business and academic organisations in place as a basis. A national quantum plan and broad government support for this ecosystem are necessary, but it also has to be encouraged to create technology for the defence industry [10].

This may be done by receiving the proper grant money or even by participating in several thematic challenges where people and entrepreneurs may contribute fresh, innovative concepts and ideas. Naturally, this will result [11] in closer collaboration between business and academia.

There is a lot of collaboration between academics and industry in the fascinating field of QTech. The first stage is to create a plan or strategy for quantum technologies. The roadmap or strategy should outline all of the following processes, starting with the identification of disruptive quantum solutions, followed by market research, technology and risk assessment, the development process itself, prototype testing, and ultimately solution implementation.

The roadmap or quantum plan may be divided into three sections: identifying, developing, implementing, and deploying are the first three steps.

Finding the most favourable and revolutionary quantum technologies for the potential military domains is the most important step. This step also involves a technological and scientific review to weigh the potential benefits of specific quantum technologies against the risks associated with technology (restricted deployability, performance below expectations [11], or impossibility of transfer from the lab to the battlefield). To be able to respond to new discoveries and disruptive ideas reasonably quickly, this identification process should be cycled through repeatedly. It's crucial to keep in mind that there are still a lot of potential uses.

The following step [10, 11] is the customary research and development procedure (R&D). R&D should have adequate financial backing and encounter few bureaucratic roadblocks. It should involve quick development cycles and close communication with the military technology's end users (specifications and performance consultations, prototype testing, preparing for certifications, ...). The new system should be prepared at the end of this phase and capable of working. Reaching full operational capability is the final step, which involves [11] changing or developing new military doctrines and developing new combat scenarios, strategies, and tactics that fully utilise the quantum advantage.

The identification phase is the subject of the last observation. In this situation, the decision maker must also adopt a long-term viewpoint. Sensors, QKD, quantum computing [11, 12], and other quantum technologies have all been taken into account separately thus far. However, the long-term plan takes into account how quantum systems interact.

28.2.2   QTech Military Applications [24, 25]

Numerous facets of human activity could be dramatically impacted by quantum technologies. The defence industry is a good example of this. All areas of contemporary warfare could be affected by quantum technologies. Instead of producing new kinds of weaponry, the second quantum revolution will increase sensitivity and efficiency, introduce new capabilities, and enhance contemporary military strategies. The text that follows maps potential QTech uses for military, security, space, and intelligence in various facets of contemporary combat [13]. Additionally, it mentions commercial uses of QTech that may provide insight into its potential and effectiveness, particularly in light of the lack of knowledge on its potential military applications.

It's crucial to remember that many applications are still more theoretical than practical. The considerable quantum progress made in the lab is not always followed by corresponding advances outside of the lab. In addition to a functioning laboratory prototype [14], the transition from the lab to a practical deployment requires other factors as well, including mobility, sensitivity, resolution, speed, resilience, low SWaP (size, weight, and power), and cost. The manufacturing and application of specific quantum technologies will depend on their viability and economics.

QTech integration into a military platform is even more challenging. With the exception of quantum computers, which will primarily be housed in data centres similar to those for civil use, the integration and deployment of quantum sensing [14], imaging, and networks face a number of difficulties because of the higher requirements of military use (compared to civil/industry or scientific requirements).

Fast measurement rates are frequently quite a constraint for the current generation of quantum inertial sensors when it comes to the military's need for precise navigation. There are more examples, and there will probably be more.

28.3   The QKD Model

Charles H. Bennett and Gilles Brassard created the idea of Qcryp in 1984 [23–25], at the IBM lab as a part of an examination into physics and information. This is the earliest known quantum distribution system. The polarization of a photon encodes the value of a conventional bit, and the distribution of single particles or photons forms the foundation of the quantum system. A photon is a fundamental unit of energy in light that carries a specific quantity of energy [8]. Light can be polarized according to physical law; polarization is a physical property that emerges, when considering light as an electromagnetic wave. A calcite crystal can be used to measure the polarization of a photon according to the direction of the photon at any chosen angle. In actuality, the laws of photon polarization and the Heisenberg uncertainty principle are two crucial aspects of quantum physics that are essential to Qcryp [8, 15].

It is argued by the Heisenberg uncertainty principle that it is impossible to distribute a system in order to measure its quantum state. This means that a photon's or light particle's polarization can only be determined at the time when it is being measured. This idea is crucial for stopping eavesdropping attempts in a quantum cryptography-based encryption scheme [8, 15].

The photon polarization principle, on the other hand, describes how light photons can be polarized in a certain direction. Additionally, due to the no-cloning theorem, which was initially proposed in 1982, unknown quantum states, or unknown qubits, cannot be copied by an eavesdropper [7]. Without the need for face-to-face contact, two communications participants can still agree on a bit string and be extremely confident that it will only be communicated by them. This is made possible by quantum cryptography.

Using polarized photons, BB84 enables dual parties—typically "Alice" and "Bob"—develop an anonymous shared key sequence. These photons are each in one of the four states indicated by one of the following symbols [8]. Figure 28.1 shows the symbols for Photons State – 1st and Figure 28.2 shows the symbols for Photons State – 2nd.

A polarizer that is oriented rectilinearly emits the initial two states of photons, and a polarizer that is oriented diagonally emits the next two states [8]. For example: +(0)= — , +(1)= | , x(0)=/, x(1)=\.

If Alice sends random sequence of photons: ++xx++xxx++xx, the binary number represented with these states is 1110010110010 [8]. Now, for Bob to receive a binary number provided by Alice, each photon must be received on the same basis.

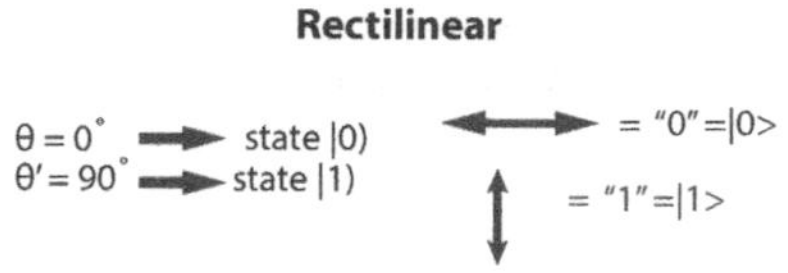

Rectilinear

$\theta = 0°$ ➡ state $|0\rangle$ ⬅➡ $= "0" = |0\rangle$
$\theta' = 90°$ ➡ state $|1\rangle$ ⬍ $= "1" = |1\rangle$

Figure 28.1 Symbols for photons state – 1st [1, 2].

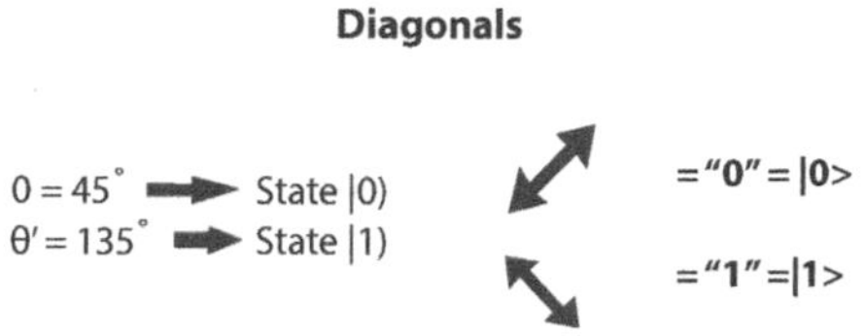

Diagonals

$0 = 45°$ ➡ State $|0\rangle$ ⬈ $= "0" = |0\rangle$
$\theta' = 135°$ ➡ State $|1\rangle$ ⬋ $= "1" = |1\rangle$

Figure 28.2 Symbols for photons state – 2nd [3, 4].

The polarization of a photon encodes the value of a conventional bit, and the distribution of single particles or photons forms the foundation of the quantum system. A photon is a basic energy carrier for light that contains a certain amount of energy. Light can be polarized according to physical law [2]; When considering light as an electromagnetic wave, the physical property known as polarization emerges.

When two parties to a communication agree on a bit string using quantum cryptography, they can do so without ever meeting in person and still be confident that the agreed-upon bit string will only be used by those two parties.

The simulation makes the assumption that Alice and Bob are two individuals who want to securely communicate. Alice starts the communication by sending Bob a key [2]. A stream of photons that move in only one direction holds the secret. Every photon is a single bit of information, either a 0 or a 1. These photons are moving linearly, but they are also vibrating or oscillating in a particular way [2]. Figure 28.3 shows the QKD details.

The photons pass through a polarizer before Alice, the sender, starts the transmission. Some photons can travel through a polarizer with the same vibrations while allowing other photons to pass through with a different vibration, potentially polarized states include 45 degrees left, 45 degrees right, vertical (1 bit), horizontal (0 bit), or diagonal (45 bits) (0 bit). In any of the schemes she employs, there are two polarizations for the transmission which indicate a single bit, either a 0 or a 1.

Now the photons are moving from the polarizer to the receiver Bob along an optical fiber. A beam splitter is used in this method to determine each photon's polarization. Bob chooses one polarization at random because he has no knowledge about proper photons' polarization when he receives the photon key. To determine the polarizer Alice used to send each

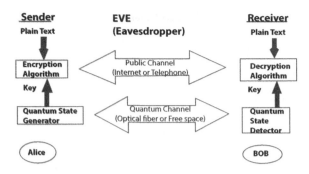

Figure 28.3 Quantum key distribution [2, 5–7].

photon [2], Bob's instruments for polarizing the key are now being compared by Alice. Bob then checks to make sure he used the right polarizer.
The sequence that is left after discarding the photons that were read with
the incorrect splitter is regarded as the key.

Consider the possibility that Eve, an eavesdropper, is present. With the
same equipment as Bob, Eve tries to listen in. Bob, however, has the benefit
of conversing with Alice to check the type of polarizer that was applied
to each photon, whereas Eve does not. Eve ultimately renders the last key
inaccurately. Bob and Alice would also be aware if Eve was listening in on
them. Alice and Bob's expected photon positions would alter as a result of
Eve viewing the photon flow [2].

28.4   Related Work

In 1969 [23, 24], Wiesner presented the idea of quantum money, which is
where Qcryp gets its name. This innovative and unique proposal cannot be
implemented due to historical limitations in technology; hence it was not
published until 1983. Bennett and Brassard proposed the first useful QKD
protocol in 2011. They were the first to use single photon polarization to
build the QKD technique. After that, QKD underwent significant improvement in terms of efficiency and security. The protocol that is based on Bell's
theorem was proposed by Ekert [25] in 1991. Keep in mind that it uses two
quantum bits, making it essentially the same as what Bennett subsequently
proposed in an enhancement of the plan in 1992. The enhancement is more
effective and straightforward when using any two nonorthogonal states.
Following that, numerous QKD techniques utilizing the fundamentals of
quantum physics have been gradually presented.

The initial network for QKD in the history of the world was the DARPA
Quantum Network. The DARPA [23–25] Quantum Network might

provide critical material produced from QKD to construct virtual private networks, to assist with IPsec or other forms of authentication, or for any other purpose. It was entirely compatible with standard Internet technologies [7]. All control methods and protocols were implemented using the Unix kernel and field-programmable gate arrays. Key content from the QKD was frequently used in applications such as video conferencing.

To investigate the properties of several QKD systems, the DARPA Quantum Network [20–24] implemented them. They were all combined into a single, high-performance protocol stack. Public keys, shared private keys, or a combination of the two were used as the basis for authentication [7].

The DARPA security paradigm is based on virtual private network encryption (VPN). In order to achieve secrecy and authentication/integrity Public-key and symmetric cryptography are both used by conventional VPNs. Public-key techniques allow for key agreement or exchange and endpoint authentication [4]. The secrecy and integrity of traffic are provided through symmetric techniques. Due to the unreliability of the public network linking the VPN sites, VPN systems can provide confidentiality, authentication, and integrity. Due to the unreliability of the public network linking the VPN sites, VPN [16–20] systems can provide confidentiality and authentication/integrity. In DARPA research, keys provided by Qcryp are supplemented or entirely replaced by current VPN key agreement primitives [4].

28.5 Preliminaries

Due to the unique properties of quantum information, compared to conventional approaches, quantum communication and information processing frequently outperform them.

28.5.1 Quantum Information Properties

Quantum teleportation, its fundamental characteristics include the uncertainty principle, the quantum no-cloning theory, and the hidden aspects of quantum information. These can be used in cyberspace communication to fend off attacks (either passive or aggressive). The uncertainty principle of Heisenberg and the theory of quantum non-cloning.

(I) Uncertainty principle: The uncertainty principle was introduced in 1927 by German physicist Heisenberg and is also known as Heisenberg's principle of uncertainty. The cornerstone of the uncertainty principle is that because a particle always exists in several places with different probabilities across the micro universe, it is impossible to pinpoint its exact location.

(II)   Quantum no-cloning theory: The unexplained quantum state's unclonable and undeleting characteristics are the basis of the No-cloning quantum theory. Cloning is the process of creating a quantum state that is exactly the similar in a different system. Scientists have established that no machines exist that can duplicate quantum systems. Any erasing or harmful effect the opponent has on the quantum information will be traced by the undeleting principle in secure communication. According to a theory put out in *Nature*, the linearity of quantum theory forbids the deletion of a copy of any given quantum state.

(III) Quantum teleportation: By measuring the original's quantum state and relaying this information in a classical manner, the sender is able to acquire the classical information. Information that is still available is quantum information that is transmitted to the recipient by measurement but is not extracted by the sender during the measurement.

(IV)   Hidden characteristics of quantum information: Information in the quantum realm has certain characteristics that classical information does not. Only joint measurements can reveal the information stored in the quantum code in the entangled state; also local measurements cannot retrieve it.

28.5.2   Quantum Communication System

There are two different kinds of quantum communication: quantum direct communication and quantum teleportation communication. The easiest method to accomplish the transmission of quantum signals between the quantum direct transmission paradigm only has two places [9]. The model for quantum direct communication is displayed in Figure 28.4. Alice wants to use a quantum channel to reach Bob. According to the quantum direct transmission paradigm, to send Bob a message, Alice must first generate a certain amount of photons through the preparation device [9]. This data also has to be handled by a quantum source encoder and a quantum error correcting code (QECC) encoder when the quantum source is

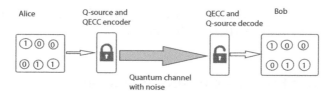

Figure 28.4 Quantum direct communication model [1, 2, 8, 9].

created. The quantum information can then be sent straight to the quantum channel after that (optical fibre or atmosphere). The Quantum Direct Communication Model is shown in Figure 28.4.

In this situation, external noise might easily interfere with the quantum channel. As a result, before applying quantum source encoding to the signal it has received, receiver Bob first applies QECC encoding. Bob finally gets the first quantum message.

Quantum teleportation is the other type of quantum communication. In contrast to conventional communication, qubits are capable of being entangled as well as a number of orthogonal superposition states [9]. The fundamental principle underlying quantum teleportation is to use two particles in their most entangled state to establish a quantum channel. Figure 28.5 shows Quantum Teleportation.

The quantum operation then transmits the message. Keep in mind that the choice of communication routes distinguishes direct communication from teleportation. Figure 28.5 shows a model of quantum teleportation in action. In this scenario [9], we show Alice trying to send Bob a one-bit quantum signal from another location. First, an EPR pair is created by the EPR entanglement source. Second, one of the particles is transferred to Alice through the quantum channel, and the other is conveyed to the recipient Bob.

Thirdly, to exchange information, Alice must measure the particles in the EPR entangled pairs and the pending bits she has. Alice then updates Bob on the measurement results. In the end [9], Bob can learn based on

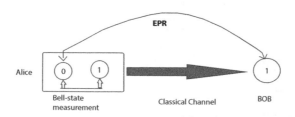

Figure 28.5 Quantum teleportation [1–3, 8, 10, 11].

the findings of Alice's measurement and his own EPR pair measurement, information about the particles to be conveyed.

28.6   QKD Protocols Implementation

We refer to the set of specialized protocols used in Qcryp as the "QKD protocols" since they are quite complex. Many of these protocols' peculiar characteristics, including their odd implementation and rationale, may be of interest to experts in communications protocols. These protocols, as depicted in Figure 28.6, are best categorized as sub-layers of the QKD protocol family [4]. Figure 28.6 shows the QKD Protocol Stack.

28.6.1   Sifting

Bob and Alice separate out all the evident "failed qubits" from string of pulses using a procedure called sifting. These failures include qubits where Bob's detectors weren't functional, Alice's laser failed to broadcast, during transmission, photons were lost, and so on. They also contain the symbols used by Alice when she chose one basis for transmission while Bob selected another for reception [4].

The worthless symbols from Alice's and Bob's internal storage are discarded. Only the symbols that Bob got and for which Bob's basis matches Alice's are left after this protocol interaction, or after a sift and sift response transaction [2].

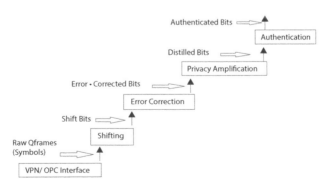

Figure 28.6 The QKD protocol stack [1, 2, 12–15].

28.6.2   Error Correction

The ability to identify and fix all "error bits" among shared, filtered bits gives Alice and Bob the ability to share the same sequence of repaired bits that Bob received as a 1 but Alice supplied as a 0, or the opposite, are called error bits. Either noise or eavesdropping can be the cause of these bit mistakes [4].

To limit the hidden entropy accessible for key material, Correction of errors in Qcryp is subject to a very unique restriction: evidence revealed in error detection and correction must be presumed to be known to Eve. Designing mistake detection and correction algorithms that make as little of their public control traffic between Bob and Alice known as possible is hence strongly motivated [4].

28.6.3   Privacy Amplifications

By using privacy amplification, Bob and Alice can limit Eve's access to their shared bits to a manageable amount. Another name for this method is advantage distillation [2].

28.6.4   Authentication

By using authentication, Alice and Bob can prevent "man in the middle attacks," or make sure they are speaking to each other and not some third party. Since Eve may interject herself into Bob's and Alice's connection at any point, continuous authentication must be carried out for all key management transactions [4].

28.7   Risk Analysis

There is a slim chance that Alice and Bob's samples in this interception, where Eve measures every qubit, won't match, leading them to attempt to send an unsecured message across Eve's channel [10]. We are evaluating the distribution of quantum keys' susceptibility.

- Alice and Bob most likely selected the same basis in order to use a qubit's result. If Eve chooses this premise as well, she will successfully block this passage without making any mistakes. This incident [10] has a 50% chance of happening.

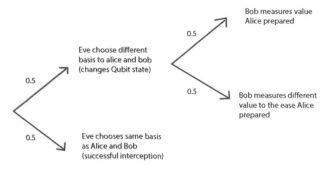

Figure 28.7 The Design Stack [1, 3, 5].

- There is still a 50% chance that [10] Bob will determine the value Alice was seeking to convey if Eve chooses an improper basis, such as one other than Alice and Bob. In this instance, the attempt to obstruct also goes unnoticed.
- However, if Eve chooses an improper basis, such as a basis different from Alice and Bob, there is a 50% chance that Bob won't measure the value Alice was trying to convey [10], which will create an error in their keys. Figure 28.7 shows the Design Stack.

If Alice and Bob each stare at 1 from their keys, there is a 0.75% chance that the bits will line up, and if they do, they won't see Eve's effort to capture them [10]. The chance that the capture attempt will be noted is 0.752=0.5625 on the odd chance that they measure 2 bits. We can see that the number of bits (q) that Alice and Bob choose to analyse can be used to estimate the likelihood of Eve evading detection [10].

28.8   Applications of Quantum Cryptography

In the public and private sectors, quantum encryption already safeguards sensitive data related to national security. Security has been evaluated and proved. Here are a few examples of recent and upcoming Qcryp applications [5].

A. Ultra-Secure Voting
Making the voting process more secure is essential given the political unrest and widespread claims of election fraud in both wealthy and developing nations. Qcryp is used to safeguard the voting results, and the most

vulnerable data transaction occurs when the vote goes from the counting station to the central repository [5].

B. Secure Communications with Space
Due to growing concerns regarding the security of communications with these entities, a company by the name of Quintessence Labs is working on a solution for NASA that would allow for secure communications with astronauts and satellites from Earth [5]. The project's aim is to create a protocol that guarantees communication security regardless of the resources or data an adversary has access to. Additionally, it contains a requirement to safeguard data "at rest" and "in transit."

C. A Smarter Power Grid
It has been suggested that one of the most exposed targets for a cyberattack is the American electricity system. In reality, cyber adversaries are "constantly" attacking some of the largest U.S. utilities. When using public data networks to regulate smart electrical grids, workers can send completely secure signals with the use of a tiny encryption device. In order to efficiently balance supply and demand, smart grids are necessary [5].

D. Quantum Internet
Although the internet of today is fairly quick, quantum encryption offers much better protection. The internet would operate much more slowly with quantum encryption. But in the future, it's likely that we may be able to seamlessly switch between "normal" and "quantum encrypted" internet, ensuring the highest level of security for even our most private transmissions. By doing this, the dream of a quick and safe internet would be realized [5].

28.9   Challenges of Quantum Cryptography

Because it is challenging to maintain their entanglement for long enough to produce the necessary outcomes, even seemingly secure entangled photons face a practical challenge. Beyond 50 kilometers, the channel becomes very vulnerable to eavesdropping as the noise increases along with the error rates. Because it is the first application of the quantum mechanism in practice, the QDP represents the basic science study.

Another challenge is a lack of a security satisfaction procedure [4]. The user demands assurance, but how can practice security be ensured? It becomes a concern. The development of a cheap optical system that is capable of creating and guiding a single proton is one of the technical difficulties.

28.10   Conclusion and Future Work

Some people propose that a satellite could detect photons in order to build a miniature telescope that could be used to communicate with any location on Earth. A major challenge for QDK is marketing quantum-based technologies to customers who frequently have limited background in physics and are accustomed to conventional cryptography [5]. Another issue is the lack of a process or standard for the equipment's security certification. To validate the security idea, fresh experiments should be conducted on the foundation of the quantum mechanism, which must first undergo a thorough review.

The capability of Qcryp to identify any third-party present between two communicating users is a crucial and distinctive feature. The security of Qcryp is based on quantum physics, which has the potential to completely transform network security. Quantum physics provides the foundation for the security of quantum cryptography. Network security (QKD) approaches may be used with conventional internet technologies to produce extremely secure communications for practical usage. QKD methods may be used in conjunction with standard internet technologies to build incredibly secure connections. It is determined that a more robust technique is required to convey sensitive information between two or more sites. QKD and other quantum encryption techniques will undoubtedly improve the security of critical data. Quantum encryption is a powerful and encouraging step toward a time when we can feel safer about how and what we exchange.

References

1. Gillis, A. S. (2022, January 28). What is quantum cryptography? Search Security; TechTarget. https://www.techtarget.com/searchsecurity/definition/quantum-cryptography.
2. Elliott, C., Pearson, D., and Troxel, G. Quantum cryptography in practice. PDFSEARCH.IO - document search engine. (n.d.). Pdfsearch.Io. Retrieved September 5, 2022, from https://www.pdfsearch.io/document/Alice+and+Bob/RLnP-show/Quantum+Cryptography+in+Practice+Chip+Elliott+Dr.+David+Pearson++Dr.+Gregory+Troxel

3. Sharbaf, M. S. (2011). Quantum cryptography: An emerging technology in network security. *2011 IEEE International Conference on Technologies for Homeland Security (HST)*, 13–19.

4. Aditya, J., & Rao, P. S. (n.d.). Quantum Cryptography. Stanford.edu. Retrieved September 22, 2022, from https://cs.stanford.edu/people/adityaj/QuantumCryptography.pdf

5. Sasirekha, N., & Hemalatha, M. (n.d.). International journal of engineering and advanced technology (IJEAT). Ijeat.org. Retrieved September 6, 2022, from https://www.ijeat.org/wp-content/uploads/papers/v3i4/D2988043414.pdf

6. Bernstein, D. J., & Lange, T. (2017). Post-quantum cryptography. *Nature*, 549(7671), 188–194. https://doi.org/10.1038/nature23461

7. Wikipedia contributors. (2022, June 2). DARPA Quantum Network. Wikipedia, The Free Encyclopedia. https://en.wikipedia.org/w/index.php?title=DARPA_Quantum_Network&oldid=1091161166

8. Sharbaf, M. S. (2011). Quantum cryptography: An emerging technology in network security. *2011 IEEE International Conference on Technologies for Homeland Security (HST)*, 13–19.

9. Zhou, T., Shen, J., Li, X., Wang, C., & Shen, J. (2018). Quantum cryptography for the future Internet and the security analysis. *Security and Communication Networks*, 2018, 1–7. https://doi.org/10.1155/2018/8214619

10. (N.d.). Researchgate.net. Retrieved October 1, 2022, from https://www.researchgate.net/publication/345675328_Quantum_Cryptography

11. Krelina, M. (2021). Quantum Technology for Military Applications. In arXiv [quant-ph]. http://arxiv.org/abs/2103.12548

12. Park, J., Anandakumar, N. N., Saha, D., Mehta, D., Pundir, N., Rahman, F., ... & Tehranipoor, M. M. (2022). PQC-SEP: Power Side-channel Evaluation Platform for Post-Quantum Cryptography Algorithms. *IACR Cryptol. ePrint Arch.*, *2022*, 527.

13. Sohma, M., & Hirota, O. (2022). Quantum Stream Cipher Based on Holevo–Yuen Theory. *Entropy*, 24(5), 667.

14. Tandel, P. H., & Nasriwala, J. V. (2022). Evaluating Hash-Based Post-Quantum Signature in Smart IoT Devices for Authentication. In *Evolutionary Computing and Mobile Sustainable Networks* (pp. 673-682). Springer, Singapore.

15. Alagic, G., Apon, D., Cooper, D., Dang, Q., Dang, T., Kelsey, J., ... & Liu, Y. K. (2022). Status report on the third round of the NIST post-quantum cryptography standardization process. National Institute of Standards and Technology, Gaithersburg.

16. Portmann, C., & Renner, R. (2022). Security in quantum cryptography. *Reviews of Modern Physics*, 94(2), 025008.

17. Kumar, A., & Garhwal, S. (2021). State-of-the-Art Survey of Quantum Cryptography. *Archives of Computational Methods in Engineering*, 28(5), 3831-3868.

18. Ahn, J., Kwon, H. Y., Ahn, B., Park, K., Kim, T., Lee, M. K., ... & Chung, J. (2022). Toward Quantum Secured Distributed Energy Resources: Adoption of Post-Quantum Cryptography (PQC) and Quantum Key Distribution (QKD). *Energies*, *15*(3), 714.
19. Bozzio, M., Vyvlecka, M., Cosacchi, M., Nawrath, C., Seidelmann, T., Loredo, J. C., ... & Walther, P. (2022). Enhancing quantum cryptography with quantum dot single-photon sources. *npj Quantum Information*, *8*(1), 1-8.
20. Chamola, V., Jolfaei, A., Chanana, V., Parashari, P., & Hassija, V. (2021). Information security in the post quantum era for 5G and beyond networks: Threats to existing cryptography, and post-quantum cryptography. *Computer Communications*, *176*, 99-118.
21. Wang, Q. K., Wang, F. X., Liu, J., Chen, W., Han, Z. F., Forbes, A., & Wang, J. (2021). High-dimensional quantum cryptography with hybrid orbital-angular-momentum states through 25 km of ring-core fiber: a proof-of-concept demonstration. *Physical Review Applied*, *15*(6), 064034.
22. Xagawa, K., Ito, A., Ueno, R., Takahashi, J., & Homma, N. (2021, December). Fault-injection attacks against NIST's post-quantum cryptography round 3 KEM candidates. In *International Conference on the Theory and Application of Cryptology and Information Security* (pp. 33-61). Springer, Cham.
23. Barbosa, M., Barthe, G., Fan, X., Grégoire, B., Hung, S. H., Katz, J., ... & Zhou, L. (2021, November). EasyPQC: Verifying post-quantum cryptography. In *Proceedings of the 2021 ACM SIGSAC Conference on Computer and Communications Security* (pp. 2564-2586).
24. Howe, J., Prest, T., & Apon, D. (2021, May). SoK: how (not) to design and implement post-quantum cryptography. In *Cryptographers' Track at the RSA Conference* (pp. 444-477). Springer, Cham.
25. Yao, K., Krawec, W. O., & Zhu, J. (2022). Quantum sampling for finite key rates in high dimensional quantum cryptography. *IEEE Transactions on Information Theory*, *68*(5), 3144-3163.

29

Cyber Crime Attack Vulnerability Review for Quantum Computing

Vaishnavi Gawde[1]*, Vanshika Goswami[1], Balwinder Kaur Dhaliwal[2],
Sunil Parihar[3], Rupali Chaure[4] and Mandakini Ingle[5]

[1]*Department of Computer Science Engineering,
Shri Vaishnav Vidyapeeth Vishwavidyalaya, Indore, India*
[2]*School of Computer Science and Engineering, Lovely Professional University
Punjab, Punjab, India*
[3]*Department of Computer Science and Engineering, Sri Aurobindo Institute of
Technology, Indore, M.P., India*
[4]*Department of Computer Science and Engineering, SIRT, Bhopal, India*
[5]*Department of Computer Science and Engineering, Medicaps University,
Indore, India*

Abstract

The frequency of cyberattacks is rising as internet usage grows more prevalent. As the race for quantum computing (QC) progresses, QC businesses and research organisations may be targeted by nation states, cybercriminals, and hacktivists for financial gain and destruction. This essay examines the state of QC technology and how cybersecurity is connected to QC. We now go into the dangers and recommended practises for preventing the quickly developing cybercrimes. Following that, we put out suggestions on how to proactively lower the cyberattack surface using threat intelligence and by ensuring that quantum software and hardware components are secure by design.

Once large-scale and fault-tolerant Qcomp(Qcomp) are built, it is projected that the security of widely used public-key science techniques (such as RSA and elliptic-curve cryptography) would worsen. Due to the fact that these algorithms are at the core of modern society's IT infrastructure, including the financial industry, the potential threat is serious. The National Institute of Standards and Technology (NIST) has been working on a technique of standardising post-quantum cryptography (PQC),

Corresponding author: vaishnavigawde28@gmail.com

Romil Rawat, Rajesh Kumar Chakrawarti, Sanjaya Kumar Sarangi, Jaideep Patel, Vivek Bhardwaj, Anjali Rawat and Hitesh Rawat (eds.) Quantum Computing in Cybersecurity, (489–504) © 2023 Scrivener Publishing LLC

which is designed to be safe against Qcomp, even if the danger is unlikely to materialise in the predictable future. NIST has been examining the performance and security of fifteen potential algorithms (seven finalists and eight alternate candidates). Standardization should hasten the transition to PQC globally, not only in the United States. In this chapter, we will discuss current developments in Qcomp analysis and development as well as the security problems associated with public-key scientific algorithms. Then we cover NIST's ongoing PQC standardisation efforts and, therefore, the responses of various organisations in favour of the migration. Finally, we discuss potential difficulties with applying PQC in the actual world.

Keywords: Quantum computing, hackivists, cyberattacks crime, quantum simulation, encryption

29.1   Introduction

Quantum information (Qinfo) science is a subfield that makes use of the capacity to create and use quantum bits, or qubits. It includes quantum networking, quantum sensing, and quantum simulation [1, 2]. In comparison to conventional or other classical computers, Qcomp have the ability to tackle some problems substantially more quickly. They conduct several processes concurrently in a manner that is fundamentally distinct from that of conventional computers by utilising the concepts of quantum physics. The fundamental concept of this work encompasses a broad range of information from academic institutions and organisations creating, producing, or working with quantum computing (QC) software or hardware, including quantum technologies connected to a network, to any sector with digital capabilities. A conversation beforehand about whether to bring secure personal technologies for drug [15, 16] users and protect their findings from relevant dangers benefits startups, university spin-offs, and merchandisers. The goal of this examination is to reflect on potential educational pathways for experts in QC while also sparking discussions and advancing ideas in multidisciplinary research.

RSA [3, 4] (Rivest-Shamir-Adleman encryption) and AES (Advanced Encryption Standard)-based encryption is being used to safeguard data. Simply put, cryptographic keys created at random decide cybersecurity. These keys' randomization serves as a gauge of their quality. When keys have weak randomness, traditional encryption techniques are vulnerable to attack by hackers. It has been demonstrated that the RSA and AES standards can be broken since they are not genuinely random. The random behaviour at the core of quantum physics is what gives quantum keys their unbreakable character. The US National Institute of Standards and

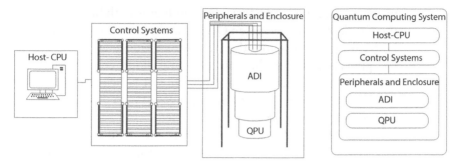

Figure 29.1 A QC architecture [1, 5].

Technology (NIST) is actively working to standardise post-quantum methods for key generation [5, 6].

Making a robust and coherent amount computer system while creating new operations for these biases marks the end of the amount computing exploratory phase. While many computers are unlikely to serve as a direct replacement for classical computers, they will be able to solve some issues that are currently essentially intractable by classical computers. Quantity processing units (QPUs) will work similarly to how plate recycling units (GPUs) [7, 8] expedite particular operations for today's computers. Previously, the community of number crunchers has connected a number of issues spanning material knowledge, biophysics and chemistry, machine literacy, and artificial intelligence that will have revolutionary effects fueled by number computers. The architecture for QC is depicted in Figure 29.1.

29.1.1 Uses of QC [9, 10]

- QC has both advantages and disadvantages for security protocols. These consequences include making the public key cryptosystems used in current security protocols (SSL, SSH, IPSec) insecure, the requirement for developing trustworthy cryptosystems in place of traditional public key cryptosystems, and the need for developing trustworthy protocols that can operate on Qcomp infrastructure.
- Qcomp are thought to provide a solution to problems with discrete logarithms, integer factorization, and search challenges in engineering fields, among others. The security of the RSA cryptosystem is directly impacted by this approach. New methods are also required to categorise challenging issues. In the current classification, discrete logarithm

problems and integer factorization problems both belong to the NP class. However, when Qcomp are taken into account, both problems move into the P class.

- In application sectors like big data and cloud computing, which are connected to data processing, it is believed that quantum techniques can change all types of data processing and security procedures that will be used.
- Near-realistic results are produced in the fields, notably in medicine and the pharmaceutical sector, by modelling quantum systems at the atomic level, and information that cannot yet be accessed is accessible in these fields.

29.2   Significance of Cyber Crime Attack for QC [15–18]

QC has become a critical part of ensuring massive changes in the fields of information science. With the rise in cyberattacks, it is believed that QC will result in cybersecurity improvement.

While it is widely anticipated that QC will remodel industries, particularly finance, it's going to additionally remodel cybersecurity. Even though QC isn't anticipated to move mainstream earlier than 2030 or later, now could be the time for organizations to start getting ready for its arrival. Why? It is expected that finally Qcomp systems could be able to factoring top numbers used with uneven encryption algorithms, which shape the idea of contemporary statistics protection systems, which means it's time for organizations to re-evaluate their cryptography systems.

Traditional encryption is based at the manipulation of big top numbers. It is tough for present-day computer systems to crack those numbers. However, for the reason that QC could be capable of parsing such complicated statistics a great deal quicker, a brand-new era of quantum-resistant encryption algorithms is wanted to keep away from capability catastrophic protection breaches throughout the enterprise world.

Today, there aren't any any Qcomp [11] systems that may control the big variety of qubits had to carry out the factoring required to crack contemporary protection. But in ten to twenty years from now, that is probably going to change, which might place organizations, which include the finance industry, at elevated risks. Therefore, scientists, coverage makers, and cybersecurity specialists are putting their attractions on growing post-quantum cryptography (PQC) [12] to cope with

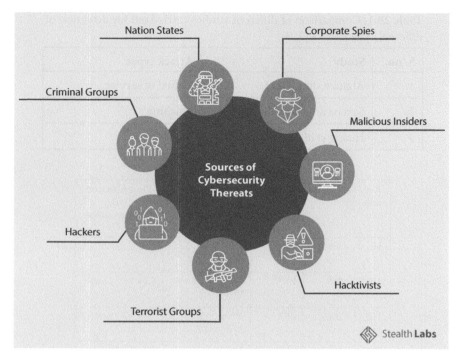

Figure 29.2 Sources of cybercrime attacks [7–9].

those anticipated issues. Figure 29.2 shows the sources of cybercrime attacks.

29.3   Related Work

Cyber technologies have the potential to significantly boost productivity and open up new opportunities that are essential to the success of our society, our economy, and our present enterprises. Our near-total reliance on cyber technology and the greater accessibility to information assets, however, creates previously unheard of vulnerabilities to cyberattacks [13] from a variety of threats. The benefit that these cyber technologies provide is kept from being undermined by these vulnerabilities thanks to cybersecurity tools. The ability of organisations to manage and safeguard crucial cyber systems and information assets against a wide range of threats, including developing QC technologies, is a must. Table 29.1 shows a comparison of different studies carried out for detection of different cyberattacks and Figure 29.3 shows the ideal time required to decrypt each algorithm using brute force attack method.

Table 29.1 Comparison of different studies carried out for detection of different cybe attacks [2, 3].

S. no.	Study	Attack types
1.	Algham die (2021)	Denial of service
2.	Saxena and Gayathri (2021)	Phishing
3.	Huang *et al.* (2020)	Malware

Key Size (bits)	Algorithm	Number of alternative keys	Time Required (105 decryption/sec)	Time Required (1013 decryption/sec)
56	DES	2^{56}	2^{55}ns = 1.125 years	1 hr
128	AES	2^{128}	2^{127}ns = 5.3 x 10^{21} years	5.3 x 10^{17} years
168	3DES	2^{168}	2^{167}ns = 5.8 x 10^{33} years	5.8 x 10^{29} years
192	AES	2^{192}	2^{191}ns = 9.8 x 10^{40} years	9.8 x 10^{36} years
256	AES	2^{56}	22^{55}ns = 1.8 x 10^{60} years	1.8 x 10^{56} years

Figure 29.3 Ideal time required to decrypt each algorithm using brute force attack method [6, 7, 12, 13].

29.4 Proposed Methodology

Cybersecurity attack improvement for QC using:

- Shor's Algorithm
- Quantum cryptography
- Quantum resistant cryptography

There are two primary types of digital encryption used today:

- Symmetric encryption
  Symmetric encryption is a sort of encryption wherein handiest one key (a mystery key) is used to each encrypt and decrypt digital records. The entities speaking through

symmetric encryption should change the important thing in order that it may be used with inside the decryption process. This encryption technique differs from uneven encryption wherein a couple of keys – one public and one private – is used to encrypt and decrypt messages.

By the use of symmetric encryption algorithms, records are "scrambled" in order that it cannot be understood by everybody who does now no longer own the name of the game key to decrypt it. Once the intended recipient who possesses the important thing has the message, the set of rules reverses its motion in order that the message is lower back to its authentic readable form. The mystery key that the sender and recipient each use might be a particular password/code or it may be random string of letters or numbers which have been generated via a stable random quantity generator (RNG) [14, 15]. For banking-grade encryption, the symmetric keys should be created the use of an RNG that is licensed in keeping with enterprise standards.

While symmetric encryption is an older approach of encryption, it's far quicker and greater green than uneven encryption, which takes a toll on networks because of overall performance problems with statistics length and heavy CPU use. Due to the higher overall performance and quicker pace of symmetric encryption (as compared to uneven), symmetric cryptography is commonly used for bulk encryption/encrypting huge quantities of statistics, e.g., for database encryption. In the case of a database, the name of the game key would possibly simplest be to be had to the database itself to encrypt or decrypt. Industry widespread symmetric encryption is likewise much less prone to advances in QC as compared to the cutting-edge [1] requirements for uneven algorithms (at the time of writing).

• Asymmetric (public-key) encryption
A publicly available key encrypts messages for recipients that have a private key for unscrambling. Public-key cryptography methods such as RSA and elliptic curve cryptography use algorithmic trapdoor functions to create keys that are relatively easy to compute in one direction, but very hard for a classical computer to reverse-engineer. Asymmetric cryptography [12], additionally called public-key cryptography,

is a method that makes use of a couple of associated keys – one public key and one non-public key – to encrypt and decrypt a message and defend it from unauthorized get right of entry to or use.

A public secret is a cryptographic key that may be utilized by any character to encrypt a message in order that it could most effectively be decrypted via the means of the supposed recipient with their non-public key. A non-public key – additionally called a mystery key – is shared most effectively with the key initiator.

When a person desires to ship an encrypted message, they could pull the supposed recipient's public key from a public listing and use it to encrypt the message earlier than sending it. The recipient of the message can then decrypt the message through the use of their associated non-public key [14–18].

If the sender encrypts the message through the use of their non-public key, the message may be decrypted most effectively with the use of that sender's public key, for this reason authenticating the sender. These encryption and decryption strategies occur automatically; customers now no longer want to bodily lock and release the message.

Many protocols [3, 4] depend on uneven cryptography, inclusive of the shipping layer safety (TLS) and stable sockets layer (SSL) protocols, which make HTTPS possible. Figure 29.4 shows public key cryptography in action.

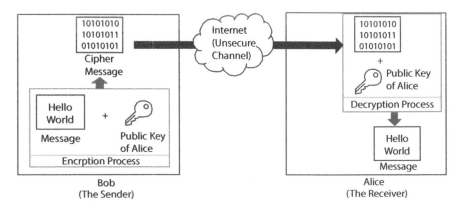

Figure 29.4 Public key cryptography in action [6, 18].

Figure 29.5 shows the entire communication process using QKD and Classical Protocols. Figure 29.6 shows the hacker attempting to crack the private key and Figure 29.7 shows the hacker attempting to retrieve the private key using QC setup with Shor's algorithm [15, 16].

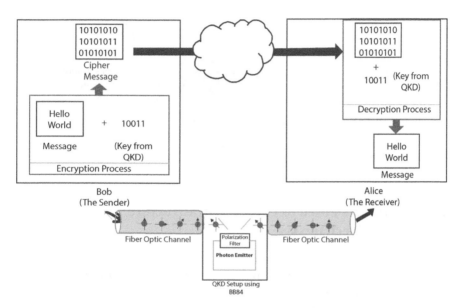

Figure 29.5 Entire communication process using QKD and classical protocols [6, 17].

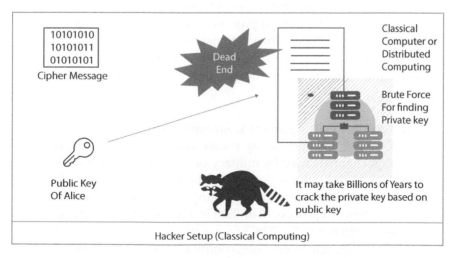

Figure 29.6 Hacker attempting to crack the private key [6].

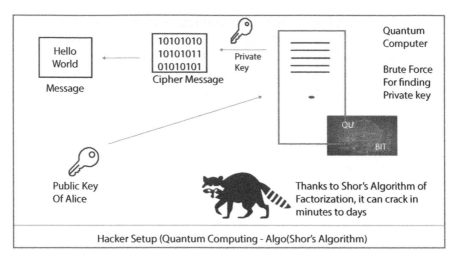

Hello World Message

10101010
10101011
01010101
Cipher Message

Private Key

Quantum Computer

Brute Force For finding Private key

QU

BIT

Public Key Of Alice

Thanks to Shor's Algorithm of Factorization, it can crack in minutes to days

Hacker Setup (Quantum Computing - Algo(Shor's Algorithm)

Figure 29.7 Hacker attempting to retrieve the private key using QC Setup with Shor's algorithm [6].

29.4.1 Threats Posed to Critical Infrastructure and Mechanisms

Brute-forcing was considered one of the effective techniques for password cracking and to perform cryptanalysis [5, 6]. A typical brute-force algorithm tries all possible combinations to figure out the correct combination to crack into the system or software. However, brute-force is one of the slowest methods of hacking since our conventional processors or cluster computing techniques are not capable of speeding up the operations. Whereas, now due to quantum processor, brute-force can now be one of the most effective methods when it comes to cracking critical information systems. Some of the possible future threats that can be introduced due to QC to critical infrastructures and communication channels are as listed below.

1. Breach of existing Secure Communication
   Channel: Compromising secure end-to-end data encryption channels used by military or financial institutions for transferring critical data would be very easy if the hacker has access to quantum processing engines which have the capability to process 10 million bits in a second. The current encryption mechanism was termed secure based on the time required to get compromised. Some of the common

algorithms used are RSA and AES algorithms which claim the fact that if the same needs to be compromised using brute-force technique, it will take several years to crack the code using the traditional supercomputers. However, using systems having quantum capabilities, the same can be cracked in a few seconds. So, if an intruder is capable to perform a "Man in the Middle" attack on a secure channel, he can sniff and collect the data and can decrypt the same, at the same time resulting in a data confidentiality breach.

2. Decrypting Encrypted Drives using Quantum Cryptanalysis: Many companies archive the data in offshore data premises and its security is maintained using "data-at-rest" encryption algorithms. Compromising encrypted data stored in overseas servers containing critical information would become an easy task if quantum capabilities are used for decrypting the same.

3. Autonomous Unmanned Explosives based on AI Object Detection, Real-time Trajectories Recognition and Object Tracking mechanisms: With the evolution of AI and its capabilities to identify real-time trajectories, object detection and recognition, there is a fair possibility of developing Unmanned Bombs which can easily bypass most of the existing security mechanisms like RADAR/SONAR sensors, motion detectors, thermal sensors, etc. Figure 29.8 shows the Quantum key Distribution Server Setup [6].

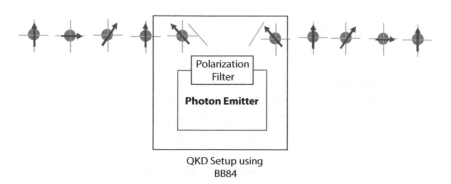

Figure 29.8 Quantum key distribution server setup [6].

29.5   Conclusion

We shouldn't wait until something goes wrong since there aren't many resources or funds available for studying QC, and there aren't many commercially available devices. We must always design and construct quantum hardware and code components with security in mind, if for no other reason. Additionally, similar services should have a leftward change in appearance. The QC industry may undoubtedly be a target for extortion, covert operations, and sabotage. Threat intelligence may transform typically reactive security measures into far more proactive defences against threat actors and system security that is foresighted. The open-source threat intelligence platform MISP (Malware Information Sharing Platform) is a good location to start gaining a grasp of the many threat actors. This innovation's benefits and drawbacks have been evaluated. The following are the studies' overall findings:

- Today, the development of computers has concentrated on minimising human effort and enhancing both the technology and the device's performance.
- The relationships between contemporary physics and matter science are evaluated in order to enhance computer performance. Nanotechnological ways of reducing the size of transistors used in traditional computers are presented as an alternative.
- Using techniques like entanglement theory and superposition, QC is a new area of study that has several advantages over traditional computers. Furthermore, given that it is capable of perfect encryption and decryption in communication (also known as cryptology), algorithmic scanning (Grover's algorithm), and polynomial time factorization (Shor's algorithm), it will have a wide range of applications in these fields. When Qcomp are assessed in terms of their application areas:
- Application contexts for quantum theories may be found in fields including deep learning, big data analytics, secure system development, attack models for security systems, and cloud computing.
- Some data mining and artificial intelligence approach models that can work on Qcomp have been created to give high-speed applications in terms of speed and performance; it is

shown when quantum methods are evaluated in terms of huge data analysis and deep learning. As a result, methodologies for deep learning and data analysis that can yield findings more quickly while being cheaper and simpler to implement have evolved.

- Existing cryptographic techniques and quantum approaches are combined to create platforms with a high level of dependability when quantum approaches are assessed in terms of establishing security mechanisms and cloud computing.
- Traditional computers are used to assess the sturdiness of security systems created using cryptographic algorithms. However, the unique benefits of Qcomp, such as their great processing power and ability to operate quickly, are evidence that these systems are less dependable than their earlier counterparts. According to Peter Shor, if you construct Qcomp, spies from all groups will be interested. They'll read our email and all of our codes will fail.

In this research work we reviewed the cybersecurity attack improvement technique for QC. The application PKI and its key exchange method can be compromised easily with the help of Qcomp. The proposed solution is to make our key exchange protocol secured, using QKD which ensures a hack-proof exchange of keys between the sender and intended receiver.

Based on the current technological advances, some of the research observation areas we can focus on, for protecting against future threats emerging due to quantum evolution, though not limited to, are as follows:

1. Focus on each PQC algorithms.
2. Making all the applications enforced to use AES 256 as a symmetric algorithm for data encryption at rest.
3. Awareness of the scope and capability of QC.

References

1. Kilber, N., Kaestle, D., & Wagner, S. (2021). Cybersecurity for Quantum Computing. *arXiv preprint arXiv:2110.14701*.
2. Hayes, J. (2019). Quantum on the MONEY [quantum computing in financial services sector]. *Engineering & Technology, 14*(4), 34-37.

3. Kaur, J., & Ramkumar, K. R. (2021). The recent trends in cyber security: A review. *Journal of King Saud University-Computer and Information Sciences.*

4. Beavers, J., & Pournouri, S. (2019). Recent cyber attacks and vulnerabilities in medical devices and healthcare institutions. In *Blockchain and clinical trial* (pp. 249-267). Springer, Cham.

5. Ahn, J., Chung, J., Kim, T., Ahn, B., & Choi, J. (2021, June). An overview of quantum security for distributed energy resources. In *2021 IEEE 12th International Symposium on Power Electronics for Distributed Generation Systems (PEDG)* (pp. 1-7). IEEE.

6. Gompert, D. C., & Libicki, M. (2021). Towards a Quantum Internet: Post-pandemic Cyber Security in a Post-digital World. *Survival, 63*(1), 113-124.

7. Wallden, P., & Kashefi, E. (2019). Cyber security in the quantum era. *Communications of the ACM, 62*(4), 120-120.

8. Moizuddin, M., Winston, J., & Qayyum, M. (2017, March). A comprehensive survey: quantum cryptography. In *2017 2nd International Conference on Anti-Cyber Crimes (ICACC)* (pp. 98-102). IEEE.

9. Rasool, R. U., Ahmad, H. F., Rafique, W., Qayyum, A., & Qadir, J. (2022). Quantum computing for healthcare: A review.

10. Cheung, K. F., Bell, M. G., & Bhattacharjya, J. (2021). Cybersecurity in logistics and supply chain management: An overview and future research directions. *Transportation Research Part E: Logistics and Transportation Review, 146,* 102217.

11. Rojasree, V., & Jayanthi, J. G. (2021, April). A Competent Intelligent Key Cryptography (IKC) Architecture. In *2021 5th International Conference on Computing Methodologies and Communication (ICCMC)* (pp. 166-173). IEEE.

12. Buchanan, W., & Woodward, A. (2017). Will quantum computers be the end of public key encryption? *Journal of Cyber Security Technology, 1*(1), 1-22.

13. Chaubey, N. K., & Prajapati, B. B. (Eds.). (2020). *Quantum Cryptography and the Future of Cyber Security.* IGI Global.

14. Njorbuenwu, M., Swar, B., & Zavarsky, P. (2019, June). A survey on the impacts of quantum computers on information security. In *2019 2nd International conference on data intelligence and security (ICDIS)* (pp. 212-218). IEEE.

15. Rohith, C., & Batth, R. S. (2019, December). Cyber warfare: nations cyber conflicts, cyber cold war between nations and its repercussion. In *2019 International Conference on Computational Intelligence and Knowledge Economy (ICCIKE)* (pp. 640-645). IEEE.

16. Lee, C. C., Tan, T. G., Sharma, V., & Zhou, J. (2021, June). Quantum computing threat modelling on a generic cps setup. In *International Conference on Applied Cryptography and Network Security* (pp. 171-190). Springer, Cham.

17. Almansoori, A., Ncube, C., & Salloum, S. A. (2021, June). Internet of Things Impact on the Future of Cyber Crime in 2050. In *The International Conference on Artificial Intelligence and Computer Vision* (pp. 643-655). Springer, Cham.

18. Chamola, V., Jolfaei, A., Chanana, V., Parashari, P., & Hassija, V. (2021). Information security in the post quantum era for 5G and beyond networks: Threats to existing cryptography, and post-quantum cryptography. *Computer Communications, 176*, 99-118.

About the Editors

Romil Rawat, PhD, is an assistant professor at Shri Vaishnav Vidyapeeth Vishwavidyalaya, Indore. With over 12 years of teaching experience, he has published numerous papers in scholarly journals and conferences. He has also published book chapters and is a board member on two scientific journals. He has received several research grants and has hosted research events, workshops, and training programs. He also has several patents to his credit.

Rajesh Kumar Chakrawarti, PhD, is a professor and the Dean of the Department of Computer Science & Engineering, Sushila Devi Bansal College, Bansal Group of Institutions, India. He has over 20 years of industry and academic experience and has published over 100 research papers and chapters in books.

Sanjaya Kumar Sarangi, PhD, is an adjunct professor and coordinator at Utkal University, Coordinator and Adjunct Professor, Utkal University, Bhubaneswar, India. He has over 23 years of academic experience and has authored textbooks, book chapters, and papers for journals and conferences. He has been a visiting doctoral fellow at the University of California, USA, and he has more than 30 patents to his credit.

Jaideep Patel, PhD, is a professor in the Computer Science and Engineering Department at the Sagar Institute of Research and Technology, Bhopal, India. He holds five patents, and has published two books and one book chapter.

Vivek Bhardwaj, PhD, is an assistant professor at Manipal University Jaipur, Jaipur, India. He has over eight years of teaching and research experience, has filed five patents, and has published many articles in scientific journals and conferences.

Anjali Rawat is a consultant for Apostelle Overseas Education, and she has over five years of consulting, teaching, and research experience. She has chaired international conferences and hosted several research events, and she holds several patents and has published research articles.

Hitesh Rawat is a faculty member in the Management Department at the Sri Aurobindo Institute of Technology and Management, Indore, India. He has over six years of consulting, teaching, and research experience and has also chaired international conferences and hosted several research events.

Index

Also of Interest

From the same editors

ROBOTIC PROCESS AUTOMATION, Edited by Romil Rawat, Rajesh Kumar Chakrawarti, Sanjaya Kumar Sarangi, Rahul Choudhary, Anand Singh Gadwal, and Vivek Bhardwaj, ISBN: 9781394166183. Presenting the latest technologies and practices in this ever-changing field, this groundbreaking new volume covers the theoretical challenges and practical solutions for using robotics across a variety of industries, encompassing many disciplines, including mathematics, computer science, electrical engineering, information technology, mechatronics, electronics, bioengineering, and command and software engineering.

AUTONOMOUS VEHICLES VOLUME 1: Using Machine Intelligence, Edited by Romil Rawat, A. Mary Sowjanya, Syed Imran Patel, Varshali Jaiswal, Imran Khan, and Allam Balaram. ISBN: 9781119871958. Addressing the current challenges, approaches and applications relating to autonomous vehicles, this groundbreaking new volume presents the research and techniques in this growing area, using Internet of Things, Machine Learning, Deep Learning, and Artificial Intelligence.

AUTONOMOUS VEHICLES VOLUME 2: Smart Vehicles for Communication, Edited by Romil Rawat, Purvee Bhardwaj, Upinder Kaur, Shrikant Telang, Mukesh Chouhan, and K. Sakthidasan Sankaran, ISBN: 9781394152254. The companion to *Autonomous Vehicles Volume 1: Using Machine Intelligence,* this second volume in the two-volume set covers intelligent techniques utilized for designing, controlling and managing vehicular systems based on advanced algorithms of computing like machine learning, artificial Intelligence, data analytics, and Internet of Things with prediction approaches to avoid accidental damages, security threats, and theft.

Check out these other related titles from Scrivener Publishing

FACTORIES OF THE FUTURE: Technological Advances in the Manufacturing Industry, Edited by Chandan Deep Singh and Harleen Kaur, ISBN: 9781119864943. The book provides insight into various technologies adopted and to be adopted in the future by industries and measures the impact of these technologies on manufacturing performance and their sustainability.

AI AND IOT-BASED INTELLIGENT AUTOMATION IN ROBOTICS, Edited by Ashutosh Kumar Dubey, Abhishek Kumar, S. Rakesh Kumar, N. Gayathri, Prasenjit Das, ISBN: 9781119711209. The 24 chapters in this book provide a deep overview of robotics and the application of AI and IoT in robotics across several industries such as healthcare, defense, education, etc.

SMART GRIDS FOR SMART CITIES VOLUME 1, Edited by O.V. Gnana Swathika, K. Karthikeyan, and Sanjeevikumar Padmanaban, ISBN: 9781119872078. Written and edited by a team of experts in the field, this first volume in a two-volume set focuses on an interdisciplinary perspective on the financial, environmental, and other benefits of smart grid technologies and solutions for smart cities.

SMART GRIDS FOR SMART CITIES VOLUME 2: Real-Time Applications in Smart Cities, Edited by O.V. Gnana Swathika, K. Karthikeyan, and Sanjeevikumar Padmanaban, ISBN: 9781394215874. Written and edited by a team of experts in the field, this second volume in a two-volume set focuses on an interdisciplinary perspective on the financial, environmental, and other benefits of smart grid technologies and solutions for smart cities.

SMART GRIDS AND INTERNET OF THINGS, Edited by Sanjeevikumar Padmanaban, Jens Bo Holm-Nielsen, Rajesh Kumar Dhanaraj, Malathy Sathyamoorthy, and Balamurugan Balusamy, ISBN: 9781119812449. Written and edited by a team of international professionals, this groundbreaking new volume covers the latest technologies in automation, tracking, energy distribution and consumption of Internet of Things (IoT) devices with smart grids.

Printed and bound by CPI Group (UK) Ltd, Croydon, CR0 4YY

27/10/2024

14580179-0001